ENDGAME F

TERESA WHITFIELD

Endgame for ETA

Elusive Peace in the Basque Country

El ojo que ves no es
ojo porque tú lo veas;
es ojo porque te ve.

The eye you see is not
an eye because you see it.
It is an eye because it sees you.

Antonio Machado

March 2014
Teresa Whitfield

HURST & COMPANY, LONDON

First published in the United Kingdom in 2014 by
C. Hurst & Co. (Publishers) Ltd.,
41 Great Russell Street, London, WC1B 3PL
© Teresa Whitfield, 2014
All rights reserved.
Printed in the United Kingdom

A Cataloguing-in-Publication data record for this book is
available from the British Library.

ISBN: 9781849043465 (paperback)

www.hurstpublishers.com

This book is printed using paper from registered sustainable
and managed sources.

For Jason, Isabel, and Harry

CONTENTS

CONTENTS

CONTENTS

ACKNOWLEDGEMENTS

In the course of the research and writing of this book, I have accumulated many debts. Since late 2008, I have travelled repeatedly to the Basque Country, Madrid and other cities of Spain. I was fortunate to be able to interview a wide range of individuals, across the political spectrum, with very different experience and perceptions of what some lived as the Basque conflict, and others had experienced only as ETA's terrorism. Many were extraordinarily generous with their time, agreeing to meet with me on repeated occasions, and providing me with information and analysis that greatly helped my understanding of the evolution of Basque politics, the impact of ETA's violence within it and the efforts made to bring it to an end.

As readers of *Endgame for ETA* will observe, some of those interviewed requested anonymity; many more did not, in several cases because they were aware of the inevitable time lag involved in the writing and production of a book. In addition to a close monitoring of the Basque and Spanish press, my understanding of the events I describe has also been enriched by the first-hand accounts of the efforts towards peace written by several of their protagonists, as well as a number of books published in Spain in recent years that have addressed different facets of the long-drawn-out process towards the end of ETA. The most significant of these are listed in the bibliography.

In addition to my sources, I would like to express my sincere thanks to those, both inside Spain and outside, who have been kind enough to read and comment on earlier drafts of my manuscript. Perhaps unusually, I have decided not to do so by name. Many of those I would like to thank will disagree with some of what is contained within this book;

ACKNOWLEDGEMENTS

none will agree with all of it. Some would not welcome their identification. These considerations would leave me with a small and unrepresentative group who should not be left to carry the burden of my gratitude on their own. But you all know who you are; so, thank you, and my apologies if, despite your best efforts, you still think I have got it all wrong.

On a more institutional level, I would like to thank the Center on International Cooperation at New York University, where I am now a Non-Resident Fellow, for hosting me during my Basque work; the United States Institute of Peace, which provided me with a grant between 2010 and 2012 that funded most of my research and writing; and Michael Dwyer and his staff at Hurst for welcoming the book when I first approached them, and shepherding it through publication. I should also acknowledge my gratitude to the two anonymous readers selected by Hurst, whose thoughtful comments were most helpful.

I need also to add a disclaimer. I have a part-time engagement as a Senior Adviser to the Centre for Humanitarian Dialogue (HD Centre) in New York, where I am responsible for liaison with the United Nations. The HD Centre, which is based in Geneva, had a significant role in the effort to bring ETA towards its end about which the individuals concerned have maintained absolute discretion. I was never involved in the HD Centre's engagement in Spain, and received no assistance from the HD Centre in my Basque work. As this book reflects, there was, however, no shortage of other sources on many aspects of the Basque story.

Finally, I would like to thank my husband Jason, and children, Isabel and Harry, for tolerating and supporting the frequent absences and long hours at my computer this book entailed. On the plus side, it did lead to summer holidays in the Basque Country and Spain that I know have contributed to a keen desire to return and the curiosity to know more.

Teresa Whitfield   March 2014

GLOSSARY OF INDIVIDUALS
AND ORGANISATIONS

This glossary has been compiled as a means to help readers navigate the large number of individuals and organisations referred to in the text. It is not comprehensive: individuals and organisations mentioned in only one section or chapter generally do not appear, and the list of organisations is limited to Spanish and Basque organisations. Individuals mentioned for the most part on the basis of their written work—fully referenced in the endnotes—are not included. Other individuals with long and complex careers are described in terms that reflect only their appearance within this book.

Individuals are listed by the first of their surnames. Organisations are listed by their acronym or full name when no acronym is commonly employed.

Individuals

Adams, Gerry: President of Sinn Féin; key supporter of Basque nationalist left in its efforts towards peace.

Albizu Iriarte, Mikel, *Mikel Anza*: Political leader of ETA from 1993 until his capture in October 2004.

Alonso, José Antonio: Interior minister in the first Zapatero government, 2004–6.

Álvarez, Joseba: Son of José Luis Álvarez Enparantza, *Txillardegi* (a founding member of ETA), and head of international relations for Batasuna.

GLOSSARY OF INDIVIDUALS AND ORGANISATIONS

Ángel Blanco, Miguel: Victim of ETA; his assassination in 1997 prompted public outrage and mobilisation against ETA.

Anza, Jon: Member of ETA; disappeared in France in April 2009, body found in a morgue in Toulouse in March 2010.

Ardanza, José Antonio: Leading member of the PNV; *lehendakari*, or Basque president, from 1985–99.

Arana y Goiri, Sabino: Father of Basque nationalism and founder of the Basque Nationalist Party (PNV) in 1895.

Arzalluz, Xabier: President of the PNV, 1986–2004.

Ares, Rodolfo: PSE politician; participated in negotiations at Loyola with Batasuna and PNV in 2006; minister of interior within Basque government, 2009–12.

Aznar, José María: President of the PP, 1990–2004; prime minister of Spain, 1996–2004.

Barreda, Leopoldo: Basque PP politician; PP spokesman in the Basque Parliament 1995–2011; deputy spokesman in Spanish Parliament from 2011.

Basagoiti, Antonio: President of Basque PP, 2008–13.

Benegas, Txiki (for José María): Basque Socialist politician; played prominent role during the transition; in González years active in the pursuit of talks with ETA.

Beñarán Ordeñana, José Miguel, *Argala*: Leader of ETA during the 1970s, killed by the BVE in the French Basque Country, 1978.

Blair, Tony: British prime minister, 1997–2007.

Bruin, Bairbre de: Sinn Féin member of the European Parliament, 2004–12, regular visitor to the Basque Country.

Carrera Sarobe, Mikel, *Ata*: Military leader of ETA until captured in May 2010.

Carmena, Manuela: Spanish judge, engaged by Basque government in 2011 to advise on policies towards victims of police abuse.

Conde-Pumpido, Cándido: Attorney general in Zapatero governments, 2004–11.

Cosidó, Ignacio: PP politician and senator during Zapatero government; director general of police in Rajoy government from 2011.

Currin, Brian: South African lawyer; involved in the Basque process since late 2003; created the International Group for Dialogue and Peace in 2007; coordinated the Brussels Declaration in March 2010; established the International Contact Group (ICG) in November 2010; participated in Aiete Conference in October 2011.

Del Río, Inés, Member of ETA sentenced to 3,828 years in prison in 1987 after being convicted for twenty-four murders; under the retroactive application of the Parot Doctrine, her release from prison—which would have been in 2008 in accordance with the 1973 criminal code—was postponed until 2017. Del Río successfully appealed the extension of her sentence before the European Court of Human Rights, which found in her favour in August 2012, and again on 21 October 2013, and ordered her release.

Diéz Usabiaga, Rafael: Leading figure within HB and the nationalist left; adviser to ETA at Algiers and secretary-general of LAB 1996–2008; associated with attempts to address the conflict by political means; was key figure in the Lizarra process and worked closely with Otegi to effect the nationalist left—and ETA's—shift away from violence between 2008–11; in September 2011 convicted as a 'leader of ETA'.

Douglass, William: US anthropologist, and founding director of the Centre for Basque Studies at the University of Nevada; in late 2003 and early 2004 helped introduce the HD Centre to ETA.

Elorza, Odón: PSE mayor of San Sebastián, 1991–2011.

Egibar, Joseba: Spokesman of the PNV in the Basque Parliament, and its leader in Guipúzcoa; participated in talks with ETA around the 1998 ceasefire.

Eguiguren, Jesús: Basque Socialist politician, president of the PSE from 2002; began secret talks with Otegi in 2001; instrumental in design and execution of Basque peace process under Zapatero; negotiated terms of ETA's March 2006 ceasefire with Josu Ternera; took part in almost all meetings with ETA between 2005–7 and in the Loyola talks held in late 2006; retired from Basque Parliament in 2012.

Espiau, Gorka: Spokesman of Elkarri, then an adviser to Ibarretxe on conflict resolution; provided advice to Currin and the ICG.

Etxebeste, Eugenio, *Antxon*: 'Historic' member of ETA; captured and deported by French authorities in 1984; in 1987, moved to Algiers to develop and take part in talks with government; from the Dominican Republic remained the regular conduit for attempts to engage in talks with ETA until returned to prison in Spain in 1997; released in 2004, and from 2009 prominent as an advocate of a political solution to the conflict.

Etxeberria, Rufino: Member of ETA in youth, then leading member of

HB and nationalist left; took part with Otegi in negotiations in Geneva in May 2007 and imprisoned later that year; after Otegi's arrest in October 2009 assumed leading role in promoting change within nationalist left and persuading ETA to abandon its armed activity.

Fernández, Jonan: HB councillor, 1987–91; founded and led Elkarri, 1992–2005; engaged in dialogue with ETA during González years; founded Baketik in 2006; from 2013 secretary for peace and coexistence in the Basque government.

Fernández Díaz, Jorge: Minister of interior in Rajoy government from 2011.

Franco, General Francisco: Leader of the military coup against the Republican government in 1936; victor of the Civil War and head of state and *Caudillo* of Spain until his death in November 1975.

Gallizo, Mercedes: PSOE politician and, between 2004–11, director general of the prison service.

Garikoitz Aspiazu Rubina, Miguel, *Txeroki*: Military leader of ETA until his capture in November 2008.

Garitano, Martín: Bildu mayor of San Sebastián from 2011.

Garzón, Baltasar: Spanish judge and investigating magistrate of the Audiencia Nacional between 1987–2010; in 1998 issued an international warrant for the arrest of General Pinochet; known for his prosecutions of ETA and nationalist left, as well as other high profile cases; suspended from judicial activity in 2010 pending resolution of charges related to his investigation of the crimes of Franco; disbarred in 2012 for authorising wire-taps of PP lawyers in a corruption case.

Gómez Benítez, José Manuel: PSOE lawyer, part of government negotiating team with ETA in Geneva and Oslo, 2006–7.

González, Felipe: Secretary-general of PSOE, 1974–97; prime minister of Spain, 1982–96.

González Peñalva, Belén, *Carmen*: Represented ETA at talks in Algiers, and in Switzerland in May 1999.

Goirizelaia, Jone: Defence lawyer for Arnaldo Otegi and others in nationalist left.

Grande-Marlaska, Fernando: Judge and investigating magistrate of the Audiencia Nacional, active in prosecutions of ETA and nationalist left during 2006 ceasefire.

Griffiths, Martin: Director of Centre for Humanitarian Dialogue (HD

Centre), 1999–2010, initiated involvement in Basque process in late 2003; facilitated talks between ETA and government in Geneva and Oslo, 2005–7.

Hottinger, Julian: Swiss mediation expert, with long experience in Basque Country.

Ibarretxe, Juan José: Leading member of the PNV; *lehendakari*, or Basque president, 1999–2009.

Imaz, Josu Jon: President of PNV, 2004–9.

Iruin, Iñigo: Nationalist left lawyer and politician; HB adviser at Algiers talks; assumed prominent role in presentation and defence of statutes of Sortu in early 2011 and defence of Otegi and others later that year.

Iturbe Abasolo, Domingo, *Txomin*: Leader of ETA, killed in a car crash in Algiers in 1987.

Iurrebaso, Jon: Member of ETA; took part, with Josu Ternera and then López Peña, in talks in Geneva and Oslo until his arrest in France on his way to Geneva in March 2007.

Jáuregui, Ramón: Leading Basque Socialist politician, vice-*lehendakari* to Ardanza between 1987–91 and minister of the presidency to Zapatero from 2010–11.

Juana Chaos, Iñaki de: Member of ETA, convicted of killing twenty-five people in 1987, given 3,000 year prison sentence, but eligible for release in late 2004; went on hunger strike after Spanish government prevented his release; a second hunger strike from November 2006 became a contentious issue in talks with ETA; released in March 2007, he was returned to prison after the end of ETA's ceasefire in June 2007 and eventually released in 2008.

Kelly, Gerry: Sinn Féin politician and former member of the IRA; active in quiet support of Basque process and present in Geneva talks of May 2007.

Kendall, Raymond: British law enforcement official and former secretary-general of Interpol, member of both the ICG and IVC.

Landa, Jon: Basque human rights academic, director of human rights in the Basque government, 2005–9.

Landaburu, Gorka: Basque journalist, son of vice-*lehendakari* of Basque government in exile during the Franco years; brother of fellow journalist Ander; victim of letter bomb sent by ETA in 2001.

Lasa, Maixabel: Director of Basque government's Office for the Attention to Victims, 2001–12; widow of Socialist politician Juan María Jáuregui, assassinated by ETA in 2000.

López, Patxi: Secretary-general of the PSE from 2002; the first non-nationalist *lehendakari*, or Basque president, from 2009–12.

López Peña, Francisco Javier, *Thierry*: Represented ETA in negotiations in Geneva and Oslo, late 2006–May 2007; captured in May 2008; died in a French hospital in March 2013.

Madina, Eduardo: Basque Socialist politician; survived car bomb attack by ETA in 2002; since 2009 secretary-general of the PSOE in the Spanish Parliament.

Madariaga, Julen: Founding member of ETA; left the organisation in 1989 and later associated with Aralar.

Manikkalingham, Ram: Coordinator, International Verification Commission; director, Dialogue Advisory Group.

Mayor Oreja, Jaime: Basque PP politician; interior minister under Aznar, 1996–2001; ran unsuccessfully for Basque presidency in 2001; member of European Parliament from 2004.

Maskey, Alex: Sinn Féin politician, active in the Basque process.

Mas, Artur: Leader of the CiU, president of the Catalan government from 2010.

Mitchell, George: Former US senator and special envoy to the Northern Ireland peace process; lent name to 'Mitchell Principles' that underpinned negotiations towards the Good Friday Agreement.

Montero, Txema: Lawyer and leading member of HB; adviser at Algiers talks; elected to European Parliament in 1987; left HB in 1992.

Mujika Garmendia, Francisco, *Pakito*: Leader of ETA; captured at Bidart in 1992.

O'Brien, Eoin: Sinn Féin politician; active in Basque process.

Ollora, Juan María: PNV politician; took part in talks with ETA around 1998 ceasefire.

Ordóñez, Gregorio: Basque PP politician; assassinated by ETA in 1995.

Ormazabal, Sabino: Basque pacifist and human rights activist; prosecuted, imprisoned and later acquitted under *macroproceso* 18/98.

Ortega Lara, José Antonio: Prison official kidnapped by ETA in 1996 and rescued in 1997.

Otegi, Arnaldo: Member of ETA in his youth; spokesman of Batasuna since 1998; played leading role in process towards Lizarra Declaration and peace process under Zapatero; participated in talks at Loyola in 2006 and in Geneva in May 2007; imprisoned after ETA ended its ceasefire; in 2008–9 initiated strategic change within nationalist left predicated on the eventual end of ETA's violence; imprisoned again in October 2009, and convicted in September 2011 as a 'leader of ETA'.

Pastor, José Antonio: PSE politician and spokesperson in the Basque Parliament.

Pagazarurtundua, Maite: President of Foundation for Victims of Terrorism (FVT), 2005–12; sister of Joseba Pagazarurtundua, assassinated by ETA in 2003.

Pérez Rubalcaba, Alfredo: Socialist politician; minister of education, 1992–3, and minister of the presidency, 1993–6, under González; campaign strategist for Zapatero and architect of policies against ETA; minister of interior, 2006–11; first deputy prime minister, 2010–11; presidential candidate, 2011; secretary-general of the PSOE and leader of the opposition from 2012.

Powell, Jonathan: Chief of staff and chief aide to Tony Blair on Northern Ireland, 1997–2007; attended May 2007 talks in Geneva and Aiete Conference in October 2011.

Rajoy, Mariano: Minister of education, 1996–2000, then deputy prime minister, 2000–3, to Aznar; leader of the PP opposition, 2004–11; prime minister of Spain from 2011.

Reid, Alec: Redemptorist priest; facilitated Adams-Hume talks in Northern Ireland; encouraged dialogue in Basque Country in advance of 2005–7 peace process.

Rios, Paul: Coordinator of Lokarri, prominent advocate of dialogue and facilitator of international efforts in support of Basque peace process.

Rodríguez Zapatero, José Luis: Secretary-general of the PSOE, 2000–12; prime minister of Spain, 2004–11.

Segura, Joseba, Basque priest; established contact with Sinn Féin in late 1980s; facilitated contacts with ETA prior to government meeting in May 1999 and supported involvement of Alec Reid in early 2000s.

Uría, Ignacio: Basque nationalist businessman assassinated by ETA in December 2008.

Uriarte, Juan María: Basque bishop; facilitated talks with ETA in May 1999.

Urrutikoetxea Bengoetxea, José Antonio, *Josu Ternera*: 'Historic' member of ETA with leadership responsibilities since 1980; detained in France in 1989, extradited to Spain and imprisoned; elected member of Basque Parliament for EH in 2001; fled Spain in 2003; in talks in Geneva and Oslo negotiated ETA's ceasefire of March 2006 with Eguiguren; took part in further talks later that year.

Urkullu, Iñigo: President of PNV, 2008–13; *lehendakari*, or Basque president, from 2012.

Vera, Rafael: State secretary (interior ministry), 1986–94; sentenced to prison for crimes related to the GAL in 1998; pardoned after little more than a year.

Zabaleta, Gemma: Basque Socialist politician.

Zabaleta, Patxi: Leading member of HB until he broke with it over ETA's violence; in 2001 founded Aralar.

Zarzalejos, Javier: Secretary of the presidency under Aznar, 1996–2004; met with ETA in Switzerland in May 1999.

Zuberbiola, Igor: Member of ETA; took part in talks in Oslo and Geneva, 2006–7; detained in 2008.

Organisations

Ahotsak (Voices): Organisation of women of diverse political identities committed to finding peace in the Basque Country; founded in April 2006.

Alternatiba (Alternative): Political party that split from Ezker Batua in 2009; member of Bildu, Amaiur and EH Bildu coalitions.

Amaiur: Left-wing and pro-independence coalition formed by Alternatiba, Aralar, Eusko Alkartasuna and individuals close to the nationalist left to contest the Spanish general election of November 2011.

ANV, Acción Nacionalista Vasca (Basque Nationalist Action): Basque nationalist party founded in 1930; member of HB from 1978; contested the 2007 local and municipal elections in the Basque Country with some lists banned; declared illegal by Supreme Court in 2008.

AP, Alianza Popular (Popular Alliance): Right-wing party founded in 1977, antecedent of Popular Party.

Aralar: Separatist and left-wing Basque political party opposed to the violence of ETA; emerged as a schism from Batasuna after ETA's violent campaign of 2000.

AVT, Asociación de Víctimas del Terrorismo (Association for the Victims of Terrorism): Spanish association of victims; prominently opposed Zapatero's policies towards ETA.

Batasuna (Unity): Established in 2001 as successor to Herri Batasuna and Euskal Herritarrok; most visible manifestation of social and political base for ETA; banned in 2003 within Spain; and included on EU and US terrorist lists; remained legal as an association in France.

GLOSSARY OF INDIVIDUALS AND ORGANISATIONS

Bateragune (Meeting point): Name of the organisation for whose formation—allegedly under the orders of ETA—Otegi, Díez and others were arrested in October 2009.

¡Basta Ya! (Enough already!): Civil society network and platform founded in 1999 to provide vigorous opposition to ETA's terrorism.

Bildu (Reunite): Left-wing and pro-independence coalition formed by Alternatiba, Eusko Alkartasuna, and individuals close to the nationalist left after Supreme Court rejected the statutes of Sortu in March 2011; contested May 2011 Basque local and municipal elections.

BVE, Batallón Vasco Español (Basque-Spanish Battalion): Right-wing paramilitary group; active between1975–1981.

CAA, Comandos Autónomos Anticapitalistas (Anticapitalist Autonomous Commandos): Armed group that splintered from ETA-pm; active in the late 1970s and early 1980s.

CiU, Convergencia i Unió (Convergence and Union): Catalan nationalist coalition of centrist tendency.

COVITE, Colectivo de Víctimas del Terrorismo en el País Vasco (Collective of Victims of Terrorism in the Basque Country): Organisation for Basque victims of terrorism; founded in 1998.

Dignidad y Justicia (Dignity and Justice): Association close to the AVT formed to promote the prosecution of cases against organisations of the MLNV.

EB, Ezker Batua (United Left): Basque expression of Spanish United Left political party, sometimes referred to as IU-EB.

EA, Eusko Alkartasuna (Basque Solidarity): Basque nationalist political party of social democratic tendencies; formed in 1986 after a schism within the PNV.

EE, Euskadiko Ezkerra (Basque Left): Political coalition mainly of former members and supporters of ETA-pm; while some affiliates joined nationalist parties, a majority allied with the PSE in 1991.

Egin: Basque newspaper closed in 1998 on the grounds that it had ties to ETA.

Egunkaria (The Daily): Basque newspaper closed in 2003 on the grounds that it had ties to ETA; Audiencia Nacional ruled in 2010 that there had been no basis to the charges against it.

EH, Euskal Herritarrok (We, the Basque Citizens): Electoral coalition formed in 1998 to replace Herri Batasuna; re-named Batasuna in 2001.

GLOSSARY OF INDIVIDUALS AND ORGANISATIONS

EHAK, Euskal Herrialdeetako Alderdi Komunista (Communist Party of the Basque Lands): Political party registered in 2002 but inactive until 2005 when the former Batasuna called its supporters to vote for it in the Basque elections; banned by Supreme Court in 2008.

EH Bildu, Euskal Herria Bildu (Basque Country Reunite): A left-wing and pro-independence coalition formed by Alternatiba, Aralar, Eusko Alkartasun, Sortu and other individuals close to the nationalist left to contest the Basque parliamentary elections in October 2012.

Ekin (Action): Both the student discussion group, formed in the 1950s, from which ETA was born, and the successor to KAS as the coordinating body within the MLNV.

ELA, Eusko Langileen Alkartasuna (Basque Workers' Solidarity): Largest union in the Basque Country; broadly affiliated with moderate Basque nationalism.

Elkarri: Basque social movement and civil society organisation founded in 1992 to defend and promote dialogue as a means to reach a solution to the Basque conflict; it was discontinued in 2006 and succeeded by Lokarri.

EPPK, Euskal Preso Politokoen Kolektiboa (Basque Political Prisoners' Collective): Organisation of Basque prisoners through which ETA exercises discipline within the prisons; a successor to Gestoras pro Amnistia and Askatasuna.

ERC, Esquerra Republicana de Catalunya (Catalan Republican Left): Left-wing and pro-independence Catalan political party.

ETA, Euskadi 'ta Askatasuna (Basque Freedom or Liberty): Separatist and revolutionary organisation, founded in 1959, that began to advocate the 'armed struggle' during the 1960s. It practised terrorist violence and claimed some 830 victims until October 2011 when it declared a 'definitive end' to its armed activities.

ETA-m, ETA *militar*: Emerged in 1974 from the most significant of ETA's many splits; insisted on the primacy of armed action and later absorbed those members of ETA-pm who chose not to demobilise in the 1980s.

ETA-pm, ETA *político-militar*: Emerged from 1974 split with ETA-m; advocated participation in democratic institutions; after 1981 negotiated reintegration with Spanish government.

Etxerat: Organisation of support of the family members of Basque prisoners.

Euskal Memoria: Basque foundation, associated with the nationalist left, established in 2009 to recover what it termed the 'stolen memory' of the Basque conflict.

Foro de Ermua (Forum of Ermua): Loosely structured civic association founded in 1998 after the assassination of Miguel Ángel Blanco to promote recognition of ETA's victims, counter ETA's terrorism and defend 'constitutionalist' positions.

Fundación para la Libertad (Foundation for Freedom): Foundation established to oppose ETA and defend 'freedom, democracy and tolerance' from the perspective of Basque constitutionalism.

FVT, Fundación Víctimas del Terrorismo (Foundation for the Victims of Terrorism): An umbrella body for organisations representing victims of terrorism; established in 2001 as a consequence of the anti-terrorist pact of 2000.

GAL, Grupos Antiterroristas de Liberación (Anti-Terrorist Liberation Groups): Shadowy death squad that between 1983 and 1987 killed twenty-seven victims; later demonstrated to have been orchestrated from within the PSOE interior ministry.

Gesto por la Paz (Gesture for Peace): Civil society organisation and movement established in 1986 to oppose all kinds of political violence; pacifist, ethical and politically independent in its approach.

Gestoras pro Amnistia (Campaigners for Amnesty): Organisation created in 1970 to advocate for the rights of Basque prisoners; became increasingly associated with ETA's control of its prisoners and was, like its successor Askatasuna (Liberty), banned in 2002 and included on the EU terrorist list as part of ETA.

GRAPO, Grupos de Resistencia Antifascista Primero de Octubre (First of October Anti-Fascist Resistance Group): Leftist armed group of Marxist origin; active in Spain from mid-1970s and disbanded in 2007.

HB, Herri Batasuna (The People United): Political coalition formed in 1978; allied to aims of ETA-m; won 150,000 votes in first Spanish general election in 1979 and remained a significant political force; re-named Euskal Herritarak in 1998.

IA, Izquierda abertzale (Nationalist left): Term used to describe the radical nationalist movement, including ETA, gathered in the MLNV, then later its non-violent expression, gathered around Batasuna and later Sortu.

ICG, International Contact Group (Basque Country): Group of independent international figures; established in November 2010 to expedite, facilitate and enable the achievement of political normalisation in the Basque Country.

IVC, International Verification Commission for the Ceasefire in the Basque Country: Group of independent international verifiers established in September 2011 to verify ETA's ceasefire.

IU, Izquierda Unida (United Left): Left-wing Spanish political party originally formed in 1986 out of a coalition of forces including the Spanish Communist Party.

Jarrai-Haika-Segi: Jarrai (Continue) was the youth organisation of KAS, associated by many with actions of *kale borroka*; after joining with a French Basque youth organisation it became Haika (Arise) and later Segi (Follow). All three were declared illegal by Spanish courts, and included on the EU list of terrorist organisations as part of ETA.

KAS, Koordinadora Abertzale Socialista (Socialist Nationalist Coordinator): Organisation responsible for political coordination within the MLNV; promoted the KAS Alternative, which in the early years of Spain's transition set conditions for ETA to enter into negotiations with the state; later banned in Spain and included on EU terrorist list as part of ETA.

LAB, Langile Abertzaleen Batzordeak (Patriotic Workers Committees): Nationalist left union.

Lokarri: Established in 2006 as successor to Elkarri and a citizen network to promote peace, dialogue and reconciliation in the Basque Country; increasingly involved in the facilitation of international efforts through support of Currin, hosting of Aiete Conference and promotion of Social Forum.

MLNV, Movimiento de Liberación Nacional Vasco (Basque National Liberation Movement): Umbrella organisation embracing ETA and a wide range of other organisations that, while not practising armed violence, shared its goals.

PNV, Partido Nacionalista Vasco (Basque Nationalist Party): Centrist Basque nationalist party; alone or in coalition headed all Basque governments between 1980 and 2009, and again from 2012.

PP, Partido Popular (Popular Party): Conservative Spanish political party; headed governments from 1996–2004 and again from 2011.

PSC, Partido de los Socialistas de Cataluña (Catalan Socialist Party): Catalan expression of the PSOE.

GLOSSARY OF INDIVIDUALS AND ORGANISATIONS

PSE-EE, Partido Socialista de Euskadi—Euskadiko Ezquerra (Basque Socialist Party—Basque Left), frequently abbreviated to PSE: Basque expression of the PSOE; headed Basque government from 2009–2012.

PSOE, Partido Socialista Obrero Español (Spanish Socialist Workers' Party): Social democratic Spanish political party; headed governments from 1982–96 and 2004–11.

Sortu (To be born): Separatist and left-wing Basque political party, founded in February 2011 as the first party of the nationalist left openly to reject violence, and ETA's violence specifically; challenged in the courts, but eventually declared legal in June 2012; member of EH Bildu coalition.

UCD, Unión de Centro Democrático (Union of the Democratic Centre): Electoral coalition that governed Spain between 1977 to 1982.

UPyD, Unión, Progreso y Democracia (Union, Progress and Democracy): Political party that split from PSOE in 2007; strongly defends 'constitutionalist' positions against regional nationalism.

UPN, Unión del Pueblo Navarro (Navarrese People's Union): Conservative regional party in Navarre; until 2008 formally linked to PP; strongly opposed to Basque nationalism.

ENDGAME FOR ETA—A TIMELINE

1952	Ekin founded as a group to study and revive Basque nationalism.
1958	Euskadi 'ta Askatasuna (ETA) founded.
1959	ETA's formation announced.
1962–7	ETA evolves, and divides, in a series of assemblies.
1967	At the second session of its V Assembly, ETA establishes four 'fronts': political, cultural, military and economic.
1968	Txabi Etxebarrieta is both the first member of ETA to kill (José Pardines, a member of the Guardia Civil, his victim) and, shortly afterwards, the first to be killed. A state of exception is declared in Guipúzcoa.
1969	The Franco regime detains numerous ETA members as the strategy of action-repression-action takes hold.
1970	The Burgos trial generates anti-Franco protests and support for ETA. ETA's VI Assembly leads to a new division between the pro-worker ETA VI and the radical nationalist ETA V.
1973	December: ETA assassinates Luis Carrero Blanco, Franco's prime minister.
1974	Internal debate after ETA's attack on the Cafeteria Rolando contributes to a division between ETA *militar* (ETA-m) and ETA *político-militar* (ETA-pm).
1975	KAS is established as a coordinating body within radical Basque nationalism. The execution of two members of ETA-pm promotes widespread protests inside the Basque Country and internationally. On 20 November Franco dies.

1976   KAS introduces platform of minimum conditions for the participation of the MLNV emerging in ETA's orbit in the reform process.

1977   Talks between radical and moderate Basque nationalists at Txiberta fail to reach agreement. June: Spain holds general elections. October: The Spanish Parliament approves an amnesty law for all political prisoners. The two branches of ETA continue attacks.

1978   HB formed as a coalition of smaller radical nationalist parties and individuals. The KAS Alternative is introduced as a series of negotiating demands. September: A new Spanish constitution is approved in a referendum. The PNV calls for abstention; in Euskadi just 31 per cent of population vote in the constitution's favour.

1979   April: In municipal elections HB emerges as the second political force in Euskadi after the PNV. October: The Basque statute of autonomy is approved in a referendum, despite the opposition of ETA-m and HB.

1980   The institutions of the new Basque autonomous community take shape. ETA's military activity reaches its high point with ninety-two mortal victims.

1981   After the attempted coup of 23 February ETA-pm declares a ceasefire and begins its process of reinsertion. The AVT is formed.

1982   October: PSOE wins an absolute majority in general elections; Felipe González becomes prime minister.

1983   The GAL makes its first appearance. Between 1983 and 1987 it kills twenty-seven in a 'dirty war'.

1984   The French government begins to collaborate more closely with Spain in its struggle against ETA.

1986   Gesto por la Paz is established. ETA assassinates María Dolores González Catarain, *Yoyes*, a former *etarra* who had separated from the organisation. Spain joins the European Union.

1987   June: In European elections HB receives 363,000 votes, the highest number in its history, ETA explodes a car bomb in the Barcelona shopping centre Hipercor, killing twenty-one.

1988   January: Basque political parties—with the exception of HB—agree Pact of Ajuria Enea, establishing a consensual basis on which to address ETA's terrorism. COVITE is founded as the first organisation of Basque victims.

1989   January: ETA declares a ceasefire and opens talks with representatives of the government in Algiers. April: The process breaks down; ETA returns to violence; Spain begins the dispersion of ETA's prisoners.

1990   State secretary Rafael Vera visits ETA in the Dominican Republic on multiple occasions. Gernika Gogoratuz encourages the visit to the Basque Country of two US experts in conflict resolution.

1991   Gernika Gogoratuz and George Mason University hold retreat for Basque political actors on conflict resolution in Virgina, USA.

1992   March: French and Spanish police capture ETA leadership in Bidart, France. Efforts to pursue channels to ETA continue. December: Elkarri founded.

1993   October: PSOE wins its fourth general election, but with a minority government. November: Jonan Fernández (Elkarri) travels to Dominican Republic to meet with ETA. December: Downing Street Declaration issued by prime ministers of UK and Ireland.

1994   Juan Alberto Belloch becomes minister of the interior and reduces the channels to ETA. *Oldartzen* document developed by HB promises to 'socialise the suffering'.

1995   January: ETA assassinates Gregorio Ordoñez of the PP. March: Elkarri celebrates its first peace conference. April: ETA attempts to assassinate José María Aznar; introduces Democratic Alternative. Government pursues contacts with ETA via Adolfo Pérez Esquivel. Elkarri and PNV visit N. Ireland.

1996   March: PP wins general elections. Aznar becomes prime minister with the support of the CIU, PNV and CC.

1997   July: Guardia Civil liberates ETA kidnap victim José Antonio Ortega Lara; days later, ETA kidnaps and kills Miguel Ángel Blanco, triggering widespread protests. December: twenty-seven members of HB's central committee sentenced to prison (sentences revoked in 1999).

1998   ¡Basta Ya! and the Foro de Ermua established. March: Ardanza Plan launched. April: Good Friday Agreement signed in Belfast. July: Garzón orders closing of *Egin*, initiates *macroproceso* 18/98. September: Estella-Lizarra agreement signed; ETA announces 'unilateral and indefinite' ceasefire. October: In Basque parliamentary elections won by the PNV, nationalist left (EH) wins fourteen seats in appreciation of ETA's ceasefire.

1999   May: Representatives of Aznar meet with ETA in Switzerland. December: ETA declares its ceasefire to be over.

2000   January: ETA returns to violence, kills twenty-three in course of the year. March: PP wins general elections with an absolute majority. December: PP government agrees anti-terrorism pact with PSOE and initiates reforms to counter-terrorism legislation.

2001   February: Elkarri launches new peace conference. May: Bitterly contested Basque parliamentary elections hand big victory to PNV, EH drops from fourteen to seven seats. HB renamed Batasuna. Eguiguren and Otegi begin meeting in secret. September: Attacks on United States met with 'global war on terrorism' and accelerate counter-terrorist measures in Spain and across EU. Aralar established as new political party.

2002   March: PSE adopts more 'Basquist' direction at extraordinary congress. June: Parliament votes to approve new law on political parties. Alec Reid becomes regular presence in Basque Country. August: After double assassination by ETA, government asks Supreme Court to ban Batasuna. Garzón orders a three-year ban to take effect immediately.

2003   Spain joins UN Security Council; Aznar allies closely with Bush and Blair to support launch of Iraq war. Batasuna added to terrorist lists in EU and Unites States and, in June, banned in Spain under revised law on political parties. October: Ibarretxe Plan approved by Basque government. November: William Douglass travels to Basque Country for HD Centre. December: PSC enters Catalan government at head of leftist coalition.

2004   February: ETA announces a ceasefire in Catalonia. March: Bombs detonated in Madrid by Islamists kill 191; the PP government attributes attack to ETA. Days later, the PSOE wins general elections. José Luis Rodríguez Zapatero becomes prime minister, supported by IU and ERC. October: *Mikel Antza* and other ETA members detained. November: Otegi introduces the Anoeta Proposal. December: Ibarretxe Plan narrowly approved by Basque Parliament.

2005   February: Ibarretxe Plan rejected by Spanish Parliament. April: ETA announces it is trying to open a peace process; Ibarretxe returned to office by Basque parliamentary elections; EHAK wins nine seats. May: Spanish Parliament passes resolution—opposed by the PP—supporting dialogue with 'those who have decided to abandon violence'; Otegi is briefly imprisoned. June–July: Eguiguren and ETA hold talks in Geneva. September: Catalan Parliament approves new statute. November: Eguiguren and ETA hold talks in Oslo. During year, victims protest Zapatero's policies towards ETA in public demonstrations.

2006   January: Batasuna suspended for further two years. February: Supreme Court approves the Parot Doctrine. 22 March: ETA announces a permanent ceasefire. April: Otegi given fifteen-month prison sentence, suspended; Ahotsak formed; Alfredo Rubalcaba appointed interior minister. June: Catalan statute approved in referendum. ETA and government delegations meet in Geneva. Zapatero declares initiation of dialogue with ETA. July: PSE meets with Batasuna; PP breaks relations with government. August: ETA warns process in crisis. De Juana Chaos begins hunger strike. September Batasuna/PSE/PNV meetings at Loyola begin. ETA defiant at *Gudari Eguna* (Day of the Basque Soldier). ETA and government meet in Geneva. October: ETA steals 350 pistols and rifles in France. EU debates Basque process. ETA and government meet in atmosphere of crisis. November: Loyola talks break down. ETA and government meet in Oslo. December: Zapatero promises that next year the situation with ETA will be 'better than today'. ETA explodes a car bomb at Barajas airport the next day, killing two; the government declares the peace process 'finished'.

2007   February: ETA offers to restart talks. Supreme Court reduces De Juana's sentence and he is released on conditional liberty.

March: Government meets with ETA in Geneva; Iurrebaso arrested on the way to meeting. May: Some ANV lists allowed to contest Basque municipal elections. 14–22 May: Government, ETA, Batasuna and international observers meet in Geneva; talks break down; municipal and local elections held. June: ETA declares its ceasefire at an end; Otegi enters prison; Ibarretxe announces plans for a new popular consultation. October: twenty-three members of Batasuna detained. December: ETA kills two members of the Guardia Civil in Capbreton, France.

2008   March: ETA assassinates Isaías Carrasco, a former PSE councillor, two days before general elections that return PSOE and Zapatero to power. May: ETA leaders Thierry and Zuberbiola detained; ETA kills member of Guardia Civil. August: Otegi leaves prison. September: ETA kills Spanish army officer. November: ETA military commander Txeroki detained. Otegi re-emerges with interview in *Gara* proposing pro-independence 'block'. December: ETA kills Basque nationalist businessman Ignacio Uría.

2009   March: Basque elections lead to PSE-PP pact and installation in May of Patxi López as first non-nationalist *lehendakari*. June: Nationalist left (IA) endorses Iniciativa Internacionalista in European elections. ETA kills Eduardo Puelles of the national police. European Court of Human Rights (ECHR) dismisses Batasuna's challenge to its dissolution under the political parties' law. July: ETA marks 50th anniversary by bombing police barracks in Burgos and killing two officers in Mallorca. October: Otegi and others in IA detained and imprisoned on charges of reconstituting Batasuna as Bateragune. *Argitzen*, a new strategy document, is distributed. November: IA commits to Mitchell Principles in Alsasua Declaration. EA proposes pact among all pro-independence social and political forces.

2010   January: ETA attack on Kio Towers in Madrid is thwarted; ETA issues a statement claiming to adopt positions of IA as its own. February: After internal consultations, IA issues new document, *Zutik Euskal Herria*, cementing the process of change. March: ETA kills French policemen after car robbery. In Brussels Declaration promoted by Brian Currin, international figures call on ETA to declare a 'permanent, fully verified ceasefire'. May: ETA commander *Ata* detained. Zapatero secures parliamentary approval for unpopular austerity measures by one vote. June: EA and IA agree pro-independence pact. Constitutional Court issues verdict on Catalan statute. July: Catalans demonstrate in protest. September: ETA declares that it had ceased 'offensive armed actions' some months previously. Pro-independence and leftist forces issue Guernica Declaration, call upon ETA to declare permanent, unilateral and verifiable ceasefire. November: Currin announces creation of the International Contact Group (ICG). December: Victims present document outlining 'model for the end of ETA without impunity' to the government.

2011   January: ETA declares a general, permanent and verifiable ceasefire. February: Etxeberria and others present the statutes for Sortu. ICG visits the Basque Country. March: Supreme Court narrowly rejects statutes of Sortu. April: Zapatero announces he will stand down at end of second term. Pro-independence coalition Bildu formed, challenged by government. May: Supreme Court upholds government challenge, but ruling is overturned by Constitutional Court, allowing Bildu to contest municipal and local elections and win 25 per cent of vote. June: Otegi and others present robust defence at Bateragune trial. September: Otegi and Díez sentenced to ten years in prison each as 'leaders of ETA'; EPPK subscribes to the Guernica Declaration; Amaiur is launched as new electoral coalition; the International Verification Commission (IVC) visits the Basque Country for the first time. October: Ekin disbands; at Aiete Conference, Kofi Annan and other international leaders call upon ETA to declare definitive ceasefire and suggest the path ahead. Days later, ETA responds and declares the definitive end to its armed activity. November: PP wins general election with absolute majority. Mariano Rajoy becomes prime minister.

2012   January: 110,000 people demonstrate against penitentiary policy in Bilbao. IVC visits the Basque Country. February: Gesto por la Paz holds last public event. Political parties reach agreement in Spanish Parliament on a joint approach to the end of ETA. IA recognises 'pain and suffering caused' at public event in San Sebastián. March: ETA calls for greater implication of French government. May: IVC visits the Basque Country, communicates ETA's readiness to engage in dialogue. ETA announces it has named a negotiating commission. June: Sortu legalised by Constitutional Court. July: ECHR rules that Parot Doctrine is in violation of European Convention on Human Rights and orders the release of Inés del Río; Spain challenges ruling. October: PNV wins Basque parliamentary elections, with EH Bildu a strong second. Izaskun Lesaka, ETA's military leader, detained in France. November: In Catalan elections CiU buffeted but support for ERC rises.

2013   February: Political representatives of ETA expelled from Norway. IVC visits Basque Country and confirms impasse. Sortu holds constituent assembly. March: Lokarri and Bake Bidea host Social Forum. May: Recommendations of Social Forum released. July: ETA responds that the recommendations are a 'constructive contribution'. September: It is reported that ETA will begin to disarm at the end of the year. October, ECHR upholds its ruling on the Parot Doctrine; Del Río and other affected prisoners begin to be released. December: ETA's prisoners distance themselves from armed struggle, recognise the harm inflicted and pledge to pursue their release from prison through the Spanish legal system.

2014   January: Sixty-three released prisoners reaffirm commitment to the democratic process and assume responsibility for 'the consequences of the conflict'. February: The IVC visits the Basque Country, announces that it has verified the beginning of an unilateral process to put ETA's arms beyond use and is summoned to testify before the Audiencia Nacional. 1 March: ETA announces that it has begun to seal its weapons dumps and will decommission all its arms in 'to the end, to the last arsenal'.

INTRODUCTION

In September 2010, as I began writing this book, ETA announced a ceasefire. I remember thinking at the time that this was a simple sentence to write. A good opening for a book whose purposes appeared straightforward: to analyse a process that I believed would see the end of the last organised armed insurgency in Western Europe, to try to explain why it had taken so long, and to extract lessons from this experience that might be of relevance elsewhere. But as I wrote those thirteen words, I ground to a halt. Inevitably the explanations necessary to qualify ETA's statement and the reactions it had spawned plunged me into controversies surrounding what ETA was, and what an end to it might look like, as well as Spanish and Basque sensitivities regarding the capacities of outsiders to understand the issue.

The ceasefire announcement was recorded on a video given to the BBC in cloak-and-dagger circumstances redolent of a different era. Clive Myrie, a reporter with sources close to ETA from his past as BBC Europe Correspondent, received a visit in London from one of them. Over coffee, he was told that ETA was considering calling a halt to its armed struggle for an independent Basque state. If Myrie was interested, he could 'break the news to the world'. Thinking that this was 'an enormous scoop' being handed to him on a plate, Myrie replied that he was. A few days later, he received a pre-arranged text message—'it was good to see you in London'—and set off for the appointed rendezvous outside the Gare du Nord in Paris, where he was handed a video.[1]

The BBC released the video on 5 September 2010. Three figures sat behind a table wearing black robes, silky white hoods and black Basque berets. Their left arms were raised, covered fists clenched in a militant

1

salute. Behind them, an ETA flag was pinned against a dark back wall. Under the letters E T A—which stand for Euskadi 'ta Askatasuna, Basque Freedom or Liberty—was the organisation's symbol: a snake, representing politics, wrapped around an axe, representing violence. The two words *bietan jarrai*—'keep up with both' in the Basque language Euskera—were written beneath. ETA was a violent secessionist organisation that had long been included on terrorist lists within the United States and European Union (EU) and excoriated within Spain as a 'terrorist band'. It had been responsible for the killing of approximately 830 people over a forty-year period, the majority carried out after the death of General Francisco Franco in 1975 and the transition to democracy that followed it. These were serious individuals. But their appearance, with echoes of both the Klu Klux Klan and costume baddies from a school play, seemed quite out of place. Why, in 2010, with international attention focused on conflicts in Afghanistan and Iraq as well as the persistent threat represented by Al Qaeda and networked international terrorism, was ETA still with us?

ETA's message was (characteristically) convoluted, opaque and less than many had hoped for. Rather than the ceasefire that had been anticipated, ETA announced that it had ceased its 'offensive armed actions' some months previously. Indeed, ETA had not killed in Spain since the summer of 2009; its only mortal victim since that time had been a French policeman gunned down in March 2010 as ETA was surprised in a car robbery. The organisation made no reference to the permanence of the ceasefire, but hinted instead at its desire for new talks.

ETA's announcement was immediately rejected as insufficient by the Spanish government and Basque political parties, including the centrist Basque Nationalist Party (PNV). 'Insufficient', again, would be the judgement in January 2011 when ETA offered a new statement. This time it heralded a 'permanent, general and internationally verifiable ceasefire', maintaining as it did so that 'the solution will come through the democratic process with dialogue and negotiation as its tools'.[2] ETA had moved on from September, but its commitment was still circumscribed by a determination to resolve its core demands of 'territoriality'—shorthand for the unification of a single Basque homeland, Euskal Herria, comprising the three Spanish provinces that form the Basque Autonomous Community, or Euskadi, recognised by Spain's 1978 constitution, the Spanish province and autonomous community of Navarre, and three Basque provinces in France—and self-determination.

The government quickly dismissed both the need for international involvement and the idea that ETA was in a position to establish political conditions. Whatever disposition to negotiate with ETA there might once have been had long since been used up. In 2005 Prime Minister José Luis Rodríguez Zapatero, of the social-democratic Spanish Socialist Workers' Party (PSOE), had launched an ambitious peace process. For contemplating talks with ETA he had been accused by the opposition Popular Party (PP) of 'betraying the dead'—ETA's victims. ETA and his representatives had met in Geneva and Oslo in talks facilitated by a private peacemaking organisation, the Centre for Humanitarian Dialogue, or HD Centre. These had led ETA to offer its first 'permanent' ceasefire. But the optimism that had greeted the prospect of an end to nearly forty years of Basque violence had been dashed when, nine months later, the organisation exploded a massive car bomb in the car park of Madrid's Barajas airport, killing two Ecuadorians asleep in their van. Since then the government had insisted that there would be no more negotiations. The only news anyone wanted to hear from ETA was that of its own demise; few expected that ETA was ready to take a step that was tantamount to surrender.

Yet something very different was underway. Despite its shortfalls in the government's eyes, ETA's shift was genuine. And on 20 October 2011, just nine months later, ETA would declare the definitive end of its armed activity—an announcement that even sceptics recognised to be of signal importance in Spain's contemporary history. The declaration came in response to an appeal made by a group of international peacemakers led by the former UN Secretary-General Kofi Annan. These dignitaries had received no formal invitation for their involvement from the Spanish government. On the contrary, the sequence of events that led them to gather in the Aiete Palace in San Sebastián for a carefully choreographed 'international peace conference' to help bring to a close what they termed 'the last armed confrontation in Europe' remained distinctly hazy. Their presence and the wording of their appeal to ETA irritated many in Spain, who saw ETA's actions solely in terms of terrorism. (The right-wing newspaper *ABC* ran a cover photograph of the smiling peacemakers; its accompanying headline read: 'In the service of ETA.')[3] Yet their brief intervention seemed to do the trick. Members of the *izquierda abertzale*, the 'nationalist left' social and political movement that had long sustained ETA,[4] including the banned political party Batasuna, subscribed to the international appeal the next morning.

ETA's response came thirty-six hours later. Fifty-two years after its creation and forty-three years after it claimed its first mortal victim, ETA declared a 'definitive end' to its armed activity. ETA itself was still out there, albeit in reduced numbers; difficult issues—regarding disarmament, but also the fate of its prisoners, exiles and 'on-the-runs', as well as other aspects of reconciliation—remained to be addressed. But a page had been turned. 'We can now say that the transition in the Basque Country is over,' wrote Josep Ramoneda, a prominent Catalan intellectual, 'the doors are open to a democratic normality that the terrorist anomaly had made impossible.'[5]

How can this be?

This book is motivated by a drive to understand the continued existence of ETA well into the twenty-first century as well as an enduring curiosity about the factors that lead men and women to take up arms against their fellow citizens, perpetuate the violence that then ensues and then, eventually, end it. Running through it is the distant echo of the foundational question recorded by the Basque anthropologist Joseba Zulaika in 1975, as ETA's violence took hold: 'But how can that be?' The question was posed by women appalled to discover that the intricacies of social and political life in the small village of Itziar had escalated to include the killing of the local bus driver, well known within the village, but suspected by ETA militants of being a *chivato*, a police informer.[6] The question was in many respects unanswerable. For Basques attuned to nationalism that had until then been peaceable in pursuit of its objectives, the eruption of violence seemed literally unfathomable.

Over the years the persistence of violence was in some respects just as impenetrable to many Spaniards—an aberration perpetrated by terrorists and criminals that defied rational explanation, especially given the extensive powers granted Euskadi in the statute of autonomy agreed in 1979. For others, mainly Basques (but only some Basques), ETA's terrorism, however unacceptable, remained the violent expression of an unresolved political conflict with origins in the distant past. These differences, with more nuanced positions between them, influenced efforts to 'defeat ETA's terrorism' on the one hand and 'resolve the Basque conflict' on the other, as well as the narratives within which Basques of diverse identities sought 'peace and coexistence' once ETA's violence was no more.

4

Whatever the understanding of what ETA was, by the early 2000s the organisation had changed beyond recognition. It had been increasingly diminished by the efficacy of police action and dwindling support for its violence, even among those who supported its political goals. Yet although evidently in crisis in structural terms, it retained a presence as a concept—the embodiment of the most radical expression of Basque nationalist and separatist aspirations—that was quite out of proportion to its operational capacity.[7] Its existence was confirmed by its capacity to kill as that capacity to kill defined its existence. And the question first asked some thirty years earlier—'How can that be?'—shadowed Spain's inability to bring it to an end.

The tortuous process towards ETA's end dates back to the immediate aftermath of the death of Franco, when many had assumed that ETA would come to a natural conclusion. Instead, the years following Franco's death were the bloodiest in ETA's history. ETA's long agony saw the organisation experience schisms and controversies, and introduce changes in both the targeting of its violence and the strategies it adopted towards negotiations. Its actions were met by the increasingly effective counter-terrorism of Spanish and French security forces. This included the capture of ETA's leadership from a French farmhouse in Bidart in 1992; the robust application of Spanish criminal law, modified after September 2001 to facilitate the illegalisation of Batasuna and the prosecution of entities perceived to be linked to ETA's terrorism; and contradictory forces within Basque society that included both a slow but powerful mobilisation against ETA's violence and polarisation between Basque nationalists and pro-Spanish or 'constitutionalist' political forces. Despite perennial controversy surrounding the very idea of negotiation with ETA, three major attempts were made to arrive at a political solution. Each involved a ceasefire that subsequently broke down. Throughout, protestations that a succession of governments would never 'negotiate with terrorists' were accompanied by a variety of back-channel and other communications with ETA, some of them facilitated by foreign third parties.

Progress towards ETA's end is thus hardly an unqualified success story. Indeed, even as successive Spanish governments aggressively pursued the organisation's demise, some of their actions—most notoriously a 'dirty war' of the mid-1980s that was later tied to officials within Spain's interior ministry—proved counterproductive. The dispersion of Basque prisoners to prisons across Spain, the expansion of counter-terrorist legislation and Spain's reluctance to acknowledge or eradicate torture contributed to militant Basques' sense of victimisation. Meanwhile, ETA's systematic abuse of human rights through assassinations, kidnappings, threats and extortion poisoned the political life of the Basque Country. Decisions taken by ETA betrayed a callous disregard for human life and were based on a consistent overestimation of the concessions that it might prove possible to force upon a Spanish government at the negotiating table.

In 1997, ETA's kidnap and assassination of the young PP councillor Miguel Ángel Blanco prompted a massive and emotional condemnation of ETA's brutality. In its wake, the response to ETA assumed increasingly moral overtones.[8] Condemnation of ETA was entirely understandable, but a Manichean view of its evils that encouraged comparisons between the Basque Country and pre-Nazi Germany did not help frame sensible policies to counter it.[9] On the contrary, it encouraged a blurring of the lines between the violent and peaceable expressions of Basque nationalism and a hardening of divisions between Euskadi and Madrid. The PP government of José María Aznar drew support from unity in opposition to Basque terrorism and revived old battle lines between Spanish nationalism and the regional nationalisms of the Basque Country and Catalonia. A pan-Basque nationalist attempt at a peace process directly modelled on the emerging process in Northern Ireland secured a ceasefire from ETA in 1998, but at a terrible cost. Moderate Basque nationalists proved unable to deliver on the promises that ETA believed it had extracted from them, and when the ceasefire collapsed in 1999 political and social animosity across the different communities of the Basque Country was at an all-time high.

Aznar's counter-terrorist strategy found reinforcement from the 'global war on terrorism' launched after the attacks of 11 September 2001. Inside the Basque Country his rejection even of the idea of dialogue grated against many Basques' intimate experience of the conflict. 'The "terrorists" and the social environment surrounding them are not socially marginalised or pathological characters, nor abstract and distant external enemies who can be portrayed as the personification of evil', wrote Begoña Aretxaga, who was born and grew up in San Sebastián, 'the "terrorists" turn out to be one's neighbours, acquaintances or family members—people who are too close and whose lives we know, and who we cannot disregard so easily'.[10] 'Nobody or almost nobody justifies torture, violence against women or hatred against immigrants,' mused Patxi López, Euskadi's first non-nationalist president or *lehendakari* in early 2012, 'yet a peculiarity of our country has been that a part of its population until recently contextualised the fact that a terrorist organisation could assassinate a citizen for thinking differently or that many others lived under threat of death.'[11]

When an end to ETA's violence eventually appeared possible, it could be attributed to many factors. Foremost among them were the decimation of the organisation by successful police action against it in Spain and France, the intensity of the legal campaign against Batasuna and others associated with the nationalist left, and the widespread rejection of ETA's violence by Basque society. But the chapters that follow also suggest that it would not have been achieved without Zapatero's initiation of the peace process in 2005, the changes set in motion by Batasuna after this process' collapse in 2007 and limited but essential assistance by international actors. Leaders of the former Batasuna, most notably the party's spokesperson Arnaldo Otegi, embarked on a determined effort to pursue the goals of the nationalist left by peaceful and democratic means. To do so involved suasion of the movement's social and political bases, a constituency that had remained remarkably cohesive through years of ostracism and legal repression, as well as politically confronting ETA itself.

Batasuna's leaders and ETA drew upon the discreet support, advice and, at times, political cover provided by a variety of international facilitators. The outsiders' involvement was repeatedly disavowed by a government that denied the need for external assistance, or any activity that could be tarnished by accusations from Spain's political right wing that it constituted dialogue with ETA or those in its orbit. There was no international mediation in a conventional sense and no direct negotiations with ETA, the Spanish government claimed. But a combination of the confusing plethora of international actors involved and the extreme confidentiality within which some of them worked should not obscure the important contribution they made to what this book suggests was an innovative kind of direct, but also 'virtual' peacemaking.[12]

The virtual nature of the peacemaking responded to political necessity. It took place within a developed European state, and in this respect it is quite distinct from Oliver Richmond's introduction of the idea of 'virtual peace' to question the extent to which liberal models of post-conflict peacebuilding in developing countries mask 'deeper cultural, social, and economic realities of violence'.[13] However, limitations intrinsic to its virtual nature quickly became evident. Indeed as a new PP government, headed by Prime Minister Mariano Rajoy, took office, the ambiguities upon which the achievement of ETA's declaration rested contributed directly to the difficulties encountered in moving forwards from the end of violence to the disarmament and dissolution of ETA.

Why the Basques?

The low levels of violence and European location of the Basque case might suggest that it is foolhardy to embark on a book that seeks conclusions that may be relevant elsewhere. Spain's sensitivity to external involvement, its governments' denial of their reported negotiating efforts and rejection of the idea that ETA's violence be considered in any way related to a 'conflict' offer little encouragement. Indeed the high level of emotion the subject of Basque violence generates within Spain and a generalised assumption that contextual analysis of ETA's violence risks conferring legitimacy upon it both offer deterrents to the unwary outsider. No other European country, the historian Fernando García de Cortázar writes in his introduction to *Vidas Rotas*, 'Broken Lives', an encyclopaedic account of ETA's victims published in 2010, has had to combine the criminal actions of terrorists with 'the infamy of a discourse of justification which converts assassins into the incarnation of a "cause"'.[14] International mediators, observes Rogelio Alonso, the most widely published Spanish author on Basque terrorism in English, 'underestimate the different factors that distinguish ETA's terrorism from the violence perpetrated in other international conflicts where negotiations between the state and armed opposition have taken place'.[15] Yet there are aspects of the Basque case that can be seen in other conflicts where negotiations have occurred, but were at first denied, just as there are others that are quite unique to it.

Such controversies fuel my interest in the Basque case and its implications for other situations in which terrorist violence may be equally loathed, but is no less likely to have originated in, and be motivated by, a 'cause', and negotiations or engagement of another kind may indeed occur, even if publicly denied. An approach to ETA and the subject of

Basque violence from a perspective informed by experience elsewhere need not be so blinkered as to make direct parallels between cases that self-evidently differ widely. Requests for interviews with Spanish officials with experience of dialogue with armed groups in more traditional conflict environments—in El Salvador, Guatemala, the Middle East and Colombia—were brushed aside when it became clear that I was working on the Basque issue. I had to understand, Emilio Cassinello, an experienced diplomat and director of a Spanish foundation dedicated to conflict resolution, explained to me early on in my research, that ETA was different. These were not insurgents, or even just terrorists, but 'barbarians of the worst kind who almost ruined our transition'.[16]

There is no justification for ETA's violence in democratic Spain. But this cannot deter efforts to understand what had sustained it for so long and the forces that struggled to bring it to an end. Zapatero's policies towards ETA and the visceral opposition they found in the PP contributed to expose fissures in Spanish society that had remained open since the transition to democracy. Among them are the ambiguities at the core of the 1978 constitution's conception of the nature of the Spanish state, and the long-term costs of what Stephanie Golob has described as 'a transition without transitional justice'.[17] Beyond Spain, they also illustrated the challenges that face a democratic state in disentangling political violence it experiences as terrorism from the grievances that fuel it so as to allow the issues in contention to be addressed by peaceful means. This return to 'normal politics' was long ago identified by William Zartman as the 'elusive peace' by which internal conflict is settled, if not resolved.[18]

As I moved forward in my research, I came to appreciate the almost neuralgic sensitivity surrounding consideration of ETA as a political as well as violent actor. Some elements of this sensitivity reflect persistent fears that acknowledgement of ETA as a political actor implies justification that its demands should have been subject to political negotiation—something no Spanish government has ever accepted, nor outside facilitator advocated. Others hold the view that to speak of 'political violence' is to deny the true nature of the terrorism that ETA has perpetrated. More broadly Spaniards outside the Basque Country have struggled to accept that the problem presented by ETA was not so much ETA itself—an organisation that practised terrorist violence—but that the social and political movement behind it consistently found support from 20 to 25 per cent of voters in Guipúzcoa and 15 per cent in

Euskadi, with the potential for more, as the 2011 elections demonstrated, once violence had been put to one side. These are small numbers in terms of Spain as a whole, but in the quite distinct environment of Basque politics, they constitute a population that cannot be ignored.

I also began to see the protracted campaign against ETA in a comparative context that would allow my investigation to contribute to two related debates. The first debate addresses the risks and opportunities presented by engagement with armed groups proscribed as terrorist organisations. The second considers the costs and benefits of counter-terrorism for the democratic states that pursue it.

Governments and other actors have long engaged with insurgent, revolutionary and other groups whose activities could be described as terrorist. Indeed the list of former terrorists subsequently recognised as statesmen is a long one (from Menachem Begin through Nelson Mandela to Gerry Adams). Yet arguments against engagement—that it is unethical, presages unacceptable compromises with the morally repugnant, or at least implies a recognition that would legitimate the terrorist organisation—inhibited negotiations in a variety of cases, including between Israel and the Palestinian Liberation Organization, or France and the Algerian National Liberation Front. After September 2001 these arguments were reinforced by rhetoric and policy rooted in a universe of moral certainty: as the world rushed to respond to the attacks on the United States, other states were either 'with' or 'against' it in the war against terrorism. As Mitchell B. Reiss, President George W. Bush's former Northern Ireland envoy, would later observe, this approach left 'not much space for engaging terrorists'.[19] Doing so would not only grant legitimacy to extremists as terrorist actors, but undermine democratic principles upon which the United States and its allies were constructed. The Taliban was most definitely excluded from the Bonn Conference held in late 2001 after the US invasion of Afghanistan.

A proliferation of lists proscribing groups and individuals as terrorists and US legislation that made it a crime to provide 'material support'— defined to include 'expert advice or assistance', 'training' and 'services' to those identified as foreign terrorist groups even when such advice and support is for wholly peaceable ends[20]—both deterred engagement. The new environment also strengthened the hand of states such as Colombia, Israel, Russia and Sri Lanka who chose military options against enemies they classified as terrorist. The level of threat represented by ETA's violence at no time could be compared to such situations. Yet Spain was no exception to this trend. Aznar recognised that he shared Bush's belief in 'leadership based on rock-solid principles and values' and quickly appropriated the discourse of the 'war on terrorism' to reinforce his campaign against ETA. His controversial support of the US invasion of Iraq and close relationship with Bush helped propel Spaniards forward as 'moral leaders in the fight against terror'. This was a battle, as Aznar conceived it, in which the stakes could not have been higher: 'between freedom, democracy and civilisation on one side, and terror, fanaticism and totalitarianism on the other'.[21]

The restriction on engagement received reinforcement from a June 2010 ruling of the US Supreme Court that upheld the 'material support' statute. But cracks had already begun to appear in the edifice represented by the counter-terrorist consensus, as the proliferating literature on 'talking to terrorists' suggested.[22] The positive example of Northern Ireland—although criticised by a number of authors who caution against its overly literal appropriation for the Basque case[23]—was one basis for advocacy of the benefits of engagement, but it was not the only one. In Iraq the United States had found it necessary to engage with leaders of the Sunni insurgency. Elsewhere in the Middle East, representatives of numerous states and private organisations flocked to meet with listed groups such as Hamas and Hezbollah, even as resistance to such contacts by Israel and the United States, as well as the increasingly complicated political dynamics in the region, limited the possibilities for progress. In the post-Bush era, and especially in the wake of the upheavals generated by the Arab Spring of 2011, the reality of a rapidly evolving world and a diffusion of violence among ideologically motivated groups, criminal actors and others whose activities straddled the two, contributed to erode the certainties of the immediate post-9/11 moment. Decision makers appeared to recognise, as Chester Crocker observed, 'that leading states also require smart power tools (e.g., intelligence, diplomacy and mediation, assistance and capacity building, and peacebuilding in civil society) as well as kinetic and coercive power in order to address the challenge of global terrorism'.[24]

In Afghanistan, a growing awareness of the limitations of a military response to move discussion beyond whether to talk to the Taliban to consideration of when and how it should be done; back channel contacts through a variety of different tracks proliferated. In 2008, Lakhdar

Brahimi, who had led the negotiations for the United Nations in late 2001, openly recognised that the exclusion of the Taliban from the Bonn Conference had been a mistake.[25] After a flurry of activity in 2010, during 2011 the United States publicly admitted meetings with the Taliban, but also a meeting with the feared Haqqani network, which unlike the Taliban it had designated a foreign terrorist organisation.[26] Changes at the United Nations delinked the listing of individuals sanctioned as members of the Taliban from known Al Qaeda operatives. And after months of discreet diplomacy involving Pakistan, Qatar, but also Germany, Norway and the UK, in mid-2013 it was revealed that the United States was prepared to begin direct talks with Taliban leaders in Doha.[27]

Push-back from Afghan President Hamid Karzai complicated the opening of the talks, but the news itself—especially when considered in the light of US support for ongoing peace talks with the Revolutionary Armed Forces of Colombia (FARC) as well as between the Turkish government and the Kurdistan Workers' Party (PKK)—suggested renewed disposition to consider engagement between government actors and non-state armed groups, as well as growing space for understanding of the difference between 'talking' and 'negotiation'.[28] Talking to Al Qaeda itself remained unthinkable for many, but that it had been openly advocated even by the former head of Britain's M15 was another indication of the changing times.[29] In a landscape of terrorism that was characterised by the proliferation of Al Qaeda affiliates, many of them primarily driven by local concerns, the possibility of combining robust security measures and law enforcement with engagement with some of them could not, as Audrey Cronin argues in *How Terrorism Ends* (2009), be easily dismissed.[30]

A growing body of work has documented the complex impact of the exceptional legal and other measures introduced by democratic states in the interests of counter-terrorism.[31] Many such measures—like the threat of terrorism itself—long pre-dated 9/11. However the new era of counter-terrorism introduced significant changes. These included a rise in international co-operation against terrorism as well as the introduction of new domestic counter-terrorist legislation. With it came risks, as Martha Crenshaw suggests in the introduction to *The Consequences of Counterterrorism* (2010), that 'a government's response to terrorism will diminish democracy more than the acts of terrorism themselves'.[32] The

Obama administration promised a shift in tone on the issue of human rights in general terms as well as the retreat by the United States from some of the most egregious practices of the Bush era, epitomised by the abuses committed within the Abu Ghraib prison in Afghanistan as well as the practice of rendition. It made an auspicious start, as the new president signed executive orders to outlaw the CIA practice of secret detention and its overseas prisons and mandated the closing of the Guantánamo prison camp within a year. However, progress soon stalled.

Fundamentally, a generalised sense of threat—exacerbated by attacks on Madrid in 2004 and London in 2005 and the slow but steady pace of other incidents in the years that followed—had encouraged the emergence of a degree of acquiescence to trade-offs between liberty and security. Liberal democracies encounter difficult choices as they seek to safeguard national security without introducing measures so restrictive to individual civil liberties that they undermine the fabric of their governance. And terrorism, as Steven Pinker observes, 'has a cockeyed ratio of fear to harm'.[33] In state after state, with Spain among them, a hard line on issues related to terrorism either did not damage, or actually bolstered political support for incumbent governments, while the actual threat represented by terrorism—statistically almost insignificant in the West—was repeatedly exaggerated.[34]

Obama greatly increased the use of pilotless drone aircrafts to target and kill suspected terrorists, including US citizens. Critical voices were raised to challenge the legality of the drone attacks in foreign countries where there is no internationally recognised armed conflict. Yet the wide acclaim Obama had received for the successful operation against Osama bin Laden in May 2011 and the apparent success of the drones in weakening Al Qaeda's capacity helped to dull concerns throughout his first term in office. Only in mid-2013 did Obama promise new measures to institutionalise the practice. A few weeks later, revelations by Edward Snowden of widespread surveillance by the US National Security Agency (NSA) introduced the most fundamental questioning of the trade-off between civil liberties and national security seen in a decade.

The two debates intersect when we turn attention to the critical issue of how conflicts or terrorist campaigns end. A number of governments drew encouragement from what has been termed the 'Sri Lanka option': the defeat and destruction of an armed group by military means (albeit after a lengthy and frustrated peace process). However, the model set a dangerous precedent, not only for its violation of the most basic laws of war, but also for its failure to address most causes of the conflict, and its contribution to new sources of resentment. Just as military options against insurgents on their own rarely succeed in creating conditions that will foster sustainable peace, so robust security measures against terrorist organisations have proven effective in reducing the levels of violence, but less so in ending it conclusively on their own. Interviewed by *The Guardian* in May 2008, Sir Hugh Orde, at the time head of the police service in Northern Ireland, commented: 'If somebody can show me any terrorism campaign where it has been policed out, I'd be happy to read about it, because I can't think of one.'[35] Rather, as Cronin demonstrates, a mix of policies and pathways generally accompany the decline and demise of terrorist campaigns and organisations. 'Negotiations rarely end terrorism by themselves,' she found, 'but adroit diplomacy can be a great strategic tool for managing the decline of a campaign.'[36]

The Basque case offers an interesting vantage point on these issues for the exceptional claims made of it within Spain, for its long duration and for its location in a democratic European state. Engagement with ETA, on the surface, seemed to fail, while the pursuit of counter-terrorism measures, especially once co-operation with France was assured, had many successes. These had been evident in the gradual erosion of ETA's operational capacity and especially since the agreement by the PSOE and PP to an anti-terrorist pact in 2000. Very significantly, this was accompanied by a decline of popular support caused by increasing rejection of ETA's violence by the Basques in whose name it was purportedly carried out. Even the highly controversial step of banning Batasuna, which was in obvious contrast to the policies adopted by the British government towards Sinn Féin, received minimal criticism. This was an exceptional measure by any standard: Israel sought to ban Hamas but was thwarted by its Supreme Court; only Turkey's banning of political parties associated with the PKK is directly comparable to the Spanish case.[37] Yet in June 2009 the European Court of Human Rights went further than Spain's Supreme Court itself when it rejected an appeal by Batasuna and ruled that the party's banning had been in response to a 'pressing social need'.[38]

The chapters that follow suggest that this version of events presents only part of the picture. ETA's very duration, and the quite disproportionate impact it has had on the development of Spanish politics, both point to the failure of policies towards it. During Zapatero's years as prime minister, the organisation killed twelve people—equivalent to the death toll of a small bus crash—yet remained at the centre of political attention and controversy. By the time ETA announced the 'definitive end' to its violence in 2011, nearly twenty years had passed since its demise was first mooted in the aftermath of the Bidart captures and fifteen years since Aznar came to power in 1996 promising to secure its defeat. Counter-terrorism achieved much in the long struggle against ETA, but it also had its limits, and other factors need to be recognised. Pro-independence forces associated with the nationalist left won 25 per cent of the Basque vote in local elections in May 2011, demonstrating the deep importance of Basque political processes. The presence of international peacemakers in San Sebastián in October of that year was one indication that committed and discreet international efforts were also part of the story.

With the violence of ETA apparently out of the picture, and the political expression of radical Basque nationalism locked into a non-violent future by its return to democratic politics, Spain faced an extraordinary opportunity to bring the rump organisation that was ETA to an orderly end. The issues that remained—prisoners, disarmament, exiles and reconciliation—were delicate from a political and emotional perspective, especially given the vocal role played by some organisations of ETA's victims. At a technical level, however, they appeared quite manageable, especially given the existence of discreet international channels to ETA, ETA's willingness to take major steps forward and a broad tolerance within the nationalist left community for a gradual process, so long as it represented a process of some kind.

This, however, was not to transpire. Economic crisis swept Rajoy and the PP to a great electoral victory in November 2011. But the Spain they governed faced multiple institutional crises—including a surging pro-independence movement in Catalonia, rampant corruption and high levels of disillusion with Spain's institutions. The PP appropriated for itself the ambiguity that had surrounded the Aiete Conference and refused to engage with ETA either directly or through the good offices of international facilitators. Instead it continued to pursue and detain the small number of ETA militants still out there in the hope that it could force ETA into unconditional surrender and dissolution. ETA dug in and appeared to do nothing.

Attention turned once more to Basque politics. Regional elections held in October 2012 saw a victory of the PNV over the pro-independence coalition EH-Bildu, which won 25 per cent of the vote in a striking confirmation of the support for pro-independence forces. The Basque Socialists and the PP, both seen as 'Spanish' parties, secured very poor results. Iñigo Urkullu of the PNV became Basque president, or *lehendakari*, with the four main expressions of Basque political life for the first time represented in the Basque Parliament without the shadow of violence. Hopes were high that they might find a way towards peace, reconciliation and eventually the still outstanding settlement of differences with each other and with Madrid regarding the nature of their relationship to the Spanish and (for some Basques if not others) French states. But instead the PP chose a policy of confrontation.

Against the backdrop of the slow progression towards the disarmament of ETA and the dismantling of its military structures, *Endgame for ETA* concludes with a return to some core questions. What led ETA to last so long, and what can we extract from the mix of counter-terrorism and political measures deployed to contest it? What does the Basque experience teach us about the benefits and risks of engagement, of counter-terrorist discourse and legislation, and the wider question of the role of the legal system in a peace process? What role can third parties play in peacemaking when political sensitivities preclude the involvement of official mediators? What, in short, are the lessons of the Basque case?

Terrorism, conflict and the Basque case

That ETA had sought an international outlet for its statement in September 2010, rather than its usual channel of the pro-independence Basque newspaper *Gara*, irritated many within Spain. It exponentially increased press coverage of the news of ETA's not-quite ceasefire and implicitly granted it a degree of credibility that many felt it did not deserve. Worse still for some was the BBC's insistence on referring to ETA as a 'violent separatist group'. Articles appeared in the Spanish and Basque press denouncing the naïvety of the BBC. Its website was so inundated with complaints that it issued an explanation that referred to internal editorial guidelines. These cautioned against the labelling of groups as 'terrorist' on the grounds that 'the word "terrorist" itself can be a barrier rather than aid to understanding'.[39] Alonso was among those who took the opposite view, denouncing the BBC's refusal to use the term 'terrorist' in a submission to *The Guardian* as 'unacceptable, since it results in a distortion of reality and misinforms the public'.[40]

The dispute points to a core challenge in approaching ETA—how to identify it—with obvious bearing on both the difficulties encountered in trying to bring its activities to an end and analysis of these efforts. It merits attention, not least as a means of clarifying the use of the loaded word 'terrorism' within this book, as well as its relation to the broader question of the existence, or not, of a Basque 'conflict'.

Language itself has become part of the battlefield. A Basque who refers openly to the existence of a 'conflict', even if only to try to explain the relationship of ETA to the distinct 'political conflict' with Madrid, may vehemently oppose ETA's violence—which at least since the late 1980s has been generally referred to as 'terrorist' even by moderate Basque nationalists—but he or she will most likely be of nationalist inclination. A pro-Spanish or constitutionalist individual will refer to the political aspects of the Basque problem as 'contentious', but in most situations go to great lengths to avoid the use of the word 'conflict'—on grounds that there is only one 'band', or armed group—even as he or she may refer in the same breath to the 'battle' or 'war' against ETA's terrorism and exhort the clear identification of 'winners' and 'losers'. This approach leaves several questions unanswered. If ETA is a small terrorist group and nothing else, like the Red Brigades, why was it able to maintain itself, and retain significant support, for half a century? And why does a pro-independence coalition, the largest party of which had clear ties to ETA, win a quarter of the Basque vote? There are political and social aspects to the Basque issue that simply calling ETA 'terrorist' does not explain.

In *Terrorism: How to Respond* (2009) Richard English describes terrorism as a method or tactic, deployed for a variety of purposes by individuals or armed groups who perceive themselves to be engaged in a form of war.[41] This is true of organisations as diverse as the African National Congress (ANC), the Red Brigades, the FARC, the Irish Republican Army (IRA), Hamas, Begin's Irgun, the Liberation Tigers of Tamil Eelam (LTTE) or Al Qaeda, and certainly in the case of ETA, which in the early 1960s declared itself to be engaged in 'revolutionary war' before it had killed a single person.[42] In each instance an understanding of the conditions in which terrorism is used and acceptance that it does have strategic purposes is a necessary basis for analysis of the phenomenon, and the first step to formulating a response.

The problem is the word 'terrorism' itself. There is no agreed definition of what it means, and thus it is inevitably confusing. But it is also, as Adam Roberts observes, a word that is both dangerous, because of its pejorative connotations, and indispensable, because terrorism exists as a serious threat.[43] Contrasting definitions of terrorism are to be found within different departments of the US government, in the foreign policies of individual states and as articulated by multilateral organisations such as the EU. During the extraordinary session it held in September 2005, the United Nations (UN) failed to arrive at an agreed definition of terrorism, in part because of member state differences over whether states as well as non-state actors could be responsible for its perpetration. The United States, the UN, other international organisations and a variety of states maintain lists of individual terrorists and terrorist groups. However, the criterion for inclusion on them is notoriously inconsistent and inherently political. It thus offers little assistance to the beleaguered researcher seeking guidance on the question of definition.[44]

For the UN—like Spain, whose criminal code defines terrorist offences but not terrorism itself—it has proven easier to think about terrorist acts than the abstract concept of 'terrorism'. UN Security Council resolution 1566 of October 2004 comes close to a definition of acts of terrorism in its characterisation of criminal acts that: (a) are committed against members of the general population, or segments of it, with the intention of causing death or serious bodily injury, or the taking of hostages; (b) have as their purpose to provoke a state of terror, intimidate a population, or compel a government or international organisation to do or abstain from doing any act; and (c) correspond to all elements of a serious crime as defined by the law. The use of the word 'terrorism' within this book reflects an understanding that those who commit acts consistent with these three criteria engage in terrorism. Such acts, the Security Council maintains, 'are under no circumstances justifiable by considerations of a political, philosophical, ideological, racial, ethnic, religious or other similar nature'.[45]

Beyond the discrepancies surrounding what terrorism is lie its negative connotations. Words matter in the waging of war and winning of peace, as well as in its analysis, and few have the capacity to distort perspectives so comprehensively. The terrorist, as Joseba Zulaika and

William Douglass put it in their study *Terror and Taboo*, published in 1996, 'becomes the paradigm of inhuman bestiality, the quintessential proscribed or tabooed figure of our times'.[46] No one likes to be called a terrorist, or would conceive their own struggle in such terms. Many professional mediators deliberately avoid use of the word without condoning the crimes committed in the course of a conflict or terrorist campaign. Some scholars of insurgent and other armed groups take a similar path and join Marianne Heiberg, Brendan O'Leary and John Tirman, in their edited volume, *Terror, Insurgency and the State* (2007), in their view that labelling insurgent organisations 'simply as "terrorist" blocks understanding and intelligent policy'.[47] Others, more attuned to the analysis of state decisions, or development of lessons for state consumption, follow William Zartman and Guy Olivier Faure in their volume *Engaging Extremists* (2011) in accepting that the term 'terrorist' means 'any movement termed "terrorist" by the state'—without limiting their analysis to this one dimension.[48] In *Endgame for ETA* I acknowledge that ETA clearly and consistently employed terrorism as a method, but I also maintain that this fact alone does little to further our understanding of its long duration and the difficulties encountered in persuading it to channel its grievances through the democratic process.

A related question is the extent to which ETA's terrorism should be considered the violent expression of a wider 'Basque conflict'. Sensitivity to the existence of a conflict is not unique to the Basque case, but a frequent occurrence in situations of internal conflict asymmetry between a state and a non-state armed group. Governments in Colombia (notably that of Álvaro Uribe), Peru, Sri Lanka and elsewhere have repeatedly insisted that the challenge to state authority they encounter be framed in terms of terrorism. Northern Ireland had its 'troubles' long before it became acceptable to speak in Britain about the Northern Irish 'conflict'. The issue is especially delicate in Spain, however, due to both a particular pride (tinged with a degree of insecurity) in the country's newly minted democracy and the extreme asymmetry represented by the low level of ETA's violence, and comparatively moderate and un-militarised response to it by the Spanish state.

Governments seek not to elevate or dignify the armed group, or groups, that oppose them with the recognition that they are engaged in armed conflict for a variety of reasons. Most immediately, it raises the problem above a matter of internal security that can be appropriately

handled by national actors and institutions. In legal terms, the designation of an 'armed conflict' has significant repercussions, as it triggers the
application of international humanitarian law as conceived in the
Geneva Conventions of 1949 and their Additional Protocols. At a
political level, meanwhile, it introduces the idea of equivalence between
conflict parties and therefore can be interpreted to impart a degree of
legitimacy to the armed group and its grievances. These, in turn, may
open the door to dialogue and negotiation—and thus the demand for
compromises to be made.[49]

There are at least two levels to the discussion of whether what is sometimes euphemistically referred to as the 'Basque problem' constitutes a
conflict. One relates to whether, even in the absence of violence, it is
correct to understand Basque nationalism—and by implication Catalan
or Galician nationalism as well—as being in 'conflict' with those
Basques and Spaniards who oppose the recognition of the Basque people
as a nation. Nearly forty years after the death of Franco, with support
for the independence of Catalonia running at an all-time high and
Basque nationalists claiming their 'right to decide' on a new status, it
would seem difficult to deny that there does indeed exist 'a serious disagreement or argument, typically a protracted one' or 'a serious incompatibility between two or more opinions, principles, or interests', as the
Oxford English Dictionary defines 'conflict'. Additional definitions
include 'a prolonged armed struggle' and 'a state of mind in which a
person experiences a clash of opposing feelings or needs'. Such political
conflict is, of course, an unremarkable occurrence: non-violent conflicts
are addressed by political means the world over, and the Spanish legal
and constitutional system is, if Spaniards so wished, well equipped with
the instruments to do so in this case as well.

But to move from acknowledgement of these underlying conflicts to
consideration of ETA as the protagonist of an 'armed conflict' is more
problematic. The concept of non-international armed conflict in humanitarian law is developed in common in Article 3 of the Geneva
Conventions and Article 1 of Additional Protocol II of 1977. Together
they determine that armed conflict 'not of international character' takes
places when at least one of the parties involved is not a government and
violence reaches a level distinct from 'situations of internal disturbances
and tensions, such as riots, isolated and sporadic acts of violence and
other acts of a similar nature' to which international humanitarian law

does not apply.[50] Case law, and in particular that practised by the International Criminal Tribunal for the former Yugoslavia (ICTY), has established that this level is reached when 'protracted armed violence' can be determined, assessed on the basis of the intensity of the violence and the organisation of the parties.[51] The ICTY introduced indicative data to help in this determination. But that some of the criteria (for example, the level of organisation of ETA) could be used to support the recognition of the Basque case as an armed conflict while others (the level of violence has not necessitated the mobilisation of Spain's army) could not, suggests that each side in the debate might find grounds to support their pre-existing position, and its resolution would not be forthcoming.[52]

Perhaps because it is far distant from the emotions and political sensitivities that determine the language, meaning and policies surrounding ETA's violence in Spain, it is helpful to turn to the cool rigour of Sweden's Uppsala Conflict Data Program (UCDP) for clarification. UCDP defines armed conflict as 'a contested incompatibility that concerns government and/or territory where the use of armed force between two parties, of which at least one is the government of a state, results in at least 25 battle-related deaths in a calendar year'. An understanding of battle-related deaths as 'armed conflict behaviour between warring parties… directly related to the incompatibility, i.e. carried out with the purpose of realising the goal of the incompatibility and resulting in deaths', explains the inclusion of the conflict between the Spanish government and ETA on the UCDP database during the years 1978–82, 1985–7 and 1991–2.[53]

The framing of the problem of ETA's violence exclusively in terms of 'terrorism'—pushing to one side its relationship to the 'basic incompatibility' that is at the heart of the conflict—has favoured a response whose dominant framework has been 'counter-terrorism'. But as the chapters that follow suggest, it has been a hard line to maintain. No one has ever challenged the ideological origins and political goals of ETA. Before 2012, all Spanish governments embarked upon talks or dialogue that implicitly accepted the existence of a conflict of some sort. In each case a failure to agree on the nature and scope of the problem to be addressed—ETA's terrorism or the Basque conflict writ large—proved a fundamental obstacle to their progression. For this reason, *Endgame for ETA* must start at the beginning, with a brief introduction to the long history of 'the Basque problem', and ETA's irruption within it.

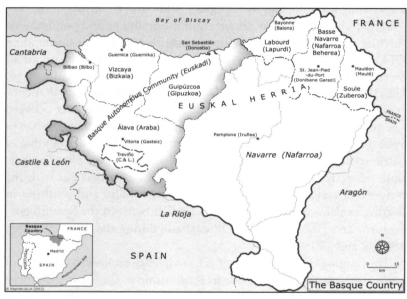

The legal and cultural geography of the Basque Country

1

THE BASQUE PROBLEM AND ETA

The Basque Country quickly induces a peculiar and quite distinctive kind of vertigo. Prosperous, self-confident and socially progressive, in many respects it represents a remarkable success. A glossy handbook produced by the Basque nationalist government in January 2009 identified Euskal Herria, the 'land of the Basque speakers', as 'a small ancient country with a strong identity and its own culture and history'.[1] Within its contours, the Basque Autonomous Community, or Euskadi, has since Spain's transition enjoyed a high degree of autonomy. It is responsible for its own taxation, education and health system, has its own police force, is zealous in the promotion of Euskera and has maintained a gross domestic product well above the Spanish average. Yet ETA and its complex relationship to an underlying 'Basque problem' with two distinct dimensions—the differences among Basques and between Basques and Madrid regarding the nature of the relationship between the Basque Country and the contemporary Spanish state—had contributed to high degrees of political polarisation and, at times, hostility. Even with its capacity to kill dramatically reduced, the armed organisation represented a defining element of Basque life.

The relationship of Euskal Herria, the territory straddling the Pyrenees that Basque nationalists claim as a homeland, to the two states, France and Spain, that hold its seven distinct administrative units, lies at the core of the dispute. The Basque government handbook did not mention the heated debates surrounding the origins of the Basques that swirl around early Basque history.[2] Yet references to Paleolithic remains and Cro-Magnon cave paintings introduce a sense of the extraordinary lengths of time that Basque forefathers had inhabited this particular corner of Europe. From these distant roots Euskal Herria had grown to a total population of approximately three million. Of these, the three Spanish provinces that compose Euskadi—Álava (Araba in Euskera), Guipúzcoa (Gipuzcoa) and Vizcaya (Bizkaia)—together accounted for 72 per cent or 2.1 million, some 4.8 per cent of that of Spain. The remaining population was divided between Navarre (Nafarroa), which nationalists claim with Euskadi as the Spanish Basque territory, or Hegoalde, with 19 per cent, and the three French Basque provinces—Basse Navarre, Labourd and Soule (Lapurdi, Nafarroa Beherea and Zuberoa)—or Iparralde, in the *département* of Pyrénées Atlantiques, with 9 per cent.[3]

The early consolidation of a centralised French state, assimilation of the Basques and relatively low levels of nationalist sentiment in the French Basque territories have placed the core of the Basque drama in Spain. There the emergence of ETA as a violent separatist group—in contrast to the largely peaceable trajectory taken by Catalan nationalism (the exception being Terra Lliure, a small separatist group that initiated armed activities in 1979, but claimed only one mortal victim before its renunciation of violence in 1991)[4]—can be traced to the complex inter-action of the distinctive form of Basque nationalism forged in Vizcaya by Sabino Arana in the latter part of the nineteenth century with the exceptional conditions created by Franco's repression of Basque identity during and after the Civil War. 'The phenomenon of ETA,' as the historian Gurutz Jáuregui has put it, is the product of these two intimately related factors: 'on the one hand Sabinian nationalism, whose funda-mental element is the consideration of Euskadi as an occupied country, and on the other, Francosim, which made such an occupation effective and real'.[5]

After Franco's death, ETA and its supporters advocated a complete break (*ruptura*) with the past rather than the agreed reform (*reforma*) that transpired. They saw a double betrayal of the Basque cause in the democratic opposition's departure from an earlier commitment to self-determination for Spain's historic nationalities and the acquiescence of the Basque Nationalist Party (PNV) to the creation of a Basque autono-mous community that did not include Navarre. Hopes that Spain's transition to democracy might undercut the rationale for ETA's existence were therefore not borne out. Instead the process by which both the constitution and the Basque statute of autonomy were approved was accompanied by a dramatic escalation in ETA's violence. ETA and the radical nationalists in its orbit held Spanish democracy to be illegitimate, Basque autonomy to be insufficient and concessions made to the Spanish right in the discussions that had preceded them to be altogether unacceptable. The violence kept going, and the transition itself remained a matter of 'unfinished business' for this community, even as the vast majority of Spaniards saw ETA as its most aggressive spoiler.[6]

In Euskadi

Euskadi in 2009 was an established autonomous community with a complex and decentralised system of government. It had benefitted from the generous terms of the Basque statute, even if its competencies had not yet been implemented to the full satisfaction of its government. Coalition governments led by the PNV had emerged from a painful and violent transition, moving away from an economy hampered by soaring unemployment and a dependency on outdated heavy industry to a more diversified economic model that mixed services with light industry. In this process the PNV had at critical moments found strength from the bargaining power its representation in Madrid's parliament gave it with Spain's minority governments.[7] In time the resilience of the Basque economy, and its reputation for innovative research and development, began to attract admiring attention. Upon leaving government in 2009, the former *lehendakari* Juan José Ibarretxe found support in the United States for a study that presented the Basque experience as a model for sustainable human development elsewhere.[8]

Yet the evidence of success in the social and economic data assiduously collected by the Basque government told but one side of a complex story. While the Basque Country prospered, its politics had been corroded by ETA's violence and vehement criticism of the complex relationship that this bore to mainstream nationalism. Prior to his departure from government Ibarretxe was one of the most controversial political figures in Spain, not least for his proposal of an ambitious plan for a new relationship of 'free association' and co-sovereignty for the Basque Country with the Spanish state.[9] The Basque Parliament narrowly approved it in late 2004, thanks to partial support offered by Batasuna. But Spain's Parliament rejected it overwhelmingly in early 2005 amid accusations that it violated the constitution and represented the 'ideological triumph of ETA'.[10]

Euskadi's three provinces had long enjoyed considerable administrative autonomy from each other. Indeed despite nationalist aspirations for the independence of Euskal Herria, Basques had to look back to the eleventh century to find the one brief moment when they could claim that all their territories had come under a single political administration—and even then the geographical space filled had been distinct. In 1029 Sancho III, 'the Great', had incorporated both the Basque territory south of the Pyrenees and some Basque-speaking lands to the north into the kingdom of Navarre. After his death in 1034 this extensive domain was divided among his sons into four distinct territories. Castile and Aragón emerged as new kingdoms, while the diminished Navarre became increasingly isolated. By the end of the twelfth century the three western Basque territories all came under the authority of Castile.[11]

Eight centuries later, Euskadi led Spain's seventeen autonomous communities in GDP per capita and was rated third in terms of standard of living after Madrid and Navarre.[12] Each province levied direct and indirect taxes, passing 70 per cent on to the Basque government in Vitoria where they formed the basis of the Basque budget. This considerable degree of fiscal autonomy was framed within an economic agreement, the *concierto económico*, that dates back to the nineteenth century and originally to medieval customs or *fueros* defended as an integral aspect of Basque political and cultural identity.[13] The terms of the *concierto económico* were unique to Euskadi and Navarre (which has a parallel agreement known as the *convenio*). They specified that Basques would pay a quota to Madrid set at 6.24 per cent of Spain's national expenditure to cover services such as foreign affairs, defence and social security. This system has favoured Euskadi in ways that exacerbated economic disparity with the rest of Spain and allowed the Basque government to extend the reach of its autonomy.[14] Catalan nationalists have made demands for an equivalent arrangement, but given the size and wealth of Catalonia—its population is 7.5 million, more than one in six Spaniards, and its economy comparable to that of Portugal—they have met adamant resistance from Madrid.

Euskera, the pre-Indo European language that is the defining element in Basque identity, was recognised as an official language—with

Spanish—within Euskadi, and in the northern parts of Navarre. Successive Basque governments promoted its use within the Basque education system and government as well as its central place within cultural traditions. Euskera's unique features and complexity represent an obvious contrast to Catalan, whose Mediterranean origins allow it to be readily acquired by Spanish or French speakers alike. By 2009 some 35 per cent of Euskadi spoke Euskera fluently and approximately 50 per cent understood it.[15] However its social use remained more limited by the ubiquity of Spanish. Meanwhile, the politics of language were complicated by tensions between Euskera as signifier of nationalist sentiment and its presence and use within Basque society more broadly conceived.[16] Particularly grating have been regulations that determine that only Euskera-speakers, *euskaldunes*, can work for Basque institutions, limiting opportunities for the two-thirds of the population fluent only in Castilian Spanish.

Basque political life is characterised by what Francisco Llera Ramo, the director of *Euskobarómetro*, an influential series of opinion polls carried out by the University of the Basque Country, describes as 'polarised pluralism'.[17] Beneath the apparent stability of the governments led by the PNV between 1980 and 2009, Basque politics was highly fragmented. Political differences were rooted in divisions between Basque nationalists and what Llera terms 'non-nationalists', of roughly equal numbers, as well as ideological variation. They were complicated by the great diversity—with regard to Basque descent, the speaking of Euskera, social class and rural/urban origin—within them, as well as the multiplicity of Basque political parties. The pro-Spanish, or non-nationalist, population generally supported the arrangements for regional autonomy introduced at the time of Spain's transition to democracy. Basque nationalists, meanwhile, broadly championed their right to self-determination (often framed as the 'right to decide') and pursued options that ranged from reform of the statute of autonomy to allow a looser association of Euskadi with Spain to full independence. Radical nationalists in the 'nationalist left' sought the independence of Euskal Herria and accepted, or at least would not publicly condemn, the use by ETA of terrorist violence as a means to achieve it. Those who favoured Basque independence oscillated over the years between 25–41 per cent, to settle by the late 2000s at approximately one in three Basques.[18]

An average of seven political parties disputed the seventy-five seats in the Basque Parliament at any time. In the period before the March 2009 elections ended the PNV's long rule, two of these seven parties were the Basque representatives of Spain's major national parties, the PSE and the PP, and a third, Ezker Batua, that of the small leftist party, United Left (EB-IU). Basque Solidarity (Eusko Alkartasuna, EA), a nationalist party that had splintered from the PNV in 1986, ran on a combined ticket with the PNV; the Communist Party of the Basque Homelands (Euskal Herrialdeetako Alderdi Komunista, EHAK) was a surrogate for the banned Batasuna, while Aralar was a new party that had splintered away from Batasuna after its explicit rejection of violence in 2001.

Basque society is further characterised both by perceptions of identity that—quite naturally—do not follow political party lines, and a highly mobilised civil society. The polls Llera had conducted since the transition revealed the prevalence of plural identities, with a majority of Basques also feeling Spanish to some degree. As elsewhere in Spain, autonomy itself—like devolution in Scotland or Quebec—had strengthened both regional identification and demands for greater autonomy.[19] In late 2010 56 per cent of Basques identified as a mix of Basque and Spanish, even as a large minority proclaimed themselves 'only Basque' (31 per cent) and a small minority identified as 'only Spanish' (8 per cent).[20] Of these diverse members of Basque society, large numbers actively participate in unions, political and cultural associations, women's and youth groups, co-operatives and ecological groups, gastronomic or sporting clubs, or other forms of organisation. This level of social mobilisation offered a contrast to the relative social and political apathy seen elsewhere in Spain.[21] It reflected an associative culture and tradition that has facilitated both the frequent mobilisation of large numbers of people onto the Basque street, and the endurance of the underground networks required to support a clandestine organisation such as ETA.[22]

The shadow of violence

The high degree of autonomy and the quality of life enjoyed by Basques sat uneasily with the persistence of violence and the tensions that underlay it. By the late 2000s, the rare drama of an ETA killing caused the spontaneous eruption of the Basque and Spanish media into a cacophony of denunciation; mini-dramas were created by each ETA statement or news of new arrests. Yet despite the apparent 'noise' of political opinions, silence on fundamental political issues that divide many Basques weighed heavily. The November 2009 *Euskobarómetro* poll found that some 49 per cent of respondents were either 'somewhat' or 'very' frightened to participate in politics, even as 35 per cent described themselves as unable to discuss politics freely with anyone and 39 per cent as able to do so only with 'some people'.[23]

ETA's violence oscillated in intensity over the years, but between 1968 and 2011 the organisation claimed approximately 830 lives, wounded more than 2,500 more and kidnapped almost eighty individuals.[24] The level of violence had been low during much of the 1990s, and ETA had no mortal victims between 2003 and late 2006. But forty years of killing and the attendant effects of extortion and the threat of physical violence had a profound impact on Basque society.

During the 1990s ETA's violence had taken new and disturbing directions as targets for assassination shifted from a preponderance of those associated with Spanish security forces to include politicians, local authorities, businessmen, academics and journalists.[25] Beyond those subjected to physical attacks were the several thousand who had been threatened and forced to curtail their activities, live with bodyguards and/or leave the Basque Country altogether, as well as the numerous businesses subjected to extortion. In the meantime, a new generation of radicalised youth embarked on a distinct form of urban street violence, *kale borroka*. This derived from the rioting that had broken out to protest against the police's violent disruption of peaceful demonstrations in the 1970s and early 1980s, but in the early 1990s assumed new forms and expression: the aggressive attack upon the Basque police and sabotage of public property such as government and court buildings, buses, rubbish bins and ATM machines with Molotov cocktails and other improvised weapons. It claimed twenty-six mortal victims, according to Spanish government figures, and contributed to high levels of social anxiety, threatening in itself, but also because the hundreds of youths it attracted were perceived as likely recruits of ETA.[26]

Extortion is estimated by Mikel Buesa, a prominent figure within Spain's antiterrorist struggle after his brother was killed by ETA in 2000, to have brought ETA approximately 3.8 million euros a year between 1993 and 2002 and 1.9 million euros a year between 2003 and 2008.[27] (In a later publication he estimated extortion and kidnapping combined to have brought in a minimum of 115 million euros at 2002 prices over the thirty-year period between 1978–2008.)[28] There has been no official verification of these figures, and it is equally hard to gauge other economic impacts of ETA's violence due to the difficulty involved in estimating the amounts lost by the flow of both population and investment away from the Basque Country, among other factors. A 1996 study on the effects of terrorism in Spain, including by groups other than ETA (the Anticapitalist Autonomous Commandos, CAA, that had splintered from ETA; the small Basque Trotskyist group, Iraulza; the Maoist-inspired First of October Anti-Fascist Resistance Group, GRAPO; and Terra Lliure), found that between 1968 and 1991 terrorism reduced net foreign direct investment in Spain by 13.5 per cent.[29] Alberto Abadie and Javier Gardeazabal developed a model that suggested that after the 'outbreak of terrorism' in the late 1960s in the Basque Country, per capita GDP declined by about 10 per cent.[30] Buesa calculated the costs to Spain of ETA's terrorist violence by combining costs associated with personal damages, pensions given to victims, material damages and security costs borne by the state. Between 1993 and 2008 these totalled just under 700 million euros a year.[31]

ETA and the broader radical nationalist community had an acute sense that they too were victims of violence and aggression. A 2010 report by Euskal Memoria, a new foundation associated with the nationalist left, documented 474 deaths between 1960 and 2010 as a consequence of extrajudicial assassinations, violent encounters with state forces or other (collateral) circumstances such as traffic accidents on the way to visit imprisoned family members that it also attributed to 'repression'.[32] The more rigorous analysis conducted by independent experts in a study of human rights violations commissioned by the Basque government in early 2013 found that those killed by agents of the state (ninety-four) or extreme right and para-police groups (seventy-three) in relation to the Basque case numbered 167, with seventy-seven cases still requiring investigation. Approximately 1,172 individuals had been wounded and 40,000 detained by the police, if only 10,000 were eventually charged with crimes related to ETA.[33] Most notoriously, in the mid-1980s a 'dirty war' conducted by a shady anti-terrorist organisation (Grupos Antiterroristas de Liberación, GAL), later proven to have direct ties to senior officials of the Socialist government, claimed twenty-seven lives, a third not associated with ETA.[34] Over the years the alleged ill-treatment and torture of ETA prisoners to extract confessions had been regularly denounced by international human rights organisations, as well as within the Basque Country, leading the authors of the Basque government study to recommend the separate investigation of 5,500 denunciations of torture.[35] Human rights groups had also questioned the dispersion of political prisoners to locations far removed from their families—in early 2010 there were 736 Basque political prisoners held in eighty-eight prisons in Spain and France[36]—as well as the sustained legal assault on the media and other organisations perceived to be sympathetic to ETA.

By the late 2000s a sense of fatigue coloured discussion of the persistence of ETA. With the onset of the financial crisis in 2009, unemployment emerged as a far more pressing concern. Yet conversations could still swirl back and forth between grievances of the Spanish Civil War, the bloody Carlist Wars of the nineteenth century, ETA and the long years of Franco's rule with disconcerting ease. Jesús Eguiguren, president of the PSE, exemplified a politician whose thirty years of political activity had been conducted in the shadow of ETA's violence. He had many friends and colleagues among its victims and had laboured long and courageously to find, if not a 'solution' to the Basque problem, then what he terms '*un arreglo*'—its 'settlement' through a series of incremental agreements.[37] From a small Euskera-speaking village in Guipúzcoa, Eguiguren had studied and taught Spanish constitutional law. In 2008, he warned against the difficulty that outsiders have in understanding both the intimacy of Basque politics ('we all know each other—we went to school together, are related, know who has killed who') and underlined the need to approach current events within a historical context. 'The last vestiges of the Civil War,' as he put it, 'are still being contested here in the Basque Country.'[38]

The narrow streets of San Sebastián's *casco viejo*, or historic centre, are crowded with shops, bars and restaurants, and had long been a theatre of action for ETA and its supporters. In 1995 the organisation assassinated the PP politician Gregorio Ordóñez while he was eating at a local restaurant. In 2009 the area remained off limits to politicians—like Eguiguren—and others viewed as potential targets for ETA. At one of the busy cafés that line the boulevard on its edge, I met in late July with José Luis Álvarez Enparantza, *Txillardegi*, one of the organisation's founders fifty years earlier. At the next table a group of French tourists discussed their options for the evening ahead, among them a choice of concerts in San Sebastián's International Jazz Festival. A noted scholar of

Basque language and culture, Txillardegi left ETA in 1968 as a consequence of an early schism between the 'culturalist' wing of the organisation he led and others who espoused a more explicitly revolutionary form of nationalism. He was now eighty. I should meet his son, he suggested—when he got out of prison. Joseba Álvarez was responsible for international relations within Batasuna but at the time imprisoned for his role in the banned party's leadership. I asked Txillardegi why the conflict persisted. 'Because the Basque people want self-determination,' he answered abruptly, 'and there will be conflict until they get it.'[39]

Until a campaign to remove pictures of ETA prisoners and 'martyrs' to the separatist cause was instituted by the new Socialist-led Basque government in mid-2009, the visual evidence of resistance had been readily apparent. Photographs were displayed on the walls of *herriko tabernas*, the bars and meeting places of the nationalist left. Family members marched to protest the dispersion of their loved ones to far-flung prisons and the conditions in which they were held. Graffiti appeared overnight, calling for prisoners to be released, or returned home. In 2009 new signs proliferated, asking *Non dago Jon?*—'Where is Jon?' Jon Anza was a member of ETA who had last been seen that April getting on a train in France and had since disappeared in mysterious circumstances (his body would be found in a morgue in Toulouse in March 2010). Village and community *fiestas*, which traditionally mixed Basque sports with dancing, music and food, were particular focuses of tension; the Basque police, the Ertzaintza, were vigilant for pro-ETA displays within them, and plain-clothes officers frequently mixed in among the crowds.

Over a cup of coffee in Bilbao's Hotel Ercilla, Kepa Aulestia—a member of ETA's *politico-militar* branch in his youth, then a leader of Euskadiko Ezkerra (EE, Basque Left) a political party formed by demobilising *poli-milis*, drew my attention to the complex mix within Basque society—so different from the stark divisions between two communities seen in a context such as Northern Ireland. Withdrawn from active politics, Aulestia was a frequent contributor of opinion pieces robustly critical of ETA in the Basque and Spanish press. Like others, he explained the presence of communities and villages identifiable for their ideological tendencies—oppressively so in some cases of radical nationalism—but also that they are rarely exclusive. More common, especially in urban areas, is diversity within families, neighbourhoods, buildings, offices and even *cuadrillas*—the tight social groups that are a mainstay of Basque social life—across the range of Basque nationalist and pro-Spanish sympathies. 'In this bar you could have a bit of everything,' Aulestia observed, looking around, 'even an ETA commander,'[40] Outside, luxury shops on the Calle Ercilla front some of Bilbao's premier office buildings; loitering in the doorways of several were the recognisable figures of *escoltas*—the bodyguards assigned to some 1,500 politicians, local councillors, journalists and others considered possible targets of ETA.

The emergence of Basque nationalism

'Our identity is formed by struggle'. A member of Batasuna was trying to explain the sense of 'imagined community', as he put it—echoing Benedict Anderson's classic work on nationalist identity of the same name—that underpins the social and political reality of the nationalist left.[41] 'Our struggle is not ethnic, and not exclusionary, but we feel ourselves to be oppressed—of being in some sense colonised or inferior.'[42] His viewpoint echoed the sense of threat experienced by minority nationalist movements in contexts as diverse as Quebec, the former Yugoslavia or Aceh in Indonesia. It was rooted in a profound sense of history and broadly shared within the nationalist community—albeit with differences among its members—if vehemently contested from outside it. Arnaldo Otegi, Batasuna's spokesperson, began an interview in 2005 recalling that the Basque nation was one in which, 'in the last two centuries there has not been a single generation that has not had first-hand experience of prison, exile, violence and repression'.[43] The sentiment was deeply felt and lived by those, such as Otegi, who had dedicated their lives to the cause of radical nationalism, but also both bewildering and offensive to those in Basque and Spanish society who had suffered the violence of ETA at first hand.

Such divisions spring from competing versions of Basque history, succinctly described by Marianne Heiberg in the preface to her study, *The Making of the Basque Nation* (1989).[44] One is informed by what Diego Muro has termed, 'the mobilising myths of Basque nationalism'.[45] It is rooted in Basques' perception of themselves as a people and nation distinguished from others by their unique language and culture (not to mention physical features such as skull structure and blood type, which have been the subject of arcane and extended debate), and with a long history of political autonomy and egalitarian tradition vested in their *fueros*. These were understood by Basque nationalists as customary rights and as the foundation for pacts with Castile entered into on a voluntary basis. By this means, Basque sovereignty, 'although partially delegated', as Heiberg put it, 'was never surrendered'. That the *fueros* recognised all Basques to be of inherently 'noble' status underpinned understanding of the unique qualities of Basque liberties. To this day the idea of the 'Basque people' as the 'political subject' of their future is central to the struggle for Basque sovereignty within which differences with Madrid— which has never accepted the unit of self-determination, or 'political subject', as anything other than Spain itself—are grounded.

The other version of history sees the trajectory of the Basque region as an integral part in the slow development of Spain as a unitary nation state, and unremarkable in the context of the nation-building of other European states (Germany, Italy and the United Kingdom) in which regional identities—in Spain's case the Basque Country, Catalonia and Galicia—were strong.[46] Within this history, individual Basques, from the explorers Lope de Aguirre and Juan Sebastián Elcano, to the founder of the Jesuit order Ignacio de Loyola, or philosopher Miguel Unamuno, had been central figures in the Spanish pantheon. And the Basque *fueros*, like those introduced elsewhere, were concessions granted by Castile, representing neither 'ancestral' rights nor the basis for particular Basque freedoms. Rather Basque society, like others, had been formed as a consequence of the evolution of distinct elite interests, at times in conflict with each other and centralising forces in Madrid, and at times in consonance with them. Unmediated by the myths and discourse of Basque nationalism, this history directly challenges the right or ability of Basque nationalists (especially violent nationalists) to speak or act in representation of 'the Basque people'.

As elsewhere, industrialisation in the late nineteenth century contributed to the rise of nationalism, and in the early decades of the twentieth century nationalist movements challenged the authority of the state. What is exceptional in the development of regional nationalisms in Spain is what happened next: the historical anomaly of Civil War, Franco and the endurance of his regime beyond 1945. While other nationalist movements collaborated with Nazism in the Second World War, and therefore lost legitimacy at its end, in Spain, as Sebastian Balfour and

Alejandro Quiroga point out, 'stateless nationalisms… gained political legitimacy precisely because they opposed a Fascist dictatorship'.[47]

Modern Basque nationalism was invented in the late nineteenth century.[48] To a remarkable extent it originated in the work of one man, Sabino Arana y Goiri, from a Carlist family in Bilbao. Arana was impelled by a sense of the imminent destruction of Basque culture and traditions as a consequence of the loss of the three Carlist Wars, the abolition of the Basque *fueros* in 1876 at the end of the last of them and the industrialisation which then quickly took hold. The Carlist Wars had been fought in the name of Don Carlos, the pretender to the Spanish crown, for the cause of rural and Catholic tradition against the liberalism first codified in Spain's 1812 constitution. The Basque provinces fiercely defended what Basque nationalists would later refer to as the 'old laws' and became a Carlist stronghold, albeit with divisions between the traditional interior and more liberal Basques from Bilbao and San Sebastián. In this respect, as Antonio Elorza has observed, 'the geography of the Carlist Wars foreshadowed the Sabinian construct of the traditional *Euskeria* [Basque Country] against a liberal and atheistic Spain'.[49]

Industrialisation built on Vizcaya's production of nearly all of Spain's iron and steel and domination of Spanish metal processing and shipbuilding. The iron ore exported from Vizcaya increased nearly eightyfold (from 55,000 tons to 4,272,000) between 1866 and 1890; by the end of the century Vizcaya provided the greater part of Spain's contribution of 21 per cent of the world's supply.[50] Open cast mines, steel mills and blast furnaces transformed the province's landscape. New social classes—a Basque industrial elite and non-Basque urban proletariat, swelled by rapid immigration from elsewhere in Spain—hastened the development of Basque nationalism as a conservative, Catholic and exclusive force that countered the modernising pressures that industrialisation brought with it. Opposing grievances among immigrant workers contributed to Bilbao's emergence as a centre of militant socialism and to the complex evolution of Basque politics in the years to come.

Arana launched the first political articulation of Basque nationalism in his 1892 pamphlet *Bizcaya por su independencia*—'Vizcaya for its independence'.[51] Within a few years he pursued a revival of Euskera— neglected and little spoken at the time—and founded the Basque Nationalist Party; invented the term '*Euzkadi*' (later modified to 'Euskadi') to refer to the Basque nation, and the red, white and green *ikurrina*, the Basque nationalist flag; and composed a Basque nationalist anthem that is still used by the PNV. Beyond these external symbols and expressions, he successfully established the ideological basis for Basque nationalism as both a social movement and a political party, deeply embedded in his mythologised vision of Basque history and in direct opposition to all things Spanish.

From the beginning, Basque nationalism faced contradictions between its conservative underpinnings and the radical aspects of a separatist— and in Arana's formulation—racist agenda. The new party's slogan *Jaungoikua eta Lagi-Zara*, 'God and the Old Laws', carried within it an implicit demand for Christian rectitude. Heroic struggles in the Basque past were epitomised by the figure of the *gudari*, the Basque soldier or freedom fighter, who offered an example of physical prowess as well as personal probity. Such rectitude was directly associated with the communitarian values of Basque society and carried with it a conception of separatist political loyalty that directly opposed all that was good and pure in Euskadi with all that was bad and impure in Spain.[52] In its emphasis on the purity of the Basque 'blood' and stated desire to drive Spanish immigrants from the Basque lands, if by non-violent means, Arana' s vision for Basque nationalism was openly exclusionary. Rather than encouraging the spread of Euskera—whose unintelligibility to others was a source of Basque pride—Arana refused to allow immigrants to learn the language.[53]

Arana's followers soon came to realise that more moderate positions were essential to the PNV's electoral viability. However, the legacy of Arana remained vivid. Both ETA and—later—the PNV formally abandoned the confessional and racial definitions of the nationalist creed. But the issue of who is 'properly' Basque is still a live undercurrent within Basque life, partially if not wholly compensated by fluency in Euskera. Over time, the rhetoric and symbols that articulated Basque nationalism in its earliest days would prove fertile ground for the sustenance of perceptions of difference, and the emergence of political violence in the specific circumstances of Franco's Spain.[54]

Civil War and Franco

Spain's loss of its colonial territories in Puerto Rico, the Philippines and Cuba in 1898 shattered the country's identity as an imperial power. It introduced a pervasive sense of national inferiority before Spain's more successful Western European neighbours and inspired a whole generation of intellectuals—the 'Generation of 1898'—to question the essence of Spain. For Catalonia, the Basque Country and Galicia, 'the disaster' was further evidence of the failure of Spain's central government.

Arana was elected to the Vizcayan provincial council that same year. Before his death in 1903 the PNV had found support among students, the urban middle classes and within the Catholic Church. Its opponents included the liberal and conservative oligarchy and socialists empowered by the backing of the immigrant labour force. But divisions soon emerged. Moderate members of the PNV renamed themselves the 'Basque Nationalist Communion'. Younger, more radical Basque nationalists, many of them inspired by Ireland's 1916 Easter Rising, formed the splinter group Aberri.[55]

The dictatorship of Miguel Primo de Rivera (1923–1930) moved promptly to repress nationalist tendencies in Spain's regions. It banned Euskera and Catalan, yet could not stem the flourishing of cultural and other traditional Basque pursuits. Mountaineering societies, in particular, assumed significant roles as a means to organise and sustain a combative sense of nationalist spirit. The Basque cultural proliferation was markedly different from the more solidly established project of cultural Catalanism, partly as a consequence of the different roles assumed by the national language in each society.[56] However, it prepared the terrain for the rise of Basque nationalism—whose two currents reunited as the Basque Nationalist Party in 1930—during the heady years between 1931 and 1936, Spain's Second Republic.

Primo de Rivera resigned in January 1930. In the months that followed, republican factions joined forces to resist the restoration of the monarchy and swept municipal elections in April 1931. A new constitution closely attuned to republican political views represented a direct challenge to the most powerful and conservative forces in Spain—landowners, the Catholic Church, industrialists and the army—and consequently a source of controversy itself, something that Hugh Thomas, in his analysis of the origins of the Civil War, would identify as a 'grave mistake'.[57] It included a clear commitment to decentralisation that acknowledged the right of Spain's regions to autonomy and prompted movement towards the development of statutes of autonomy in Catalonia, the Basque Country and Galicia. These established an important precedent that would contribute to the regions' recognition as 'historical nationalities' after Franco's death.

In the Basque context, the Second Republic exposed an inherent contradiction between the confessional and conservative aspects of Basque nationalism, and liberal and secular forces pushing for change. Despite its active pursuit of regional autonomy, the PNV remained outside government.[58] Meanwhile, its more radical members again moved away to form a new group, Jagi-Jagi. While Catalonia achieved its statute of autonomy in 1932, differences among Basques delayed agreement of the Basque statute until 1 October 1936. Its adoption was achieved with the decisive support of the Basque Socialist Indalecio Prieto and marked a critical shift from the Catholic and anti-republican majority present in Basque politics in 1931 towards pro-autonomy and republican sentiment.[59] José Antonio Aguirre became the first *lehendakari* of the provisional Basque government formed a few days later.

But broader political dynamics across Spain had moved on. A coalition of centre right and right-wing parties had won the elections of 1934 and set about suspending many of the previous government's reforms. Armed forces led by General Francisco Franco, a veteran of the Rif War in Morocco, repressed a general strike and miners' uprising in Asturias; a rebellion calling for independence in Catalonia was also put down. In 1935 the monarchist politician José Calvo Sotelo famously gave voice to the rising passion with which the autonomous tendencies of the republic were resisted in San Sebastián: '*antes una España roja que una España rota*'—'better a red Spain than a broken Spain'.[60] Socialists, communists, and Catalan and Madrid-based republicans joined together and won elections in January 1936. Violence soon escalated. On 18 July 1936 Franco launched a military rebellion against the new government from Moroccan Spain that quickly spread to other parts of the country. Forces loyal to the republic resisted and the Civil War began.

Basques responded to Franco with divided loyalty. Navarre and Álava found affinity in the rebels' conservative Catholicism and aligned themselves accordingly. Vizcaya and Guipúzcoa reacted against the fiercely anti-Basque tenor of the rebellion and sided with the republicans. The division ensured that the particular tragedy of Civil War played out among Basques, as well as between Basques and the advancing rebel front. The new Basque government was short-lived. San Sebastián had surrendered to Franco's forces before its formation, and in the spring of

1937 a major assault on Vizcaya began. On 26 April 1937 Luftwaffe aircraft bombed Guernica, combining Nazi support for the rebel cause with a test run of the latest in destructive airpower. It was the first instance of the aerial bombardment of a civilian population and remains etched in European history as a horrible foretaste of the warfare to come. Bilbao fell in mid-June, a major prize as both the largest city yet to succumb to Franco's forces and the seat of Basque nationalism, itself 'an affront to the concept of national unity espoused by the rebel generals of 18 July', as Juan Pablo Fusi put it.[61] Bilbao's new mayor, the Basque Falangist José María de Areilza, proclaimed: 'The revolting, sinister, heinous nightmare known as Euskadi has fallen forever.'[62]

An estimated 25,000 Basques were killed between 1936 and 1939, 16,000 loyal to the republic and 9,000 to the rebellion; thousands more were imprisoned.[63] These numbers were not exceptional in light of the extraordinary losses in other areas of Spain, but the Basques had experienced the Civil War as a nationalist war, and for this reason its scars would linger.[64] Elsewhere in Spain the Civil War dragged on until April 1939 as Franco pursued the eradication of the communists, Jews, freemasons and separatists he saw as opposing his cause and the consolidation of his own power. Although no official reckoning of the casualties of the Civil War and the immediate post-war period has ever been undertaken, most historians assess them to number some half a million, with nearly 200,000 executed by both sides—many more of them by rebel than republican supporters. More than half a million people, including some 150,000 Basques, fled into exile.[65]

The relentless pursuit of a country divided into the *vencedores y vencidos*, 'victors and vanquished', of 1939 continued into Franco's rule. Under cover of the Second World War, within which Spain remained officially non-belligerent, Franco rounded up republican sympathisers, imprisoned or forced them into labour camps and, in their tens of thousands, killed them. He secured his regime by bringing the different factions among the rebel forces together into an official state party, the Falange Española Tradicionalista de las Juntas de la Ofensiva Nacional y Sindicalista ('Traditionalist Spanish Phalanx of the Juntas of the National Syndicalist Offensive') and established himself as *Caudillo* and head of state. His national Catholicism prized God and the unity of the Spanish state ('*España una, grande y libre*—'Spain one, great and free', as the call and response slogan of the Falange had first put it); manifestations of cultural and linguistic difference were not tolerated.

After the rapid conclusion of open conflict, Franco embarked on a determined effort to destroy all evidence of Basque culture and political organisation.[66] His regime prohibited the use of Euskera in public—even on the streets—and in all religious activities, closed the only university, raided libraries and burned books. It banned the use of Basque names and purged all of those who had supported the Basque nationalist cause. It branded Vizcaya and Guipúzcoa 'traitorous' provinces, confiscated property, imposed fines, fired teachers, closed businesses and expropriated industries. Catholic priests and other officials who had openly opposed rebel violence pursued as a crusade to 'save' the Church from the Marxist hordes of the republic were particularly vulnerable. Sixteen priests were executed and more than three hundred priests and monks were imprisoned or deported to other parts of Spain.[67] Yet the Basque church remained active. As Euskera retreated into the private realm of the home, the family and the *cuadrilla*, some Basque priests defied the Catholic hierarchy to remain vital, if clandestine, points of reference for nationalist identity.

ETA takes shape

After the fall of Bilbao, the Basque government moved first to Barcelona and then into exile, pinning its hopes on Western powers rallying against Franco in the aftermath of the Second World War. This was not to be. *Realpolitik* in fragile post-war Europe quickly set in and recognised the utility of Franco's Spain as an anti-communist bulwark in the Cold War. From 1945 Aguirre, now president of the Basque government-in-exile, lobbied Washington. He was respectfully received, but achieved nothing. The United States began to shift its policy to Spain to one of 'normalisation' as early as 1947.[68] In 1951 it began discussions regarding the opening of military bases on Spanish soil. The bases opened in 1953, and in 1955 Spain was admitted to the UN.

In retrospect, it is difficult to see how the Basque government-in-exile could have impressed upon the United States and other Western powers a sense that, in the larger scheme of things, the Basque fate mattered. But this was not how it seemed to some among the younger generation of Basque nationalists that began to meet as a group called Ekin, 'Action'. The group discussed Basque history, language and culture, and how to resist what they perceived as the imminent disappearance of the Basque nation. With an ethnic understanding of Basque identity at its core, Ekin was influenced by existentialism, but also anti-colonial and other liberation struggles. In 2010, Julen Madariaga, a founding member of both Ekin and ETA, would remember a particular fascination with Irgun, the Jewish paramilitary organisation that had been responsible for the bombing of the King David Hotel in 1948 and was later absorbed into the Israeli Defence Forces. The Cypriot and Irish rebellions against Britain, and the Algerian liberation struggle against French colonialism were also closely analysed.[69] Ekin collaborated with the PNV's youth sector Egi, but its advocacy of an independent Basque republic in which Euskera would be the sole official language was dismissed by the PNV as 'incredibly utopian'.[70] Ekin argued that the PNV was too passive. As discussions among Ekin and some members of Egi turned towards operational issues, the divisions became more profound.

A decision was taken to form a new and clandestine organisation in December 1958; Euskadi Ta Askatasuna was formally constituted in July 1959. ETA defined itself as a 'political organisation that practices the armed struggle'.[71] It rejected the idea of race as an indication of Basque identity in favour of more flexible sense of 'ethnos', rooted in Euskera and a dedication to Basque cultural ideals; committed itself to the exclusion of the Catholic Church from politics; and advocated an independent socialist state embracing both the Spanish and French Basque territories. From an early period it also looked beyond the constraints represented by France and Spain to Europe as 'the ideal structure in which Euskadi might develop its own sovereign identity'.[72]

Developing this ambitious and, in some respects, contradictory platform would prove a difficult task. ETA's early years saw dramatic social change in the Basque Country as the revival of its economy spurred an increase in immigration comparable to that of the late nineteenth century. Within the organisation extensive discussion of its ideology, orientation and strategy accompanied a gradual escalation of propaganda, sabotage and armed action. Attention to third-world liberation struggles (especially in Algeria, Cuba and Vietnam), most of which were wholly unsuited as models for the Basque Country's industrialised society, promoted a mystical sense of engagement in a kind of pre-insurrectionary guerrilla warfare.[73] In circumstances in which conditions for a mass insurrection did not exist, in 1964 ETA shifted its attention to a progressive struggle through an escalating spiral of 'action-repression-action'. Two

41

important doctrinal documents of this period, 'Open letter to Basque intellectuals' and 'Theoretical bases of revolutionary war', foresaw ETA's own actions prompting state repression that would, in turn, galvanise support for wider action by the militant nationalist community.[74]

In time ETA deliberately sought access to, and support from, other liberation movements, receiving arms and training from Algeria and elsewhere. Northern Ireland was of interest for reasons that extended from the historic links between Basque nationalism and Irish republicanism to the lessons that could be gleaned from it regarding the practice of armed conflict. Contacts were established with the IRA—initially through Egi—and over the years the operational and political ties between the respective armed organisations and their political proxies would follow a complex trajectory. The military to military connections between the two organisations have never been fully revealed, but the IRA is suspected of having been a significant source of weapons for ETA during the 1980s and 1990s, including in the period after the Good Friday Agreement of 1998.[75] Basques retained a special consideration of what could be learned from the 'brother conflict', even as many assumed that a solution would be found more readily for their own situation, clearly distinct from the stark sectarianism of Northern Ireland.[76]

ETA was identified by Spain's authorities as a terrorist organisation from its earliest days.[77] Repression came quickly, and most of ETA's leadership was forced into exile in 1961. However, in a series of assemblies held between 1962 and 1973 the organisation gradually took shape. Differences over the relative importance of the ethno-national and class struggles quickly emerged, contributing to a series of divisions and splits. The issue was particularly challenging for ETA because of the non-Basque immigrants who made up most of the Basque working class. The first of two major schisms during the Franco period erupted in 1966 during ETA's Fifth Assembly. Three distinct factions emerged: one prioritised the socialist struggle over the goals of Basque nationalism and advocated greater ties to revolutionary movements elsewhere in Europe; a second argued for the maintenance of Basque nationalist ideals and the rejection of Marxism; and the third favoured armed action as a means to achieve independence within a broad commitment to 'revolutionary socialism'. The expulsion of the first two by the third left the hardliners in charge and established the central tenets of the organisation for years to come.[78]

It would not be until 1968 that ETA claimed its first victim and suffered its first loss.[79] On 7 June two ETA members were detained at a road block in Guipúzcoa and killed José Pardines, a member of Spain's militarised police force, the Guardia Civil. Txabi Etxebarrieta, one of the *etarras* in the car, was immediately pursued and killed. ETA's next victim was carefully selected: Melitón Manzanas, a police commissioner notorious for his brutality. His assassination in August prompted Franco to declare a state of emergency in Guipúzcoa that was later extended across Spain. Many of ETA's leaders were arrested and nearly 2,000 Basques would be detained in the course of the year.[80] The virulence of the state response nearly destroyed ETA. As the organisation struggled to respond, new divisions emerged between those largely identified by their prioritisation of armed action (the *frente militar*) and the revindication of workers' rights (the *frente obrero*).[81]

That ETA survived was a consequence of a number of different factors. These included the safe haven it found in France, where opposition to Franco and thus a degree of sympathy to his opponents was widespread; the compatibility of the Basques' mountainous terrain with guerrilla activities; and the considerable support ETA received from the Basque population, especially the young and some elements of the Basque clergy. In this respect, the spiral of action-repression-action proved remarkably successful. ETA found legitimacy for its existence, ideology and actions in Franco's repression of Basque culture and identity and targeted excesses against it—the result of a policy that Franco's biographer Juan Pablo Fusi would describe as 'one of the great historic errors of recent times in Spain'.[82]

Two events catapulted ETA onto the international stage and rallied public opinion in Spain to its support. The first was the trial of sixteen members of ETA arrested after the killing of Manzanas. The 'Burgos trial' took place in December 1970 in a charged and chaotic atmosphere; it provoked demonstrations in Spain and abroad, and was complicated by the kidnapping of the West German consul in San Sebastián by the faction of ETA now known as the *milis*. The consul was eventually released unharmed, but the kidnapping contributed to the pressure on Franco to treat the Burgos prisoners with some leniency, and he commuted the death sentences handed down to six of them. The second was ETA's spectacular assassination of Admiral Luis Carrero Blanco, Franco's prime minister, whose car it blew up as he was being driven to church in Madrid on 20 December 1973. The operation—which was applauded by many who were far removed from ETA in ideological terms—confirmed ETA as the most audacious and effective force in opposition to the aging Spanish regime. It had a lasting impact on the course taken by post-Franco Spain.

In 1974 ETA experienced its second major split, in part as a consequence of differences over the impending political change. ETA *politico-militar* (ETA-pm) advocated a dual-functioned political and military organisation answering to a unified command. Many of its members supported a political path towards self-determination and independence, and would be active in Basque politics in the late 1970s and 1980s. ETA *militar* (ETA-m), meanwhile, favoured a clear separation between the military wing of the organisation and cultural, political and workers' fronts that might be able to operate openly in a post-Franco democracy. In the short term both factions of ETA continued military actions in a competitive cycle that sought to influence and/or undermine a process they believed to be incompatible with their goals. Divisions within ETA-pm that led to the appearance of the Anticapitalist Autonomous Commandos (CAA), which undertook armed actions independent of ETA-m, further complicated what was already an increasingly confused situation.

A contested transition

The orthodox view of the path taken by ETA's violence is that while it might have been understandable as a response to Franco's repression, during the transition to democracy a Rubicon was crossed. Until 1975, as José Luis Corcuera, later a Socialist minister of the interior, would remember, 'it seemed that they were fighting against the dictatorship, and even if you weren't in favour of their methods, this mitigated revulsion at the cold assassination of any individual'.[83] The argument is succinctly expressed by Gregorio Morán: after the transition 'the political violence of a political organisation became terrorist activity'.[84] There are both methodological and political problems with this reading of Basque history. As a tactic, terrorism is terrorism regardless of its political context, as Louise Richardson points out.[85] And the nature of the transition as it was experienced in the Basque Country—violent, actively rejected by a small but significant part of the population, and qualitatively different from that experienced elsewhere in Spain—militates against the possibility of drawing a clear, Rubicon-like line.[86]

That the transition to democracy did not undercut the reasons for ETA's existence and hasten the organisation's end suggested a signal error of the period. 'We all believed that ETA would end with Franco,' recalled Josep Ramoneda, who as a young journalist in the 1970s interviewed ETA militants: 'That it did not happen showed that we all got our analysis wrong.'[87] ETA's mobilisation as an armed group, although triggered by Francoism, drew on a wellspring of Basque nationalist opposition to Spain itself, as manifested in the government—any government—in Madrid. Important numbers of ETA militants maintained their commitment to the armed struggle, sustained by an enabling community of support, new recruits and an existential need for relevance. For ETA the failure of the pacts upon which the transition was based to recognise Basque self-determination invalidated all that was done in their name.

Viewed within a broader perspective, Spain's transition was an extraordinary achievement. It has been studied as 'a unique case of the democratisation of a dictatorship "from the inside out"', as well as a broadly smooth transformation of 'one of the most centralised regimes in Western Europe into a quasi-federal monarchy', and 'the paradigmatic case for the study of pacted democratic transition and rapid democratic consolidation'.[88] Change built on shifts within the dictatorship in the latter years of the regime and was pursued by consensus and through existing legal mechanisms. Individuals either hand-picked by Franco (the new head of state, King Juan Carlos I) or having held senior positions within his regime (including Adolfo Suárez, Spain's prime minister from 1976–81) played leading roles in a difficult balancing act between opposing political forces. By the end of 1978 negotiations between the government and opposition political parties had paved the way for Spain to approve a new constitution. In early 1981, the country successfully weathered an attempted coup. In 1982 it elected a Socialist government, headed by a dynamic young politician from Andalucia, Felipe González. And on 1 January 1986 Spain joined the European Community.

The transition was, however, more violent than many care to remember—by one account 773 people were killed by groups of the extreme right, extreme left or ETA between 1972 and 1982, 450 of them in the

Basque Country[89]—and contingent upon two unwritten arrangements. One has a name, the *pacto de olvido* or 'pact of forgetting'. Rather than forgetting, Spain drew a veil over its recent history. No formal accounting was ever made of the violence meted out upon Franco's enemies during and after the Civil War; no 'truth' was established, or 'reconciliation' pursued. The second was unnamed, but was the arrangement that left many institutions—including the army, police and judiciary—in the hands of Franco's officials. Both reflected a process that was one of an agreed and limited 'reform' rather than an abrupt 'rupture' with Spain's past.

These arrangements can be attributed to the threat represented by the army and other forces resistant to the coming change, including concessions made to demands for regional autonomy. They also reflected a fear of reviving the old divisions and terrible bloodshed of the Civil War.[90] Silence was preferable, and indeed perceived by many as essential to moving on. However, it exacerbated the opposition of those who had held out for more. Moreover, as the years passed and Spain, in contrast to other countries that had made the difficult transition away from dictatorship or authoritarian rule, failed to take steps to introduce measures of what came to be known as 'transitional justice' ('the set of judicial and non-judicial measures that have been implemented by different countries in order to redress the legacies of massive human rights abuses', as the International Center for Transitional Justice defines it) arguments for Spanish exceptionalism in this area became increasingly difficult to sustain.[91] 'Thirty years after what was supposed to be a model transition,' Rafael (Rafa) Diéz Usabiaga, a leading figure in the Basque nationalist left, observed in 2010, 'we confront the flagrant contradiction that in the Spanish state they still have not addressed something so fundamental as the crimes of Francoism.'[92]

Pragmatism saw the most prominent of the parties in opposition to Franco, the PSOE and the Spanish Communist Party, abandon long-held positions on the critical issue of self-determination. Self-determination had been part of the PSOE platform agreed in 1974; two years later the party still maintained that 'all nationalities and regions' had the right to break free from the Spanish state.[93] The shift experienced by Basque Socialists was particularly wrenching. As late as 1977 the Basque Socialist Party (PSE), led by Txiki Benegas, had supported Basque self-determination and championed a constitutional and federal Spain that would 'acknowledge the political, economic and administrative personality of Euskadi and the rest of the peoples of Spain'.[94] But in the following year the PSE, already enmeshed in a struggle between a specifically 'Basque' identity and responsibility to class politics, moved sharply towards more overtly centralist positions. The PSOE abandoned all pretensions to support self-determination within a constitutional drafting committee (*ponencia constitucional*) that had been established without the presence of the PNV. It was left to a Catalan, Miquel Roca i Junyent, to argue in favour of federalism on regional nationalists' behalf, while Basque nationalists—in a slight they would long remember—pressed their case from outside.[95]

ETA had claimed six mortal victims in 1973; its annual tally would stay below twenty through 1977 then suddenly escalate to sixty-six in 1978 and seventy-six in 1979, before reaching its historic high in 1980, the year that saw the government of Euskadi installed, at ninety-two.[96] A desire for change and the more immediate goal of the release and amnesty of Basque prisoners, most of them ETA militants or collaborators, brought thousands onto the streets in demonstrations and strikes. Yet many blamed ETA for bringing the still fragile democratic process into jeopardy and provoking the re-emergence of the extreme right.[97] In some instances right-wing and paramilitary groups—such as the Basque-Spanish Battalion (BVE) and Triple A—maintained ties to elements within the police and armed forces in a form of 'dirty war'. In others, violence was more directly attributable to the state. On 3 March 1976 the Guardia Civil opened fire on striking workers seeking refuge in a church in Vitoria, leaving five dead and approximately 150 wounded. Radical Basque nationalists still refer to events that day as 'our Bloody Sunday'.[98]

The year 1975 was one of extraordinary upheaval. A state of emergency was declared in Guipúzcoa and Vizcaya in April and more than 5,000 Basques were detained by Franco's forces. In August ETA-pm and a number of political parties and labour organisations created the Koordinadora Abertzale Socialista (Socialist Nationalist Coordinator, KAS), a coordinating committee that developed a platform of minimum conditions for the participation of the Basque National Liberation Movement (MLNV) emerging in ETA's orbit in the reform process. And in September, in the last major political drama of Franco's lifetime, two ETA militants—Juan Paredes Manot, *Txiki*, and Ángel Otaegui—together with three Maoists, were executed, despite intense domestic and international pressure for their lives to be spared.

During 1976 ETA-pm created a political party that quickly joined the coalition Euskadiko Ezkerra to contest the Spanish elections of 1977. Basque nationalist forces—from ETA to the PNV—met in April and May in Txiberta, near Biarritz, in an attempt to develop a common nationalist position from which to negotiate with the state. The meeting was a failure and left the two main expressions of Basque nationalism bitterly opposed. Each, predictably, blamed the other. In November 2011 ETA would look back and recall that 'the end of the armed conflict' had been 'on the table' for discussion at Txiberta, until the PNV had spoiled the possibility by accepting the 'partition imposed by Spain'.[99]

Suárez' Union of the Democratic Centre (UCD) won the general elections held in June 1977 with a strong showing by the PSOE. Organisations associated with KAS and others within the MLNV created a new coalition, Herri Batasuna (HB, Unity of the People)—this time closer to ETA-m—in order to contest future elections and push for a statute of autonomy for the four Spanish Basque provinces. A revised version of KAS' platform known as the KAS Alternative listed five conditions necessary for ETA to give up the armed struggle: amnesty for all Basque prisoners; the legalisation of Basque pro-independence political parties; the withdrawal of Spanish police from the four Basque provinces; an improvement in basic living conditions for the working classes; and an autonomy statute that recognised the national sovereignty of the Spanish Basque territories, established the use of Euskera as the principal language within them and allowed for Basque self-determination.[100] A general amnesty law covering all 'crimes of a political nature' was passed in 1977. It released Basque (as well as other) political prisoners even as it provided a legal basis for the *pacto de olvido*. But the direct negotiations with Madrid that ETA demanded, as well as the terms spelled out within the KAS Alternative, were unacceptable. ETA launched a series of provocative attacks, and Spain began what Robert Clark would describe as 'the long road back to Francoism without Franco'.[101] A new anti-terrorist law was introduced in 1978 and with it a number of Franco's methods for dealing with terrorists.

The negotiation and referendum of Spain's new constitution was achieved by 1978.[102] At its centre was an effort to address the tension between the centre and periphery that was inherent in Spain's identity. The solution found sought to respond to the regions' demands for autonomy and the guarantee of linguistic rights. It was a compromise conditioned by the threat of intervention by the army that rested on a fundamental ambiguity. Representing a difficult balance between nationalism and federalism, Article 2 defends 'the indivisible unity of the Spanish nation, common and indivisible fatherland (*patria*) of all the Spaniards' while acknowledging 'the right to autonomy of the nationalities and regions which form it and the solidarity among them'. Article 3 recognised Castilian as the official language of the Spanish state, but allowed for other languages to be 'official in their respective autonomous communities according to their own statutes'. Article 8.1 included the assurance that Spain's sovereignty and territorial integrity would be guaranteed by its armed forces. As these were still under the control of Franco's generals, Basque nationalists understood this as a provocation—and the more radical among them viewed it as the continuing 'occupation' of the Basque Country.

Only representatives of the Popular Alliance (AP), a new right-wing party formed by Franco's former minister Manuel Fraga, and the PNV resisted the constitution.[103] The AP objected to the recognition of the existence of distinct 'nationalities' within Spain and the dual-track process of the development of a 'state of autonomies' that it looked forward to. This foresaw an accelerated route to autonomy for those regions with greater claims to self-government under Article 151 and a slower route for others, under Article 143. The PNV, on the hand, opposed it on the basis of its ambiguities regarding Basque rights, but also in order not to lose support to radical nationalists.[104] After arguing for the restitution of the Basque *fueros* and the institutional arrangements necessary to implement them, it achieved recognition of 'historical rights' sufficient to protect the fiscal regime, but was blocked in its demand that these rights form the basis for autonomous government. Basque nationalists consequently called for abstention from the constitutional referendum.

Abstention topped 55 per cent; although 75 per cent of those who did vote voted to approve the constitution, this represented only 31 per cent of the Basque population, a little over half of the 59 per cent approval the constitution found across Spain.[105] Interpretation of opposition to the constitution was complicated by the likely existence of a high rate of natural abstention, but Euskadi remained the one region in the country in which a majority of the electorate did not support the foundational document of Spain's democracy.

The negotiation by the PNV—and all political parties other than HB—of the Basque statute of autonomy the following year contained within it an implied acquiescence with the constitutional framework that Llera Ramo would characterise as 'semi-loyal'.[106] Latent in the arguments of the PNV was the idea that a high degree of self-rule would not only address the inequitable treatment of the Basques by Franco but also help undercut the demands of ETA.[107] The party reluctantly accepted that Navarre—which retained strong Basque sentiment in its northern areas, but was much more inclined to Spain in its central and southern regions, and was controlled by conservative forces—would be established as a distinct autonomous community. Critical concessions to Basque nationalists' desire that, in time, the autonomy statute should be renegotiated and full self-determination pursued included Article 2, which left the door open for Navarre to join Euskadi if it so chose, and an 'additional provision' which spelled out that acceptance of the statute did not imply the renunciation of Basques' historical rights, which could be updated in accordance with the legal code.[108] The statute provided for autonomous education and health systems, Basque television channels and radio stations. In 1980 a further agreement created an autonomous police force, the Ertzaintza. Together these competencies would constitute the highest degree of autonomy seen anywhere in Europe.

The statute was approved by 95 per cent of those who took part in its referendum in October 1979.[109] No political project has ever gained greater support in Euskadi. But with an abstention rate of 41 per cent, it fell far short of a consensus reached among Basque political forces, and the Basque problem, like ETA, remained very much alive.

2

VIOLENCE, TERROR AND TALKING

The possibility of negotiation shadowed ETA's long history. Exploratory contacts began soon after Franco's death, but with the exception of a successful effort to reintegrate former members of ETA-pm, attempts to establish channels for dialogue did not prosper.[1] It would be more than a decade before sustained face-to-face 'conversations' between representatives of ETA and the Spanish government took place in Algiers. In their latter stages these talks were accompanied by a ceasefire from ETA, and great expectation that they might be able to advance towards peace. But it soon became clear that neither side was prepared to enter into a serious process of negotiation.

A number of elements worked against addressing ETA's violence by political means. Three stand out. The first was ETA itself and its conception of the terms of the KAS Alternative as a pre-condition for negotiations and armed action as a means of forcing the government to accept them. The second was the extent to which the idea of negotiation became an issue of political contention. Writing in 1998, Florencio Domínguez described 'negotiation' and 'repression'—understood as incompatible and mutually exclusive alternatives to the problem presented by ETA's violence—as having been at the centre of political debate in the Basque Country for more than twenty years, creating stark divisions between their proponents.[2] Finally, conceptual and tactical confusion on the part of Spanish governments fostered incoherent and at times counterproductive policies. After 1982, the Socialist government

51

turned to individuals and practices of the Franco era in its own counter-terror campaign. These galvanised opposition both within the mainstream of Basque nationalism and among its more radical and violent expressions. In an improvised and scattershot fashion, the government also pursued contacts with ETA that fuelled expectations that political negotiations represented a realistic goal when this was never the case.

ETA drew on substantial support from the complex web of political and social organisations that developed within the orbit of the Basque National Liberation Movement (MLNV), as well as significant ambivalence towards it among the mainstream of Basque nationalism. The organisations of the MLNV were not all created by ETA or directly bound to it, but their emergence as a radical nationalist community in opposition to the Spanish state was predicated on its existence and military activity. Much the most significant among them was Herri Batasuna (HB). Its decision to contest all Basque elections after 1978 gave the MLNV an effective means to demonstrate the 'accumulation of forces' behind the separatist cause, even as ETA insisted on the primacy of armed action as the 'most genuine expression of our force'.[3]

The PNV never supported the use of violence, but ideological as well as other ties to ETA encouraged a degree of understanding of its militants as 'wayward children' (*los hijos descarriados*). A reluctance to condemn ETA with the vehemence demanded by pro-Spanish parties and a perceived indifference to victims largely representative of its political opponents came to be seen as implicit—and culpable—collusion.[4] That many nationalists shared an antipathy to police action in the Basque Country by Spanish security forces they still associated with Franco encouraged their support of dialogue with ETA. But it also tainted this support in the eyes of pro-Spanish 'constitutionalists' who upheld the legitimacy of a democratic state to defend itself against acts of terrorism directed at it.

Basque political parties other than HB finally reached consensus towards ETA in the Pact of Ajuria Enea agreed in 1988. The pact included both strong commitments to counter ETA's terrorism through police action and the possibility of dialogue with those who had decided to abandon violence, so long as political questions were addressed only among the population's legitimately elected representatives—i.e. not at a negotiating table with ETA.[5] It was on this basis that formal talks began in Algiers in early 1989, but soon broke down. In their wake,

ETA returned to violence with a new determination to force the government back to the negotiating table, while the government strengthened its efforts against it. A major success came in 1992 when the capture of ETA's leadership at Bidart forced the organisation to contemplate the possibility of its military defeat for the first time in its history. ETA and the MLNV embarked on a lengthy period of reflection, the outcome of which ensured the continuity of violence for decades to come.

Contacts and killing

In his pioneering study of early efforts to negotiate with ETA, Robert Clark recorded that between November 1975 and mid-1988, 'there were between twenty and thirty serious attempts to negotiate an end to insurgent violence in the Basque provinces in Spain'.[6] Clark was writing as the Cold War ended, but before the boom in negotiated conflict settlements that its conclusion triggered had taken hold. We would no longer characterise all contacts with, or attempts to open channels to ETA as 'serious attempts to negotiate'. The passage of time has sharpened sensitivities to the use of language around contacts, dialogue and negotiations with ETA, as indeed with armed groups elsewhere. Moreover Clark's own detailed account of these various attempts questions whether the intention, capacity and cohesion necessary to advance in a political process were present either within ETA or the Spanish governments of the day. More than twenty years later, it would be difficult to quantify the number of occasions in which Spanish or Basque officials have reached out to ETA or its surrogates, either directly or through third parties, and their relation to the multiple proposals for peace that would emanate from Basque society.[7] Efforts to engage in dialogue were a constant accompaniment to ETA's long history of violence.

ETA's move towards a political process was inhibited by the primacy of armed action within an overall strategy that purported to be both military and political, as well as by differences between its two branches. In broad terms, in the early years of the transition, ETA-pm conceived its violence as a means to exert pressure on the government to negotiate, while ETA-m consciously provoked further repression consistent with the cycle of action-repression-action and thus opposed pursuit of a settlement. 'Until late in the 1980s,' Domínguez observed, 'ETA remained convinced that there was no possibility of negotiating with the government of Spain in the medium term.'[8] But there were differences within ETA-pm, and in time ETA-m's position evolved towards a more instrumental use of its violence to pressure for political concessions from the state. In both cases the political strategy rested on the mobilisation of Basque society—through strikes, protests and demonstrations—around the core KAS demands: amnesty for Basque prisoners; the legalisation of political parties; the reunification of the Basque territories; and self-determination.

ETA drew upon a ritualised approach to the violence it inflicted and suffered. This sense of ritual—memorably explored by Joseba Zulaika in his book *Basque Violence* (1988)—derived from the origins and subsequent evolution of the cultural aspects of Basque nationalism as well as the residual effects of the deep religiosity of Basque life. Mythologisation of the organisation drew upon both the clandestinity within which ETA's members operated and the absolutes with which their struggle was conceived. The ETA slogan *iraultza ala hil*, 'revolution or death', suggests a world in which you are either right or wrong, either a hero or a traitor—and either alive or dead. No room was left for compromise, negotiation or equivocation. Each violent action, or *ekintza*, implied 'a ritual condensation of action invested with premises of almost magical efficacy'.[9] 'Martyred' *etarras* were celebrated in elaborate public funerals, their virtues cultivated as examples for the young revolutionaries who aspired to follow in their footsteps.

The tangibly individual aspects of the violence—the tally of victims of ETA could be disputed, but the numbers were small enough to be counted and the victims identified—meant that each action, or mistake, could be assessed for its political repercussions. Under Franco, the ready identification of the enemy made this easier than it became as Spain moved towards democracy and ETA became less discriminating in its target selection. Most armed actions were against the 'occupying forces' of the Spanish police or Guardia Civil. In 1978 ETA began killing representatives of the Spanish army in what could be seen as the deliberate provocation of a response that might justify its assertion that the forces of Franco were alive and well. Attacks on civilians—such as an attack on the Cafeteria Rolando in Madrid in 1974 that killed thirteen people—led to internal disputes and contradictions.[10] As Spain's counter-terrorism became more effective, the broadening of ETA's targets would be a central element within its evolution, and the hardening of public opinion against it.

The introduction of the KAS Alternative in February 1978 appeared to offer an opportunity for political engagement with ETA. (Tentative meetings between representatives of the Spanish government and both factions of ETA had been held in Geneva in late 1976 and early 1977 with no obvious outcomes.)[11] But ETA's insistence that its terms were conditions for it to give up the armed struggle, rather than an opening position within a negotiation, prompted a firm rejection from the government. A strengthened ETA-m, led by José Miguel Beñarán Ordeñana, *Argala*, increased its violence in an effort to exert pressure upon Madrid. At least two separate channels of communication to ETA were developed. ETA-m killed one of the intermediaries, the Basque journalist José María Portell, in June 1978.[12] The Basque Socialist Txiki Benegas opened a second channel, but the continuing violence undermined any progress. In December Argala was killed by a car bomb in the French Basque Country by the rightist armed group the Basque-Spanish Battalion (BVE).[13]

ETA responded to the approval of the constitution and the negotiation of the Basque autonomy statute by ratcheting up its violence, fortified by the wave of new recruits with which it had been flooded.[14] During 1979 it exploded bombs in tourist areas on the coast, usually with advance warnings to prevent casualties. Levels of violence built again during 1980, with tension peaking in the tumultuous month of February 1981. This saw popular mobilisation against ETA's kidnapping and killing of José María Ryan, an engineer in the Lemóniz nuclear plant whose installation had become the object of a violent campaign by ETA;[15] a general strike; the largest demonstration yet seen against ETA in Bilbao; the death of ETA prisoner Joxe Arregi after clear indications of his torture; and the kidnapping of three foreign consuls by ETA-pm. Frustration within the army and Guardia Civil was but one element in what Javier Cercas has evocatively described as the rich 'placenta' of aggravating conditions from which the attempted military coup of 23 February was born.[16]

The coup, its rebuttal by King Juan Carlos and the immediate reinforcement of the antiterrorist forces deployed against ETA led ETA-pm to conclude that the limits of its armed action had been reached. It declared a unilateral ceasefire on 28 February, freed the kidnapped consuls and embarked on a process of 'social reintegration' that would allow its members to re-join Basque society. Those within ETA-pm who continued to advocate for violent resistance joined ETA-m and a single organisation emerged. This ETA, steadfastly dedicated to the unification of the Basque territories, self-determination and the defence of Basque rights through armed struggle, would remain the hegemonic force within the MLNV for decades to come.

ETA found a narrative that helped justify the continuation of its armed struggle in the measures used against it. When arrested, alleged *etarras* continued to be held *incommunicado*, denied legal representation and subjected to torture with a degree of regularity. They were tried before the Audiencia Nacional, a high court created in 1977 to address crimes related to terrorism under an exceptional legal regime. Its establishment represented a significant advance on the military courts that had addressed terrorist crimes under Franco, but its status as the heir to Franco's Tribunal de Ordén Público (Public Order Tribunal) meant that decades later it was still seen by Batasuna as a 'modified' version of the Francoist court.[17] Meanwhile, even peaceful demonstrations were violently repressed with tear gas, rubber bullets and widespread arrests. Injuries were frequent, and occasionally led to death. The affected community was much larger than ETA itself. It saw its enemy—Madrid and the state it represented—as 'Francoism light': unresponsive to demands for Basque rights, persistently repressive and illegitimate in democratic terms.

Juan María Bandrés and Mario Onaindia, leaders of Euskadiko Ezquerra (EE), and Interior Minister Juan José Rosón negotiated the reintegration of ETA-pm. The government agreed to address cases of the reintegrating ETA militants on an individual, rather than collective basis, and took some pains to avoid their humiliation. Taking a pragmatic approach, it granted amnesty on the grounds that it was 'for the public good', and forced no prisoner or exile to repent or reject their past militancy.[18] By 1986, after a PNV senator, Joseba Azkarraga, had initiated a new phase of the programme—those who subscribed to it had to sign a document breaking their links 'to any armed organisation' and rejecting violence 'as a means of political action'—nearly 250 former ETA militants, most of them from ETA-pm, had been reincorporated into Basque life either through programmes of reinsertion or individual pardons.[19]

Success in the negotiations depended on ETA-pm's acceptance of a distinction between the technical or 'tactical' issues that were available for negotiation—principally the release and/or return of prisoners and/ or exiles—and the raft of political issues that remained its core demands. This distinction, and the perception that the reintegrating members of ETA-pm had surrendered to the state, would lead to threats against them from ETA-m and the hostility of the nationalist left to EE, which many of the former *poli-milis* would join, for years to come. But as Clark pointed out with prescience, the negotiations had introduced 'what would prove to be one of the key conceptual distinctions between what Madrid would discuss [with ETA] and what they would not, between what could be gained through armed struggle and what could not'.[20] This distinction would complicate all future efforts to engage in dialogue and remain a point of contention for ETA to its end.

The Socialists and the GAL

The Socialist government arrived in office in December 1982 with a huge parliamentary majority. Its young leaders were a world away from Spain's past and promised great things for Spain's future. They also proved surprisingly pragmatic. Upon assuming power, Felipe González moved promptly to implement austerity programmes to address the economic crisis and performed a U-turn on the contentious issue of Spain's May 1982 entry into NATO.[21] A hard line on ETA and an effort to secure the co-operation of France against it developed alongside an uncertain start in putting into practice the autonomy arrangements foreseen in the constitution. Together, these led to measures that in some respects made things worse. Foremost among them was the disastrous decision to reactivate targeted assassinations performed by illegal groups as a means of destabilising the comfortable sanctuary Basque refugees enjoyed in the French Basque provinces. The new measures were accompanied by continual efforts to reach out to individual ETA members through a variety of channels. But as González remained adamant that he would not negotiate with terrorists, they did not add up to a coherent strategy for political engagement.

Complicating relations between Madrid and Euskadi were pressures from other autonomous regions. During the early 1980s decentralisation followed an improvised path. Bilateral negotiations between Madrid and individual regions led to wide variation in the competences awarded to the newly autonomous communities that together made up *el estado de autonomias*, the 'state of autonomies'. Some regions resented what they saw as the unfair rewarding of Basques and Catalans for their militant nationalism, while Basque and Catalan nationalists understood the distinctive aspects of their own rights and privileges to have been diluted by a policy that was derided as *café para todos*, 'coffee for everybody'.[22] Working with the outgoing UCD government, the PSOE tried to address this situation through the introduction of a new law for 'the harmonisation of the autonomy process' (LOAPA). The PNV and Catalan nationalists criticised the new law as an illegitimate imposition by the Spanish state and in 1983 the Constitutional Court dismissed it almost in its entirety. The PSOE's inability to reach an agreed vision on the future shape of Spain helped to prevent the introduction of an alternative. But the dynamics of competitive grievance between, and escalating demands within, Spain's seventeen autonomous communities were already in place. In time they would emerge as a major flaw in the country's development.[23]

Counter-terrorism policy under the PSOE was both more robust and more coercive than that of the UCD. José Barrionuevo, the new minister of the interior, had been a member of the Francoist student union, and deputy mayor of Madrid.[24] His appointment reflected acquiescence with what González would later describe as a 'state apparatus inherited in its entirety from the dictatorship'.[25] Barrionuevo failed to capitalise on the Socialists' popular mandate to purge the security forces of officials with the experience, methods and mindset of the past. A new security plan, the *Plan de Zona Especial Norte*, or Plan ZEN (for the 'Special Northern Zone'), was introduced in 1983. It recommended counter-insurgency activities that ranged from improved police methods to psychological operations to confuse ETA and win over Basque public opinion, but was contested by Basque nationalists and rejected by the Basque Parliament.[26] Writing in *El País*, Eduardo Uriarte of EE complained that the government had paid little attention either to what it knew to be the political foundations of the Basque problem or to the fact that 'police action in the past has created more ETA militants than every pamphlet written since Sabino Arana'.[27] Detentions and arrests continued apace, and escalated after the introduction of a tough new anti-terrorist law in 1985.[28] Torture remained widespread, as was documented in an Amnesty International report published that same year.[29]

A desire to secure French co-operation against ETA had been an early preoccupation of the new government. By the 1980s the organisation's military, political, financial and propaganda operations were primarily run out of the hospitable villages of the Basque riviera. They offered the double benefit of a comfortable refuge beyond the reach of Spanish law that was nonetheless part of the Basque homeland. French policy towards the Basque refugees had been forged under Franco and had changed little to reflect Spain's transition, to the great irritation of the government. Socialist officials embarked upon a series of meetings with their French counterparts, bent on persuading them to withdraw the tacit support they were offering to ETA. From late 1983 these diplomatic contacts ran in parallel to a series of targeted assassinations and kidnappings, mostly carried out in French territory, in a new manifestation of a 'dirty war'.[30]

October 1983 was a turning point. Holdouts from ETA-pm kidnapped an army medical officer, Captain Alberto Martín Barrios, and threatened to kill him—an action that aroused public sympathy for their victim and infuriated the army. While Barrios was held captive (but before he was killed, as he would be shortly afterwards), two young ETA militants, José Antonio Lasa and José Ignacio Zabala, were kidnapped in Bayonne and never seen alive again. Only many years later would it emerge that they had been held for three months, tortured, and then shot and buried in quicklime in Alicante.[31] A note found in the pocket of the next victim, Segundo Marey—a man of no known political affiliation, kidnapped from his home in the border town of Hendaye in December 1983 and released alive ten day later—left the identity and purposes of the perpetrator in no doubt. Claiming responsibility for the kidnapping, the Grupos Antiterroristas de Liberación ('Anti-terrorist Liberation Groups') stated that it had 'decided to eliminate' the situation created by the 'increase in the murders, kidnappings and extortion committed by the terrorist organisation ETA on Spanish soil, planned and directed from French territory'. It promised to respond to each of ETA's murders with 'the necessary reply' and warned: 'you will hear news of the GAL'.[32]

Between 1983 and 1987 the GAL claimed at least twenty-seven mortal victims, a third of them without ties to ETA, and wounded some thirty-five more. Its actions were always rumoured to be tied to state security forces and were later demonstrated to have been ordered from within the interior ministry. Barrionuevo, Rafael Vera, the director of state security, Ricardo Damborenea, secretary-general of the PSE in

Vizcaya, and General (then Colonel) Enrique Rodríguez Galindo of the Guardia Civil were among the senior officials convicted of crimes related to the GAL, while speculation swirled around the identity of a supposed mastermind, *Señor X*. Paddy Woodworth's chilling account of the evolution and subsequent investigation of the GAL, *Dirty War, Clean Hands*, demonstrates that the actions of the GAL helped shift French policy towards ETA. As lines between the terrorism of ETA and the GAL became blurred, so the Basque refugees were increasingly understood as a problem. France started extraditing *etarras* in 1984—initially to distant third countries—and later in the year to Spain itself. By the time GAL's activities ceased in 1987, the arrest, imprisonment and extradition of ETA militants had become a routine feature of French security policy that would permanently undermine ETA's operational capacity.

But the saga of the GAL had other consequences too. The GAL attacks created a whole new pantheon of ETA martyrs, bolstered its recruitment and support among the nationalist left, and undermined the legitimacy of Spain's democracy. Particularly dramatic was the assassination of Santiago Brouard, a popular paediatrician and prominent leader of Herri Batasuna, shot and killed by the GAL in Bilbao in November 1984. The possibility of dialogue with ETA had been once more in the air. In August a surprise offer by the government for direct negotiations between Barrionuevo and Domingo Iturbe Abasolo, *Txomin*, ETA's foremost leader, had appeared to offer a radical shift in government policy. But it had been quickly modified by the explanation that the offer was restricted to the 'police' and not 'political' orbit, and was rejected by ETA.[33] Brouard had flown to the Dominican Republic shortly afterwards to brief the exiled ETA leader Eugenio Etxebeste, *Antxon*, on the proposal. He also discussed a (different) possible process with the French ambassador to Spain, and was viewed by many as the individual within the nationalist left with the greatest capacity to prepare or lead any eventual negotiation with the government.[34] His death prompted an immediate response by ETA, which attacked a Spanish general in Madrid the next day, and brought thousands of people onto the streets of Bilbao to take part in his funeral procession.

No less damaging than the GAL attacks was the slow unravelling of the legal cases against the officials charged with their organisation. These gathered pace only in the 1990s and were resisted every step of the way. They would therefore sustain the GAL as a mobilising force against the

Socialists long after its activities ceased in 1987. Convictions were achieved as a consequence of the courage and persistence of individual journalists and judges—notably the crusading magistrate Baltasar Garzón—but for the most part they were overturned with unseemly haste (Barrionuevo and Vera served just three months of their ten-year prison sentences).[35] Scandals surrounding the GAL exposed deep-rooted problems in the country's security and counter-terrorist structures that were eagerly exploited by the opposition PP. They combined with well-founded charges of financial corruption within the PSOE to ensure its defeat in the general elections of 1996. But the court cases rumbled on well into the 2000s and—together with the fact that the Socialists offered no formal apology for their role in the GAL—kept the increasingly distant 'dirty war' a live issue in Basque politics.[36]

ETA and its world

After the ideological debates that had characterised ETA's early years and the shift away from dreams of insurrection to a long war of attrition, a kind of stasis set in.[37] The organisation was rigid in its core precepts and its prioritisation of revolutionary—understood as armed—action to achieve them, even as the political changes around it and its tendency towards more indiscriminate violence led many associated with it to move away. Although formally not exclusive it ethnic terms, it ignored and assaulted the plural nature of Basque society with an insistence on a stark choice: being with the radical nationalist community it identified as *el pueblo vasco*, the Basque people, or against it, and thus effectively 'Spanish'. It claimed to be acting on behalf of the 'popular majority' even as the actual Basque majority increasingly resisted its attempt to impose its views by violent means. And it refused to accept that 'constitutionalist' Basques—some of whom held prominent positions in Spanish life (between 1957 and 1980 three of Spain's six foreign ministers—Fernando María Castiella, José María de Areilza and Marcelino Oreja Aguirre—were Basque)—were 'Basque' at all.[38]

ETA's own structure would vary over the years, with changes made in response to arrests and in the interest of greater security.[39] Most significant was a move away from a structure that included a single figure at its apex to a collective leadership resident in France. For many years ETA's activities were divided into three main areas—politics, logistics and military operations—each with its own support structures and commander on the organisation's executive committee. This vertical structure sought to establish authority over ETA's small operational cells, but also exposed the organisation to security problems. Members of operational cells lived and worked in clandestinity; communication was only possible upwards through ETA's hierarchy to the executive committee. Arrests at any level thus exposed the chain of command in each direction. Over time, the size of the executive committee grew to oversee eleven distinct sections: logistics; politics; international affairs; military operations; reserves; prisoners; extortion—or 'revolutionary taxation' as ETA termed it; information; recruitment; negotiation; and finances. However, as the arrests of successive ETA leaders mounted, a reduced number of individuals constituted the committee's inner 'permanent' core, *el permanente*.[40]

ETA's militants included those who operated 'legally' (*legales*) and those, the *fichados*, who were already 'charged' or identified by the security forces. The *legales* were untarnished by a criminal record and maintained legitimate employment and lifestyle until activated in ETA's service. The *fichados* operated in small clandestine cells; also known as *liberados* ('liberated'), they were paid by ETA and generally carried out the most dangerous assignments. The number of ETA members has been necessarily difficult to determine with any accuracy; for much of its existence, however, they were estimated as being in the hundreds, with several hundred more in Spanish and Basque prisons or in exile at any one time.[41]

Recruitment to ETA followed no formal process. Recruits were frequently drawn from families with a long history of Basque militancy, as well as the many youth, cultural or social organisations that populated radical nationalist circles. They were characterised by their dedication to the cause, and belief in the inherent rightness of actions undertaken in its name, however violent. 'ETA is a movement of political roots and political motivation,' Patxi Zabaleta, a leading member of Herri Batasuna before he rejected ETA's violence to form Aralar, recalled in 2010, 'there are no mercenaries in ETA.'[42]

In the early 1970s ETA had generally attracted men in their twenties from the towns and villages of Guipúzcoa and Vizcaya, frequently from Euskera-speaking families. The specific conditions of the mountainous but densely populated regions of Guipúzcoa such as the Goeirri, which combined an intense rural life with burgeoning light industry, had long proved a particularly rich source of future *etarras*. In such circumstances familial and social bonds were tight, and the influence of the *cuadrilla* strong, contributing to the high levels of social cohesion and control that would characterise ETA and the nationalist left as a whole. By the mid-1980s, however, both the average age and the tendency to be Euskera-speaking of the recruits had dropped. New *etarras* were younger and more likely to come from urban areas. Fernando Reinares' research suggested that ETA's membership began to show more resemblance to the radical youth drawn to anti-system violence in other European contexts than had been the case in the past.[43] Twenty years later, the slew of documents captured from the organisation during the assault upon ETA after the end of the 2007 ceasefire revealed new worries about the calibre of its cadres, as well as evidence of their incompetence.[44]

From the earliest years of the transition, ETA was sustained by a complex web of other organisations. These included both the electoral coalition, and later political party, that was HB but also a wide range of other organisations given specific ideological and political identification by the umbrella of the MLNV. Initially linked to ETA through the coordination of KAS, this disparate collection of forces was conceived in Maoist terms as carrying forward an armed struggle, a political struggle and a struggle of the popular masses. Together it constituted the *izquierda abertzale* or nationalist left community. In such a context, HB was much more than a political party. As Begoña Aretxaga described it, it was a 'way of life': 'With its own bars, social events and rituals, associations and groups, Herri Batasuna… responded to the social and political pressure by becoming an ever more intense social microcosm and thereby perceiving itself as a metonym for the Basque nation—the model of the imagined national community.'[45]

As a social as well as a political movement—indeed a universe of surprising ideological heterogeneity—the nationalist left gained strength from the leading role it played in mobilisation against issues such as the construction of the nuclear power station at Lemóniz (halted in 1993) or Spain's determination to enter NATO in 1986. Over time it grew to include networks of lawyers and businessmen, the trade union Langile Abertzaleen Batzordeak (LAB), youth groups (Jarrai, later renamed as Haika and Segi), pro-amnesty and prisoner solidarity organisations (Gestoras pro Amnistia, later Askatasuna, Etxerat), an international solidarity group (Askapena), and cultural societies, feminist and ecological organisations, mountaineering and other sporting and culinary associations, and its own network of bars (*herriko tabernas*).[46]

During the 2000s the extent to which this broad milieu represented a world in which 'everything is ETA' became highly controversial. While it was ETA that set the strategic limits as to what the MLNV could or could not do, the organisations within it varied over time, as did their economic and political ties to ETA. Individuals within the nationalist left acknowledge that there were always some among their number who practised a 'double militancy' that included participation in or abetting of ETA's violent actions, even as the positions of others on ETA's violence varied widely. A number of those who moved away from this close-knit world but remained sympathetic to its goals cited its 'undemocratic', 'totalitarian' or 'Stalinist' forms of internal control as instrumental in their decision to leave it behind. Those who remained make a clear distinction between sharing the same ideological substrata as ETA and a more instrumental relationship.[47] 'In organisational terms,' as Rafa Diéz, for many years secretary-general of LAB, explained, 'one thing is ETA and another is the multitude of other organisations that developed. The trade union [LAB], Batasuna or other organisations have links with ETA; these links might be ideological, might be organic, or might only reflect their shared revindications for the Basque people.'[48]

The most critical relationship was with HB. After an initial period of greater autonomy, HB subordinated its political activities to ETA's tactical needs and neither challenged nor condemned its use of violence. ETA's dominant role could from the beginning be attributed to two distinct factors: the acceptance within HB that if the militants of ETA were prepared to kill and be killed ('contributing blood') for the struggle, then they should be in charge; and the practical consideration that ETA was already organised with a plan of action and functioning clandestine structures, while HB was initially much more diffuse. ETA ended up strengthening its hold over the entire MLNV, albeit with tensions within it. This process, as Txema Montero, a leading member of HB for many years, recalled, 'was curiously accelerated when the *poli-milis* split and dissolved. Those *poli-milis* who joined ETA-m strengthened its position in the political vanguard.'[49] Some of the tensions, perhaps counter-intuitively, were rooted in the fact that there were many in ETA who instinctively distrusted HB, particularly at moments when its electoral support appeared the strongest. José Felix Azurmendi, the former editor of the nationalist left newspaper *Egin*, explains that at times ETA even came to think that, 'it did not matter that its assassinations took votes from HB, because it was better to have fewer, but more solid [supporters]'.[50]

HB was ETA's political surrogate, but also its interlocutor, including for those wishing to pay their extortion dues. A decision to take part in elections but not to occupy the institutional positions to which its representatives had been elected was taken early. On this basis, the party erupted onto the political scene in the Basque provincial and municipal elections in 1979 and participated in all elections held in the Basque Country until it was banned in 2003. HB won more than 20 per cent of the Basque vote in its first provincial elections and 15 per cent at the municipal level. Between 1979 and the end of 1999 it contested five additional provincial and municipal elections, six autonomous elections, six (Spanish) legislative elections and two European elections. Its support oscillated between 12 and 20 per cent of the Basque vote, peaking in the late 1980s and 1990s, while the local council seats it won grew from 260 in 1979 to 669 in 1987. This meant that between 150,000 and 220,000 people regularly voted for a party aligned with ETA that challenged the legitimacy of the Spanish state.[51] This was a force, representative of a community, which could not be dismissed as 'terrorist' and nothing more.

Although the ties between the MLNV and Irish republicanism were always present—and both movements were for many years characterised by the pursuit of their goals through the combination of a 'ballot paper in one hand and the Armalite in the other', to cite the memorable phrase of Danny Morrison—there were considerable differences between them.[52] Most obvious was the gradual ascendance of Sinn Féin from the late 1980s on and its subsequent capacity to act as interlocutor between other political actors and the IRA's Army Council (an achievement that would be closely studied by Batasuna's leaders after 2007). Political relations between Sinn Féin and HB were of high priority for each organisation. As Eoin O'Brien, Sinn Féin's director for European Affairs during the mid-2000s observed, for Irish republicanism the relationship with the Basques was 'unique in a European context'.[53]

Early connections to the republican movement had been managed by the *poli-milis*. In the late 1970s, ETA-m had no interest in maintaining them, so it had fallen to Montero to rebuild relations from inside HB.

He met a number of individuals who would rise to very prominent positions in Sinn Féin and found an immediate affinity with them: 'the *poli-milis* had a very elaborate Marxist-Leninist discourse whereas we had a sort of revolutionary nationalism that was more comprehensible to Sinn Féin', as he would later recall.[54] O'Brien agreed: 'we inhabit the same cosmos in all sorts of ways—the sense of self, place, party, relation to other stateless nations and so forth'. The relationship was based on strong personal ties and on respect for the strengths and weaknesses of the other. HB's electoral presence in the early days, the nationalist left's projection through the media and capacity for social mobilisation were quite unlike anything Sinn Féin achieved; HB, meanwhile, looked up to Sinn Féin's negotiating capacity, international networks and institutional projects.

As Spanish democracy took hold, and ETA's military goals settled into a long war of attrition against the state, so its violence began to change, alienating some of its own supporters. An early shock was the assassination of María Dolores González Catarain, *Yoyes*, in September 1986. As head of ETA-m's military front between 1978 and 1980, Yoyes had been one of the few women to have held a senior position in the organisation. She had broken with ETA in 1981 and had lived in exile in Mexico and Paris, from where she returned to Spain under the reintegration programme. Like others before her she was perceived by some within ETA to be a traitor. Her cold-blooded assassination in the Guipuzcoan town of Ordizia in front of her three-year-old daughter was nevertheless unprecedented. The crime sent reverberations around the nationalist community, profoundly disturbed by what ETA was prepared to do to one of its own.[55]

Worse was to come. In the following year, HB won one of its greatest electoral victories when it emerged as the most voted Basque party in elections to the European Parliament. At the head of HB's list, Txema Montero received 240,000 votes from within the Basque Country and 120,000 more from elsewhere in Spain, including 40,000 from Catalonia. Days later ETA appeared to repay this support by exploding a large bomb in the car park of the Hipercor supermarket in Barcelona, killing twenty-one people and injuring forty-five. A sense of revulsion swept through Spain. ETA struggled to counter what was clearly a public relations disaster. Admitting its 'error', it offered its sympathy to the people of Catalonia and the families and friends of the victims. It had not meant to kill. It had repeatedly telephoned in warnings of the bomb's existence to the Barcelona Police. It would do everything possible to ensure the selectivity of its targets in the future.[56] But there could be no excuses for exploding a bomb in a crowded supermarket. Hipercor would mark a point of inflection at which ETA lost a significant degree of social cover it had long enjoyed from sectors of Basque society beyond the nationalist left.[57]

The 'two souls' of the PNV

In 1980 Carlos Garaikoetxea became *lehendakari* at the head of the first of a series of PNV-led governments. Encompassing a variety of coalition arrangements, these would extend to 2009. During this nearly thirty-year period the party built on its deep roots in Basque society. Bilbao remained its political stronghold and spiritual home. Sabin Etxea, the birthplace of Sabino Arana that in the early 1990s was converted into a gleaming new party headquarters, embodied the power and money of its Vizcayan delegation, the Bizkai Baru Batzar. A sense of the omnipresence of the PNV was reinforced by its habitual control of the three provincial governments, a party structure that kept its powerful presidency—for many years held by the imposing figure of Xabier Arzalluz—outside the government, and its successful promotion of trade unions, media, and a wide range of sporting, cultural, youth and other associations.[58]

The PNV was institutionally committed to the full realisation of the autonomy statute and disposed to enter into a series of pacts and agreements with Madrid to further it. But it was difficult for a Basque nationalist to renounce self-determination, or even independence. These 'two souls' of the PNV, described by Santiago de Pablo and Ludger Mees as the swing of a 'patriotic pendulum' between autonomy and independence, had been present in the party since its birth.[59] Meanwhile, a continuing perception of the PNV's 'calculated ambiguity' inevitably complicated its relations to the Spanish political parties, especially with respect to ETA.[60] Ramón Jáuregui, a Socialist who would serve in the Basque government alongside the PNV for many years, recalled its politicians as playing 'a game, sometimes disloyal, always a bit roguish, a little cunning, of saying "yes, but no", of committing themselves but leaving the door open to a configuration that reflects their millenarian ideal of Euskadi as the seven territories'.[61]

In the early 1980s 51 per cent of PNV supporters perceived ETA militants as 'patriots' or 'idealists', and the party was unable to condemn ETA as a purely terrorist organisation to the extent demanded of it by Spanish politicians.[62] Suspicion of emotional sympathy for those willing to kill and be killed for the Basque cause was compounded by fears of a more instrumental relationship. Many believed that, just as the PNV had achieved more from the statute of autonomy, with the threatening presence of ETA looming over its shoulder as it negotiated with Suárez, than it would have if the armed organisation had not existed, so it continued to benefit from ETA's violence in its negotiations with Madrid. Arzalluz himself did much to stoke these fears, most notoriously by observing that 'while some shake the trees others gather the nuts'. He would later insist that his remark had referred to HB—not the PNV—and ETA, but his explanation gained little traction with his critics.[63] The distinction between the doctrinal ambiguity of the PNV and responsibility for violence was nonetheless a stark one. 'The responsibility of a killer is the killer's,' observed Eduardo Madina, a Basque Socialist a generation younger than Jáuregui who lost a leg to a car bomb of ETA's in 2002: 'The existence of a nationalist party more pro-autonomy than independence—we should be clear—does not justify, create conditions or facilitate the existence of a group of people who kill'.[64]

A clear understanding of the political origins of ETA led the PNV to support the idea of dialogue. However, it was also consistently wary of the possibility that ETA's political demands might be discussed with the Spanish government to its own exclusion. In early 1983 Garaikoetxea launched a peace initiative that sought to bring together the PNV, HB and the PSOE. But the mutual distrust—HB was too close to ETA for the PSOE, the PSOE too representative of the state for HB and the PNV had the full confidence of neither—was too great, and his idea for a *mesa de paz*, a 'peace roundtable', never prospered.[65] Instead he pushed for implementation of the provisions of the autonomy statute, with emphasis on the creation of a Basque police force, the Ertzaintza, that might eventually replace the unwelcome presence of the Spanish police and Guardia Civil. The PNV's hope was that Basque police would prove effective both in countering ETA and undermining its arguments against the 'occupying forces' of Spain. But it would not be easy; the Spanish security services did not trust the Ertzaintza as reliable partners in counter-terrorism, while ETA and the nationalist left came to oppose the Ertzaintza as *cipayos*—a word taken from 'cipoys', the name for Indian soldiers serving in the British colonial army, that implied a nationalist betrayal.[66]

Other differences with Madrid—like the so-called 'war of the flags', which suddenly flared up in the summer of 1983—revolved around the all-important symbolic representation of the Basque nation. A delay in the legalisation of the public display of the Basque *ikurrina* had been a cause of tension during the transition.[67] Basque nationalists now either tore down or refused to fly the Spanish flag—for radical nationalists not only the symbol of Spain but 'the same as under Franco… a symbol of torturers'[68]—mandated by the constitution to be displayed alongside regional flags on public buildings. Violent protests broke out as *ikurrinas* fluttered alone in Basque town halls, and on the institutions of the Basque government. Years later, public display of a Spanish flag continued to be charged with political implication, as the celebration of Spain's triumph in the World Cup in July 2010 would illustrate. Basques, like Catalans, had long demanded the right to field national sports teams in international competition. Ardent football fans, their range of responses to the triumph of Spain's national team, *La Roja*—the squad heavily populated by Catalan and Basque players—mirrored their ideological diversity (some nationalists supported the Netherlands in the final only for being 'not' Spain, as a member of Batasuna explained). For days afterwards the extent to which Spanish flags had or had not been visible in Euskadi after Spain's win, and what it meant, was hotly debated. One Basque PP politician recalled sadly that he had hung a Spanish flag from his apartment window in a spirit of defiance, only to have it pelted with eggs.[69]

Relations with Madrid improved in 1985. The PNV signed a legislative pact with Madrid that included the condemnation of terrorism and, after ETA's assassination of the head of the Ertzainza, the Basque Parliament explicitly condemned ETA's violence for the first time.[70] Meanwhile, an internal crisis concluded in a painful split that saw Garaikoetxea leave the PNV to found a new nationalist party, Eusko Alkartasuna (EA, Basque Solidarity). Like the PNV, EA was committed to non-violent Basque nationalism, but it identified itself as a social-democratic party and as such to be distinguished from the more conservative and Christian democratic PNV. Garaikoetxea's departure prompted new elections in Euskadi; when these were won by the PNV with a slim margin, it entered into a coalition government with the PSE. José Antonio Ardanza became *lehendakari* with Ramón Jáuregui as his deputy, initiating a coalition that held for more than a decade and did much to build the foundations of Euskadi as a functioning autonomous community.

Prominent among the coalition's achievements was agreement amongst Basque political parties—with the obvious exception of HB—on the approach to be taken towards ETA.[71] The Pact of Ajuria Enea built on an anti-terrorist agreement reached in Madrid in November 1987, movement towards the derogation of the 1985 anti-terrorism legislation, and noted improvement in the efficiency and discrimination of counter-terrorist operations.[72] The final text was firmly rooted in defence of the autonomy statute. It acknowledged that there was an unresolved dispute between the Basque people and the Spanish state, and recognised the possibility of a solution through dialogue. But it also reaffirmed that only the Navarrese could decide whether Navarre should be united with Euskadi, rejected any dialogue or negotiations until violence had ceased, and denied ETA the legitimacy to address political questions.[73] A distinction between an end to violence and political dialogue was caught in the agreement's formal title: 'Agreement on the Normalisation and Pacification of Euskadi.' To the extent that it proposed a hard division between proponents of democracy and the supporters of terrorism, the MLNV saw the Pact of Ajuria Enea as a 'a declaration of war against the nationalist left'.[74] For others it would remain the cornerstone of Spanish and Basque policy towards ETA. Alfredo Pérez Rubalcaba, who would oversee policies towards ETA for the PSOE from the late 1990s and throughout the seven and a half years of Zapatero's government, would look back on it in 2012 as 'the best thing democratic parties did' against ETA, 'the best'.[75]

Conversations in Algiers

In 1986 the PSOE comfortably won its second general election. From a position of strength the government embarked on the most sustained attempt to date to engage ETA in dialogue. A disparate set of contacts and overtures in 1987 and 1988 gradually coalesced into direct talks in Algiers. These took place in early 1989 with the good offices of the Algerian government and against the backdrop of a temporary ceasefire.

A complicated mix of factors led a democratic European state to talk in Algeria with an entity it perceived as a terrorist organisation. Among them were the benefits to be gained from Spain's relations with both France and Algeria.[76] President Mitterand encouraged negotiations in part because they would strengthen domestic support in France for security co-operation with Spain. Algeria, meanwhile, had friendly relations with ETA; it had hosted military training in the past and still provided a refuge for some thirty exiles. Spain knew that it could more credibly ask Algeria to break those ties if it demonstrated willingness to talk to ETA—and also that Algeria had an interest in securing Spanish support in its conflict with Morocco over Western Sahara and in limiting the activities of an illegal opposition party, the Algerian Democratic Movement, with a presence in Madrid. With this array of factors in the background, Spain could accept Algeria's good offices, but it would be uncomfortable with the parity Algeria offered the two delegations in the talks and consistently reject the idea that its role should grow into that of a mediator.[77]

ETA had been weakened by the involvement of France and the increasing cohesion among Spanish and Basque political parties. Yet it was still strong enough to put the government under pressure. Txomin had been arrested in April 1986 and moved first to Gabon and then Algeria, facilitating the contacts upon which the talks would be based. He was killed in a car accident in early 1987, but would be quickly replaced by Antxon. Contacts from within the interior ministry and by police officials continued despite the escalation of terrorist attacks and Antxon's suspicion that the government's prime concern was to explore the possibility of fissures within ETA.[78] The ETA leader Santiago Arrospide Sarasola, *Santi Potros*, was captured in late September 1987. In December ETA exploded a huge car-bomb in the Guardia Civil barracks at Zaragoza, killing eleven, including five children, and wounding many more. Outrage at this new atrocity prompted the government temporarily to break off contacts with ETA, but also increased public pressure upon it to explore every avenue to bring about an end to the violence.

In January 1988 ETA offered a two-month ceasefire if the government were to agree to a preliminary meeting with the MLNV and political negotiations.[79] The government offered no formal response to the proposal even as consultations with Antxon continued. At the end of February they finally broke down. ETA kidnapped Emiliano Revilla, a wealthy businessman, and the government suspended its contacts with the organisation. Revilla was released in October after the payment of a large ransom, and ETA once again offered to talk. The government was under pressure from trade unions, which had called a general strike in December 1988, and popular opinion was coalescing around the benefits of engaging directly with ETA. Formal talks began in Algeria in early 1989 after ETA offered a unilateral fifteen-day ceasefire—the first official ceasefire in its history.

Six meetings were held between the two delegations: Rafael Vera in addition to the Basque politician Juan Manuel Eguiagaray, on the government's behalf, and Belén González Peñalva, *Carmen*, and Iñaki Arakama Mendia, *Makario*, in addition to Antxon, on that of ETA.[80] Each had advisers—ETA representatives of HB and LAB in addition to several lawyers—outside the negotiating room and maintained frequent telephone contact with Madrid, on the one hand, and ETA's leadership in France, on the other. Media speculation on developments within the talks was intense, and demonstrations in the Basque Country confirmed that other representatives of Basque society had much at stake. Particularly influential was the massive demonstration against ETA convened in Bilbao by the parties to the Ajuria Enea Pact on 18 March. ETA considered it an act of sabotage of the talks by the PNV, which it understood to have assumed the counter-terrorist discourse of the state while still fearing that Spain might reach agreement with ETA behind its back.[81]

The government had entered the talks with no confidence that a positive outcome would be possible. It wanted 'peace in exchange for nothing… or peace for prisoners, in the best case', as Eguiagaray recalled, and therefore understood ETA's refusal to address the issue of prisoners as an indication that it was not serious.[82] ETA demanded political negotiations on the core issues it had outlined so long ago in the KAS Alternative and, failing this, the political recognition it could derive from direct talks with the Spanish government. Discussions were at once 'political' and not, ranging far and wide over Basque history and culture and the parties' different perspectives on the transition. They ended in April with the gap between the two sides evident to both, and as ETA alleged that the government in Madrid had made unacceptable changes to agreements reached with its negotiating delegation in Algiers.[83]

ETA returned to violence. It sent letter bombs to a number of those involved in the process and assassinated a member of the Guardia Civil in the outskirts of Bilbao. The government prevailed upon the Algerians to expel ETA's negotiating delegation to the Dominican Republic. In a major shift in prison policy, it also began sending about 500 ETA prisoners to a wide range of prisons across Spain, including in the Canary Islands, and subjected them to harsh new regimes once they got there. The dispersion was designed to counter the political cohesion that had been so successfully demonstrated by IRA prisoners in Northern Ireland (especially since the hunger strikes of 1981). It sought to disrupt ETA's control over its prisoners through its lawyers and entities such as Gestoras pro Amnistia, thereby undermining what Mercedes Gallizo, the director general of the prison service under Zapatero, would describe as ETA's use of its prisoners as 'an instrument of its political action'.[84] Dispersion had no basis in Spanish law; indeed Article 12.1 of the general penitentiary law establishes that there should be sufficient prisons to avoid prisoners having to be incarcerated outside their own communities.[85] Rather it was part of what Manuela Carmena, a Judge of Prison Supervision (*Juez de Vigilancia Penitenciaria*) at the time of dispersion's introduction, described as the government's 'political war' against ETA.[86] Consequently, it was experienced as an additional punishment by ETA prisoners and their family members, who now had to travel extensively for brief prison visits.

The end of the Algiers talks was bruising, but both sides considered that they had gained something. The government had used the talks to maintain unity with the political opposition and cement international co-operation; it had been seen to go the extra mile for peace without engaging in what it considered political negotiation, and ETA had got the blame for the talks' collapse.[87] For ETA the benefits were less obvious, but considerable. The 'great achievement' of Algiers, as Batasuna's Arnaldo Otegi would observe, was that 'the Spanish state consented to sit with an armed organisation in a neutral country and talk about politics… [It] recognised ETA as an interlocutor, and gave it legitimacy as a political actor'.[88]

As an exercise in peacemaking the Algiers talks were evidently immature. There had been no consideration on either side that a process of negotiation involves concessions, and no real expectation that any might have been given. From ETA's perspective the government had violated commitments made at the table and avoided either a sustained discussion of elements that would be required for a political solution or the involvement of other actors (HB) with whom it would have been forced to address issues that extended beyond the violence of ETA. Under such circumstances consideration of a more permanent cessation of its hostilities was unthinkable.

Turning point

The 1980s had been a turbulent and bloody decade for the Basque Country. ETA had claimed nearly four hundred victims. It was weakened by the efforts against it, but it had also been able to draw on a depth of support that ensured its survival. In the aftermath of Algiers, ETA sought to impose new negotiations upon the government by force. Firmly within its sights was 1992, the five-hundredth anniversary of Columbus' journey to the Americas. Madrid was to be cultural capital of Europe and Spain to host the summer Olympics in Barcelona as well as an International Expo in Seville. Together these events represented an extraordinary opportunity for the 'new Spain'—the Spain of social and political progress, a booming economy, the cultural riches of *la movida* and the plaudits won by Felipe González as an international statesman—to show itself off.[89] They also represented an irresistible target for ETA.

Between the breakdown of the talks in Algeria and the end of 1992 ETA claimed 115 lives in 386 armed actions, in addition to high profile kidnappings and a series of attacks in Italy and Germany, launched in an attempt to raise international awareness of its conflict.[90] This wave of violence was countered by police action that thwarted ETA's ambitions to disrupt the 1992 festivities. On 29 March 1992, French and Spanish security services achieved one of their most spectacular successes when they captured José Luis Álvarez Santacristina, *Txelis*, Francisco Mujika Garmendia, *Pakito*, and Joseba Arregi Erostarbe, the three leading members of ETA's executive committee, in Bidart, in southern France. A few months later ETA's substitute leadership was also detained.

The shock to ETA and HB was immediate, and real. For the first time in its history the MLNV was forced to contemplate the possibility that ETA might be defeated by police means. In the short term ETA's military capacity was severely restricted and its strategy and predicament subjected to an unusual degree of internal criticism—including from two of the three commanders captured at Bidart, Txelis and Pakito, and from Antxon in Santo Domingo.[91] There were also rumblings from within HB, which in late 1991 had embarked on a process of internal reflection, *Urrats Berri*, in which some of its members questioned the party's dependence on the actions of ETA. Several prominent members of HB—including Txema Montero—left the MLNV. But the crisis was contained without a more fundamental questioning of ETA's violence; KAS assumed control of the MLNV and a dominant position within the executive direction of HB.[92]

Throughout this period counter-terrorism was accompanied by a confusing number of initiatives to re-open channels to ETA. The confusion reflected growing rifts within the Spanish interior ministry, where Vera continued to promote contacts with ETA—at times without the authorisation, or even knowledge, of his superiors. It also suggested a startling absence of any overarching strategy. In order to avoid contacts primarily directed towards fomenting internal divisions and gathering intelligence, ETA repeatedly insisted that Antxon was the sole authorised channel. It appealed for more 'seriousness' from the government and from December 1993 began to call for international mediation (Antxon would later recall that ETA, with a close eye on the role being played by the UN in the Central American peace process, had hoped for the involvement of the world organisation).[93] Disarray within the government was accelerated by revelations regarding the GAL, as well as the eruption of a scandal involving the financial corruption of Luis Roldán, the long-time director general of the Guardia Civil, who in April 1994 fled Spain to avoid charges against him.

The unedifying tale of the multiple contacts and channels to ETA pursued in this period is vividly recounted by Carlos Fonseca.[94] They included an initial effort by Vera to work through Antxon in the Dominican Republic, abandoned because Vera believed Antxon had lost credibility within the organisation; a channel through Roldán to the HB leader Patxi Zabaleta, which did not prosper; Vera's attempts to work through two HB lawyers who had been present in Algeria to establish a channel to a senior ETA member imprisoned in France; and the involvement of two civil society organisations, Gernika Gogoratuz, a centre for peace studies which had been created in 1987 under the auspices of the Basque government, and Elkarri, an organisation founded in December 1992 with the specific desire to encourage dialogue as a means to end the violence.

Gernika Gogoratuz and its director Juan Gutierrez facilitated the first involvement of external actors in efforts to encourage dialogue (although not initially with ETA) by making introductions for two US academics, Christopher Mitchell and John Paul Lederach. The two men were both prominent for their role in developing—and putting into practice—some of the core principles of conflict resolution and transformation, including problem-solving workshops, informal or 'Track II' dialogue, and efforts to introduce changes in conflict parties' relationships through improved mutual understanding.[95] Mitchell had first been approached by Robert Clark, a colleague at George Mason University in Washington, DC, after the collapse of the Algiers talks. From his own study of ETA and the various efforts to pursue negotiations to date, Clark had concluded that the Basques might benefit from outside assistance. Mitchell brought in Lederach, and the two began a series of visits in 1990, meeting with a wide array of Basques, and in Madrid with Vera. They found that 'nobody talked to anybody', so in late 1991 they invited representatives of all Basque political parties, including the PP and HB, to a retreat centre in Virginia in order to encourage dialogue between them and explore the possibility of reaching some sort of pact.[96] The PNV politician Juan María Ollora would remember the meeting for the first exposure it provided participants to some of the basic elements of conflict resolution, but also that 'neither the Spanish government nor the nationalist left was interested in international involvement at that time'.[97] Returning to the Basque Country after the Bidart captures, Mitchell remembered being told that ETA was 'finished'. He and Lederach met with the PSOE and PP and tried to explain that 'they may have been rounded up, but this can't be "over" because you have not dealt with underlying issues'.

Elkarri's director, Jonan Fernández, was a former member of HB who maintained good contacts within the MLNV. His experience of a bitter conflict over the route to be taken by a new Basque motorway—which the ecological organisation (Lurraldea) with which he had been involved had fiercely resisted—had led him to believe that in the Basque Country, 'a whole lot of effort is put into the extremes and not much into the idea of dialogue'.[98] He consulted regularly with Benegas, who remained eager to explore the possibility of engaging with ETA, and in October 1993 travelled to the Dominican Republic. There Fernández met with Antxon, who designated a three-man negotiating team from HB to carry talks forward. Rafa Díez (who had been an adviser to ETA in Algiers), José Luís Elkoro and Karmelo Landa met with Vera and

Benegas in early 1994, but the initiative was on uncertain footing within the interior ministry. A new minister, Antonio Asunción, prevented Vera attending a second meeting and was then forced to resign by Roldán's flight after just five months on the job. Juan Manuel Belloch succeeded him and immediately announced his rejection of dialogue with ETA. But the door was not quite closed. Margarita Robles, one of Belloch's deputies, would herself soon become involved in developing a secret channel to ETA.[99]

Fernández was also pursuing another track. Enlisting the assistance of the anthropologist Joseba Zulaika, by then affiliated with the Center for Basque Studies at the University of Reno, Nevada, he began to think about developing international involvement in the pursuit of talks. Fernández and Zulaika persuaded William Douglass, the Center's director, to host an International Committee for the Basque Peace Process, and to sanction their contact with the Carter Center. The International Committee proved a short-lived effort—an appeal for funds to some 10,000 contacts produced just $300, effectively demonstrating the dearth of interest in ETA among the Basque diaspora in the US—but the contact with the Carter Center prospered.[100] Fernández and Zulaika met with Harry Barnes, at the time overseeing the conflict resolution activities of the Center. With Elkarri's assistance, Barnes met several times with Antxon in the Dominican Republic and also with Benegas. But, as Fernández would recall, his efforts ran into what was becoming a familiar problem: 'the expectation generated by our interlocutors was one thing, but the reality within ETA was another. Antxon and Rafa Díez seemed willing to move ahead, but their views weren't aligned with what was going on inside ETA.' A recurring problem in talks with ETA, Fernández would conclude, 'is that you never knew who you were talking to or what power they actually had'.[101]

Belloch, who also served as minister of justice, renewed efforts to encourage the reinsertion of ETA's prisoners. In mid-1995, despite his assurances to the contrary, he also allowed Robles to exchange messages with the Argentinian Nobel Peace Prize Laureate, Adolfo Pérez Esquivel, whom ETA had asked to assume a role as interlocutor with the Spanish government. These contacts, which included ETA's transmittal of a written proposal for negotiation, as well as visits by emissaries of both the ministry of interior and Peréz Esquivel to Santo Domingo, would be the last attempt at anything approaching a negotiation with ETA during the

González years.[102] They took place against the backdrop of an escalation of ETA's violence—in late 1995 and early 1996 ETA's rate of assassination increased markedly and ETA kidnapped the prison official José Antonio Ortega Lara—but for reasons that in retrospect seem unfathomable the government maintained hope that talks might still be possible. Like other channels to ETA this one abruptly ceased when the PP came to power in 1996 and criticised their internal contradictions as evidence of the decadence of the Socialists' counter-terrorist policies.

Bidart had demonstrated to ETA and the MLNV the limitations of a purely 'military' struggle. It followed in the wake of the pacts of 1987 and 1988 and the Algiers talks, which had effectively framed what the MLNV saw as its 'liberation process' as an 'exclusively bipolar conflict between ETA and the state'.[103] This was a structural approach to the Basque problem that aligned 'democrats' against 'terrorists' to the evident disadvantage of the MLNV. The nationalist left had thought that 'ETA was going to resolve everything,' as Otegi would recall, 'that everything depended on the military strength of ETA, that one day ETA would force the state to a negotiating table and an agreement and the next day Basques would live happily ever after.'[104] This was now quite clearly not a realistic objective.

In a shifting international context the impact of the end of the Cold War was felt only indirectly, but it contributed to a change of direction. Radical nationalists found encouragement in their demands for independence from the break-up of the former Soviet Union. They also began to pay close attention to the peace processes that were developing in El Salvador, South Africa and, especially, Northern Ireland. A new orientation for ETA and the MLNV would materialise gradually in the early 1990s around a decision to extend the fronts for conflict to involve a broader popular base but also to ensure that its impact was more widely felt within Basque society. This involved renewed attention to the myriad civil, social and political organisations of the nationalist left and the role that they could play in the daily task of building the imagined community of the Basque nation, but also the decision, put forward by HB in the *Oldartzen* document it developed in 1994 and 1995, to 'socialise the suffering' caused by ETA more widely within Basque society.[105] ETA's violence would never again claim the numbers of victims seen in the 1980s, but its political and social impact was about to take a new and destructive direction.

3

AZNAR, COUNTER-TERRORISM
AND ESTELLA-LIZARRA

The eight years in office of Prime Minister José María Aznar saw radical change in the strategies adopted against ETA. At their core lay a determination to defeat terrorism by police means and not to countenance contacts, dialogue or negotiation with its perpetrators. The consequences of this harder line were complex and contested. Aznar recalled his struggle against ETA as 'the most demanding and the most difficult, but also... the most creditable' of his responsibilities.[1] Yet progress against ETA did not break either its demands or its ties to the radical nationalist community. Moreover Aznar's policies, and the revival of an assertive form of Spanish nationalism of which they formed a part, increased the level of polarisation and political animosity in the Basque Country, rendering anything approaching a peaceful settlement of the Basque problem a distant prospect.

Twenty years after the death of Franco, the PP's capacity to attract the centre of Spain's political spectrum in the elections of 1996 was a significant achievement in the consolidation of Spain's democracy. In a notably tough campaign, the PP fully exploited the corruption and other scandals—especially the GAL—swirling around the PSOE, suggesting that the sins of the Socialists had stained their regime so comprehensively as to undermine their legitimacy to govern. Its electoral triumph—although short of an absolute majority—therefore represented what Juan Luís Cebrián, the founding director of *El País*, would describe as a 'golden opportunity' for Spanish conservatives both to dislodge the PSOE and to launch a 'second transition' in which they could cleanse the first one of its ills. 'The true Spain was reborn,' Cebrián wrote in a polemic attack on the 'democratic fundamentalism' that flourished under Aznar, 'it came with the sacred fire of purification to cast out the moneychangers from the temple of democracy'.[2]

Aznar's messianic approach to government found the perfect foil in ETA. In its 'all or nothing' response to its post-Bidart crisis, the organisation shifted towards actions designed to have the maximum destabilising impact.[3] These included *kale borroka*, which became the primary form by which radical nationalists imposed their presence upon the streets of the Basque Country, and an expansion in the targeting of its victims. This new and disastrous course was suggested in January 1995 when ETA gunned down the PP politician Gregorio Ordóñez, an elected representative of the 'Basque people' it purported to represent. In April ETA went after Aznar himself, then leader of the opposition, and came close to killing him with a car bomb. Aznar escaped relatively unscathed, but was deeply affected by the experience.

In a communiqué that assumed responsibility for the attack on Aznar, ETA introduced a new political strategy with the optimistic title of the 'Democratic Alternative'. In this updating of the KAS Alternative, ETA proposed two orbits for negotiation: one between ETA and the state, and the other open to 'all citizens of Euskal Herria'. This second track promised 'a democratic process without limits, with the capacity to choose amongst all options', and pre-figured work towards a broad nationalist front. But, as in Algiers, progress remained conditioned on ETA and the government reaching agreement on the core political questions: 'the recognition of Euskal Herria, the recognition of the right to self-determination, and territorial unity'.[4] ETA and Batasuna would both look back on the Democratic Alternative as the first step in the MLNV's long transition towards democratic politics.[5] Others saw only the continuation of ETA's profoundly undemocratic attempt to impose its views by force.

Social opposition to ETA increased dramatically after July 1997, when ETA kidnapped Miguel Ángel Blanco, a young PP councillor from the Vizcayan town of Ermua, and two days later killed him. The shift was one of a number of factors that contributed to movement towards a new peace process, this time structured along pan-nationalist lines in reflection of the influence of the developing process in Northern Ireland. ETA declared a ceasefire in September 1998, but the group was no more disposed to compromise on its core demands than it had been in the past and it ended it fifteen months later. The bloody campaign that followed worsened the rift between Basque nationalism and constitutionalist forces and plunged Basque politics into crisis. Tough legal measures complemented police action against ETA and would help to secure what some analysts claimed as ETA's 'political defeat' by 2003.[6] Yet that ETA still had the capacity to kill on a sporadic basis and continued to condition the development of Basque politics was not in question. ETA was down but not out.

Pursuing the defeat of ETA

During his first government Aznar reached agreements that secured the legislative support of nationalist parties from the Canary Islands, Catalonia and Euskadi, and introduced immediate changes to the style and substance of counter-terrorism. The economy boomed, helped by the successful preparations for Spain's adoption of the euro in 2002, and in the 2000 elections the PP achieved a majority government. Already deteriorated relations with the PNV sank further, and were accompanied by open antagonism with Catalan nationalists and a controversial reorientation of Spain's foreign policy away from its traditional European allies and towards the United States. After 9/11, Aznar became the most eager of allies in George W. Bush's 'war against terrorism' and—despite widespread public opposition within Spain—a vocal advocate of military intervention in Iraq. By the end of his second term in 2004 these sweeping changes in domestic and international policy had left Spain deeply divided.[7]

The PP was acutely aware of the gravity of the threat represented by ETA. The organisation killed eighteen people in 1995; in 1996 the tally would drop to just five but *kale borroka* peaked at a high of 1,100 incidents.[8] Government policy towards ETA was based on four central ideas: that it is possible to end terrorism; that this should be pursued by waging what Aznar would describe as, 'an open war... standing strong and showing no mercy'; that the government should act within the rule of law; and that it would also aggressively pursue greater international co-operation.[9] In a laudatory account of Spain's 'road to freedom', as they describe the PP's efforts against ETA, Ignacio Cosidó and Oscar Elía explain how this was to be achieved: 'democratic resolve, an absolute refusal to pay any political price to ETA or cede a millimetre to blackmail by terror, and the firm conviction that there could be neither dialogue nor negotiation with terrorists'.[10] The legal campaign against the MLNV was modelled in part on the strategies adopted by the Italian magistrate Giovanne Falcone against the mafia and justified on the basis that 'everything is ETA'. 'We knew that we couldn't distinguish between a terrorist organisation and its purportedly non-violent setting,' Aznar would recall, 'it's all the same.'[11]

The changes had been prefigured in a document on terrorism adopted during the PP's national assembly in 1993. They were framed within a searing critique of the PSOE's oscillation between a 'dirty war' that legitimised ETA while damaging the integrity of the institutions of the state and pursuit of dialogue and negotiation that the PP believed had both reinforced ETA and besmirched the memory of its victims.[12] The PP was strongly opposed both to the early release of ETA prisoners—no parole for good behaviour or political reasons—and to negotiation. This position represented a direct challenge to the consensus upon which the Ajuria Enea Pact had been constructed. Once in government it put the PP on a collision course with the PNV, which demanded that all Basque prisoners—more than 550 at the time—be transferred to Basque prisons, refused to accept that ETA's violence was not political, and continued to defend the validity of dialogue in a context of non-violence and, if necessary, the preliminary contacts and meetings necessary to secure it.[13]

The forceful Basque politician Jaime Mayor Oreja became Aznar's first minister of the interior and immediately rejected existing channels to, or contacts with, ETA. 'This idea of taking the temperature of ETA,' Mayor Oreja recalled telling his PSOE predecessor Belloch, 'I will never do it.'[14] Like his two successors, Mariano Rajoy (February 2001–July 2002) and Ángel Acebes (to April 2004), Mayor Oreja set much store by concrete actions, *hechos*. None was more spectacular than the rescue of José Antonio Ortega Lara, the prison official kidnapped in January 1996 after a series of kidnappings had ended in the payment of ransoms. On 1 July 1997 the Guardia Civil extracted Ortega Lara from a windowless underground hole in which ETA had kept him. Photographs of his emaciated body and accounts of his traumatised state were prominently reported by newspapers across Spain in vivid representation of the cruelty of ETA and the determination of the new government to counter it.

Popular mobilisation against the kidnapping of Ortega Lara had been led by Gesto por la Paz, 'Gesture for Peace', a civil movement founded in 1986 that rose to prominence for the role it assumed in organising silent protests against all kinds of political violence. After 1993, it held weekly vigils for kidnap victims, its members united by displaying blue ribbons shaped into an 'A' for *Askatu*, 'liberty', in Euskera and frequently confronted by militants of the nationalist left or acts of *kale borroka*.[15] In the charged atmosphere that gripped the Basque Country, the phenomenon of Basques confronting Basques in the streets—at its most dramatic in violent encounters between masked groups of Basque youth engaged in aggressive rioting and sabotage and the Basque police force, the Ertzaintza—was an indication that something had gone very badly wrong in Euskadi's plural society.[16]

Worse was to come. On 10 July, ETA kidnapped Miguel Ángel Blanco and announced that it would kill him in forty-eight hours if all Basque prisoners were not moved to prisons within the Basque Country. An estimated six million people took to the streets across Spain in mass demonstrations calling for Blanco's release. ETA resisted all public entreaties for mercy, shot Blanco in the head and left him for dead in the woods a few miles outside San Sebastián. Spain was left, 'with its heart broken and its eyes reddened with tears', as José Luis Barbería remembered ten years later.[17] Spanish and Basque society responded to Blanco's death with the unambiguous rejection of ETA's confrontation with the state. A photograph published in the newspaper *El Mundo* showed leaders of HB above a caption stating 'They pulled the trigger.' Demonstrations in Ermua and elsewhere resounded to the cries of '*A por ellos!*'—'Go get 'em!'[18] In a symbolic gesture Antxon and other ETA prisoners were moved from Santo Domingo to Spanish prisons. In Madrid a massive event was held in Blanco's memory in the Las Ventas bullring. That condemnation of terrorism now bled into opposition to Spain's regional nationalisms was certainly the message when the Valencian singer Raimón was booed for singing in Catalan.

Blanco's cold-blooded assassination shifted the social and political dynamics within which ETA's terrorism would be addressed in dramatic fashion. It deepened divisions between pro-Spanish constitutionalists and Basque nationalists, and drew new attention to the plight of ETA's victims. With a particular affinity for victims of terrorism shaped by his narrow escape in 1995, Aznar's policies towards them rested on the obligation to respond to their material needs, but also on a determination to provide them with the social and political support that had until then had been lacking. 'Victims are always right,' Mayor Oreja would often remark.[19] He was regularly applauded when he attended the funerals of ETA's victims and became Spain's most admired politician. The PP's standing within the Basque Country, as across Spain, rose.[20]

The change was the more notable because of the surprising invisibility of ETA's victims before the mid-1990s. An Association for the Victims of Terrorism (AVT) had been founded in 1981 but its profile remained low. The selectivity of ETA in picking targets and the latent hostility still evident towards victims associated with Franco had contributed to a degree of public indifference. Some Basque nationalists' dismissal of reports of a new assassination with the phrase 'algo habrá hecho' ('he must have done something') came to epitomise what critics would describe as a 'moral gangrene'.[21] Prominent politicians—including the former lehendakaris Ardanza and Ibarretxe—would reject such a charge, but also acknowledge that they did not do enough on victims' behalf.[22] There was no dedicated office to provide attention to victims within the Basque government until 2002. And Basque society paid little attention to victims on an individual basis until ETA deliberately shifted its targets from relatively anonymous Spanish policemen to politicians, academics, journalists and others.[23] Spectacular crimes of the past—at Hipercor or Zaragoza—had been widely decried for the indiscriminate use of violence they represented. But nothing touched the small world of Euskadi as much as the tragic loss of friends, colleagues or familiar public figures, and rioting in its streets.

In 1998 the Collective of Victims of Terrorism (COVITE) was established as the first organisation specifically dedicated to Basque victims. In the following year the Spanish Parliament approved its first law on solidarity with the victims of terrorism.[24] This legislation and subsequent policies on victims—significantly amplified during the 2000s—would be recognised as best practice in important respects.[25] Individual victims and the organisations they chose to be associated with (by 2010 about half of ETA's victims were active members of victims' organisations, according to the director of the office for attention to victims within the Basque government)[26] advocated for their rights and core demands of truth, memory, justice and dignity. The prominence of victims reinforced the legitimacy of the government's stance against ETA and the nationalist left. However, as the public aspects of the campaign against ETA gathered strength, some organisations adopted positions and pursued activities that transformed 'victims of ETA' into a vocal anti-terrorist lobby and political force in its own right, prefiguring a complex and sometimes controversial role in the years ahead.

The emerging visibility of victims was but one aspect in the growing importance of civil society in the confrontation between ETA and the Spanish state. This was evident in the silent protests of Gesto and the more political work of Elkarri but also included the contribution made by new organisations created as an expression of the passionate rejection of ETA that followed the assassination of Blanco—a phenomenon that became known as the 'spirit of Ermua'. In an effort to capture and extend the mood on the street, the Foro de Ermua, a loosely structured opinion-setting forum, and the activist platform ¡Basta Ya! encouraged radical opposition to terrorism, support to its victims and defence of the rule of law, the constitution and the Basque autonomy statute. They acknowledged the work of Gesto that had preceded them, but also differed markedly in demanding more robust action against what the Foro de Ermua, in its founding manifesto, defined as 'a fascist movement that seeks to hijack democracy and attack our most essential rights and freedoms'.[27]

This 'constitutional movement' drew on the work of a number of influential intellectuals, many of them Basque—including José María Calleja, Jon Juaristi and the philosopher Fernando Savater—as well as the 'constitutional patriotism' that had emerged as a form of Spanish nationalism untainted by association with Franco. Anchored in the 'democratic contract' represented by the 1978 constitution, constitutional patriotism drew on the 'triad of new national myths'—that Spain was a peaceful, democratic and modern nation—identified by Sebastian Balfour and Alejandro Quiroga as a significant legacy of the González era.[28] Adopted and then adapted by the PP into the 'fundamentalism' criticised by Cebrián, this civil patriotism became the bedrock of opposition to Basque—and Catalan—nationalism, which were implicitly identified with an inferior and outdated form of ethnic nationalism. The spirit of Ermua intellectuals denounced ETA's violence and the fanaticism within the nationalist left as antithetical to the principles of freedom and tolerance upon which democracy rested. But, especially after moderate Basque nationalists entered into alliance with the nationalist left in 1998, commentary on the Basque drama extended from censure of ETA as 'postmodern totalitarianism', as Savater put it, to criticism of Spain's regional nationalisms as 'damaging to democratic coexistence and—in the Basque case—potentially criminogenic'.[29] In nationalist circles this current of thinking was widely perceived as propaganda reflective of the conflict's dynamics, if not actually 'fascist' itself.[30]

From Northern Ireland to Estella-Lizarra

Increasing social isolation and tougher counter-terrorism policies pursued by Madrid both contributed to impress upon the MLNV the limits of ETA's Democratic Alternative. But the growing polarisation within Basque society and breakdown of the Ajuria Enea Pact also forced others to look for a new solution to the Basque problem. In a period of great political and social effervescence, internal criticism of the path taken by ETA's violence, the emergence of a 'third space' located somewhere between the maximalist demands of ETA and the Spanish government's refusal to countenance movement of any kind, and the growing influence of the peace process in Northern Ireland, all encouraged movement towards the announcement of a joint declaration by a wide array of nationalist forces in the Navarran town of Estella (Lizarra in Euskera) in September 1998, and a ceasefire by ETA soon afterwards.[31]

Tensions within the MLNV were expressed through distinct channels of dissent. Julen Madariaga spoke out against the assassination of a member of the Ertzaintza in 1993 and left HB in 1995 after ETA killed Ordoñez. In the weeks following Blanco's death Txelis and five other senior ETA prisoners denounced ETA's armed action as discredited and called for it to end.[32] With increasing doubts about ETA's violence came pressure for change from an alliance developed between Eusko Langileen Alkartasuna (ELA), the Basque Country's largest labour union, broadly associated with moderate nationalism, and LAB, where Rafa Diéz and others were working quietly to introduce new thinking. In October 1997 the two unions joined other nationalist forces—including HB—in a public meeting in Guernica that was the most visible manifestation to date of a potential 'third space'. José Elorrieta, ELA's leader, delivered a powerful speech announcing the 'death' of the autonomy statute. He called for a new struggle towards sovereignty and Basques' right to decide their future, while serving ETA notice that 'we don't need them'.[33]

Legal action against the MLNV was another source of pressure. In December 1997 all twenty-three members of HB's central committee were sentenced to seven-year prison terms for 'collaboration with an armed terrorist group'. The grounds for imposing such a harsh sentence were thin—the charge of 'collaboration' was based on HB's attempt to promote a video introducing ETA's Democratic Alternative within the 1996 electoral campaign—and would in July 1999 be revoked by the Constitutional Court.[34] But the case suggested a new direction in legal action against the nationalist left that would be confirmed when Baltasar Garzón ordered the pre-emptive closure of the newspaper *Egin* in July 1998 on the basis that it was 'an instrument of the criminal network of ETA-KAS'. The charges against *Egin* were dropped the following year; it was too late for the newspaper to re-open, but a new paper, *Gara*, had already been established in its stead.[35]

By late 1997 the divide between Madrid and Basque nationalism was growing and the PNV and others were increasing their efforts to find new ideas to address the conflict. Many came from Northern Ireland, where in 1993 Gerry Adams of Sinn Féin and John Hume, the leader of the moderate nationalist Social Democratic and Labour Party (SDLP), had signed a joint declaration that was a critical step forward on the road to peace. Basque nationalists of different orientations began to wonder whether such a model was applicable in the Basque Country too. At the end of the year the British and Irish prime ministers, John Major and Albert Reynolds, issued the Downing Street Declaration. Their recognition of the right of self-determination, 'on the basis of consent freely and concurrently given, North and South, to bring about a united Ireland if that is their wish', was a remarkable development to Basque ears.[36]

Gerry Adams would credit Father Alec Reid, the Redemptorist priest who had facilitated his conversations with John Hume, as being the person who first interested HB in the Irish peace process. But he also noted that it had been the Basque priest Joseba Segura who had approached Reid in the late 1980s, having been sent to Belfast by his bishop, Juan María Uriarte. Reid secured meetings for Segura with Adams, and from the early 1990s Sinn Féin began to involve itself more directly in sharing experience of its efforts towards peace, including by sending its negotiating team of Bairbre de Bruin, Gerry Kelly and Alex Maskey to hold discussions with HB.[37] Elkarri too reached out to Northern Ireland. 'From the beginning we saw that we had to learn, that we had to be very close to the Irish process,' Jonan Fernández would recall.[38] In1995 (a year in which Elkarri organised a first peace confer-ence) Fernández and his colleague Gorka Espiau began travelling to Belfast and encouraging those they met there—including Reid—to come to the Basque Country. The PNV also made the Belfast trip. In 1996, Juan María Ollora published a much-discussed book, *Un vía hacía la paz* ('A Road to Peace'), that sought to reconsider the Basque conflict in light of ideas he had gleaned from travel to Northern Ireland, the Middle East and Quebec.[39]

The Northern Ireland model became more interesting in 1997 when a new Labour government, led by Tony Blair, was swept to power in Britain with a large majority. Blair was determined to make progress in advancing the Northern Ireland peace process and his readiness to engage with Sinn Féin—in full knowledge of its close ties to the IRA—was a critical aspect of Northern Ireland's appeal to the MLNV. British policy was built on clandestine channels the government had long main-tained to Irish republicanism, cross-nationalist ties developed during the Adams-Hume talks and an evolution in the thinking of both the IRA and the British government.[40] The IRA's strategy of 'long war' had shared with the armed struggle of ETA the goal of attrition. But effective counter-terrorist work by the police as well as loyalist paramilitary vio-lence had both taken their toll. The IRA had come to accept that it could never drive British troops from Northern Ireland. New ways of building support for a united Ireland had to be considered, and pursued by peaceful means. The British government and army had similarly come to realise that they could contain, but never defeat, the IRA. The essential conditions of the 'mutually hurting stalemate' identified by William Zartman as suggesting a 'ripe mount' for peacemaking were therefore in place. (Zartman's concept of ripeness 'is based on the notion that when the parties find themselves locked in a conflict from which they cannot escalate to victory and this deadlock is painful to both of them [although not necessarily in equal degree or for the same reasons], they seek an alternative policy or Way Out'.)[41] What followed was a complex peace process that involved both the British and Irish states, but also the judicious involvement of an outside mediator, the former US senator, George Mitchell.

ETA's continuing campaign against PP councillors (it killed five more between December 1997 and May 1998) starkly illustrated the corrosive effect of violence: with each assassination, Basque nationalists from the

PNV to HB saw support for the PP grow. While the conflict in Northern Ireland appeared to be heading towards a solution, the Basques risked being left behind. Rufino (Rufi) Etxeberria, of HB's central committee, met with the PNV leader Joseba Egibar in late 1997, shortly before entering prison. He told him that HB had moved away from the positions outlined in the *Oldartzen* document and was now committed to dialogue. HB's new leadership, with Arnaldo Otegi as its spokesperson, would take up the baton. Otegi—whose past included a period in ETA-pm, exile in France and prison in Spain on charges related to kidnapping—contacted the PNV in January 1998, initiating a series of meetings between the two parties that consciously echoed the discussions between Adams and Hume.[42]

Meanwhile, in early 1998, Ardanza made a final effort to rebuild a consensual approach to the Basque problem. What became known as the Ardanza Plan accepted the need for a strategy against ETA that combined pressure with dialogue; foresaw talks between Basque parties, including HB, as opposed to the government/ETA axis of the past; and admitted that the 'national question' would be at the centre of the agenda, and could include the possibility of self-determination and a referendum.[43] At its core was an insistence that what was freely and democratically decided by Basque society should be accepted by Madrid. Despite the mathematical certainty that no majority for independence would emerge within Euskadi—still less in Navarre or the French Basque territories—this 'Basque sphere of decision making' (the untranslatable *ambito vasco de decisión*) was inherently threatening to the non-nationalist members of Basque society, as well as Madrid. The proposal was consequently rejected by the PP and, in a decision that would be much debated in later years, by the weakened and increasingly divided PSE as well.

On 12 September 1998 twenty-three Basque nationalist and leftist forces, including the PNV, EA, HB, the United Left, LAB, ELA, Elkarri and a variety of organisations from the MLNV, signed the Estella-Lizarra Declaration, shocking Spain's political system. The declaration followed numerous meetings between the PNV and HB, the constitution of a broad Ireland Forum to study the implications of the peace process in Northern Ireland, especially after the Good Friday Agreement was reached on 10 April 1998, and secret meetings between the PNV, EA and ETA. In the course of this process the PNV's deepening engagement with radical nationalism had led the PSE to abandon the coalition on which the Basque government had rested for more than a decade.

The Estella-Lizarra Declaration reflected a partial reading of the Northern Ireland process.[44] It listed seven factors which contributed to the Good Friday Agreement, beginning with an observation that on its own suggested the yawning gulf between the circumstances in Northern Ireland and the Basque Country in the late 1990s: 'All of those involved in the conflict have accepted its political origin and nature, and consequently that its resolution must also be political.' The declaration continued by outlining the potential application for Euskal Herria of the characteristics of the Irish process. These were parsed to include the need for political solutions to the core issues of territoriality, the 'subject' of decision-making and political sovereignty; a two-stage process encompassing a preliminary phase without pre-conditions and a second phase 'of resolution' requiring the permanent absence of all expressions of violence; and elements of a solution that would include respect for the plurality of Basque society and give the final word to the citizens of Euskal Herria. The final scenario was left open-ended, but would respond to these citizens' aspirations of sovereignty.[45]

The declaration prompted inevitable discussion of the extent to which the Irish process was or was not a 'mirror' of Basque efforts towards peace.[46] Perhaps predictably, the debate was both intensely polarised and overly literal. Some sought to develop direct parallels: If the PNV was ready to play the SDLP, was Otegi 'the Basque Gerry Adams'? Would Madrid accept the legitimacy of the aspiration for Basque independence as Britain accepted that of a united Ireland? And could ETA be persuaded by the very significant concessions made by Irish republicans to assume a degree of flexibility in the interests of peace? Others emphasised the obvious differences between the two cases. Foremost among them were the high level of self-government already enjoyed in Euskadi, Northern Ireland's sectarian divide between Catholics and Protestants, and the interest in, and role available to, outside third parties, including the United States.[47] Most fundamental was the structural difference between Spain and Britain regarding the unit of self-determination and therefore the issue of consent. The UK's comfort as a multinational state was very far removed from the 'indivisible unity of the Spanish nation' claimed by Spain's constitution. Blair could pronounce himself 'easy either way' as to what the people of Northern Ireland decided, a sentiment literally inconceivable to any Spanish prime minister in the Basque or Catalan context.[48]

Basque nationalists were at the very beginning of what they saw as a democratic process that could open the way to an end to violence and a 'right to decide'. Its flaws, however, were evident. The declaration had been negotiated by and for nationalists in parallel, as it would later turn out, to talks with ETA regarding the conditions necessary for a ceasefire, and behind the back of the constitutionalist political parties. It rested on a fundamental contradiction between a process of nation-building among Basque nationalist forces and the aspirations of an inclusive peace process, as had been seen in Northern Ireland. There the SDLP had rejected a nationalist front and acted as a moderating force upon Sinn Féin. The Good Friday Agreement had been hammered out in multiparty talks and concluded only after significant concessions on all sides.[49] For many nationalists Estella-Lizarra represented the realisation of a long-held dream of 'all nationalists against Madrid', as Otegi recalled.[50] For the excluded pro-Spanish parties, on the other hand, it was nothing less than 'the betrayal by Basque nationalism of eleven years of collaboration, the Pact of Ajuria Enea, and the path laid out by the statute', as Ramón Jáuregui would put it.[51]

The ceasefire and beyond

On 16 September ETA announced that the first unilateral and indefinite ceasefire in its history would begin two days later. Aznar was in Peru. Surprised by the news, he struggled to articulate a coherent response. Mayor Oreja, meanwhile, immediately dismissed the ceasefire as a 'tactical manoeuvre' by ETA.[52] To the immense disappointment of many Basques and others across Spain who responded to the ceasefire with an outpouring of hope and expectation, fifteen months later he would be proven to be right. As details emerged of the contacts between the PNV, EA and ETA in the weeks preceding the ceasefire, the unstable grounds upon which the ceasefire rested became evident to all. ETA returned to violence with its capacity reinforced by the rearmament and reorganisation it had undertaken during the truce, and dialogue or negotiation deeply discredited.

It would later emerge that in August 1998 ETA had held a meeting with the PNV—represented by Gorka Agirre, Joseba Egibar and Juan María Ollora—and EA. It had presented a text that contained commitments to work towards a 'single and sovereign institution', embracing the whole of Euskal Herria, and to break all existing agreements with 'the forces whose objective is the destruction of Euskal Herria and the construction of Spain (PP and PSOE)'. Agreement was a condition for ETA's declaration of an 'indefinite' ceasefire that was itself qualified by the statement that it would be reviewed after four months.[53] Ludger Mees aptly described the proposal as a 'poisoned chalice' for the PNV.[54] With discussion of the political dimensions of the Basque problem with Madrid blocked, the process under way appeared to offer an opportunity to end ETA's violence and pursue Basque nationalist aspirations by democratic means. The three parties signed the text, but the PNV and EA added qualifications on the other side of the paper in an attempt to relegate ETA's demands to a long-term goal.[55] In early October, however, the negotiators were summoned to a meeting with ETA in France. They were told that their amendments had been rejected. This meant, as Egibar would recall, that 'there was no agreement'.[56] The PNV was left in an unenviable position. It knew from the start that the ceasefire was heavily conditioned. By entering into secret and ambiguous talks with ETA it had put its name to a document that directly challenged Spain's national parties and the state and left itself extraordinarily vulnerable to its exposure.

In October's elections to the Basque Parliament voters rewarded HB, which had renamed itself Euskal Herritarrok (EH, 'We, the Basque Citizens') to avoid the risk of illegalisation, for its efforts towards peace and ETA's ceasefire. The number of its seats rose from seven to fourteen (out of the total of seventy-five), equalling that won by the PSE. But the polarising effects of the past eighteen months were also in evidence: the PP had its best result to date and won sixteen seats, while the forty-one seats held by nationalist parties remained the same as in the outgoing parliament.[57] The PNV, with twenty-one seats (a loss of one) was unable to command a majority. With relations with the PSE broken, Juan José Ibarretxe found support for his election as *lehendakari* from EA, but also EH—further antagonising Madrid.

Aznar responded to the ceasefire determined neither to make political concessions, nor to be seen to miss opportunities the new situation presented.[58] Although both *kale borroka* and extortion continued during the ceasefire, between September 1998 and September 1999 the government adopted a new flexibility in its penitentiary policy by releasing 180

Basque prisoners, moving 135 closer to the Basque Country and allowing the return of more than 300 exiles.[59] Breaking with the PP's opposition to any communication with the 'terrorists', in October 1998 Aznar's state secretary for security, Ricardo Martí Fluxá, initiated quiet consultations with international figures (including Blair's chief of staff Jonathan Powell, Kofi Annan and George Mitchell, according to Ángeles Escrivá) in a position to advise on the benefits of talking.[60] In November 1998 Aznar authorised contacts with interlocutors he identified as 'from the world of the so-called MLNV' in order to explore the disposition of ETA to open a peace process 'grounded in the definitive cessation of violence'.[61] Aznar's secretary of the presidency, Javier Zarzalejos, Martí Fluxá and Pedro Arriola, a personal adviser to the prime minister, met with HB in Burgos in December and then established contact with ETA through Bishop Uriarte. With the assistance of Joseba Segura, Uriarte made quiet arrangements with Swiss authorities for a meeting to be held outside Geneva in May 1999 between the government delegation and two representatives of ETA, Mikel Albizu, *Mikel Antza*, and Belén González Peñalva, *Carmen*.

Aznar and his officials insisted that they did not negotiate with ETA in Switzerland. But, as the record of the meeting kept by ETA suggests, in direct talks undertaken without pre-conditions or insistence on the verification of the ceasefire, they held exactly the kind of meeting with ETA that Mayor Oreja had long disavowed and on several occasions directly blocked.[62] (Most recent had been his rebuff of an overture from ETA delivered by a representative of the Community of Sant'Egidio, a lay Catholic organisation that had played an active peacemaking role in Mozambique and a number of other conflicts in Africa. In early 1998 a priest from Sant'Egidio who had met with ETA in Paris had brought him the organisation's request for 'dialogue and negotiation'. Mayor Oreja had sent him packing with the instruction that he should tell ETA that 'their message was not received'.)[63] ETA reported statements that reflected an attempt to understand its position that was entirely antithetical to government policy: 'We have made an effort to assume the logic of the other and within this logic we don't think ETA will surrender,' a government representative was reported as saying. 'We know that ETA still has the capacity to kill. We don't think that what we can say to you about the armed struggle, about violence, can modify actions of the organisation... *No venimos a la derrota de ETA...* We are not here for the defeat of ETA.'

Aznar had agreed to talks in order to test ETA's disposition to consider the old formula of 'peace for prisoners'. But, as Zarzalejos recalled, his representatives found no evidence of the 'unequivocal will to give up violence' on which any process would have to be based. Against the backdrop of Lizarra, ETA's priorities were elsewhere. It was quickly evident that neither side was going to get what it wanted or had an interest in probing other possibilities. The discussion turned instead to consideration of how and when to make the news of the meeting public, and a confused debate over the nature of the problem that the two parties had supposedly met to resolve. (The notes from the meeting record a government representative saying: 'If Aznar did not admit the existence of a conflict that is evident—all you have to do is look at history and the newspaper archives… we would not be here.')[64] They also discussed arrangements for a second meeting, but it would never take place. Any sense of the seriousness with which the government approached the talks was undermined, in ETA's eyes, by the exposure of Uriarte's role in the meeting through leaks to the press, and the arrest of Belén González in October.[65]

In the meantime, developments in the Basque Country were not encouraging. It was simply not possible to pursue both 'national construction' among Basque nationalist forces and a 'peace process' that would inevitably have to include pro-Spanish parties, and eventually the government in Madrid. Criticism of the PNV's ties to radical nationalism mounted, while it was both unwilling and unable to proceed at the speed demanded by ETA. For a party with inherently conservative roots and significant internal differences it was unnerving to be in partnership with individuals with proven ties to terrorism. Most controversial was the presence of José Antonio Urrutikoetxe, or *Josu Ternera*, as one of EH's elected members—with a position on the Human Rights Commission, no less—in the Basque Parliament. Ternera had been a military commander within ETA and responsible for both the organisation's political and international apparatuses before being imprisoned in France, deported to Spain and then imprisoned again.[66] He had been accused of ordering the attack on the barracks in Zaragoza in 1987, as well as involvement in several other violent crimes.

At a meeting in July, ETA presented representatives of the PNV and EA with the draft of a new agreement that proposed the dissolution of Euskadi's institutional structures and the renegotiation of the full seven territories of Euskal Herria with Spain and France. Egibar dismissed it as 'ridiculous'.[67] ETA informed its interlocutors that the ceasefire was all but over. Over the following months Otegi and others in EH worked hard to try and rescue the situation. But even the creation in September of Udalbiltza, an organisation of nationalist municipal representatives that for the first time included all of the territory claimed as Euskal Herria, could not halt the deterioration of the political process.

ETA declared its ceasefire at an end in December 1999, and in January 2000 assassinated Lt. Colonel Pedro Antonio Blanco in Madrid. His death marked the beginning of a brutal campaign. ETA killed twenty-three people in 2000 alone. It was the highest number for eight years and a clear indicator of the extent to which ETA had abused the ceasefire by preparing for future operational activities. Arrests of ETA militants had dipped and their re-armament had proceeded apace.[68] ETA's victims included the Socialist politician Fernando Buesa and his bodyguard; the former PSE civil governor of Guipúzcoa, Juan María Jáuregui; and the Catalan academic Ernest Lluch, a former Socialist minister who had been a prominent supporter of dialogue with ETA and active with Elkarri. Several victims associated with the PP were killed, as well as a journalist and founding member of the Foro de Ermua; a PNV business-man who spoke up against extortion; local councillors; a judge; and members of the security forces. Other judges, academics and journalists, as well as politicians, suffered attacks and threats. Rioting in the streets, and attacks on public property and political party offices again became a frequent occurrence.

Basques looked on in horror, struggling to understand what appeared to many as 'political madness' largely incomprehensible to the majority of the population. In addition to appearing as a 'traumatic breach of the moral community', as Begoña Aretxaga would write, the violence of ETA's campaign seemed counter-productive in political terms, 'reinforc-ing the anti-nationalist Spanish right-wing in the Basque Country as well as debilitating the social fabric that constitutes Basque nationalism at the local level'.[69] Ibarretxe lamented that ETA was 'out of reality'; many left the Basque Country as political cleavages deepened.[70]

The PNV suspended its agreement with EH when ETA ended its ceasefire and cancelled it once ETA starting killing again; EH left the Basque Parliament. The campaign for the March general elections took place under the shadow of violence and amidst accusations that the

PNV was 'sheltering' ETA and the PP hewing to its Francoist roots.[71] Criticism of the PNV's secret dealings with ETA escalated. Relations with the PSE were particularly difficult, in part as a consequence of the targeting of the PSE by ETA that specifically sought to undermine understanding between them. The PSE found itself increasingly divided. On the one hand it was aware of the limitations of the security approach pursued with such zeal by Aznar (a poll taken in November 2000 found 94 per cent of Basques in favour of dialogue, and 75 per cent favouring means of countering ETA in addition to police measures).[72] On the other, its politicians and party members were being killed with the PP. Under assault from ETA, the two parties instinctively clung together. A situation in which officials of the Basque government went about their business in relative safety while members of the opposition were being killed, threatened or living with bodyguards made normal political relations quite impossible.

Aznar's offensive and 9/11

Aznar triumphed in the general elections held in March 2000 and began his second term with a comfortable majority. As ETA's post-ceasefire campaign took hold, he strengthened co-operation with France and introduced changes in Spain's legal framework that facilitated the prosecution of the web of social and political organisations associated with radical nationalism and the MLNV. ETA, Aznar's third minister of the interior Acebes was fond of repeating, 'could be defeated with the law, only with the law, but with all of the law'.[73]

Doubts regarding the loyalty of the PSOE were assuaged in September 2000 when José Luis Rodríguez Zapatero, the party's new secretary-general, proposed an anti-terrorist pact. Some within the PP questioned whether a new agreement was necessary: Aznar's deputy, Mariano Rajoy, dismissed Zapatero's proposal as a 'rabbit pulled out of a hat', a phrase that Zapatero would throw back at him when Rajoy berated him, as prime minister, for violating the pact.[74] Yet the 'Agreement for freedoms and against terrorism' reached in December would provide Aznar with an instrument that synthesised his counter-terrorist policies. The agreement began with the statement that it was the responsibility of the government to direct the anti-terrorist struggle. The responsibility was nevertheless one shared by all democratic political parties—as the agreement implicitly suggested, acting in loyal support of decisions taken by the government. It bound the principal opposition party to the idea that ETA could be defeated by police means, while also taking a broad side swipe at the Basque nationalist parties who remained outside it by criticising them for their willingness to put a 'political price'—identified as 'the imposition of self-determination as a means to arrive at the independence of the Basque country'—on the end of ETA's violence. The agreement stated that 'victims of terrorism are our principal concern' and, in clear contrast to the Ajuria Enea Pact, left no room for dialogue with terrorists.[75]

Political tension in the Basque Country peaked in the weeks preceding bitterly fought elections to the Basque Parliament in May 2001. The campaign pitched Mayor Oreja, running for the PP but with the agreed support of the PSE, against Ibarretxe as part of a determined attempt to dislodge the Basque nationalists from power.[76] Aznar's electoral strategy made partisan use of the victims of terrorism and deliberately confused the means and ends of ETA in order to attack the PNV and Basque nationalism itself.[77] Basque nationalists, meanwhile, understood the PP's assault as a direct attack upon their identity and turned out to vote in their droves. The PNV and EA, running together, received some 600,000 votes and thirty-three seats in the Basque Parliament, while the vote for the radical nationalists in EH plummeted. The party lost seven out of the fourteen seats it had previously held in a dramatic indication of the erosion of its support after ETA's return to violence. Ibarretxe was returned to power at the head of a minority government that included EA and IU-EB, and with his personal authority greatly enhanced.[78]

The attacks on the United States in September 2001 and its subsequent declaration of a 'global war on terrorism' prompted many countries to strengthen existing domestic counter-terrorism legislation or enact new emergency measures.[79] The reasons, as John Finn suggests, were varied: many states had direct connections to the 9/11 attacks, either through its perpetrators or victims; some introduced changes for their symbolic value; others rushed to comply with UN Security Council Resolution 1373's demand for states to introduce measures such as the criminalisation of terrorist acts and the financing of terrorist networks. Finally, the combination of the attacks and UNSCR 1373 'gave some advocates of security legislation an opportunity to further a legislative agenda that preceded 9/11'.[80] Spain was prominent among them. The consequences, as elsewhere, were complex, and deeply contested, raising clear concerns regarding civil liberties, but also regarding the implications of their erosion for the rule of law and democracy more broadly.[81]

Spain assumed an assertive role at home and internationally on the basis of the authority it had accrued from its long history with ETA as well as the consonance of Aznar's conviction that there was no distinction to be made between domestic and international terrorism, and thus ETA and Al Qaeda, with the dominant discourse in Washington.[82] 'Spain, like Britain, embraced the American approach,' observed Alan Riding in *The New York Times* in the days following the terrorist attack on Madrid's commuter trains in March 2004, 'principally in order to place its fight against ETA in the context of a global war on terrorism'.[83] The approach differed markedly from the clear distinction maintained by the British government between the domestic threat represented by the IRA, rooted in British and Irish history, and the global threat of Al Qaeda. Indeed Blair's government went to considerable pains not to allow the gradual accommodation of the IRA underway within the Northern Irish peace process to be derailed by the exceptional counter-terrorist measures introduced in the post-9/11 environment.[84]

In his memoirs, Aznar recalls that the terrorist attacks on New York and Washington in September 2001 proved a boon in two respects. They brought welcome international legitimacy and assistance to his determination to destroy ETA, while paving the way for a reorientation of Spanish foreign policy that propelled Spain to a new international prominence. Aznar had offered Spain's full support for US efforts against Islamic terrorism; when he also asked the EU and United States to do more against ETA, he found that he was pushing at an open door. 'We'd been fighting for years to make changes internationally on things like police co-operation, legislation and classifying terrorist groups,' he would recall, 'and just a few months after September 11th, we achieved more than we had over the course of all those years.'[85]

Aznar pursued enhanced co-operation with France with determination. A summit meeting held in Santander in May 2000 had provided an early opportunity for Spain to seek a new level of French engagement in counter-terrorism.[86] The rate of extradition of members of ETA from France to Spain began to rise (France extradited nine and ten *etarras* in 2000 and 2001 as opposed to two in each of the previous two years).[87] However, Spain only achieved the immediate handover of ETA suspects it had long desired after September 2001 and real-time access to information and materiel captured from ETA in France after a new summit meeting held in Málaga in September 2002.

Beyond bilateral co-operation, Aznar found particular gratification in the agreement in December 2001 of a European Arrest Warrant creating a single judicial space, a measure that he had advocated in previous years without success.[88] Spain was also a leading actor in the EU's adoption of a common definition of terrorism with unusually broad scope and promoted a new EU list of terrorist organisations modelled on the list maintained by US State Department (on which ETA had been included since its creation in 1997). The EU list approved in December 2001 included not just ETA but KAS, Xaki, Ekin, Jarrai-Haika-Segi and Gestoras pro Amnistia, all identified as 'part of the terrorist group ETA'.[89] The government had lobbied to have Batasuna—as EH had been renamed—included too, despite the staunch opposition of the Socialists. 'The terrorist is not only the one who kills,' interior minister Mariano Rajoy argued, 'but also whoever helps, shelters, finances or politically encourages the group.'[90] Other EU members had balked. Batasuna was legal in Spain at the time, and indeed had a representative, Koldo Gorostiaga, in the European Parliament.[91]

Aznar had established a basis for co-operation with the United States during the Clinton presidency, but the relationship shifted to a new level during the presidency of George W. Bush. After 9/11, it had counter-terrorism co-operation as its cornerstone. US officials betrayed occasional frustration with Spain's 'fixation' with ETA, to the detriment of the looming threat posed by Islamic extremists. However, they shared actionable intelligence with Spanish counterparts, and co-operated on border security as well as in countering terrorist financing networks.[92] US assistance also helped Spain decipher encoded documents seized from ETA, reinforce surveillance of ETA militants and improve its ability to intercept the organisation's communications.[93]

Spain's membership of the UN Security Council in 2003 and 2004 helped it become a crucial third leg to the United States and United Kingdom as they advanced towards military intervention in Iraq; it also assumed a prominent role as the chair of the UN's Counter-Terrorism Committee. Bush welcomed Aznar at his Crawford ranch in February 2003 as 'my good friend… a strong fighter in the war against terror'[94] and included him—with Tony Blair—in the Azores Summit meeting on

16 March 2003 that set the deadline for the assault on Iraq. Spain would eventually send some 1,400 troops to Iraq, a contribution of relative military importance. However it implied a reorientation of Spanish foreign policy away from its traditional concentration on the EU and Latin America, and a perceived loss of independence that would be bitterly criticised at home. Aznar had pursued his policy on Iraq in defiance of overwhelming public opposition (a series of polls found approximately 90 per cent of Spain's population to be opposed to it) and a tradition of consensual foreign policy that had held steady since the transition.[95]

Aznar achieved significant successes in his counter-terrorist offensive. The period to the end of 2003 saw numerous detentions in Spain and France as well as the capture of large quantities of weapons and other materiel. During his two terms in office a total of 634 alleged ETA members and associates were detained in Spain (a rise from thirty-nine in 1996 to 126 in 2003 suggesting the mounting pressure under which ETA found itself during this period), 331 in France and forty in other foreign countries, among them significant numbers of ETA's ever-evolving leadership.[96] ETA's armed actions, which had been running at just under eighty a year in 1996, had dipped during the ceasefire, before rising again to seventy in 2000. But by 2003 relentless police action, the escalating campaign against ETA's financial and other support structures, and changing dynamics within ETA after 9/11 had reduced them to twenty, even as the organisation killed just three victims. The government offensive brought ETA's lucrative kidnapping industry to an end and progress was also made in countering *kale borroka*, which fell to a level of a little over 200 incidents in 2003.[97]

'All of the law' and the banning of Batasuna

Aznar's efforts were reinforced by a package of legal reforms that drew upon the conflation of Basque nationalism with terrorism in the minds of many Spaniards. His government did not introduce specific anti-terrorism laws, but rather reforms to the criminal code, criminal procedures code and the law on minors, in some cases after overcoming objections by the PSOE and other political parties. The reforms substantively broadened both the concept of terrorism in Spain and the measures that could be used to punish it. Modifications were made to key articles of the criminal code to extend its application to include the 'urban terrorism' of *kale borroka* (this meant, as Patxi Zabaleta pointed out, that burning a rubbish bin in Pamplona was a terrorist offence and carried a prison sentence of up to twelve years, while doing the same thing eighty kilometres away in Logroño carried a fine of 300 euros)[98] as well as to expand upon the crimes of 'glorification' of terrorism and 'collaboration' with terrorist groups.[99]

Changes to the criminal procedures code included an extension of the period for which those charged on terrorist-related offences could be held in *incommunicado* detention from five to thirteen days. Amendments to the law on minors increased sentences for youths convicted of crimes related to *kale borroka* and ruled that they should be tried by the Audiencia Nacional.[100] Those to the penitentiary code modified penal legislation to ensure that prisoners serving sentences for terrorist-related sentences fulfilled the full terms of their sentences—to a new maximum of forty years—while also restricting their privileges. Article 76.2 introduced tough new criteria that this class of prisoner— Spain would always deny their 'political' status, even as it increased legislation distinguishing them from common criminals—would have to meet before acceding to the privileges associated with the 'third grade', or a regime of semi-liberty.[101]

Human rights defenders argued that a number of the changes fell short of international standards. In a 2008 report, the UN Special Rapporteur on the promotion of human rights while countering terrorism, Martin Scheinin, expressed the view that elements of Spain's criminal code 'do not fully respect the requirement of legality' as it is spelled out in Article 15 of the International Covenant on Civil and Political Rights.[102] Among the language he singled out for criticism is that of Article 574 of the criminal code, which punishes 'any other crime' committed with the aims of subverting constitutional order or altering public peace; that of Article 576, which includes among acts exemplifying the crime of collaboration with terrorism 'any other equivalent form of co-operation, assistance or complicity, economic or otherwise'; and that of Article 577, which defines 'urban terrorism' as comprising offences committed by persons acting with the aims of subverting the constitutional order or seriously altering public peace. Amnesty International would similarly caution that Spain risked broadening an understanding of terrorism 'to include crimes that do not comprise or have sufficient relation to the intentional element of causing deadly or serious bodily injury to, or terrorising of, a population'.[103]

The extensive legal changes facilitated the prosecution of individuals and organisations identified as being part of ETA's network of support and in the process amplified the universe of those considered 'terrorist' by the Spanish state. The legal process with the widest ramifications was the '*macroproceso*' known as 18/98, which had been launched in 1998 as Garzón closed *Egin* and led to the conviction of a wide range of individuals for 'collaboration' with a terrorist organisation as very broadly conceived by Article 576 of the criminal code. But it was not alone. Indeed, a series of cases initiated during the Aznar period would result in the prosecution of more than 170 individuals, according to the estimates of Daniel Portero, the director of Dignity and Justice, an organisation formed from within the AVT to prosecute cases against the MLNV under a provision of Spanish law that allows private actors to initiate court action.[104] The cases included charges brought against organisations and individuals of widely varying political and social profiles. Among them were KAS and its successor Ekin, an entity at the heart of the MLNV for its coordinating role between ETA and other bodies; the youth movements Jarrai/Haika/Segi, prosecuted for their involvement in *kale borro*ka; Gestoras pro Amnistia, the prisoner support movement; the *herriko tabernas*, the nationalist left bars accused of acting as a fundraising network; but also Udalbiltza, the organisation of Basque municipalities; the Basque language newspaper *Egunkaria*, whose editor and some journalists claimed to have been tortured and mistreated as they were arrested for maintaining ties to ETA; and the Joxemi Zumalabe Foundation, a civil society organisation committed to non-violence but accused of civil disobedience.

Many of these cases would conclude in the imposition of lengthy prison sentences. In several, legal challenges led to appeals and the eventual acquittal of the accused. In May 2009 Sabino Ormazabal, a pacifist recognised as a prisoner of conscience by Amnesty International, and seven other men charged under the 18/98 process were finally acquitted.[105] The case against *Egunkaria* was dismissed in 2010, and the allegations of torture made by its defendants sustained; that against Udalbiltza was dismissed in 2011.[106] From the perspective of the nationalist left, as well as many more moderate nationalists overtly opposed to ETA's violence, these cases prosecuted on the basis of association rather than individual responsibility and for crimes that either did not exist or fell far short of internationally accepted standards for the serious crimes associated with terrorism, spoke only of injustice. At a minimum they perpetuated a sense of victimisation and ingrained suspicion of the law as another weapon in the armoury of the Spanish state. As Jone Goirizelaia, one of Batasuna's leading defence lawyers, maintained in 2010, many of the cases drew on police reports that 'gave juridical form to political decisions that already had been taken'. As such, she argued, they represented a fundamental perversion of Spain's rule of law.[107]

The failure to secure Batasuna's listing as a terrorist organisation within the EU in late 2001 had encouraged the government's efforts towards the fulfilment of a goal long cherished by Aznar and the PP: its illegalisation as a political party. In June 2002 the Spanish Parliament voted to amend the law on political parties to establish that a party will be declared illegal when its 'grave and continuous' activity 'makes democratic principles vulnerable'. As it did so it introduced a list of prohibited activities that represented a catalogue of actions attributable to Batasuna. These included many that were not previously proscribed by the law, such as the inclusion in electoral lists of former prisoners 'who had not publicly rejected the ends and means of terrorism', or 'the use of symbols identified with conduct associated with violence'. By including 'tacit political support of terrorism' within the conduct that could trigger illegalisation the law also introduced the demand that any legal political party should explicitly condemn ETA.[108]

In August, amid heightened tension caused by ETA's killing of two victims (one a child of six) with a car bomb and Batasuna's refusal to condemn the double assassination, the Spanish Parliament asked the Supreme Court to dissolve Batasuna in accordance with the newly revised law. The government submitted a brief outlining twenty-three reasons for Batasuna's illegalisation to the Supreme Court, which would rule in its favour in March 2003.[109] However, on the same day as the parliament took action under the new law, Garzón ordered a three-year ban on Batasuna's political activities. He argued that he had established the financial and organisational links between Batasuna and ETA that proved they were one and the same. He had already moved to seize $23 million in assets from Batasuna, and now issued orders to have the party's offices closed down.[110]

Banning a political party rather than the prosecution of individuals within it responsible for criminal offences was a drastic measure by any means. It directly challenged freedoms of expression, assembly and association, and effectively disenfranchised those individuals—some 10–15 per cent of Basque voters in this instance—who constituted its electorate. It was vehemently opposed by the PNV on these grounds (in September 2003 the PNV formally accused the Spanish state of violating the European Covenant of Human Rights; its case was rejected on the grounds that an autonomous entity cannot sue its own state), even as the PSOE—after a heated internal debate—supported it. Alfredo Rubalcaba had strongly championed this support. Ten years later he would describe it as the consequence of a deep frustration. The PSOE had previously considered that Batasuna was 'the place in which *etarras* ended up when they had finished with violence'.[111] The problem was that this was not how things worked out. At the time of its banning there were some one hundred and thirty-two elected Batasuna officials who were standing trial or had been convicted of involvement in terrorist activities. Meanwhile, polls in the Basque Country suggested that four out of ten Basques believed it was impossible to hold truly democratic elections in Euskadi because of the degree of threat exerted upon constitutional politicians and their supporters.[112] Batasuna, Rubalcaba maintained, had become 'the political arm of ETA, simply complying with the instructions of ETA'. Far from attracting ETA to democracy, 'it defended ETA within it'. And this was unacceptable.

Internationally, the measure was viewed with concern. An editorial in *The Economist* argued that the banning was a mistake: '[Batasuna's] views may be odious, but free speech should be valued to protect not anodyne views but offensive ones. Moreover, measures short of a complete ban could, and should, have been taken against it.'[113] Outside Basque nationalism, the reaction in Spain was largely positive, particularly as the violent protests in the Basque Country that had been feared failed to materialise. Banning Batasuna was understood as an action in favour of the human rights of those assailed by ETA that might temper the oppressive presence that Batasuna represented at the community level. Analysts for the most part expressed the hope that, as the Barcelona newspaper *La Vanguardia* put it, 'things will be more difficult for ETA without a lawful sphere which gives it oxygen'.[114] However, those able to step back and consider the measure in comparative perspective were not so sanguine. The Basque journalist Javier Ortiz raised a somewhat lonely voice against the banning in an informal canvassing of intellectuals undertaken by *El Mundo*. Ortiz cautioned that Batasuna represented 'a social phenomenon that it would be a mistake to identify with ETA'. He was against the banning 'for the same reason that the government and courts in the UK have never promoted the illegalisation of Sinn Fein'.[115]

The decision to ban Batasuna represented the culmination of the counter-terrorist policies pursued by Aznar and clearly favoured the police and judicial defeat of ETA. It would help secure the party's addition to the terrorist lists in the EU and the United States in mid-2003. As Ortiz's reference to Sinn Féin suggested, it also confirmed that Spain was ready to give up on any prospect of dialogue with radical nationalism. Rather than finding ways to build trust and communication with the political expression of a violent problem, it had pushed it further away.

4

THE BASQUE CRISIS

LOOKING FOR A WAY OUT

By the early 2000s the Basque Country was in its deepest political crisis since the transition. In its proximate causes the crisis could be traced back to the end of ETA's ceasefire and the stark political, ideological and emotional divisions exposed by the changes within Basque nationalism with which the ceasefire had been accompanied. These had set in motion what José Luis Barbería and Patxo Unzueta identified as a process of 'internal rupture' within Basque society.[1] In the introduction to their study of this period the authors recall how, on 20 February 2002, Basque political activists gathered to protest against ETA's attack on Eduardo Madina, the young Socialist politician who had lost a leg to a car bomb the previous day. 'How could we come to this?' the protesters had asked the older politicians, echoing the question Joseba Zulaika had heard in Itziar so long ago, 'How can that be?'. How was it possible that there were young Basques in ETA who considered it legitimate to try to assassinate another young Basque solely because he was a Socialist?[2]

The May 2001 election had seen Basque voters reject the alternative to Euskadi's post-transition trajectory offered by Mayor Oreja, even as it had exposed the inherent contradictions of the status quo. Moderate Basque nationalists had benefitted from an autonomy statute they openly questioned. They were also perceived by many to share at least some of the goals of an armed organisation whose terrorist violence they were committed to thwarting. Yet despite a campaign of unprecedented vehemence against it strongly backed by Madrid, the Basque Nationalist Party had been returned to lead the new Basque government, while the radical nationalists had been weakened. In the election's aftermath, with ETA's violence still all too present, Basques of all ideological persuasions found themselves 'confused, with sentiments of despair and incredulity', as Elkarri put it in late 2001.[3]

Aznar's offensive against ETA and the MLNV, deep antagonism to the PNV and growing intolerance of regional demands—also evident in the deterioration of relations with Catalonia—widened the gulf with Madrid and among the democratic forces in the Basque Country. But even unpropitious circumstances could not stall intense activity within the Basque government, political parties and civil society directed towards the exploration of pathways out of, or beyond, the double bind of the increasingly conflictive issue of Euskadi's relationship to the central state and the continuing violence of ETA. Most prominent among the new initiatives was Ibarretxe's controversial proposal for a relationship of 'free association' for Euskadi with Spain that in time became known as the 'Ibarretxe Plan'.

Neither Spain's domestic politics nor the international moment offered hope for innovative approaches to a problem tainted by its association with terrorism. Basques nevertheless turned to experience elsewhere for new ideas. Elkarri launched a peace conference in 2001 as an effort to build support and momentum for dialogue. It invited international figures and experts to visit the Basque Country in recognition of its perception of the benefits to be gained from the involvement of outside third parties who would encourage dialogue.[4] The ongoing peace process in Northern Ireland remained an important model, but the Ibarretxe Plan also drew upon Quebec's quest for independence from Canada and new thinking elsewhere in the EU. Meanwhile, as Batasuna and ETA reflected upon the Lizarra process, they began to place increasing focus on the international projection of their cause, both to undermine the legitimacy of policies pursued by the government and as a means to build support for a future peace process.

From Madrid came consistent opposition to these efforts. Any possibility of outside involvement was robustly resisted as an unacceptable infringement of Spanish sovereignty. However, while Spain could draw on a well of international sympathy in its struggle against terrorist violence, this was not sufficient to counter concern with its human rights record in some quarters. To the government's frustration, international human rights organisations and bodies, while not wavering in their criticism of ETA's abuses, were troubled by allegations of torture or the threats to freedom of association and expression implicit in the legal campaign against the nationalist left. In broad terms the government saw this interest as reflecting, or at least assisting, an international propaganda campaign mounted by ETA and its supporters in the MLNV.[5] It therefore presented robust resistance in the UN Human Rights Commission and elsewhere. However, the crudity of some of the tools Madrid employed to lobby against any criticism of its record in the struggle against terrorism—as was demonstrated by its rebuttal of the work of the UN's Special Rapporteur on torture in 2004—did little more than confirm outsiders in the positions they already held on either side of the Basque divide.

Over time, opposition to the Ibarretxe Plan within the Basque Socialist Party would combine with changes within radical nationalism to contribute to the emergence of a new approach to the Basque crisis. As this thinking quietly took shape in confidential talks, a number of external actors seeking to encourage or support nascent efforts to foster peace began to venture in.

Beyond impasse

In the days before the 13 May 2001 election, ETA exploded a large car bomb in one of the most elegant neighbourhoods in Madrid, the Barrio Salamanca, and killed the president of PP in the autonomous community of Aragón. On 15 May it sent a letter bomb to the journalist Gorka Landaburu, who wrote for the weekly magazine *Cambio 16*. The explosion wounded him in the face, abdomen and hands. Days later, Santiago Oleaga, the financial director of the newspaper *El Diario Vasco*, was shot to death in the parking lot of a medical centre in San Sebastián. The organisation would claim seven more mortal victims in the course of the year, most of them members of Spain's security forces. The government's efforts against it were encroaching upon its operational capacity: ETA's structures were increasingly infiltrated by Spanish and French intelligence and arrests were mounting. Yet how to move beyond the presence of ETA in Basque political and social life remained an elusive goal.

Ibarretxe returned to the Basque government facing a conflictive political environment. He had been able to establish a 'tripartite' government that meant he did not have to rely on the nationalist left for support. But the presence of EH in the wings represented an unstated—and inevitably controversial—guarantee. (As the *Gara* journalist Iñaki Iriondo would observe, in the course of his government Ibarretxe was able to move ahead with his most ambitious projects only 'thanks either to a favourable vote or the agreed abstention of the nationalist left.')[6] After the illegalisation of Batasuna, Ibarretxe was legally bound to take police action against the party; the Ertzaintza closed Batasuna's offices and conducted arrests and raids on other premises, increasing the hostility of the nationalist left to the Basque government as it did so. But the Basque Parliament refused to dissolve its parliamentary group, incurring the wrath of the PP and the indictment of its PNV president Juan María Atutxa, by Basque and Spanish courts.[7]

No less complicated were Ibarretxe's attempts to address the delicate issue of ETA's victims. The Basque government was acutely aware of the debt it owed the victims, but many within it continued to see them in antagonistic terms. Ibarretxe elevated a small existing office into a 'Directorate for the Attention to Victims' and appointed Maixabel Lasa, the widow of the Socialist politician (and ETA victim) Juan María Jáuregui, to head it. Her deputy was Txema Urkijo, who had been a spokesperson for Gesto por la Paz. The office was intended as a bridge between the Basque government and the victims, yet began work not fully trusted by either.[8] (At this point 'victims' were implicitly understood to be limited to the victims of ETA. In 2000 the Basque Parliament's Human Rights Commission, under the chairmanship of Iñigo Urkullu of the PNV, had commissioned a report on 'all the victims of the violence generated in our country'. The report failed to win support of the PP and the PSE and had to be put to one side.)[9] The office promoted the approval of a first law on victims in 2003, but it was only in 2007 that the Basque government finally celebrated a day in recognition of victims. The proceedings included a formal apology by Ibarretxe to victims for their past neglect, but were boycotted by the PP and some of the victims' organisations.[10]

Ibarretxe would recall that after the collapse of the Lizarra ceasefire he had 'felt challenged to come up with a new way to sort this out'.[11] At his investiture as *lehendakari* in July 2001 he announced that he would propose a reform of the Basque statute of autonomy and a popular consultation.[12] The obstacles that lay ahead were immediately obvious. Aznar met Ibarretxe later that month and bluntly stated: 'The right to self-determination is not recognised anywhere in the world... Mr. Ibarretxe better be aware that no part of Spain will be segregated.'[13] Undeterred, in October 2001 Ibarretxe introduced the basic principles of his programme for 'self-government' in the Basque Parliament. They included the recognition of the 'Basque people' or Euskal Herria as a 'political subject' and the affirmation of their right to be able to 'freely and democratically' decide on their own future.[14] This was interpreted by the PP and PSOE as a direct challenge to the constitution.

Other social and political forces also began to articulate their own ideas for a possible way out of the Basque impasse. In February 2001 Elkarri initiated a new peace conference. It gathered signatures and financial contributions from more than 50,000 supporters and established an international honorary committee.[15] In a second phase, which ran to October 2002, it organised public seminars and discussions in parallel to indirect dialogues involving all political parties other than the PP and its Navarrese associate, the Navarre People's Union (UPN). Elkarri could not claim agreement at the conclusion of its peace conference—rather it had exposed the depth of divisions over ETA's violence and the 'anti-democratic response' by the Spanish state—but it was able to point to the strengthening of a social network committed to peace, as well as incipient international support.[16]

A confidential attempt to develop understanding of points of agreement and disagreement promoted by a Catalan peace institute also hit problems. Between September 2000 and April 2003 this 'Contrasts' exercise sent a series of questionnaires to representatives of all the Basque political parties, including EH/Batasuna, in order to try to build consensus around elements that might facilitate understanding of a way forward.[17] The project was directed by Viçenc Fisas, a Catalan specialist in conflict studies who brought with him both deep knowledge of the Basque Country and peacemaking elsewhere. However, while it made progress, it also exposed serious differences between its interlocutors and had to be abandoned in 2003 after the illegalisation of Batasuna. Meanwhile, the contentious nature of the political moment took its toll upon those who aspired to fill the role of intermediary. The PP accused Elkarri of being in the 'vanguard of the non-defeat of ETA'.[18] Batasuna, on the other hand, complained that Elkarri had conducted a 'hostile takeover' of some of its own ideas, while resenting both the extent to which it focused on ETA's armed action as 'the only problem' to resolve and its growing ties to the PNV.[19]

In 2001 the Basque Socialists had been at low ebb. The decision to contest the May 2001 election in alliance with the PP had been a difficult one, and it had clearly not paid off. The party had presented itself as the strategic partner of the Spanish right, increasingly aligned with a virulent form of Spanish nationalism that many Basque Socialists believed to be anathema to their political identity. A further problem was what outspoken individuals such as Jesús Eguiguren charged was the manipulation of the anti-terrorist pact signed the previous year. 'It is inadmissible,' wrote Eguiguren in *Cambio 16* in October 2001, that the government should accuse the opposition of weakening the struggle against terrorism every time anyone in the Basque Country 'takes a political decision or makes a declaration that the government does not like'. An example was Aznar's request that representatives of the PSE who attended meetings of Elkarri's peace conference should clarify 'whether they are on the side of the victims or perpetrators' of terrorism. Many constitutionalist politicians, like Eguiguren himself, lived under permanent threat from ETA, and now they were being accused 'almost of collaborating with terrorism' for attending a peace conference.[20]

In March 2002 the PSE convened an extraordinary congress that proved extraordinarily divisive. It concluded with the resignation of its secretary-general, Nicolás Redondo, and the adoption of a new political platform. Establishing a position on core issues that rejected both the PNV's view that 'to finish with terrorism', as Eguiguren put it, 'it is first necessary to solve the Basque problem', and the PP position that 'there is no problem other than terrorism', was not easy. In an attempt to do so Eguiguren drafted a strategy paper that offered a rigorous defence of the PSE as an autonomous political force with a history of support for Basque self-government that dated back to the first Basque autonomy statute in 1936.[21] His paper drew on the experience of Quebec to offer a measured but comprehensive critique of Ibarretxe's proposals. But it was interpreted by some as offering a defence of self-determination. (In an article titled 'Oxygen for ETA', Fernando Savater characterised the PSE's new position as confirming that 'to be a Socialist in the Basque Country you have to resign yourself to wearing nationalist camouflage'.)[22] The PSE that emerged from the party congress had Eguiguren as the party president and his Vizcayan ally Patxi López as its new secretary-general; it would set a very different course from that pursued in advance of the 2001 elections.

The collapse of the Lizarra process and ETA's return to violence had contributed to confusion within the MLNV that was confirmed by EH's poor electoral results in May 2001. Until the ceasefire, supporters of the liberation movement had believed, as Urko Aiartza and Julen Zabalo put it, 'that the armed struggle would continue until some minimum rights were recognised'.[23] The prospect of an end to violence and progress in achieving nationalist political goals had energised its social base. Many within the MLNV had questioned the circumstances of the ceasefire's end as well as ETA's bloody campaign in its wake in a significant shift towards the recognition that armed action might be a choice and not an essential requirement to the separatist struggle. This shift was reinforced by external developments. The split from Batasuna of Aralar, which was established in September 2001 as a political party clearly committed to both independence and non-violence, was inevitably perceived as a 'betrayal'. But as the first institutional schism from the nationalist left in many years, it could not lightly be ignored. In the meantime the attacks of 9/11, the launch of the 'global war on terrorism' in their wake and the continuing onslaught of the Spanish and French security services all contributed to underline real limitations to ETA's armed action.

With the threat of its illegalisation already rumbling in the political background, Batasuna presented a new position paper, 'A scenario for peace', in January 2002. The document began with a familiar account of the two hundred years of repression suffered by 'the Basque people', but it also contained a number of new departures. Most significant was Batasuna's clear statement that it 'has abandoned, abandons and will abandon the idea of imposing its own political agenda' upon the Basque Country and avowal of respect for the Basque plurality 'as a determining factor of cultural and political enrichment'.[24] Batasuna encouraged the discussion of its new position among Basque political parties. It also began to promote it abroad, conscious that one of the weaknesses' of the Lizarra process—despite its direct links to Northern Ireland—had been the absence of the international community and, in general terms, international understanding of its cause and grievances. (Before September 2001 Batasuna had even considered opening a liaison office in New

York.) Several party leaders travelled to Brussels. And in October 2002 Arnaldo Otegi, Josu Ternera and Joseba Álvarez presented Batasuna's position in a press conference at the United Nations in Geneva, to the outrage of the Spanish government.[25] It would be Ternera's last public appearance before he disappeared into clandestinity to avoid his possible imprisonment under new charges related to his activity with ETA.

The Ibarretxe Plan

Ibarretxe introduced his ideas for 'a new political agreement for coexistence' in September 2002.[26] A more fully developed proposal for a new 'Political Statute for the Community of Euskadi' was approved by the Basque government in October 2003 and submitted to the Basque Parliament for its consideration.[27] The Ibarretxe Plan looked towards a new status of 'free association' for the three provinces of Euskadi, with provision for Navarre and the French Basque provinces to join if they should so decide. Basque citizenship would be open to all residents of the community, in addition to those of Basque ancestry outside it, with all Basque citizens also recognised as holding Basque nationality. With a nod to the flexibility of arrangements in Northern Ireland, where citizens can hold both Irish and UK passports, Basque citizens would be entitled to carry both Basque and Spanish passports, while the king of Spain would remain head of state. A revision of the allocation of administrative powers between Euskadi and Spain was envisaged as well as, in somewhat more hazy terms, the 'direct representation' of the new community in the organs of the EU.

Ibarretxe's proposal claimed to combine respect for Spain's existing legal framework with a reassessment of the understanding of national identity in Spain. It aspired to a nuanced interpretation of the concepts of sovereignty and nationhood that drew upon a somewhat amorphous combination of Basque foral traditions and new thinking among Europe's stateless nations, as well as the experience of Quebec (in 1980, in the first of two referenda, the Partie Québécois had proposed replacing Quebec's federal ties to Canada with an arrangement of 'sovereignty-association').[28] For many of its critics, however, it represented a direct challenge to Spain's constitutional identity as a single nation state. The plan's claim of the right of Basques 'to decide their own future' implicitly suggested that they were already sovereign. And the means by which this was to be done—through consultation within Euskadi, negotiation with the state and, most controversially, a referendum—was quite unacceptable to Spanish nationalists.[29] Discussion of the Ibarretxe Plan's substance was quickly overwhelmed by the entrenched ideological positions that characterised the political environment. As a consequence, far from offering the basis for a peaceful settlement of the differences that divided Basques, and the Basque government from Madrid, Ibarretxe's efforts served to reinforce existing divisions.[30]

Basque nationalists had paid close attention to Canada where, in 1995, a motion for Quebec's unilateral declaration of independence had been narrowly defeated (49.4 per cent to 50.6 per cent). Shocked by this slim margin of victory, the federal government sought legal clarification from the Supreme Court on three questions: the legality of the secession of Quebec under Canada's constitution; the existence under international law of a right of self-determination that might allow Canada to effect Quebec's secession; and, in the event of conflict between national and international law on this question, guidance as to which would take precedence.[31] The ruling delivered two years later was welcomed by Canadian federalists and Québécois secessionists alike, each of whom immediately sought to spin its contents in their favour.[32] To the relief of the government, the Court decided that unilateral secession was not legal under either domestic or international law. Meanwhile, Québécois nationalists were greatly encouraged by its ruling that if a 'clear majority' (how clear was not specified) within Quebec responded positively to a 'clear question' (also not specified) asked in a referendum on secession, negotiations between Quebec and the federal government would have to take place.[33]

In the strategy paper he prepared for the PSE, Eguiguren had argued that the Canadian Supreme Court's ruling had included much that was relevant to the Basque situation. The ruling upheld the inexistence under the Canadian constitution and international law of an innate 'right' to self-determination, but also the democratic legitimacy of the opinion of a qualified majority of the citizens of Quebec. These considerations bolstered Eguiguren's controversial view that, while Ibarretxe's ideas were based on a misunderstanding of the Quebec case, there could be conditions in Spain under which the independence of Euskadi could be accepted: it would have to represent the clear choice of a qualified majority of Basques and its pursuit be achieved through legal procedures.[34] A pre-condition was circumstances that allowed for political discussion to take place freely. Ibarretxe's proposals were predicated on a situation of 'total absence of violence', but they ignored the very obvious point that violence still existed in the Basque Country, constituting a direct threat to individual Basques as well as a more existential assault on the 'normal politics' of a democratic society.

In the course of the plan's development, Ibarretxe and his government sought to redefine the relationship between the Basque Country as a region and Spain as a state within the context of new thinking within the EU.[35] As they did so they drew on the PNV's long ties to European structures as well as the activism of pro-independence nationalist parties gathered in the European Free Alliance (EFA), of which EA was a member. These parties, which included the Catalan Left Republican Party (ERC), Sinn Féin and Flemish, Corsican and Scottish nationalist parties, supported the idea of the 'internal enlargement' of the European Union through recognition of its hitherto stateless nations or, failing that, a 'Europe of the Regions'—an old idea that had first been advanced to support a European federation—that recognised self-governing territorial entities such as the Basque Country and Catalonia as 'partners in the governance of the Union'.[36] However, the parallel discussion of the new European constitution—and the hard reality that the EU was, first and foremost, an entity whose actions were determined by its member states—contributed to dilute the European aspirations of Ibarretxe's ideas considerably.

The elements of ambiguity that remained in the new political statute were rapidly overwhelmed by criticism from the PP and PSOE of what they perceived as the proposal's exclusive and sectarian tendencies. Ibarretxe's ambitions were dismissed as 'treason' by the PP's Mariano Rajoy and his plan described as sharing 'the same objectives as ETA'.[37] The Socialists confirmed that they would 'never' support the Ibarretxe Plan, which they held to be 'the messianic product of an exclusive nationalist ideology'.[38] The PP tried to block the discussion of the new statute even within the Basque Parliament and, having failed to do so, introduced a reform to the criminal code that threatened anyone who called a referendum without the authorisation of the government with prison.[39] Attitudes towards the Ibarretxe Plan from within the nationalist left, meanwhile, were understandably complex. ETA and Batasuna saw it as a belated response by the PNV to the demands that ETA had made of it during the Lizarra ceasefire, as well as a deliberate attempt to capitalise on radical nationalism's political weakness after the 2001 elections.[40] Batasuna had to welcome the direction taken by Ibarretxe in general terms and in particular the broad sweep of his proposal's preamble, which recognised the 'Basque people' and Euskal Herria as well as Basques' right to decide in accordance with the principle of self-determination. But it repeatedly criticised the detailed development of the plan and would continue to view the initiative with suspicion.

On 30 December 2004, the Ibarretxe Plan was finally put to a vote in the Basque Parliament. Ibarretxe needed an absolute majority for its approval (thirty-eight out of seventy-five votes). Despite all his efforts to the contrary he had failed to win a single vote outside his governing coalition. The 'key' to any majority therefore lay in the seven votes commanded by Batasuna. As the debate began, only a very few people were privy to Batasuna's voting strategy. With a packed parliament hanging on his words, Otegi finally announced that Batasuna would split its vote, offering three votes in favour—enough to allow Ibarretxe's proposal to pass by thirty-nine to thirty-six votes—as a means of saying 'yes to Euskal Herria, yes to self-determination and yes to a broad agreement that will allow us to open the doors to a process that will overcome the conflict', but three votes against in a clear 'no' to reform of the statute and 'the errors of twenty-five years ago'.[41]

Ibarretxe would take his plan to Madrid, where his opponents were quick to point out that its approval had been achieved only thanks to the votes of a political party banned for its ties to a terrorist organisation.[42] He went with little real hope that it would become a political reality. However, in its presentation and debate the Ibarretxe Plan had had an impact that even some of its critics acknowledged. 'Nothing is going to be exactly the same as before the about-turn taken by nationalism,' Jésus Eguiguren would write in 2004. 'Although we might defend the validity of the statute of Guernica [autonomy], and denounce its unilateral abandonment by nationalism, the fact is that we are not where we were before. The nationalists want something else, something different.'[43] And in the Basque Country the views of the nationalists could neither be simply ignored nor dismissed on the basis of their alleged affinity with ETA.

'Basquist' socialism and the Txillare channel

Jesús Eguiguren would always be a controversial figure both inside and outside Euskadi. But between the May 2001 elections and the elections to the Basque Parliament held in April 2005, his thinking and writing led the way in establishing the primacy of the *vasquista* or 'Basquist' wing within the PSE and pre-positioned the Socialists for the peace process with ETA launched by Prime Minister Zapatero in 2005.

The 'Basquism' that Basque Socialists defended—some more than others—would be described at the party congress held in late 2005 as 'connecting in a profound way with the distinguishing characteristics of the [Basque] Country'. Drawing upon the successful evolution of 'Catalanism' within Catalan socialism, especially after the Catalan Socialist Party, the PSC, entered the Catalan government at the head of a leftist coalition in December 2003, the PSE claimed ground at the centre of Basque political life. From there it sought to attract voters from beyond its traditional constituencies and position itself as a party capable of mounting credible opposition to the Basque nationalist hegemony and eventually leading a Basque government. Shunning the essentialist preoccupations of Basque nationalism, it worked 'to articulate, from a post-nationalist perspective, a country of plural identities and diverse feelings of belonging, expressed through the linguistic richness of Euskera and Spanish'.[44] Such positions were viewed warily from Madrid but in the starkly polarised environment of the Basque Country in the Aznar years, they gradually gained traction.

A central element of the articulation of 'Basquist' views was the responsibility that Basque Socialists believed they carried. To be a Basque Socialist politician meant to live with the loss of friends and colleagues who had fallen to ETA's violence, to be subjected to threats and shadowed by bodyguards, and to be accosted by *kale borroka* and other expressions of the radical opposition. Unlike Basque representatives of the PP—a number of whom lived outside the Basque Country—and members of the PSOE elsewhere, Basque Socialists did not deny the existence of conflict within Basque political life or the complex relationship that ETA's terrorism bore to it, even if, the use of the word 'conflict' itself remained sensitive. Nor were some of them closed to the possibility of revising the Basque statute to accommodate pressures for change, so long as any changes were made in accordance with existing legal procedures. In 2002 the Guipuzcoan politicians Gemma Zabaleta and Denis

Itzaso wrote a book, *Con mano izquierda* ('With the left hand'), which defended the idea that all political projects could be championed democratically and did not rule out a popular consultation, so long as it was crafted as an instrument of cohesion and consensus. They also advocated dialogue between the PSE and the nationalist left and consequently opposed the banning of Batasuna (on this point they differed from the official position of the PSE).[45]

As both Eguiguren's opposition to the Ibarretxe Plan, and development of an alternate proposal for *un arreglo*—the 'settlement' of the Basque problem—took shape, he wrote numerous articles in the Spanish and Basque press. These were gathered together in 2003 in a volume that also included a far-sighted and at the time quite unrealistic proposal for settlement. A more considered set of proposals published in 2004, 'The Basque crisis: between rupture and dialogue', set out the conditions and contents of a new 'internal pact' between the Basque Country's political forces.[46] Eguiguren's bottom line was two-fold: constitutionalists would need to commit the state to respecting what was agreed among the Basque political parties; nationalists that these changes should be implemented in accordance with established legal processes, including ratification by the Spanish Parliament.

Eguiguren's political vision was grounded in his understanding of Basque history and its culture of 'pacts' as well as his own Basque identity. That this had been formed in the Euskera-speaking environment of 'deep Guipúzcoa' was significant. It meant, for example, that Eguiguren could openly acknowledge that Euskal Herria existed as a socio-cultural reality that was distinct from the political construct that was Euskadi, but not in itself threatening. Growing up, Euskal Herria had been, as Eguiguren recalled in 2008, simply 'the words we [speakers of Euskera] used for the Basque Country (*el País Vasco*), whereas now people think that Euskal Herria is an invention of ETA and Batasuna'. Eguiguren approached the Basque problem from a vantage point that recognised ETA and the nationalist left as 'a social sector with deep historical roots that derive from a specific and integral vision of the country, its politics and other things, which was not included at the time of the transition and has remained outside the system'. As such, it represented a problem that 'cannot be solved by elimination; what we call the nationalist left is not going to disappear'.[47]

Back in 2003, Eguiguren had drawn on an example from the Carlist Wars to illustrate what he viewed as the appropriate way to approach the

Basque problem. He recalled that it was when the Spanish General Baldomero Espartero was militarily dominant, advancing inexorably through the Basque provinces against the Carlist forces, that he had put most emphasis on the need for negotiation with the enemy. 'Fighting and doing politics is how we will finish with this,' he is reported to have said, as the contending parties moved towards the 'embrace of Vergara', the agreement reached in 1839, based on peace and a compromise on the *fueros*, that brought an end to the first Carlist War.[48] Eguiguren's own commitment to 'fighting and doing politics' had some practical consequences. Indeed since 2001 he had been meeting on a regular basis with Arnaldo Otegi. These meetings represented a considerable risk, given the strictures of the anti-terrorist pact and the illegalisation of Batasuna, and took place with the knowledge of only a few individuals within the PSE. They had begun at a difficult political moment, but not exactly from nothing. Eguiguren and Otegi had been among delegations of the PSE and Batasuna that met during the 1999 Lizarra ceasefire. In 2000, Otegi began to hold the occasional meeting with Francisco (Paco) Egea, a member of the PSE who, like him, was from the Guipuzcoan town of Elgoibar. Their *rendezvous* took place in a remote farmhouse called Txillare, outside Elgoibar, with the help of its owner and their mutual friend, Pello Rubio. In 2001 the two decided to elevate the conversations to include Eguiguren, and a pattern soon developed. Eguiguren would ascend the rough country road to Txillare with Paco Egea, while Otegi would usually be accompanied by another noted leader of Batasuna, Pernando Barrena.[49]

Eguiguren and Otegi were motivated by a need to do something to extract the political situation from its current impasse—'Are we going to leave this to our children? Is this absurd fight going to continue for them as well?' Eguiguren recalled them asking—but to begin with they had little idea as to how this might be achieved. A first step, as Otegi would remember, was recovering an ability to listen: 'We'd spent decades shouting at each other and making each others' lives much harder. So the first thing we learned was to listen to each other and understand that neither was in possession of the whole truth, or all of the suffering.' They quickly agreed that they would protect their meetings in Txillare from whatever happened around them. This agreement held firm, even as political relations between them were complicated by ETA's continued violence (ETA killed fifteen people in 2001, including a PSE councillor; five people in

2002; and three in 2003); the campaign to ban Batasuna, which was supported by the PSE and Eguiguren personally; and the difficult local and municipal elections of 2003, the first electoral event that Batasuna was not able to contest. (Batasuna called upon its voters to enter a blank vote; it achieved some 165,000 votes in circumstances in which its supporters knew their votes to be of purely symbolic importance.)[50]

In 2002 Eguiguren and Otegi reached a written agreement on the basis for their meetings. This specified that Eguiguren attended them as a leader of the PSE-EE, but did not represent the PSOE; Otegi was there for Batasuna, but did not speak for ETA. The two would try to agree the conditions upon which a process for the resolution of the political conflict and the construction of peace could be based. They began by analysing the past attempts to reach peace represented by the talks in Algiers and the Estella-Lizarra Declaration; they also devoted considerable attention to extracting the lessons from Northern Ireland. Their analysis concluded that the Algiers talks had failed because ETA had brought political issues to the negotiating table. Lizarra, on the other hand, had excluded a significant part of Basque society from the process, and it was impossible to conceive of a future for Euskadi that marginalised half its population. In Northern Ireland they saw the benefits of including all political sentiments within the process and a shift from an exclusive focus on the principle of self-determination to the idea of 'consent'.

Eguiguren's proposal for a settlement of the Basque problem ('*Bases para un arreglo*') was published when he was already two years into talks with Otegi. It was received with indifference by the public at large, but attracted a lot of attention within the nationalist left and circles such as Elkarri. Eguiguren suggested that 'all political options should be able to have access to the means and possibility of bringing into practice their democratic objectives... our society is free to decide its future following democratic procedures'.[51] The distance between this position and that of Batasuna—which recognised the need to look for a political agreement among different actors, and accepted that the key to the solution of the conflict lay not in achieving independence, but in the possibility that all political projects, including independence, could be realised and Basque society free to choose between them—suddenly did not seem insurmountable.[52] For the moment, however, with Aznar still in power and the existence of the Txillare channel swathed in secrecy, exactly what might come of the conversations in this remote Basque farmhouse remained far from clear.

The great taboo

Elkarri's peace conference and the debate surrounding the Ibarretxe Plan had highlighted the sensitivities involved in an internationalised approach to the Basque problem. Both built on the interest and disposition to help of a number of outsiders—among them political actors from Northern Ireland, US-based conflict resolution specialists who had followed the Basque situation from the early 1990s and interested individuals from within Europe—even as they danced around what they knew to be a central taboo: the involvement of an external third party, or third parties, in the Basque issue.

Eguiguren addressed the issue in a piece he wrote in May 2002, but did not publish at the time on account of its political sensitivity. He had been motivated by an article by Felipe González in *El País* on the Palestinian problem.[53] In the early 1990s, González had been a keen proponent of the role that Spain could play in international efforts to resolve conflicts elsewhere, notably in Central America. He had actively championed the Madrid Conference that in 1991 had been an important precursor of the Oslo agreements on the Middle East. And he now argued that a solution to the differences between Israel and Palestine could only come from outside, and that the EU, among others, should fully involve itself in trying to find it. Eguiguren read the article and immediately wondered: Why not in the Basque case?

Even to ask the question, Eguiguren knew, was something that 'no one will dare to do in public, because it is political-fiction, politically incorrect or simply unrealisable in political terms'. But he went on to ask it anyway. If it was a good thing that the EU became involved in those parts of the world where it could contribute to the resolution of conflicts, was it not reasonable to demand that it first concern itself with what happened within its own territory? The Basque Country, after all, was the only place in the EU where people were regularly assassinated for their political ideas and other freedoms were routinely assaulted. Basque citizens were Spanish and European—did not the obligation to guarantee their rights and freedoms extend from the Basque government, to the Spanish government and European institutions as well?

Eguiguren accepted that the prospect of EU involvement in the Basque Country was at this point something of a fantasy. Appealing for help from outside, 'internationalising the problem', would at once dignify it as an issue requiring a mix of security and political measures and expose Spain's incapacity to resolve it on its own. In the current context, the 'abyss of fear and distrust that separate the ruling parties in Vitoria and Madrid', as Eguiguren put it, left little room to move beyond mistaken policies that contributed to perpetuating the problem.

Sensitivity to the involvement of outsiders in internal conflict perceived through the lens of terrorist violence was by no means unique to Spain. Other governments, Russia and Turkey among them, carefully protected their own capacity to address internal insurgencies as they saw fit, while even those—such as Colombia, Indonesia and Sri Lanka—who did countenance the involvement of outsiders tightly circumscribed its extent. They selected 'weak' mediators—the non-governmental organisations the Centre for Humanitarian Dialogue (HD Centre) and the Crisis Management Initiative, in the case of talks between the Free Aceh Movement (GAM) and the government of Indonesia; the government of Norway in those that developed between the government of Sri Lanka and the LTTE—and limited their role to one of 'facilitation'.[54] In Colombia, despite a long history of negotiation with guerrilla groups, successive governments had for many years shied away from international mediation.[55] Under the presidency of Andrés Pastrana (1998–2002), a variety of states, including Spain, did become involved in supporting dialogue with both the Revolutionary Armed Forces of Colombia (FARC) and the National Liberation Army (ELN).[56] However, the government made it clear that their primary function was to help it overcome its terrorist threat.

In July 2009, Otegi attributed Spanish resistance to international involvement to a 'pure inferiority complex'. Spain was, in his view, unwilling to contemplate the kind of assistance that the Irish had received from George Mitchell and others, in large part, he believed, because of an emotional conviction that 'no one can come here and tell us Spaniards how to resolve our own problems'.[57] Spanish sovereignty was informed by its imperial history, the ambiguous legacy of Francoism, the constitutional patriotism that had quickly replaced it, and anxiety surrounding a possible loss of identity accentuated by both the demands of regional nationalisms and the encroaching powers of the EU.

Outsiders who broached the subject of engagement with Spanish governments would be met with repeated protestations that Spain was different; their concern for the Basque problem was appreciated, but they would have to understand that this was a problem of purely internal dimensions that Spain would resolve for itself.[58] That the Basque conflict had, as the Sinn Féin MP Alex Maskey put it, 'no international cachet' did not help.[59] A lack of interest among the Basque diaspora, the strategic irrelevance of Basque violence to any state other than France and the strong bilateral relations that other Western countries maintained with Spain, all conspired to ensure that interest in formal international involvement in the Basque issue was minimal.

International engagement in an asymmetric conflict is inherently sensitive, not least for the difficulties implicit in maintaining the 'impartiality' that the UN 'Guidance for Effective Mediation' recognises as one of eight 'mediation fundamentals'.[60] 'Neither party trusts the other but both must trust the mediator for the mediation to work,' as a US Institute for Peace peacemaker's 'toolkit' put it.[61] A non-state armed group—especially if proscribed as a terrorist organisation—will fear the pro-state bias of any external actor and the international legal system it is being asked to rejoin.[62] Meanwhile, the initial recognition of the armed group as an interlocutor and the degree of levelling of the playing field required for an effective negotiating process—for example with regard to the respect with which the parties may be treated by the mediator or through the development of the capacity of the armed group—will likely be interpreted as favouring the non-state armed group by the state concerned.[63] In the Basque context, where the asymmetry was extreme and the political calculations of engagement influenced by the emotional issue of the victims, even the idea of international mediators—who as Michael Ignatieff has observed 'are impartial without being fair; it is not their task to make moral distinctions between aggressor and victim'— and the impartiality they would have to demonstrate to ETA was considered quite unacceptable in many quarters.[64]

An element of double standards in Spain's attitude to efforts to resolve conflicts (and indeed engage with recognised terrorists) was nonetheless evident from its involvement in Colombia. This was for many years led by an experienced Spanish diplomat, Yago Pico de Coaña, who, as Felipe González's top adviser on Latin America in the 1990s had been closely involved in the Central American peace process. Pico de Coaña had arrived in Colombia as Spain's ambassador in 1996 and assumed an influential position among Bogotá's diplomatic community. Spain was Colombia's largest external investor and took a leading role in Pastrana's efforts to pursue separate negotiations with the FARC and the ELN. Spain was a member of the group of facilitators of the first process, and the group of friends of the second. Pico de Coaña met on several occasions with the leadership of the FARC and promoted a visit to Madrid by the FARC and several Colombian officials in February 2000, as part of a 'Eurotour' designed to introduce the guerrillas to the modern world and encourage them towards flexibility in the peace process.[65]

Such activities were predicated upon an understanding that there was no military solution to the Colombian conflict; that the depth of the humanitarian crisis and civilian suffering demanded a response from the international community; and that Pastrana's peace process, although flawed, merited support.[66] They also reflected a Spanish engagement in Colombia that was far removed from the approach to ETA pursued by Aznar at home. Photographs of PP officials welcoming Raúl Reyes, the FARC's leading negotiator (killed in Ecuador in 2008 in possession of computer files that yielded a trove of information about the ties between ETA and the FARC) in February 2000 openly contradicted Aznar's statements regarding the need to defeat, not enter into dialogue with, terrorists.[67] The collapse of Pastrana's peace process and the electoral triumph of Alvaro Uribe a few months later, promising a much harder military line against the guerrillas, brought about an abrupt shift. Aznar developed a close relationship with Uribe based on fulsome support of his attempt to defeat the FARC that was wholly consistent with Spain's efforts to combat international terrorism. Spain played a leading role in ensuring that the ELN, as well as the FARC, was included on the EU terrorist list, and for the first time gave Colombia military assistance to help prosecute its war against terrorism and drug trafficking.

More bruising for Spain than the inconsistencies of its policies on internal conflict were its battles over the issue of human rights. Spain remained unable to address—or even fully acknowledge—the abuses committed under Franco.[68] It nevertheless took pride in its status as an advanced democracy that had ratified all major human rights instruments and treaties, and actively championed full respect for human rights and the rule of law at home and abroad. Within this broad, rights-respecting panorama, the Basque issue represented a thorn in Spain's side capable of inflicting small but recurring pain. International attention was encouraged, as successive Spanish governments saw it, by the efforts of radical Basque nationalists to exploit the issue of human rights in fora such as the UN Human Rights Commission.[69] These efforts—which were understood as seeking to undermine the legitimacy of the Spanish state—were robustly, if at times crudely, resisted by all Spanish governments, with important differences of degree between those of Aznar and Zapatero, but not in the fundamentals of the approach.

Resistance to international attention drew on both a broad consensus within Spain (outside Euskadi) supporting counter-terrorist policy as well as the intense politicisation of human rights among and around the Basques. This cut so deeply into Basque society that it was difficult to speak of a 'culture' of human rights consistent with international norms.[70] Ideological battles marked the history of the Human Rights Commission in the Basque Parliament; outside official structures human rights associations were either immediately identifiable by their political affiliation (the Basque Observatory of Human Rights is an expression of the nationalist left)[71] or dodged the issue altogether. In July 2009, for example, the director of the Pedro Arrupe Institute for Human Rights in Bilbao's University of Deusto explained the difficulties the institute encountered in addressing human rights within the Basque Country as attributable to the varied positions on identity held by its staff.[72]

Since the early years of Spain's transition, international human rights organisations had regularly monitored the abuse of human rights in the context of the Basque problem. Their most vehement criticism had of course been reserved for ETA. Over the years abuses by representatives of the Spanish state had diminished as democracy took root and Spain's security sector became more professional. However, reports of Amnesty International, Human Rights Watch, the European Committee to Prevent Torture (CPT) and a variety of UN human rights bodies continued to point towards serious concerns deriving from issues such as the persistence of torture, as well as the new concerns raised by the modifications to the criminal and penitentiary codes and the law on political parties introduced in the early 2000s. Recommendations were made to address issues that did not conform to Spain's international responsibilities, such as the extensive period in *incommunicado* detention permitted under Spanish law, which human rights bodies considered 'facilitates the commission of acts of torture and ill-treatment', as the UN Committee Against Torture put it in 2002.[73] Improvements were made—the Ertzaintza and later some but not all individual judges on the Audiencia Nacional, following the lead of Baltazar Garzón, introduced measures such as the videotaping of prisoners in order to protect the integrity of *incommunicado* detentions—but the response by Spanish governments continued to be considered 'inadequate' in some areas.[74]

A particularly sensitive issue were the allegations of torture regularly made by Basque prisoners accused of terrorism or crimes associated with it. The nationalist left perceived torture as a deliberate element of the government's counter-terrorist strategy, designed to instil fear, but also as a means of extracting confessions that would later be used to build cases against defendants in court, and detain other ETA members they had implicated. Torture had been used, as a Spanish judge with a deep knowledge of the campaign against ETA explained, 'as one way in which the police gather material to convict them'.[75] The Spanish authorities, however, maintained that the allegations of torture reflected standing instructions by ETA to its militants to claim torture as a means of countering arrest.[76] The lack of an accepted narrative regarding the extent to which torture existed or not (and the hard fact that many Spaniards and indeed Basques were indifferent on the matter) was compounded by the problem that ETA's allegations were rarely investigated, and when they were, and grounds were found for prosecution, that prosecution was usually not sustained. On the rare occasion when it resulted in a conviction, it was frequently overturned, or the case dismissed, resulting in almost complete impunity.[77]

This background fuelled the controversy sparked by the presentation in 2004 of a report on Spain by the UN Special Rapporteur on torture, Theo van Boven.[78] Van Boven by 2004 had some thirty years' experience at an international level. His invitation to Spain responded to the government's wish that he prove the 'falsity of the denunciations that arrive at the [UN Human Rights] Commission from the world of ETA'.[79] Once in Spain, van Boven found that, 'with all honesty and integrity I could not do that'.[80] He concluded that allegations of torture and ill-treatment 'cannot be considered to be fabrications'. Although such treatment did not constitute a 'regular practice', its occurrence was 'more than sporadic and incidental'.[81] His report contained ample material to support this assertion, while also revealing the depth of the distortion of official thinking where issues related to Basque terrorism were involved.

In response to a question about the freedom of the press to discuss torture, for example, the interior minister (Ángel Acebes at the time) had told him that, 'if there was a credible complaint of torture it would be discussed publicly; however, in counter-terrorism cases it was standard practice for a person who had been detained systematically to allege that he/she has been tortured. Consequently most press agencies did not report the case as they knew the claim to be false, except for those newspapers linked to terrorism.'[82]

The Spanish government was outraged by van Boven's report and took steps to discredit his work and reputation, even alleging that he favoured terrorism. Its eighty-seven page rebuttal (of his twenty-three page report) judged van Boven's report to be 'virtually unacceptable in its entirety, being unfounded and lacking in rigour, substance and method'.[83] The Spanish delegation walked out of the UN human rights chamber in Geneva as van Boven was presenting his report—an unprecedented step—having already persuaded EU member states not to participate in the debate, a development that took van Boven by surprise. 'EU countries can be very firm when there are violations of human rights elsewhere,' he would recall of the episode, 'but in one of their own countries they can be very evasive and protective of their own relations.'[84] Asked whether the reaction of Spain was consistent with that of other countries that came under his purview during his four years as UN Special Rapporteur, van Boven would recall that no other country had reacted as strongly. The only parallel he could draw with regard to the vehemence and level of denial—albeit with due respect to the vast disparity in abuses committed—was to the military government of Argentina in the early 1980s.

Outsiders venture in

By late 2003, political attention in Spain had turned to the general elections expected for March 2004. Aznar had been faithful to a promise that he would only serve as prime minister through two legislatures and had handed over leadership of the PP to Rajoy, by now first vice-president of the government. Despite the antagonism generated by Aznar's defiance of Spanish public opinion on Iraq, his government's poor handling of an oil spill from a tanker off the coast of Cantabria in the autumn of 2002, and a growing dislike of the arrogance of his governing style, the strength of the economy underlay broadly shared predictions that the PP would be returned to government for a third term.[85]

In these rather unprepossessing circumstances, and in ignorance of the conversations in Txillare, a small number of outsiders began to put their toes in the water of the Basque conflict to see if they might be of assistance in facilitating contacts in efforts to end it. The involvement of Alec Reid built on his ties to HB, Elkarri and others he had met in the late 1990s. That of the Geneva-based HD Centre was, in contrast, self-starting, but soon found take-up inside the Basque Country. In the background to both was the widespread demand for change felt within Basque society as well as some still largely subterranean movement within the nationalist left and ETA.

ETA's leadership, whose most prominent figure was Mikel Albizu, *Mikel Antza*, who had led the political front since the early 1990s, was operating from deep clandestinity in France, but had been kept informed of Otegi's meetings with Eguiguren. From late 2002, these developed in parallel to a process of reflection within the organisation conducted by a form of 'postal assembly' because of the difficulties involved in convening meetings. This, as ETA indicated in its internal publication *Zutabe*, began from the realisation that, with a broad nationalist front unlikely to materialise, 'it was time to re-visit the Democratic Alternative'.[86] In accounts of this process based on documents captured from ETA, Florencio Domínguez described the organisation as in crisis. It was severely weakened by the assault upon it by the government forces, conscious that it had the capacity to keep on killing, but also internally divided and troubled by issues of discipline. Questions about the purposes of violence contributed to what was, from ETA's perspective, an unwelcome diversity of opinions within the nationalist left. ETA insisted on the need to 'regain the political value of the [armed] struggle' and, in this context, 're-affirmed its decision to continue its terrorist activity', as Domínguez put it. But in practical terms the internal questioning aligned with external pressures upon ETA to reduce its operational activity.[87] ETA assassinated two members of Spain's national police on 30 May 2003. They would be its last mortal victims until December 2006.

In its attempts to find a 'way out' of the Basque crisis, Elkarri had found affinity within sectors of the Basque Catholic Church. The Basque church's complex history included both the controversial involvement of some priests with ETA in the organisation's early days and battles between its more progressive members and the entrenched conservatism of the Spanish Catholic hierarchy. These had left the church wary of venturing into the treacherous waters of Basque politics at an institutional level, even as a small number of individuals remained committed to efforts to pursue a peaceful resolution of the conflict. One of them was Joseba Segura, who had maintained his lines of contact to the nationalist left since the Lizarra ceasefire.[88] With the support of his bishop, Monseñor Blázquez, Segura decided to ask Alec Reid if he could be persuaded to come to the Basque Country and explore the possibility of encouraging dialogue. In mid-2002 Segura, Jonan Fernández, Gorka Espiau and another representative of Elkarri travelled to Belfast. Over a period of three days in the Clonard Monastery—where Hume and Adams had met repeatedly many years before—the Basques explained the impasse they were facing and asked Reid to come and help them move beyond it. A few weeks later, and with the encouragement of Sinn Féin, although not its direct sponsorship, Reid agreed.[89] He would spend much of the following three years in the Basque Country, engaging with a wide variety of political actors, including Ibarretxe, Eguiguren, Rafa Diéz and, eventually, ETA itself.

The involvement of the HD Centre would follow a very different course. In 2003, the Centre was four years old. It had been founded in 1999 by Martin Griffiths, a former UN official with deep humanitarian experience who had soon taken the Centre from an original focus on 'humanitarian dialogue' to a more political involvement in conflict mediation. A formative experience for the HD Centre had been involvement in Aceh, Indonesia, which had begun in late 1999 as it sought to prevent a humanitarian crisis in the province. Initial meetings with representatives of the GAM in Malaysia and Sweden and consultations in Jakarta and Aceh had quickly thrown the Centre into the facilitation of talks between the GAM and representatives of the government of Indonesia. The process broke down in December 2002, five months after the signing of a Cessation of Hostilities Agreement—to be resumed in early 2005, when the former president of Finland, Martti Ahtisaari, and his Crisis Management Initiative were able to bring it to a successful conclusion—but the HD Centre had discovered a niche.[90] As a private actor able to draw upon the skills and contacts of the official world, it was well placed for the discreet promotion of engagement between armed groups and governments reluctant to embark on visible processes of international mediation. By mid-2003 the HD Centre was engaged in the promotion of dialogue in Nepal—having first reached out to that country's Maoist insurgents in 2000—and in early talks with rebels in Darfur.

The HD Centre's involvement in the Basque process developed out of a chance remark to Martin Griffiths by Nancy Soderberg, in mid-2003 vice-president of the International Crisis Group.[91] As a member of Clinton's National Security Council, Soderberg had been closely involved in the Northern Irish peace process. In the course of this engagement she had had been introduced to Basques pursuing links between the two situations. She asked Griffiths why the HD Centre had not considered involvement in the Basque conflict. It seemed a hard target with significant interests at stake which would prevent the entry of a small private organisation. But the idea did not go away. A short while later Griffiths mentioned to a Swiss colleague that the Centre was thinking of looking at the Basque conflict. Switzerland had long maintained quiet channels to individuals in the nationalist left and ETA, many through contacts maintained since the late 1970s by Julian Hottinger, an adviser on peace processes within the Swiss foreign ministry.[92] Talks had been held in Switzerland in 1999—without any involvement of the HD Centre—and ETA had recently approached the Swiss government and asked it to assume a mediating role. With an important bilateral relationship at stake Switzerland would have required approval from Madrid to move ahead. But this had not been forthcoming. Perhaps there was a role for a non-governmental actor instead.

Staff at the HD Centre identified William Douglass, the founding director of the Center for Basque Studies in Reno, Nevada, as a leading international expert on Basque issues and invited him to visit its Geneva headquarters. Douglass politely declined. He had retired from his position in Reno, and recalled his disappointment at the joint attempt of his Center and Elkarri to engage the Carter Center in the mid-1990s. The HD Centre persisted, and in November 2003 Douglass travelled first to Geneva to brief Griffiths and his deputy, Andrew Marshall, on the origins and context of the Basque problem, and then, discreetly, to the Basque Country to explore attitudes towards the possibility of a negotiated settlement. In conversations with all of those he met with except Ibarretxe—to whom he openly explained his assignment—Douglass maintained that he was researching an article on the Ibarretxe Plan. From this he segued easily into discussion of the possibility of negotiations. Rather to his surprise, he found that such an idea 'would likely find considerable support across a broad spectrum of the Basque public'.

Douglass arranged for Griffiths and Marshall to meet with Ibarretxe and a colleague from the Basque government who were visiting Geneva on other business. They were interested in what Ibarretxe had to say, but non-committal as to what the HD Centre might be able to do. After the meeting, however, the HD Centre asked Douglass to return to the Basque Country and try to contact ETA. Assuming he could, Douglass suggested that the HD Centre should be absolutely clear in proposing that it would only be willing to mediate discussion of the key humanitarian issues that were a consequence of the conflict, while remaining scrupulously impartial regarding the resolution of political disputes. This advice was given on the basis of Douglass' knowledge of previous negotiation efforts in the Basque Country, as well as his strong conviction that ETA could not be encouraged to think it would have a role in the negotiation of political issues. Neither Douglass, nor anyone he spoke to during this period, was aware of or referred to ongoing discussions between Eguiguren and Otegi.[93]

Back in the Basque Country, Douglass sought advice from a friend he would describe as 'a reasonably prominent figure within the Basque radical left'. His friend proposed a person in the labour movement who, 'while probably not a member *per se* of ETA, was certainly able to communicate with it'. Douglass met with this 'possible emissary of ETA' and was informed that ETA would require a letter from the HD Centre specifying the details of its proposal and outlining its commitment. He relayed the message to Griffiths and Marshall, and then returned to Reno. In January 2004, Griffiths flew to Bilbao. In an anonymous hotel near the airport he met with an intermediary and handed over a letter to an organisation clearly identified as terrorist by every European government. He would subsequently inform Douglass that the HD Centre had received a reply from ETA and met briefly with two of its messengers in Geneva. With the intensity of the electoral campaign gathering pace, Douglass remained in Reno, monitoring the Basque and Spanish press. As he would later recall, 'it had seemed unlikely that we could undertake a serious peace initiative until the electoral dust had settled and the true magnitude of the PP's victory was known'.[94]

5

ZAPATERO'S MOMENT

On 11 March 2004 Islamic extremists launched a massive terrorist attack on Madrid commuter trains only days in advance of Spain's general election. The PP had run an aggressive campaign in which its successes against ETA had featured prominently, couched in an anti-Basque rhetoric that at times appeared to paint all Basques as either terrorists or their supporters. Public opinion polls had predicted that it would return to power with a comfortable victory, if short of the absolute majority Aznar had enjoyed since 2000.[1] Following the bombing it quickly became evident that whether this was the case or not could be determined by the identity of the culprits. ETA had had several recent attempts to commit attacks on Madrid thwarted. If it had been responsible, popular revulsion at the unprecedented scale of the assault (the count of 191 dead was almost a quarter that of all those killed by ETA since 1968; 1,400 more had been wounded) and confidence in Aznar's tough stance on terrorism would have reinforced the PP's support. If, on the other hand, the bombs had been placed by Islamic militants protesting against Aznar's support for US policy in Iraq, voters were considered likely to favour the PSOE and its relatively untried leader, José Luis Rodríguez Zapatero.

In the immediate aftermath of the bombings Aznar's officials declared ETA to be responsible and urged others—from the Basque government to the UN Security Council—to follow their lead. Only Arnaldo Otegi insisted from the outset that ETA had nothing to do with the bombing and that its characteristics suggested Islamic terrorism.[2] As evidence accumulated to support this assertion, the government held fast. Suspicions quickly mounted that this was a manipulation of public opinion for political ends. The Spanish electorate sensed that it had been lied to and on 14 March handed Zapatero a solid victory at the polls.[3]

Zapatero assumed office in mid-April at the head of a minority government. His first four years as prime minister benefitted from continued economic stability. They were characterised by the introduction of significant social changes and more controversial attempts to reform the state of autonomies and address the neglected issue of Spain's 'historical memory'. Scarred by the loss of the 2004 election, the PP offered a brutal opposition that became known as *crispación*. It involved the deliberate pursuit of political confrontation through insults, personal attacks, alarmism and exaggeration to an extent that went 'further than what might be considered normal in advanced democracies' as Ignacio Sánchez-Cuenca put it with studied understatement.[4]

At the centre of the storm was the dialogue with ETA for which Zapatero sought and received the formal approval of parliament in May 2005. This was framed in accordance with proposals put forward in November 2004 by Otegi, on Batasuna's behalf, in terms that built on his discussions with Jesús Eguiguren. Initial talks conducted in conditions of almost total secrecy prepared the way for ETA's announcement of a permanent ceasefire in 2006. From that time forth the process would be beset by a permanent trickle and at times deluge of leaks and speculation that fed the seemingly ceaseless appetite of Zapatero's political opponents. The PP and victims' organisations led a series of demonstrations not against terrorism, but the government's policies towards it. Zapatero was assailed as a traitor of ETA's victims and an enabler of terrorist violence, and accused of presiding over the break-up of Spain.

Seen from a different perspective, the new government had inherited a promising set of circumstances with regard to the Basque issue: ETA was a weakened force and had not killed for more than a year; it had the possibility of killing again undermined by public revulsion at the slaughter in Madrid in March; and popular mobilisation within the Basque Country in favour of dialogue was at a high. The evolution of the Ibarretxe Plan represented a major headache, but the retirement of Xabier Arzalluz, the president of the PNV, was seen as a welcome development. Josu Jon Imaz, a pragmatic politician who would prove a reliable partner to Madrid, had replaced him. Moreover, within weeks of the election Zapatero had been briefed by Patxi López on Eguiguren's conversations with Batasuna and encouraged to believe that real change might be in the offing. The particularities of the Basque case, and especially the debilitation of ETA, meant that there was nothing approaching a 'hurting stalemate' propitious to the resolution of a classically configured conflict. Instead what appeared to be present was the related phenomenon of a 'mutually enticing opportunity' (defined by William Zartman as the 'pull of an attractive outcome without the push of a mutually hurting stalemate').[5] A peace process with ETA was nowhere in his campaign promises or plans, but Zapatero would later comment that 'it would have been a crime against the state not to try a negotiation with ETA when it seemed to be served up on a plate'.[6]

A second transition?

The sweeping changes introduced or attempted in the early years of Zapatero's government prompted renewal of the talk of a 'second transition' that had (briefly) accompanied Aznar's arrival in power in 1996. The idea was prominently promoted by *The Economist* in a survey of Spain published in June 2004. The magazine's foreign editor, John Grimond, suggested that the 2004 election would come to be seen not 'as the by-product of a terrorist attack... but as the natural end of the first era of Spain's post-Franco transition to democracy'.[7] The question, of course, was whether Zapatero would be up to the job of leading Spain towards the second one. Writing a little over a year later, Paddy Woodworth highlighted the aspects of Spain's first transition that still maintained their grip upon its political life. He likened Zapatero's blithe intention to 'change Spain's present by refusing to accept the realities of the recent past' to the quest of Don Quixote and posed a slightly different—and prescient—question: 'whether this upheaval will permit the creation of new and improved democratic institutions, or simply put the old ones under severe strain'.[8]

Spain's successes since the transition had been remarkable. Yet there were aspects to the country that still belied the modern democracy to which it aspired. Even putting to one side the persistence of ETA (twelve years after Bidart, and eight years after Aznar had promised its defeat), Spain was not quite as confident as it seemed. Institutions that might elsewhere be independent—the judiciary, think tanks and the media—remained staunchly beholden to political masters. The tight grip on social mores maintained by the Catholic Church meant that Spain lagged in areas such as the role of women and homosexual rights. It had yet to develop adequate policies to accommodate the changes precipitated by its sudden boom in immigration. Overall, its politics were suffused by an unwritten agreement to uphold the consensus on core issues established during the early days of the transition. Any threat of intervention by the army had long since disappeared, but successive Spanish governments had been shadowed by the fear that to depart from this consensus would unleash differences between the 'two Spains' of the Civil War still latent in Spanish society.

As so often in Spanish history, the regional issue represented the greatest challenge. Spain had already devolved more power and resources from its centre than any other country in Europe, and indeed by 2004 the central government controlled just 40 per cent of public spending.[9] The state of autonomies was under strain: it had created expensive and unwieldy regional governments, headed by political barons whose first priority was the accumulation of power and influence at the regional level even when issues of national identity and difference were not at stake. But while many Spaniards thought the state had conceded too much (or at least conceded too much to 'others'—the historical nationalities and the newer autonomous communities consistently saw each other as unnecessarily greedy/privileged and profligate) many others, and Basques and Catalans especially, were demanding more.

Aznar's neglect of the autonomies as a political issue had contributed to demands for reform. These extended from the Ibarretxe Plan to a new Catalan statute and included petitions for modifications to their statutes from other autonomous communities.[10] Zapatero was an eloquent champion of a 'plural Spain'. His campaign included promises to reform individual statutes of autonomy, to transform the Senate into a chamber of regional representation, to create a new 'conference' of the presidents of the autonomous communities to increase liaison with the central government; and to improve the integration of the autonomous communities into the EU.[11] Together these proposals represented the most ambitious agenda for change in the articulation of Spain since the transition. However they found mixed support even within the PSOE, where there had long been deep divisions regarding Spain's asymmetric federal model and there was little agreement on how it should be reformed.[12]

Civil society had led the challenge to 'the pact of forgetting'. Since 2000 the Association for the Recuperation of Historical Memory (ARMH) had drawn attention to the 30,000 unidentified republican victims estimated to be still buried in unmarked graves, and had succeeded in exhuming 300.[13] In 2002 the opposition parties had eventually managed to persuade the PP to agree to a declaration that condemned the military uprising that had started the Civil War and offered 'moral recognition' to its victims. All other judicial and non-judicial efforts to address the past had been rebuffed. Yet Spain's prosecution of crimes against humanity committed by military dictatorships elsewhere suggested an inconsistency in its position. Baltazar Garzón's 1998 indictment of General Augusto Pinochet and the events that followed it had triggered an 'irruption of memory' in Chile's transition to democracy.[14] In Spain, meanwhile, the memories of the victims of the Civil War and Franco remained constricted to the private domain while the country was still replete with the symbols of Francoism. Some dozen statues of the man himself, and many more of his generals and political associates, were to be found in villages, towns and cities across Spain together with plaques commemorating those 'proto-martyrs' who had 'fallen for God and for Spain'. Most bizarre of all was the massive mausoleum that Franco ordered built for him (by 1,200 political prisoners) in the Valley of the Fallen, outside Madrid, which was expensively maintained at the cost of the Spanish taxpayer.[15]

Zapatero was in some respects well suited to address this far-reaching set of challenges. Born in 1960, his generation of politicians had lived through the transition but not been among its architects. Yet he had a strong sense of the past and referred frequently to his grandfather, Juan Rodríguez Lozano, a captain in the Spanish army who in 1936 had been sentenced to death for his loyalty to the elected republican government.[16] The young José Luis had followed in his father's footsteps into the PSOE, entering parliament in 1986 to represent León as Spain's youngest deputy. His rise through the party was steady, but unspectacular. Certainly he had been a surprise winner of the PSOE's internal elections in 2000, for which the party heavyweight José Bono had been the favourite. He was rewarded for his pragmatism, for his capacity to build bridges with others and for his eternal—he would call it 'anthropological'—optimism. This disarming sense that anything was possible, that he had what in Arabic is referred to as *baraka*, a golden touch, travelled with Zapatero to the palace of Moncloa, the official residence of the Spanish prime minister. It was much in evidence as he introduced a raft of new policy initiatives. But to many even in the PSOE it was disquieting. His critics were alarmed by what they saw as naïvety, rather than political audacity, and wondered where it all would end.

The PP would continue to believe that the circumstances that had delivered Zapatero to office were accidental, and thus an illegitimate foundation for government, even as a succession of poor results in European and regional elections confirmed that the PSOE's 2004 victory had not been an aberration. A parliamentary commission established to investigate the circumstances surrounding the Madrid bombing eventually asserted that Aznar's government had 'manipulated and distorted' information for its own interests to an extent that was 'improper for any democratic government'.[17] But its work did not quell the persistence of a range of bizarre conspiracy theories. These included suggestions that ETA was somehow behind the attack all along, and extended to a theory that police officers with PSOE sympathies had played a part in facilitating the Islamist bombings and thus the PP's removal from power.[18]

Once in government Zapatero moved forward with a series of actions—maintaining his campaign promise to withdraw Spanish troops from Iraq; legalising gay marriage; offering a hand in dialogue to the Arab world by proposing an 'Alliance of Civilizations' at the United Nations; and reforming the state of autonomies—with a decisiveness that variously pleased and alarmed many who had expected a more cautious approach. He appointed women to half the positions in his cabinet. Other policies were anchored in a vigorous defence of civil rights and influenced by the 'civic republicanism' of the political philosopher Phillip Petit, who would write admiringly—if not uncritically—of Zapatero's efforts.[19] In September 2004, he created a parliamentary commission to address the rehabilitation of Franco's victims. Over the next two years, amidst heated public debate that fuelled the climate of *crispación*, parliament moved towards approval of a law of historical memory—the phrase suggests the difficult fit between the rigorous documentation of history and the subjective phenomenon that is memory—that managed to please almost nobody.[20] It notably failed to respond to recommendations from outside Spain (from Amnesty International and the Council of Europe) that Spain establish some kind of an investigative body, or truth commission, to throw light on the crimes of the past.[21]

With a few exceptions such as Bono, who became defence minister, the most prominent veteran of the González era was Alfredo Pérez Rubalcaba, whom Zapatero appointed government spokesman in the Parliament. A brilliant, ascetic and notoriously driven man—a chemist by training, he had been a noted athlete in his youth—Rubalcaba was one of the most experienced and able politicians in any political party. As minister of the presidency in the mid-1990s he had doggedly resisted the accusations of government responsibility for the GAL. Once in opposition, he had assumed a leading role within the party on terrorist issues, and in this capacity he had masterminded PSOE strategy during the difficult days between 11 and 14 March 2004. Rubalcaba would remain a critical figure throughout both Zapatero's governments, assuming responsibility for policies against ETA even before Zapatero named him interior minister in 2006, and in 2010 becoming first vice-president of the government as well. When economic crisis threatened the survival of Zapatero's government in 2011, it was Rubalcaba the PSOE put forward as its most plausible candidate to lead it into the general election held that November.

The reform of the Catalan statute would have a particular impact on developments in the Basque Country.[22] Catalan votes had been essential to Zapatero's election, and his minority government relied on the former communists in the IU (Initiative for Catalonia, IC, in its regional incarnation) and the pro-independence Catalan Republican Left (ERC) that supported the Catalan Socialist Party (PSC) in the tripartite regional government. On the campaign trail he had—perhaps rashly—promised that, if elected prime minister, he would respect whatever revised statute could be agreed upon within Catalonia. A new draft statute was already shaping up to be radical not only in its redefinition of Catalonia as a 'nation' but also in proposals to decrease the fiscal contribution made by Catalonia to the rest of Spain. Basque nationalists of all kinds viewed the statute's evolution as a test of Zapatero's reforming mettle. Spain's political right, meanwhile, criticised the new statute as unconstitutional and argued strongly for negotiation of a comprehensive agreement to reform all the autonomous communities at once. Outside Catalonia the contentious passage of its statute was used to stoke fears as to what Zapatero might be tempted to concede to ETA at the negotiating table, particularly with regard to the future status of Navarre.

Towards Anoeta

There was nothing in the 'useful opposition' that Zapatero had presented to Aznar that suggested a radical change in his approach to ETA.[23] He had proposed the anti-terrorist pact of 2000, backed the law on political parties and offered consistent support of the government's effort to defeat ETA through robust policing and the full force of the law. The Basque Country had never been a personal priority for Zapatero, nor was he particularly well versed in its politics. The position of the PSOE rather reflected the broad consensus shared across Spain on the evils of ETA and the virtues of robust counter-terrorist measures against it.

It was therefore not surprising that Zapatero retained many aspects of Aznar's counter-terrorism policies, with the fundamental distinction that a firm commitment to the pursuit of ETA was accompanied by cultivation of a political process. Although criticised—by Washington as well as the PP—for bowing to terrorist pressure as he kept his campaign promise to withdraw troops from Iraq, Zapatero adopted a strong stance on terrorism. His government supported the Club of Madrid in hosting a major international summit meeting on 'Democracy, Terrorism and Security' to commemorate the one-year anniversary of the Madrid bombings.[24] At home and abroad Zapatero provided vocal support for human rights as the bedrock of counter-terrorism. However, although his government introduced a new human rights plan in 2008, it made no obvious effort to amend the draconian changes to the criminal and penitentiary codes introduced by Aznar.[25] Rather, as the legal cases against organisations of the nationalist left opened under Aznar gradually came to court, the PSOE reaped the benefits they brought in undermining structures and organisations of the radical nationalists in ETA's orbit.

In the context of the continued assault against ETA, a combined French and Spanish operation brought notable success in early October 2004 with the capture of Mikel Antza and his partner, Soledad Iparragirre, *Anboto*, who was only the second woman (after Yoyes) to serve on ETA's executive committee. 'Operation Sanctuary' led to the arrest of nineteen other individuals and uncovered the most significant weapons and explosive caches ever captured from ETA, as well as an archive containing extensive documentation of ETA's history and current operations, including plans for the peace process to come.[26] A few weeks later the publication of a letter addressed to ETA's leadership by six senior ETA prisoners—Pakito among them—represented a new blow to the organisation. The letter offered a scathing analysis of ETA's circumstances and prospects, concluding that the organisation had never in its history been in such a poor state and that its political-military strategy 'has been overcome by the enemy's repression'. 'It is not a question of fixing the rear view mirror or a burst tyre,' the prisoners wrote, 'it is the motor which does not work.' In seeking to move forward from this nadir, they argued that 'it ought to be the nationalist left as a whole that defines the strategy and tactics to be followed'.[27]

That the results of the March 2004 election changed the game in the Basque Country was immediately obvious. For ETA and Batasuna the defeat of the PP meant that, quite simply, a wall had come down.[28] In the days after the election, ETA issued a communiqué that welcomed Zapatero's victory and asked him to make 'brave gestures towards Euskal Herria'.[29] Jesús Eguiguren, meanwhile, recalled that he had always expected the PP to win the 2004 election.[30] He did not know Zapatero personally, but on election night he had excitedly tried to reach him on the telephone, hoping to tell the prime minister-elect about the opportunity that awaited him. He had been unable to get through, but his call would later be returned to Patxi López. López informed Zapatero of the years of secret meetings with Otegi, and the PSE's belief that there existed the possibility of working jointly with Batasuna to explore a process that would bring ETA's violence to an end. Zapatero authorised the conversations to continue, on the condition that if news of their existence leaked, responsibility would remain solely with the PSE—any connection to the central government would be disavowed.[31]

The conversations between Eguiguren and Otegi moved from the realm of theoretical discussion to design of a peace process, the broad contours of which would be introduced by Otegi at a public meeting in San Sebastián's Anoeta football stadium in November 2004. In the meantime, seeking a third party to facilitate contacts between ETA and the new government and recalling the role played by Bishop Uriarte in the past, the two had turned to the Church. They first approached Cardinal Roger Etchegaray, a French Basque bishop. Eguiguren arranged an appointment in Rome in late May, but when he got there Etchegaray told him that the Vatican could not become involved in such a delicate issue. Eguiguren then sought a meeting with Uriarte, who advised him to pursue contacts with ETA 'in the simplest way possible, without third states and international mediators'.[32] In consultation with Otegi, Eguiguren assumed the role of postman and in August collected a letter from ETA addressed to Zapatero and duly passed it along.

In the meantime, Alec Reid had installed himself in the Basque Country on a semi-permanent basis. ETA had insisted that he disassociate himself from Elkarri, but met with him at its most senior level (Antza) before the election. Reid reportedly asked ETA whether, if the government was ready to negotiate, it would consider a ceasefire. ETA's answer was only a very qualified yes. Through the good offices of the British government, Reid later secured a meeting with the new government; there he asked whether, if ETA was ready to declare a 'total and definite' ceasefire (which was not what ETA had said), the government would be prepared to contemplate negotiations.[33] Beyond these direct contacts, Reid would be credited with encouraging the idea of dialogue. But he did not speak Spanish, and his knowledge of the political situation was strongly influenced both by Northern Ireland and what even some within Batasuna would recognise as a degree of wishful thinking about the intentions of ETA.[34]

With the assistance of Segura, Reid would be closely involved with the preparations for a broad Forum for National Debate launched in early 2005, largely at Batasuna's instigation. However, despite his willingness to facilitate direct talks, neither ETA nor the nationalist left considered him suitable for this role. Indeed, captured notes from a February 2004 meeting of ETA's executive committee revealed that the mediating services Reid—whom ETA referred to as *Aurelio*—had offered had already been declined. ETA had decided that if it should be approached by the PSOE with a request for a meeting, it would accept. But before doing so it would be necessary to find, 'a space which gives sufficient security to both parties'. In addition to Reid and a mediation option identified only by the word *níspero*, two institutions were discussed: the Centre for Humanitarian Dialogue, or HD Centre, in Geneva (from whom ETA had just received Griffiths' letter) and the University of Uppsala, in Sweden. The HD Centre was selected.[35]

Elkarri launched a new dialogue initiative and peace conference in May. It again sought to be as inclusive as possible, and invited all Basque political parties to participate. Only the PP refused from the outset, but Batasuna attended just the first of more than a dozen meetings held over the following year. Elkarri placed emphasis on the involvement of international actors and in November 2004 organised a visit by a group of experienced experts and practitioners in conflict resolution.[36] Like the conference as a whole, their presence was seen as contributing to build confidence in dialogue as a means to resolve the conflict. But the lack of trust between Elkarri and Batasuna meant that its efforts remained at some remove from the front line of the 'pre-dialogue' consultations under way.

Of more durable impact would be the role played by Brian Currin, a lawyer recommended to Batasuna by Sinn Féin when it visited South Africa in late 2003.[37] Batasuna had recently been banned, and it was interested in learning how the African National Congress (ANC) had existed in clandestinity for decades. Those in Batasuna responsible for its international relations had also been told by Sinn Féin how useful the lessons learned from South Africa had been to the Northern Ireland process. Understanding the likely centrality of the issue of prisoners to any Basque peace process, Sinn Féin had thought that the Basques might benefit from Currin's specialist knowledge in this area. Currin had been appointed by Nelson Mandela to head a Prison Audit Committee and had then been involved in the establishment of the Truth and Reconciliation Commission in South Africa; his expertise on prison issues had brought him to Northern Ireland where he still served on the Sentence Review Commission.

In conversations with Batasuna, Currin quickly understood that the challenges in the Basque case were particularly difficult. In 2004 there were more than 700 prisoners in French and Spanish prisons, a higher number than at any time since Franco.[38] Unlike in Northern Ireland, however, the only prisoners were those of ETA and the nationalist left: the option of negotiating some kind of reciprocal prisoner release was therefore quite out of the question.[39] Moreover, the possibility of the courts displaying the kind of flexibility adopted by the British courts on Northern Ireland was extremely unlikely. The Spanish judiciary, although formally independent from executive power, is in practice politicised by the appointment of senior judges by the party in government. Individual judges, who are vested with huge personal power as a consequence of a Napoleonic system constructed around the figure of the investigating magistrate, have the capacity to defy expectations in the prosecution of individual cases. However, since the time of Franco the judiciary as a whole has been heavily weighted towards the PP.

Batasuna had been impressed by Currin. In April 2004 its representatives met with him again in the picturesque Catalan town of Cadaqués, just south of the French border. Currin returned to Catalonia in December, this time to participate in an international seminar in the Catalan Parliament addressing lessons to be learned from the handling of prisoner issues in Northern Ireland for a possible Basque peace process.[40] Delegations from Batasuna—most frequently some combination of Joseba Álvarez, Pernando Barrena and Urko Aiartza, a lawyer who spoke good English and was in frequent liaison with Sinn Féin, but which at times also including the former ETA prisoner Jon Anza—would visit South Africa regularly during 2005 and 2006. Their initial work with Currin focused on prisoners, but as time went by it extended to broader questions of negotiation strategy. Currin facilitated training sessions and introduced Batasuna to several others with experience of the South African process, including the former government negotiator, Roelf Meyer, and the secretary-general of the ANC, Kgalema Motlanthe.[41]

The government had reason to be extraordinarily nervous about any kind of direct talks with ETA. Although every government since the transition had tried them, the failure of both the Algiers process and Estella-Lizarra had left deep scars. Rubalcaba, in particular, would recall that he was haunted by memories of the Lizarra ceasefire, which he had lived through very directly. From the opposition the PSOE had provided support to the PP throughout 1998 and 1999. As Rubalcaba remembered there had been times when both parties had believed that ceasefire might hold, 'but while the state was thinking it all might finish, ETA was filling Spain with commandos'. The result had been ETA's bloody campaign of 2000 and 2001.[42]

Aznar's demonisation of dialogue and the bombings in Madrid both suggested that talking to ETA would come at a high political cost. The example of Josep Lluis Carod-Rovira, secretary-general of the ERC, stood out as a cautionary tale. In January 2004, Carod-Rovira had held a secret meeting with Mikel Antza and Josu Ternera in Perpignan, France, which soon leaked to the press. In July 2011 he recalled that he had used the opportunity to berate ETA for the organisation's insistence in including Catalonia as a target (in contrast to the IRA, which never launched attacks on Scotland or Wales).[43] As an ardent Catalan nationalist, he was particularly incensed that his own town, the seaside resort of Cambrils, should be threatened by ETA's summer campaigns against the coast of

'Spain'. Carod-Rovira maintained that he had no intention to negotiate with ETA. But when news of the meeting leaked to *ABC*, he was portrayed as having asked ETA to kill Spaniards instead of Catalans—a charge that gained new salience when ETA declared that it would cease its armed actions in Catalonia.[44] Amid the ensuing outcry, he was forced to resign his position as vice-president of the Catalan government.

In November 2004 the prospect of talks came considerably closer as Otegi introduced a proposal for a two-track peace process to some 15,000 people thronging the Anoeta football stadium in San Sebastián.[45] The proposal contemplated one negotiation towards an agreement on pacification between ETA and the Spanish and French states—to address the technical issues of demilitarisation, prisoners, deportees and refugees, and victims—and another between Basque political and social forces on future political arrangements for Euskal Herria. The nationalist left remained focused on its two core demands of self-determination and territoriality. However Batasuna could now accept the former as the 'right to decide' and the latter as a subject for negotiation. Implicit was the recognition that the democratic exercise of decision—an eventual referendum on terms to be agreed among all Basque political sensibilities—was only likely to take place in a distant future.[46] For the first time the methodology proposed adhered to the existing legal framework and was consistent with the bottom line in all Spanish governments' dealings with ETA since the early 1980s: the negotiation of political issues would not be conducted with ETA.

The Anoeta Proposal drew on the years of discussion with Eguiguren, months of work since the March elections and a long process of consultation with ETA, in which Mikel Antza had been the principal interlocutor. The consultation had concluded in a document jointly agreed between ETA and Batasuna in the summer of 2004, the *Ponencia Udaberri*, whose major lines of thinking were consistent with what was publicly presented at Anoeta.[47] But the ideas put forward at Anoeta—framed as following on from the KAS Alternative and Lizarra as the third distinct strategy pursued since the transition—were presented as those of Batasuna, and shared in advance with the PSE. Otegi used language he would acknowledge as being 'very Irish' to suggest a process that would 'bring conflict from the streets to the negotiating table' and 'seek the embrace of our adversaries and the complicity of our enemies'.[48] As he did so he was suggesting the predominance of the political over the military in the political-military strategy long maintained by the MLNV and a new relationship between Batasuna and ETA. This was the obvious outcome if the process was to lead to the eventual disappearance of ETA. But in Basque terms, it promised a revolution.

Green light and broken bridges

On 14 January 2005, Otegi addressed a public letter to Zapatero. 'Mr. President, you have in your hands the real possibility of beginning a course of action that would permit a definitive solution of this historic conflict of political dimensions,' he wrote, while also spelling out with great clarity what Batasuna was not proposing. Batasuna was not proposing a scenario that would lead to independence, but a new political framework in which all political options, including that of independence, could be considered. It was not proposing a nationalist front, but an agreement between nationalists and non-nationalists on which the views of 'all of those who live and work in Euskal Herria' would be sought. In publicising the letter, Otegi said that if Zapatero decided to be the 'the Spanish Tony Blair' and negotiate a peace agreement he could count on Batasuna's support.[49] Zapatero responded the next day during an appearance at the Kursaal, San Sebastián's sea-front conference centre. He said that that he was ready to listen to Batasuna once the 'noise of the bombs and pistols has quieted' and asked that Batasuna publicly condemn ETA's violence.[50]

The response reflected what Eguiguren would recall, in an account of the peace process he co-authored with the *El País* journalist Luis Aizpeolea, as the 'complicity' between the PSOE and Batasuna in this period. This was grounded in the conviction of Eguiguren and Otegi, who had 'really believed [the process] would work'.[51] Their confidence was at least partly responsible for the unrealistic degree of optimism that flowered in Zapatero. Eguiguren recalled that in early 2005 the prime minister had believed that the peace process would begin imminently, and that ETA would declare a ceasefire by Easter.[52] Others who spoke to Zapatero in 2005 and 2006 would be struck by the confidence he betrayed, even in private conversations.[53]

More immediately, Zapatero faced the political challenge represented by the discussion of the Ibarretxe Plan within the Spanish Parliament. With the Catalan statute also advancing, the PP and its allies in the media went on the offensive. 'Now it is time for [Zapatero] to respond,' demanded an editorial in *El Mundo*. 'This is without a doubt the greatest challenge presented to the Spanish state and the democratic parties since the transition.'[54] The Ibarretxe Plan was put to the vote in the Spanish Parliament on 1 February and, as expected, roundly rejected. On the day after the debate Ibarretxe called for the Basque elections due in May to be brought forward to 17 April, framing the vote as an opportunity for Basques to have their say on his proposal and asking that Batasuna be allowed to present itself at the polls.

ETA responded to the growing sense that things were on the move by making its presence felt. During December it had exploded more than a dozen small bombs in Madrid and elsewhere in Spain. On 15 January it issued a statement formally announcing its commitment to the Anoeta Proposal. Three days later it exploded a large car bomb in Getxo, an affluent suburb of Bilbao, and the following month another in Madrid, injuring forty people outside a convention centre. It was actively seeking a negotiation with the government. If successful this would conclude with the disappearance of violence that ETA understood, as its January statement reiterated, to include the repression and violence it attributed to the Spanish state.[55] But for the moment violence was a means to exert pressure towards negotiations, and the government responded with pressure in kind. Amidst a continuous back and forth over the legality of the public activities of the nationalist left, in February forty-two members of the youth organisations Jarrai, Haika and Segi were brought to trial, charged with contributing to *kale borroka* and membership of ETA.[56]

In early April ETA admitted that it was 'trying to open a process of resolution and negotiation with the government'.[57] In February it had written to ask whether the government was willing to meet, and offered to find an international organisation to facilitate a meeting. The government had responded positively in March, with the caveat that any such meeting would be incompatible with violence. ETA wrote again in April, this time suggesting the HD Centre. The letters and the response to them were given not to the minister of interior, José Antonio Alonso, but to Rubalcaba.[58]

In a climate of increasing expectation, the PSE kept talking to Batasuna, Batasuna met frequently with the PNV (usually Imaz and Iñigo Urkullu, president of the Vizcayan delegation of the party, but also

147

Ibarretxe), and the PNV maintained direct channels to the PSOE in Madrid. Batasuna had the April elections within its sights. It tried to participate both by presenting its own candidates and, more seriously, through the creation of a new platform, Aukera Guztiak ('All the Options'), that was promptly rejected by the Supreme Court. It appeared that Batasuna had been thwarted. But those who opposed its participation had not counted on what Karmelo Landa of Batasuna would refer to as its 'Trojan horse': the obscure and vaguely Soviet-sounding 'Communist Party of the Basque Lands' (EHAK), whose registration during the Aznar period had passed largely unnoticed.[59] Batasuna called for its voters to support EHAK only on 8 April; nine days later it won more than 12 per cent of the vote and nine seats in the Basque Parliament, two more than it had achieved in 2001.

The presence of EHAK in the Basque Parliament—which some would attribute to the government's deliberate encouragement of the secret process it was on the point of launching—[60] complicated the political scenario. Running in partnership with EA, Ibarretxe's PNV remained the largest party with twenty-nine seats, but it was seven short of an overall majority, a blow to any further aspirations for the Ibarretxe Plan. With the PNV reluctant to form any kind of pact with the PSE, it also left Ibarretxe—again—dependent on support from the nationalist left, in addition to the smaller parties of EA and IU-EB. The PSE had been rewarded for its more 'Basquist' direction and the efforts it was evidently making towards peace, overtaking the PP as the second largest party in parliament with eighteen seats. But in Madrid the PSOE's relations with the PP deteriorated when the party leader, Mariano Rajoy, refused to attend a meeting of the anti-terrorist pact scheduled for April unless the government promoted the illegalisation of EHAK.[61]

On 17 May 2005 Zapatero took the unprecedented step of asking for authorisation from the Spanish Parliament for a process of dialogue with 'those who have decided to abandon violence' just a few days after parliament's annual debate on the state of the nation. Much of this three and a half hour confrontation between Rajoy and Zapatero had focused on the struggle against ETA. Rajoy charged Zapatero with 'betraying the dead' for having allowed ETA to gain strength and return—through EHAK—to the Basque Parliament and for considering dialogue with terrorists. He accused the government of being responsible for the 'biggest problem with the autonomies' seen since the transition and having dedicated its first year in office to 're-opening the wounds of the past'.[62] The government went ahead, confident that it had the support of 61 per cent of Spaniards for contacts with ETA if the organisation announced a ceasefire, as well as all political parties other than the PP, and anxious to obtain the political cover that the resolution would bring.[63] But the pursuit of the resolution was also problematic. It raised expectations regarding the extent to which parliament would be consulted regarding a process that was being conducted in strict confidentiality. And it formalised the opposition of the PP, encouraging its use of the government's policies towards ETA for political purposes.

The text of the resolution drew heavily on the Pact of Ajuria Enea. It condemned terrorist violence, and expressed support for the efforts of the security forces and solidarity with ETA's victims. It affirmed that 'political questions should be resolved solely by legitimate representatives of the people' and, in an echo of the anti-terrorist pact itself (in its criticism of the Basque nationalist parties for the price they had appeared willing to pay for peace during the Estella-Lizarra process), clearly stated that 'violence has no political price'.[64] This last point would remain a central tenet of Zapatero's somewhat ambiguous approach to the entire process. It would become a common refrain, qualified by the observation that 'politics can and should contribute to an end to violence', even as the fundamental inconsistency of the pursuit of a peace for which the government had publicly committed to bear no cost would become more evident.

Rajoy vowed to work with all his might to 'defeat and not negotiate with ETA'. He charged that Zapatero had put himself 'in ETA's hands' and violated the anti-terrorist pact (overlooking the pact's insistence that it is the government that determines anti-terrorist policy). The PP embarked on a public campaign to undermine Zapatero's policies through the abuse of public sympathy towards ETA's victims that had no precedent in Spanish democracy, supporting and participating in a series of demonstrations—most called by the Association of the Victims of Terrorism (AVT)—to protest against the government's policies towards ETA. Zapatero struggled to respond, hamstrung by the obvious taboo represented by criticism of victims on any count. He appointed Gregorio Peces-Barba, one of the seven 'fathers' of the Spanish constitution, to a new position of High Commissioner for the Support of Victims of Terrorism and met with victims' organisations himself. But his efforts never captured the public imagination and Peces-Barba resigned his position in September 2006.[65]

In Geneva and Oslo

In conditions of utmost secrecy, Zapatero authorised initial meetings between Jesús Eguiguren and ETA, facilitated by the HD Centre, in June and July 2005. In Geneva, and at a second round of meetings held in Oslo in November, the negotiators worked towards confidential agreements. They sought to provide ETA with the assurances it would need to declare a ceasefire and the terms under which the government would respond in a manner that would allow the parties to move towards a formal dialogue: 'point zero'. For ETA this response had to include a public declaration of respect for a decision to be taken on their future by the Basque people in 'a kind of Downing Street Declaration', as Otegi had put it to Eguiguren.[66]

In late 2008 Eguiguren explained that the meetings represented the second part of a process that had been conceived as comprising four distinct phases: his pre-dialogue conversations with Otegi; this dialogue with ETA, at which he was still not representing the government, but the 'party in government'; a third phase in which two distinct 'tables' would be formally established, one between the government and ETA to address the 'technical' issues that ETA framed as 'consequences of the conflict' and a second composed of political parties to address political arrangements with Madrid; and a fourth period of implementation, which would involve seeing the agreements through both the Basque and Spanish Parliaments. Taking into consideration that the critical third phase might take two years, Eguiguren had calculated that the process as a whole might extend over eight years to its full fruition.[67]

Eguiguren's elaboration of this complex architecture was at some odds with the description of the process given by the more sceptical Rubalcaba, carefully circumscribed by what he would in 2012 describe as a 'double strategy' of talking, but also pursuing ETA with every available instrument.[68] This involved a very careful delineation of what, exactly, Eguiguren represented: 'the Socialist party but', as Rubalcaba put it, 'if pushed, only the Basque Socialist Party'. This was consistent with the decision taken by Zapatero and Rubalcaba that no member of the government—neither a ranking official nor a representative of the police or intelligence services—should ever sit down with ETA, in order 'never to contaminate the state with a terrorist band'.

When Eguiguren's written account of the process emerged in late 2011, the contrast between the years of work that pre-dated the 2005 meetings, the enormous risk taken by Zapatero in pursuing talks with ETA and Madrid's ambivalence towards them, was striking. Eguiguren attended the first meetings in Geneva, and all meetings before the cease-fire, on his own. He arrived without instructions or advisers from Madrid—or even a laptop ('I had everything in my head,' as he put it)—conscious that there were those in Madrid who had hoped he could achieve agreement on a ceasefire with ETA within a day but also of how unlikely this would be.[69] His actions reflected an extraordinary degree of improvisation (making up the list of guarantees to be demanded of ETA's ceasefire in a few minutes in his hotel room in Oslo, for example), which was occasionally abruptly halted by the imposition of red lines from Madrid. Yet even as Madrid put limits on what was agreed, it retained a distance that suggested his efforts—and the process they anchored—would be easily dispensable if they came to naught.

William Douglass had been surprised to be told in April 2004 that the HD Centre had decided not to engage in the Basque conflict any further, as its plate was too full. 'Stunned and chagrined,' he found it difficult to understand why, with the doors to ETA opened and the opportunities presented by the changed circumstances in Spain, the Centre would want to drop it at that time. Only after the ceasefire would he learn that this was far from the case. A lie to him had been the necessary price for the absolute discretion with which the Centre had decided it must continue its involvement. To Douglass' credit, when Martin Griffiths told him the whole story after ETA's announcement of its ceasefire he 'could not have been more euphoric'.[70]

That ETA trusted Griffiths and his colleagues with its members' security, and the government with its facilitation of meetings of extreme political delicacy with ETA, represented a quite exceptional degree of confidence in the HD Centre. (After an early meeting in France, an internal ETA report had described the Centre's representatives as 'very professional': 'They don't have prejudices, they don't take postures against us, they won't make inappropriate comments about armed actions (except to know whether they have taken place), they won't "sell" a process in advance.')[71] However, what each actually wanted—logistical and security arrangements for the meetings and a technical role as note-taker with responsibility for formal records (*actas*) of the meetings interspersed, on occasion, with careful 'steering' of the discussion—was, at least to begin with, quite limited. The government and ETA shared a concern to keep the HD Centre from the development of a political role. The facilitators held periodic consultations in Madrid and remained in contact by other means, but they did not make proposals within the meetings, nor did they communicate with other actors essential to a full understanding of the Basque problem and its solution—even Batasuna.[72]

Between 21 June and 14 July, Eguiguren and a two-man ETA delegation met almost on a daily basis, all in the presence of the HD Centre and often in the comfortable environment provided by Geneva's Hotel Palais Wilson, overlooking Lac Leman and the Alps. Eguiguren had arrived without knowing whom ETA would send to meet him. Somewhat to his surprise the members of the HD Centre introduced him as *Miguel* to *George*—as a security measure all participants in the talks would be known by pseudonyms throughout. But 'George' was none other than Josu Ternera, whom Eguiguren recognised from his time in the Basque Parliament but did not know personally. Like others within the Socialist party, Eguiguren considered Ternera to be the maximum authority within ETA; his presence was therefore proof of the seriousness with which the organisation was taking this initiative. No less important, Ternera was a man of similar age to Eguiguren with a long political trajectory and a familiarity with Eguiguren's thought and writings. The two might not agree, but they could talk, and, as with Otegi, Eguiguren knew that they could talk straight.[73]

This confidence, and the bedrock of the prior conversations with Otegi, underlay the relative speed with which the talks progressed. Eguiguren worked from the government's two-fold bottom line: in order for anything they discussed to happen, there had to be 'a definitive end' to ETA's terrorism; and nothing agreed could violate the laws and constitution of Spain. At the same time he saw that no terrorist organisation was going to accept 'unconditional surrender'. Rather it needed to be able to 'dress-up' its end in 'dignity', to point to the results of its struggle and the prospect of a political channel to pursue its goals.[74] Ternera was accompanied by Jon Iurrebaso, *Robert*, another senior member of ETA. Iurrebaso would play a secondary role within the meetings but take copious notes. For the highly disciplined ETA, formed by long years of collective decision-making, it would have been unthinkable for one man to come to such a significant meeting on his own. However, as Ternera repeatedly insisted to Eguiguren, the two men were in Geneva as 'interlocutors' and not 'leaders' of ETA with decision-making authority; the police intelligence that suggested otherwise was quite wrong.[75]

The two sides quickly agreed that the purpose of the meetings was to discuss the way forward towards 'point zero', the beginning of substantive dialogue on the 'consequences' of the conflict after ETA declared a ceasefire. They sought agreement on how to move ahead, but also on the text of declarations to be made by ETA announcing a ceasefire and by the government when it was willing to open a formal process of dialogue. This was originally contemplated as occurring six months after ETA's statement, in order to give the negotiating table time for what was described as 'house work'.[76]

On 25 June discussions were abruptly interrupted when ETA exploded a large car bomb outside the Olympic sports stadium in Madrid in order to disrupt Spain's bid for the 2012 Olympics. Eguiguren received instructions to return to Madrid but instead threatened—through the HD Centre—to break off talks if they were further interrupted by violence. After overcoming this hiccup, the negotiators moved towards draft documents containing texts of the two statements, agreeing that these would be accompanied by a series of clarifications and guarantees that would remain confidential. The next stage would be a new round of talks to confirm the decisions they had reached, once each had had the chance to consult with their respective constituencies—ETA's leadership, and the government of Spain. For Eguiguren, this meant Rubalcaba, who would be his conduit to Zapatero throughout. (Remarkably, he never discussed the process with the prime minister directly, nor was he kept apprised by Rubalcaba of the government's continuing counterterrorist activity against ETA.)[77]

Talks resumed in November just outside Oslo. The Norwegian foreign minister, Jonas Støre, and several officials made brief appearances, but facilitation remained in the hands of the HD Centre. Eguiguren would recall the Oslo meetings as surprisingly difficult. He had arrived suggesting no further changes to the drafts agreed in Geneva. ETA, on the other hand, had 'problems'—the most serious of which was Ternera's demand that Madrid accept what the Basques agreed at the political table without discussion, which the government could not accept. The talks were shadowed by a difficult discussion of the new Catalan statute in the Spanish Parliament, as well as Rubalcaba's increasing impatience from Madrid. The HD Centre was now assuming a more active intermediary role. At the two delegations' request, for example, it proposed ideas for the conduct of the formal government-ETA talks that both readily accepted. These included an agenda, methodology and suggested roles for both observers and a verification commission that looked towards the growing involvement of third parties.[78]

The document agreed in Oslo was modified by ETA in February 2006, with the government's agreement secured by consultations conducted by the HD Centre. The original and only copy of the agreed document was left with the HD Centre for safekeeping, and has never been made public. However, its existence was leaked to the press soon after the ceasefire's announcement and, after its formal end in June 2007, ETA released its version of the document to *Gara*.[79] ETA's version of the agreement was never directly challenged, but it is clearly not without some editing: most obviously it did not include the negotiated text of ETA's declaration of its ceasefire.[80] The published document is nonetheless revealing, particularly with regard to the 'clarifications' specifying what was meant by a number of terms used within the declaration, the 'guarantees' agreed to facilitate forward movement and a number of issues regarding the third phase of the process. These included the size and composition of the parties' delegations, as well as what to do about possible 'accidents' (breaches of the ceasefire by ETA) and leaks, and what would happen in case of a hypothetical breakdown of the process.

ETA's guarantees included commitments not to realise 'actions' (including letters or other communications) against individuals or public or private property, and not to replenish supplies of weapons and explosives or materials for their fabrication. No mention is made of an agreement not to carry out extortion, although subsequent accounts of the process imply that this was indeed part of ETA's commitments.[81] That there is no reference to a commitment to halt *kale borroka* was explained by *Gara* as responding to ETA's longstanding, if somewhat unconvincing, assertion that this lay beyond its control.[82] The government guarantees, meanwhile, were so broad and unrealistic that it is difficult not to interpret them as a form of trap. In the period following ETA's announcement of the ceasefire, the government committed to promote a 'pact of state'—a phrase implying agreement among all Spain's major political forces, including the PP, to uphold the validity of agreements reached even in the event of a change of government; 'palpably to lessen' police presence, which would include the disappearance of police pressure on the political activities of the nationalist left; to accept *de facto* that Batasuna and other organisations of the nationalist left could carry out political activities; and that the Spanish national police, Guardia Civil, Ertzaintza, or French security forces would not undertake detentions except in cases of criminal activity—a commitment the government estimated it would need seven to ten days to implement.

Six years later, Rubalcaba observed that there were, from the beginning, 'many ambiguities' in these confidential pre-agreements: 'everyone interpreted them as they wanted'. For Rubalcaba their purpose was clear—'to get to the ceasefire'—and the most important phrase within them that 'police forces would continue their normal work with regard to criminal activities (the theft of cars, assaults, homicides etc.)'. This was a hard guarantee that gave the government leeway to ignore almost everything else, so long as criminal activity of some kind continued: 'either there is a definitive ceasefire, a serious ceasefire', as Rubalcaba put it, 'or there is nothing, and what we had at the beginning were the conditions for such a ceasefire'.[83] ETA, on the other hand, understood the guarantees as a package. It insisted from the beginning that, 'if the agreements are breached, the ceasefire will break down'. On this basis it looked to the government to lessen police presence and promote the *de facto* legalisation of Batasuna and cross-party agreement with the PP. That neither Spain's legal framework nor the political circumstances, or even the government's intentions, made any of this very likely suggested that the government and ETA had intentionally contradictory approaches to the pillars upon which ETA's ceasefire would rest.

To a 'permanent' ceasefire

The experience of Estella-Lizarra had soured the government—as well as public opinion—on the idea of an 'indefinite' ceasefire. ETA was not yet ready to commit to the 'definitive' end of its violence, but in the course of the discussions in Geneva and Oslo, it eventually accepted that 'permanent' was possible.[84] Getting to the point at which this 'permanent ceasefire' could be made public was still not easy. Eguiguren met with Ternera in Geneva on 29 December. The ceasefire announcement had been expected by mid-February. Ternera warned that it would likely take longer. The delay suggested a complex process of internal consultations within ETA. As would later emerge, the arrest of Antza and other senior figures within ETA's political leadership had contributed to differences within the organisation that would have a lasting impact on the course the peace process would take.

In the latter months of 2005 and early 2006, amidst rumours that a ceasefire was imminent, victims' organisations began to mobilise against a peace process. The AVT led the charge, but even more moderate entities such as the Foundation for the Victims of Terrorism (FVT) took a vocal position against dialogue. The FVT was headed by Maite Pagazaurtundua, a former PSE councillor and the sister of Joseba Pagazaurtundua, a municipal police officer in the Guipuzcoan town of Andoain who was assassinated by ETA in 2003. Pagazaurtundua met with Zapatero in February and presented him with a 'decalogue' of principles 'for the construction of peace' to which Rajoy and the PP quickly subscribed. First and last among the ten points made were: 'Terrorism is defeated' and 'There must be victors and vanquished' (the Spanish phrase *vencedores y vencidos* still evokes the divided Spain that emerged from the Civil War). 'The terrorists are not a social interlocutor,' the decalogue insisted, 'they are criminals organised to achieve political gains through the use of terror and silence and fear that infuse society.'[85]

The progress of the Catalan statute contributed to heighten the tension. Ninety per cent of the Catalan Parliament had approved the new statute in September 2005 (only the PP had voted against it), raising a storm of opposition from the right, who charged that it was unconstitutional. Difficult negotiations between the PSOE in Madrid and the Catalan parties continued through the autumn months, illustrating the considerable distance that separates the PSOE from its Catalan branch.[86] In January 2006, Zapatero and Artur Mas, the leader of the moderate Catalan nationalist party Convergence and Union (CiU)—which was outside the Catalan government at the time—reached an agreement on a 'cleaned-up' version of the statute that included the relegation of a reference to the Catalan 'nation' to the statute's preamble. Many Catalans considered the changes unacceptable, and a direct betrayal by Zapatero of the Catalan Socialists. The revised statute lost the support of the ERC, which—like the PP—would campaign against ratification of the statute when it came to its referendum in June 2006.[87] For Basque nationalists, none of this was a good precedent.

Batasuna had long been worried that the judicial system would put obstacles in the way of dialogue—indeed the party's illegal status represented the most obvious structural impediment to the entire process. Developments since mid-2005 were not encouraging. On 25 May 2005, just days after the parliamentary resolution giving the green light to dialogue with ETA, Otegi had been briefly imprisoned by the Audiencia Nacional as he attended what he had expected to be routine hearings in one of the multiple cases in which he was charged with a crime of opinion. A few days later he was released on bail. In the following months, the Audiencia Nacional began investigating EHAK to see if grounds existed for its illegalisation—it would eventually be banned in 2009—and began the first phase of the government's 'show trial' against the nationalist left, the *macroproceso* 18/98. In January 2006, Judge Fernando Grande-Marlaska suspended the activities of Batasuna for a further two-year period on top of Garzón's original ban, hugely complicating the coming peace process. In February Otegi, Joseba Permach and Joseba Álvarez were summoned to testify before the Audiencia Nacional, somewhat bizarrely accused of 'glorifying terrorism' at the Anoeta meeting that they—and Zapatero—had seen as an important step forward on the path to peace.[88]

Events within the prisons exacerbated the climate of uncertainty. A Basque prisoner had committed suicide in October 2005. In February 2006 the Supreme Court introduced a constitutionally questionable new measure known as the Parot Doctrine—after Unai Parot, the ETA prisoner to whom it was first applied. This retroactively provided for prisoners who had been convicted under the 1973 criminal code to serve consecutive rather than simultaneous sentences. Sentences served in parallel and reduced for good behaviour had until then led to prisoners' release before the maximum time allowed for thirty years (later extended to forty years) even when, like Parot, they had accumulated sentences of many thousands of years. The new doctrine extended Parot's time in prison by ten years and triggered the review of the sentences of more than 180 ETA prisoners.[89] Another prisoner committed suicide and a third died a few days later of a heart attack. On 5 March the nationalist left called a general strike in protest.[90] Five days later Attorney General Cándido Conde-Pumpido demanded that Otegi be imprisoned for incidents related to the strike. Only the fact that he had pneumonia prevented his detention.

Against this backdrop, ETA increased its military activity, committing twenty-one actions of various kinds in the last two months of 2005 and twenty-four in the first weeks of 2006. Most involved the infliction of material damage against those who had not paid extortion demands, suggesting that the organisation was trying to stockpile its finances before an imminent period of inactivity.[91] No less disturbing, for those anxiously waiting news of a ceasefire, was a tough communiqué that ETA issued on 18 February 2006, claiming responsibility for recent armed action and denouncing the continued illegalisation of Batasuna and the judicial campaign against the nationalist left.[92]

Finally, on 22 March 2005 ETA released a video in which three masked militants announced that the organisation would enter into a permanent ceasefire in two days time. Grounds for optimism were found in both what ETA did and did not say. The communiqué was relatively short by ETA's standards and it avoided direct reference to the organisation's traditional demands—independence, or even self-determination, and Navarre. Instead ETA explained the ceasefire as being to advance the democratic process in the Basque Country and construct a new framework 'in which our rights as a people will be recognised' alongside the expression of 'all political options'.[93] At the end of the process, the results of which ETA demanded should be recognised by the Spanish and French states, Basque citizens should 'decide on their own future'. That the ceasefire offered was 'permanent', and came at a moment at which ETA had not killed for almost three years—the longest period without an assassination since Spain's transition to democracy—added to the optimism with which the announcement was greeted.[94]

Within the Basque Country, ETA's announcement was met with relief, open celebration in many quarters—even tears of joy—but also apprehension. Could this time be for real? Txiki Benegas, the veteran Socialist politician who had been, one way or another, involved in efforts to promote an end to the ETA's violence since the transition, began a diary chronicling the ceasefire. 'When I heard the news I imagined thousands of guns with their barrels doubled over, forcefully thrown into the Cantabrian Sea. ETA had just announced "a permanent ceasefire",' his first entry began: 'Once more a dream of peace…'[95]

6

THE CEASEFIRE UNRAVELS

In retrospect, ETA's announcement of its ceasefire would be seen as a high point. ETA and representatives of the government met four times between June and December 2006, but they never arrived at 'point zero', the beginning of substantive talks. Rather their discussions remained mired in mutual recrimination and crisis management, as each side's confidence in the process eroded.

Three clear phases could be distinguished between the beginning of ETA's 'permanent' ceasefire and its end, in early June 2007. The first marked the time between ETA's announcement and Zapatero's formal declaration of the initiation of dialogue on 29 June 2006. Contradictory understandings of the purposes and structure of the process were exacerbated by the opposition encountered from the PP and the spike in activity against ETA and Batasuna by Spain's judges that was related to it. The problems became more serious in the second period, which ran until ETA's explosion of a car bomb in Barajas airport on 30 December 2006, killing two Ecuadorians. ETA's violations of the ceasefire multiplied, and in September and October the PSE, Batasuna and the PNV held a series of confidential meetings in an attempt to move towards an outline of a political agreement. But when ETA pressured Batasuna to introduce changes unacceptable to the other two parties, the talks broke down. After the bomb at Barajas, the government pronounced the process finished. Yet in a third period it maintained contact with ETA through the HD Centre and, in May 2007, agreed to sit down with it again. This time a new format allowed the presence not just of Batasuna but also international actors—representatives of Sinn Féin and the governments of Norway and the United Kingdom—as well as the HD Centre.

Four overarching difficulties undermined progress. The first was the difference in perception of what the process actually was, a difficulty exacerbated by the deep distrust between the parties. Between the clarity of the positions espoused by the PP, for whom the problem was one of terrorism and the solution was its defeat, and ETA and Batasuna, who saw themselves mired in a political-military conflict whose solution lay through classically-structured negotiations and a political agreement, the government assumed an ambiguous position. By entering the peace process at all it acknowledged that the 'surrender' long perceived by the PP as ETA's only acceptable end-state was unobtainable without addressing the situation of the prisoners and some of the demands for change articulated within the Basque Country. Yet it was unacceptable for this process to be conditioned by ETA. The ceasefire with its *quid pro quo*—a political dialogue in the Basque Country—was therefore perceived as a face-saving exit, a soft landing, even as what the government actually wanted was ETA just to disappear.

A second problem was the status of the agreements between the parties that underpinned ETA's declaration of its ceasefire. ETA understood the commitments and guarantees agreed with Eguiguren as establishing the terms of a mutual ceasefire between parties in conflict. But the government remained the executive of a democratic state engaged in the preservation of law and order in the face of a continuing terrorist threat. The confidential status of the guarantees and the government's own ambivalence towards the assumptions on which they were based created ample room for confusion regarding implementation of the ceasefire and the sequencing of the two tracks of dialogue it was supposed to lead to. It also contributed to problems for the government when, inevitably, the existence of the guarantees began to leak.

Thirdly, the illegal status of Batasuna had a contradictory impact on the process. The government had entered into talks with a radical nationalist movement with identifiable political and military expressions. As Stacie L. Pettyjohn observes in a review of US policy towards 'nationalist terrorist organizations', this organisational structure suggested possibilities in itself, not least that 'the political wing provides an interlocutor that is more acceptable than the armed branch'.[1] Yet

Spanish policy, far from pursuing engagement with Batasuna as a natural partner in dialogue, had been to render it illegal. This inevitably complicated any effort for representatives of Spanish or Basque political parties to meet with it, let alone enter into a sustained process of dialogue that might strengthen the more moderate forces within Batasuna. While the illegalisation of Batasuna would be defended as an effective means to force Batasuna to exert pressure on ETA, in the short term it had the opposite effect: it made the kind of political process Otegi had outlined at Anoeta almost impossible and reinforced ETA's hegemony over the nationalist left.

Finally, the political conditions under which the process was undertaken were adverse in the extreme. The hostility of the PP inhibited anything approaching the 'pact of state' ETA believed it had been promised. In addition to direct attacks on Zapatero, the PP increased its pressure on the government through victims' organisations, the media and the judiciary. The government was revealed as being unable to push back and explain the process with conviction. Vehement opposition from the right-wing press was yet more strident in the Catholic radio station COPE, or on the private television channel *Intereconomía*. Accusations that dialogue with ETA risked the loss not only of Navarre, but 'the nation, liberty and justice', were patently inaccurate.[2] They also exaggerated the influence of ETA beyond its wildest dreams.

The shadow of Northern Ireland

On 26 March 2006, four days after ETA's announcement, Zapatero gave a long interview to *El País*. He exuded confidence that, however difficult the process Spain was facing, it would indeed be possible. Among the elements sustaining this confidence was the experience of Northern Ireland. In July 2005 the IRA had pledged to end its armed conflict; two months later the decommissioning of the IRA's weapons had finally been certified.[3] Zapatero observed that ETA's ceasefire announcement echoed the terms of the IRA's 1994 ceasefire (which had promised a 'complete cessation of military operations') and referred to the encouragement he had drawn from conversations with both Tony Blair and the Irish prime minister Bertie Ahern.[4]

Zapatero's remarks reflected a pattern of references to Blair's advice consistent with his desire to affirm the legitimacy of his actions on the international stage as well as the shadow that the Northern Irish experience continued to cast across the Basque process. Both were important elements of the approach taken by the government to the 'internationalisation' of the peace process. This was quite different to the closed door maintained by the PP to any question of international involvement, even as limits on outside engagement were tightly proscribed.

Putting to one side the core issue of counter-terrorism co-operation, the international aspects of Spain's policies towards ETA had at least two different dimensions. In the first instance Spain worked confidentially—albeit with varying degrees of proximity—with a small number of individuals from the HD Centre, more remotely Norway and at a later stage the United Kingdom, directly involved in facilitating the talks with ETA, in addition to France and Switzerland, whose co-operation was required for the movement of ETA personnel to Geneva. At the same time, and conscious of the great importance ETA and Batasuna placed upon their international support networks, the government sought to 'use the world against ETA'.[5] In addition to a controversial effort to secure the formal support of the European Parliament for the peace process, this involved briefing key partners, including the EU, United States and other states—especially those, such as Cuba, Mexico and Venezuela, which had long had friendly relations with ETA and other Basque exiles—on all that the government was doing to end ETA's terrorist violence. This had a double purpose: to secure international support and pressure on ETA and to ensure that if the ceasefire broke down, the whole world would understand that the responsibility was ETA's alone.

Northern Ireland was important because of Sinn Féin, which remained the nationalist left's most significant international partner. Its members spoke to Batasuna, as Joseba Álvarez recalled, 'with the legitimacy of their own struggle and process'.[6] The government kept close watch on travels to and forth from Belfast. Leading representatives of Sinn Féin, including Gerry Adams, Alex Maskey and Gerry Kelly, arrived in the Basque Country with some regularity and varying levels of publicity (Kelly—a former adjutant general of the IRA, with a history that included bombing the Old Bailey in 1973, enduring a lengthy hunger strike and leading a breakout from the Maze prison in 1983—tended to visit discreetly). Alec Reid remained a visible presence while other Irish and South African politicians, to Madrid's considerable irritation, also continued to interact with Ibarretxe and the Basque government. Meanwhile in Brussels Sinn Féin's Bairbre de Bruin—another regular visitor to the Basque Country—played a prominent role within the Basque Friendship, a group of Euro-parliamentarians, many of them representing small nationalist parties, that had been formed in late 2005 to encourage the developing peace process.[7] In a curious historical role reversal, Sinn Féin now offered the banned Batasuna the kind of support in Brussels that Batasuna had given Sinn Féin in the years before the former was rendered illegal and the latter had its own representation in the European Parliament.

The Spanish government's contacts with Blair and his officials were at this stage considerably more limited than this multi-faceted activity. The two prime ministers discussed the Northern Irish process when they met; Zapatero's first interior minister, José Antonio Alonso, had been briefed over a dinner in London by British officials with experience of Northern Ireland; and in mid-2005 Blair had, at Zapatero's request, sent a report outlining lessons learned from Northern Ireland. British advice had reportedly included maintaining a dedicated channel for communication with ETA; achieving the support of the PP; not putting too much emphasis on disarmament, but rather concentrating on the public commitment of ETA to a ceasefire; and linking prison measures to ETA's commitment to end violence.[8] But British offers for further assistance had not yet been taken up, and it was only in the spring of 2007 that the British prime minister would become more directly involved.

Members of Sinn Féin spoke from their own experience and on this basis encouraged a political path to peace. 'No one was telling [the Basques] what to do,' as Alex Maskey would recall.[9] Adams had written to Zapatero to offer encouragement before the ceasefire; he had also spoken to both Blair and Bill Clinton on the Basque process. His advice that the most difficult negotiation is 'always that with your own band', as he put it in April 2006, had broad resonance in the Basque context. It also echoed experience elsewhere regarding the importance, but also challenges, for an armed group of maintaining internal unity through a peace process.[10] Relations between the leadership of Batasuna and ETA were maintained by a direct channel of communication between Batasuna and ETA's negotiators in Geneva. But they were markedly different from those between Sinn Féin and the IRA in the Northern Ireland's peace process, where Sinn Féin's negotiators, Adams and Martin McGuinness, had the authority to 'talk the IRA into peace', as Jonathan Powell would put it.[11]

The strategy presented at Anoeta had followed extensive internal deliberations. However, problems encountered throughout the process, which were exacerbated by the absence of Antza and others arrested with him in October 2004, reflected persistent differences within ETA and the nationalist left more broadly. 'We began the dialogue process,' as Otegi would recall some eight years later, 'with two substantially different visions at our core.'[12] ETA's executive committee was deeply divided at the prospect of ending violence.[13] There was also resistance in KAS' successor, Ekin, the prisoner support organisation Gestoras pro Amnistia, now renamed Askatasuna, and among the young in Segi, although this resistance was neither limited to nor uniform within these organisations.[14] The government had pinned its hope on the authority wielded by Josu Ternera—despite Ternera's caution to the contrary—and its understanding of his alliance with Otegi.[15] In the process it paid too little attention to the horizontal nature of ETA's leadership and the possible divergence of views within ETA that later became all too evident.

Meanwhile, Zapatero himself found mixed support even within the PSOE. Distrust of the more 'Basquist' wing of the PSE represented by Eguiguren was widespread; those reported to be sceptical included Bono, who left government in April 2005, as well as other senior figures from the González era. In contrast to Eguiguren and Zapatero, Rubalcaba would admit that he 'honestly, never believed' in ETA's commitment to its ceasefire. The ceasefire of 1998 remained engraved in his memory, 'it was my obsession'. To make sure that what had followed it 'would never happen to us' he was determined 'not to let [ETA] breathe'. In time Spanish intelligence, and ETA's own actions would reveal that it too had what Rubalcaba had termed a 'double strategy'—a plan B to try make sure that the armed organisation would not be wrong-footed if the ceasefire broke down. Speaking with the benefit of hindsight, and recalling that the government had later discovered that ETA's military commander Miguel Garikoitz Aspiazu Rubina, *Txeroki*, had ordered an ETA commando unit into San Sebastián soon after the ceasefire announcement, Rubalcaba would make the parallel explicit: 'ETA had Josu Ternera sitting there but it also had Txeroki sending commandos into Spain, while I had Jesús Eguiguren sitting there but I also had the Guardia Civil hunting down the commandos.'[16] The strategy was securely anchored in a single bottom line: 'If it turns out well—good; but if it doesn't then at least it should be clear that it is ETA's fault and not the state's.'

Zapatero's frequent invocations of Northern Ireland were much more abstract than the concrete desiderata extracted by ETA and Batasuna from its peace process (a government talking to terrorists, recognising self-determination, agreeing to formal international mediation, releasing prisoners etc.). They contributed to a revival of the discussion of the merit and de-merits of the 'Irish mirror' that had had first emerged in the margins of the Lizarra process. One difference was the entrenched opposition of the PP, which was in clear contrast to the critical support provided to Blair by the Conservative party. Among the critics of the Irish example was Rogelio Alonso, who had spent several years in Northern Ireland researching a book on the IRA. He emerged firmly opposed to the concessions made to Irish republicanism by the British government as well as any attempts to draw simplistic parallels between the two cases. His writing questioned the idea of a 'happy ending' to the Irish process and reinforced the position maintained by the PP that Zapatero had squandered the opportunity presented by the near-defeat of ETA, and would contribute to strengthening not weakening the armed organisation.[17]

A more pragmatic stance was taken by John Carlin, the international affairs correspondent of *El País* and a journalist with long experience of both Northern Ireland and South Africa, who published a series of articles that analysed the achievements and challenges of the Northern Irish process. The implicitly pedagogical aspect of Carlin's work was most evident in two articles published in early July 2006. He took as a starting point that all the Spanish parties, including the PP, had studied the peace process that had begun in Northern Ireland three months after the IRA had declared its 'complete' ceasefire in 1994. The articles explained, 'how and why almost four years went by—four years of distrust, frustrated hopes, heated recriminations and outbursts of violence—before in 1998 the Good Friday Agreement finally established the basis of a lasting peace', but also the difficulties encountered in the implementation, over eight more years, of the provisions it had contained.[18] By implication, the Basque process was likely to be—as Zapatero would regularly repeat—'long, hard and difficult' as well.

Off to a shaky start

In no aspect of the process was Zapatero's optimism more evident than in his hope that the PP would eventually come around. This confidence, 'led him to believe that the criticism of the PP did not matter much', Luis Aizpeolea would recall, as 'they would board the train as it moved forward'.[19] In this he was clearly misguided. Eguiguren would similarly remember that the government had been 'unprepared' for the depth and virulence of the PP's opposition. 'I—and the PSE/PSOE—have always supported police, security, justice approaches against ETA. We signed the anti-terrorist pact and never saw the attempt by security forces to achieve the defeat of ETA as incompatible with a need to design new political frameworks... Looking back, the fact that there was no political consensus was one of the errors. I thought that, little by little, the PP would come closer—that they could not, would not, take against the PSOE on this issue.'[20] 'It really wasn't normal,' was Rubalcaba's conclusion, 'there isn't a country in the democratic world in which a government tries to end a conflict in which you will find the opposition behaving with such complete disloyalty.'[21]

Public opinion was solidly committed (nearly 64 per cent) to exploring the possibility of dialogue with ETA. However, the same poll found near equal (62 per cent) opposition to any leniency towards ETA's prisoners—a serious problem for a process that, ultimately, contemplated 'peace for prisoners' and a dichotomy that the PP would ably exploit.[22] Meanwhile, the PP's differences with the PSOE on the legitimacy of dialogue were compounded by distrust on the issue of information. Zapatero had briefed Rajoy on the meetings in Geneva in the late summer of 2005, but after the PP leaked information to *El Mundo* he had decided not to share further details of the process.[23] Rumours of contacts between ETA and the government proliferated in the months that followed, but a degree of discretion had prevailed until the ceasefire was announced. At that time the walls of restraint appeared to break and a series of reports appeared in the press, laden with details of the meetings that had preceded it.[24] In the absence of full disclosure, Zapatero was vulnerable to accusations that he was lying to the Spanish people even as every twist and turn was subjected to discussion, dissection and at times distortion by media hungry for news of this most sensational story.

What confidence ETA and Batasuna had held in the process was quickly dented. 'The curious thing,' as Otegi would recall, 'is that we had been having secret talks for many years. We reach an agreement and as soon as the process becomes public we have problems. This led to all sorts of extreme analysis.... [including] that the only thing the government wanted was a ceasefire and once it had got it was prepared to ignore everything else.'[25] A first problem was presented by Zapatero's announcement of a period of 'verification'—something far beyond the internal 'house work' discussed with ETA. Meanwhile, on 29 March, Otegi entered prison under an order from the Audiencia Nacional. He would be released on bail a few days later, but his detention was the first in a series of judicial actions that appeared to be deliberately sabotaging the peace process. Old cases were resurrected from the archives and new ones pursued in what was the highest rate of prosecution of cases related to Basque terrorism (some eighty during the ceasefire) during Spanish democracy.[26] Particularly active in their prosecution was Fernando Grande-Marlaska, the conservative Basque judge who had replaced Baltasar Garzón in the Audiencia Nacional while the latter was on leave in the United States. He prohibited Batasuna's participation in a number of public activities as actions against ETA proceeded apace.

The sudden legal activism took the government by surprise and was to prove a vivid example of the tensions between peace and justice that have characterised other recent attempts to negotiate the end of violent conflict, with important differences introduced by Spain's status as a developed democracy.[27] Spain's legal system is formally independent, but there is a provision within the civil code that allows juridical norms to be interpreted with a certain degree of flexibility according to the circumstances of the moment.[28] Beyond this, the close ties between governments and the judicial system contributes to an expectation of tacit support for government policies. As Javier Zarzalejos, Aznar's adviser, put it, 'the judicial system instinctively does not undermine the position of a government'.[29] On 22 March Attorney General Cándido Conde-Pumpido appealed to judges to take into consideration 'the new situation' that prevailed after ETA's ceasefire.[30] But the automatic alignment of the General Council of the Judiciary with the PP proved too much. The spokesmen of the various judicial bodies immediately responded to Conde-Pumpido's appeal by saying that ETA's ceasefire would not alter their criteria in cases in which terrorism was involved.[31]

Inside the nationalist left the judicial onslaught was profoundly disconcerting. On 27 April, Otegi was sentenced to a new fifteen-month prison term for 'glorifying terrorism' at an event held in 2003 to commemorate the death of the former ETA leader Argala. He was again released on bail. In late May, together with seven others, he was once more summoned before Grande-Marlaska and threatened with imprisonment, this time for having participated in an event presenting Batasuna's leadership on 24 March. Meanwhile, in early June the Basque High Court accepted a lawsuit filed by the Foro de Ermua against Ibarretxe for the 'crime' of having met with members of the banned Batasuna. Later in the month a large operation against ETA's extortion network (it would subsequently emerge that this had been delayed as a result of a controversial *chivatazo*, or tip-off, by the police of the owner of the Bar Faisán in Irun, alerting him of the imminence of the raid) led to the arrest of twelve individuals in Spain and France and the implication of many others.

By June, the government and ETA had not met for six months. Channels of communication were kept open through the HD Centre, while all parties waited for Zapatero's declaration that dialogue could begin. The articulation between the two separate tracks had emerged as a serious problem. Zapatero and Josu Jon Imaz, the PNV president, both publicly favoured a clear sequence—'first peace, then politics'—which meant there could be no consideration of any political track until the end of ETA's violence had been determined.[32] But a long-winded interview with ETA in mid-May suggested that this would be difficult. ETA warned that the attacks it perceived to be directed against the process by Spain and France threatened the continuity of the process.[33] Otegi and his colleagues asked for a confidential meeting with the PSE to address this 'evident crisis'. They demanded assurances that their leadership would not go to prison and clear steps towards dialogue in the political track, including a public meeting between the PSE and Batasuna. In a significant concession, Patxi López announced that it was time to move a phase of contacts to that of negotiation, and that the PSE intended to meet shortly with representatives of the nationalist left he recognised as a 'necessary interlocutor'.[34]

The phrase was immediately and vehemently contested ('recognising Batasuna as a "necessary interlocutor" would inevitably involve legitimising violence to a certain degree', read a statement issued by ¡Basta Ya!).[35] Days later, in a bitter parliamentary debate on the state of the nation, Mariano Rajoy took a step unprecedented in Spain's years of democracy and announced that the PP would formally break 'all relations with the government' to protest against the 'ignominy' of the government's agreement to the meeting. Ángel Acebes, Rajoy's deputy, declared that Zapatero now shared the political project of ETA.[36]

Failure to launch

At ETA's request, a meeting with the government—which was now represented by Javier Moscoso, a retired politician from Navarre who had been minister of the presidency in Felipe González's first government, as well as Eguiguren—was held in Switzerland in late June.[37] A new communiqué suggested a hardening of the organisation's position. Rumours of the existence of the government's ceasefire commitments were beginning to percolate in political circles and would be confirmed in July, when *Gara*, at ETA's instigation, went public.[38] ETA demanded that the government 'de-activate all the measures of repression and exception'.[39] The government responded with a brief statement that reiterated that Spain would pay no political price for peace, and that the road map for any process lay in the parliamentary resolution approved in May 2005.

Discussion in Geneva, according to the version of events that ETA conveyed to *Gara*, which is largely corroborated by Eguiguren's account of the talks, was consumed by ETA's complaints of violations of the Oslo guarantees. The violations included the continuing detention of ETA militants, the failure to ensure the *de facto* legalisation of Batasuna and the legal campaign that had instead been unleashed against it. ETA had prepared a letter for Zapatero warning that the violation of the guarantees was motivation for the breakdown of negotiations.[40] The representatives of the government complained that ETA ignored the fact that judges acted independently of the government, and in this instance appeared to be 'instruments of the PP'. They also protested that ETA was both continuing to issue extortion letters and unwilling to prevent incidents of *kale borroka* (both would continue throughout the ceasefire).[41] ETA insisted that *kale borroka* was beyond its control and argued that the extortion letters no longer contained explicit threats. Moscoso and Eguiguren countered that the fact that these letters were from ETA and bore its seal—the serpent wrapped around the axe—was threat enough.[42]

Against this somewhat inauspicious background came Zapatero's declaration to parliament, opening the way for the formal process of dialogue. Instead of being delivered in the parliamentary chamber, as ETA had expected, Zapatero spoke in the vestibule outside it. The declaration contained many of the elements that had been agreed in 2005, including the all-important commitment of the government 'to respect the decisions that Basque citizens freely adopt'. By accepting that 'reaching peace, achieving the end of violence will be a task that will take us some time' and that 'this is not going to impede that the political dialogue begins', Zapatero also moved beyond limitations imposed by the government's earlier insistence on 'first peace, then politics'.[43] It was a watershed moment in the process, and, given the difficulties already present, a calculated risk.

The PP predictably heaped criticism on Zapatero's declaration, while Otegi welcomed it on Batasuna's behalf as being, 'of the greatest importance'.[44] The response reflected a deliberate decision to concentrate on the big picture—a viewpoint that was not shared with ETA. The organisation instead focused on elements Zapatero had added to his statement that had not been agreed between the parties. These would be subjects of complaint when Ternera and Iurrebaso next met with representatives of the government in September. ETA objected to a specific reference to Euskadi and thus the apparent exclusion of Navarre. It saw this and the insertion of references to the political parties' law and the framework of the 1978 constitution as deliberate provocations, and was concerned by Zapatero's failure to secure the support of the PP, as it believed it had been promised.[45] The government defended the statement as equivalent to the Downing Street Declaration and explained the differences between what was agreed and was said as attributable to the fact that Zapatero spoke from memory. But ETA and Batasuna would dismiss this excuse as ridiculous. 'They said, well Zapatero has a photographic memory and he did not write it down, but he made a few mistakes,' Otegi would recall, with a laugh, in July 2009. 'Well, we may be terrorists and *independentistas*, but we are not fools.'[46]

Back in June, one of the few positive developments in ETA's eyes had been the commitment by the PSE to meet publicly with Batasuna. The meeting between Patxi López and Rodolfo Ares, a leading member of the PSE of somewhat hawkish disposition, and Otegi and Rufi Etxeberria, whom the PSE viewed warily as a hardliner close to ETA, took place in San Sebastián on 6 July. It epitomised the contradictions of the process. The Socialists had recognised the nationalist left as a 'necessary interlocutor', yet Batasuna remained an illegal actor. The PP asked the attorney general to prohibit the meeting and Dignity and Justice brought the issue to the Audiencia Nacional. In a pragmatic ruling Garzón—now back in Spain—allowed the meeting to go ahead.[47] Yet López and Ares would, like Ibarretxe before them, have a lawsuit filed against them in the Basque High Court for meeting with members of an illegal party—a development that seemed ironic given their insistence within the meeting that Batasuna seek legalisation through compliance with the political parties' law. This demand led to a stalemate at least partly attributable to differences within the nationalist left. The Batasuna lawyer Iñigo Iruin drew up proposals for the party's legalisation, but further movement was stopped by ETA. It suspected 'a new argument destined to delay the beginning of a multiparty dialogue' and in any case doubted that legalisation would work given the extension of the ban on Batasuna introduced at the beginning of the year.[48]

The government had wanted the first formal meeting of the technical track to take place immediately after Zapatero went to parliament. But in the summer months ETA and Batasuna conducted an internal review of the process. In a communiqué released in mid-August ETA described it as 'immersed in an evident crisis' and threatened that 'if the attacks against Euskal Herria continue, ETA will respond'.[49] Its doubts translated into a series of actions that marked a turning point in the ascendance of the military preoccupations of Txeroki—already readying ETA to break the ceasefire—and the more political concerns of Ternera: the continuation of extortion letters and *kale borroka*, as well as the theft of a large number of cars and the unprecedented display of threat at a celebration of *Gudari Eguna* (the day of Basque soldier) in Oiarzun, Guipúzcoa in late September. Three hooded ETA militants, two of them brandishing, and then firing, assault rifles, defended ETA's struggle as 'not a thing of the past, but of today and for tomorrow'. They vowed to pursue it 'with our weapons in our hand, until we achieve independence and socialism in Euskal Herria'.[50]

The HD Centre convened meetings in Geneva in late September that both sides attended with an expanded negotiating team. The government delegation of Eguiguren and Moscoso now included José Manuel Gómez Benítez, a hard-driving PSOE lawyer who was close to Rubalcaba. ETA's delegation was also three strong: Ternera and Iurrebaso were joined by Francisco Javier López Peña, known within ETA as *Thierry*, and within the talks as *Marc*. Thierry had a long career on the military and training side of ETA (only months later he would be identified as the organisation's 'political head').[51] He represented positions that were sceptical of what the peace process might yield and soon sidelined Ternera; these meetings would turn out to be the last time the latter appeared at the talks.

A spate of leaks preceded the meetings.[52] Within them, ETA emphasised its unhappiness with Zapatero's June declaration and warned that it would not move forward until the government fulfilled its obligations. It also demanded resolution of a series of issues related to prisoners, a subject that quickly became complicated by the case of Iñaki de Juana Chaos. De Juana was an ETA militant who had been condemned to prison in 1997 for more than 2,500 years for his part in twenty-five assassinations. Under existing sentencing guidelines, he had been due for release in October 2004. However, fearing public outcry, an appeal was filed to prevent it. In January 2005 Grande-Marlaska charged de Juana with membership of ETA and making terrorist threats in two articles he had published in *Gara* the month before. The case was shelved in June but revived after the justice minister, Juan Fernando López Aguilar, recommended that a new criminal charge be made against him.[53] In August 2006 de Juana began a hunger strike to protest against his treatment and on 19 September he had been admitted to hospital. The government feared the repercussions of his death in custody and was force-feeding him while binding him to a bed with shackles.[54] Opinion within the nationalist left mobilised against the perceived perversion of justice in his case; on the other side, victims and others protested against the introduction of anything that smacked of special treatment for a notoriously violent terrorist.

In addition to the immediate release of de Juana, ETA asked for the release on medical grounds of other prisoners, the repeal of the Parot Doctrine (now extending the length of prison sentences being served by dozens of ETA prisoners) and for the government to start moving prisoners dispersed across Spain closer to the Basque Country. These requests were outside the framework of the guarantees. However, ETA sought them as a means to regain some confidence in the process and thus help prevent *kale borroka*. The government had commissioned studies from the prison service and from judicial experts contemplating the legal possibilities for the transfer of prisoners, and in some cases their release.[55] However, it insisted that moving prisoners closer to the Basque Country would be contingent on concrete steps from ETA.[56]

A brief moment of optimism followed this meeting. Both sides had renewed their commitment to the process. *Kale borroka* was reduced; de Juana abandoned his hunger strike while awaiting his trial, and political discussions between the PSE, Batasuna and the PNV made much better progress than might have been expected. In early October Zapatero received a boost from a visit by Tony Blair—his first to Spain since Zapatero took office. The two men had not met since the preceding December. Blair encouraged Zapatero's efforts and counselled 'patient determination'.[57] In late October, however, a series of developments suddenly imperilled the situation: ETA was the obvious suspect for the robbery of 350 pistols and revolvers reported in Nimes, France (the intelligence suggested that Txeroki was the author of this crime in the expectation that the peace process would break down);[58] the Basque police conducted raids on more than a hundred *herriko tabernas*; and the trial of de Juana got underway. Meanwhile, Zapatero's effort to seek international legitimacy for the peace process through a resolution of the European Parliament came perilously close to backfiring. Instead of the overwhelming endorsement he had hoped for, the PP's insistence that the resolution gave legitimacy to ETA led to protests in Spain, a stormy debate in Strasbourg—where the PP had galvanised its European allies—and a narrow margin of victory (321 to 311 with twenty-four abstentions) that gained little political mileage.[59]

A new meeting between ETA and the government took place in late October in an atmosphere of crisis. Both sides spoke in terms that suggested the breakdown of the process. ETA asked whether the government had decided to end it; the government charged that the robbery represented the process' 'rupture'. Thierry reportedly warned that ETA had a judge within its sights as a possible target for assassination.[60] The intervention of the HD Centre helped cool tempers: the government rephrased its characterisation of the robbery as 'blocking' the process and Gómez Benítez defended the government's determination to keep it on track. One example he cited, according to notes from the meeting taken by ETA and later captured with Thierry, was collaboration with the police to effect the 'tip-off' at the Bar Faisán in June—an allegation that would be jumped upon by the PP and lead to the launch of a highly politicised legal case against the senior police officers said to be involved.[61] Despite the evident difficulties the parties both faced, they agreed to keep working through the HD Centre, and to meet again in December.

The political track

The six months between Zapatero's declaration at the end of June and ETA's explosion of the car bomb at Barajas airport in late December marked a disconcerting period in Basque political life. Things were self-evidently not going at all well by June, and by the time ETA issued its August statement the process was in serious trouble. In the public eye, the major unfolding drama was that of Zapatero's government, constantly on the defensive against the PP. A relatively fluid relationship between the PSOE and the sectors of the PNV led by Imaz masked resentment by Ibarretxe that the Basque government was being kept out of the process. Meanwhile the nationalist left itself was wrought by internal differences, as the more progressive political leaders around Otegi and Rafa Díez struggled to counter those sectors, in ETA and elsewhere, that were rapidly losing faith in the possibilities the ceasefire held out for them.

Less prominent than in earlier periods was the activity of the social movement, which took a back seat to the complex processes playing out among and within the Basque Country's various political forces. Elkarri had disbanded in March 2006, in part as a consequence of a belief that its job—the promotion of the benefits of dialogue and negotiation—had been completed. A new organisation, Lokarri, was established to continue with some aspects of its work, but it would take some time to assume a public profile.[62] Gesto por la Paz remained active, but its attempt to pursue an apolitical stand rendered it something of a bystander at this critical moment. Indeed given the enormous civic investment in the pursuit of peace, and the bedrock of opposition to ETA's violence, the absence of social support of the peace process, let alone public voice and reaction to the clamour against it emanating from the right, was a significant problem. It was in part attributable to the bitter political divisions that surrounded the process, but also to the government's failure to invest any effort in building public support for its efforts.

A platform for political dialogue among women, Ahotsak, emerged as the most visible of the unofficial entities working for peace. The initiative grew out of the friendship between Gemma Zabaleta of the PSE and Jone Goirizelaia of Batasuna quietly formed while both were in the Basque Parliament in the early 2000s. On 8 April 2006 Ahotsak had issued a declaration that offered a firm commitment to peace and reconciliation.[63] In the following months it sought to build support among its members—representatives of parties and social forces from Navarre and the French Basque territories as well as Euskadi (although not the PP or its allies in the UPN)[64]—on a series of agreements that might be a starting point for an eventual multiparty table. Demonstrating a capacity to work across political divisions that was not possible at the formal party level, in December 2006 Ahotsak convened 4,000 Basque women in Bilbao's Euskuldun convention centre. For a moment they appeared to hold out the hope of what a broad consensus on the way ahead might look like.[65]

In practice, by December hopes for the political track of the peace process had been badly dented. Back in the summer Otegi had suggested to Eguiguren that Batasuna and the PSE work towards a pre-accord that might give ETA confidence that the government was 'not tricking them—that there is a genuine will to move ahead'.[66] Thinking that this pre-accord would later require the formal approval of the Basque Parliament and citizens (and eventually the Spanish Parliament), the two agreed that the PNV had to be there too. The PNV accepted the invitation to join the talks. But it remained somewhat sceptical. More reluctant still was Rubalcaba in Madrid. However, with the PSE and PNV behind him, Eguiguren prevailed, and the talks went ahead. In obvious contrast to the process under way in Geneva, they took place without any international involvement at all.

'The meetings we had in Loyola,' Otegi would remember, 'were because we told them that this is getting away from us.'[67] The twelve meetings held at the Jesuit sanctuary of Loyola between late September and mid-November represented the first time that the three primary political forces in the Basque Country had together addressed the political aspects of the Basque problem. The composition of the different delegations—the Loyola 'triangle' analysed by Imanol Murua—remained consistent.[68] Otegi, Etxeberria and one of two younger party leaders represented Batasuna. The delegation had prepared assiduously for the talks and, in a manner typical of the nationalist left, maintained tight discipline at the negotiating table; any differences between its representatives were addressed in private. In this respect it differed from the PSE, which was represented by Eguiguren, but also Ares, whom Eguiguren and both the other delegations assumed had been put there by Rubalcaba to keep an eye on him. The PNV delegation, which was composed of Imaz and Iñigo Urkullu, reflected the more pragmatic wing of the party. The two men briefed Ibarretxe regularly, but also remained in close touch with Madrid; to Batasuna's frustration, their baseline loyalty to what the government could or could not contemplate was never in doubt.

The lack of Navarrese participation at Loyola was an evident flaw. It was on 'territorial articulation' that the parties would have the hardest time reaching agreement, even as the extreme sensitivity of the question of Navarre outside the talks shadowed their deliberations. The Socialists were content with the arrangements established in the course of the transition: the Basque statute of autonomy, and Euskadi and Navarre as distinct legal entities. Batasuna, on the other hand, approached the subject of the four Spanish provinces with its sense of historic betrayal. Realising that it could not ask the government of Spain to resolve the issue of the French Basque territories, it nonetheless insisted that, as the 'territorial division' within Spain had been the fault of the government of the day, its successor had the responsibility to fix it.[69] The PSE was prepared to accommodate solutions that were consistent with the existing legal framework and democratic practice, but it had little room for manoeuvre. A conservative coalition governed in Navarre; from Madrid the PP stoked fears that Zapatero was prepared to cede to Basque nationalist pressure and let Navarre go.

On 31 October the PSE, PNV and Batasuna agreed in principle on a document outlining 'Bases for dialogue and a political agreement.'[70] The document represented significant concessions on all sides. It recognised the identity of the Basque people as a 'nation', and Euskal Herria as a 'reality composed of social, linguistic, historic, economic and cultural bonds' and looked forward to the creation of a Basque 'euro-region'. The document mentioned neither self-determination nor the right to decide. However, the three parties agreed to defend the idea 'that the decisions on their political future freely and democratically adopted by Basque citizens should be respected by the institutions of Spain'. These decisions included the possibility that independence could be realised, if it was the 'desire of the majority of Basque citizens expressed through legal processes'. On the critical question of territory, the document committed the three parties to promoting the creation of a new 'common institutional entity' encompassing Euskadi and Navarre, whose establishment was subject to approval in separate referenda in each of the two existing autonomous communities. However it included little definition as to what, in practical and political terms, this 'common entity' would do.[71]

The three delegations withdrew from Loyola for consultations. Before they reconvened on 8 November, Otegi summoned Eguiguren to

Txillare to tell him that there was a problem. Batasuna, after consultations with ETA and others in the nationalist left, had changes that Otegi knew to be substantive. In a stormy meeting back at Loyola, Batasuna now pushed for detailed attributes of the 'common institutional entity', including its elaboration within a period of two years of a single statute binding Euskadi and Navarre in a new autonomous community.[72] With this the political track foundered. The PSE attempted a counter-proposal, but the proposal for a single statute, and a hard deadline of just two years to reach it, was qualitatively different to anything discussed at Loyola, or ever before it. With the PNV behind it, the PSE dismissed it as unconstitutional and unacceptable.

The breakdown of the talks on 10 November 2006 represented a deep blow to the effort to shift from the ascendance of ETA to the political logic of the more progressive sectors of the nationalist left. In this respect it was a disaster for Batasuna. Two and half years later, in July 2009 it was still a sensitive subject for Otegi. He recalled that Batasuna had gone to Loyola to establish a 'base camp' in terms of the aspirations of the nationalist left, 'not to reach the summit'. He had believed that this 'base camp' had been achieved in the draft agreed on 31 October, even as he was aware that it contained no guarantees as to the process' eventual outcome. If confidence in the process had been greater within the nationalist left, he still believed that this draft would have been acceptable. However, consultations with ETA had revealed 'such a high degree of distrust throughout the organisation that there existed a fear that… this base camp might be the summit of our achievements. So the decision was taken to go for the summit right away—now.' This had been a mistake.[73] Eguiguren would dismiss any suggestion that ETA had wanted to 'push one step further' in the negotiations at Loyola as 'absurd'. The demand for a single autonomous community was not 'an addition to the existing agreement', as he saw it, 'but its complete destruction'. It was 'an unrealisable demand that ETA put on the table to undermine the draft negotiated by Batasuna and break the process'.[74]

Oslo, Barajas and bust

Preparations for new meetings between the government and ETA took place in an environment tainted by the collapse of the Loyola talks, new reports from French security forces of ETA activity, rapidly evaporating public confidence in the peace process (by early December 67 per cent of Basques believed it to be stuck or deteriorating)[75] and a spike in political antagonism between the PP and the government. Much later it would emerge that ETA had already given orders for the ceasefire to be broken, and that it was only as a consequence of the incompetence of the commando cell charged with car-bombing of the palace of justice in Burgos that it had not already happened.[76] The PP backed a demonstration called by the AVT on 25 November to protest the government's 'surrender' to ETA. Aznar and Rajoy both took prominent positions within it. The PSOE responded by releasing a polemic video recalling the actions of the Aznar government during the ceasefire of 1998–9, fuelling a bizarre public competition over which government had done less for peace. The video sought to highlight the hypocrisy of the PP by recalling that in the interest of peace Aznar had moved prisoners closer to the Basque Country, released others and encouraged Basque exiles to return to Spain. He had even promised that his government was open to 'hope, pardon and generosity' if ETA's violence were to end—for all of which, the implication was, the PP should now be ashamed.[77]

Among the very few voices venturing that these were precisely the kind of gestures required were those who drew on experience from elsewhere. In mid-November, Matteo Zuppi of the Community of San Egidio, Julian Hottinger of Switzerland and Roelf Meyer of South Africa, spoke at a conference on the peace process in Bilbao. Their remarks drew attention to critical issues in any peace process, but the gulf between the suggestions made—for inclusivity, for taking advantages of the small window of opportunity available to the Basques, for pursuing win-win solutions—and the prevailing political climate was extreme.[78] More advice came from Brian Currin and other experts cited by John Carlin in *El País* in early December. Their suggestions that an imaginative approach to prisoner issues or the repeal of the law of political parties was exactly what was required to build confidence were not welcomed. Carlin's articles caused disquiet within *El País*. The following day the paper ran a commentary by Francisco Tomás y Valiente Lanuza, the son of the former president of the Constitutional Court assassinated by ETA in 1996. 'Are we mad?' he asked. 'The government is doing what it should, not accepting the blackmail that seems so natural to these "experts" who know so little, those "experts", who, without identifying themselves, are allowed to advise contempt of democratic legitimacy and the rule of law.'[79]

Talks in Oslo began on 11 December. The government was again represented by Moscoso, Eguiguren and Gómez Benítez, while Thierry led an ETA delegation comprised of Iurrebaso and a younger man, Igor Zuberbiola. With the possibility of breakdown shadowing the meetings—*ABC* now predicted that ETA would suspend the ceasefire before the end of the year[80]—the parties struggled to move ahead. The HD Centre facilitated the talks within an atmosphere fraught with tension; Norwegian officials were again present in the wings. But the challenges facing the negotiators were daunting. The political and technical tracks were both blocked, but also increasingly interlinked. The government— and especially Rubalcaba from Madrid—struggled to keep them apart. After Loyola this was difficult, and ETA was pushing the interdependence of the two tracks hard, putting forward a written proposal that identified the key to the resolution of the conflict as an agreement between the political parties on a single entity embracing Euskadi and Navarre.[81] ETA now insisted that the legalisation of Batasuna would not be pursued before a political agreement and demanded the withdrawal of the political parties' law after the municipal elections due in May.[82]

The accounts of these talks offered by Eguiguren and Aizpeolea in their book and that of ETA in *Zutabe* and *Gara* give some indication of the conflicting impressions that they may have created. Both Eguiguren and ETA reported hitting a wall on the issue of the political agreement that ETA demanded and the government refused to contemplate; but they also admitted that the talks had been more honest and substantive than any held to date. Eguiguren was convinced at the time that the process was 'broken', and that ETA was going to strike again. Yet when the talks ended on 14 December the two parties agreed to re-convene in late January 2007. This modest achievement, as well as the government's lack of intelligence pointing to the preparation of an armed action, may have contributed to the up-beat assessment given by Zapatero on 29 December. In the most damaging phrase of his government, Zapatero promised that in a year's time the situation with ETA would be 'better than today'.[83]

The massive car bomb that ripped through Barajas airport's Terminal Four (T4) less than twenty-four hours later plunged Zapatero's government into crisis. The peace process, Rubalcaba declared, 'is broken, liquidated, and finished'.[84] ETA had not issued a public statement on its rupture of the ceasefire before Barajas, although it had telephoned in warnings in advance of the bomb's explosion. In this respect only its actions differed markedly from the parallel bomb attack against Canary Wharf with which the IRA had ended a two-year ceasefire in February 1996. Like ETA, the IRA had not meant to kill, but had claimed two victims. Unlike ETA, however, the IRA had announced earlier that day that its ceasefire was in suspension.[85] ETA's action would prove a dramatic mistake, not only because of the deaths it caused. The organisation had violated its own ceasefire, unilaterally ended the talks, put Batasuna in an impossible position and—once again—disappointed the overwhelming majority of Basques who had hoped that its violence was already a thing of the past.

Batasuna struggled to understand ETA's action. 'For us,' Otegi recalled, 'the term "ceasefire" is more or less incompatible with a right to respond.'[86] With its credibility shattered, Batasuna met separately with the PNV and the PSE in the days following the bombing. It passed a message to the government asking it to avoid the 'temptation to accelerate the repression of the nationalist left' and to 'maintain open and stable (in the manner and form it considers appropriate) its channels of communication with the organisation ETA'.[87] In a press conference on 8 January it made a direct appeal to ETA—the first in its history—to respect the commitments it had entered into in the ceasefire and to confirm that any future dialogue would take place 'in the absence of any type of violence'.[88] ETA issued a lengthy, and somewhat contradictory, communiqué the next day, claiming responsibility for the Barajas bomb, but insisting that it had not meant to kill. ETA reaffirmed the objectives of the ceasefire but also emphasised its 'determination to respond' if the current situation of 'attacks against Euskal Herria' continued.[89]

Rubalcaba would long remember a photograph taken in the hours following the Barajas bomb. It shows Otegi and other leaders of Batasuna standing inside a lift, their faces stunned in a shock that Rubalcaba read as recognition of the depth of the damage done. 'It took a few more years,' he would recall in 2012, 'but I always thought—and you can imagine T4 was terrible for us—I always said to Zapatero, "Remember that photograph—it's the end."'[90] Otegi's assessment was not much different. Years later, writing from prison, he would recall that Barajas had put the nationalist left, 'not at the edge of a precipice, but falling directly into it'.[91]

Limping forward

During the months between the bombing of Barajas airport and the local and municipal elections held on 27 May 2007 the government publicly disavowed any continuing engagement in the peace process but nevertheless maintained channels of communication to ETA through the HD Centre. When these contacts later emerged they would be the subject of particularly heated criticism, and point-blank accusations of lying.[92] With public opinion in broad revulsion against ETA's action, measures against the organisation and its affiliates were stepped up (thirty-four alleged ETA militants were detained during the ceasefire in 2006; fifty-eight between 1 January and its end of 6 June 2007).[93] In January, the Supreme Court ruled that the youth groups Jarrai and its successors Haika and Segi be considered terrorist organisations linked to ETA as its 'appendices'. The decision immediately increased the sentences against those members of the groups already charged, and led to new arrests.[94]

Communication with ETA was renewed some time after the organisation wrote to the government in February offering to restart talks.[95] The government continued to maintain that the bombing of Barajas had ended the process, but it agreed that Gómez Benítez would meet with ETA at the end of March. In a long interview with *El Mundo* in January 2008 Zapatero attributed his controversial decision to continue the contacts with ETA to the influence of 'international actors'.[96] The example of Britain was widely reported to have played a key role. However, it is difficult to see this explanation as entirely convincing. The government did not consult the British government before the March meeting, and if it had it can be surmised that the advice it received might have been different. In his account of the Northern Irish peace process, Jonathan Powell, Blair's chief of staff, is strongly critical of the response of the Major government to the Canary Wharf bombing. This 'should have been that they would never deal with the IRA again until they had put violence aside for good, but instead officials were in touch with Sinn Féin two weeks later'.[97]

Spain would not have maintained its contacts with ETA if had not had good reason to do so. Zapatero told *El Mundo* of his determination to explore every last possibility of bringing ETA's violence to an end. Rubalcaba referred in 2012 to quite distinct reasons for maintaining 'open lines' to ETA. There were advantages to be reaped from ETA's post-Barajas disgrace and this uncertain period of semi-ceasefire: police work that contributed to the arrests of ETA's leadership after the end of the ceasefire, and the possibility of further complicating relations between Batasuna and ETA, as well as with Sinn Féin.[98] Unstated, but nevertheless obvious, was the benefit of delaying any terminal breakdown in the process until after the local elections due in May.

In November de Juana had been sentenced to a further twelve and half years in prison; he returned to his hunger strike and by early February was close to death. On 12 February the Supreme Court reduced his sentence to three years, which meant—as over half this time had already been served in pre-emptive custody—that he was eligible for release into conditional liberty. With the whole country hanging on his fate, the government transferred de Juana to a hospital in the Basque Country, where he abandoned his hunger strike. In response the PP, with the support of most Spanish media, accused Zapatero of ceding to blackmail, and siding with terrorists against their victims.[99] On 10 March it convened a massive demonstration in Madrid to 'defend Spain' and protest against the government's anti-terrorist policy.[100] In a revealing conversation with the US ambassador, Rubalcaba explained the government's decision as having prevented de Juana becoming a 'decades-long martyr for radical ETA youth'. But he also acknowledged that the justice minister's decision to prevent de Juana's release in 2005 by slapping on an additional charge, 'with flimsy merits', had been a mistake for which the government now was paying.[101]

More controversy surrounded the participation of the nationalist left within the May elections. Batasuna was working every angle to try to run in a political context in which the government knew that ETA could 'put the PP in the driver's seat' by returning to targeted assassinations, as Rubalcaba had said to the US ambassador. The government had a clear preference to keep Batasuna out of the elections, but an even greater concern to avoid violence by ETA that might tip the balance of political power towards the PP. Although the Supreme Court had quickly ruled against the legalisation of a new party proposed by Batasuna, it proved harder to take legal action against a long established non-violent radical nationalist party, Basque Nationalist Action (ANV) when it became evident that its candidates would carry the support of the nationalist left.[102] In late April Garzón ruled that ANV's participation in the elections was permissible, but warned that there existed the possibility that it could be 'used' by ETA.[103] The PP and others imme-diately demanded that all ANV's candidates be banned.[104] The govern-ment eventually banned some candidates but not others (133 out of a total of 256 ANV lists presented), with the distinction made on the basis of which candidates were 'contaminated' by ties to Batasuna. Like the decision on de Juana, this was an improvised solution that proved difficult to defend on legal grounds. It revealed the difficult position that the continuing effort to engage ETA had placed the government, as well as the contradictory, and short-term, impulses now driving its policy.

Iurrebaso was arrested in southern France on the way to the meeting in Geneva, so Gómez Benítez met only with Thierry. His sole interest was whether ETA was prepared to take the steps necessary to start the process again, beginning with a communiqué that included an explicit rejection of violence. Thierry quite clearly had a different agenda: he held fast to the need for a political agreement and demanded the imme-diate release of Iurrebaso.[105] By the end of the meeting, the two men had achieved nothing other than an agreement that they would meet again. In early May Thierry attempted to present Gómez Benítez with a new proposal from ETA, but Gómez Benítez refused even to consider it. Leaving it in the hands of the HD Centre he had indicated that, from the government's perspective, the process had broken down.[106]

After a series of contacts involving the HD Centre, the government and ETA, but also British officials, Sinn Féin and the government of Norway, the parties agreed to meet again. Unlike in the past, the talks would bring the 'two tables' originally proposed at Anoeta under one roof: the government (Gómez Benítez and Eguiguren) and ETA (Thierry and Zuberbiola) would meet to discuss technical issues, while political questions would be addressed in talks between Batasuna (Otegi and Etxeberria), and the PSE, represented by Eguiguren and Ares. (The PNV had been neither invited to nor informed of the meetings.) In addition to the HD Centre, which retained its facilitating role, the meetings would be attended by five international observers: two from the British government, including Jonathan Powell; two senior members of Sinn Féin, including Gerry Kelly; and a representative of Norway.[107]

The presence of these international actors was welcomed by Batasuna and ETA, who saw the legitimacy of the process, and thus their own demands, boosted by the change in the talks' format. But exactly what the government hoped to achieve—in addition to staving off the threat of ETA's violence before the municipal elections due on 27 May—remains unclear. The accounts of the meetings that took place on 14, 15, 16 and 21 May suggest that the encouragement offered by the HD Centre, Gerry Adams and Tony Blair—who telephoned Zapatero before the government agreed to attend the talks—was key to the decision to go ahead with them. But broadening participation within them also appeared to reflect both an understanding that the presence of Sinn Féin, including individuals such as Kelly, who had made the hard transition away from violence himself, might be helpful, and that there were advantages of having the international actors present witness ETA's intransigence.

Looking back at the May meetings, Eguiguren and Otegi gave quite different accounts of what happened within them. In Eguiguren's version of events, the government knew the process was over, but had been told that ETA had something 'new to offer'; it came to see whether this was the case, and if not to make sure that the international observers understood ETA's responsibility for the breakdown of the talks.[108] Otegi's version is quite different. Batasuna, although invited to participate only at the last minute, went to Geneva 'wanting to work'. The government arrived in Geneva at least saying that it was willing to make a final attempt to reach a solution, even if in practice Batasuna would find that it was not prepared to engage with the seriousness required.[109] What transpired in the course of the meetings in Geneva—even in the confused account given by Eguiguren—suggests that this indeed was the case.

ETA presented its proposal when the parties met on 14 May. It offered to end its armed struggle and dismantle its military structures under the supervision of a verification commission in exchange for a political agreement that would guarantee the territorial unity of Álava, Guipúzcoa, Vizcaya and Navarre within a single institutional framework; the right of the citizens to decide their future as the basis for consensus; and the steps that each side would need to take in order to get there by 2012. These included specific demands that the government legalise political parties of the nationalist left before the May elections, repeal the political parties' law after them and address ETA's requirements on prisoners in the interests of humanising the conflict.[110]

The government quickly rejected ETA's proposal, but in a lengthy discussion Batasuna expanded on the position of the nationalist left for the benefit of the internationals present. Conscious of the wide gulf separating the parties, some of them undertook to prepare a compromise document. Their proposal was rapidly rejected by the PSE, but Eguiguren took to the blackboard to explain, as he would recall it, the legal steps necessary to bring Batasuna's ideas into practice. Batasuna remembered his presentation as being a proposal outlining a process that the PSE—and government—could itself accept. Hopes were briefly raised, although fell on 16 May, when word came from Madrid that this was not the case, and Eguiguren's ideas were dismissed. In a tense meeting between ETA and the government, ETA presented a half-page proposal in which it stated that, if there was a political agreement—and it now did not specify what was in it—it was ready to abandon its armed struggle and dismantle its military structures. Batasuna's notes of the meeting record that the PSE remarked that ETA's proposal was 'very positive' and that the government had asked for a recess of a few days to consult in Madrid while also taking part in the electoral campaign. Eguiguren, on the other hand, recalled that the talks broke only for purposes related to the campaign—an explanation that is simply not credible.[111]

When the parties met again on 21 May it was in the format of the 'political' table only as Thierry, a menacing presence outside the room, refused to engage with the government without a political agreement. Despite warnings from Sinn Féin about the serious consequences of rupture—Kelly told Thierry that the IRA only ever got up from a negotiating table if it believed it would be in a condition to return to it with its negotiating position strengthened[112]—he also introduced an ultimatum: if there was no agreement to ETA's demands that night it would end the process. Otegi would recall that the government presented a counter-proposal so much weakened that breakdown appeared imminent. In a final effort to avoid it, a mediator from the HD Centre prepared a new draft 'road map'. This one-page document divided the process ahead into three phases, and outlined the steps to be taken in each. Eguiguren's version of events confuses the origins of this document (he claimed to recall that it was Batasuna's), but for Otegi the situation was clear: the facilitators presented their proposed road map and Batasuna, with ETA behind it, was prepared to accept it.[113]

A point of contention, however, remained ETA and Batasuna's insistence that a provision be added to the road map that stated that the PSOE, the PSE and the Socialist Party of Navarre publicly commit to the common entity and single statute, and campaign for this outcome. This was quite unacceptable to the government and, as those with experience of Northern Ireland observed, an echo of the old demand for the British government to be a 'persuader' for Irish unity. Blair had rejected the demand when he took office on grounds that, as Powell explains them, had direct applicability to the Basque case: 'a democratic government cannot agree, under pressure from a terrorist organisation and under the threat of violence, to argue for a position it does not itself hold'.[114] But Batasuna and ETA were adamant.

The talks broke down amidst bitter acrimony in the early hours of 22 May. In several respects they had had little chance of succeeding. The Spanish government had lost all confidence in assurances from ETA, while ETA was no longer disposed to believe any of the promises that might be made to it by the government. The government had been pushed, or had slid, into discussion of political issues that lay well beyond the remit it had received from parliament in 2005, or could expect to find support for in public opinion. And the calculations of electoral politics stacked up against this uncertain and risky process with ETA. Local and municipal elections were due within days, and the polls predicted a near tie between the government and the PP. General elections were due in a less than a year and were likely to be close fought. All present in Geneva knew the end of the talks meant that a return to violence by ETA was imminent, and that the leaders of Batasuna would soon be imprisoned. But while the collapse of the process was a deep blow, the closing of the door on dialogue and a return to an all-out counter-terrorist campaign was much easier for the government to contemplate than a political settlement put on the table by ETA.

7

AFTERMATH

On 6 June 2007 ETA issued a statement ending its ceasefire. It blamed the 'fascism' of Zapatero for the breakdown of the peace process and declared all fronts open for armed action.[1] Although hardly a surprise, this was a defining moment in Zapatero's first government, as well as a deep disappointment to those individuals and organisations who had invested years of hope and work in the prospect of a Basque Country without violence, at peace with itself and with Spain.

The government clamped down hard and fast on ETA and the nationalist left. De Juana went back to prison the next day. Otegi was detained in San Sebastián on 8 June and sent to Martutene prison to complete the fifteen-month sentence he had been given for commemorating the death of Argala. In October Garzón ordered the detention of twenty-three members of the leadership of Batasuna, the single largest legal action against the party since the introduction of the political parties law. ETA returned to killing in December 2007, with an opportunistic assassination of two members of the Guardia Civil. But with exemplary co-operation from French security forces, arrests soon mounted up. Thierry and Zuberbiola were both detained in May 2008; Txeroki, in November 2008; his replacement, Aitzol Iriondo, *Gurbitz*, just three weeks after that; and the latter's successor, Jurdan Martitegi, *Arlas*, in April 2009. Mikel Carrera Sarobe, *Ata*, the final member of the organisation's leadership during the ceasefire still at large, was arrested in May 2010.

The inevitable debate over who was to blame for what was accelerated by an avalanche of information on the peace process released in the Spanish and Basque press. This began in late May 2007 and quickened after ETA's announced end of the ceasefire. It drew on the detailed records of the talks that the organisation had passed to *Gara*.[2] A multitude of expert and less expert observers offered competing analyses of a process that did not improve under the harsh inspection of a highly politicised media, heavily weighted towards the right. More positively, the Socialists—especially in the Basque Country—reaped benefits from the recognition that Zapatero had done all he could for peace, despite the constant hostility of the PP and in the face of ETA's increasingly incomprehensible determination to keep on killing.

Rubalcaba would explain the government's strategy after the ceasefire as a simple one: 'by police means pursue them fully, and politically give them nothing'.[3] It built on a broad consensus that ETA could never again be trusted to abide by a ceasefire. Zapatero's critics sustained that the peace process had legitimised ETA as a political actor, provided breathing space for it to regroup and rearm, and encouraged it to raise the demands it made of the state.[4] The government found solid ground on which to resist these charges. ETA's public and international standing was at an all-time low, police successes confirmed its weakened state and the dynamics set in motion by the peace process would gradually be shown to have had long lasting impact. The general elections in March 2008 were closely fought, but a degree of public backlash against the more extreme positions of *crispación* the PP had assumed against Zapatero's policies on ETA, the Catalan statute and in the social realm, helped return the PSOE to power, buoyed by Basque and Catalan votes, for a second four-year term.[5]

Inside the Basque Country the aftermath of the frustrated process was complex. Ibarretxe emerged from the sidelines with an attempt to launch a new popular consultation on Basques' right to decide. His initiative was abruptly dismissed by Madrid and deepened divisions within the PNV. The PNV fared well in the Basque autonomous elections held in March 2009, but the poor performance of its coalition partners led to the loss of the Basque government. Patxi López of the PSE became the first non-nationalist *lehendakari*, sustained by a startling alliance with the PP that found common cause in the struggle against ETA. His government acted firmly against terrorism, seeking to delegitimise ETA and its supporters in Basque society and move on from the bitter divisions of the Ibarretxe years. However, an air of unreality clouded its claims to the 'normalisation' of Basque politics in that it rested on an alliance that many Basques found unnatural—and the continuing exclusion of the nationalist left.[6]

The end of ETA's ceasefire exposed internal contradictions within the MLNV. It marked the frustration of the first attempt to resolve the Basque conflict since Lizarra, despite years of internal reflection, the conversations with Eguiguren, the proposal put forward at Anoeta and unprecedented international involvement. The intensity of the government campaign against it reduced Batasuna's capacity to reflect on what had happened and consider its next steps. But when Otegi re-emerged from prison in August 2008 he and others began a process of significant change. Building on a critical assessment of what had gone wrong in the past, it had at its centre the realisation that unless the nationalist left collectively was able to find a way to move beyond the armed struggle it was 'inexorably heading for a precipice of political marginalisation and ideological drift', as Otegi later would put it.[6]

Post mortem

In the short term, the breakdown of ETA's ceasefire represented humiliation for Zapatero and Rubalcaba, and an implicit political victory for the PP. It also marked the end of the road for classically structured negotiations between any government of Spain and ETA. The government's motives for engagement had been opportunity—rather than need—based. They stemmed from recognition that, contrary to the views of the PP, the 'defeat' of ETA could not be achieved without dialogue, and confidence that the moderating tendencies within Batasuna and ETA could deliver peace. ETA, however, had showed bad faith throughout. It never fully broke with extortion or *kale borroka* or abandoned the idea that it could use violence to exert pressure on the government. 'The process failed,' as Eguiguren and Aizpeolea put it, 'because there was never a decision within ETA to end its terrorism. As ETA did not take this decision the process acquired an infernal dynamic which led to its breakdown.'[7] More broadly, as Imaz had stated soon after the breakdown of the Loyola talks, ETA had refused 'to abandon its old role as tutor or guarantor of political agreements between Basque parties'. The peace process had therefore exposed 'fear and vertigo within the radical left to engage in politics without the tutelage of violence'.[8]

Yet condemnation of ETA could not quiet questions regarding the conduct of the peace process by the government.[9] Despite the years of preparation by Eguiguren, the government demonstrated little strategic depth in its approach to ETA, and no capacity to address the very serious difficulties it encountered. Negotiations over terrorism, Zartman and Faure observe, 'lie on the fragile, delicate edge of the possible and exemplify the most tentative aspects of the general negotiation process'.[10] Like other negotiations between conflict parties, they involve a deal or a pact between the more moderate forces on each side, and the construction of broader support to secure the legitimacy and implementation of what has been agreed. In a democratic state, with an open press and an independent judiciary, let alone the highly polarised environment of Zapatero's Spain, in which hatred of ETA represented one of the few unifying features of public life, the challenge represented by this already difficult task was multiplied.

After the breakdown of ETA's ceasefire, it was hard to avoid the conclusion that neither Zapatero's actions nor the underlying conditions in Spain had been up to this challenge. Patxo Unzueta, the leading commentator on ETA in the opinion pages of *El País*, recalled that 'the big secret' of the peace process had turned out to be that, 'there wasn't any': 'when things were going badly in the autumn of 2006, we trusted that Zapatero knew more than we did—but he didn't'.[11] Basque analysts Kepa Aulestia and José Luis Zubizarreta charged that he had acted with 'naïvete' and a 'lack of professionalism' and wondered how he could not have paid more attention to information from the police and French and Spanish intelligence services regarding ETA's activities.[12] Zapatero was reviled by the right for having praised Otegi as 'a man of peace' (what he had actually said was that Otegi offered 'a discourse of peace')[13] and for his heedless observation in October 2006 that Iñaki de Juana was among those *etarras* who favoured the peace process.[14] Such statements seemed to confirm his essential *frivolidad*—a word with wider resonance in Spanish than 'frivolity' that nevertheless captures the lightness or lack of seriousness that many saw as one of his greatest flaws.

ETA was an organisation with a notoriously opaque organisational structure; it inhabited an enclosed and largely clandestine environment in which its increasingly anachronistic world view was justified by what it saw as the heroism and sacrifices of its past, both intrinsically bound to the practice of violence. Battered though it was by a string of arrests, a decision to bring the armed struggle to an end—and thus negate its very existence—was always going to be extremely difficult. That Zapatero embarked on a formal peace process in the face of the openly declared hostility of the main opposition party, and judges who held the capacity to ratchet up the legal campaign against ETA and those in its orbit in their hands, made it almost impossible.

Rajoy made an attack upon the process with ETA the centrepiece of a debate on the state of the nation in early July 2007. He accused Zapatero of 'lying to an unprecedented extent' and charged that ETA had been 're-constituted, emboldened and strengthened with the hope of seeing us one day on our knees'. He called upon Zapatero to return to the anti-terrorist pact and unity between political parties based on a determination to 'defeat ETA'. Citing his 'embarrassment' that the government had used outside mediators to engage with ETA, Rajoy also demanded that the government publish the records of the conversations prior to the 2006 ceasefire held by the HD Centre in a secure location—a request that the government had no intention of heeding.[15] This aggressive stance put ETA at the centre of political discussion. Journalists and intellectuals who had written little about ETA while it was killing on a regular basis crowded Spain's media, calling for a heroic struggle against the terrorists that would only culminate when their 'final defeat' was achieved.[16] As in the aftermath of the Lizarra ceasefire, a hard line against terrorism, the championing of victims and a defence of the constitution provided clothing for a familiar form of Spanish nationalism. Outrage at the perfidies of the Socialists fuelled criticism that the 'so-called' peace process had 'weakened the moral fibre with which societies and institutions should contemplate and combat the terrorist phenomenon', as José Antonio Zarzalejos, the former editor of *ABC*, fulminated.[17]

In the battle for public opinion the government projected somewhat contradictory narratives. Across Spain, it sought to emphasise what it had not done: it had not made political concessions to ETA on self-determination, on Navarre or the constitution; nor had it demonstrated any clemency at all towards ETA's prisoners, with the confused exception of de Juana. In the Basque Country, in contrast, it was important to show that it had gone to the greatest lengths possible in pursuit of peace, especially as most Basques (75 per cent) believed that the government had failed to explain the peace process adequately.[18] The PP and the nationalist left were—as could be expected—largely critical of the government's actions. Others appreciated the effort demonstrated by the PSE and Zapatero, even as plenty of Basques believed that more could have been done to build confidence in the process. This might have included moving prisoners closer to the Basque Country—something still supported by 69 per cent of Basques[19]—relaxing the special regimes that Basque prisoners were subject to or pursuing the repeal of the Parot Doctrine. A bolder gesture would have been to take unilateral action to comply with its commitment to facilitate the activities of Batasuna and engagement with it.

Differences in the narratives reflected the ambiguity that had clouded the process from the beginning, on the part of the government as well as ETA. This was most evident in its acceptance of the two-track model proposed at Anoeta, predicated on a political as well as 'technical' process, despite the affirmation that peace could be achieved without a political price. But it was present also in the confused status of the 2005 talks between Eguiguren and Ternera, and thus the unrealistic nature of the confidential agreements with which they concluded. Rubalcaba's scepticism, never fully hidden within political circles despite his loyalty to Zapatero, had proven well founded.

Eguiguren and Otegi separately sought to analyse what went wrong.[20] ETA and Batasuna had entered the peace process believing they had obtained assurances on its development from Eguiguren and the PSOE. They had not fully appreciated either the fragility of Zapatero's position or the gulf dividing Eguiguren from Madrid. Eguiguren and the government, meanwhile, had been ignorant of ETA's internal dynamics and paid little attention to a dissonance between ETA and Batasuna that was not helped by the isolation, until May 2007, of the latter from the international mediators. Ternera—whom Eguiguren remembers as a deeply serious negotiator, 'austere and methodical, sober in his words'[21]—had negotiated agreements that ETA had understood in a literal sense. ETA and the nationalist left more broadly had been both surprised and confounded by the fact that the government had not approached the process with what they considered an equal degree of rigour.

Otegi was particularly critical of what he termed the 'improvisation' of the Socialists. 'They're Spanish and have a particular culture,' he recalled, '"I have a problem today and the important thing is that I resolve it today. If it creates more problems for me tomorrow, then I will sort them out tomorrow."' This approach, which he believed had applied to issues as diverse as the Parot Doctrine, the government's handling of the de Juana case and its commitments with regard to the *de facto* legalisation of Batasuna, had been hugely destabilising. 'If the government had been able to say, "we are not going to be able to guarantee that Batasuna can freely act even though we'd like to because we have these judges", well then, there would be no agreement, but at least we'd have been able to know what we were working with.'

Most fundamental were the differences over the balance between the two tracks proposed at Anoeta. For Batasuna it had been clear all along that the process would conclude with an end to violence—even if this central point had not been fully assumed by ETA. But the government, as Otegi put it, 'did not understand that we needed to construct an alternative to the armed struggle at the political level'.[22] It would later emerge that Thierry had lambasted both Otegi and Ternera for 'not having properly established the pillars for the political agreement amongst the parties', and for putting the technical track 'in the frontline of the process'.[23] While the government had thought it might be possible to achieve an end to violence on the cheap ('no political price'), for ETA it was, in the end, all political. Otegi and Rufi Etxeberria had been confronted with the depth of these differences in the meetings between the government and ETA held in Geneva in May 2007. On the long train ride back home, Etxeberria had turned to Otegi to say: 'This model of negotiation and strategy is finished.' Otegi would later recall the remark as triggering reflections that would lead to a profound change in the direction taken by the nationalist left—and ETA.[24]

Terror and counter-terror, again

The documents captured with Thierry received wide publicity in early 2011.[25] In addition to providing salacious details of the talks themselves, they added substance to the reports of divisions within the leadership of ETA that had been percolating through the Spanish media. Elaborate and unverifiable accounts of betrayals, coups and counter-coups within the organisation's leadership were at first riddled with inconsistencies: Thierry was the military leader, then political leader of ETA; he had been the hardliner responsible for breaking the process, or not; aligned with the actual military leader Txeroki, or locked in a bitter power struggle with him. In time, however, a clearer picture began to emerge, albeit one still derived from documents and recordings that had fallen into police hands. The level of detail conveyed by some of these reports—and especially books published by Florencio Domínguez and Ángeles Escrivá in 2012 (*La Agonía de ETA*, 'The Agony of ETA', and *Maldito el País que Necesita Héroes: Cómo los Demócratas Acabaron con ETA*, 'Unhappy the Land in Need of Heroes: How Democrats Finished with ETA')—was a consequence of the curiously bureaucratic nature of ETA. Whether for reasons of internal distrust or out of a sense of responsibility to the historical record, ETA wrote everything down. The elevated rate of its militants' capture had obvious consequences. 'The history of ETA,' concluded Domínguez, who had dedicated his entire career to its chronicling, 'ended up in the hands of the police.'[26]

ETA's return to violence came quickly. It exploded bombs in July and August 2007, targeting the route of the Tour de France, Durango in Vizcaya and Castellón in Valencia. In September it issued a statement warning that its violence would continue until it achieved self-determination, vowing 'to strike at Spanish state structures on all fronts'.[27] ETA attributed some of the blame for the process' failure to its own military weakness. The absence of killing for the three years before the ceasefire had, ETA believed, weakened its bargaining capacity. It could accept that bombing Barajas had not been successful as a means of putting pressure on the government but, employing a logic that at this point seemed delusional, it still believed that not sitting down to talk 'with bodies on the negotiating table' had been a mistake.[28] An interview with *Gara* in January 2008 confirmed a discourse of self-justification rooted in old claims that 'the Spanish state has not experienced a true democratic transition'.[29]

Constant surveillance and a string of arrests, including that of the organisation's suspected logistics chief, limited ETA's operational capacity. It did not kill until December, when a three-person commando cell chanced upon two members of the Guardia Civil having breakfast in a bar in Capbreton, France. *Etarras* followed the two into the parking lot and opened fire once they were back in their car. The incident was a rare example of the assassination of Spanish security forces on French soil and prompted the creation of permanent joint intelligence teams between Spanish and French police forces in January 2008.[30]

In the eighteen months that followed the end of the Lizarra ceasefire, ETA had claimed thirty-two victims. Between June 2007 and December 2008 its toll was just six. Despite threats to the contrary, ETA's actions had little effect on the Basque elections held in March 2009, and it did not act on the explicit threat it issued against members of the Basque government a few weeks later.[31] A further three victims were killed during the summer of 2009, two of them in a spate of attacks to mark ETA's fiftieth anniversary, before ETA's final victim, a French policemen, fell in March 2010. In the meantime a string of arrests dismantled the five operational cells ETA had activated after the end of the ceasefire as well as three successive leadership structures. By early 2010 an internal intelligence report described ETA as being 'at the edge of the abyss'.[32] At this point some 310 alleged members of ETA had been detained in Spain and France since the end of the ceasefire and the organisation was struggling with recruitment.[33] A high proportion of new recruits had long come from Segi and the world of *kale borroka*; many of these were lying low to avoid detention and did not want to join ETA. The calibre of those ETA was able to recruit had consequently fallen, contributing to perpetuate a cycle of detention and arrest, often before operations could materialise. ETA's 'insecurity and confusion' was viewed with alarm from inside the prisons, where the government had initiated a new campaign to encourage the disaffection of ETA prisoners from the rigid structures with which the organisation had long maintained internal cohesion.

The intelligence report suggested that the post-Antza leadership of ETA had been composed of a nucleus of five.[34] As Ternera had insisted to Eguiguren, he had not been within it. In 2007 Thierry, Ainhoa Ozaeta and Zubierola had formed one faction, heading the fronts responsible for its political and financial direction and the fabrication of false documents, while Txeroki and Ata commanded its military activities and logistics. During the peace process divisions had emerged as a consequence of a power struggle over how the process should be conducted. Txeroki and Ata had reportedly demanded greater speed and more concrete concessions from the government, while criticising Thierry for his comportment within the negotiations. An internal crisis threatened the first split in the organisation since 1974. It was precipitated by Ata in early 2008 when he presented a blistering written critique of the performance of Thierry and the two commanders aligned with him, calling for their removal. They responded with a three-two vote expelling Txeroki and Ata. But the arrest and detention of the victors in May 2008 (suspecting that they had been betrayed by Txeroki and Ata) turned the tables again. Txeroki and Ata expelled Thierry and those detained with him from ETA and—briefly—assumed the leadership of the organisation. After Txeroki's arrest in late 2008, Ata remained as the last of the original five.

Otegi had fully expected to be returned to prison at the ceasefire's end. But the extent of the legal assault upon others in Batasuna unleashed in early October 2007 was unprecedented. On 4 October Garzón ordered the detention of twenty-two members of the nationalist left who had gathered for a secret meeting in Olaberría, in the Goierri region of Guipúzcoa. Those detained—seventeen would be charged with membership of ETA—included Rufi Etxeberria, Joseba Permach and most of Batasuna's leadership (Joseba Álvarez had been arrested earlier in the week). Pernando Barrena remained at large; he denounced the detentions as 'an act of war' against the Basque independence movement.[35] Processes to ban both EHAK and the ANV had been opened and would be successfully completed in September 2008, and in December 2007 the Audiencia Nacional concluded its controversial eight-year 18/98 *macroproceso* with the conviction of forty-seven people for their ties to ETA.

One obvious result of the crackdown was a marked rise in the number of Basque prisoners accused of, or serving sentences for crimes related to, activities of ETA or associated with the broader nationalist left. The new arrests, compounded by the changes in the penal legislation that had ushered in longer sentences, brought the total number of those in the Basque Political Prisoners Collective (EPPK) to 755 by late 2008—the highest number since 1969. These 755 prisoners were dispersed across eighty-two prisons in Spain and France, with only sixteen of them within Basque prisons.[36] Authority within ETA or the nationalist left more broadly, as in the past, was shed when a militant entered prison. However, that the weight of the organisation—in terms of experience as well as numbers—was behind bars created a complicated dynamic. The prisoners had neither been consulted nor informed of the details of the peace process.[37] Rumblings of discontent grew in the post-ceasefire period, as on the one hand the prospects of some kind of negotiated solution to the prisoners' situation began to fade, and on the other the relative failure of ETA's military campaign exposed its incapacity to achieve its goals through violence.

Dispersion had disrupted ETA's ability to mobilise the prisoners as a political block, but it had not succeeded in breaking its control. Rather, a small nucleus of EPPK lawyers worked assiduously to communicate instructions to counter any inclination to engage with prison authorities on an individual basis and to coordinate sit-ins and other protests.[38] This left the prisoners, as Mercedes Gallizo, the director of prisons, recalled, as 'hostages to their organisation' rather than individuals serving out a sentence 'who have to start thinking about how to rebuild their lives'.[39] The special measures applicable to those imprisoned on charges related to terrorism kept the Basque prisoners in isolation modules, with many in solitary confinement for extended periods of time. They were unable to participate in usual prison activities, and lived within what Gallizo termed 'an invented reality'. Seen from inside the nationalist left, this reality was of struggle and sacrifice, in the service of the cause of Basque liberation. To Gallizo, on the other hand, they appeared, 'like robots of some kind… waiting to fulfil the orders that come from outside in the hope that this would help the great revolution that one day would arrive'.

The end of the ceasefire restored violence to the top of the list of concerns cited by Basques (21 per cent) in a *Euskobarómetro* opinion poll released in November 2007. The poll also revealed a rise in the number of Basques who expressed their 'total rejection' of ETA—although that this was to a figure of only 58 per cent indicated the complex emotions and allegiances that pervade Basque society. More than a quarter of Basques had once justified ETA's violence but could do so no more (18 per cent) or shared ETA's ends but not its violent methods (10 per cent). The poll's authors characterised these positions as 'remote support' for ETA, even as they noted the 'practical disappearance' of 'total and explicit support' (to 0.4 per cent) as an important finding. It was accompanied by evidence that only 2 per cent of Basques—and 8 per cent of those who had voted for the nationalist left (EHAK) in 2005—offered 'critical support' to ETA. The clear implication was that the vast majority of those within the nationalist left no longer supported ETA's violence, but retained allegiance to its political goals.[40]

Both the identity of the victims in the post-ceasefire period and the circumstances of their killing heightened this dissonance. Logistical and operational weakness meant that ETA was for the most part limited to 'easy' targets. Meanwhile the charged political atmosphere and extensive media attention to the organisation's straightened circumstances elevated the impact of its violence to an unprecedented degree. Each new killing prompted a massive and emotional condemnation of ETA. Particularly shocking were the two victims individually targeted in the course of 2008. ETA assassinated Isaías Carrasco, a former PSE councillor close to Eguiguren, two days before the general elections held on 9 March. It gunned down the Basque nationalist businessman, Ignacio Uría—who had ties to the Eusko Alkartasuna (EA) party—in Azpeitia, Guipúzcoa, on 3 December. Between them ETA killed a member of the Guardia Civil, in May 2008, and a brigadier in the Spanish Army, in September 2008.

The government suspended all election campaigning in response to Carrasco's assassination—a reaction that appeared to hand ETA exactly the kind of publicity it craved. The killing of Uría, ostensibly because of his company's involvement in a planned new high-speed train, the *Y vasca*—so called because it was to provide a long overdue link between Euskadi's three provincial capitals—was no less destabilising. The *Y vasca* had been subject to attacks by ETA reminiscent of its earlier campaigns against the Lemoníz nuclear power plant and Leizarán motorway for their broad anti-capitalist and ecological goals. But support for the campaign within the nationalist left was not rock solid, even before ETA killed Uría.[41] ETA's action led to the collapse of Azpeitia's municipal government, which had been run by an alliance between EA and the ANV, after the latter refused to condemn the assassination. It also created 'many internal contradictions', as one young member of Batasuna carefully put it, 'because of his age, because of his status, because he was a nationalist'.[42] Several prominent members of the nationalist left—among them Iñaki Antigüedad, a former deputy in the Basque Parliament, and Mikel Álvarez, Joseba's brother—publicly spoke out against the assassination, calling for ETA to stop its 'tutelage of Basque society'.[43] Many more voiced their criticism more quietly.

'Thou shalt not negotiate'

'"Thou shalt not negotiate", the candidate's first commandment'—was the title of an article written by Ramón Sola in *Gara* in early 2008.[44] The phrase represented the bottom-line of the anti-terrorist policies espoused by both the PSOE and PP as they campaigned for the March 2008 general elections. Sola's point was that it always had been thus. Every aspiring prime minister since Spain's transition had vowed never to negotiate with ETA, yet every elected prime minister had ended up trying to do so.

There were indications suggesting that this time things would be different. Zapatero and Rubalcaba could not have been clearer in their demands for ETA to renounce violence and accept defeat, and for Batasuna either to persuade ETA to do so, or split from the armed organisation, choosing 'bombs or votes'. Electoral logic dictated that the PSOE had everything to gain from maintaining a hard line on this issue. And in March 2008 the PSOE was returned to power with a slightly increased vote over 2004, burying forever the idea that Zapatero's government was illegitimate.[45] Zapatero and Rajoy reached a formal truce at a meeting on 23 July. 'Goodbye to *crispación*' read the editorial in *El País* the next day.[46] At the truce's core was a pact on anti-terrorist policy that included a commitment to promote a reform of the law of solidarity with victims of terrorism, the removal of street names and other visible symbols perceived to glorify terrorism, and five principles that should govern anti-terrorist policy. The two parties agreed to unite behind a shared strategy, to enhance support to victims, to rely exclusively on the rule of law and the security forces, not to pay a political price for the end of ETA and on international co-operation.[47]

Before the elections Zapatero had confirmed his appreciation of the limits of counter-terrorism. Asked by *20 Minutos* (in an interview whose headline statement was the unfortunate observation that 'there is no risk of an economic crisis') to clarify whether he believed police action could 'end' or would only 'weaken' ETA he had stated: 'Weaken a great deal. I think we have to be honest. We have been using police means against ETA for more than forty years and it has not been easy.'[48] Such frankness was missing from the agreement with Rajoy, which included no reference to the possible end of ETA. But controversy was not so easily avoided. 'We said there is no place for dialogue with ETA,' Rajoy claimed straight after the meeting. 'The government has changed its position—it has accepted ours and I will support it.' His statement prompted the agreement's immediate rejection by the PNV, which continued to insist that some sort of dialogue with ETA would in the end be necessary (a position supported by some 84 per cent of Basques).[49]

Only after Zapatero personally explained to Josu Erkoreka, the PNV spokesman in parliament, that the agreement did not include the explicit rejection of dialogue with ETA once it had acknowledged defeat—and in this respect was in conformity with the Ajuria Enea Pact—did the PNV come around.[50]

Debate over the legitimacy of dialogue found further fuel from the spectacle created by the prosecution of Ibarretxe, Patxi López and Rodolfo Ares for meeting with Batasuna in the course of the peace process. The cases proceeded despite a November 2006 decision by the Supreme Court to reject charges against Zapatero and other officials filed by the far-right pseudo-union Manos Limpias ('Clean Hands') for the meeting the previous July that was now a subject of investigation.[51] As the cases dragged on towards their predictable dismissal in early 2010, they presented a sorry picture of the knots into which the justice system was prepared to tie itself over Basque issues. They also helped preserve an unrealistic and at times hysterical sensitivity around the question of dialogue. In this environment any admission that 'one day' there might be a need for talks, even if current circumstances rendered them impossible, was immediately jumped upon (as Eguiguren found to his cost when he conceded as much in an interview with *El Correo* in October 2008 and was vehemently criticised by the PP).[52]

Rajoy and Zapatero had found it easy to agree to work together to block the popular consultation proposed by Ibarretxe. The *lehendakari* had announced his intention to pursue a new political proposal in the summer of 2007. The was pre-emptively subjected to a barrage of criticism, including from within the PNV; Imaz took the unusual step of issuing a written critique of Ibarretxe's plans that brought into public the party's divisions.[53] Ibarretxe conceived his consultation as consisting of two questions that in other circumstances might have been considered eminently reasonable: one asked if the respondent would support a solution to violence through dialogue, if ETA had previously expressed its unequivocal intention to end violence; the other if Basque political parties should initiate negotiations to reach a democratic agreement on the right to decide.[54] He consciously drew upon the text of the draft agreement that ETA had rejected at Loyola. But the circumstances had changed dramatically. The consultation was put to a vote in the Basque Parliament in June 2009 and, like the Ibarretxe Plan before it, passed only because of the support of the nationalist left. However, a single vote from EHAK—of the nine at its disposal—was not much of an endorsement. The government had already prepared its legal challenge and in September the Constitutional Court unanimously ruled the consultation unconstitutional.

Imaz resigned from his position within the PNV in September 2008, unwilling to contemplate the kind of schism that the party had seen in the mid-1980s. Urkullu became the PNV's new president, but Imaz's departure left Ibarretxe the dominant force, to the great discomfort of Madrid. The Basque elections of March 2009 were rapidly approaching, and the Socialists scented an opportunity to do what had long seemed impossible: unseat Basque nationalism from the autonomous government it had lead since 1980. Clearly in their favour was the fact that Batasuna and its surrogates would be out of the electoral picture: in February 2009 the Supreme Court accepted the government's submission that new political platforms formed by the nationalist left, D3M (Demodrazia 3 Milioi) and Askatasuna, were successors of Batasuna and banned them both.

Batasuna digs in

Over the winter of 2008–9 the nationalist left was at low ebb. Comprehensively discredited by the end of the peace process, Batasuna was an illegal political party with most of its leadership behind bars. ETA was actively pursuing a violent campaign that found dwindling support among its social and political bases, and had successfully united all other Basque and Spanish political forces against it. Counter-terrorist policies had never enjoyed wider backing or greater operational success, while complaints about their intrusion on Basques' rights fell on deaf ears. Cross-community dialogue was all but silent, and comparisons with Northern Ireland muted. Hopes for a new peace process, or anything approximating it, were at a low. Visiting the Basque Country in September 2008, the Irish journalist Paddy Woodworth was shunned by long-time contacts. 'I had never seen such pessimism amongst those characterised by different ideologies as on this visit,' he would recall in the article he wrote for the Spanish edition of *Vanity Fair*. He found the nationalist left, in particular, 'disoriented and lacking leadership after the judicial offensive [against it]'.[55]

The disorientation reflected profound internal divisions and a looming internal struggle between a group of individuals gathered around

Arnaldo Otegi and other leaders of Batasuna, and ETA and hardliners in other entities of the nationalist left. An Ekin document of this period exposed the breach between those who were resigned to a long-term struggle (and violence) with negotiations between ETA and the government as the eventual goal, and those who maintained that it was necessary to begin working towards 'a new political cycle' for which the strategy should not remain limited to a 'hypothetical' process of negotiations.[56] Batasuna described this split in a document it released in 2010: 'Those in the first position considered that after the breakdown of the negotiations attempted between 2005 and 2007 there was no means by which to find a solution in the short term. They therefore foresaw a long cycle of confrontation/resistance. The second position gave priority to the fact that the work carried out in the past decade—concretely what had taken root in the last negotiation process—had opened up the possibility of political change.'[57] Resolving these divisions would be a slow and difficult process.

Otegi, whom Woodworth had known since 1998, had been among those who had refused to meet with him. Any hope that he would be elevated above ETA by the peace process had been dashed. Instead of growing into the role of peacemaker ('man of peace') he had been imprisoned before, during and after the talks between the government and ETA. He had been humiliated by ETA at Loyola and again by ETA's return to violence at Barajas. For many outside the nationalist left his refusal to break with ETA at that point had been a disappointment, the moment at which he had failed to display what the veteran Basque journalist Ander Landerburu would describe as the 'courage and authority' of a true leader. By the summer of 2009, Otegi had re-emerged onto the political scene but perceptions of him outside his political orbit remained low. Landaburu claimed many people now saw him as a 'clown'; Kepa Aulestia, who knew Otegi many years earlier in the *polimilis*, described him as a *trilero* or a 'card-sharp', capable of trying to sell you anything.[58]

Otegi would try to deflect attention from his own persona by referring to the nationalist left as a 'collective Gerry Adams', partly in deference to the puritanical streak within the movement that looked gravely on any cult of personality. But the strength of his character, political and communication skills made such self-effacement difficult. During the months he spent in Martutene prison after the end of ETA's ceasefire, he had dedicated himself to an analysis of the frustrated dialogue process and its implications for the future. As he would describe in the book-length interview he wrote from prison in 2012, *El Tiempo de las Luces*, ('The Time of Lights'), he became convinced of the need to begin a profound debate on the future of the nationalist left, conscious that it would need to question much 'of what had been held to be immutable for decades'.[59] To unblock the situation, Otegi believed it was necessary to do three things: to conduct a rigorous personal and collective self-criticism of the actions taken by ETA and the nationalist left as a whole in the previous processes; to understand that only by political and democratic means would it be possible to try to build the majority support necessary to reach their goals, and therefore continuing the armed struggle—besides giving the government 'the perfect excuse to distort the political conflict and place it in a scheme of "anti-terrorism"'—was directly counter-productive; and, perhaps most critically, to embark on a path towards a new process unilaterally, without 'waiting for anyone or anything'.[60]

Otegi emerged from prison in August 2008, conscious that he might have a limited time to lay the groundwork for a new process before being detained again. He spent three months out of the public eye, consulting widely within the nationalist left regarding ideas that he knew represented a direct confrontation with the official strategy promoted by ETA. On 30 November he re-emerged onto the Basque political scene in an interview with *Gara* he gave in a personal capacity.[61] He explained that he had used the time since his release from prison to talk to people, and to listen. The conclusion he had come to was the need to create a pro-independence political block or 'pole', combining the nationalist left but also other political forces to the left of the PNV. Such a block would change the balance of nationalist politics within the Basque Country and allow for decisive steps to be taken towards a situation in which Basques would be able to exercise their right to decide. Otegi's proposal built on a central lesson of the peace process: ETA and the nationalist left alone could not take on the government and nor, after Lizarra and Loyola, could they rely on support from the PNV.

The interview reflected Otegi's conviction that violence had become an obstacle to the political goals of radical nationalism. Most obviously, any proposal for a pro-independence block in itself pre-supposed the end to ETA's violence that would be demanded by other political parties. The idea for a 'block' drew in part on conversations with Unai Ziarreta, the leader of EA, who had announced his party's split from the PNV as a result of Ibarretxe's passive acceptance of the prohibition of his proposed consultation.[62] Ziarreta had visited Otegi in prison, and conversations with EA had continued after his release. ETA endorsed the idea of the pro-independence alliance, but had not absorbed what it would mean: as its killing of Uría in early December—obviously damaging the talks with EA—had illustrated, it still conceived the alliance as being compatible with a broader political-military strategy. The nationalist left had issued a statement that observed that the 'blockage, confrontation and the abuse of rights demand efforts to reach definitive solutions' and called for 'a debate and strategic reflection that will allow Basque society to open a cycle of conflict resolution by political and democratic means'. Although widely ignored amidst the condemnation of the Uría killing, the statement was seen as 'really significant' within the enclosed world of its militants.[63]

As Batasuna struggled to formulate the means by which it would present itself to the Basque elections held in March, Otegi's ideas gained support. Otegi himself spoke forcefully at an event held at San Sebastián's Kursaal in January on the need to 'confront the state on its weak point, the political terrain'. Rafa Diéz had long seen no hope of a political process with Madrid in the presence of ETA's violence.[64] He was a friend of Otegi's and now began calling openly for 'an accumulation of forces' to move towards a democratic process. But their efforts met opposition from ETA. A letter Díez wrote in March to a friend in prison described a 'positive evolution' but warned that there still existed a 'tendency to believe that everything is compatible, and that this reflection and discourse can complement other things' ('everything' and 'other things' both referred to ETA's armed action)—something that 'would lead to another monumental mess'.[65] Discussions took root within wider circles within the nationalist left, as Otegi reached out to influential younger leaders and former ETA prisoners. One prominent ally was Eugenio Etxebeste, *Antxon*, the former ETA leader who for so many years had been the organisation's principal interlocutor with any real or would-be mediators. Released from prison in early 2004, Antxon had returned to San Sebastián after three decades outside the Basque Country. No longer a militant of ETA, he saw himself as involved in 'another kind of struggle', and immersed himself in the effort.[66]

But it was not easy. Otegi, Antxon and others were derided as *los gandhis* by some of the younger and more hard-headed members of the nationalist left.[67] Some still saw that violence offered the greatest potential for exerting pressure on the state, others experienced doubts as to what the proposed change could achieve, or quite simply just confusion. The broad contours of political-military struggle had been established so long ago that envisioning what might lie beyond them, and how this could be conceived other than in terms of 'defeat' was difficult; the options offered by the government appeared to be, as one member of Batasuna put it in May 2009, 'surrender or surrender'.[68] Moreover, the results of Basque elections—which ETA and Batasuna both criticised as 'anti-democratic' for their exclusion of the nationalist left—had proven a disappointment. D3M had received some 100,000 null votes, 50,000 less than the votes received by EHAK in 2005. At less than 9 per cent of the votes cast, this was the nationalist left's weakest electoral performance in its history. Deepening the blow was the strong performance of Aralar, which had emerged as a non-violent radical nationalist alternative to win 62,500 votes and four seats in the Basque Parliament.[69] Writing in *El País* Luis Aizpeolea cited phrases from disillusioned ETA prisoners, 'I didn't expect it. I am flipping out. For me it is a big disaster.'[70]

At a press conference after the election Otegi was surrounded by other significant figures within the nationalist left as he announced a round of contacts with 'those who want to build a state for this country' (the pro-independence forces) and delivered an assessment of the election results as a tribute to a capacity for resistance in the face of a 'brutal [campaign] of persecution, repression and imprisonment'.[71] But he also acknowledged that there was no room for self-congratulation: 'we are more than 100,000… we know that with 100,000 we don't win a democratic scenario nor, in the long term, a Basque state, so we will have to grow'.[72] Already planned as a means of building support for the nationalist left's new proposals were actions for *Aberri Eguna* (the Basque day of independence, celebrated on Easter Sunday), and the first of May, a 'general strike' by pro-independence forces later that month, and some form of participation within elections to the European Parliament to be held in June. On the horizon was the hard deadline represented by the local and municipal elections due in May 2011: if Batasuna or some version of it was not able to contest these elections it would be left outside all political institutions and perhaps terminally marginalised from political life.

The PSE and the PNV had both performed well in the Basque elections: the PSE received over 30 per cent of the vote, and twenty-five seats, far exceeding all its previous results, and the PNV more than 38 per cent and thirty seats. But support for the PNV's former allies in government, EA and IU-EB, had almost disappeared, and they won just one seat each in parliament.[73] In the absence of EHAK or any successor the PNV was no longer in a position to lead a nationalist coalition. After a few days of back-room conversations with Madrid the contours of a new Basque political reality emerged. This saw Patxi López become *lehendakari* at the head of a government formed with the support of the Basque PP, which had experienced something of a revival since 2004 under the leadership of Antonio Basagoiti. The alliance was in many respects unlikely. The PP and the PSOE were at loggerheads on almost every political, economic and social issue other than their policies towards ETA, and memories of the divisive policies pursued by the Aznar government were fresh. Many Basques—including many Socialist voters—had a much higher degree of comfort with the centrist PNV-PSE coalitions they had seen in the past.[74] But others, and certainly most Spaniards outside the Basque Country, greeted the new government as a breath of fresh air after the long period of nationalist hegemony. The first days of May 2009 remained 'engraved in the memory of many', as Ángeles Escrivá would observe, 'as the most emotional of the last thirty years in Euskadi'.[75]

The election results represented a personal triumph for Jesús Eguiguren, although one not without some irony. The PSE had been rewarded for the 'Basquist' direction he had encouraged it to pursue and his—and its—efforts within the peace process, but now entered government on the basis of a platform whose unifying feature was an approach to ETA exclusively concentrated on counter-terrorism. Eguiguren remained president of the PSE but stayed outside government, surfacing at regular intervals in the Basque press with opinions that were not always to the liking of his party. Otegi had briefed him on the changes he and others were trying to introduce, but in late May 2009 Eguiguren saw their path ahead as difficult.[76] The 'national strike' in his view had fallen flat; ETA's actions and statements—it had just announced internal consultations 'to establish an effective political and armed strategy'[77]—limited relations with other political forces; and the PSE-PP alliance had strengthened the hand of the Basque and national governments against both

Batasuna and ETA. Otegi was openly advocating a return to dialogue in campaign appearances for the Iniciativa Internacionalista, a leftist political party that the Constitutional Court had allowed to contest European elections. Eguiguren reaffirmed the government position that no such dialogue would take place. Yet he remained convinced that, by one means or another, the 'problem' represented by ETA's violence would come to an end. 'It will finish one way, or it will finish another… if there is no dialogue, Batasuna will have to disentangle itself from the violence, or it will disappear.'[78]

International dimensions

Rubalcaba's determination to shore up international support for Spain's efforts against ETA went hand-in-hand with an attempt to undermine ETA and Batasuna in the eyes of the international community. 'ETA broke the ceasefire,' as he recalled, 'and found that democratic governments blamed it.'[79] Other governments, just as he had expected, had no hesitation in heaping opprobrium on ETA for the end of the process and offering sympathy and continued counter-terrorism co-operation to Spain. The Batasuna-friendly political parties in the 'Friendship Group' within the European Parliament entered a period of confusion and even Sinn Féin adopted a degree of coolness, careful not to complicate its own profile as a party that had made a definitive break with violence.

Batasuna had been keenly aware of the risks of its isolation. 'One of our greatest fears,' explained one of its senior representatives in July 2010, was that when the peace process ended, 'we would close all the doors we had opened.'[80] The spate of arrests and uncertainty over its political future necessarily led to a period of retrenchment. However, carefully and quietly, Batasuna took steps to ensure that its communication with the most significant international actors the last process had brought it into contact with—not least the somewhat heterogeneous grouping that Otegi and Etxeberria had met for the first time in Geneva in May 2007—was never broken. Geneva had opened the door for Batasuna to international contacts that had until then solely been managed by ETA; it had also allowed Batasuna to demonstrate to them that there was a considerable gulf between their ideas and ambitions and those of ETA. Although contacts were necessarily managed in deep secrecy, Otegi would later recall that, as the May meetings were ending, he had formally asked the internationals present in Geneva that, whatever might happen in the future, they should 'not cease their efforts to find an agreed solution to the conflict'. He also confirmed that 'never again (even in prison) did we not maintain a fluid communication with them'.[81]

In June 2008 José Luis Barbería sharply countered a claim by Zapatero that international support to ETA had been 'radically reduced' in an extensive report in *El País*.[82] He described Spain as a 'pole of attraction for international experts in conflict resolution—the well known "mediation industry"', as well as a parade of human rights rapporteurs. The nationalist left's capacity to engage with international interlocutors extended from the traditional kind of solidarity and advocacy work conducted by Askapena—an organisation originally formed to provide solidarity to Central American revolutionaries—in Latin America, to advocacy with the human rights community, and outreach to Europe's minority parties. A new grouping of European parliamentarians, the Guernica Network for Self-Determination, had held its first meeting in November 2007. Meanwhile, the nationalist left had stayed closely attuned to the rise of Flemish nationalism in Belgium, pressures for autonomy from Denmark in Greenland and the active campaign of the Scottish National Party for independence from Britain. Batasuna maintained bilateral contacts with other minority groups such as the Kurds and a continuing engagement with South Africa, all in addition to its constant ties to Northern Ireland.

Spain was in a strong position to monitor and limit the nationalist left's interactions with other states or multilateral bodies. But it had a much harder time restricting contacts with sympathetic individual officials, parliamentarians, human rights bodies or NGOs. It made intermittent efforts to do so, at times enlisting partners such as the Basque Fundación para la Libertad ('Foundation for Freedom') to offer a 'constitutionalist' view of the Basque Country in opposition to the decidedly partial vision presented by the nationalist left.[83] In September 2007, two representatives of the foundation, Javier Elorrieta and Teo Uriarte, took the by now well-travelled route between the Basque Country and South Africa to try to counter what they saw as the distortion of Basque reality by the ties that had developed between South Africans and Batasuna, but also Ibarretxe and Basque nationalism more broadly.[84] The foundation also visited Geneva in an effort to assert its views within the UN Human Rights Council. In March 2009 it offered a critical response to the report—much maligned by the Spanish government, which also offered its own formal rebuttal—on his visit to Spain the previous year by Martin Scheinin, the UN Special Rapporteur on the promotion and protection of human rights and fundamental freedoms while countering terrorism.[85] However, its efforts had only limited impact on the effective lobbying of Batasuna, or concerns of the international human rights community.

Brian Currin was among those individuals who remained involved in efforts directed to the revival of some kind of peace process. After the end of the ceasefire Batasuna had asked him to help sustain international involvement and the channels to other Basque parties it had established during the peace process.[86] Currin formed an International Group for Dialogue and Peace in the Basque Country, whose other members were Roelf Meyer, Nuala O'Loan, the former police ombudsman in Northern Ireland, and Raymond Kendall, the former secretary-general of Interpol. The group visited the Basque Country several times, but it was a bleak period and it achieved little. Currin concluded that only a fundamental change of direction would bring dividends and proposed to Batasuna that he draw on South African experience to suggest 'why it is important for the nationalist left to move into completely new political space'. The paper he subsequently delivered in September 2008 set out to explain how a political opposition movement—South Africa's United Democratic Front (UDF)—'created space for itself to operate legally in a highly conflictual, repressive political environment by renouncing violence and using solely peaceful means to achieve its political objectives'.[87]

Currin prepared himself with some nervousness for a meeting with Otegi in November 2008. He intended to say that unless Batasuna could commit to 'a process where you can be legalised—and we know what the implications of that are—there is nothing more I can do'. To his surprise he had found Otegi 'already there'. Currin was convinced that Otegi's change on the core issue of violence was for real, and began to work from outside, as well on periodic visits to the Basque Country, to support it. As he did so, he met discreetly with a number of officials across Europe who had followed the earlier process to brief them on developments in Batasuna's thinking. Working from the principles established by George Mitchell as the basis for Northern Ireland's peace process—the first was that all involved in negotiations had to affirm their commitment to democratic and exclusively peaceful means of resolving political issues; others related to disarmament and its verification by an independent commission[88]—he also began discussing a draft of a statement that Batasuna might make as it sought to move towards legalisation. Currin's efforts were evidently disquieting to the government; it requested representatives of other states neither to meet with him, nor fund his activities. He believed that it saw him as trying to rally international support against Madrid, but insisted this was not the case. Rather, what he was trying to do, as he explained in August 2009, was 'to help Batasuna and ETA end, and to provide that end with international support'.[89]

How difficult this was going to be had been demonstrated by a resurgence of ETA's activity in June and July that was indicative of serious tensions within the nationalist left. ETA had opposed Batasuna's decision to endorse the Iniciativa Internacionalista within the European elections, having originally favoured an electoral alliance with EA. When that became obviously impossible (EA had been battered by its poor results in the elections to the Basque Parliament and was in any case not about to agree to an electoral alliance with the nationalist left) it had wanted Batasuna either to secure legalisation for a new political initiative or to abstain. ETA had been forced to accept Iniciativa Internacionalista as a *fait accompli* but had written to Batasuna afterwards to complain: 'Where are decisions being taken? Is there someone taking their own line outside that of the direction? We are not trying to look for "the internal enemy", but having read the communications and meeting notes it is difficult for us to see where this decision came from.'[90] Batasuna had emerged somewhat strengthened by the dispute as, after its energetic campaigning, Iniciativa Internacionalista won nearly 140,000 votes in Euskadi and Navarre in the European elections, a considerable improvement on the null votes cast for D3M in March.[91]

ETA, however, made its presence felt. On 19 June, just two weeks after the elections, it killed Eduardo Puelles, a Basque inspector in the national police with a brother in the Ertzaintza. His assassination prompted a frenzy of outraged condemnations. In the following days López, newly installed as *lehendakari*, led an emotional demonstration in Bilbao alongside Puelles' grieving widow, and the Basque Parliament offered a formal homage to his memory. This combination of events—in parallel to a widely criticised communiqué from the nationalist left that equated Puelles's death to detentions and the recent disappearance of the *etarra* Jon Anza in France—was seized upon as an indication of the changes afoot in Euskadi.[92] Rodolfo Ares, now the Basque government's interior minister, mounted a campaign of 'zero tolerance' against *kale borroka*, photographs of prisoners and other manifestations of support for ETA as part of a wider effort to delegitimise violence and promote *convivencia*, 'coexistence', in Basque society.[93] This involved considerable harassment of the nationalist left, including in the village and community fiestas that are a mainstay of the Basque summer. Those detained even for displaying an imprisoned relative's photograph were charged with 'glorification of terrorism'.

For Batasuna worse was to come. On 30 June 2009 the European Court of Human Rights issued a long-awaited ruling on its challenge to its dissolution by the Supreme Court under the political parties' law. Batasuna was not expecting to win its appeal outright, but had held out hopes for the recognition of liberties related to political participation and free association.[94] In this respect it had been encouraged by the nuanced critique of the law given by Scheinin in his recent report to the UN Human Rights Council. Scheinin had noted that Article 9 (2) of the law might be interpreted to 'include any political party which through peaceful political means seeks similar political objectives as those pursued by terrorist groups' and insisted that 'all limitations on the right to political participation must meet strict criteria in order to be compatible with international standards'.[95] The European Court, however, upheld the position of the Spanish government in terms that legitimised some of the most questioned aspects of its counter-terrorist legislation. Its judgment acknowledged that the Supreme Court's findings had to be placed 'in the context of an international wish to condemn the public defence of terrorism' and confirmed that the illegalisation of Batasuna had responded to a 'pressing social need' and the existence of links between the 'applicant parties' (Herri Batasuna and Batasuna) and ETA. Those links could 'objectively be considered a threat to democracy'.[96] The court's ruling maintained—and in this point it went further than Spanish jurisprudence—that even though the illegalisation of Batasuna did not rest solely on its refusal to condemn ETA's terrorist attacks, this 'would not have been in contradiction with' the European Convention on Human Rights'.

The ruling, as Otegi acknowledged, was a 'catastrophe' for Batasuna—both for what it meant in political terms and for its symbolic value. It had demolished years of work against the political parties' law on human rights' grounds as well as the idealisation of Europe within the MLNV since the time of Franco as 'the bastion of great liberties'. In the short term it represented an obvious setback to the launch of a new political process.[97] 'It couldn't be worse,' was the Batasuna lawyer Jone Goirizelaia's bleak verdict.[98] For Spain's constitutionalist parties, of course, it could not have been better. The judgment represented a milestone in the long struggle against terrorism, all the sweeter because of the complicated position in which it put the PNV, whose criticism of the political parties' law had become more ringing in the months since it lost control of the Basque government. It also offered unprecedented reinforcement to the government's position that Batasuna could only return to legality by breaking with ETA, or persuading it to end its violence. 'Strasbourg buries Batasuna', ran the headline in *El País*.[99]

ETA conspired to help in this burial by marking its fiftieth anniversary on 31 July 2009 with a bombing campaign that destroyed the family quarters of a police barracks in Burgos in which 120 people, a third of them children, were sleeping—as the photographs of the devastation it wrought demonstrated, the large truck bomb was intended to kill multiple victims—and killed two officers with a more targeted car bomb in Mallorca, close to the summer residence of Spain's royal family. After extensive arrests and amidst conviction of ETA's weak, demoralised and divided status, the attacks came as a shock: they took place on consecutive days, outside the Basque Country, and evidently after long and careful planning. ETA, it would seem, was not done yet.

8

LEAVING VIOLENCE BEHIND

Two weeks before the bombs in Burgos and Mallorca in late July 2009, the reflections of Txema Matanzas, a lawyer in prison for membership of Ekin, surfaced in the press. Matanzas offered a blunt analysis of the situation facing ETA and the nationalist left and concluded that 'the state is not going to negotiate'. The time had come, he said, 'to close the shutters' on ETA's violence.[1] Matanzas' assessment was much commented on outside the nationalist left; from within, however, it was not news at all. Its leaders were in the midst of a bitter internal debate on exactly this issue, conscious that their future—indeed whether they had a political future—depended on its outcome. Like Matanzas, Arnaldo Otegi recognised that the government and public opinion more broadly were both 'fundamentally against the idea of negotiation' even as it seemed that, 'it is only through some kind of negotiation that we can get anywhere'. The challenge he and others were struggling to address, with the assistance of a number of the international actors who had supported the earlier process, was to find 'some creative way to get over this impasse'.[2]

What then transpired drew upon a rigorous analysis of the nationalist left's inability to achieve peace in the past, as well as the dire situation in which the most recent attempt had left it. Change was influenced by peace processes elsewhere and had elements in common with the shift from armed struggle to non-violent political action that made those processes possible. 'One of the key factors defining the success of Civil

War endings,' observed Jeroen de Zeeuw in an assertion robustly supported by the wider literature on civil war termination, 'is the ability of former rebel movements to transform themselves into "normal" political organisations.'[3] In all cases external factors—among them military pressure and the degree of popular support and legitimacy with which a rebel movement was able to pursue the armed struggle—played their part. However, in a project that invited leading associates of the ANC, the IRA, the M-19 in Colombia, the GAM in Aceh and the Maoists in Nepal to reflect on their respective organisations' experience, the Berghof Foundation found that their transition away from violence was 'primarily directed by their decision to shift and reconsider their overarching goals, ideology, strategies and tactics'.[4] As the possibility for the kind of negotiated process seen in these cases was blocked, the Basque nationalist left was forced to pursue a path that was not directly comparable to any of them.

With its attention focused on its counter-terrorist campaign, the government was slow to acknowledge the changing dynamics within the nationalist left and slower still to believe in them. Each statement by the nationalist left or ETA was greeted with the mantra that it was 'insufficient'; the demands of what it required of them began to rise. Deep distrust, vulnerability to the PP within the Basque government and across Spain, and reluctance to countenance the possibility that Batasuna might derive benefits from an end to terrorist violence it did not fully condemn, all contributed to inhibit flexibility. Meanwhile, as the likelihood of ETA's end began to approach, a kind of collective vertigo affected the Spanish right and the media it controlled. A return to tactics of *crispación* most obviously suggested a desire to thwart the possibility of the PSOE's possible electoral benefit from ETA's end. But it was hard to avoid the conclusion that it also reflected the latent but deeply institutionalised belief that ETA at a low intensity was a lesser threat to the state than Basques demanding independence by peaceable means.

And Zapatero had other problems to worry about. In 2008 he had campaigned for the general elections on a platform that had promised full employment. He had denied the possibility of economic crisis—in Spain's case largely rooted in the bursting of the property bubble upon which its spectacular economic growth had rested—as it threatened, reacted slowly when it broke and then, when the EU debt crisis hit, succumbed to pressure from Brussels to introduce austerity measures that betrayed his party's principles by slashing programmes that had the most impact upon Spain's poor. Unemployment rose sharply until more than one in five Spaniards were out of work, and nearly half of those aged between twenty and thirty. This was a generation that, for the first time since the Civil War, faced economic prospects worse than their parents. The appearance of non-violent demonstrators—known simply as *los indignados*, 'the indignant'—in May 2011 gave shape and voice to the malaise and uncertainty faced by increasing numbers of Spaniards.

By early 2011 things were self-evidently on the move in the Basque process. ETA declared a general, permanent and verifiable ceasefire and Batasuna presented the statutes for a new political party, Sortu ('To be born'), which clearly rejected violence and ETA's violence explicitly. In Madrid the opposition to any party that shared ETA's goals being able to pursue them while ETA was still alive was intense. In the Basque Country, in contrast, demands for the recognition of the changes underway were becoming more pressing. The Supreme Court rejected Sortu's statutes by a narrow margin, angering many Basques. The nationalist left's next move—to contest the municipal and local elections in May 2011 in a coalition, Bildu ('Reunite'), formed with legal political parties—was again opposed by the Supreme Court. A last minute approval by the Constitutional Court allowed the nationalist left to return to democratic politics with its electorate energised by the obstructions that had been put in its path. Rufi Etxeberria had taken over the leadership of this effort after Otegi was imprisoned in October 2009. In July 2011 he described the strategic change that underpinned the move away from violence as comparable in importance to ETA's original adoption of a political-military strategy in the mid-1960s, and the path to ETA's eventual end.[5]

Zutik (Stand up) Euskal Herria

Shock and anger at ETA's spectacular attacks in July 2009 reinforced the government's determination to combat both ETA and the incipient initiatives within the nationalist left. Rubalcaba left no room for ambiguity in a widely reported interview in early August. He had, he said, 'something more' than an impression that within a few months Batasuna might try to secure its legalisation by 'distancing itself more or less explicitly from violence' while asking for time to convince ETA to stop killing. If this was the case, 'the answer will be radically no. This is a farce directed by ETA and the courts have already demonstrated that ETA and Batasuna are the same.... we must tell Batasuna with the utmost clarity that it will never return to institutions while ETA remains alive.'[6]

On 13 October, under instructions from Baltazar Garzón, Otegi and several other leaders of the nationalist left were detained in the offices of the trade union LAB. A few days later Otegi, Rafa Diéz, Arkaitz Rodríguez, Sonia Jacinto and Miren Zabaleta—the daughter of the Aralar leader Patxi Zabaleta who was prominent within Ekin but supportive of the changes proposed by Otegi—were sent to prison. They were charged with reconstituting the illegal Batasuna as a new entity, 'Bateragune', under instructions from ETA and in order to execute its 'political-military strategy'.[7] 'No one is going to engage in politics and violence at the same time,' Rubalcaba stated categorically from Madrid.[8]

The detentions caused outrage in Basque nationalist circles, where the determination of Otegi and some of his colleagues to move away from violence was widely known and the allegation that they had been acting under ETA's instructions simply not credible. The charges released by Garzón a few days later did little to alter this view. Deriving from the old mantra that 'everything is ETA', they drew on casuistic reasoning that because ETA had in December 2008 endorsed the idea of a pro-independence block, all those who worked towards it (regardless of whether their actions constituted a crime or not) were doing so under its orders.[9] They suggested either a fundamental failing in the intelligence and police work upon which they had been based, or an action of deliberate sabotage of the last opportunity to achieve an end to ETA's violence. On 17 October, some 47,000 people demonstrated against the arrests in San Sebastián, among them representatives of the PNV. The party, which was simultaneously negotiating the terms under which its six deputies in Madrid would provide a lifeline of support to Zapatero's budget, had been encouraged to participate by Joseba Egibar. Still the PNV's closest link to the nationalist left, Egibar accused those who had ordered the arrests of not wanting ETA to disappear because they feared the resurgence of the nationalist left once it was gone.[10] Rubalcaba countered by lambasting the PNV for 'defending a political-military strategy designed by ETA'.[11]

Far from being under the thumb of ETA, Otegi and his colleagues were in fact at loggerheads with it. New differences had emerged over the summer months as Batasuna had worked on a strategy paper suitable for consultation with the movement's bases, *Argitzen* ('Clarifying the political phase and strategy'). When Batasuna refused to accept amendments introduced by ETA, ETA had complained that it was 'enormously irritated that a model of the process that is not shared by the organisation continues to be debated' and argued that it was not the place of the nationalist left [ie other than ETA] 'to get involved in the high levels of definition of the democratic process'.[12] A compromise was found by which ETA drafted its own document, *Mugarri*, which questioned the viability of a political process in the absence of the 'guarantee' of armed struggle. It was agreed that it would be presented for consultation as a document of Ekin in parallel to *Argitzen*.[13]

Differences with the positions espoused by Batasuna's leadership—which were already producing a leakage of individuals away from Ekin and some of the other hard-line entities of the nationalist left such as Segi, as well as considerable support in the prisons—came to a head with the October arrests. Ekin tried to take advantage of the moment by circulating its *Mugarri* document. Batasuna responded quickly by making the full text of *Argitzen* public. On 1 November, Etxeberria told *Gara* that it was 'time to gather the fruit of long years of struggle and not to let it go to waste'. The following week the newspaper published an upbeat letter from Otegi and the others imprisoned with him encouraging the formation of a broad pro-independence alliance. On 15 November, in public events held in Alsasua, Navarre and Venice, the nationalist left launched a declaration summarising the proposals that Otegi and the others had been reviewing at the time of their arrest and committing itself to an 'exclusively' peaceful and democratic process.[14]

International support and advice had continued behind the scenes, with a particularly intense period of contacts and strategy sessions taking place in the early summer. Contacts with the HD Centre and some of the others involved in the May 2007 meetings in Geneva were maintained in the strictest confidentiality.[15] They were known to the government, but according to Ángeles Escrivá, dissuaded in mid-2009 on the grounds that outsiders should for the moment pay no heed to what were termed 'the siren songs' of Batasuna.[16] The contacts cooled in the weeks after ETA's July attacks, but picked up again in the autumn, contributing to the design of a clearly planned set of actions to support the series of steps that Batasuna knew to be necessary to bring about the fundamental change it pursued. Although the international actors were not directly involved in the nationalist left's internal reflection, Otegi would recall that periodic visits by 'the Irish' to share their experiences (some of whom included individuals with direct experience of some of the IRA's most bloody actions) had helped in terms of 'pedagogy with our most militant structures'.[17]

Brian Currin worked apart, and had been particularly engaged in providing elements for a draft statement that would inform the Alsasua Declaration. After the October arrests, however, he decided that something more public than his discreet advice to Batasuna was needed: 'a spin doctor—somebody who was speaking up the process and encouraging it along'.[18] He chose a conference in San Sebastián on 28 October to break his silence and from this point forward became a vocal advocate of the path taken by the nationalist left, speaking publicly in the Basque Country, Madrid and Barcelona, and meeting with a range of Basque actors, most of them associated with nationalist parties, on his regular visits to the region.[19] He found support from Lokarri, which assumed a new prominence in its promotion of public participation in efforts towards peace, as well as from Gorka Espiau who, like Lokarri's director Paul Rios, was a former member of Elkarri.[20] Currin's increasingly visible presence prompted a mix of appreciation and criticism in the press. It was fuelled by confusion as to his role (although not a 'mediator' he was regularly described as such), complaints that his understanding of Basque politics was overly determined by the nationalist company he kept, and resentment that he should not only presume to tell Basques and Spaniards what to do, but encourage others to do so as well.[21]

Neither the strategy document *Argitzen* nor the Alsasua Declaration referred to ETA in terms convincing to those not familiar with Batasuna's opaque discourse. *Argitzen* proposed to open a 'democratic process' that would take place 'in the absence of any violence or internal interference'. This would not 'be limited to negotiation and does not depend on negotiation' but would follow its own 'gradual' dynamic, with no guarantees other than those that it generated itself. In a significant advance, the document included concessions on Navarre, accepting that the 'right to decide' could not be imposed from outside, while 'independence and socialism' remained on the horizon.[22] The declaration simultaneously launched by Etxeberria in Alsasua and Jone Goirizelaia at a conference in Venice, also attended by Currin and representatives of Sinn Féin and

Kurdish nationalism, stated that the democratic process it proposed 'has to be conducted in accordance with the Mitchell Principles'. The formulation was weaker than in earlier drafts but represented a direct threat to those in ETA who still defended armed action.[23]

Gerry Adams and the Friendship Group within the European Parliament each offered praise.[24] In Madrid, Rubalcaba quickly dismissed the declaration as 'more of the same and a road to nowhere'.[25] The parties—Eusko Alkatarsuna (EA) and Alternatiba, a small leftist party formed after a split within Izquierda Unida-Ezker Batua—already in discussion with the nationalist left recognised it as a step forward, if not enough. Significant, however, was the response of Egibar, who publicly hailed Alsasua as 'an important qualitative change' and, in private, prepared analyses for the PNV to drive home its implications.[26] Alsasua did not give 'full satisfaction', but it was 'conclusive', as he put it in December: 'We are looking at the end of the armed struggle and the beginning of something else.'[27]

In late November a massive police operation against Segi led to the detention and arrest of thirty-four of its members. Out of public sight, the consultation of Batasuna's base took place in two hundred and seventy meetings. Resistance from ETA was real, and rooted in the fear that—just as the government wanted—it would get nothing in return for abandoning violence. Ekin was already a weakened force and had little success in circulating *Mugarri* except within the prisons. ETA, under the military leadership of Mikel Carrera, *Ata*, nonetheless made a last attempt to assert itself, initiating an operation that was to have concluded with a massive car-bomb attack on the Kio Towers in the heart of Madrid. The attack, according to Florencio Domínguez, was conceived as a 'resounding response' to the Alsasua Declaration.[28] If successful, it would have had a profound—but unpredictable—impact on the consultations underway within the bases of the nationalist left. It was thwarted on 9 January, when a Guardia Civil patrol intercepted a lorry laden with explosives on the border with Portugal.

Days later ETA released a statement accepting that 'the nationalist left has spoken' and adopting 'its words as its own'.[29] But it offered little reassurance. The statement was issued before the conclusion of the nationalist left's consultations (it hadn't 'spoken') and made no reference at all to the Alsasua Declaration. Whatever the message it had been designed to send, its coincidence with the planned attack on Madrid suggested that there was a long way to go before ETA would be able to support the new directions being pursued by the nationalist left. These, in the meantime, had found a level of endorsement that surprised even some of their advocates. In February, after 7,200 activists had been consulted and in their great majority (80 per cent) offered their support, the nationalist left released a new document, *Zutik Euskal Herria* ('Stand-up Euskal Herria') cementing the change.[30] Its importance was both the direction it marked and the means by which it had been reached. 'The shadow of ETA over the nationalist left had been very important, determinant', Etxeberria acknowledged in 2011. The process begun in 2009 and concluded with *Zutik Euskal Herria* was 'the first time in the history of the nationalist left that it evaluated, debated and adopted a position on ETA's armed struggle'.[31]

Inching forwards

The flurry of documents and statements met with a mix of indifference and scepticism from outside the nationalist left. Reports of divisions within ETA as well as the continuous string of arrests—there would be more than a hundred alleged *etarras* detained in 2010 alone—encouraged the impression that the organisation was still active, even before the attack on the Kio Towers was detected and stopped.[32] Many Basques had accepted the repression of Batasuna. If they did not actually welcome its absence, they did not necessarily mind that it was not present in Basque institutions. For those paying attention, however, the struggle between the nationalist left and ETA was now evident, even as its outcome remained uncertain.[33] Two questions presented themselves: whether Batasuna would be able to persuade ETA to end its violence and thus assume the leadership of the political process it aspired to; and would—could—the government accept such a process it if actually transpired?

ETA had informed Batasuna that it required three things to be persuaded that a non-violent path was viable: political alliances with other pro-independence forces, mass support and international involvement. These demands created what a leading member of Batasuna would describe in March 2010 as a classic 'chicken and egg' dilemma.[34] ETA held out for the proof of support from within Basque society and evidence of international interest and recognition. But political and other social forces were ready to support a new, pro-independence platform only with the assurance that ETA's violence would be no more. Batasuna's allies in Sinn Féin and the Friendship Group were on board (Gerry Adams wrote an article in *The Guardian* that highlighted the echoes of Northern Ireland in the process underway).[35] Yet in Currin's efforts to promote the process internationally, he found the government representatives with whom he had been in contact in the past unimpressed. With Batasuna's leaders under pressure from ETA and keen to offer reassurance to their base that they retained access to international interlocutors, he began to think about approaching 'prominent international peace leaders' who might be able to make a statement in their individual capacities.[36]

EA, Aralar, Abertzaleen Batasuna (the French Basque expression of the nationalist left) and Alternatiba had sponsored a demonstration in support of prisoners in Bilbao in January. Yet they were still far apart with regard to the nationalist left's new direction. In November 2009 EA had publicly proposed a pact among all pro-independence social and political forces. Other political actors viewed EA's continuing discussions with Batasuna as risky and primarily driven by concerns for its own political survival. But their positions were no less bound by consideration of the implications of the nationalist left's possible return to legal politics. The latest *Euskobarómetro* poll had found that 71 per cent of those consulted had little or no confidence in the Basque government.[37] The presence of the nationalist left would bring a nationalist majority into the Basque Parliament to the clear advantage of the PNV, whose primary goal was to ensure its return to power. But the PNV was wary of competition for its own votes and, after its experience at Lizarra and Loyola, not prepared to help. 'Every time you lend them a hand they cut off a finger,' quipped Andoni Ortuzar, the party's president in Vizcaya, 'and we have already lost two or three.'[38] Aralar, meanwhile, had good reason to fear the annihilation of the political space it had carefully cultivated since its split from Batasuna a decade ago.

While the political parties demanded more, the nationalist left felt exposed and vulnerable. Its leaders were under close surveillance and had difficulties meeting. Political activities were banned, and detentions continued apace. Three prominent *etarras* were captured in France in late February. Others captured in Spain denounced serious incidents of torture (including attempted anal rape, continuous body blows and

221

threats of the use of the 'bag' and electrodes).[39] Government policies within the prisons—which combined a continuing campaign to coax dissidents to break with ETA and the prisoners' collective (EPPK), the movement of prisoners within and between prisons to fuel rumours of disloyalty to ETA, the modification of conditions within them and an increase of measures such as body searches for visitors—placed prisoners and their families under stress.[40] In March Otegi was sentenced to two years in prison and a sixteen-year prohibition on holding political office for 'glorification of terrorism' at an act of homage to *Gatza*, ETA's longest serving political prisoner (a retrial would be ordered on the basis of the judge's partiality and Otegi was acquitted in 2011). Outstanding cases—notably one alleging the illegal financing of Batasuna through the *herriko tabernas* in which Otegi and some forty others faced charges of membership of ETA that carried lengthy prison sentences—constituted additional threats.

Contributing to the low standing of the judicial system was a case brought against Garzón by the Falange and other extreme right entities. They accused him of abusing his judicial powers in an investigation he had launched into the thousands of deaths and disappearances during the Franco period as possible crimes of humanity. Nationally and internationally, the case had drawn widespread condemnation, and a degree of incredulity: this was Spain's response to the first attempt to open the door on its long-distant past by judicial means, and thus the first time relatives of victims had the opportunity to be recognised as such before a Spanish court. There was no love lost towards Garzón within the nationalist left, but this case was 'literally unbelievable', as Batasuna's Joseba Álvarez put it, 'as if a Nazi organisation challenged a German judge for investigating the Holocaust'.[41]

The absence of Otegi was sorely felt. Etxeberria had a unique position inside the nationalist left. He had been an adviser at Algiers, had passed the baton to Otegi when sent to prison with other members of HB's leadership in 1997 before Lizarra and, before his involvement in the Anoeta process, had a reputation as 'ETA's commissar' within Batasuna (Spanish officials considered him an active member of ETA until around 2000). But he was not comfortable in the public eye and did not have Otegi's communication skills or obvious qualities as a salesman. Otegi's stature as an unjustly imprisoned 'martyr' to the effort to move away from violence gave his absent figure a particular cachet that was enhanced by his periodic appearances in court or interviews in the press. In time, however, Etxeberria's quiet but unyielding authority would prove a powerful element in maintaining both the cohesion and momentum of the process that Otegi had initiated.

A critical question was what the nationalist left might do if ETA attacked again. Whether condemnation would be possible remained untested until 16 March 2010 when ETA killed a French policeman, Jean Serge Nérin, who had surprised a car robbery on the outskirts of Paris. The nationalist left put out a statement that managed to be both a step forward and disappointing. It regretted the killing of Nérin, asked ETA to 'ratify' its earlier support of a 'democratic process' and stated that this should be conducted 'in absence of all forms of violence'. But it did not ask ETA to abandon its arms, and linked the killing to the appearance of Jon Anza's body in a morgue in Toulouse as parallel occurrences in 'the reality of a political conflict'.[42] Much worse was the statement eventually released by ETA, which contained a self-serving account of the circumstances of Nérin's death and no commitment to forswear future violence. Rubalcaba angrily dismissed it as 'an intolerable insult' to the family of the slain policeman and 'vile, repulsive and repugnant cock-and-bull', as he promised to send the statement to Brussels so that the Friendship Group could understand ETA in its true colours.[43]

On 29 March Currin introduced the brief statement that became known as the 'Brussels Declaration' in a conference room of the European Parliament. Securing signatories had involved delicate negotiations with individuals with widely ranging knowledge of the Basque process. At their conclusion, however, the declaration's sponsors included four Nobel peace prize winners (Betty Williams, John Hume, Desmond Tutu, President FW de Klerk), the former President of Ireland, Mary Robinson, other dignitaries associated with the peace processes in Northern Ireland and South Africa or previously involved with Currin in the Basque Country, as well as a selection of US conflict resolution specialists. Their statement welcomed the steps taken by the Basque 'pro-independence (*abertzale*) left' and appealed to ETA to support its commitment by 'declaring a permanent, fully verified ceasefire'. 'Such a declaration appropriately responded to by [the Spanish] government,' it concluded, with careful use of the passive voice, 'would permit new political and democratic efforts to advance, differences to be resolved and lasting peace attained.'[44]

Even before the launch of the Brussels Declaration, *El Correo* published an editorial decrying the manipulation by ETA and its world of 'naïve and interested defenders'.[45] The criticism that followed the declaration's release was informed by the belief that its demand for a ceasefire from ETA was made in terms 'favourable to the terrorists, by reinforcing the narrative of conflict they propagate' as Rogelio Alonso put it. Its signatories 'support the tactics with which the political representatives of ETA depict a simulated but inexistent distancing from terrorism' and 'transfer to the government responsibility for the resolution of a terrorist conflict for which only the band is responsible'.[46] Such criticism neglected that the existence of conflict was not a 'narrative' but a reality for the nationalist left, whatever the views of others, and therefore needed to be addressed. Nor did it consider the possible benefits of the Brussels Declaration's attempt to alter the structural antagonism within which this unusual process risked becoming stuck. In addition to its own arguments, the nationalist left could now draw upon a clear appeal for ETA to declare a permanent and verifiable ceasefire from 'the international community'. This offered ETA, when it chose to move, the possibility of doing so without appearing to cede to demands from Madrid. It would also make it much harder for ETA to break any commitments it did make.

Government pressure on ETA was constant. In mid-April, in an operation described by Rubalcaba as 'of great importance' to the counter-terrorist campaign, it arrested three EPPK lawyers and seven collaborators found to be acting as liaisons to the prisoners 'in the name of ETA [and] under ETA's orders'.[47] Meanwhile, the first fruit of the nationalist left's new effort was seen at the end of a month in a large event in Pamplona. Etxeberria introduced a document that recognised that ETA and the government shared blame for the failure of the last peace process, chastised ETA for returning to armed action in its wake ('far from resolving the obstacles to dialogue' it had 'only made these obstacles worse'), and called upon ETA and the government to respond to the Brussels Declaration.[48] In a small if indirect recognition that things were on the move, Rafa Díez was released on bail a few days later, ostensibly to look after his ailing mother. In May the French police arrested Ata, whom the government considered to be the last *etarra* with significant operational capacity. Rubalcaba would recall that this was the moment when he began to believe the end was in sight: 'It was a question of time, and of pressure, of not letting up on the pressure to make sure that ETA had no oxygen to recover.'[49]

Hesitation and resistance

By the summer of 2010 the nationalist left had completed a strategic shift it believed to be irreversible and ETA appeared to be in *de facto* ceasefire—the government knew from international interlocutors that it had been in a 'technical halt' from the end of February.[50] The nationalist left's contacts with other political forces—Etxeberria met with Iñigo Urkullu of the PNV in June—were growing and rumours abounded that ETA would respond to the Brussels Declaration that month. When it didn't, the process entered a strange hiatus, blocked by resistance within ETA and complicated by the deterioration of the political climate in Spain.

That a weakened Zapatero was belatedly coming to terms with the economic crisis did not augur well for bold gestures from the government. In May he managed to get parliamentary approval for an unpopular series of austerity measures by just a single vote, narrowly averting the collapse of his government. But the nationalist left knew it had no option other than to keep going. 'Whoever has the initiative wins society,' one leading proponent of change had explained in July 2009. A year later, he likened the process on which Batasuna had embarked to a bicycle, echoing a metaphor employed by Jonathan Powell, who would recall telling Tony Blair at the worst moments of the Northern Ireland process, 'no matter what, we have to keep things moving forward, like a bicycle'.[51] 'We can't stop riding the bicycle or it will fall over,' as this member of Batasuna put it, 'we need to maintain an adequate rhythm, to keep the wheels turning around, even if we have to sweat a bit.'[52] 'Batasuna can't get there before it gets there,' explained Oscar Matute of Alternatiba. Demanding otherwise 'would be like asking someone making the Compostela pilgrimage to be in Compostela when they are only in Burgos'.[53]

Progress in the political terrain came in late June when EA and the nationalist left launched a formal pro-independence pact in the Euskalduna conference centre in Bilbao.[54] Other political parties greeted the agreement with opprobrium: it made no demands of ETA and immediately raised the spectre that the nationalist left might ride EA's coat-tails back into democratic politics. As the PP started making oblique references to the possibility of illegalising EA, the government agreed to tighten the electoral law to complicate the presentation of candidates 'contaminated' by their links to banned parties.[55] One consequence of such measures was to help galvanise Basque social forces in support of the changes underway. Adierazi EH, a social platform broader than the nationalist left, began planning a large demonstration in favour of civil and political rights for mid-September.

Outside the emerging pro-independence block there was a solid consensus that the best way of helping the nationalist left move forward was by not helping it at all. Those outsiders who suggested otherwise were dismissed as being 'at the service of Batasuna… confused individuals who don't understand what is happening here' as Gorka Maneiro of Union, Progress and Democracy (UPyD)—a small party that had splintered from the Socialists and held strongly constitutionalist views—put it, or 'mugs lining their pockets by defending a terrorist band' in Antonio Basagoiti's more colourful phrase.[56] Currin became a visible lightening rod for many of these frustrations. Joseba Arregi, a former member of the PNV who was now an outspoken critic of nationalism, lambasted him as 'an embarrassment, an embarrassment, someone who comes here saying that democracy will come to Spain when Batasuna can join the political institutions, as if the rest of us have not been democrats since 1978'.[57] Reports that Currin's work was funded by the Joseph Rowntree Foundation—for some reason this was considered 'news'—fuelled analysis of the 'Currin enigma' (he was 'cold, cautious and in the pay of the Quakers'), allegations that he 'lived at the cost of the victims of terrorism', as the AVT put it, and a demand that he should be investigated under US laws that forbid 'material support' of terrorism.[58]

Jesús Eguiguren was another target. His public statements, compounded by captured ETA documents that referred to the existence of a *via Txusito*, 'a Txusito channel' ('Txusito' being the Basque diminutive of Jesús) led to noisy complaints from Jaime Mayor Oreja and others in the PP that he was involved in secret talks or negotiations.[59] He wasn't, although he continued to maintain his regular channels to the nationalist left. However, frustrated by the PP's opposition to its legalisation, even if it was to distance itself from violence, in June he released some 'reflections and proposals' on the future.[60] The ideas that Eguiguren put forward were considered, thoughtful and, although widely criticised as unwelcome in their political timing, entirely coherent. He presented them on the assumption that in the near future major change—a cease-fire from ETA or a statement from the nationalist left clearly distancing itself from terrorism—was coming. He had not departed from his conviction that there was nothing to negotiate before this shift took place. However, he urged López and Basagoiti to lead the coming change by forging a pact that might offer incentives to Batasuna in its efforts to persuade ETA to move ahead, including the possibility of legalisation.

The outrage was immediate. Dolores Cospedal, second in the PP hierarchy, called for Eguiguren to be relieved of his position as president of the PSE. The Basque PP threatened to break off its support of the PSE in the Basque government. López publicly disavowed his ideas, claiming, 'I'm in charge of the battle against terrorism in this government.'[61] The PSE soon closed ranks around Eguiguren, dismissing his proposals as just 'cosas de Jesús'—'Jesús' ideas'.[62] But the reaction demonstrated both the limitations to government action imposed by the PP's manipulation of the subject of terrorism and the extent to which the discourse of the right had been internalised. The possibility of creative thinking about the benefits of an orderly end to ETA's violence and the return of its grievances into the channels of normal politics was almost non-existent. 'We are all paralysed by fear,' wrote Eguiguren, 'that the usual forces will bring out the battle axe if we try any kind of movement on this issue.'[63]

The fragile space within which the Spanish government was operating was again illustrated in late July when a series of articles addressed its policies in the prisons. The numbers of prisoners the government had successfully encouraged to distance themselves from ETA was small in comparison with the efforts it had exerted for two distinct reasons. Social pressure from the EPPK and the broader world of the nationalist left made dissidence from the encompassing reality it represented difficult. Meanwhile, many prisoners (upwards of a hundred, according to prisons' director Mercedes Gallizo) whom the government had believed ready to distance themselves from ETA—a goal pursued as a means to 'break' ETA from within—had held back from doing so as Otegi's efforts towards a new strategy for the nationalist left took hold.[64] The government had rewarded some twenty dissident prisoners in total, several of whom had separated from ETA many years previously, with transfer to the prison of Nanclares de Oca, in the Basque province of

Álava.[65] But reports that these prisoners had been granted permission to leave the prison at regular intervals—in line with legal provisions for rewards for good behaviour—prompted immediate protests from the PP and aggrieved victims' organisations. 'Playing games' with ETA's prisoners, Basagoiti complained, distracted from what should have been the government's priority: 'making them lose all hope'.[66]

In this difficult environment movement within ETA slowed. The organisation had never contemplated the circumstances of its ending except as the negotiation of its core demands. Its leaders were finding it difficult to absorb what Patxi Zabaleta described as a 'Copernican change': the idea that stopping was not in exchange 'for something' but a political decision 'without any concrete achievement'.[67] In July members of Batasuna confirmed that 'as a collective ETA is moving, just not all at the same time'. They were not yet sure how things would turn out, or whether a shift within ETA was one that would leave 'remnants' behind. However, they saw it as 'logical and normal', as Rafa Díez put it, that 'doubts and questions' existed. The wave of arrests had brought younger, less experienced individuals into the leadership. Having just got there, they were 'frightened to flip the switch; they don't want to go down in history for shutting [ETA] down after fifty years'.[68]

The Constitutional Court's verdict on the Catalan statute, handed down in late June, was another disincentive. The court had rejected many of the PP's complaints of unconstitutionality but it had accepted others. Most significantly, it struck down the carefully parsed reference to Catalonia as a 'nation'—'the parliament of Catalonia, reflecting the will and sentiment of the people of Catalonia, has with a broad majority defined Catalonia as a nation' (a statement followed by the reminder that Catalonia was defined as a 'nationality' in the constitution) that had already been relegated to its preamble—on the basis that 'the constitution only knows one nation, Spain'.[69] It was a blow to a progressive understanding of the idea of a 'plural Spain' on which Zapatero had campaigned, and illustrative of the fear that still lurked within the right if so much as a shadow should threaten the unity of Spain. On 10 July more than a million Catalans took to the streets in defence of the statute in the biggest demonstration seen in Barcelona since the transition. 'What can we expect after Catalonia?' asked Joseba Álvarez. If in the short term ETA presented a problem for the political aspirations of the nationalist left, the core issue was clearly still Spain. The government 'understands perfectly well', Rafa Díez had drily observed, 'that if this goes ahead in a certain direction the political conflict will emerge with greater force'. [70]

Have we all gone mad?

ETA responded to the Brussels Declaration and the pressure on it from within the nationalist left through two different communiqués and an interview in *Gara* in September 2010, setting in motion a flurry of analyses, initiatives and political positioning that became increasingly fevered as the months of the autumn went by. Against the backdrop of the very serious challenges facing Spain—Zapatero's austerity measures had stayed but not halted the economic crisis, unemployment continued to rise until it reached 21 per cent, twice the European average, with youth unemployment at an unprecedented 45 per cent—the paroxysm into which the possibility of a ceasefire from ETA threw the political world was a strange thing to behold. 'Anyone would think we'd all gone mad,' wrote José Luis Zubizarreta in *El Correo*.[71]

In the video it released to the BBC on 5 September ETA announced what the government knew already—that it had called a halt to its 'offensive armed actions' some months previously. It also demanded a role in 'agreeing (with the government of Spain) the minimum democratic conditions necessary to embark on the democratic process'.[72] The nationalist left and Gerry Adams issued upbeat but not fulsome responses. Sinn Féin sent Bairbre de Bruin and Alex Maskey on a public visit to the Basque Country to encourage the process along. But the government and other political parties quickly dismissed ETA's communiqué as 'clearly insufficient'.[73] Worse, in some respects, was the statement ETA issued on 19 September, which indicated ETA's disposition to discuss 'the steps required for the democratic process' with the Brussels Declaration's international signatories.[74] The demand was inconsistent with positions maintained by Batasuna and a complicating factor for the external actors involved: neither the Brussels Declaration nor they had advocated talks, but they were tainted by ETA's request for them. Contributing to the confusion was the interview published in *Gara* at the end of the month. ETA acknowledged that it would be ready to declare a 'permanent and verifiable ceasefire', once 'conditions' for it were in place, and called for the opening of negotiations in accordance with the two-track model at Anoeta, long ago rejected by the government, and put to one side by Batasuna.[75]

ETA's unusually visible vacillations suggested both the gap that still existed between its positions and those of Batasuna, and the consequences of the pressure upon it. The courts had banned the large demonstration called by Adierazi EH on 11 September to defend political and social rights. In mid-September some 300 police detained nine members of Ekin. Later in the month further arrests led to the detention of the leaders of Askapena. The nationalist left accused the government of 'sabotage of the new phase'.[76] It was nonetheless able to take a major step forward when, on 25 September, it joined with EA, Alternatiba, Aralar, LAB and a wide range of other leftist and pro-independence forces to introduce a formal statement in the symbolic location of Guernica.

The Guernica Declaration gave shape and purpose to the pro-independence block first suggested by Otegi in late 2008. It spelled out demands for 'a scenario of non-violence with guarantees and progressive political normalisation' as the necessary pre-conditions for 'dialogue and political negotiation' that should take place in accordance with the Mitchell Principles. And for the first time it contained an explicit request to ETA to declare a ceasefire that was permanent, unilateral and verifiable by the international community as an expression of its will to 'definitively abandon its arms'.[77] 'Normalisation' was understood to include the derogation of the political parties' law; the disappearance of threats, persecution and torture; substantial modification to penitentiary policies (including an end to dispersion, the release of sick prisoners, those held in preventive detention and those who had completed legally required sentences), the revision and derogation of exceptional (ie. anti-terrorist) legislation and the disappearance of *incommunicado* detention; and the involvement of international actors to verify the absence of human rights abuses. Political dialogue would seek agreement on the recognition of the 'Basque national reality' and the right to decide, and respect for 'popular democratic will' on institutional arrangements 'including independence'. It would encompass the 'recognition, reconciliation and reparation of all the victims of the political conflict and the reality of multiple violences'.

The agreement was notable both for those who subscribed to it—especially Aralar—and for what they subscribed to. It would be criticised for introducing 'unacceptable parallelism' between the responsibility of 'the terrorist band' to end its violence and the steps demanded of the state, for its insistence on the existence of 'multiple violences' and its equation of ETA's victims with its own.[78] But in clear and direct terms it answered the amorphous and unrealistic declarations made by ETA. The message was unequivocal: within the nationalist left it was Batasuna that was imposing the policy, and doing so in partnership with other actors who promised a politically viable future. With the clock ticking before the May 2011 municipal elections, securing ETA's commitment to a unilateral, permanent and verifiable ceasefire was the absolute priority. On 2 October some 46,000 people filled the streets of Bilbao in a demonstration in favour of the 'new political scenario'.[79]

The PNV had strongly denounced ETA after the September statements and demanded a complete end to ETA's armed activities. It offered support to the government, even as clear differences remained regarding its insistence that, once violence was out of the way and the nationalist left was legalised, all-party dialogue would be necessary to resolve the political conflict. On the basis of this position Urkullu would parlay the party's votes in the Spanish Parliament, which were required by Zapatero to pass Spain's budget, against the 'transference' of outstanding benefits under the autonomy statute. The agreement appeared to offer a guarantee that Zapatero could maintain his hold on the government until the end of his term in March 2012, and thus won time to secure peace in the Basque Country.[80] It also brought Urkullu benefits: he marginalised López and the Basque government from the essential business of the Basque Country's relationship to Madrid and established himself as a critical interlocutor with Zapatero with regard to ETA. From the end of the year, Urkullu also began to meet regularly with Mariano Rajoy. In a radical change from the days of Aznar and Ibarretxe, the meetings suggested that the PNV could be a reliable partner to a likely PP government, while allowing Urkullu to brief Rajoy on developments within the nationalist left.[81]

The Basque government took only timid steps to engage with the emerging process. How difficult it was to do more was suggested when reports of a meeting between the PSE and Batasuna leaked out, prompting threats from the PP to break its pact with the PSE unless all involved denied it—which they did.[82] Small signs of encouragement from the PSOE—including agreement that *El País* could publish a long interview with Otegi in mid-October under the headline 'The pro-independence strategy is incompatible with armed violence'[83]—were subjected to vigilant scrutiny by the PP, which had responded to the possibility of progress towards ETA's end with the politics of *crispación*. Uproar followed Zapatero's statement on 20 October that Batasuna's change of direction 'would not be in vain'.[84] The PP suspected that the PSOE was preparing to negotiate the legalisation of the nationalist left, so Basagoiti suggested that ETA and Batasuna be placed in 'quarantine' for four years to test their commitment to democracy.[85] Next up was Eguiguren, who, together with the journalist Gorka Landaburu, made an appearance before the Audiencia Nacional as a witness for Otegi's defence as he, Joseba Permach and Joseba Álvarez faced trial for 'glorifying terrorism' during the meeting in the Anoeta stadium that launched the 2005 peace process. At the trial—which led to acquittal—Eguiguren shook Otegi's hand; on the witness stand, he described Otegi as someone with whom he had developed 'normal friendly relations'.[86] It was a brave performance for which he was subjected to a lynching in the press.

As ETA continued to stall, speculation about the possibility of a split either with Batasuna or within ETA itself mounted. In the interview in *El País*, Otegi had dismissed the idea of a splinter group equivalent to the Real IRA as 'highly improbable, if not to say impossible'.[87] That 'everything' was not ETA had never been clearer as Batasuna sought to assert itself over the armed organisation, but the complex bonds that had so long sustained the movement as a whole could not easily be untied. 'What would a break with ETA mean?' one member of Batasuna would ask in November, while confirming his belief that it was a primary goal of government strategy. 'I don't know how we'd do it even if we wanted to.' Facing a weak but immobile government, Batasuna was resigned to working on the basis of two different timeframes. The 'fast route' could be taken if ETA declared its ceasefire, at which point the nationalist left would seek legalisation of a new political party whose contours—beginning with strict adherence to the political parties' law—were outlined at a public event held in Pamplona in late November.[88] The 'slow route' would be the only option if ETA delayed and the process dragged on until after 2012. At that point the nationalist left assumed it would be facing a PP government, which would be 'much harder'. Given how bad everything else looked for the PSOE, the hope was that it would want to take advantage of the opportunity to end ETA's violence—if ETA moved first.[89]

Drawing on the experience of Northern Ireland, and the tacit assumption that if ETA offered a permanent and verifiable ceasefire the government would accept it, the nationalist left had worked towards a 'verifiable' ceasefire as an essential guarantee. The idea raised obvious questions about who would do the verifying. With Currin viewed as partial (if there had been any question regarding what the PP thought of him it was dispelled by a letter of quite remarkable rudeness with which Basagoiti in October rejected a request for a meeting)[90] and the other international actors trusted by Batasuna shrouded in secrecy, discussion turned to the creation of an international verification commission equivalent to that led by the Canadian general John de Chastelain in Northern Ireland. The intense resistance to outside involvement suggested that this would be difficult for Spain to countenance. An editorial written to accompany *El País*' interview with Otegi maintained—without offering analysis of why this was the case—that Spain could 'under no circumstances delegate functions which affect the security of threatened citizens to international personalities or organisations, however respectable they might be'.[91] The government's position was that any verification would be carried out by its security services, a prospect that offered no encouragement at all to ETA and the nationalist left.

In mid-November Currin announced the creation of an International Contact Group (ICG) to take forward the work of the Brussels Declaration. He introduced the 'mandate' of the group, which he had crafted after a round of consultations—but not with the Basque government, the PP or even the PSE in a formal fashion—as being to assist 'political normalisation in the Basque Country' once ETA declared a permanent and verifiable ceasefire through the promotion of the legalisation of the nationalist left, reform of penitentiary policy and assistance to multi-party dialogue to resolve the political conflict.[92] However, in launching the ICG, he strayed beyond the sphere of action conceived for it by calling on the government to verify the permanent ceasefire he predicted would be announced before the end of year and suggesting that, if it was not prepared to do so, the ICG could do it instead.[93] The nationalist left quickly clarified that Currin was in no position to offer assurances as to what ETA might or might not do. Others—including Urkullu—appealed publicly for greater 'discretion' or privately questioned exactly from whom or what the ICG presumed to claim its 'mandate'.[94] More critical still, predictably, was Rubalcaba, who dismissed

Currin as being, at most, a mediator between Batasuna and ETA, and of no interest to the state because 'there is no dialogue with ETA and nor will there be'.[95]

Back in May, Maite Pagazaurtundua, the director of the Foundation for Victims' of Terrorism, had made the startling observation that the 'the one thing the victims of terrorism don't want is to end up being the victims of peace'.[96] This fear of being forgotten, of having victims' demands for truth, memory, justice and dignity swept aside, grew more acute as speculation regarding the imminence of a permanent ceasefire mounted. In November the foundation brought representatives of almost all the victims' organisations together to develop a common position with respect to a possible end to ETA. A document sent to the government in December set out principles for a 'model for the end of ETA without impunity'.[97] The victims rejected the early release of ETA prisoners as part of end-state agreements, or the use of prison policy as a means of 'grace'. They also demanded that ETA condemn its entire history, something quite unthinkable for an armed organisation that, however weakened, retained a deeply ingrained sense of its 'heroic' trajectory and unwavering dedication to its goals.

Crossing the Rubicon

ETA issued its long awaited declaration of a 'permanent and general ceasefire, which can be verified by the international community' in January 2011.[98] As so often in this tortuous process its statement was a step forward, if not quite the step forward desired. It responded to the petition contained in the Brussels Declaration and included a reference to the word 'definitive' introduced at Guernica ('This is ETA's firm commitment to a process of definitive solution and an end of the armed confrontation'). But it also suggested that ETA had not entirely abandoned its habitual tutelage of the political process. The statement asserted that the 'democratic process' had to resolve the old goals of territoriality and self-determination, and ended by offering the ominous assurance that 'ETA will not cease in its effort and struggle to move the democratic process forward and bring it to conclusion', intimating that the possibility of a return to armed action remained in reserve.[99] More positively, the ceasefire was described as 'general'. This suggested that it extended to all areas of ETA's activity, including extortion, which would be formally cancelled in April when ETA wrote to Basque businessmen to inform them that it was ending the practice.

The communiqué suggested that ETA had moved forward, but was still trying to respond to multiple internal constituencies. Politicians and pundits reacted predictably with responses that were upbeat from those whose first priority was to encourage the process forward, much more critical from those who remained resolutely sceptical of ETA's position and utterly dismissive from the PP, victims' organisations and others who appeared resistant to any change in the status quo.[100] But the distance travelled by ETA, the clearly rhetorical nature of some aspects of the declaration and the by-now transparent determination of the nationalist left to leave violence behind were beginning to undermine the validity of doing nothing more than berating the 'insufficiency' of ETA's communiqués. Raising the bar with respect to what was required from the organisation—as Rubalcaba did by stating that the only acceptable communiqué 'is that ETA announces its end and it does so in an irreversible manner'—prompted intense frustration. 'To hear phrases such as "this is easy to do, a communiqué that says 'we're stopping' will suffice",' wrote Iñaki Iriondo in *Gara*, 'is an insult to the intelligence as no political-military conflict has ended this way.'[101]

The first visit to the Basque Country by the newly constituted ICG—whose members included Raymond Kendall, Nuala O'Loan, the criminologist Silvia Casale, and Pierre Hazan and Albert Spektorowski, Swiss and Israeli academics, in addition to Currin himself—took place in mid-February with the facilitation of Lokarri. It was abruptly dismissed by both the central and Basque governments, but welcomed by others who appreciated international help in building confidence in the changes underway. The pressure was real. Some 65,000 people had joined a demonstration that called for the movement of prisoners to the Basque Country in early January as a prelude to a year of remarkable activity by pro-independence and leftist forces.[102] An increasing number of voices—including from within the PNV and Eguiguren—were, like the ICG, openly calling for the legalisation of the nationalist left.

The dilemma facing the government had become more acute in early February, when Etxeberria, the veteran lawyer Iñigo Iruin and other senior members of the former Batasuna introduced a charter for a new political party, 'Sortu'. The 'beauty and sincerity' of the charter, as the Basque analyst Ramón Zallo described it, took everyone by surprise.[103]

A legal team led by Iruin had drawn up a document that clearly rejected violence, and ETA's violence specifically, in terms that scrupulously reflected the demands of the political parties' law. 'The new political party will develop its political activity,' it read, 'on the basis of the rejection of violence as an instrument of political action or method for the achievement of political objectives, whatever its origin or nature, a rejection that, openly and without ambiguities, includes the organisation ETA.'[104] Consciously modelled on the internal organisation of the PSOE, Sortu would be a party whose internal structures represented a radical departure from the amorphous practices of Batasuna and the MLNV. It undertook to expel from its ranks, for example, those affiliates who did not maintain its commitment to non-violence. 'Monday was the first day of peace in Euskadi,' was Eguiguren's prompt verdict. 'Processes of this kind, of transition from violence to peace, tend to reach a red line which you can't see, but is there, and which, if crossed, means there is no going back. And in this case we have crossed it.'[105]

The introduction of Sortu's charter vividly illustrated the extent to which Madrid and the Basque Country were two different worlds where Basque politics were concerned. In Madrid, popular opinion remained largely uninformed about the evolution of relations between the nationalist left and ETA, not least because it had for years been told they were one and the same. The government, still haunted by the bombing of Barajas, publicly questioned Sortu's credibility and faced an opposition party, the PP, which threatened to break with it if Sortu should be legalised, and anxious, angry and mobilised victims organisations. In the Basque Country, meanwhile, most political actors recognised the change within the nationalist left to be genuine and its legalisation as a step that would favour the end of ETA. This position was strongly championed by Urkullu, who had been convinced of the sincerity of the change within the nationalist left by a confidential meeting he had held with the PSE and nationalist left in early January. In the following months he stepped up his contacts with the PSOE and PP in Madrid, as well as economic and social actors in the Basque Country, in an effort he saw as internal 'facilitation' of the process towards ETA's end.[106]

Sortu's charter made it immediately obvious that the new party's fate was primarily a political rather than a juridical question. The government referred Sortu to the Supreme Court, together with a brief from the attorney general's office advising against legalisation on the grounds that Sortu was 'a continuation and successor' of the illegal Batasuna.[107] Its position reflected a formal hardening of the earlier demand that Batasuna had to choose between 'votes and bombs'. There had been new detentions of ETA militants (followed by more allegations of torture, later deigned 'credible and consistent' by the Council of Europe's Committee for the Prevention of Torture)[108] and a sudden appearance of reports that ETA had the previous year planned to kill Patxi López. These were categorically denied by ETA, but had encouraged Zapatero to insist that 'with ETA alive, [Sortu] will have a hard time' becoming legal.[109] The government's arguments against Sortu were patently weak. The brief maintained that Sortu 'complied with the law in order to defraud it' and drew on police reports to argue the obvious: that Sortu bore an integral relationship to the former Batasuna and represented an effort by the nationalist left to contest the May elections. It also attempted to prove that legalisation of Sortu responded to a strategy of ETA and that its rejection of terrorism was consequently 'cosmetic, rhetorical and manipulative'. Overall, it suggested that however effective the political parties' law might have been as an instrument for banning a political party of the nationalist left, little thought had been given to what its un-banning might look like.

On 23 March 2011 the Supreme Court announced its support for the government's petition on grounds that Sortu would later appeal to the Constitutional Court. In a decision handed down by an almost evenly divided court—nine judges against legalisation and seven in favour, a dramatic contrast to the unanimous verdicts on all other cases regarding the legality of political formations associated with the nationalist left—the Supreme Court decided that Sortu 'was an unacceptable threat… to Spanish democracy'.[110] The majority opinion drew heavily on the government brief and reflected its weaknesses; that written by the minority, on the other hand, accepted that Sortu's rejection of ETA was 'firm and unequivocal' and argued against its 'preventive illegalisation'.[111] The solidity of its arguments suggested that when consideration of Sortu's case eventually reached the Constitutional Court—where, in contrast to the Supreme Court there was a majority of judges considered 'progressive'—it stood a good chance of approval. This reading of the Supreme Court's ruling reflected a pragmatic application of the 'democratic quarantine' demanded by the PP, as well as the preference of Socialists for the nationalist left to 'demonstrate' its firm commitment to a peaceful and democratic future.[112] But it angered many Basques—including many who were far from supporters of the nationalist left—who believed that Sortu had complied with what had been asked of it, only to have the government and courts change their demands.

In the days following the Supreme Court's ruling, ETA issued a communiqué lowering its request for international verification to an 'informal mechanism'.[113] The request reflected discreet discussions on the formation of a verification mechanism clearly distinct from the ICG. Implicit within them was the importance that ETA and the nationalist left continued to attach to verification that was not conducted by security forces they could only consider their enemy, and the echo that this concern was finding with their international interlocutors.

Plummeting polls—in one Zapatero received the lowest rating ever achieved by a Spanish prime minister, below González at the height of the GAL scandal or Aznar during the war in Iraq[114]—suggested that the PSOE was in for a drubbing at the May elections. On 2 April Zapatero announced his decision to stand down at the end of his second term. Rubalcaba was favoured to replace him as the PSOE's candidate for prime minister, which explained the decision by the PP to bring out the heavy guns against him. The publication of ETA's notes of its talks with the government in 2006 (captured with Thierry in 2008), and the revival of the allegations deriving from the Bar Faisán case regarding the 'tip-off' allegedly given to ETA, created one of the Spanish press' periodic feeding frenzies.[115] The accusations against Rubalcaba were bruising but inflicted no lasting damage. They were, after all, based on the reporting of ETA, which in other circumstances the entire Spanish establishment dismissed as unreliable. Charges that the government had made unacceptable concessions to ETA were countered by the fact that the dénouement of the 2005–7 peace process had demonstrated that it had not.

With the deadline for filing candidates for May's elections fast approaching, individuals close to Batasuna joined Bildu, a pro-independence coalition formed with EA and Alternatiba. In mid-April Bildu filed lists of candidates individually vetted as 'clean' of any former association with Batasuna or its predecessors to contest elections in 254 communities across Euskadi and Navarre, after discarding the extraordinary figure of 40,000 'contaminated' candidates. Bildu's desire to participate in the elections was predictably challenged by the government, which charged that the new formation responded to a 'strategy' directed by the Batasuna-ETA conglomerate.[116] The Supreme Court upheld the challenge on 1 May by nine votes to six and banned all Bildu's lists including those of EA and Alternatiba, democratic parties with no association with ETA at all.

The ruling prompted outrage in the Basque Country and, as Bildu's lawyers prepared their appeal to the Constitutional Court, a complicated combination of public statements and private pressure on Madrid. Patxi López trod a particularly delicate line: clearly in disagreement with the positions assumed by the PSOE in Madrid—which were openly challenged by prominent Basque Socialists such as Txiki Benegas, Odón Elorza, the long-serving mayor of San Sebastián, and Gemma Zabaleta—he limited his dissent to the hope that the Constitutional Court would 'defend the rights of the candidates of Bildu'.[117] Urkullu went much further, threatening to withdraw the PNV's support for Zapatero's budget if the Supreme Court's verdict was not reversed. In a series of 'very difficult' telephone conversations with Zapatero and Rubalcaba, he insisted that it was 'absolutely essential' that Bildu be able to contest the elections.[118] On 5 May, a last-minute ruling handed down by the Constitutional Court by a five-four majority some minutes after the midnight deadline overturned the decision of the Supreme Court and allowed Bildu to run. Thousands of supporters of Bildu had been waiting beside the river Nervión on Bilbao's Arenal and in the central square in Pamplona. As the news arrived they erupted in jubilation. They would long remember what they christened the 'magic night' when the nationalist left returned to electoral politics.[119]

The right responded with virulent attacks upon the justices and their alleged influence by the government. Rajoy claimed the decision a 'step backwards in the fight against terrorism' and Frederico Trillo, the PP's justice spokesperson, that the Constitutional Court had lost the confidence of the party, the Guardia Civil, the police, the parliament and 'all Spanish citizens'.[120] The victims' organisations called a demonstration to protest about 'treason against Spain' and demanded the resignation of both Zapatero and Rubalcaba.[121] Bildu too understood the Constitutional Court's ruling in political terms: 'we knew the court would do what the government wanted', Santi Merino, a Bildu lawyer, would recall.[122] The government naturally denied any suggestion of its influence on the legal process. But it was hard not to see the move to legalise Bildu as representing both the outcome of a somewhat reluctant choice between two potentially destabilising situations, and a significant gamble on the future.

9

VIRTUAL PEACEMAKING

Bildu exploded into Basque politics by winning 25.5 per cent of the vote in Euskadi's May 2011 elections, a better result than ever before achieved by the nationalist left and one that effectively ended its internal debate with ETA. Second only to the PNV in the popular vote, the coalition won more elected officials than any other party and its candidates were appointed governor of Guipúzcoa and mayor of San Sebastián respectively.[1] Spaniards were left struggling to comprehend that a counter-terrorist campaign that had seemed destined to conclude with the 'defeat' of ETA had been accompanied by a resurgence of radical nationalism. 'Until recently,' Rufi Etxeberria observed that July, 'people were talking about the nationalist left as defeated, as at the gates of ruin, and now we see that it has been reborn like a phoenix.'[2]

The election result challenged the narrative of 'victors and vanquished', *vencedores y vencidos*, underpinning Spain's long counter-terrorist struggle and suggested a new terrain for conflict: peace. 'After winning the war,' Alfredo Rubalcaba, now confirmed as the Socialists' prime ministerial candidate, told *El País* in early July, 'what we cannot allow is that they win the peace.'[3] 'In peace, winning is collective,' countered Otegi from prison, 'and the very fact of beginning to talk of peace brings the first tangible dividend: the collective hope of believing that achieving it is possible.'[4]

The debate highlighted the very different conceptions of what peace—as conflict—in the Basque context might mean. While for most Spaniards,

241

'peace' meant the absence of terrorist violence, the defeat—and ideally the disappearance—of ETA, for the nationalist left, imbued as it was in its experience of a long armed conflict in the past, and animated by the prospect of a continued political struggle in the years ahead, this would not be enough. As the moment for ETA to announce the end of its violence approached, lines were drawn for the 'battle' for *el relato*—the story, the history of all that had happened and why: 'The construction of *el relato* depends on the end of ETA,' argued Iñaki Gabilondo in his influential daily video blog carried by *El País*, 'If ETA ends reasonably well, having achieved the legalisation of its political arm… and maintaining the idea that its fundamental goals are on track, *el relato* will without doubt represent the triumph of its epic thesis.' To prevent this, 'democracy', meaning the state, had to act: 'It is essential that the end of ETA is sufficiently clear to ensure that there is no room to invoke even an indirect victory. It has to be the triumph of democracy.'[5]

Central to this goal was the idea that the end of ETA should be 'an end without a process', the culmination of the government's intense persecution of ETA by police means and through the courts.[6] This was going to be difficult. Members of Batasuna confided in July that they believed they had reached the end of what they could achieve with ETA without movement from the government. The nationalist left—and ETA—had travelled far, but the government, in their view, had done nothing.[7] ETA, although a severely weakened force—the security services estimated its active militants to number between fifty and seventy, while there were some 700 Basque prisoners—was insisting that it required assurances from the government on the terms of cessation of its armed activities. Far from the old demands for self-determination and territoriality, these centred on the legalisation of Sortu and the securing of conditions to benefit the situation of its prisoners. While a maximalist demand for amnesty was still out there, Batasuna maintained that the circumstances of the prisoners and the list of measures included in the Guernica Declaration meant that there were many measures that could be taken—bringing prisoners closer to the Basque Country, releasing sick prisoners, a revision of the Parot Doctrine—on humanitarian grounds and within existing laws.

In other contexts, none of this might have been that difficult. As Vicenç Fisas pointed out in late August, elsewhere, armed groups end and states decide what concessions must reasonably be given to them.

Such concessions are understood as in the interest of the greater good that the end of violence represents and the terms of the group's dissolution are negotiated—'it is how things are done across the world'.[8] Spain, however, was different. The history of ETA and the efforts to achieve its end, the stigmatisation of dialogue and the sense of exceptionalism with which Spain approached Basque terrorism, the weakness of the outgoing PSOE government, strength of constituencies of the right and triumphalism now evident within the nationalist left all conspired to complicate what would have been a reasonable, even an obvious course of action elsewhere.

Instead what was taking place was an unusual form of peacemaking, never acknowledged by the government, but involving communication between the nationalist left, ETA and the government through trusted international facilitators, but not direct talks. There was nothing remarkable in the confidentiality itself, as early contacts between governments and armed insurgencies or terrorist groups are frequently conducted in secrecy. However, in other circumstances these contacts, if they prosper, almost all develop into face-to-face meetings and emerge into the public eye (in Colombia, for example, where the announcement of talks between the government of Juan Manuel Santos and the FARC in September 2012 came after a year of secret contacts).[9] In Spain, however, conditions for the 'surfacing' of what went on in secret were not present. Rather, the existence of a 'virtual' form of peacemaking was hinted at in the occasional press leak,[10] but confirmed only by what it produced: a tightly choreographed international conference in October 2011 in the Aiete Palace in San Sebastián, where Franco used to pass his summers. In what appeared to the public as a hastily assembled event, distinguished international leaders, with the former UN Secretary-General Kofi Annan at their head, called upon ETA to announce a definitive end to its armed activities. ETA responded promptly to this appeal, and three days later issued a statement that brought to a formal end more than forty years of violence.

Winners and losers

Martín Garitano—a former *Gara* journalist whom the elections had swept into office as Bildu's governor of Guipúzcoa—was pleased to show a curious visitor around San Sebastián's elegant Palacio de la Diputación.

The wood panels, red carpets and hushed rooms spoke of a history heavy with Guipuzcoan pride and wealth, and the province's complex bonds to Spain: here a stained glass window depicting King Sancho VI of Navarre presenting the Basques with their *fueros*; there a portrait of Queen Victoria Eugenia, the grandmother of the current King Juan Carlos; or chairs sat on by the royal family and Franco. The contrast to the functional offices of *Gara*, which are to be found in a boxy modern building on the Calle Portuetxe a few miles away, was stark, and the challenges ahead—first off 'to govern Guipúzcoa', as Garitano put it— immense.[11] Bildu's elected officials were inexperienced; they were governing from a position of minority and knew that the other political parties would work together to impede their efforts at every turn.

Bildu's election results had exceeded even its own most optimistic expectations. The coalition, strongly weighted towards 'independent' candidates suggested by the nationalist left (some 70 per cent), won some 313,000 votes in municipal and local elections across Euskadi and Navarre.[12] Its success produced a realignment of Basque politics into the four blocks—progressive and more conservative in both the constitutionalist (PSE and PP) and nationalist (Bildu and PNV) spheres—that broadly represented Basque society, while also illustrating the considerable fluidity that existed between them.[13] As could be expected, Bildu's presence within the institutions provoked mixed reactions; the Basque PP's spokesman, Leopoldo Barreda, attributed it to the 'incapacity of democrats to prevent its legalisation' and consequently viewed it 'a serious democratic setback'.[14]

The hiring by Bildu's officials of a raft of more experienced advisers 'contaminated' by their past association with Batasuna was a concern to some, and encouraged comparisons of Bildu's arrival in the local town councils to the advent of Nazism to Germany.[15] The coalition came under pressure to demand ETA's end, and found no good reason to explain why it couldn't. It raised hackles when it introduced a series of symbolic changes—removing a portrait of the king from a public office in San Sebastián, and the Spanish flag from some municipalities—and Garitano revealed an early insensitivity towards the victims of ETA. But as the months went by the great majority of complaints fell within the realm of the messy business of democratic politics. And it said something that at the end of Bildu's first year in office, Garitano's most urgent political challenge was a bitter dispute sparked by his plans to introduce a new system of rubbish collection.

Representatives of the nationalist left knew that Bildu had attracted new voters whose future support would not be assured, and would therefore have to be won by its performance in office. The coalition had benefitted from conditions that approached a perfect electoral storm. In addition to Batasuna's core voters, elements favouring its electoral success had included: the rewarding of the nationalist left's internal evolution and effort to bring peace; the perverse effect of the battle for legalisation of Sortu and then Bildu, which had galvanised voter support; the ability of a coalition to attract more votes than would have been possible for its constituent parts ('in this case', as Etxeberria put it, 'two plus two plus two made more than six');[16] a vote against establishment political parties, and especially the PSOE, across Spain; and a vote for Bildu as something 'new', 'clean', and 'anti-system', especially attractive to the young and consonant with the movement of *indignados* which had made its sudden appearance on the streets of Madrid just a week before the elections.

In Euskadi, as across Spain, where the PSOE vote fell behind the PP by 10 per cent, the Socialists were the big losers, winning just 16 per cent of the vote, down from 24 per cent in 2007. Oscar Rodríguez, secretary-general of the PSE in Álava, acknowledged that the party—with the notable exception of Eguiguren—had been too slow to understand the profundity of the changes under way with the nationalist left, and had consequently handled them badly. It had been a mistake 'not to celebrate the statutes of Sortu with champagne' and present them as Batasuna's 'surrender to institutional Spain and the constitution'.[17] Odón Elorza had lost his job as mayor of San Sebastian to Bildu's Juan Karlos Izagirre in a surprise upset. He had supported the legalisation of both Sortu and Bildu because 'it was the democratic thing to do', but, like Rodríguez, he was frustrated that the government's inability to act had strengthened radical nationalism. 'We did the campaigning for them,' he observed. Elorza believed that Bildu was 'like a soufflé' and would soon deflate, but in the short term Otegi and Bildu had managed to 'turn history on its head'. They had created the idea that they had 'somehow brought peace' when it had been the weakness of the nationalist left—and not its conviction—that had forced change upon it.[18]

Otegi's appearance in the Bateragune trial, which came before the Audiencia Nacional in late June, contributed to the problem. Otegi, Rafa Diéz and six other members of the nationalist left were charged

245

with forming Bateragune in order to promote a 'sovereigntist block subordinated to the ends and means of ETA'—something that the passage of time had demonstrated was not true. Bateragune, the case against them maintained, was 'the structure that developed the different actions of the terrorist organisation in order to achieve the integral ends of the political and social project it had for Euskadi through terrorist violence'; its members 'lacked any margin of manoeuvre outside the channels established by ETA'.[19] The evidence to support this theory was thin: police reports drew on the documents captured from ETA that had informed the case against Sortu, as well as reports of Otegi's visits to France, allegedly to confer with ETA, which revealed nothing about what had transpired in their meetings. It was, moreover, presented to a court presided over by Ángela Murillo, whose trial of the Anoeta case had been dismissed on grounds of her 'partiality' against Otegi.

The defence offered by Iñigo Iruin and Jone Goirizelaia was built around a detailed account of the defendants' efforts to do exactly opposite of that with which they were charged: develop a strategy to move the nationalist left away from the 'means' employed by ETA for good. The defence team had hoped to call both Brian Currin and Gerry Adams as witnesses able to testify to the positions assumed by the defendants before their arrest—Currin could have described his conversations with Otegi and others; Adams how he had sent Sinn Féin representatives Eoin O'Brien and Gerry Kelly to discuss the need for change within the nationalist left—but had had the requests turned down.[20] They nonetheless introduced a robust defence around a narrative that, to the great frustration of the state, made no reference to the role played by police action against ETA in what Rubacalba would term 'clearing the landing strip' for Batasuna.[21]

Otegi began his testimony with a rhetorical flourish, announcing that 'if encouraging a solely peaceful and democratic strategy is a crime, then we are guilty'.[22] The elections, he claimed, had demonstrated that while those who had promoted this strategy had 'started out as four or five... we are now 313,000'. It emerged in the trial that the police had not had an arrest warrant for Rafa Díez, but had detained him when they found him meeting with the others and then built a case against him. Díez volunteered that he had contacted Otegi when the latter was released from prison in the summer of 2008 and worked with him to encourage 'a historic debate' that had concluded with the pursuit of 'an exclusively political and democratic path, and consequently the rejection of violence'.[23] This debate, far from being subordinated to any strategy of ETA, had led to direct confrontation with an organisation that was 'not sufficiently mature for what we were discussing', as Otegi put it: 'ETA thought that it was possible to accumulate forces maintaining the armed struggle and we thought not.' The defendants now saw violence as a direct threat to their goals. 'You have defended your thesis here and I have defended mine,' Otegi claimed to the prosecutor Vicente González Meta. 'But between the two there is a difference: what has happened in these two years confirms what I am saying and not what you say.'

Otegi had ended his courtroom appearance saying, 'Smile, because we are going to win.' Leaders of the nationalist left similarly assessed, soon after the trial closed, that they would 'win' whatever its outcome: acquittal would be seen as a great triumph, offering further vindication that the theory—already severely eroded by ringing victories won when the Audiencia Nacional had upheld appeals in the Egunkaria and Udalbiltza cases and dropped all charges against the defendants[24]—that 'everything was ETA' no longer was valid and returning Otegi and the others to freedom. If they lost, on the other hand, the status of Otegi, Díez and their colleagues as martyrs to the inequities of the Spanish justice system would only grow. 'They are making a new Mandela of Otegi,' observed Gorka Espiau, the former member of Elkarri, in July, 'the longer he stays in prison, the better for Batasuna and him.'[25]

In September Otegi and Díez were found guilty and sentenced to ten years each in prison as 'leaders of ETA', and Miren Zabaleta, Arkaitz Rodríguez and Sonia Jacinto each were given eight years. The sentences handed down to Otegi and Díez—who would be promptly returned to prison—were unlike anything either had received before. Since Otegi had left ETA he had faced prison terms of one to two years largely for crimes of opinion; Díez had never been convicted of any crime at all and was known as one of the most long-standing and consistent advocates of a move away from violence within the nationalist left. The sentence itself was a bizarre amalgamation of insinuation and non-sequiturs that tried to maintain that ETA had developed the strategy that would lead to its own end and imposed it on Bateragune.[26] While the editorialist of *ABC* rejoiced that the 'man of peace' who had been an interlocutor of the Zapatero government had been recognised as a 'pure and simple terrorist',[27] the conviction of Otegi prompted outrage from the nationalist left and its allies, and incredulity in other circles.

The PSE and the Basque government it led were placed in an indefensible position. Patxi López weakly admitted that the verdict could create 'surprise or even frustration' in some sectors of Basque society and warned against again 'campaigning' for the nationalist left by making Batasuna a 'victim'.[28] Others with less institutional responsibility—such as Eguiguren and Elorza—were more forthright in expressing their dismay. The problem was evident: like it or not, Otegi and the others were victims of the blatant politicisation of the justice system and their conviction galvanised opposition to the establishment parties. The verdicts against them did not make sense on legal grounds but instead could be explained, as Javier Pradera suggested in *El País*, by 'logical incoherences'.[29] These pointed to a conviction within the most conservative bowels of the state that the leaders of Batasuna were somehow still ETA, hesitation on the part of others to admit otherwise and a desire to use the legal system to force Batasuna to confront ETA more directly, avoiding the prospect that ETA could claim victory by declaring a definitive end to its violence with Otegi a free man and Sortu legal. Attorney General Cándido Conde-Pumpido admitted as much by stating that, if Batasuna had demanded the dissolution of ETA or ETA had already disarmed, Otegi's sentence might have been different.[30]

Towards endgame

Urkullu would recall that it was only in May or June 2011 that the intelligence reports received by the government offered it full reassurance of the validity of ETA's ceasefire. They had confirmed the end of extortion and thus ETA's willingness to accept the end of its violence.[31] An internal circular distributed by ETA in the summer finally acknowledged that the 'vanguard' now lay within the political structure of the nationalist left, as police action impeded it from exercising political leadership.[32] In July Zapatero received a message from ETA through international interlocutors that it wanted to establish a road map with the government before moving ahead. Zapatero had insisted that any message from ETA had to be that of a definitive end to its violence and Urkullu had issued a series of public statements urging ETA to take that step.[33] But the organisation was not yet ready.

At the end of the month a struggling Zapatero announced that general elections would be held on 20 November. For the nationalist left, time now seemed too tight to expect favourable verdicts from the Constitutional Court on appeals lodged with regard to Sortu and the Parot Doctrine—a ruling that the latter was unconstitutional would have led to the immediate release of dozens of *etarras* from prison— before the elections. Moreover, the enormous pressure imposed on individual judges by politicians and other forces of the right after their ruling on Bildu suggested that further movement would be difficult. (This suspicion was confirmed in mid-September, when government lawyers filed a petition to the Constitutional Court to prevent its con- sideration of Sortu. They argued that while ETA existed and the nation- alist left had not broken with it, Sortu 'cannot be a normal political actor, equivalent to other parties'.)[34] Instead the nationalist left decided to try to take advantage of the opportunity presented by the PSOE's likely desire to secure a single piece of good news at the end of Zapatero's otherwise disastrous second term. Etxeberria and others therefore redou- bled their efforts to elicit a formal declaration from ETA announcing the end of its armed action.

To do so required the assistance of the international actors who had, to differing degrees, been accompanying and encouraging the nationalist left's internal transition. This entailed, as Etxeberria put it in July, raising their involvement 'to another level'.[35] The Brussels Declaration had played a critical role—certainly much greater than its signatories, most of whom had had no further involvement in the process, could have conceived—in the internal debates with ETA and in shaping the public steps forward taken by the nationalist left, including the achievement of the Guernica Declaration. In the months since its signing, international actors had remained closely engaged. The ICG had continued quiet consultations with a variety of sectors—unions, the Catholic Church and business associations, in addition to political parties—on the forma- tion of a verification mechanism, while others had begun engaging directly with ETA. In the new phase, Etxeberria hoped that interna- tional actors would assume a more active role in monitoring ETA's ceasefire—after the establishment of a verification mechanism—as well as in direct facilitation. Moving forward in both areas, however, 'would depend on the willingness of the Spanish state'.

After the municipal elections, and with the knowledge that the future of Sortu and of the Parot Doctrine would be decided by the courts, Currin considered his work with Batasuna on the 'political situation' to be essentially over.[36] He had no access to ETA or to the government and his public profile was controversial. His prominent role in a television documentary on the role of 'international mediators in the Basque Country' and his authorship of a long article in the international edition of *Le Monde Diplomatique* had prompted renewed criticism of his involvement.[37] The documentary seemed to belie repeated reassurances that he was not a mediator. Within it his revelation of a strange episode by which he had received a threatening letter from ETA in mid-2008, later denied by the organisation (Currin suggested that it had either been fabricated by Spanish intelligence or a dissident faction of ETA) and a portrayal of the role of external actors considered lacking in nuance, had irritated the nationalist left, as well as Currin's more usual critics.

No less damaging was the article in the *Le Monde Diplomatique*, which some believed reflected both over-reach in the recounting of Currin's achievements and partiality in analysing the 'conflict' in 'exactly the same terms as those used by one of the parties involved'.[38] Particularly grating was the apprehension he expressed that ETA might fear that, even if it renounced violence definitively, the government would refuse to address the 'political aspects of the conflict'. Currin noted that 'the constitution of the ICG was intended, in part, to impede this'. This was a statement that, to many Basques and Spaniards, promised unacceptable interference in their internal affairs. It also seemed insensitive to the ambivalence within an increasingly broad political spectrum—including some within the PNV—regarding the need for political talks to take place in a framework other than the Basque Parliament. After the May elections it was evident that the nationalist left would, in time, be represented within it with strength. A return to the old contours of the Pact of Ajuria Enea, which had specified that political issues could only be addressed by legitimately elected representatives, was not just the only means to secure the participation of the PP, but a formula with which both the PNV and PSE felt comfortable.

Together with Raymond Kendall, in July 2011 Currin continued consultations on the formation of an International Verification Commission of which—in deference to the sensitivities he raised—he would not be a member.[39] In a press conference he also gave voice to the concern expressed privately by the nationalist left: that the limits of a unilateral process had been reached and that, in order for ETA to move ahead, something 'multilateral' would now be required.[40] The concern did not question the validity of the unilateral process pursued by Batasuna—on the contrary its unilateral nature had allowed the nationalist left to advance thus far without being dependant on what the government would or would not agree to—nor did it suggest that ETA required political guarantees before it announced the end of its violence. However, representatives of the nationalist left insisted that ETA needed 'more' than the 'nothing' it had received so far from the government with regard to assurances on legalisation and the technical 'consequences of the conflict'—especially the fate of the prisoners—that would be the province of ETA and the government alone.[41]

In early 2012 Urkullu and senior members of the nationalist left acknowledged the critical role that a confidential 'road map' had played in getting to ETA's October declaration. Rubalcaba, however, flatly denied its existence.[42] As even ETA's account suggested, the process that preceded its declaration was opaque, not least to avoid the levelling of accusations against the government—on other fronts locked in bitter pre-electoral competition with the PP—that it had offered concessions of any kind ('paid a price for peace') to ETA. And indeed in early September, in response to new demands from the nationalist left for movement by the government on legalisation of Sortu and guarantees for the prisoners, it was made quite clear, as Luis Aizpeolea reported, that 'neither Patxi López, nor Rubalcaba, nor [Antonio] Camacho [the new minister of the interior], nor Ares want… "to take risks or commit the mistakes of the past, such as embarking on a policy of mutual gestures, or still less open a process of conversations"'.[43] However, in November 2011, in a long interview in *Gara*, ETA explained its prompt response to the Aiete Conference as consistent with commitments it had made to 'the international community' beforehand. Rather than a 'concrete agreement' there had been a 'sequence of steps to be taken' that had amounted to 'a kind of road map'. It added that while there had been no 'direct meeting' between ETA and the government of Spain, in recent months there had been a 'mutual understanding' of which, as far as ETA knew, the PP had been informed.[44] Otegi would later confirm that the PSOE and the government were 'totally and faithfully informed of all that was to take place in Euskal Herria'.[45]

The existence of a 'road map' of sorts helped explain the rapid acceleration of developments in late September. Critical steps forward had included the long-awaited subscription of the prisoners' collective,

EPPK, to the Guernica Declaration on 23 September. This, as Urkullu recalled, was an important marker for the government: 'at that moment the light, which until then might have been red or yellow, switched to a flashing yellow'. The following week saw a remarkable pace of events: on 27 September Amaiur was launched as a new electoral coalition (Bildu with the addition of Aralar) to contend the general elections; on 28 September a newly formed International Verification Commission (IVC) gave a press conference in Bilbao; on 29 September, in a deca-logue of proposals for 'unity, concord and coexistence' he presented to the Basque Parliament, Patxi López accepted the possibility of the move-ment of Basque prisoners closer to Basque Country and changes in penitentiary policy if ETA abandoned violence;[46] and on 1 October Ekin announced its disbanding—a very significant step forward in sym-bolic terms despite the fact that internal divisions and police action against it meant there was not much left of it to disband.

Representatives of the nationalist left would recall the actions they took in this period as balanced against steps taken and promises made by the government to 'other actors' in the road map. Neither they, nor still less ETA was ever involved in direct negotiations with the govern-ment or its representatives, but they believed they had secured assur-ances with regard to measures to ameliorate conditions in the prisons, and to promote the legalisation of Sortu and repeal of the Parot Doctrine. While some positive steps were seen before the Aiete Conference within the prisons—in addition to López' statement—they would later maintain that most of the measures they understood to have been agreed to by the government were never fulfilled.[47] The ambiguous status of the road map—and indeed the virtual nature of the process that had produced it—inevitably gave them little solid ground from which to defend this position.

In the absence of visible movement from the government, its toler-ance of the formation of the IVC took on particular importance. Back in July there had been indications from Madrid that it would offer no formal objection to its formation—something deemed encouraging in itself. In advancing this far, the support of Urkullu—who had intro-duced the members of the commission to the PSE and other sectors of Basque society—had been key. As on other issues related to the emerg-ing process, he also tried to ensure that the PP might at least temper its resistance. 'They could adopt a negative posture,' he would recall, 'but not frontal rejection.'[48]

The apparent acceptance, however tacit, of the IVC—even as the government and the PP held fast to the public line that no verification other than that of the security forces was required—reflected a variety of different factors: the consultations that had preceded the commission's formation and its strong support by the PNV; the identity of its members; a careful delineation of its scope of work; and the timing of its launch, which to many seemed ripe for taking engagement with ETA's ceasefire to a new level. Chaired by Ram Manikkalingham, director of the Dialogue Advisory Group, based in the Netherlands, and a former senior adviser to the president of Sri Lanka, its other four members brought with them a wide range of experience. They included Kendall himself, who had had a distinguished career in the Special Branch, the UK police counter-terrorist unit linked to the secret services, prior to joining Interpol; Ronnie Kasrils, a former deputy defence minister and minister of the interior in South Africa and veteran member of the ANC; Chris McCabe, a former political director of the Northern Ireland Office in the British government as well as head of prison regimes in Northern Ireland; and Lt. General Satish Nambiar, who had been deputy chief of staff of the Indian army. Fleur Ravensbergen, also of the Dialogue Advisory Group, would serve as the IVC's coordinator.

As Manikkalingham explained at a press conference on 28 September, the IVC's formation and specific technical expertise responded both to the demand from Basque actors for assistance with verification of ETA's ceasefire and to the sense of the ICG that 'they had neither the competence nor desire' to do this themselves.[49] The latter, he added, was because 'they felt some people perceived them to be partial to one side'. He reported that before beginning work the members of the IVC had 'needed to know' that ETA accepted their interpretation of the ceasefire. They felt that both 'permanent' and 'verifiable' were insufficient and so had sought—and received—confirmation from ETA that the ceasefire was 'unilateral and without conditions'. Announcing that the IVC planned to develop 'links to the authorities in the Basque Country and in the national government in Madrid', Manikkalingham acknowledged that there would be some information only a government would have access to as well as the sensitivity of timing with regard to elections. Finally, he explained what the IVC would not do: it would not address political issues, or all issues related to ETA or its members—its task was limited to the technical one of 'ETA's adherence to the ceasefire'.

Although attracting less attention than the simultaneous news of Ekin's dissolution, on 1 October ETA issued a communiqué announcing its commitment to collaborate with the IVC and welcoming its formation as 'an important step' towards the end of violence.[50]

ETA and its prisoners

What ETA was at this critical moment in its history was of course integral to the steps taken towards the ending of its armed activity. A decade on from 2002, when Aznar's stepped-up counter-terrorism policies beat back its post-Lizarra offensive, ETA was reported to have just several dozen active militants and was a shadow of the organisation it once had been. There had been reports that Josu Ternera had returned to the leadership, but none suggested that he was in a position of ultimate command.[51] The organisation had been in permanent ceasefire for six months, and had effectively ceased its offensive operations a year before that.

The summer of 2011 had been notable for the absence of *kale borroka* and other incidents of violence on Basque streets; confidence in the ceasefire was such that the 1,500 bodyguards employed by politicians, judges, journalists and other potential targets of ETA were worrying about unemployment. With extortion no longer a source of income, *etarras* were reportedly living on the organisation's savings and 'voluntary contributions' from sympathisers.[52] As ETA faced the end of its armed activities—and thus the prospect of the leverage over Basque and Spanish politics that it long believed these brought it—the prisoners, a community within which the weight, experience and history of the organisation had long been vested, loomed large. ETA's existence would necessarily be bound to theirs.

Batasuna's understanding of what went on in the prisons was anecdotal rather than systematic—each prisoner maintained communication with his or her lawyer and network of family and friends—fractured by the government's prison policy, and complicated by the control still exercised by the EPPK. In the summer of 2011, Etxerat, the support organisation for prisoners' families, documented 707 prisoners within the EPPK in eighty prisons in four countries; in Spain there were 549 prisoners in forty-nine different prisons, while a further 149 were in twenty-nine prisons in France.[53] The government had intensified surveillance in the course of its broader effort to encourage dissidence; Batasuna suspected that it had a better sense of what was going on within the prisons than it did. The grip maintained on the prisoners by ETA had been weakened by the arrest of the EPPK lawyers in April 2010. Yet the leadership of the prisoners' collective remained resistant to change, and dispersion represented a serious obstacle to any process of consultation.

The EPPK included many prisoners who had never militated within ETA—those awaiting trial or serving sentences for crimes of association and opinion attributed to defendants in the 18/98 *macroproceso* and other political entities of the nationalist left—but their influence was necessarily muted. As one former prisoner explained, many prisoners did not support the hard line EPPK pursued or welcome the tight controls it exerted, but they dared not reject its membership. These individuals did not necessarily want to assume public dissidence against ETA—the prisoners gathered in Nanclares had signed letters of repentance and rejection of ETA drafted for them by the government—but nor did they feel able to face the lonely prospect of being a Basque 'terrorist' in a Spanish prison without the protection and solidarity offered by the EPPK.[54]

Since 2009, there had been continuing speculation regarding the positions assumed by the prisoners on the changes taking place within the nationalist left, fuelled, and frequently manipulated, by the government's leaking of intercepted conversations. Differences among the prisoners were generally summarised as distinguishing between positions assumed by those in open dissidence with ETA—twenty-four gathered in Nanclares by September 2011[55]—a majority of prisoners supportive of the changes within the nationalist left but waiting to see how they would develop, and a smaller, but never precise, number of prisoners aligned with the holdouts inside ETA, who retained influence over the EPPK as a whole. During 2010 and 2011 the positions assumed by the Nanclares prisoners were frequently reflected in the media, raising the profile of this still relatively small number of individuals. Relations between the Nanclares group, inevitably seen as 'traitors' by some, and the EPPK and the nationalist left more broadly, deteriorated.

Etxerat had been a signatory of the Guernica Declaration, but not the EPPK. (The Nanclares group had wanted to sign but had been prevented from doing so by the nationalist left). The collective had issued a statement in December 2010 that had expressed its intention to take an active part in the process developing in the Basque Country in only the vaguest terms. It had instead offered criticism of government manipulation and 'blackmail' in the prisons through offers of 'options to get out of prison and improve our quality of life if we leave the EPPK, undertake political repentance and let them show us off like trophies gathered on a safari'.[56] Leaders of the nationalist left had subsequently embarked on an intense effort to gain the support of individual prisoners for the Guernica agreement.[57] They had been helped both by the 2010 arrest of the EPPK's lawyers and by a change in its leadership to individuals more attuned to the new direction they were advocating. A further contributing factor was the degree of 'anxiousness and concern' on the part of prisoners' families. The demonstration in support of the prisoners in January 2011 had been the largest in a year of remarkable social mobilisation. But the electoral success of Bildu had made families feel that things had moved very fast on the political process while no progress at all had been made with regard to prisoners' demands.[58]

These antecedents gave particular resonance to the event in the Teatro Liceo of Guernica, on 23 September. Two former ETA prisoners, Gloria Rekarte and Jon Agirre Agiriano—the latter released in May after serving thirty years in prison for two assassinations—signed the Guernica Declaration on its one-year anniversary on behalf of the EPPK.[59] Immediately recognised as an 'important step' by the PSOE—'unheard of' Rubalcaba put it—although dismissed as 'nothing new' by the PP, the shift on the part of the prisoners was rightly identified by José Luis Zubizarreta as the 'penultimate piece in the puzzle'.[60] The impenetrable prose of the EPPK communiqué suggested considerable difficulties ahead. It referred to the need for a 'complete amnesty' and reiterated the importance of the 'political and collective' nature of the EPPK, suggesting that the prisoners would continue to demand a collective solution to their situation that would be quite unacceptable to any Spanish government. But in the immediate future, the clear priority was to build on the momentum created by this historic renunciation of violence by ETA's prisoners and move ahead.

Aiete

The subterranean process that concluded in the Aiete Conference built upon the unilateral path towards an end to ETA's violence taken by the nationalist left, but it also reflected its limits. It represented a creative use of international contacts that Batasuna had developed over the years, as well as a creditable disposition on the part of international actors to assume prominent roles in the scenography required for ETA to take the irrevocable step towards its end. The government's role remained shrouded in ambiguity. Only a few within it were appraised of arrangements for the Aiete Conference, and none have openly discussed them. That Zapatero and Rubalcaba—and even Rajoy—had been informed of and had tacitly allowed arrangements for the international conference to go ahead was evident. 'The government did not organise it,' the Socialist politician Eduardo Madina explained, 'but it gave its approval through people who were very highly regarded internationally with good connections in Spain.'[61] The decision to do so rested on a hard-won belief that, this time, Batasuna would deliver ETA, as well as a steely pragmatism that recognised that the reputational risk incurred by the prominent internationals who attended the conference was greater than that taken by government officials who remained at a public distance from their effort—and could always condemn it as a misguided initiative by naïve do-gooders if it all went wrong.

The idea for an international peace conference had first been mooted in the discussions at Loyola in 2006. The thinking at the time was that it would be hosted by a Basque institution—Eusko Ikaskuntza (the Society of Basque Studies)—but involve international participants. These would both provide public legitimacy to the agreements reached in confidence between the PSE, PNV and Batasuna, and give a degree of cover to the inclusion of participants from across Euskal Herria—including Navarre and the French Basque provinces of Iparralde—that was a core requirement of the nationalist left.[62] Batasuna and its international advisers had for some time considered the possibility of a similar international conference providing a setting in which it might be possible to stage manage an acceptable end to ETA's violence. The idea now was to hold an event in San Sebastián in which credible international figures would join together to ask ETA to declare a definitive end to its armed violence in terms that would allow it to offer a positive response. As such, the conference undoubtedly included an element of theatre: the invisibility of the contacts that necessarily preceded it allowed the government, which was conceding nothing, to hold firm to its rejection of negotiations, while ETA achieved a means to lay down its arms on terms that, while gaining nothing, it could consider its own, with the added advantage of the legitimacy offered by the involvement of distinguished international figures and their presentation of a statement that could indicate the way ahead.

The preparations and organisation of the Aiete Conference were veiled in secrecy and a deliberate degree of confusion. Both were deemed necessary to protect the government and the conference itself from the onslaught of criticism that was deemed likely to torpedo its existence if its planning should become public. Lokarri took care of the conference's logistics and officially promoted it, together with the ICG, the Berghof Foundation, Conciliation Resources—both highly regarded non-governmental peacebuilding organisations which had been previously involved in the Basque Country through the provision of workshops and commissioning of research that had won the trust of the nationalist left[63]—the Desmond and Leah Tutu Legacy Foundation, and the Norwegian Peacebuilding Resource Centre. Currin and the ICG, as the best known of the international entities in the Basque context, were publicly credited with the organisation of the conference.[64] However, those closely attuned to the conference's planning knew that Currin and his colleagues had no direct communication with ETA or credibility in Madrid. They noted instead the key role of Jonathan Powell, who retained the confidence of interlocutors in Madrid from his period as Blair's chief of staff and connections to the Basque case and the HD Centre since his involvement in the talks in Geneva in May 2007. Although it had maintained the lowest of profiles, they also acknowledged the discreet backing of Norway, which had been recognised by Gerry Adams in an interview with Paddy Woodworth and was evident in the presence at Aiete of a former Norwegian prime minister, Gro Harlem Bruntland.[65]

Arrangements for the conference were put in place only at the very last minute, in deference not only for the need for secrecy but also to divisions apparently present within the PSOE regarding the desirability of its going ahead. Even once the decision was taken, doubts remained at a senior level until Zapatero himself approved it. Ramón Jáuregui, for example, Zapatero's minister of the presidency, recalled being 'sceptical' to the end. 'Despite being involved in this so long I had lost hope that something so clear, so convincing [as ETA's declaration] could be produced.'[66]

Powell spoke at a press conference held in San Sebastián on 11 October to announce that the international conference would take place on 17 October 2011. He made his first public declaration on the Basque process flanked by representatives of Lokarri and the other institutional sponsors of the event. His remarks were carefully limited to lessons he had learned in Northern Ireland. Even so, what he said came as a breath of fresh air to those accustomed to the extraordinary contortions into which any discussion of the Basque issue had been driven by the peculiarities of Spanish politics. He noted the international community's concern for the 'last armed conflict in Europe'—a red flag to many from the beginning—and stressed that the international leaders, unnamed at this stage, who were to attend the conference would speak only from their experience. 'No conflict is resolved without leadership and risk,' he told the assembled journalists. 'It is time to move beyond a situation in which one party believes it has won and that the other has lost. Everyone has to think that they have won.'[67]

Which international leaders—and which Basque politicians—would attend the conference was a subject of mystery and high drama. Until the very last moment it was rumoured that Powell's former boss, Tony Blair—who indeed had agreed to attend the conference but had to cancel his participation—would be present. Other names, including that of Kofi Annan, former secretary-general of the United Nations, were kept secret because of a complex process of consultation undertaken with Madrid and strong push-back from Aznar, who remained a potent force within sectors of the PP. As *ABC* reported, Annan, as could be expected of a diplomat of his experience, did not take his participation in the conference lightly. He had called the Moncloa palace with three questions on which he had wanted reassurance from Zapatero: 'if he should come, if his presence would be useful, and, above all, if this really was the end of ETA'. He received a positive response to all three, and decided that it was worth the trip.[68]

The PP's refusal to participate in the conference was no surprise, but a fierce discussion took place within the PSOE regarding whether it should participate and at what level. The Basque government—like the central government—stayed away while the PSE was in the end represented by Eguiguren and Carlos Totorika, the mayor of Ermua. Patxi López held fast to existing plans for a trade trip in the United States, and was thus out of the country. (He had been reportedly keen to avoid it in part to protect his prospects for advancement within the PSOE.) In his absence Rodolfo Ares paid a courtesy call on Annan and the other international participants at Aiete. But questions remained regarding why the *lehendakari*—even if had not attended the conference itself—would not at least have wanted to take the opportunity to present Annan and the international community with his new proposals ('you'd have thought he might have wanted to invite Kofi Annan to lunch', recalled one representative of the nationalist left with an abrupt laugh, 'he left Martín Garitano to host the UN secretary-general!'). The PSE's ambivalent stance towards the Aiete Conference contributed to an intemperate outburst by Eguiguren that the Socialists 'have lost the opportunity to lead the peace'.[69] But the real damage came when news of ETA's declaration of the end of its violence caught López on a train somewhere between Washington and New York, thousands of miles from home.

The international leaders who gathered in the Aiete palace on 17 October included Annan; Gerry Adams of Sinn Féin; Bertie Ahern, the former prime minister of Ireland; Gro Harlem Bruntland; Pierre Joxe—as French interior minister during a period of intense ETA activity in the Mitterand years his presence had particular resonance for the nationalist left—and Powell. Basque political parties and social forces, including representatives from Navarre and the French Basque territories, each made brief statements before the visiting dignitaries took to the floor.

At the conference's conclusion, Ahern read the carefully worded declaration that was its purpose on the steps of the Aiete palace. Echoing Powell a week earlier, he explained that the international leaders were in San Sebastián to help bring to a close 'the last armed confrontation in Europe'. They called upon ETA to make a public declaration of the definitive cessation of all armed action and to 'request talks with the governments of Spain and France to address exclusively the consequences of the conflict'. If such a declaration was made, they urged the governments of Spain and France to welcome it and to agree to such talks, as well as 'major steps' to promote reconciliation; to recognise, compensate and assist all victims; to acknowledge the harm that had been done; and to seek to heal personal and social wounds. Drawing on their own experience, they suggested that 'non violent actors and political representatives meet and discuss political and other related issues, in consultation with the citizenry, that could contribute to a new era without conflict'. They recalled that that third-party observers or facilitators frequently help such dialogue and could do so in this case 'if it were desired by those involved'. They also indicated their willingness to form a committee to follow-up on their recommendations.[70]

Nationalist social and political forces in the Basque Country immediately welcomed the Aiete Conference as a landmark contribution to
the effort to secure the end of ETA's violence, initiate the social reconciliation required within the Basque Country and lay the groundwork
for the difficult political discussions that would eventually need to take
place first among Basques, and then between Basques and Madrid,
regarding the Basque Country's future relations to the Spanish state. On
behalf of the nationalist left, Rufi Etxeberria offered a formal endorsement of the conference's declaration and called upon ETA to respond.
From outside Spain, Tony Blair, Jimmy Carter and George Mitchell all
quickly issued public statements supporting the declaration.[71] From
France came careful support 'of all the efforts of the Spanish government
to bring an end to violence in the Basque Country'.[72]

In Spain, other reactions reflected resentment that international leaders considered dupes of ETA had unapologetically adopted the language
of the nationalist left—nowhere did the declaration use the word 'terrorism'—and that they failed to ask for the immediate and unconditional dissolution of ETA demanded by the PP, mixed political issues in
with the demand for an end to ETA's armed action and raised the sensitive issues of political talks.[73] The declaration also troubled victims'
organisations: the AVT branded the conference 'another pantomime' of
ETA's; Maite Pagazaurtundua quipped 'perhaps only Apple sells its
products better'.[74] Basagoiti immediately dismissed the conference declaration as 'unacceptable to any democrat' and sent each of the international leaders a long letter explaining the many ways in which they had
misunderstood the nature of Basque reality.[75]

But while Basagoiti and others within the PP piled on the criticism—
the party's deputy director of communications, Esteban González Pons
claimed of Annan and Adams, 'they think this is South Africa, they don't
have a damn idea'[76]—this too had a certain theatricality about it. Direct
criticism of the PNV and the PSE for their participation in the conference was absent. Rajoy himself declined to comment on the conference,
reflecting both the shared desire by the PSOE and PP not to politicise the
issue of ETA during the electoral campaign and the extent to which he
had been fully briefed on events in San Sebastián. For its part the government assumed a studiously distant tone that verged on the comical. It
was, 'not concerned or challenged' by the conference's declaration,
explained Jáuregui, who of course had been involved in the difficult discussions that had preceded it, 'we think it just another piece of paper'.[77]

The definitive end to armed activity

ETA responded three days later by announcing 'the definitive end of its armed activity' and calling upon the governments of Spain and France to enter into a process of direct dialogue to resolve the 'consequences of the conflict'.[78] This was a signal moment in Spain's democratic history, to be savoured and appreciated in the Basque Country and across Spain. Doubts, of course, remained, but both the very public transition within the nationalist left and the very private pre-cooking that had preceded the Aiete Conference upon which the end of ETA's violence rested gave the announcement a degree of credibility distinct from anything else in ETA's history. 'I am personally convinced that ETA will never kill in Spain again. It is over,' Rubalcaba told *The Washington Post*.[79] In early 2012, Rubalcaba would refuse to be drawn into discussing any of the arrangements that had preceded Aiete and the statement from ETA that had so quickly responded to it. But he interpreted the conference—as he had no doubt done from the beginning—in functional terms: 'if the price to pay for ETA to abandon its violence is that Kofi Annan comes to San Sebastián, I would buy the ticket myself'.[80]

The scenography of the end was such that a number of individuals knew that the statement from ETA was coming. As a year earlier, when ETA's not-quite ceasefire of September 2010 had been prominently reported by the BBC, ETA was acutely aware of the value of international projection of its news. The BBC and *The New York Times* as well as *Gara* and *Berria* had received copies of ETA's communiqué early on 20 October, but they were embargoed until 7 pm in Spain. News of the capture and death of Mohamed Qaddafi, in the outskirts of Sirte, Libya, that morning, was a distraction, even a concern—would ETA want to lose its last opportunity to dominate international headlines? But ETA's announcement went ahead. Once again, three hooded figures sat behind a table, surrounded by the organisation's symbols and flags. A commander later identified as David Pla, flanked by Isaskun Lesaka and Iratxe Sorzábal, read the communiqué and ETA's violence was no more.

The headline news was more than welcome, but there were elements of the communiqué that gave pause. There was no reference to victims, or the suffering caused by ETA's violence. And the communiqué was suffused by a tone of self-justification that seemed to imply that thanks were due to ETA's forbearance from the violence that it had inflicted on Basque and Spanish society for so many years. There was no sign at all—as no one close to the process that lay behind this hard-won communiqué would have expected—of the softening of the epic narrative that ETA had managed to maintain to the end.

Reactions came quickly, with a confidence on the part of both the government and the PP that reflected their shared knowledge that ETA's statement was solidly grounded. Zapatero welcomed 'the definitive and unconditional triumph of the rule of law' while promising 'democracy without terrorism, but not without memory'.[81] Rajoy recognised ETA's communiqué as 'great news, there have been no concessions', even as he cautioned that 'the tranquillity of Spaniards only will be complete when we achieve the irreversible dissolution of ETA'.[82] Rubalcaba, who had been more deeply invested in the long process towards this moment than any other Spanish official, gave an emotional statement with an emphasis on what the violence itself had meant: 'Decades of death and suffering have come to an end; they have broken the lives of many people and caused anguish for many more. They have been a constant threat to Spanish democracy. Years of the assassination of innocents, of shots in the head, of car bombs. Of decent citizens who each morning have had to check beneath their car; of honest people who each day leave home with great uncertainty; of mornings in flames and streets taken over by the violent.'[83]

Much, obviously, remained to be done. The Socialists—especially in the Basque Country—were already showing signs of recognition that flexibility on the issue of prisoners would be a key issue in moving towards the desired dissolution of ETA. But the positions of ETA and any government in Madrid would likely to be far apart. ETA wanted dialogue and verification. The victims were adamant in resisting anything that smacked of impunity and demanded the condemnation by ETA and Batasuna of the armed organisation's history. Coexistence and then, eventually, reconciliation, remained distant goals. These issues threatened to open up difficult divisions between the candidates, and the parties, immersed in an electoral campaign forced upon Spain by the dire condition of its economy.

Zapatero, Rajoy and Rubalcaba all quickly announced that it would fall to the new government to manage the end of ETA—to the disappointment of those within the nationalist left who had believed they had an agreement on a road map that would yield more. Zapatero reiterated this position to Urkullu during the final meeting he held with the PNV president. Urkullu urged movement of prisoners to the Basque Country, the revision of the Parot Doctrine and the provision of prison benefits to those prisoners who took the necessary steps to achieve them. He was told that with the exception of the movement of sick prisoners for humanitarian reasons—some had been recently been returned home—nothing related to the end of ETA could be expected to happen in the remaining weeks of the Socialist government.[84]

In the Basque Country, reactions to ETA's declaration had in some respects been muted.[85] The pages of *Gara*—closely aligned with those sectors of the nationalist left that had struggled to move beyond violence since the end of the last ceasefire—were predictably triumphant in welcoming ETA's 'historic decision' and looking forward to 'a new time for Euskal Herria'.[86] But elsewhere the reaction was more complex. It had been more than two years since ETA had killed in Spain, and a year since it had first announced its ceasefire. Although the news of the 'definitive end' was qualitatively different—for an organisation whose identity had so long been defined by the *ekintza*, the armed action, it was in many respects the only news that mattered—a sense of triumph was tempered by the weight of ETA's history and the recognition of the deep divisions in Basque society that remained. So much time had gone by, so many lives had been lost, such rancour and hatred had poisoned Basque political life—and what had it all been for? Above all it was hard not to wonder why ETA had not been able to take this step ten, twenty or thirty years before.

At the end, as at the beginning, Basque society was left to face both its very different narratives and the political and social challenge implicit in the hard fact that while the majority of Basques felt very Basque, but also a bit Spanish, and only a small minority felt not Basque at all, there was a sizeable minority of Basques who did not want to be Spanish and a large number that would demand not independence—not yet—but the right to decide, among Basques, how to sort it all out.

10

UNFINISHED BUSINESS

Mariano Rajoy was swept to power in general elections held in November 2011 at the head of a PP government with an absolute majority. The results represented the most devastating loss by the Socialists and the PP's greatest victory since the transition. But the Spain that Rajoy set out to govern was in a sorry state as, it would soon be shown, was his own political party. Economic woes came accompanied by a profound institutional crisis. Public confidence in the judiciary, politicians, the banking sector and even Spain's royalty was buffeted by blatant politicisation, endemic corruption and incompetence at a moment when individual Spaniards faced unprecedented economic stress. The failures of the judicial system were among the most obvious. Three cases against Baltazar Garzón, including the challenge to his investigation of the crimes of Franco, came to trial in early 2012 in circumstance that smacked of a judicial vendetta. Garzón was disbarred for ordering wire-taps of lawyers of PP officials facing corruption charges—a practice that directly echoed the means by which he had successfully built the case against ETA's lawyers in 2010—and the Franco case was dropped. The politics of Garzón's prosecution were keenly debated, but the case represented a humiliating demonstration of the murky depths into which Spanish justice had fallen and, as Reed Brody of Human Rights Watch put it, 'an affront to principles of human rights and judicial independence'.[1]

When the PP assumed government in December 2011, what Rajoy was or was not prepared to do to secure the end of ETA had been largely unknown. Expectations were hostage to the ambiguity that had swirled around the Aiete Conference and ETA's declaration that quickly followed. ETA and the nationalist left had moved forward on the basis of the confidential road map they had agreed with the outgoing government and of the international encouragement of the 'process' spelled out at Aiete. This had looked towards direct talks between the government and ETA on the consequences of the conflict as well as the possibility of broader political dialogue on the underlying differences among Basques. They were aware that Aiete offered no guarantees, but had understood ETA's declaration as a 'kind of beginning'.[2] However, the agreement that the new government would manage the next phase towards ETA's end had allowed the Socialists to mask undertakings they had given to the nationalist left and left the incoming Rajoy government with its hands free.

From a technical perspective, what remained to be done was not, in some respects, that difficult: ETA had declared an end to its violence, and the security services quickly confirmed this to be genuine. The much-reduced organisation had communicated its willingness to cede discussion of political issues to other actors and wanted to discuss questions of disarmament and the fate of its prisoners and exiles. Moreover, as the PSOE had confidentially informed Rajoy, there were reputable international actors with open channels to ETA willing and able to help advance the process towards ETA's dissolution. The prisoner issue was complex, and ETA's prisoners demanded amnesty and remained beholden to the strictures of the EPPK. Yet there was a strong argument to be made for reversing some of the exceptional legal measures introduced to combat ETA's terrorism and much that could be done (moving prisoners closer to the Basque Country, releasing sick prisoners, repealing the Parot Doctrine, extending prison privileges) within existing laws to build confidence and encourage ETA to move ahead. ETA itself sent clear messages that it was willing to be flexible; conditions existed to permit fully discreet discussions to begin to disband ETA forever and to bring much needed resolution to the Basque region.

But it soon became clear that forward movement was unlikely. That ETA had stopped killing meant that it was objectively not a problem for most Spaniards, while those with most to lose from any relapse into violence were its political associates in the nationalist left. Bildu had joined with Aralar to contest the general elections as Amaiur, won 24 per cent of the Basque vote and was now represented by seven deputies and three senators in Madrid, fuelling criticism that the Socialists had allowed the 'terrorist movement' to snatch victory from the jaws of the defeat inflicted by Aznar.[3] The government did not take steps to reverse the political progress made in 2011. But under mounting pressure from victims' organisations and right-wing sectors of the party gathered around Aznar and Jaime Mayor Oreja, it refused to assume the flexibility in penitentiary policy advocated by the PSOE and PNV, held fast to demands for ETA's dissolution, and rejected all offers of international assistance to facilitate it while pursuing ETA with the full force of the police and law. In doing so it undermined the best opportunity to end ETA that had so far existed in what appeared an almost inexplicable rejection of all that experience elsewhere—and indeed common sense—suggested about the value of building confidence in the shift of violent actors towards peace.[4]

In Euskadi the separate but related challenges of how to move forward to the dissolution of ETA and the re-alignment of Basque politics that the end of its violence had precipitated could neither be wished away nor addressed too quickly. The governing pact between the PSE and PP faltered over irreconcilable differences on Rajoy's economic policies and broke down in May. Basque politics plunged into pre-electoral mode, invigorated by the legalisation of Sortu that was finally approved by the Constitutional Court in June. In late July Patxi López announced that parliamentary elections would be brought forward from early 2013 to 21 October, just a year after ETA's declared end to its violence. They would be the first democratic elections held in the Basque Country without the threat of violence since 1932.

Rajoy's Spain, and ETA

In a pattern that was beginning to sound familiar the arrival of a new prime minister prompted reflection on the need for Spain's 'second transition'.[5] This time around the vulnerabilities of the first one were more clearly in evidence than ever before. Zapatero had failed to live up to the ambition of his first term. In trying, his government had exposed both the need for major reform and obstacles to achieving it deeply engrained within Spanish society. A crisis in the state of autonomies rooted in the unbridled expansion of regional governments and the inability of some of them to curb their spending was one of the core elements of the Spanish drama.

In Catalonia, Madrid's rejection of proposals for a new fiscal pact to address what Catalans perceived as their unjust subsidy of the national budget (Catalans transferred up to ten times more to Madrid than Basques on a per capita basis) combined with frustration at the long saga of the new autonomy statute and threats of re-centralisation to encourage separatist tendencies. In a public opinion poll conducted in June 2012, support for independence stood at a historic high of 51 per cent.[6] On 11 September, Catalonia's *Diada*, or national day, a million and a half people took to the streets of Barcelona to demand 'Catalonia, a new state in Europe'. As in the Basque Country, pro-independence forces found encouragement from the prospect of a referendum on Scottish independence in Britain. Artur Mas, leader of the Convergence and Union (CiU) party called early elections for November 2012 as a step on the way to an eventual referendum. The prospect of the break-up of Spain appeared a more imminent threat to Spanish nationalists than at any time in the country's modern history.

The problems facing Spain in 2012 exposed perils intrinsic to general elections won by default: the big swing to the PP (which won 44.6 per cent of the vote across Spain to the PSOE's 28.7 per cent) had been a swing away from the Socialists rather than a vote inspired by the leadership or platform offered by Rajoy. The campaign had done its best to reinvent the candidate, a cautious politician who had twice lost elections to Zapatero, as a steady hand. But the indecision and public reticence that characterised Rajoy's political style were unsuited to the challenges he faced. In his first few months in office Spain agreed to a bail-out of its troubled banking sector and Rajoy was forced to announce cuts and tax increases totalling 65 billion euros. Unable or unwilling to explain austerity measures inflicted upon an already reeling economy to meet demands from European lenders, the prime minister hid from journalists, avoided appearing in parliament except when legally bound to and cancelled the annual debate on the state of the nation.

Those in the nationalist left working to convince ETA to make its declaration before the PP arrived in power had understood that they could put the 'key in the door' to the resolution of the conflict, but could not know whether Rajoy would turn it. They recognised that the PP could choose whether to move forward in accordance with the Aiete

Conference, aggressively pursue its reversal—for example by arresting leaders of the nationalist left and seeking to illegalise Bildu and Amaiur—or simply just 'stop' and do nothing.[7] By early 2012 it was clear that the government had opted for the latter even as the possibility for small steps forward remained open.

Emphasis was put on the pursuit of unity among democratic parties in forging polices towards ETA. In meetings with López and Urkullu in late January Rajoy responded cautiously to demands that both made for flexibility on the issue of prisoners.[8] Opposition from the party's right, the more vocal victims' organisations and sectors of the media (*ABC, La Razón, Intereconomía*) drew on the fundamentals of counter-terrorism established under Aznar and the antagonistic politics cultivated by the PP during the Zapatero years. Rajoy and his officials were, as Rubalcaba observed, 'prisoners of what they themselves had created'.[9] In time the contradictions between policies rooted in the determination to cede nothing to ETA or those who might share its goals and social pressure to move forward to consolidate peace became evident. Any movement at all was held to be 'irreconcilable' with the concerns of many PP voters and 'following the road map agreed with ETA by Zapatero'.[10]

An agreement reached on 21 February among all Spain's political parties other than Amaiur, the Catalan Republican Left (ERC) and the UPyD on a joint approach to management of the end of ETA held out the hope that some progress would be possible. The agreement signalled the PP's acceptance that there were now no grounds to challenge the legality of Bildu, its successor Amaiur or indeed Sortu when it eventually came before the Constitutional Court and looked forward to measures that might favour 'social coexistence'. These were understood to imply some flexibility with regard to ETA's prisoners, but came with a steep price: the agreement committed the PSOE and the PNV to the PP's demand for the 'unconditional' dissolution of ETA, something the PP understood as running directly against the possibility of discussion with ETA of anything.[11]

This minimal level of agreement among politicians in Madrid was insufficient for the demands of the Basque Country. In early January Etxerat's annual rally against prison policy had brought as many as 110,000 people into the streets of Bilbao—one of the largest demonstrations in the Basque Country's long history of public protest. A poll conducted in early February found that 72 per cent of Basques supported the reinsertion of prisoners who renounced violence and 69 per cent favoured moving them to the Basque Country.[12] These figures were in stark contrast to a Spain-wide poll conducted in November 2011, which had revealed the deep level of hostility towards any concessions. Even once an end to terrorist activity had been confirmed, 60 per cent of participants were against the moving of Basque prisoners closer to the Basque Country, and 66 per cent against their being allowed benefits equal to those available to other prisoners.[13] For most Spaniards, ETA remained the terrorist 'other', and as such to be subjected to punishments above and beyond those given ordinary criminals.

The appearance of consensus among the political parties was soon tested. In broad terms, the PSE and PNV advocated the prompt legalisation of Sortu and accepted the logic of the Ajuria Enea Pact. 'The legalisation of Sortu now,' as López explained in March 2012, 'would demonstrate that Batasuna was not banned for defending independence, but for supporting a political-military strategy that implied the assassination of political adversaries.'[14] The Ajuria Enea logic held that once the end of ETA's violence had been established it should be possible to address issues of prisoner reinsertion and disarmament through dialogue, so long as any steps taken were within the law and no political discussions were held outside the framework of the Basque Parliament. The PNV and PSE also supported movement of prisoners to, or closer to, the Basque Country, the release of sick prisoners and the repeal of the Parot Doctrine. Although to a differing extent—and in public they were coy on the subject—both parties accepted the utility of some degree of international assistance with technical issues. International actors, as one PSE parliamentarian acknowledged, had 'the great advantage of being able to talk to ETA'.[15]

Many within the PP believed that the PSOE's cardinal error had been allowing Bildu to participate in the May 2011 elections, both facilitating the return of the nationalist left to public life and relieving the pressure on ETA exerted by its continuing illegal status.[16] The new minister of interior was Jorge Fernández Díaz, an ally of Rajoy who was close to the Opus Dei and without a long trajectory in the campaign against ETA. Other appointments assured continuity in the PP's counter-terrorist policies. Angel Yuste, who had been director general of the prison service between 1996 and 2004, returned to his old post; Ignacio Cosidó, chief of staff of the Guardia Civil under Aznar and then a PP senator, was appointed director general of the police. Nine months into his new job, Cosidó described how 'the unconditional defeat' of ETA was to be achieved. The government had maintained the anti-terrorist capacities of the past and kept up the pressure on ETA with a steady rate of arrests (by the end of February 2014 the interior ministry reported the detention of sixty-eight members of ETA and seven individuals on charges relating to *kale borroka*).[17] In the international sphere counter-terrorist co-operation remained the priority (*etarras* had been arrested in Belgium, Italy and the United Kingdom, as well as France and Spain), even as the government severed all channels 'of negotiation, dialogue, engagement, takings of temperature, and other communication' opened by international actors.[18]

As thus articulated, the policy was remarkable for its scant reflection of the fact that an end of ETA's armed activities had changed the situation dramatically. Vigilance was imperative, yet conditions in the Basque Country were quite distinct from those present while the organisation retained the will to kill. Basque political parties recognised that they offered an opportunity to work towards a degree of coexistence—even tolerance—long absent from Basque political life. In Madrid the priorities, however, lay elsewhere: an end of ETA that Cosidó likened to that of GRAPO, the Maoist-inspired 'First of October Anti-Fascist Resistance Group' active in Spain from the mid-1970s on and disbanded in 2007, although never formally dissolved. But ETA, unlike GRAPO, had consistently drawn upon social support, and the end of its military activity could not be dissociated from its political consequences. Now that it had abjured violence, the former Batasuna—whose dual identity as the political arm of the nationalist left (and thus ETA) and an expression of radical nationalism deeply rooted in Basque society had been distorted by the over-simplification that 'everything is ETA'—formed the backbone of a coalition that challenged the PNV as the largest political force in the Basque Country.

'What do they all think they are doing here?'

For ETA and the nationalist left Aiete brought the promise of greater international involvement. It had looked towards the creation of a follow-up committee, international facilitation of talks between ETA, Spain and France to address 'the consequences of the conflict', as well as support for dialogue among 'non violent actors and political representatives' on 'political and other related issues', all in addition to the existing involvement of the International Verification Commission (IVC) and International Contact Group (ICG). Over coffee in the French Basque village of Ciboure in the thin winter sunshine, in February 2012 a representative of the Basque refugees' collective—a former *etarra* who had been a close associate of Argala in years gone by—recalled the conference as 'a before and after in the recognition of the existence of a Basque people and conflict'. He described contacts with ETA maintained by international actors as preparing for 'technical' talks to address the situation of the estimated three hundred exiles and refugees, in France, Latin America and elsewhere, as well as the prisoners and disarmament. Such continuing international involvement was 'a form of guarantee' of what might happen next.[19]

Lokarri had assumed responsibility for the promotion of the Aiete Conference's conclusions. It identified three major conditions for 'the peace process to be irreversible': the end of ETA's violence, the legalisation of Sortu and citizen participation in its support.[20] With the press erroneously attributing Aiete's organisation to the ICG, the latter was assumed by some to be the conference's 'follow-up committee'. This impression was reinforced by the invisibility of the 'international leaders' who had been the figureheads at Aiete. They were on the one hand kept busy by their day jobs (Kofi Annan served as the UN and Arab League's envoy to Syria between March and August 2012), and on the other, reluctant to take public positions critical of Spain's new government. In addition to Gerry Adams, Bertie Ahern and Jonathan Powell represented partial exceptions. Ahern accepted a prize awarded to the Aiete Conference by the Sabino Arana Foundation in January 2012. In late March Powell spoke in Brussels at an event hosted by the Basque Friendship and the Greens/EFA Group in the European Parliament. In remarks carefully framed around his experience of Northern Ireland, he advised that 'peace is a process not an event' and that 'you can't just wish a conflict away... you need to have engagement, you have to have talking if the problem is to be solved'.[21]

The IVC visited the Basque Country publicly in both January and May 2012. In January it met with a wide array of political actors—including, discreetly, Rodolfo Ares, the Basque government's minister for the interior—individually and in a large meeting that brought together all political parties other than the PP, and representatives of the Catholic Church, business associations and others. It stated its conviction that the end of ETA's violence was 'part of an irreversible process' and that ETA had 'no intention of committing or organising acts of terrorism or violence in the future', even as it remained 'a clandestine and armed organisation'. ETA continued to commit illegal acts such as the falsification of documents and maintenance of arms caches; these however were 'not necessarily related to the preparation of violent acts'. The IVC reported that it had told ETA that its continued possession of weapons and explosives, and especially its militants' insistence on carrying side arms (*etarras* in France carried weapons in order to ensure that if detained they would automatically be handed over to the French justice system rather than deported across the border to Spain) could give rise to 'potentially dangerous situations'.[22]

Relations with the government became more complicated during the May visit. As before, the commission held a wide variety of meetings, including with Ares and Jesús Loza, López's newly appointed commissioner for memory and coexistence. But its communication of ETA's readiness to engage in dialogue with the government raised sensitivities that it was advocating on the organisation's behalf. Rajoy predictably reiterated that he was not prepared to move, while Fernández declared that the government did not recognise 'any legitimacy' of the IVC and had refused to meet with it.[23] The government's stance, as Cosidó would explain, was both a question of principle—'you don't negotiate with terrorists'—and one of trust. The PP's voters expected 'coherence and responsibility' from the government they had elected. The government was resolved not 'to give [ETA] now what we did not give them when they were killing', nor betray its 'moral and political commitment to ETA's victims'.[24]

Public criticism of the more visible international involvement was accompanied by less visible surveillance and obstruction. How international contacts with ETA were managed would become evident in March 2013 when press reports asserted what had been whispered informally for some time: at the request of the former Socialist government, Norway had been sheltering the political leadership of ETA—David Pla, Iratxe Sorzábal and Josu Ternera—and in this capacity facilitating their meetings with the international verifiers and members of the nationalist left.[25] ETA would later state publicly that the creation of this 'dialogue table' had been the result of an agreement it had reached with the Spanish government before its October 2011 declaration, 'with the support of international actors'. The PP government had been informed all along about the existence of 'a space for dialogue to address the consequences of the conflict' but had ignored it, when not, according to ETA, 'sabotaging it and attacking it with its intelligence service'.[26] Faced with the government's refusal to meet with ETA, in mid-February 2013 Norway had reportedly expelled the three *etarras*, who were said to be in hiding in France.

Currin and the ICG sought to encourage the legalisation of Sortu and multi-party political dialogue, at least until discouraged from the latter by Urkullu. As there was no possibility that the PP would agree to such talks, seeking to suggest otherwise, as Urkullu explained to them in early 2012, might only complicate future discussions.[27] Currin's frank observation in April 2013 that it might be more helpful for the management of outstanding issues if ETA did not in fact disband (as the IRA has not disbanded) prompted a particularly vehement response.[28] Basagoiti claimed that if international facilitators such as Currin had not become involved, ETA 'probably would not exist today'.[29] The PP lobbied against the funding of the ICG, and in late May boycotted a session of the Basque Parliament addressed by Albert Spektorowski, one of its members. 'The verifiers and contact-ers are filling their pockets while ETA goes around with weapons,' claimed Basagoiti. 'There is no better verification than that ETA hands over its weapons and leaves us in peace. What do they all think they are doing here?'[30]

Two communiqués issued by ETA reflected the hope that a Socialist government headed by François Hollande might favour French engagement. The first came in March 2013, after then President Sarkozy stated in Bayonne that he considered the moving of prisoners closer to the Basque Country to be desirable.[31] Acknowledging the increasing activity among social and political actors in the French Basque Country, ETA called for greater implication of the French government in the changes underway, but met with little response.[32] Soon after Hollande took office, ETA announced that it had 'nominated its delegation to enter into direct dialogue with Spain and France'.[33] The communiqué was rapidly dismissed inside Spain, while France confirmed an 'absolute solidarity' with Spanish policy towards ETA that would be formalised later in the year.[34] France's new interior minister, the Catalan-born Manuel

Valls, went out of his way to continue counter-terrorist co-operation. On 27 May 2013 a joint operation detained two *etarras* in south-western France. In late October Spanish-French co-operation achieved its greatest prize with the arrest in Mâcon of Izaskun Lesaka, ETA's military leader, and her lieutenant Joseba Iturbe. Lesaka had been one of the three ETA commanders to read ETA's declaration of the end of its violence the year before; her detention was understood by the nationalist left as a direct assault on Aiete and its promise.[35]

In mid-July 2012, ETA issued a new communiqué.[36] Taking stock of the eight months that had passed since the end of its violence, it criticised the Spanish and French governments for trying to 'paralyse and impede the process'. No one was willing to discount the possibility of isolated violence by disgruntled *etarras*, but the government was not worried. Reinforced by the knowledge that a return to violence would provoke the immediate condemnation of the nationalist left, in August Fernández argued that those who advocated 'dialogue' with ETA were doing so based on faulty analysis.[37] Government policy remained fixed on the dissolution of ETA. This he saw as developing along similar lines to the path taken by the Red Brigades in the 1980s, whose demise had been founded on its members' cultivated 'repentance' or 'disassociation' from the organisation.[38] Time, he argued, was proving the government right. However, as with GRAPO, the parallel was by no means exact: the Red Brigades were not comparable to ETA and the nationalist left in social and political terms—indeed their end had been encouraged by the backlash against them from other leftist forces as well as the absence of any possibility of the kind of proletarian revolution in Italy they advocated.[39] The political costs of the management of their demise were thus quite distinct.

The prisoners as touchstone

Throughout ETA's history, efforts to end it had been predicated on the understanding that some form of the old formula of 'peace for prisoners' would be necessary. The prospect drew on the central position in the penitentiary system Spain's constitution (Art. 25.2) gives to the re-education and reinsertion of prisoners as well as tacit recognition that *etarras* who conceived themselves as disciplined members of a military organisation would pose no threat once the organisation had renounced the use of violence. The more classically configured conflict in Northern Ireland had facilitated the rapid release of distinct communities of prisoners as a means of reinforcing the end of the violence.[40] In the Basque context the amnesty demanded by ETA as a 'collective' solution to the prisoners' future was never a remote possibility. However, individual solutions grounded in separation from ETA, or the 'repentance' demanded by victims and some other social sectors, were always going to be complicated. As a practical way forward the nationalist left worked to promote a solution that blended aspects of both collective and individual measures. 'The problem is collective and so the solution has to be collective as well,' explained Antxon in early 2012, 'we are pursuing solutions for the collective, but that can be applied in an individual manner.'[41]

The dispersion of prisoners had been an exceptional measure with no basis in Spanish law that gave the government a new tool in its counter-terrorist armoury. Aznar famously released prisons during the Lizarra ceasefire and moved others closer to the Basque Country.[42] Proposals for the movement of prisoners were prepared in parallel to the 2006 talks with ETA. They were never implemented, but at a later date, as an end to ETA's violence became more likely, new plans had been drawn up to bring the prisoners closer to home.[43] And now that ETA's violence had ended there was a broad consensus—outside the PP—that the prisoners should be moved. 'I would bring the prisoners closer,' reasoned the Socialist Eduardo Madina, who since 2009 had been secretary-general of the PSOE in the Spanish Parliament. 'I think the government has to do it. It doesn't cost anything, its reversible—if there is a problem you can always move them back—and it would generate a degree of confidence. Just as dispersion was useful at one specific time, so taking this step could be useful at this moment.'[44]

Obstacles came from within the PP, the victims' organisations and the media, but also from the leadership of the EPPK. After a reshuffle in early 2012 this was mostly held by veteran leaders of ETA with little possibility of release from prison in the short or medium term.[45] They were subject neither to the direct authority of the nationalist left, nor, necessarily, that of the less experienced leadership of ETA that remained on the outside. Complicating their calculations was their isolation from Basque political life, but also the legacy of the effort to 'break' ETA from inside the prisons initiated by Rubalcaba after the end of the 2007 ceasefire. This had found its most visible expression in the 'Nanclares route', which had promised individual paths to reinsertion to those willing to defy the EPPK and accept the conditions outlined by the 2003 reform of the penitentiary law. In the new circumstances after 20 October 2011, ETA's prisoners assumed that a more favourable arrangement could be negotiated. Meanwhile the victims' organisations and others critical of the steps taken by the PSOE opposed the Nanclares route and certainly anything more lenient.[46]

The conditions for prisoners charged with terrorist offences to be elevated to a 'third grade' regime of semi-liberty spelled out by Art. 76.2 of the penitentiary law were stringent, and 'almost impossible' for most militants in the nationalist left to contemplate.[47] Jon Landa, former director for human rights in the Basque government, argued cogently that their mix of ethical and political demands was both inappropriate for the many prisoners serving sentences for crimes of opinion and questionable in terms of the violation of prisoners' rights to 'freedom of opinion, ideology and thought'.[48] Prisoners were required to reject violence and break not only with the 'means' of terrorism but its 'ends', ask forgiveness of their victims, pay civil indemnities, collaborate with the authorities and provide assurance that they were separated both from the terrorist organisation and from its 'environment'.[49] These demands are unprecedented. Public reports of the series of workshops offered to the prisoners in Nanclares in late 2011, and moving accounts of the encounters that several of them had held with victims, provided an impressive example of the steps towards repentance and reconciliation that a few individuals had been able to take. But they also encouraged confusion between what Landa termed a 'juridical minimum' that should be demanded of all prisoners desiring reinsertion—the rejection of all violence and firm commitment to forswear it in the future—and an 'ethical maximum' that would only be possible in a few cases and could then be rewarded with exceptional benefits and privileges.

In March 2012 the Constitutional Court ruled on forty-seven Basque cases affected by the Parot Doctrine. To the disappointment of the nationalist left and others who now agreed that it was unconstitutional, the court re-affirmed the validity of the Parot Doctrine and opted to review the affected cases on an individual basis.[50] A few weeks later the PP announced a plan designed to encourage the return of prisoners to the Basque Country and their eventual reinsertion.[51] The plan specified that prisoners would need to reject violence and separate themselves from ETA, but not in the first instance ask for the forgiveness of their victims or pay indemnities. It was immediately attacked by victims' organisations, Mayor Oreja and the right-wing media.[52] Rajoy's response—that the plan did not represent 'any penitentiary benefit' and the government had not and would not change its anti-terrorist policy—did little to inspire confidence in a proposal that in any case had demanded that prisoners break from ETA just to be re-located to a Basque prison.[53] A new blow to the nationalist left came in May, when a bitterly divided Supreme Court upheld the verdict of the Audiencia Nacional in the Bateragune case against Otegi, Díez and the others, albeit with a reduction in the sentences imposed (Otegi and Diéz saw theirs reduced from ten years to six and a half). The ruling struck many in the Basque Country as the perpetuation of an injustice, and was openly criticised by López, Urkullu and their political parties.

The EPPK concluded a period of internal debate with a disappointing public statement in early June. The collective recognised both the end of the armed conflict and the suffering it had caused (without acknowledging responsibility for its part in it), but linked its demands to an old appeal for 'amnesty and self-determination'.[54] The statement had been preceded by pressure from the nationalist left for the EPPK to follow Sortu in acceding to the existing legal framework. Loza had been the Basque government's interlocutor with the nationalist left on this issue. He had believed that agreement had been found on a text that required a prisoner only to admit that he or she was in conformity with ETA's declaration of 20 October 2011, and to request transfer to a Basque prison as the first step towards reinsertion. But this proposal had been blocked by 'radicals' in the EPPK's leadership, a development that suggested a breach between the political leadership of the nationalist left and those calling the shots inside the prisons.[55] The prisoners did not move, as Fernando Etxegarai and Nagore Mujika, both former ETA prisoners, explained in September, 'because we've seen no steps taken by the government'.[56] Timid initial discussions regarding the return of Basque exiles had also ground to a halt as distrust deepened.

The legalisation of Sortu by the Constitutional Court had been widely expected, but none the less anxiously awaited by the nationalist left. When it finally came in mid-June 2012 it represented a milestone of great importance to both sides in the conflict divide. It was a source of jubilation and relief to the nationalist left, but the reaction from some sectors of the PP was illustrative of the deep antagonism to the political 'normalisation' it promised. Dolores Cospedal, the party's secretary-general, described 'the immense majority of democrats' as 'saddened and deceived' by the ruling. Esperanza Aguirre, the powerful PP president of the community of Madrid, went so far as to suggest that the Constitutional Court should be eliminated. 'Never has ETA caressed power so closely,' proclaimed Mayor Oreja.[57]

A further setback to the government came on 10 July, when the European Court of Human Rights issued its first ruling on the Parot Doctrine. The Court found that the application of the doctrine to Inés del Río—a member of ETA imprisoned in 1987 for her role in multiple murders, who had been due for release in 2008—was in clear violation of the European Convention of Human Rights ('domestic courts could not apply retroactively and to the detriment of the persons concerned the spirit of legislative changes that occurred after offences had been committed'). It ordered Spain to release del Río 'at the earliest possible date' and pay her 30,000 euros in damages.[58] In contrast to the praise heaped on the court when it had ruled against Batasuna in 2009, the government—acutely aware of the implication of this case for the dozens of others still imprisoned only because of this discredited doctrine—refused to release del Río and vowed to appeal against the ruling. 'It is an offence to the victims, Spanish society and the Spanish courts,' claimed interior minister Fernández, 'it is unacceptable that this tribunal says that Spanish courts violate human rights.'[59] 'Letting such people out of jail,' he later told *The New York Times*, 'would mean not only freeing unrepentant terrorists but also allowing them to claim a victory on human rights grounds.'[60]

By late July 2012 the prospect of progress towards either the dissolution of ETA demanded by the government or the bilateral process of dialogue and concession pursued by the nationalist left had dissipated. No episode exposed the depth of emotions impeding forward movement before the Basque elections now due in October more acutely than the drama surrounding Josu Uribetxeberria Bolinaga, an ETA prisoner suffering from terminal cancer.[61] In early August Uribetxeberria had embarked on a hunger strike to demand early release on compassionate grounds. Article 92 of Spain's criminal code allows, but does not oblige, a judge to concede conditional liberty to prisoners who are 'seriously ill with incurable diseases'. Over the years twenty-three Basque prisoners had been afforded early release, eighteen of them during Aznar's first term in office when Mayor Oreja had been minister of the interior. Uribetxeberria was suffering from kidney cancer that had metastasised to other organs and his central nervous system; his release was never seriously in doubt.

Uribetxeberria was released to a hospital bed in San Sebastián in early September after a drawn-out process that was mishandled by the government and manipulated by the nationalist left. The high tensions surrounding the case had their roots in who Uribetxeberria was: not just any ETA prisoner doing time for multiple assassinations, but one of the kidnappers of Ortega Lara, whose emaciated appearance as he emerged from the underground hole in which he had been held captive remained one of the quintessential images of ETA's brutality. Several hundred other prisoners joined Uribetxeberria in his hunger strike. There were reports of widely different degrees of adherence to the strike, as well of pressure on Uribetxeberria to maintain it until his family insisted that he call it off. However his eventual release, and the intervention of sectors of the radical right who appeared more bent on vengeance than justice in their dealings with ETA, allowed the nationalist left to claim victory in its campaign. Outrage from victims and others that leaders of the nationalist left (including Otegi, who had joined the strike) offered no recognition of the suffering inflicted on Ortega Lara shifted to accusations that the government had succumbed to ETA's 'blackmail'.[62] Demonstrators claimed Rajoy to be 'a traitor like Zapatero', as the AVT demanded 'voice and vote' in future decisions related to penitentiary policy.[63]

Coexistence and 'el relato'

In some respects, Basques adapted quickly to the end of ETA's violence. Those who had spent years shadowed by bodyguards gladly returned to freedoms small and large they had long ago surrendered. Basagoiti was photographed on 21 October 2011, sitting on a step and savouring the first cigar he had smoked in the street since 1997; Gorka Landaburu would recall that, driving himself for the first time in twelve years, he had to re-learn to park a car. At the political level too, the changes were dramatic. Mikel Errekondo, spokesperson of Amaiur in the Spanish Parliament, held a cordial meeting with King Juan Carlos—the first encounter between a representative of the nationalist left and the monarch in eighteen years. Other deputies and senators travelled to Madrid to take their place within Spanish institutions whose legitimacy they had challenged their entire lives. As attention turned to the elections due in Euskadi in October, political parties threw themselves into haggling over electoral lists and developing party platforms and campaign strategies with deceptive ease.

Gesto por la Paz held its final public event in February 2012: a march under the banner *Lortu duku*, 'We've done it.' But healing the wounds inflicted on Basque society would require the work of many years. Isabel Urkijo had been involved with Gesto for more than two decades. She, as so many others, carried memories of violence and the sense of threat and fear in the Basque streets—cars and buses burning, rocks hurled from behind barricades, and young Basque radicals shouting, *¡Eta, matenlos!'*, 'ETA—kill them!'—permanently within her. 'Killing here in Euskadi was part of the landscape,' she recalled, 'as it rains, there are trees, there is *bocce* ball in Bilbao in the summers, people killed.'[64] Attention turned, necessarily, to the past. 'We will never construct the future if we don't see and analyse the past,' Landaburu, long active in Gesto as well, observed. He recalled that in his own life he had lived through 'two dictatorships'—that of Franco and that of ETA—and experienced the full trajectory of recent Basque history: exile in France, Franco, early militancy in ETA, the transition, threats from the rightist armed group Triple A, an attack by ETA. 'When we speak of coexistence and reconciliation,' he continued, 'I say take it slowly (*tranquilos*). Before reconciling, we are going to coexist. *Convivencia*, coexistence first.'[65]

A variety of initiatives had been launched with coexistence as their goal. They ranged from the Basque government's public efforts to 'delegitimate violence', to the establishment of Euskal Memoria as a foundation dedicated to the recuperation of the 'stolen' memory of the nationalist left.[66] The promotion of meetings with victims and other workshops for the Nanclares prisoners had taken place in parallel to a series of discreet encounters between victims of different provenances that became known as the Glencree initiative.[67] And the Basque Parliament, at its third attempt, had finally begun to address the sensitive issue of what were termed 'other victims' through approval of a decree addressing the victims of abuses committed by the police between 1960 and 1978—the first formal recognition of this long-neglected population.[68] Victims' organisations such as COVITE and the foundations established in the memory of Gregorio Ordoñez and Fernando Buesa held roundtables, meetings and seminars. Other civil society bodies including Lokarri, Baketik—a peace centre run by Jonan Fernández, the former director of Elkarri—and Argituz, a human rights association established in 2010, redoubled their efforts to contribute ideas and expertise. In April 2012 family members of those killed as a consequence of the 'repressive strategies' of France and Spain, formed a new foundation, Egiari Zor.[69]

Basques held widely differing interpretations of what had happened and why. Many of their efforts to promote coexistence were coloured by a partisan construction of the history and violence they had experienced that were together subsumed within 'el relato'. They shared a desire to arrive at 'the truth', and a determination that there should be no return to the dark days of the past. But their very great differences revealed a gulf in understanding of what that 'truth' might be, and thus the role of memory. A central distorting factor was an understanding of victims, and the violation of human rights, 'according to who had been the perpetrator', as the former prisoner of conscience Sabino Ormazabal observed.[70] Most Spaniards wanted a truth that told of senseless terrorism that had extended for thirty years too long, and achieved nothing. The nationalist left, on the other hand, wanted the truth of a conflict in which there have been victims on both sides—and 'martyrs' on theirs—and social and political achievement in the survival of their political demands. Whether it would be possible to work towards a 'shared memory', an 'inclusive' or 'collective memory', or accept the existence of multiple truths as the prism through which the Basque experience would have to be understood was itself an issue of contention.

A Basque Parliament whose composition all knew would be changed by the coming elections adopted initiatives with short- as well as long-term objectives. The exclusion of the nationalist left from discussion of 'memory and coexistence' made no sense in substantive terms (if there was any sector that should have been included as a priority, it was that associated with violence in the past). Yet it responded to a logic that held that it was easier as well as ethically important to forge agreement on 'principles for a peace with memory' among other parties now, and hope that Euskal Herria Bildu (EH Bildu), as the pro-independence coalition had been renamed to contest the coming elections, might subscribe to it in the future. A document that advocated a 'collective', 'not neutral' and 'active' memory was agreed between the PNV, PSE and PP in July 2012 as an 'ethical baseline', *suelo ético*, for the Basque parties' approach to the past. 'Future peace and coexistence require recognition of the injustice of the violence', it stated, 'recognition of the harm caused and of the dignity of the victims, all of them deserving of the right to truth, justice and reparation.' Immediately problematic for the nationalist left was its assertion that 'memory is an essential tool for the ethical, social and political de-legitimation of terrorism'.[71]

A lack of clarity even in the term 'victim' contributed to the confusion.[72] Victims of ETA, so long neglected, had come to dominate the public space of suffering, while those of the state or parapolice structures ETA associated with it had been ignored. The organisations that most visibly represented ETA's victims held that 'to talk of reconciliation and inclusive memory now does a lot of damage to victims'. They rejected the Basque government's attention to 'other victims' as suggesting 'an unacceptable equivalence' between ETA's terrorism and the actions of the state.[73] ETA and the nationalist left, meanwhile, had an acute sense that the treatment of human rights violations and violent crimes had been unjust: while their crimes had been pursued with the full force of the Spanish justice system, those against them had remained publicly invisible. They demanded 'all the truth' and not 'equivalence' but an equal treatment under the law with regard to the rights due victims, a distinction that many in Spain found difficult to stomach.[74]

This sense of victimisation fuelled a tendency to confuse violations of human rights with suffering. Euskal Memoria's list of 474 victims of 'state repression' mixed in extrajudicial assassinations and deaths caused by police abuse with deaths attributable to other circumstances such as traffic accidents related to the dispersion of prisoners, or death from illness in exile, as if they were all the same.[75] Many close to ETA adopted criteria distinguishing between victims of ETA—police and military officers were considered 'combatants', distinct from 'civilian' victims or bystanders who might themselves be 'consequences of the conflict'— that complicated the widespread demand for ETA to recognise the harm inflicted by its violence.[76] Also delicate was the effort to explore means to register those whom violence had forced to leave as voters in Euskadi.[77] The nationalist left did not formally oppose such a measure— those who could prove that they were victims of threats from ETA had the right to return and vote—but suspicion of the 'colonisation' of the Basque Country from outside was rife.[78]

Movement on these issues was slower and more limited than others demanded, but significant. On 26 February 2012 the nationalist left issued a statement on the transition towards a 'scenario of just and lasting peace' at an event attended by representatives of Sinn Féin and the ANC. The statement represented a determined effort to recognise the 'pain and suffering' caused by the violence of ETA and the nationalist left's own lack of sensitivity in the past.[79] It called for measures of transitional justice, including an international and independent truth commission, and dialogue and agreement as a guarantee that the violence of the past would not be repeated in the future. It was broadly criticised in the press ('Without dissolution, nothing,' was the headline of an editorial in *El País*)[80] even as those who followed the nationalist left most closely could appreciate its significance. The problem, once more, was one of narrative. The nationalist left sought reconciliation after what it had experienced as a long and bruising conflict, and considered that it had come a long way to be able to contemplate this possibility. The experience of many other Basques and almost all Spaniards, meanwhile, had been of terrorist violence that was morally and ethically *wrong* in the deepest sense.

The idea of a Basque truth commission had been debated within nationalist circles for several years, although initially conceived as addressing only the Civil War and the Franco years.[81] It developed in the context of the intense debate across Spain of the law of historical memory, Garzón's attempts to investigate the crimes committed under Franco and the constitution of a truth commission in Valencia in February 2007, prompted by the discovery of common graves in the city's cemetery that were estimated as holding as many as 26,300 bodies.[82] In early 2009, Jon Landa submitted a report on the subject to the Basque Parliament, which was quickly shelved when Patxi López took office as *lehendakari* a few months later.[83] Landa had identified a number of challenges that would complicate investigation of the Franco period, including the amount of time passed since 1936 and the political sensitivities involved in addressing the Civil War; the period after 1968, when ETA became active; and the transition itself. After the end of ETA's violence, such sensitivities loomed, if anything, even larger. In addition to fears of legitimating ETA's struggle, Spain's national parties had no desire to open Pandora's box on the country's past at the instigation of the nationalist left.

A sense of deep and enduring wrong—and a culture still suffused by a Catholic sensibility—contributed to the demand for ETA and the nationalist left to do 'more' than recognise the suffering they had caused. In the weeks before the Basque elections, Arnaldo Otegi offered a broad, if carefully limited, apology within the interview published as *El Tiempo de las Luces* ('The Time of Lights'): 'If, in my capacity as spokesman (and I speak in the name of all of the spokespersons of Batasuna), I have added a trace of pain, suffering or humiliation to the families of the victims of armed action by ETA, I would like to apologise most sincerely, and say "I am sorry" from the bottom of my heart.'[84] Otegi's words carried resonance for some, but did not assuage a demand for a more sweeping 'repentance' in political terms. What was needed, Loza suggested, soon after Otegi's remarks became public, was a statement along these lines: 'We were wrong. We should have stopped at the time of the 1977 amnesty, or with the *poli-milis* in 1983… We should have stopped then because since then it has made no sense. It was a mistake'.[85] For ETA and the nationalist left, acutely conscious that Spain had still neither fully acknowledged nor apologised for the crimes committed by and under Franco, such a blanket apology was quite impossible. 'You cannot ask us to repent of our cause,' countered the former *etarra* Nagore Mujika, 'it would mean denying our own being.'[86]

As yet unaddressed was the controversial issue of torture in the years of democracy. The magnitude of the challenge it would represent—compounded by the evident difficulty of investigating allegations of torture, especially when long in the past—was clear. The nationalist left claimed the extraordinary figure of 11,000 alleged torture incidents.[87] Spain, on the other hand, had not—as acknowledged in a refreshingly blunt article by Manuel Altozano published in *El País* in September 2012—secured the binding conviction of a single police official for mistreatment of members of ETA between the introduction of the criminal code of 1995 and 2012.[88] In this 'effective impunity', as Amnesty International labelled it, officials were either not investigated, found not guilty, or found guilty and later released.[89] Sensitivity to the subject was such that Spain had delayed publication of a critical report by the Council of Europe's Committee on the Prevention of Torture on a visit to Spain it conducted in September 2007 for three and half years.[90] Its courts, meanwhile, had overturned even proven cases such as that of the torture of Igor Portu and Martín Sarasola, the two *etarras* convicted for the bombing of Barajas airport, who had been visibly battered at the time of their arrest (Portu required emergency medical attention and a hospital stay for a broken rib that had pierced his lung).[91]

Two distinct aspects of the torture issue, identified by Euskal Memoria as its 'moral' and 'utilitarian' dimensions, compounded its sensitivity.[92] That credible reports of torture had continued over decades and had been confirmed by leading human rights organisations and other international actors was shocking in itself and fuelled demand for the truth. But former members of ETA in the orbit of the nationalist left also draw attention to the extraordinary difference between what had happened to *etarras* arrested in France and those in Spain: ETA members, they claim, were not tortured in France.[93] The truth of this may be seen in the strange fact that French police almost never found an ETA weapons cache or arrested more ETA members based on detainees' confessions, whereas in Spain it had been commonplace for police to find weapons or arrest other members of ETA within days or even hours of detentions. It is difficult to explain the disparity on the basis of police effectiveness alone. ETA and the nationalist left, however, claim that the answer is easy: Spanish police had been effective at extracting information under duress. If this is true, it would mean that a significant number of ETA prisoners have been imprisoned under testimony extracted under torture. And if ever proved, and this was the only evidence against them, international standards would suggest these prisoners would have to be released.

'Normal politics' and the challenge of an orderly end

As Rajoy entered his second year in government, unemployment topped 25 per cent, while youth unemployment stood at the staggering figure of 52 per cent.[94] In deference to demands from Brussels, Rajoy had implemented cuts and raised taxes in an effort to balance the largest budget deficit in the region, but the economy remained stuck in recession. Disillusion with the government surged as corruption scandals swirling around the PP reached the prime minister himself. During the early months of 2013, revelations stemming from the pre-trial investigation of Luis Bárcenas, the PP's former treasurer, led to allegations that senior party figures, including Rajoy, had received payments from a secret slush fund. By early July Rajoy's refusal to speak publicly about the case fuelled demands for his resignation.

The most acute crisis was in Catalonia. The Catalan elections held in late November 2012 had produced a disappointing result for CiU, but support for the more radical ERC had surged. In September 2013 the *Diada* was again celebrated by massive social mobilisation: some 1.6 million Catalans turned out in support of a human chain, the *Via catalana para la independencia* ('Catalan route to independence'), which stretched 400 kilometres across Catalonia to demand a referendum—a demand that was now supported by 80 per cent of Catalans.[95] Rubalcaba denounced the situation in Catalonia as the most dramatic manifestation of the 'fully fledged territorial crisis' facing Spain and reiterated calls that he had made the year before for a reform of the constitution and the introduction of federalism.[96]

It was hard not to see the proposal as offering too little, too late. Spain's state of autonomies had offered a quasi-federal arrangement from the start, and it was in the nature of regional nationalisms that their drive for recognition of their difference would demand more. The Basques, for the moment, remained simultaneously protected from the urgency of the Catalan drama by the financial autonomy they were assured by the *concierto económico* and inhibited by the complexity of moving forward from their conflictive past. Both lay behind the news in September 2013 that the PNV and PSE had reached a pact on fiscal issues that bound them together in a manner reassuring to those who remembered the relative stability of the Ardanza years. But this did not stop Basque nationalists of a variety of tendencies looking forward to the possibility of one day following the *Via catalana* with their own *Via vasca*.[97]

A year earlier, candidates had campaigned for the Basque parliamentary elections held on 21 October 2012 with unprecedented freedom. López and Basagoiti held rallies in the heart of San Sebastián's *casco viejo*, something unthinkable with ETA still active. The Basque PP opened street-level party offices for the first time in its history, and the candidates for *lehendakari*—Basagoiti, López, Urkullu, Laura Mintegi, a former university professor, of EH Bildu, and representatives of UPyD and Ezker Batua—together participated in a televised debate as if such 'normal politics' were a regular occurrence. In substance the campaign was surprisingly subdued. Basques had so far avoided the worst effects of the economic crisis (unemployment in Euskadi stood at 15.5 per cent, a figure lower than that of any autonomous community other than Navarre).[98] However, its consequences had been felt in 2012 as never before and further cuts in 2013 were inevitable.

Developments in Catalonia gave independence a more prominent place in the campaign than might have been suggested either by EH Bildu's electoral platform—in which the core issue of sovereignty seemed overwhelmed by its extensive, but somewhat incomprehensible, goals for government[99]—or the demand from Basques. This had never approached the level now seen in Catalonia (the *Euskobarómetro* poll of May 2012 recorded little change in the figure of 33 per cent of Basques who harboured a strong desire for independence).[100] And with the PP eager to whip up fear that the PNV was intent on following the path taken by the CiU in order 'to break Spain', Urkullu had played a cautious hand.[101] The PNV set 2015 as the date by which it would bring forward a proposal to facilitate the development of a 'new status' for Euskadi and its emergence as a 'European nation'.[102] Firmly in its sightlines was the agreement reached before the elections between the British Prime Minister, David Cameron, and Alex Salmond of the Scottish National Party to hold a referendum on the independence of Scotland. For Basque and Catalan nationalists of all ideological hues, a central government calmly negotiating with minority nationalists the means to advance towards the 'right to decide' through a clear choice on independence was no small source of envy.

EH Bildu was an uneasy mix of quite disparate ideologies ranging from social democrats in EA, to the leftists in Alternatiba, Aralar—whose relationship with the former Batasuna was still complex—and the 'historic' nationalist left, which remained the coalition's behemoth. Sortu, which held its founding congress in February 2013, was a work in progress. In its journey away from violence the nationalist left had drawn on a dizzying array of ideological and political influences—Irish republicanism, European separatists in Scotland, Flanders and elsewhere, but also proponents of the Bolivarian form of 'new socialism' in Latin America—as encouraging examples of a political future even as it had remained faithful to its own deep roots in the pursuit of Basque liberation. It was not surprising that its shift towards institutional politics, complemented by social mobilisation and civil disobedience, had fuelled internal tensions. Neither the internal or external manifestations of democratic policies would come easily to all militants of a movement formed by decades of popular mobilisation and the authoritarian practices of a revolutionary organisation.[103]

Otegi was badly missed. With the publication of *El Tiempo de las Luces* in September 2012 he had sought to bring new energy to the bases of the nationalist left in the closing weeks of the campaign. Characteristically upbeat, he countered disappointment regarding progress made since Aiete with a re-affirmation of the value of unilateral action as the 'keystone' of political strategy. He claimed his 'only confidence' was in mass struggle and the capacity of 'left-wing patriots' to generate pressure to force the state to adapt more constructive positions.[104] In this process, the nationalist left had to be ready to accept 'scenarios of agreement, or non-agreement' with Spain and France, maintaining the political initiative even if—for the moment—the bilateral process hoped for after Aiete had not materialised: 'We should not understand the process in static and rigid terms,' he suggested, 'but rather as dynamic and flexible. Strategies, stages and road maps are only instruments to achieve our ends… instruments should always be open to modification.'[105]

The election brought a clear win for the PNV, with twenty-seven out of the seventy-five seats in the Basque Parliament (and 34.6 per cent of the popular vote). EH Bildu confirmed its position as Euskadi's second political force with twenty-one seats (25 per cent). It was the strongest performance in history for the nationalist left in parliamentary elections, but also somewhat disappointing: it lost votes in Guipúzcoa, and elsewhere failed to build on its spectacular results of 2011. The PSE and the PP both fared badly—the PSE dropping from its high of twenty-five seats in 2009 to sixteen (19.1 per cent) and the PP down from thirteen to ten seats (11.7 per cent)—while UPyD retained the one seat it had held in the previous parliament.[106] Voters punished PSE for a pact with the PP that much of its base had always considered unnatural, and for having missed opportunities to distinguish itself in the process towards the end of ETA. Jesús Eguiguren had withdrawn from active politics in the run-up to the election; the departure of other Socialists with a 'Basquist' vision for the party left the PSE closer to Madrid at a moment when the PSOE as a whole was in profound crisis. The PP was left to contemplate its worst loss ever in the Basque Country. Never had its views on ETA seemed further removed from the mainstream of Basque public opinion. Never had Basque voters seemed so far removed from Spain and Madrid.

The result paved the way for Urkullu's election as *lehendakari* at the head of a minority government. It gave nationalists two-thirds of the Basque Parliament, but promised a new chapter in the long history of contention between the two expressions of Basque nationalism. A first priority was the possibility of forging consensus on steps towards the 'orderly' end of ETA that, for different reasons, both deemed necessary. Shortly after the elections, reports had surfaced of ETA's readiness to dissolve if the government would amend its policies towards the prisoners. Rajoy—unlike the Basques—was in no hurry, and again said no.[107] Urkullu emphasised his firm commitment to the 'normalisation of coexistence' in a press conference he gave after his first meeting with Rajoy in January 2013, insisting: 'it has to be normal to engage in dialogue amongst opposed ideologies'.[108] To further this end he appointed Jonan Fernández commissioner of peace and coexistence, despite opposition from victims and the PP, who recalled not only Fernández' long service in Elkarri, but the time he had spent as an HB councillor some thirty years previously.

A new visit by the IVC in February 2013 confirmed the depth of the impasse with ETA. In meetings with Urkullu and other Basque political parties (not the PP, which still refused to meet with them), Ram Mannikalingham, the commission's coordinator, countered rumours that ETA was about to disarm by saying that the IVC had no information that this was the case. He reported that there had been no advance in ETA's position on victims, and no change on either side with respect to prisoners. Looking ahead, two options presented themselves: the first was 'an orderly end in which all actors and authorities know what they have to do and how to do it… in order to consolidate peace'. The second was 'disorderly and complicated, with no order or understanding'.[109]

News of the expulsion of ETA's political representatives from Norway, and ETA's angry response a few weeks later comprehensively sealed any possibility that an orderly end could be derived from the negotiations that ETA had aspired to. Other mechanisms, as Otegi had intimated six months earlier, would have to be found. In the coming months two avenues for political and social engagement opened up. The first was in the context of efforts by the Basque government to build on the work begun the previous year and promote 'peace and coexistence' from inside the Basque Parliament; the second was the work of a 'Social Forum' promoted by Lokarri and Bake Bidea, a civil society organisation of the French Basque Country, with the participation of a wide range of other social actors and the support of international non-governmental organisations and experts.[110] By summer, the Social Forum had suggested the means by which the blockage impeding progress since Aiete might finally be overcome, while the Basque government's efforts were foundering on the deep emotional and political divisions that still characterised Basque politics.

The Basque government presented a preliminary outline of its plan for peace and coexistence in March 2013, and a detailed document, open for comments for a further three-month period, in June.[111] A first outcome was a 'baseline' report on violations of human rights in the Basque case. Released in late June 2013, this had been prepared as a rigorously empirical account that could 'be assumed as true by any interlocutor of good faith'.[112] Building sufficient consensus to move ahead with a broader programme to foster peace and coexistence was to prove much harder. Differences on the proposals rumbled on through July and August. In September the PSE insisted that it would withdraw from the plan's discussion—which the PP had already rejected—unless EH Bildu openly assumed as its own the *suelo ético*, the 'ethical baseline' first agreed the year before and in March 2013 adopted as a resolution of the new Basque Parliament.[113] EH Bildu had abstained from the March vote, but tacitly accepted the existence of the *suelo ético* as a starting point. However, the demand that it should publicly subscribe to the idea that memory was 'a tool for delegitimation of terrorism' was untenable.[114] For the PSE, which had its eye on how a hard line on this issue would play elsewhere in Spain the *suelo ético* was non-negotiable, and it withdrew from the discussion of the plan on that basis.

The plan had included a component specifically dedicated to penitentiary policy. The Basque government had limited competences in this area; hope for movement came instead from the Social Forum, an initiative developed outside formal institutions, which, rather like the Aiete Conference, had both public and more discreet manifestations. Over two days in mid-March in Bilbao and Pamplona, international experts spoke publicly about issues such as prisoner reinsertion, transitional justice and disarmament, being careful as they did so to reflect only on their experience from elsewhere.[115] The substance of their contributions was then drawn upon for the extended consultation and negotiation of a text composed of twelve recommendations 'to encourage the peace process'. This text, which had been agreed with social forces that included the nationalist left—it could be assumed in communication with ETA—was eventually released in May.[116]

At the recommendations' core was the pursuit of consensus on a 'controlled and orderly' process that would conclude with the dismantling of ETA's weapons and military structures and 'an integral solution' for prisoners and exiles. In addition to proposals for reform of penitentiary policy, this included the all-important recommendation that prisoner reintegration be realised through legal channels and on an individual basis.[117] The recommendations were immediately welcomed by the Basque government, openly encouraged by Sortu and then, in July, welcomed by ETA as a 'constructive contribution' that could, 'with the commitment of all', constitute a point of departure for a new 'road map'.[118] Rumours abounded that ETA was—finally—ready to move ahead towards disarmament. Predictably, such a step was dismissed as 'cock and bull' and a 'false disarmament' by *ABC* in late August, even before it had taken place.[119] A few weeks later a new report, attributed to 'sources knowledgeable of the process', intimated that ETA was indeed readying itself to move, and would begin handing over its weapons to an independent international 'notary' before the end of the year.[120]

This report was ostensibly a means to lower expectations of what ETA might announce on *Gudari Eguna*, the 'day of the Basque soldier' celebrated on 27 September. However, the political climate was such that it could not lower them far enough. In its communiqué ETA made no mention of disarmament and instead introduced unwelcome views on a future political process. It insisted on the right of Basque citizens 'to know the truth, but all the truth' and claimed that it was ready to take part in a collective exercise that would acknowledge 'all the suffering and the responsibilities of each party'. ETA defended its struggle as 'just and legitimate'. It could understand and respect that others would not share its views. But it also insisted that it 'did not accept that we have to deny our history of struggle and assume *el relato* of the oppressors'. The communiqué was roundly dismissed by all political parties other than EH Bildu. By this point there was no tolerance at all for a statement from ETA on anything other than the steps it might take towards its dissolution.

CONCLUSION

WHAT CAN WE LEARN FROM THE BASQUE CASE?

By some strange coincidence, while I was revising this book's proofs, ETA released another video to the BBC. This time it marked a historic step towards its disarmament. The video appeared on 21 February 2014 to corroborate the announcement in Bilbao by the International Verification Commission (IVC) that ETA had 'sealed and put beyond use a specified quantity of arms, ammunition and explosives'.[1] Gone were the white hoods and black berets in evidence back in September 2010, when ETA had broadcast its still tentative ceasefire; the identity of the two ETA militants visible was instead disguised by masks. A small collection of a rifle, three pistols, two grenades, explosives, ammunition and detonators had been laid out on a table in front of a reproduction of Picasso's Guernica. Ram Manikkalingham and Ronnie Kasrils of the IVC solemnly inspected the assembled hardware; then Manikkalingham signed a piece of paper to certify that all was in order.

As an initial gesture, the relatively limited nature of ETA's offerings was unsurprising. However, months of anticipation had raised expectations and contributed to a sensation of anticlimax. Things went from bad to worse as the Spanish right mobilised to belittle the news. Members of the IVC were accused by a senior member of the PP of 'working for ETA and not for Spain'.[2] On the initiative of some of ETA's victims in COVITE, they were summoned to testify before the Audiencia Nacional and account for their contacts with the terrorists. They were confident that the weapons and material they had seen had been 'put beyond operational use'—in contexts as distinct as Aceh and

Nepal, as well as Northern Ireland, this had been a prelude to full disarmament—but also revealed that they had later been taken away by ETA
in a box. Critical voices condemned what had been a huge advance for
ETA and a complex and risky endeavour for the verifiers as 'a farce',
'vaudeville-esque', comparable to a scene from the Quentin Tarantino
film *Pulp Fiction*, and a 'fiasco for the verifiers'.[3]

That it was also much more than this was confirmed on 1 March
2014. ETA issued a communiqué in which it announced that it had
begun to seal its weapons' caches and undertook to decommission its
weapons, munitions and explosives in a process that would go 'to the
end, to the last arsenal'.[4] This was very significant. It pointed towards
the end of the last major armed movement in Western Europe and represented a milestone in this unique process. The steps towards the eventual end of ETA had all been taken unilaterally; no political concessions
had been made, and the organisation now sought to move forward to
disarmament and its eventual dissolution. It was a mark of the extraordinarily contorted political environment in which the Basque peace
process was taking place that this could not be unambiguously welcomed as an achievement.

The messy business of the video and the challenge to the IVC underlined the limits of both unilateral action and the informal structures
established in its support. Decommissioning and disarmament need a
recognised recipient—an institution or entity with the authority to
certify that weapons and munitions have been put beyond use, and the
capacity to receive any that might be handed over for destruction. The
decommissioning and disarmament of ETA, as Jonathan Powell argued
in the *Financial Times*, would require the involvement of the Spanish
government.[5] ETA still had substantial amounts of explosives, as well
as hundreds of pistols, semi-automatic rifles and grenades, hidden in
secret weapons' caches. Its militants included explosive experts with
specialised skills in car bombs, remote-controlled detonators and fuses.
There was real work to be done. But independent international verifiers
could not do it if witnessing the decommissioning of weapons meant
risking arrest.

In the case of Northern Ireland the British and Irish governments had
passed legislation that had allowed the Independent International
Commission on Decommissioning to oversee the IRA's acts of decommissioning legally. In the Basque case, an equivalent step was unlikely.

For over two years the Rajoy government had refused to move the hundreds of Basque prisoners scattered across Spain and France to prisons closer to their home; it had rejected appeals for an 'orderly end' to ETA made by the Basque government and others, and it had left the members of ETA's admittedly depleted ranks in limbo, whilst offering no provision for the future of the explosives and weapons at their disposal. The vacuum had been partially filled by international actors and Basque political and social forces, which had been pushing hard for peace. But as the clamour for ETA's dissolution had risen, practical consideration of the arguments to be made for the maintenance of ETA's control of its militants and material as it carried out the complex process of its own dissolution had been overlooked.

There was no precedent for a government offered an opportunity to secure and put beyond use the weapons of a deep-rooted terrorist group to reject it outright. No one who had followed the long-drawn out process towards ETA's end could deny the possibility that Spain might prove an exception. Yet as all political parties other than the PP and UPyD welcomed ETA's commitment to put its arms beyond use and offered support to the IVC, the obduracy of the Spanish and French governments appeared increasingly irrational. With Basque public opinion running strongly in favour of moving ahead, Iñigo Urkullu stepped forward to say that he would be willing to engage in dialogue with ETA if it was 'to talk of peace'.[6] Implicit within his offer was the expectation that ETA would have to recognise the harm it had caused, as Basque and Spanish society demanded, and that at least a quiet nod from Madrid would be required.

ETA's not-quite end

The shift towards the beginning of ETA's disarmament had been a long time coming. By late 2013, ETA had declared an end to its violence and the nationalist left was back in the Basque parliament in force. But movement towards decommissioning and the dismantling of ETA's military structures had slowed as the government had refused to accept that a 'process' of any kind was warranted. The PP had found itself riven by internal conflict over this issue, and in early 2014 experienced its first split. Rebels on the party's right wing—including the ETA victim José Antonio Ortega Lara—formed a new party, Vox, that vowed to push a harder line on the subject of ETA, as well as against Basque and Catalan separatism.

Perhaps paradoxically, the single biggest jolt to this strange peace process that wasn't had come from outside Spain. On 21 October 2013, the European Court of Human Rights upheld its earlier decision that the retroactive extension of prison sentences introduced by the Parot Doctrine violated the European Convention on Human Rights and ordered that Inés del Río be freed immediately.[7] The ruling and its consequences—the imminent release of dozens of ETA members affected by the doctrine—was entirely predictable, not least because it was consistent with recent decisions by the Spanish courts. It was welcomed in the Basque Country by those who had long perceived the Parot Doctrine as unconstitutional, and as an opportunity to unblock the stalled peace process.

The uproar from the AVT and other victims' organisations was immediate, and the government's response entirely inept. Rajoy refused to speak publicly on the ruling for several days, and dithered in deciding whether or how the PP would be represented in a demonstration called by the AVT to protest it. He had no choice other than to leave the judges to comply with the European Court, but he did so grudgingly, labelling the ruling 'unjust and wrong'.[8] Casting itself as the 'last bulwark of democratic dignity in Spain', the AVT claimed 200,000 people attended its demonstration; PP members aligned with Rajoy were heckled and Rajoy himself branded a 'traitor'.[9]

Sixty-three prisoners were released before the end of the year. Compliance with the ruling of the European Court remained deeply disturbing to many of ETA's victims, but it also gave new animus to the remaining prisoners' consideration of the recommendations of the Social Forum. On 28 December, the prisoners in the EPPK issued a statement in which they distanced themselves from armed struggle and recognised the suffering and harm inflicted by decades of violence. They also pledged to pursue their release from prison through the Spanish legal system, abandoning their old demand for amnesty.[10] A few days later the newly-released prisoners held a press conference. The former prisoners—hard men and women, responsible for more than 300 of ETA's assassinations—expressed their conformity with the positions taken by the EPPK and their 'total commitment to the new political scenario' established at the initiative of the nationalist left. They accepted full responsibility for what they termed the 'consequences of the conflict'.[11]

Although short of the repentance and open demand for ETA's dissolution that many had wished to hear, the prisoners' *de facto* recognition of the legitimacy and authority of the French and Spanish states was an important advance. The government, however, rejected the prisoners' communiqué as irrelevant and the meeting of the ex-prisoners as 'repugnant' and a 'witches' sabbath'.[12] It then arrested several of the EPPK lawyers. A judge in Madrid banned the annual demonstration to be held in support of the prisoners. When another march was approved, the PNV joined ranks with Sortu to lead it. On 11 January 2014 more than 100,000 people took to the streets of Bilbao to demand 'human rights, agreement, peace' in a potent display of opposition to the government's intransigence toward ETA.

Following these events from afar, I was again drawn back to the question recorded by Joseba Zulaika so many years ago: How can that be? The strange story of ETA's not-quite end had taken directions that I had not envisaged when I began it, and now appeared more intertwined with the greater drama of Spain itself than had at first been apparent. Spain's economy had finally begun to grow again, but the credibility of its politicians and institutions remained at an all time low. The challenge represented by Catalonia was immediate and the possibility of the country facing a constitutional crisis more serious than any seen since the transition was real. The long process towards ETA's end had moved far further than had seemed possible when I began my research in 2008, but it had also exposed the deep divisions that still scarred Spanish and Basque society.

Business as usual in the campaign against the nationalist left meant that Arnaldo Otegi and Rafa Díez were still in prison as 'leaders of ETA' despite it being widely recognised that they had led the nationalist left towards peace after a difficult internal confrontation with the actual leaders of ETA. The mayor of Guernica, who had presided over a committee that had awarded the 'Guernica Peace Prize' to Otegi and Jesús Eguiguren for their efforts towards peace, had been prosecuted for the 'glorification of terrorism'.[13] In September 2013 the Guardia Civil had launched a shock assault on Herrira, an organisation created in early 2012 to support the Basque prisoners that had consistently expressed itself in support of human rights, arresting eighteen of its members on the grounds that it was a 'tentacle of ETA'.[14] In October trials began in two *macroprocesos*—one against members of Segi, and the other, the *herriko tabernas* case against leaders of the nationalist left that had been rumbling through the legal system since 2002.

Other stray pieces of news, like the report back in June of right-wing pressure to tear down the small monument in Madrid to the members of the International Brigades—while a large triumphal arch to the Civil War's victors remained standing, and numerous streets, parks and plazas in Madrid still bore the names of members of Franco's regime—continued to provide a jarring reminder of Spain's inability to address its past.[15] In November 2013 the UN Committee on Enforced Disappearances called on Spain to do more to pursue justice for the relatives of the disappeared. As a coalition of civil society organisations submitted, Spain had not yet opened a single judicial process to pursue of 'truth, justice and reparations' despite the more than 150,000 disappeared, more than 30,000 stolen children, and more than 2,232 mass graves—of which only 390 had so far been opened—that stained its history.[16]

ETA remained a divisive issue in Spanish politics. Yet few in the Basque Country or Spain could ignore the metamorphosis that had taken place. After years of determined police work, widespread rejection of ETA's violence, and a surprisingly public struggle over the validity of armed action, those within the nationalist left supporting a non-violent and democratic path toward Basque independence had emerged triumphant, to the obvious discomfort of those who celebrated ETA's defeat. Sortu had been legalised. EH Bildu had demonstrated that it had everything to fight for by political means, and no desire at all to have the obstacle of violence cast in its way. The resolution of the 'Basque problem' was a distant prospect, but the violent ETA that had been a defining feature of Basque and Spanish life for decades was no more—an achievement, however late in coming, of true worth.

The long road to peace

Considerations of 'peace' are determined by the conflict that has preceded it. In the Basque case, the persistence of ETA's violence through Spain's transition to democracy and the high degree of political, social and economic development of Spain impose particular parameters. Debates in the peacebuilding literature, pioneered by the work of Roland Paris and Oliver Richmond, regarding the benefits and limitations of 'liberal peacebuilding'—understood to include an end to violence, but also the establishment of liberal democracy and free and globalised markets—are in many respects not relevant.[17] Instead, the exceptional nature of ETA's violence and the return to the democratic framework of those in its political orbit lend weight to arguments that the 'elusive peace' that emerges from internal conflict had been achieved through the transformation of the means by which radical nationalists pursued their political goals. The conflict, it could be argued, had been returned to 'normal politics'.

Through an incremental process, the nationalist left had come to accept that all members of Basque society had a voice and vote in their future; that different rhythms and processes for the distinct territories—Navarre and the French Basque Country as well as Euskadi—they claim as the Basque homeland, Euskal Herria, were valid; and that the goal of independence could be pursued by peaceful and democratic means, and thus within Spain's existing legal framework. But, as the difficult progression of events in the more than two years since ETA's renunciation of violence suggested, how much this peace owed to a more profound transformation of the actors concerned remained an open question. The disarmament and dissolution of ETA were still to come; complex issues regarding its prisoners and exiles also remained outstanding. And the consolidation of peace, pursued through coexistence and reconciliation grounded in an accommodation with the past, would be an endeavour of many years duration.

Endgame for ETA chronicles the history upon which the achievement of the end of ETA's violence was built within a framework determined by interlocking preoccupations regarding the risks and benefits of engagement with armed groups proscribed as terrorist and the costs and benefits of counter-terrorism for democratic states. It is in many respects a story suffused with sadness—a story of lives lost and threatened, the traumatisation of the public space, the erosion of trust, denial of rights, the poisoning of political dialogue and failed negotiations—and also one intimately interwoven with Spain's difficult and ambiguous posttransition evolution.

The legacy of Franco tainted Spain's democratic transition, as well as ETA and the efforts by Spain to force it to an end, contributing to almost uniquely difficult circumstances for the conflict's resolution. After its peak in 1980, ETA's violence was gradually reduced by actions taken by Spain. Yet its continuing existence accentuated flaws in the pacts and compromises upon which Spain's transition had been constructed and continued to inflict real harm on the 'new Spain' that had emerged from it. ETA's terrorist violence and the attendant extortion, threats and oppressive presence on the Basque streets represented a comprehensive violation of the freedom and rights promised by Spain's constitution. The harm done, however, was exacerbated by at least two other elements: ETA's actions provoked a Spanish over-reaction that had damaging consequences for its democracy; and the presence of ETA, even as it lost popular support, appeared to have little impact on the fact that an important sector of Basque society continued to seek independence from Spain. Basque nationalism suffered too: inside Spain it was perceived as culpably ambivalent towards ETA's terrorism; outside, it was tainted by association with a separatist organisation whose sporadic lethal violence seemed ever more inexplicable.

ETA endured for a complex combination of reasons that do not detract from its responsibility for the suffering it caused. It was more deeply committed to a distinct and intolerant Basque identity and a 'rupture' with the Spain of Franco than those who negotiated the pacts of the transition had realised. An assumption that a high degree of autonomy would encourage it to abandon the armed struggle therefore was proven wrong. ETA never conceived of its end except in terms of its absolute objectives and missed opportunities to pursue it on a more favourable basis than it achieved in 2011. It adopted a strategy of negotiation from the earliest days, but insistence on the imposition of its goals and Spain's refusal to countenance political negotiation with a terrorist organisation doomed formal talks to failure. A major crisis after the arrests at Bidart in 1992 prompted difficult internal reflection. However, the leadership of the moment did not have the vision to realise that, while Spain might not have had the capacity to inflict a total defeat, it could limit the organisation's operational capacity so completely as to render any possibility that it could extract substantive political gain from negotiations beyond question. ETA instead took the decision to double down and embark on a strategy of 'all or nothing' through a deliberate expansion of its target base and the 'socialisation of suffering'.

A full range of political, legal and security measures were thrown at ETA over the course of its lifetime. At different moments, and to differing extents they worked, and didn't. Actions taken against an organisation primarily identified by the state as terrorist were framed as counter-terrorism. Initially pursued through repressive measures, police action against ETA grew in efficiency as Spanish democracy, including the largely successful experiment that was the Basque autonomous government, took hold and the democratic political parties reached consensus in the Pact of Ajuria Enea. It found support from cross-border co-operation from France, the robust application of targeted counter-terrorist legislation, including the banning of political parties, and the waning legitimacy of ETA's violence within the broader Basque nationalist community.

However, early excesses—including the GAL—indifference to credible and repeated allegations of torture, the deliberate confusion by Spain's 'constitutional fundamentalists' of the peaceable with the violent strains of Basque nationalism and an expansive conception of terrorism validated by the 'global war on terrorism' introduced after September 2001 all contributed to create conditions that undermined Spain's democratic development, fuelled radical nationalism's sense of its persecution and helped deepen rather than bridge the polarising forces in Basque society. These polarising forces and an understandably emotional reaction to the pain inflicted by ETA inhibited the introduction of coherent policies to counter ETA's violence that could retain the support of moderate Basque nationalists, and demonised the idea of dialogue as a means of pursuing them.

Lurking beneath Spain's long struggle against ETA was a persistent ambivalence regarding the problem it presented and the benefits that would accrue by bringing it to an end. On the one hand ETA was a terrorist band, an illegal armed group guilty of the perpetration of the most horrible assassinations, kidnappings and other attacks, as well as a campaign of threats and extortion quite unacceptable in any law-abiding country. On the other was the more inconvenient truth that ETA was not the core problem. ETA represented, as Alfredo Rubalcaba candidly observed in February 2012, 'a certain "guarantee" for those of us who are not [Basque] nationalists'.[18] It prevented the formation of a broad alliance among Basque nationalists and allowed successive governments in Madrid to dismiss those nationalists' demands, with a tacit understanding that the continuation of ETA's violence at a manageably low level was the least bad option available. In the crudest form of this line of thinking, Luis María Ansón, during the 1980s the editor of *ABC*, famously compared ETA to 'a small ulcer, which sometimes bleeds but doesn't kill'.[19] By extension, if ETA was an 'ulcer' afflicting Spain as a persistent irritant, the true 'cancer' and mortal threat to Spanish nationalists such as Ansón was Basque nationalism itself, which remained, as

ETA's end approached, as deeply rooted in Basque society and politics as it ever had been.

These considerations go some way to explain the view, articulated by Florencio Domínguez in late August 2013, that Mariano Rajoy's 'immobility' with regard to the end of ETA, had been 'effective', despite the criticism heaped upon the government's refusal to move from all sectors of Basque society other than the PP itself.[20] The results were, in fact, two-fold. Firstly—and this was the point made by Domínguez—it put ETA under pressure to undertake unilateral steps to move forward to its dissolution from across the political spectrum, including the nationalist left, as well as its international interlocutors. But Rajoy's 'immobility' had other consequences as well, certainly 'effective' from the point of view of the PP, but disorienting for Basque society and short-sighted in terms of the long-term relationship between the Basque Country and Spain. From the perspective of the PP in Madrid, it was difficult to see the downside of a long drawn out and contentious path towards ETA's dissolution. The organisation represented no real security threat, and its existence helped ensure continuing divisions within the Basque polity. Perhaps most significantly, it complicated relations between the nationalist left and the PNV, thereby contributing to impede the development of a joint position articulating Basques' 'right to decide'.

Historically, intolerance and the refusal to recognise difference lie deep in Spanish culture. The Inquisition, the Counter Reformation, and the expulsion of both the Jews and the Arabs are distant, but nonetheless striking, examples of Spanish resistance to compromise with internal critics and opponents. Beneath the upbeat rhetoric of the 'new time' for the Basque independence movement prevalent since its electoral successes in 2011, the hard truth remained that the issues, demands and key arguments at the heart of the political conflict had remained essentially unchanged since the institutions of the transition were put in place by the constitution in 1978 and the Basque statute of autonomy that quickly followed it. In decades of Spanish democracy, the nationalist left had not become more tolerant of a shared Spanish identity or abandoned its dream of independence, even if it espoused ideas that were non-violent, and infinitely more pragmatic—and law-abiding—than those it had advocated in the past. The political establishment in Madrid had become no less intolerant towards the demands of Basque (or Catalan) nationalism, and no less adamant in defence of constitutional provisions that set the bar for change very high. All hoped and believed that ETA's violence was a thing of the past, yet even on this issue the gulf separating public opinion in the Basque Country and the rest of Spain—for example with regard to the movement of Basque prisoners—yawned wide. Far from making an enduring relationship to the central Spanish state more appealing, the actions and rhetoric assumed by Madrid and Spain had pushed regional nationalisms further away.

Endgame and its lessons

'The end and the endgame matters,' was one of the conclusions reached by the multi-case study of the ending of protracted conflicts led by Heiberg et al. in the mid-2000s.[21] It is fitting that ETA's endgame, when it eventually came into sight, should be as singular as the conflict it had waged and the state had refused to recognise. No negotiations took place and no peace agreement was reached in a process that saw unilateral change within a political-military organisation and the broader structures of its political and social support, directly informed by actions of the state, pressure from Basque society and the involvement of international actors.

Much about the Spanish-Basque case complicates the extraction of lessons from it. It is exceptional in terms of the degree of asymmetry of the violence, the high degree of autonomy granted Basques at the time of Spain's transition to democracy and the 'polarised pluralism' that characterises Basque politics, all factors that impeded a negotiated outcome. It is exceptional also in the nature of Spain, an established Western democracy, but one shadowed by the combination of pride, insecurity and intolerance that remained the less-celebrated legacy of its transition to democracy. No less exceptional, of course, was ETA itself, which shared characteristics with other violent ethno-nationalist groups but was distinguished by the specific identity and history that drove it and the social and political movement in its orbit from which it drew legitimacy and support.

Although notable for its longevity, ETA was far from exceptional as an organisation that conceived its struggle as being both political and military and used terrorist violence not as an end in itself but as a tactic in what it perceived as a war waged to further its political cause. There was nothing exceptional, either, in its vilification as a 'criminal terrorist band', or the difficulties encountered by democratic Spain in arriving at a durable end to the violence conducted against it. Spain's reluctance to countenance the involvement of outsiders in the resolution of a problem of evidently internal origin was shared by many other states, as were the domestic benefits it reaped for maintaining a firm hand against the terrorist threat. This complex mix suggests that, just as there are many elements in common between ETA and other violent armed groups perceived by governments as terrorist organisations and the peace processes or campaigns that eventually bring about their end, so there are aspects of the Basque case that are quite distinct.

The literature on conflict termination and the decline and demise of terrorist campaigns is rich in both individual case and comparative studies. Research pursued from varying perspectives—ranging from analyses of engagement with 'the enemy', 'extremists' or 'terrorists' undertaken with a view to determining options for state policy to studies focused on the internal choices made by 'armed groups', 'insurgents', or 'resistance and liberation movements'—has greatly expanded knowledge of how and why violence may be reduced, or end, as a contribution to more enduring processes of conflict transformation and peacebuilding. Although the framing of the different elements and processes that will contribute to such change inevitably vary, some important common findings emerge.

Perhaps most centrally, conflict termination, as the decline and demise of terrorist campaigns, is overdetermined and only explicable by some combination of factors both internal and external to the parties concerned. In 1991 Martha Crenshaw attributed 'the decline of terrorism' to three: 'the physical defeat of the extremist organization by the government, the group's decision to abandon the terrorist strategy, and organizational disintegration'.[22] These are expanded into the six patterns that collectively cover the full range of paths towards a group or campaign's end identified by Audrey Kurth Cronin in her 2009 study *How Terrorism Ends*: the capture or killing of the group's leader; the entry of the group into a legitimate political process; the achievement of the group's aims; the implosion or loss of the group's public support; the defeat and elimination by brute force, and transition from terrorism into other forms of violence.[23] Crenshaw observed that 'decisive defeats are rare' in the absence of other factors, a finding shared by Cronin, who concludes that 'repression alone seldom ends terrorism'.[24]

Analysts of the internal dynamics of armed groups or insurgents who have 'political programs, legitimacy amongst a significant portion of the populace, and objectives that may include the overthrow or re-shaping of the existing regime or outright secession' (as the groups, including ETA, studied by Heiberg et al. are described) similarly find that they 'cannot easily be defeated by strong militaries from democratic states' but may instead conclude their violent activities as a consequence of a combination of policies pursued by governments and other elements.[25] These were categorised by Véronique Dudouet, in the Berghof Foundation's study of resistance and liberation movements in transition, as embracing internal dynamics and leadership within the movements; inter-party dynamics (i.e. relations with the state); the movement's relations with its constituency and other social and political forces; and the international arena.[26] As Clem McCartney observed in an earlier article examining why, when and how armed groups choose to move 'from armed struggle to political negotiations', the question each group engaged in violence faces has two components: 'when its transition to a conflict transformation paradigm is appropriate and whether it can manage that transition effectively'.[27] This choice will be strongly affected by the military situation in which the group finds itself (its recognition of a 'mutually hurting stalemate', to return to Zartman's term) but also its perception of marginalisation from its community of support either because its ideology has become irrelevant, or its targeting of victims has prompted a backlash against it.[28]

This brief and inevitably inadequate overview suggests how centrally the Basque case—despite Spanish protestations of its exceptionalism—sits within the study and practice of conflict resolution or other efforts to prise armed groups away from their violence. But it is not intended to belittle the unique features, explored at length within *Endgame for ETA*, of the long journey towards ETA's decision to abandon the military dimensions of its political-military struggle. Together these two elements suggest that, despite and in some respects because of its singularity, there are lessons that can be drawn from the Spanish-Basque case that will have resonance in other contexts. Without being in any sense exhaustive, ten stand out:

1. It is difficult, if not impossible, to solve a problem without first acknowledging what it is.

Disagreement on the nature of the problem represented by ETA had direct impact upon Spain's difficulties in establishing a clear strategy, broadly shared among all democratic parties, to address it. There were good reasons for confusion, rooted in opposing perceptions and experiences of Basque history and identity that are never likely to be resolved. But the confusion was extended, manipulated and distorted by discourse of the war on terrorism appropriated by the government of José María Aznar. This both fed on and fed the fanaticism of ETA and contributed to conditions in which contending views regarding whether the goal was to bring an end to ETA's terrorism or resolve the Basque conflict made progress in a formal setting of negotiations all but impossible.

The truth, of course, was that terrorism and the Basque conflict were not mutually exclusive: ETA used terrorism to further the ends of what it perceived and experienced as a conflict. And the fact that it operated on the basis that it was engaged in a conflict with the Spanish state that was obviously ideological in both its origins and ends could not be ignored by any attempt to solve the problem represented by its violence. The structure of the two-track process introduced by Otegi at Anoeta in late 2004 attempted to overcome the state's consistent and understandable refusal to discuss political issues with ETA, but as later events demonstrated, neither side was either able or prepared to follow it through.

It is perhaps worth observing that this is a lesson that seems to have been learned in the very different context of Colombia. For years President Alvaro Uribe—a close political ally of Aznar's—had defined the Colombian conflict only in terms of terrorism and refused any prospect of negotiation. When his successor, President Juan Manuel Santos, launched a peace process with the FARC in 2012, it was on the understanding that a first priority was the need 'to recognise that one does not cure a sickness, or resolve a problem, if one does not call things by their name'. And in the case of Colombia—where the military had long been engaged in combat operations with the FARC—'the name of this problem is "internal armed conflict"'.[29]

2. Robust security or counter-terrorist measures have their role, but politics is what brings sustainable peace.

Groups formed for organised resistance embark on a violent path—and may employ the tactic of terrorism—when they conclude there is no political option available to them. If outright victory is impossible, they end it if and when they can accept this fact and be assured that a political future once more extends before them. It is unrealistic to think that armed groups that still command social support will end their violence without such police—or when the scale of the conflict determines it—military pressure. However to be effective this pressure must be accompanied by a conflict resolution strategy that allows for political goals to be pursued by peaceful and democratic means.

The founders of ETA established it as a political-military organisation to oppose the repression of Franco and because there was not a democracy that allowed fair debate of its demands. ETA continued through the transition, even as many militants reintegrated into civilian life or joined Basque political parties, because it continued to hold Spanish democracy to be illegitimate, and armed action as the most effective means to force its objectives upon Spanish and Basque society. Increasingly effective police action, buttressed by strong leadership from successive ministers of the interior, robust intelligence and growing international co-operation, lay at the core of Spain's assertion of the rule of law against criminal and terrorist violence. This pressure eroded ETA's operational capacity, inflicting what Spanish security forces would claim as its 'defeat', but never eliminating its capacity to kill at a reduced level or vanquishing the political potency of the cause of Basque national liberation.

No consideration of ETA can be separated from an understanding of the social and political movement that formed its base. This was intimately related to the dense associational life of the Basque Country, and the Basque nationalist community in particular, and grew into a network of extraordinary resilience. It drew on the mobilisation of successive generations of Basque youth, reached across many walks of life—from political organisation to social mobilisation and cultural activities—and demonstrated a capacity to animate conflict around a wide range of issues (from a nuclear plant to the construction of a new highway, for example). Although the view that 'everything was ETA' was a gross oversimplification, the ties of the nationalist left to the armed organisation were deep and enduring (and in many instances criminal). These ties played a essential role in sustaining ETA for so many years, but also in ensuring a political way out in the future. ETA was policed down but, to borrow the phrasing of Hugh Orde cited in the Introduction, not 'out'. Albeit in a severely weakened state, it took the decision to end its violence only once the nationalist left had demonstrated that it could more effectively continue its struggle by political means.

3. The law is central to counter-terrorism, but should be tightly circumscribed to the serious crimes that constitute a terrorist offence; it can also complicate a peace process.

Exceptional measures of counter-terrorism bring operational benefits to a state's counter-terrorist campaign, but also risks related to the protection of human rights and the institutions charged with their implementation. As John Finn demonstrates in his review of counter-terrorism regimes introduced in the aftermath of 9/11, such regimes can directly undermine the protection of civil liberties, while they also impact upon other constitutional norms of 'accountability, transparency and deliberation, and proportionality'.[30] Spain, which was not considered within Finn's review, is no exception. An expansive understanding of terrorist activities allowed for prosecutions based on association rather than individual responsibility and of activities addressed under vaguely defined understanding of 'collaboration' or 'glorification' of terrorism that at times fell short of the serious crimes that should constitute a terrorist offence.

Actions such as the closure of *Egunkaria*, the introduction of the Parot Doctrine, the spike in arrests during 2006, the mishandling of the de Juana Chaos case, the arrest and prosecution of Otegi and the others detained in October 2009, and the contested legalisation of Sortu, were widely understood to have been motivated by short-term political needs. They contributed to an erosion of the credibility of Spain's democratic institutions—especially its tarnished judiciary—in the interests of counter-terrorism that will not easily be remedied. Between 2005 and 2007 the intense hostility displayed by many judges to Zapatero's efforts to launch a peace process highlighted the tensions between peace and justice that frequently manifest when peace is sought with individuals and entities responsible for violent actions. The problem takes on particular dimensions in a functioning democratic state—perhaps especially in a situation such as Spain in which the 'independence' of individual judges may be directly influenced by political allegiance or inclinations.

As the centrepiece of the legal battle against ETA, the political parties' law was an effective but blunt instrument. Over a decade it isolated Batasuna in social terms, dramatically curtailed its access to public finances and eventually contributed to the pressure on ETA to call a halt to its violence for good. However, the ingenuity of the nationalist left kept its participation—or not—within every election held in the Basque

Country after 2002 a live issue. In the meantime, banning the political expression of a movement articulated around both a political and military strategy hindered efforts to resolve the conflict more quickly while disenfranchising a sector of the electorate infinitely larger than could be directly linked to ETA. Batasuna's illegal status was one of the primary obstacles to the peace process launched by Zapatero in 2005. It undermined dialogue and directly inhibited the logical course of action in any peace process, which would be to strengthen the 'moderates' at the expense of their violent associates.[31] Far from eroding support, a sense of the injustice inflicted upon the nationalist left by the political parties' law galvanised its bases once a return to politics became possible in 2011.

A problem inherent in the introduction of exceptional legislation that then becomes the norm was exemplified by Spain's policy of prisoner dispersion and the Rajoy government's unwillingness to reverse it. Dispersion had sought to disrupt the privileges available to Basque prisoners and break ETA's hold upon them. It was more successful at the former than the latter. But it also inflicted hardship on prisoners' family members, met with broad opposition within Basque society and, in practical terms, slowed the process of internal consultation necessary to engage the support of the prisoners of the new direction taken by the nationalist left after 2009. Changes to the penitentiary law in 2003 compounded the exceptional circumstances applicable to those imprisoned for terrorism-related offences. Once ETA had formally renounced the use of violence, and this had been confirmed by the security services, a more pragmatic government might have welcomed the opportunity to modify the exceptional measures applicable to prisoners—with dispersion foremost among them—as a means to cement ETA's move away from violence and build confidence in the possibilities offered by peace.

4. Victims should be afforded full respect and rights, but not given a veto role over policy decisions.

ETA's victims were for a long time wrongly neglected by the Basque and Spanish governments and civil society. This isolation was followed by the introduction of robust legislation to address the rights and reparations due to victims of terrorism, consistent with international best practice, and their welfare remained a central preoccupation for successive governments. Throughout the years of ETA's existence its victims acted with admirable restraint towards the armed organisation—never engaging in acts of vengeance for example. However, their collective elevation to a position of moral arbiter undermined efforts to develop coherent policies towards ETA or grant recognition to the victims of the state, the GAL or other rightist armed groups. The primacy some of the ETA victims' organisations came to assume in the counter-terrorist struggle undermined government policy towards ETA pursued by Zapatero and had a disproportionate influence over discussion of counter-terrorist strategy in much of Spain's media. In the period after ETA's renunciation of violence, positions assumed by ETA's victims constrained Rajoy from demonstrating greater flexibility towards the prisoners, even through the implementation of measures that would have been wholly consistent with the law.

Meanwhile, the legacy of Spain's inability to address the issue of victims (including Basque victims) under Franco, its fear of establishing equivalence between two sides in a conflict that it did not acknowledge and antipathy to the idea that terrorists or those associated with them could be victims too, led to the neglect of victims of the state and contributed to the hardening of the conflict divide. Spain refuses any forgiveness or partial amnesty for ETA's crimes and killings. Yet Spain fully amnestied all the killers and torturers of the Franco regime and—even years later—refused all appeals by victims of the dictatorship and their family members for recognition and some form of justice. Spain, almost uniquely in the world—much less Europe—has even been unwilling to fully identify and uncover graves of leftist forces and victims of Franco during the Civil War.

A state's responsibility to respect and respond to the rights and needs of victims is clearly established; the Basque experience, however, highlights the risks inherent in ceding a veto role in policy formation to those motivated by grief and outrage and vulnerable to political manipulation. Victims are not always 'right' nor should they—however deep the suffering or admirable their behaviour at an individual level—serve a role in the determination of policy formation. Ending violent conflict requires hard political decisions that may include compromises and concessions that victims find unpalatable. In some circumstances—as in Northern Ireland, where the British government agreed to keep releasing IRA prisoners even as the IRA was failing to decommission its weapons—the exigencies of peacebuilding have led strong governments to take decisions difficult to justify except on political grounds, and impossible to defend to victims. Such solutions cannot be rammed through in a situation of such asymmetry as that of the Basque case, and are likely to be increasingly difficult in other cases (Colombia comes to mind) in which exceptions in the application of the rule of law, even for the sake of peace, may meet with opposition. But nor was the rigidity adopted in the Basque case the only available option.

5. A normative approach to human rights, founded on the principle that there should be equal protection for equal violation, could help build trust.

The obstacles to adherence to a normative approach to human rights in the Basque case, consistent with internationally accepted standards—notably but not exclusively with regard to the contested issue of allegations of torture—were intimately related to the difficulty Spain has encountered in addressing the human rights violations of the Civil War and Franco era. Discussion of human rights violations in the Basque context was understandably dominated by criticism of the serious and consistent abuses perpetrated by ETA. Yet censure of ETA contributed to a distortion inherent in the consideration of human rights in terms of authorship rather than violation and thus the invisibility of 'other victims' in Basque and Spanish society. Efforts to redress this tendency underway within the Basque government in 2013 suggested the utility of a 'back to basics' approach to human rights as a means by which Basque society could begin to acknowledge the past, as a necessary step towards social and political coexistence in the future.

One of the more surprising aspects of Spain's actions was its reluctance to engage more actively on the issue of human rights, including with the international community, in order to undermine the nationalist left's sense of its own victimisation. This was perhaps most obvious in its resistance to the recommendations of international bodies such the European Committee to Prevent Torture, Amnesty International, Human Rights Watch, a variety of UN special rapporteurs and the European Court on Human Rights (for example with regard to the Parot Doctrine). The tolerance of torture suggested by the failure to investigate its allegation or adopt measures—notably with regard to *incommunicado* detention and the use of testimony extracted under torture—

to prevent its occurrence contributed to degrade the human rights protections that Spain is committed to uphold. In political terms it also represented a missed opportunity to demonstrate Spain's democratic credentials, and counter the view of the nationalist left that the value of confessions extracted by torture outweighed any benefits Spain might have gained by taking steps to demonstrate that torture is a violation of human rights unacceptable in any circumstance.

In an environment in which all parties—from the victims' organisations to Sortu—demand 'truth', even as their conceptions of what that 'truth' might be vary widely, a rigorous approach to human rights violations offers one possible way forward. Consideration of a mechanism such as a truth commission is complicated by both the wider context of Spain—in which there is no desire to shine light on all that has remained unexamined in the Franco era, the murky violence of the transition and some of the actions of Spanish state in the democratic period—and the fact that it has been articulated as a demand of the nationalist left. Yet, at an appropriate time, establishing a record of human rights violations that, as the baseline report prepared by the Basque government in early 2013, could 'be assumed as true by any interlocutor of good faith', could have multiple benefits. Not least among them would be an attempt to shift the discussion of such violations away from debates regarding the 'equivalence' or not between the actions of ETA and the Spanish state—there is after all no conceivable way in which a rights-based approached to ETA's violence would legitimate its terrorist actions—to acknowledge publicly that in Spanish democracy, all such violations are unacceptable.

6. Dialogue and engagement should not be stigmatised by opposition to 'talking to terrorists' or confusion with negotiation.

The possibility of negotiation with ETA and contacts, messages, channels, 'takings of temperatures' and talks accompanied its long history. The idea of negotiation was progressively degraded by the failure of the formal processes—most notably the evidence that later emerged of ETA's offensive activities during both the Lizarra and Zapatero ceasefires—but also stigmatised by the escalating rhetoric of counter-terrorism. Whether or not Zapatero's government had contacts with ETA became an issue of contention out of all proportion to the seriousness of the threat such talks represented, and in noted contrast to the relative calm with which news of contacts with the FARC, the PKK in Turkey or indeed the Taliban in Afghanistan has been greeted. In such a highly charged political environment, the point that there are many forms of engagement with a non-state armed group, conferring very different levels of recognition, and in any case quite distinct from the formal negotiation of political issues, was almost entirely lost.

Despite its atypical trajectory, and its origins in the breakdown of a more conventional process of negotiation, the Basque case as it developed from 2009 onwards nevertheless confirms the value of engagement and dialogue at multiple levels. Indeed it suggests that more rather than less engagement with ETA—a closed, extremist organisation inherently suspicious of outsiders but urgently in need of greater communication with those capable of giving a blunt assessment of the possibilities open to it in the real world—would have been desirable throughout its history, and perhaps especially during its period of greatest isolation under Aznar. It is, of course, difficult for democratic governments to talk to terrorists, and usually necessary for them to begin to do so through third parties or in secret. The challenge, as Zapatero found, is how to bring such contacts—if and when they leak or develop into a more formal process—into the public domain.

Very little of what happened in the Zapatero years would have been possible without the extended conversations between Eguiguren and Otegi, and Zapatero's bold decision to launch a peace process on their basis. The two men had different priorities and visions for the future of the Basque Country but shared a desire to end the conflict that had shaped their lives and a willingness to listen to the other. Engagement with Batasuna, by a range of Basque forces and international actors, was also a vital element of the transition it embarked on. The discreet channels between Batasuna—and later ETA—and the government played a positive, indeed essential, role in bringing this process to fruition. Zapatero and Rubalcaba held a firm line against ETA during the PSOE's second government. However, they would not have achieved its declaration of the end to its violence if they had not also been prepared to maintain channels of communication with Batasuna and ETA and to act on the opportunity to move ahead when it eventually was presented to them. The issue, the Basque case suggests, is not if contacts with an illegal armed group are desirable, but how, when and to what end they should be pursued.

7. Change is difficult, and requires leadership and a clear and unambiguous strategy.

There are lessons to be learned by other political-military organisations from the Basque experience and indications, for example, that both the FARC and the PKK have paid it close attention.[32] ETA's long history, and certainly its progression since 2004, illustrates how difficult it is for groups whose existence has been defined by the armed struggle to leave violence behind. A diffuse and opaque leadership structure contributed to complicate efforts to engage with ETA or understand its decision-making process. Meanwhile the successive decapitation of the organisation by the death, capture or detention of its leaders facilitated the ascension of more intransigent and less experienced individuals to its executive committee. Change when it did come was, nonetheless, intimately related to the leadership of top ETA commanders and representatives of Batasuna. The ability of Otegi, Etxeberria and their associates to construct a new strategy after the end of the ceasefire in June 2007, and eventually to persuade ETA that this was viable was the direct catalyst of ETA's decision to call a definitive end to its violence. Their strategy drew on a series of unilateral steps, carefully planned and executed by a widening group. It depended on their ability to maintain internal cohesion, and was continuously assisted by discreet and unofficial international engagement.

The effort they led was anchored in self-criticism of what went wrong in the earlier process. It represented recognition of the need to move beyond the ambiguity on which it had been founded—both within ETA and the nationalist left and in the agreements entered into with the Spanish government—given the total breakdown of trust between the parties and the very unambiguous determination by the government never to return to negotiations. It confirmed an important lesson identified by Jonathan Powell from his experience in Northern Ireland: ambiguity can have a place in the early stages of a peace process as 'an essential tool to bridge the gap between irreconcilable positions', but if things do not advance it ceases to be constructive and can become instead 'the enemy of progress'.[33]

Internal consultation, concluding with the approval of the document *Zutik Euskal Herria* in early 2010, underpinned a strategy built around the twin axes of unilateralism and alliances with other social and political forces. A unilateral process was, on the one hand, all that was available to the nationalist left. On the other, it was a constructive response to the frustration of the bilateral process that had preceded it. Unilateral action gave the nationalist left autonomy of decision, initiative and action that was impervious to the disappointment of unfulfilled agreements with the government. As events between 2012 and early 2014 demonstrated, it also imparted a degree of resilience in the face of Rajoy's refusal to take up the opportunities presented by the Aiete Conference. From an early stage Otegi and the nucleus around him also began reaching out to those who might join a broad pro-independence and leftist platform once violence was out of the way, greatly increasing the viability of the political option they put forward. Without such leadership within the nationalist left—and ultimately in ETA as well—the end of ETA's violence would not have been achieved.

8. Civil society and social forces have a responsibility and role.

Civil society and broader social forces play multiple roles in the validation of, or opposition to, armed struggle. In the Basque case, organised civil society was slow to mobilise against ETA's violence. However, it became an important vehicle for wider public rejection of ETA while also actively pursuing the possible ways out of the impasse into which political parties had become locked. The social and intellectual frameworks through which civil society engaged were quite distinct, but organisations ranging from those dedicated to victims' rights and demands, the ethically-based Gesto por la Paz, and more overtly political ¡Basta Ya!, led the way in articulating the demand for an end to terrorism, including through public demonstrations that sought to counter the oppressive presence of the nationalist left in the Basque streets. Overall, the mobilisation of social forces against ETA's violence played an essential part in denying the organisation the legitimacy it required to pursue a struggle it always conceived as being undertaken on behalf of 'the Basque people'. Not to be overlooked in this process was the central role played by the nationalist left's own constituency: opinion polls over the years suggested increasing doubts within this community regarding the efficacy of ETA's violence. When the time eventually came for ETA to shift, it was only able to do so in response to the firm position taken against violence within its own social and political base.

Elkarri and later Lokarri introduced and championed a 'third way' in Basque politics that prioritised the role that could be played by dialogue as an alternative to violence, and encouraged perspectives derived from other peace processes.[34] In its turn Ahotsak provided a forum within which women of diverse political and ideological persuasions could articulate their concerns. The activities of Elkarri and then Lokarri took various forms. These ranged from Jonan Fernández's direct engagement in dialogue with ETA to the convening of international peace conferences and the promotion of dialogue between political parties, other social forces and interested individuals. They included Elkarri's encouragement of the engagement of Alec Reid and others with experience of peace processes in Northern Ireland, South Africa and elsewhere, and Lokarri's facilitation of the work of Brian Currin, hosting of the Aiete Conference and promotion of the Social Forum in 2013. Although the timing of the demise of Elkarri contributed to Basque civil society appearing curiously muted during the critical year of 2006, Elkarri and Lokarri together should be recognised as having represented a strong and consistent social and political influence for peace.

Over many years' work civil society actors were able to embark on initiatives and promote public participation, as well as the involvement of actors—international experts and advisers, but also representatives of social and political sectors in Navarre and the French Basque territories—that would not have been possible at an institutional level. Their endeavours were facilitated by the high degree of social mobilisation within Basque society and the myriad of organisations through which this mobilisation found expression. After the end of ETA's violence, a number of civil society organisations whose existence had been directly linked to their active opposition to terrorism brought their activities to an end. However, as discussion of 'peace and coexistence' encountered serious obstacles within the Basque Parliament—under both the governments of both Patxi López and Iñigo Urkullu—the value of civil society fora as a means to take work in this area forward, in consultation with the broadest possible spectrum of Basque society, came to the fore.

9. Even in circumstances when formal international involvement is not possible, international actors can play a variety of useful functions.

Overall, an international involvement that reached its apogee at Aiete in October 2011 was as ambiguous as the process it supported, but a remarkable example of the possibilities for informal third-party involvement in dialogue of different kinds when conditions inhibit a more established process. The Zapatero government had trouble in mounting a peace process during its first legislature. International facilitation was essential to its progression, but given sensitivities that held that recurrence to international assistance represented a betrayal of Spanish sovereignty, it was easier to contemplate when offered by a discreet private organisation such as the HD Centre than by a state. To secure the unilateral process it embarked on in 2009, the nationalist left made adroit use of its international contacts to boost its leverage with ETA and to develop a channel of communication to an initially sceptical Socialist government. This concluded in the agreement of a 'road map' that the government never acknowledged, and could push to one side with impunity as a consequence of the electoral timetable and the informal nature of the facilitation upon which it had rested. But, before this time, the road map and the direct international assistance that had secured it had been able to build a momentum for peace that held firm even when the nationalist left's hopes of what the road map might bring had been thwarted.

In the development of its strategic shift away from violence Batasuna drew on a partnership with international actors quite distinct from the Northern Ireland 'model' adopted in the Estella-Lizarra process. Zapatero's government, meanwhile, maintained a public position of distance, interspersed with open criticism of international involvement, even as Zapatero himself praised—and at times hid behind—the influence of Tony Blair, and a very small number of government officials maintained relations of trust with a similarly small number of individuals in direct communication with ETA, Batasuna, and later ETA again. More distant initiatives, most prominently the Basque Friendship group in the European Parliament, offered undeniably partisan solidarity with the efforts of the nationalist left while unequivocally calling upon ETA to end its violence.

During 2005–2007 the HD Centre had been limited to the facilitation of the talks between the government delegation and ETA, while Batasuna developed a distinct relationship with Brian Currin. However, the May 2007 talks widened the frame of international participation considerably, bringing representatives of Sinn Féin and the British and Norwegian governments to the table and in the process fostering contacts with Batasuna, ETA and the HD Centre. After the end of ETA's ceasefire, Batasuna worked hard to rebuild the support of what would be referred to as 'the international community' but in truth was a small number of committed individuals and entities, able to operate in ways that a state could not. Their involvement included both the relatively public engagement of Currin, the International Contact Group and International Verification Commission—which were significant for their direct engagement of Basque actors outside the nationalist left, in addition to the latter's access to ETA—as well as others whose efficacy was inextricably interwoven with the discretion within which they operated. And herein lies another lesson of this process: the absolute necessity of discreet work by international actors. It was only this discretion that allowed them to maintain access to Batasuna and ETA and to influence both to take steps towards peace, while also being able to reassure Spain and France that this work would not lead to embarrassment.

The existence of parallel tracks of public and confidential engagement brought complementary benefits, but also a useful degree of confusion regarding what was actually happening at any given moment. The reported backing of Norway, publicly invisible even at Aiete, echoes other long-term commitments of Norway to peacemaking—in some cases, as in Sri Lanka and Colombia with more public recognition—in its commendable patience, discretion, consistency and willingness to take risks. None was greater than its disposition to host the political leadership of ETA after Aiete. This it did at the request of the Spanish government, in the hope that the Rajoy government would then take the logical step forward and establish some means of contact—quite possibly far short of direct talks—to secure the final dissolution of ETA. One feature of Norway's role, evident in the 'buffering' of its presence by the more front-line engagement of others such as the HD Centre, was its apparent willingness to develop relations, and a partnership, of deep trust with non-governmental peacemakers.

For the nationalist left, the layered international involvement had both internal and external dimensions. As the receptor of advice and encouragement—interlaced with home truths that were sometimes unpalatable—the leadership of Batasuna was able to display to its bases, and to ETA, that its move away from violence would find international support. Most fundamentally, the experience of its old allies in the IRA and Sinn Féin helped convey that 'it was possible to move towards politics, without achieving all goals, and still come out ahead'.[35] Externally, the decision by Currin to 'talk up' the changes underway within Batasuna after the arrests of 2009, and the bluff he risked with the Brussels Declaration both played important roles. The structural shift introduced by the Brussels Declaration offered the possibility that ETA could respond not to the government's desire for surrender, and not only to the appeal to it made by the nationalist left but also to the demand of the 'international community' for it to end its violence. These public gestures and steps could then be reinforced and built upon directly by international actors in contact with ETA and Batasuna. This multi-level, multi-actor, both public and discreet effort by committed international actors could be of use in other conflicts.

10. A process is necessary, but peace does not come without a political price.

Finally, the a-typical trajectory taken in the Basque case confirms the need for a peacemaking process. Insistence on ETA's unconditional 'defeat', it is true, left room for a process that appeared to be one of only 'virtual' peacemaking. But it was in fact quite real. The most significant aspect of the end of ETA's armed activities was that, even in the absence of a formal peace agreement, the organisation could claim ownership of its decision. It may have been a weakened force, but it was an active ETA that responded to the appeal made to it at Aiete. The decision to abandon 'the use of the armed struggle as a political strategy', as the veteran ETA leader Antxon explained in early 2012, in this respect had to be understood as distinct from the campaign against it.[36] This observation is not to deny the structural pressures of the Basque process—in which the ascendency of the political over the military logic was facilitated by the effective work of Spanish and French police, the rejection of ETA by Basque society and the political opportunities secured by the nationalist left. But as even Socialist officials could quietly accept, if ETA was, as they had been assured, really readying itself to abandon its armed activity for good, it required a degree of 'cover' to be able to do so with some dignity intact.

The need for a process did not evaporate after Aiete. While hopes that the road map the nationalist left had agreed with the outgoing Socialist government were dashed by the immobility of Rajoy, the pressure for forward movement still remained. The problem was political but also practical—how could an armed organisation dissolve clandestine structures, weapons, explosives and other resources on its own? In this respect, those inside and outside the Basque Country working to promote the benefits of 'an orderly end'—rather than a disorganised mess that might leave the prisoners and exiles stranded, provoke the appearance of armed splinter groups, or deny Basque society the possibility to be satisfied by ETA's admission of the harm done its victims and other steps towards peace and coexistence—were on solid ground. The reluctance of the Rajoy government to concede ETA the recognition that would be afforded by an assisted ending was rooted in old concerns about what ETA was, as well as an obsessive need for 'total victory' over it. Implicit was the fear that acknowledgement that peace is worth working for, or a process necessary to achieve it, might imply that some kind of price or concession would therefore be required to be 'paid' for it.

A response would seem self-evident. Spanish intransigence may uphold Spanish 'principles', but it also helps ensure that Basque society will remain deeply polarised and significantly hostile to Spain and Madrid. Over many years, ETA had inflicted great suffering on its victims and damage to the Basque Country and Spain. The ending of its armed activities had been unanimously welcomed, and its dissolution would be too. Peace is not worth any price, but nor does it come free.

NOTES

INTRODUCTION

1. Myrie, Clive, 'Eta ceasefire scoop: how the BBC got the story', 5 September 2010, http://www.bbc.co.uk/news/world-europe-11195595, last accessed 10 Sep. 2010.
2. Rodríguez, J.A. and L.R. Aizpeolea, 'ETA anuncia un alto de fuego "permanente y verificable"', *El País*, 10 January 2011.
3. 'Al servicio de ETA', *ABC*, 18 October 2011.
4. The phrase 'nationalist left' went through a subtle process of evolution—reflected in its use within this book—from a generic description of the membership of the Basque National Liberation Movement (MLNV) comprised of ETA and those organisations in its orbit, to a more specific association with the political party Batasuna and the other components of the liberation movement other than ETA.
5. Ramoneda, Josep, 'La última herencia del franquismo', *El País*, 21 October 2011.
6. Zulaika, Joseba, *Basque Violence: Metaphor and Sacrament*, Reno: University of Nevada Press, 1988, pp. 74–101.
7. Douglass, William A. and Joseba Zulaika, 'On the interpretation of terrorist violence: ETA and the Basque political process', *Comparative Studies in Society and History*, 32, 2 (April 1990), p. 252.
8. Sánchez-Cuenca, Ignacio, 'Moral y política ante ETA', Dominio público blog, *El Público*, 2 November 2011, http://blogs.publico.es/dominiopublico/4202/moral-y-politica-ante-eta/, last accessed 12 Apr. 2012.
9. See, for example, Varela Ortega, José, 'Del nacional-socialismo alemán y del vasco', *Fundación Papeles de Ermua no. 2*, 2001.
10. Aretxaga, Begoña, 'The intimacy of violence', in Zulaika, Joseba (ed.), *States of Terror: Begoña Aretxaga's Essays*, Reno: Center for Basque Studies, University of Nevada, 2005, p. 166.
11. Author interview (written), Patxi López, March 2012.
12. Whitfield, Teresa, 'Virtual peacemaking: the end of ETA's violence', *World Politics Review*, 31 October 2011, http://www.worldpoliticsreview.com/articles/10504/virtual-peacemaking-the-end-of-etas-violence, last accessed 6 Nov. 2011.
13. Richmond, Oliver, *The Transformation of Peace*, Basingstoke: Palgrave, 2005. p. 205.
14. García de Cortázar Ruiz de Aguirre, Fernando, 'Demasiadas voces y demasiadas veces', in Alonso, Rogelio, Florencio Domínguez and Marcos García Rey, *Vidas Rotas: Historia de los Hombres, Mujeres y Niños Víctimas de ETA*, Madrid: Espasa Libros, 2010, p. xiii. See also Calleja, José María, *Algo Habrá Hecho: Odio, Muerte y Miedo en Euskadi*, Madrid: Editorial Espasa Calpe, 2006, p. 14.

15. Alonso, Rogelio, 'The International Dimension of ETA's Terrorism and the Internationalization of the Conflict in the Basque Country', *Democracy and Security*, 7, 2 (2011), p. 193. See also Alonso, Rogelio, 'Leaving terrorism behind in Northern Ireland and the Basque Country', in Bjørgo, Tore and John Horgan, *Leaving Terrorism Behind: Individual and Collective Disengagement*, Oxford and New York: Routledge, 2009, pp. 103–5.

16. Conversation with the author, Emilio Cassinello, Virginia, April 2010.

17. Golob, Stephanie R., 'Volver: the return of/to transitional justice politics in Spain', *Journal of Spanish Cultural Studies*, 9, 2 (July 2008), pp. 127–41.

18. See Introduction to Zartman, I. William (ed.), *Elusive Peace: Negotiating an End to Civil Wars*, Washington, DC: The Brookings Institution, 1998, pp. 3–33.

19. Reiss, Mitchell B., *Negotiating with Evil: When to Talk to Terrorists*, E-book, Open Road Integrated Media, September 2010.

20. U.S. Code, Title 18, §2339B, 'Providing material support or resources to designated foreign terrorist organisations', United States Code, Supplement 3, Washington, DC, 2006 edition.

21. Aznar, José María, *Eight Years as Prime Minister: A Personal View of Spain*, Barcelona: Planeta, 2004, pp. 128–82 and 218.

22. Bew, John, Martyn Frampton and Iñigo Gurruchaga, *Talking To Terrorists: Making Peace in Northern Ireland and the Basque Country*, London: Hurst, 2009; English, Richard, *Terrorism: How To Respond*, Oxford and New York: Oxford University Press, 2009; Perry, Mark, *Talking To Terrorists: Why America Must Engage With Its Enemies*, New York: Basic Books, 2010; Powell, Jonathan, *Great Hatred, Little Room: Making Peace in Northern Ireland*, London: The Bodley Head, 2008, and *BBC Radio Four*, 'Talking to the enemy', August–September 2010; Quinney, Nigel and A. Heather Coyne, 'Talking to groups that use terror', *Peacemaker's Toolkit*, Washington, DC: United States Institute for Peace, 2011; Reiss, *Negotiating with Evil*; Ricigliano, Robert (ed.), 'Choosing to engage: armed groups and peace processes', *Accord Issue 16*, London: Conciliation Resources, 2005; Whitfield, Teresa, 'Engaging with armed groups: challenges and opportunities for mediators', Geneva: Centre for Humanitarian Dialogue, 2010; Støre, Jonas Gahr, 'Why we must talk', *New York Review of Books*, 7 April 2011; and Zartman, I. William and Guy Olivier Faure (eds), *Engaging Extremists: Trade-Offs, Timing and Diplomacy*, Washington, DC: United States Institute of Peace, 2011.

23. Bew et al., *Talking to Terrorists*, but also Alonso, Rogelio, 'Leaving terrorism behind', and 'Pathways out of terrorism in Northern Ireland and the Basque Country: the misrepresentation of the Irish model', *Terrorism and Political Violence*, 16, 4 (2004), pp. 695–713.

24. Crocker, Chester A., 'Thoughts on the conflict management field after 30 years', *International Negotiation*, 16, (2011), p. 5.

25. Ackerman, Spencer, 'Diplomat lends credence to talks with Taliban', *The Washington Independent*, 18 December 2008, http://washingtonindependent.com/22577/lakhdar-brahimi, last accessed 15 Jul. 2013. On the various tracks to the Taliban, see Ruttig, Thomas, 'Negotiations with the Taliban', in Bergen, Peter (ed.), *Talibanistan: Negotiating the Borders Between Terror, Politics and Religion*, New York: Oxford University Press, 2013, pp. 431–82.

26. Dougherty, Jill, 'U.S. met with Haqqani terrorists this summer', 21 October 2011, *CNN*, http://security.blogs.cnn.com/2011/10/21/u-s-met-with-haqqani-terrorists-this-summer/, last accessed 6 Nov. 2011.

27. Roberts, Dan and Emma Graham-Harrison, 'Taliban peace talks: "Peace and reconciliation" negotiations to take place in Qatar', *The Guardian*, 18 June 2013.

28. See Zartman and Faure, 'Conclusion: when and how to engage', *Engaging Extremists*, p. 277.

29. 'UK should talk to al-Qaeda, says former head of MI5', *BBC News*, 20 March 2011, http://www.bbc.co.uk/news/uk-12770153, last accessed 6 Nov. 2011. See also Manningham-Buller, Baroness Eliza, 'BBC Reith Lectures 2011: Securing Freedom, Lecture One: Terror', *BBC Radio*

4, 6 September 2011, http://downloads.bbc.co.uk/rmhttp/radio4/transcripts/2011_reith3.pdf, last accessed 6 Nov. 2011.

30. Cronin, Audrey Kurth, *How Terrorism Ends: Understanding the Decline and Demise of Terrorist Campaigns*, Princeton and Oxford: Princeton University Press, 2009, p. 195.

31. The literature in this area is extensive. See, for example, Cole, David and James X. Dempsey, *Terrorism and the Constitution*, London and New York: The New Press, 2006; Crenshaw, Martha (ed.), *The Consequences of Counterterrorism*, New York: Russell Sage Foundation, 2010; Walker, Clive, *Terrorism and the Law*, Oxford: Oxford University Press, 2011; and Wittes, Benjamin, *Law and the Long War: The Future of Justice in the Age of Terror*, New York: Penguin, 2008.

32. Crenshaw, 'Introduction', *The Consequences of Counterterrorism*, p. 2.

33. Pinker, Steven, *The Better Angels of our Nature*, New York: Penguin Books, 2012, p. 344.

34. Ibid., pp. 344–53; Anderson, David, Q.C., 'The Terrorism Acts in 2012: Report of the Independent Reviewer on the Operation of the Terrorism Act 2000 and Part 1 of the Terrorism Act 2008', July 2013, para. 2.84.

35. Dodd, Vikram, 'Time to talk to al-Qaida, senior police chief urges', *The Guardian*, 30 May 2008.

36. Cronin, *How Terrorism Ends*, p. 201.

37. On the banning of political parties in Turkey, see Human Rights Watch, 'Questions and answers about the case against the Democratic Society Party', 9 December 2009, http://www.hrw.org/print/news/2009/12/09/questions-and-answers-about-case-against-democratic-society-party, last accessed 15 Jul. 2012.

38. Registrar of the European Court of Human Rights, Press Release 531, 'Chamber Judgments: Herri Batasuna and Batasuna v. Spain, et al', 30 June 2009.

39. Fernandez, Adrián, 'La BBC y ETA', *BBC Mundo*, 7 September 2010, http://www.bbc.co.uk/blogs/mundo/blog_de_los_editores/2010/09/la_bbc_y_eta.html, last accessed 10 Sep. 2010; See also Conlan, Tara, 'BBC warns staff over "terrorism"', *The Guardian*, 16 December 2005.

40. Alonso, Rogelio, 'The BBC and Eta's deceitful games', *The Guardian: Comment is Free*, 7 September 2010, http://www.guardian.co.uk/commentisfree/2010/sep/07/bbc-eta-deceitful-games, last accessed 10 Sep. 2010.

41. English, *Terrorism: How to Respond*, p. 23.

42. 'Bases téoricas de la guerra revolucionaria' was a key strategy document of the period. See Garmendia, José María, 'ETA: nacimiento, desarrollo y crisis (1959–1978)', in Elorza, Antonio (coord.), *La Historia de ETA*, Madrid: Temas de Hoy, 2006, p. 118.

43. Roberts, Adam, 'The "War on Terror" in historical perspective', *Survival*, 47, 2 (Summer 2005), pp. 101–30.

44. De Jonge Oudraat, Chantal and Jean-Luc Marret, 'The uses and abuses of terrorist designation lists', in Crenshaw (ed.), *The Consequences of Counterterrorism*, pp. 94–129; Haspelagh, Sophie, '"Listing terrorists": the impact of proscription on third-party efforts to engage armed groups in peace processes—a practitioner's perspective', *Critical Studies on Terrorism*, 2013, pp. 1–20.

45. UN Security Council Resolution 1566, 8 October 2004, Op. para 3; Roberts, 'The "War on Terror"', p. 102, and UN Human Rights Council, 'Report of the Special Rapporteur on the promotion and protection of human rights and fundamental freedoms while countering terrorism, Martin Scheinin, Addendum, Mission to Spain', A/HRC/10/3/Add.2, 16 December 2008, para. 6.

46. Zulaika, Joseba and William A. Douglass, *Terror and Taboo: The Follies, Fables and Faces of Terrorism*, New York and London: Routledge, 1996, p. 6.

47. Heiberg, Marianne, Brendan O'Leary and John Tirman (eds), *Terror, Insurgency and the State: Ending Protracted Conflicts*, Philadelphia: University of Pennsylvania Press, 2007, p. 7. See also Dayton, Bruce W. and Louis Kriesberg (eds), *Conflict Transformation and Peacebuilding:*

Moving from Violence to Sustainable Peace, London: Routledge, 2008; De Zeeuw, Jeroen (ed.), *From Soldiers to Politicians: Transforming Rebel Movements After Civil War*, Boulder: Lynne Rienner, 2008; and Dudouet, Véronique, 'From war to politics: resistance and liberation movements in transition', *Berghof Report no. 17*, Berghof Research Centre for Constructive Conflict Management, April 2009.

48. Zartman and Faure, *Engaging Extremists*, p. 3. See also Bjørgo and Horgan, *Leaving Terrorism Behind;* Cronin, *How Terrorism Ends;* and Germani, L. Sergio and D. R. Karthikeyan, *Pathways out of Terrorism and Insurgency: The Dynamics of Terrorist Violence and Peace Processes*, Elgin: New Dawn Press, 2005.

49. Philipson, Liz, 'Engaging armed groups: the challenge of asymmetries', in Ricigliano (ed.), 'Choosing to engage', pp. 69–71.

50. Article I (2), Additional Protocol II of the Geneva Conventions (1977). International Committee of the Red Cross (ICRC), 'How is the Term "Armed Conflict" Defined in International Humanitarian Law?', Geneva: ICRC Opinion paper, March 2008; and Vité, Sylvain, 'Typology of armed conflicts in international humanitarian law: legal concepts and actual situations', *International Review of the Red Cross*, 91, 873 (March 2009), pp. 69–94.

51. ICTY, Prosecutor v. Tadic, Case No. IT-94-1, Decision on the Defence Motion for Interlocutory Appeal on Jurisdiction, 2 October 1995, para. 10, cited in Ibid., p. 76.

52. Ibid., pp. 76 and 83.

53. Spain country profile, *Uppsala Conflict Data Program*, UCDP database, Uppsala University, Sweden. http://www.ucdp.uu.se/gpdatabase/gpcountry-n2.php?id=143&regionSelect=8-Western_Europe, last accessed 9 May 2011.

1. THE BASQUE PROBLEM AND ETA

1. Zallo, Ramón and Mikel Ayuso, *The Basque Country: Insight into its Culture, History, Society and Institutions*, Vitoria-Gasteiz: The Basque Government, January 2009.

2. Collins, Roger, *The Basques*, Oxford: Basil Blackwell, 1986; Kurlansky, Mark, *The Basque History of the World*, New York: Penguin Books, 2001; and Woodworth, Paddy, *The Basque Country: A Cultural History*, Oxford and London: Oxford University Press, 2007.

3. The map on page 22 introduces place names in their Spanish or French forms with the name in Euskera in brackets. Elsewhere in the book I use Spanish or French place names—at times adopting the English form (ie. Castile not Castilla) when it will be more familiar to the reader— with a few exceptions such as references to Euskadi (understood as the Basque Autonomous Community) and Euskal Herria (the full Basque Country of the seven territories claimed by nationalists). An exception, however, is the place of publication of some of the books and other materials cited in these notes and in the bibliography. Where this is identified by its name in Euskera, I do so as well.

4. Sánchez Soler, Mariano, *La Transición Sangrienta: Una Historia Violenta del Proceso Democrático en España (1975–1983)*, Barcelona: Ediciones Península, 2010, pp. 295–8.

5. Jáuregui, Gurutz. 'ETA: orígenes y evolución ideológica y política', in Elorza, Antonio (coord.), *La Historia de ETA*, Madrid: Temas de Hoy, 2006, p. 173.

6. On radical Basque nationalists' perception of the 'unfinished business' of the transition, see Aiartza, Urko and Julen Zabalo, 'The Basque Country: the long walk to a democratic scenario', Berlin: Berghof Conflict Research, *Berghof Transitions 7*, 2009, pp. 14–21.

7. Six out of the eleven Spanish governments elected between the adoption of the 1978 constitution and 2013 have been minority governments.

8. Ibarretxe Markuartu, Juan José, '"The Basque Case": a comprehensive model for sustainable human development', Executive Summary, Washington, DC: George Mason University, School

for Conflict Analysis and Resolution, February 2012, http://scar.gmu.edu/sites/default/files/The%20Basque%20Case.pdf, last accessed on 18 Apr. 2012.

9. The Ibarretxe Plan is discussed in Chapter Four, pp. 114.

10. Cited in Cala, Andrés and Keith Johnson, 'Basque vote draws interest', *The Wall Street Journal Europe*, 15 April 2005.

11. Payne, Stanley G., *Basque Nationalism*, Reno: University of Nevada Press, 1975, pp. 13–6.

12. Instituto Nacional de Estadística, Contabilidad Regional de España, Base 2000, Data from 2009, http://www.ine.es/jaxi/menu.do?type=pcaxis&path=/t35/p010&file=inebase&L=0, last accessed 19 Apr. 2012.

13. Payne, *Basque Nationalism*, pp. 17–18, 49.

14. Balfour, Sebastian and Alejandro Quiroga, *The Reinvention of Spain: Nation and Identity since Democracy*, New York: Oxford University Press, 2007, p. 14; Lecours, André, *Basque Nationalism and the Spanish State*, Reno and Las Vegas: University of Nevada Press, 2007, pp. 114–34. Martínez Churiaque, José Ignacio, 'La situación económica del País Vasco', in Fundación para la Libertad, *Breve Guía Para Orientarse en el Laberinto Vasco*, Bilbao: Fundación para la Libertad, 2007, pp. 33–40.

15. Ibarra, Pedro, and Ramón Zallo, 'El Papel de Egunkaria y las consecuencias de su clausura', in *Egunkaria: la Verdad de un Sueño*, Txema Ramirez de la Piscina, Teresa Agirreazaldegi, Pedro Ibarra and Ramón Zallo (eds), Donostia: Ttarttalo, 2010, p. 81.

16. Consejo Asesor del Euskera, 'Bases para la política lingüística de principios del siglo XXI: Ponencia base', Vitoria-Gasteiz: Gobierno Vasco, 29 April 2008, http://www.euskara.euskadi. net/r59–738/es/contenidos/informacion/7041/es_2447/adjuntos/PonenciaBase.pdf, last accessed 23 Jul. 2010.

17. Llera Ramo, Francisco J., 'La Transición y la autonomía actual', in *Historia del País Vasco y Navarra en el Siglo XX*, de la Granja, José Luis and Santiago de Pablo (eds), Madrid: Biblioteca Nueva, 2002, pp. 129–36 and Llera Ramo, Francisco J., 'El País Vasco una sociedad plural', in Fundación para la Libertad, *Breve Guía*, pp. 21–31.

18. *Euskobarómetro*, 'Evolución del deseo de independencia para el País Vasco', Series Temporales, November 2011, pp. 128–31, http://alweb.ehu.es/euskobarometro/index.php?option=com_docman&task=cat_view&gid=15&Itemid=97, last accessed 18 Apr. 2012.

19. Balfour and Quiroga, *The Reinvention of Spain*, especially, 'Houses of many nations: identities in Catalonia and the Basque Country', pp. 127–60.

20. *Euskobarómetro*, November 2010, p. 40, http://alweb.ehu.es/euskobarometro/index.php?option=com_content&task=view&id=98&Itemid=118, last accessed 23 Jan. 2011.

21. Encarnación, Omar G., 'Spain's new left turn: society driven or party instigated?', in *Spain's 'Second Transition'? The Socialist Government of José Luis Rodríguez Zapatero*, Field, Bonnie N. (ed.), London and New York: Routledge, 2011, pp. 23–4.

22. Bullain, Iñigo, *Revolucionarismo Patriótico: El Movimiento de Liberación Nacional Vasco (MLNV)*, Madrid: Editorial Tecnos, 2011; Irvin, Cynthia J., *Militant Nationalism: Between Movement and Party in Ireland and the Basque Country*, Minneapolis: University of Minnesota Press, 1999; Muro, Diego, *Ethnicity and Violence: The Case of Radical Basque Nationalism*, New York and Abingdon: Routledge, 2010.

23. *Euskobarómetro*, November 2009, p. 9, http://alweb.ehu.es/euskobarometro/index.php?option=com_content&task=view&id=81&Itemid=115, last accessed, 4 Jan. 2011.

24. The Spanish ministry of the interior identifies 829 mortal victims of ETA and a further twenty-six attributable to *kale borroka*, http://www.interior.gob.es/prensa-3/balances-e-informes-21/ultimas-victimas-mortales-de-eta-cuadros-estadisticos-630, last accessed 12 Sep. 2011. Alonso, Rogelio, Florencio Domínguez and Marcos García Rey, *Vidas Rotas: Historia de los Hombres Mujeres y Niños Victimes de ETA*, Madrid: Espasa, 2010, list a total of 857 victims of ETA,

including those of *kale borroka*. A report prepared at the request of the Basque government in early 2013 documented 837 mortal victims of ETA and associated organisations, between 2,365 and 2,600 wounded and seventy-seven kidnappings (fifteen of which had led to the death of the victim). Carmena, Manuela, Jon Mirena Landa, Ramón Múgica and Juan María Uriarte, 'Informe-base de vulneraciones de derechos humanos en el caso vasco (1960–2013)', Vitoria-Gasteiz: Gobierno Vasco, June 2013, http://www.eitb.com/multimedia/documentos/2013/06/14/1145758/INFORME-BASE-PDF.pdf, last accessed, 25 Jun. 2013.

25. Politicians and state officials represented only 2.6 per cent of ETA's victims between 1977 and 1992; between 1992 and 2007 this figure rose to 21.7 per cent. Sánchez-Cuenca, Ignacio, 'Explaining temporal variation in the lethality of ETA', January 2009. *Revista Internacional de Sociología*, 67, 3 (September–December 2009), pp. 609–29, http://www.march.es/ceacs/proyectos/dtv/papers.asp, last accessed 3 Nov. 2010.

26. Aretxaga, Begoña, 'States of terror and the political imaginary in the Basque Country', and 'Before the law; the narrative of the unconscious in Basque political violence', in *States of Terror: Begoña Aretxaga's Essays*, Joseba Zulaika (ed.), Reno: Center for Basque Studies, University of Nevada, 2005, pp. 140 and 183.

27. Buesa, Mikel, 'El coste económico de la violencia terrorista: El caso de ETA y el País Vasco,' Documento de Trabajo No. 6, December 2009, Universidad Complutense de Madrid, Cátedra de Economía del Terrorismo, p. 3, http://www.ucm.es/info/cet/documentos%20trabajo/DocTrab%20CET%206-Coste%20economico%20violencia%20terrorista.pdf, last accessed 4 Jan. 2011. See also Buesa, Mikel, *ETA, S.A*, Barcelona: Editorial Planeta, 2011 and Domínguez, Florencio, *La Agonía de ETA: Una Investigación Inédita Sobre los Últimos Días de la Banda*, Madrid: La Esfera de los Libros, 2012, pp. 241–7.

28. Buesa, *ETA, S.A*, p. 82.

29. Enders, Walter and Todd Sandler, 'Terrorism and foreign direct investment in Spain and Greece', *Kyklos*, 49, 3 (1996), pp. 331–52.

30. Abadie, Alberto and Javier Gardeazabal, 'The economic costs of conflict: a case study of the Basque Country', *American Economic Review*, 93, 1 (March 2003), pp. 113–31.

31. Buesa, 'El coste económico', p. 6.

32. Agirre, Joxean (coord.), *No les Bastó Gernika: Euskal Herria 1960–2010*, Andoian: Euskal Memoria Fundazoa, 2010, p. 184.

33. Carmena, Manuela, et al., 'Informe-base de vulneraciones de derechos humanos en el caso vasco (1960–2013)'.

34. Woodworth, Paddy, *Dirty War, Clean Hands: ETA, the GAL and Spanish Democracy*, Princeton: Yale University Press, 2002.

35. See in particular reports of Amnesty International, the Council of Europe, European Committee for the Prevention of Torture, Human Rights Watch and the UN Human Rights Commission, especially those of the Commission on Torture and of the Special Rapporteurs on torture, on human rights and counter-terrorism. A report on the incidences of torture of *incommunicado* detainees was submitted to the Basque government by the director of its human rights office in March 2009. Landa Gorostiza, Jon-Mirena, 'Documentación de la tortura en detenidos incomunicados en el País Vasco desde el 2000 al 2008: Abordaje Científico', Vitoria-Gasteiz: Gobierno Vasco, Dirección de Derechos Humanos, 31 March 2009, http://www.lokarri.org/files/File/PDF/Dictamen%20tortura_cast.pdf, last accessed 19 Apr. 2012.

36. 534 prisoners were held in fifty-three Spanish prisons, at an average distance of 630 kilometres from the Basque Country. '736 familiares y allegados forman el colectivo de presos y presas políticas vascas', *Etxerat*, 11 February 2010. http://www.etxerat.info/albisteak.php?id_edukia=703&id_saila=9&lang=es, last accessed 6 Jan. 2011.

37. Eguiguren's ideas are further developed in Chapter Four. See also Eguiguren, Imaz, Jesús, *Los Últimos Españoles sin Patria (y sin Libertad): Escritos Sobre un Problema que no Tiene Solución (Pero sí Arreglo)*, Sevilla: Editorial Cambio, 2003 and *El Arreglo Vasco: Fueros, Constitución y Política en los Siglos XIX y XX*, San Sebastián: Hiria, 2008.

38. Author interview, Jesús Eguiguren, San Sebastián, December 2008.

39. Author interview, José Luis Alvarez Enparantza, *Txillardegi*, San Sebastián, July 2009.

40. Author interview, Kepa Aulestia, Bilbao, August 2009.

41. Anderson, Benedict, *Imagined Communities*, London and New York: Verso, revised edn, 2006.

42. Author interview, San Sebastián, March 2010.

43. Iriondo, Iñaki and Ramón Sola, *Mañana, Euskal Herria: Entrevista con Arnaldo Otegi*, Bilbao: Gara, 2005, p. 18.

44. Heiberg, Marianne, *The Making of the Basque Nation*, Cambridge and New York: Cambridge University Press, 1989, p. xi.

45. Muro, *Ethnicity and Violence*, p. 137.

46. Balfour and Quiroga, *The Reinvention of Spain*, p. 43–4; Fusi, Juan Pablo, *Identidades Proscritas: El no Nacionalismo en las Sociedades Nacionalistas*, Barcelona: Seix Barral, 2006; Muro, *Ethnicity and Violence*, pp. 41–4; Ruiz Soroa, José María, 'El canon nacionalista: la argumentación del "conflicto" vasco', in Fundación para la Libertad, *Breve Guía Para Orientarse*, pp. 13–20.

47. Balfour and Quiroga, *The Reinvention of Spain*, p. 44.

48. The literature on the emergence of Basque nationalism is extensive. See for example, Conversi, Daniele, *The Basques, the Catalans and Spain: Alternative Routes to Nationalist Mobilisation*, London: Hurst, 2nd edn, 2000; Corcuera Atienza, Javier, *Orígenes, Ideología y Organización del Nacionalismo Vasco, 1976–1904*, Madrid: Siglo Veintiuno, 1977; Heiberg, *The Making of the Basque Nation*; Mees, Ludger, *Nationalism, Violence and Democracy: The Basque Clash of Identities*, New York: Palgrave Macmillan, 2003; Muro, *Ethnicity and Violence*; and Watson, Cameron, *Basque Nationalism and Political Violence: The Ideological and Intellectual Origins of ETA*, Reno: University of Nevada, Center for Basque Studies, Occasional Papers Series, No. 14, 2007.

49. Elorza, Antonio, 'Sabino Arana and the dynamics of ETA terrorism', in Germani, L. Sergio and D.R. Kaarthikeyan (eds), *Pathways out of Terrorism and Insurgency*, New Dawn Press: Elgin, 2005, p. 240.

50. Conversi, *The Basques, the Catalans and Spain*, p. 49 and Payne, *Basque Nationalism*, p. 61.

51. Ibid., p. 65.

52. Elorza, 'Vascos guerreros', in Elorza (coord.), *La Historia de ETA*, p. 43.

53. Conversi, *The Basques, the Catalans and Spain*, p. 60.

54. Watson, *Basque Nationalism and Political Violence*, p. 23.

55. Ibid., p. 103.

56. Conversi, *The Basques, the Catalans and Spain*, pp. 11–43.

57. Thomas, Hugh, *The Spanish Civil War*, London: Penguin Books, 3rd edn, 1986, p. 74.

58. Muro, *Ethnicity and Violence*, p. 85.

59. De la Granja, José Luis, 'La II República y la Guerra Civil', in De la Granja and De Pablo (eds), *Historia del País Vasco y Navarra en el Siglo XX*, pp. 66–8.

60. Cited in ibid, p. 70.

61. Fusi, J., trans. by Fernández-Armesto, Felipe, *Franco: A Biography*, New York: Harper and Row, 1987, p. 30.

62. Cited in Preston, Paul, *The Spanish Civil War: Reaction, Revolution and Revenge*, New York and London: W.W. Norton, revised edn 2006, p. 271.

63. Sanz-Marcotegui, Angel García, 'La población vasco-navarra entre 1930 y 1960. Los efectos de guerra y los cambios demográficos', *Boletín del Instituto Gerónimo de Usariz*, 4 (1990),

pp. 99, 102, cited in Watson, Cameron, *Modern Basque History*, Reno: Center for Basque Studies, University of Nevada, 2003, p. 308. See also Preston, Paul, *The Spanish Holocaust: Inquisition and Extermination in Twentieth-Century Spain*, New York and London: W.W. Norton, 2012, pp. 429–40.

64. Conversi, *The Basques, the Catalans and Spain*, p. 224.
65. Preston, *The Spanish Holocaust*; Thomas, *The Spanish Civil War*.
66. Clark, Robert P., *The Basques: The Franco Years and Beyond*, Reno: University of Nevada Press, 1979, pp. 80–8; Preston, *The Spanish Holocaust*, pp. 429–40.
67. Thomas, *The Spanish Civil War*, p. 698.
68. Clark, *The Basques*, p. 98.
69. Author interview, Julen Madariaga, Irun, November 2010. On the origins and development of ETA see Casanova, Iker, *ETA 1958–2008: Medio Siglo de Historia*, Tafalla: Txalaparta, 2007; Clark, Robert P., *The Basque Insurgents: ETA, 1952–1980*, Madison: University of Wisconsin Press, 1984; Garmendia, José María, *Historia de ETA I*, San Sebastián: Haranburu, 1979; Garmendia, José María, 'ETA: nacimiento, desarrollo y crisis (1959–78)', and Jáuregui, Gurutz, 'ETA: orígenes, y evolución ideológica y política', in Elorza (coord.), *La Historia de ETA*, pp. 83–170 and pp. 173–270; Heiberg, Marianne, 'ETA: Euskadi 'ta Askatasuna', in *Terror, Insurgency and the State: Ending Protracted Conflicts*, Heiberg, Marianne, Brendan O'Leary and John Tirman (eds), Philadelphia: University of Pennsylvannia Press, 2007; Ibarra Güell, Pedro, *La Evolución Estratégica de ETA (1963–1987)*, San Sebastián: Kriselu, 1987; Unzueta, Patxo, *Los Nietos de la Ira: Nacionalismo y Violencia en el País Vasco*, Madrid: El País-Aguilar, 1988.
70. Clark, *The Basque Insurgents*, p. 26.
71. Cited in Casanova, *ETA 1958–2008*, p. 9.
72. Jáuregui, 'ETA: orígenes, y evolución', p. 199.
73. One influential source of ETA's thinking was Federico Krutwig's book, *Vasconia* (1963). A number of his ideas were reflected in ETA's 1963 document, 'La insurrección in Euskadi,' Jáuregui, 'ETA: orígenes y evolución', pp. 222–6.
74. 'Carta abierta a los intelectuales vascos' was published in *Zutik* 25 in September 1964; 'Bases teóricas de la guerra revolucionaria' was the central document for discussion during ETA's IV assembly, held in July 1965. Casanova, *ETA 1958–2008*, pp. 51–4 and 62–4.
75. Domínguez, *La Agonía de ETA*, pp. 15–21.
76. Author interview, Txema Montero, Bilbao, July 2010.
77. Garmendia, 'ETA: nacimiento, desarrollo y crisis', p. 104.
78. Douglass, William A. and Joseba Zulaika, 'On the interpretation of terrorist violence: ETA and the Basque political process', *Comparative Studies in Society and History*, 32, 2 (April 1990), p. 245.
79. A number of sources, including Alonso et al., *Vidas Rotas*, but not the Spanish ministry of interior, claim the first of ETA's victims to be a 22-month old girl killed by a bomb in 1980 at San Sebastian's train station; the strong arguments against this being the case are addressed by de Pablo, Santiago, 'La primera victim de ETA?', *El Correo*, 19 June 2010.
80. Garmendia cites 1,953 detentions without trial in the course of 1969. 'ETA: nacimiento, desarrollo y crisis', p. 146.
81. Clark, *The Basque Insurgents*, pp. 48–56.
82. Fusi, *Franco*, p. 139.
83. José Luis Corcuera, in Iglesias, María Antonia, *Memoria de Euskadi*, Madrid: Aguilar, 2009, p. 494.
84. Morán, Gregorio, *Los Españoles que Dejaron de Serlo: Cómo y por qué Euskadi se ha Convertido en la Gran Herida Histórica de España*, Barcelona: Editorial Planeta, revised edn, 2003, p. xxvi.
85. Richardson, Louise, *What Terrorists Want: Understanding the Terrorist Threat*, London: John Murray, 2006, p. 25.
86. Moran, *Los Españoles que Dejaron de Serlo*; Llera, Ramo, 'La transición y la autonomía actual',

pp. 117–44; Muro, Diego, 'The Basque experience of the transition to democracy', in Alonso, Gregorio and Diego Muro (eds), *The Politics and Memory of Democratic Transition: The Spanish Model*, New York and London: Routledge, 2011, pp. 159–80.

87. Author interview, Josep Ramoneda, Barcelona, July 2011.
88. Payne, Stanley (ed.), *The Politics of Democratic Spain*, Chicago: Chicago Council on Foreign Relations, 1986, pp. 3–4; Conversi, Daniele, 'The smooth transition: Spain's 1978 constitution and the nationalities question', *National Identities*, 4, 3 (2002), p. 223; Linz, Juan L. and Alfred Stepan, *Problems of Democratic Transition and Consolidation*, Baltimore and London: Johns Hopkins University Press, 1996, p. 87. See also Alonso and Muro (eds), *The Politics and Memory of Democratic Transition*; Carr, Raymond and Juan Pablo Fusi Aizpurua, *Spain: Dictatorship to Democracy*, London: Allen and Unwin, 2nd edn, 1981.
89. Muro, 'The Basque experience', p. 178; See also Sánchez, Soler, *La Transición Sangrienta*.
90. Tremlett, Giles, *Ghosts of Spain: Travels Through Spain and Its Silent Past*, New York: Walker and Company, 2008; Humblebaek, Carsten, 'The "Pacto de Olvido"', in Alonso and Muro (eds), *The Politics and Memory of Democratic Transition*, pp. 183–97.
91. 'What is transitional justice', website of the International Center for Transitional Justice, http://ictj.org/about/transitional-justice, last accessed 10 Sep. 2013; Golob, Stephanie R., 'Volver: the return of/to transitional justice politics in Spain', *Journal of Spanish Cultural Studies*, 9, 2 (July 2008), pp. 127–41.
92. Author interview, Rafael Diéz Usabiaga, San Sebastián, July 2010.
93. 26th Congress of the PSOE, held in Suresnes, France, in October 1974, cited by Balfour and Quiroga, *The Reinvention of Spain*, p. 72.
94. Euzkadi Sozialista VI, 1977, 7. Cited in Quiroga, Alejandro, 'Salvation by betrayal: the left and the Spanish nation', in Alonso and Muro (eds), *The Politics and Memory of Democratic Transition*, p. 151.
95. Ibid., p. 169.
96. These figures are from the ministry of interior's list of ETA's victims.
97. Carr and Fusi, *Spain: Dictatorship to Democracy*, p. 246.
98. Author interview, Antxon Gómez, San Sebastián, July 2010.
99. Interview with ETA, 'Euskadi Ta Askatasuna nunca será una amenaza para el proceso de resolución política', *Gara*, 11 November 2011.
100. Clark, *The Basque Insurgents*, p. 253.
101. Ibid., p. 246. See also Reinares, Fernando and Oscar Jaime-Jiménez, 'Countering terrorism in Spain', in Reinares, Fernando (ed.), *European Democracies Against Terrorism: Governmental Policies and Intergovernmental Cooperation*, Aldershot: Dartmouth Publishing Company, 2000, p. 124.
102. Balfour and Quiroga, *The Reinvention of Spain*, pp. 45–60; Conversi, *The Smooth Transition*, pp. 226–9.
103. Llera Ramo, 'La transición y la autonomía actual', p. 119.
104. Muro, 'The Basque experience', p. 169.
105. Electoral results from the website of the Basque government, http://www.euskadi.net/q93TodoWar/eleccionesJSP/q93Contenedor.jsp?idioma=c&menu=li_2_1_1&opcion=menu, last accessed 10 Jul. 2013.
106. Ramo, Llera, 'La transición y la autonomía actual', p. 124.
107. Muro, 'The Basque experience', p. 169.
108. The Basque statute of autonomy, translation of Basque government, http://www.basques.euskadi.net/t32–448/en/contenidos/informacion/estatuto_guernica/en_455/adjuntos/estatu_i.pdf, last accessed 8 Sep. 2010.
109. Electoral results from the website of the Basque government.

2. VIOLENCE, TERROR AND TALKING

1. Clark, Robert P., *Negotiating with ETA: Obstacles to Peace in the Basque Country, 1975–1988*, Reno and Las Vegas: University of Nevada Press, 1990; Domínguez Iribarren, Florencio, *De la Negociación a la Tregua: El Final de ETA?* Madrid: Taurus, 1998; Fonseca, Carlos, *Negociar con ETA: Del Proceso de Argel de Felipe González a la Paz Dialogada de Rodríguez Zapatero*, Madrid: Temas de Hoy, 2006; Sánchez-Cuenca, Ignacio, *ETA Contra el Estado: Las Estrategias del Terrorismo*, Barcelona: Tusquets, 2001.

2. Domínguez Iribarren, *De la Negociación a la Tregua*, p. 9.

3. ETA, Internal circular of executive committee, January 1984, cited in ibid., p. 22.

4. Calleja, José María, *Algo Habrá Hecho: Odio, Muerte y Miedo en Euskadi*, Madrid: Espasa Calpe, 2006, especially pp. 113–36.

5. 'Pacto de Ajuria Enea, Acuerdo para la normalización y pacificación de Euskadi', Vitoria-Gasteiz: 12 January 1988, op. para. 10, http://www.elmundo.es/eta/documentos/pacto_ajuria_enea.html, last accessed 14 Jun. 2010.

6. Clark, *Negotiating with ETA*, p. 3.

7. Fonseca, *Negociar con ETA* provides a detailed account of the many contacts maintained by the PSOE government after the Algiers talks. See also Fisas, Vicenç, *Llegó la hora? Promesas de Paz Para el País Vasco*, Barcelona: Icaria, 2010, for a succinct account of proposals emanating from within the Basque Country.

8. Domínguez Iribarren, Florencio, 'El enfrentamiento de ETA con la democracia', in Elorza, Antonio (coord.), *La Historia de ETA*, Madrid: Temas de Hoy, 2006, p. 297.

9. Zulaika, Joseba, *Basque Violence: Metaphor and Sacrament*, Reno: University of Nevada Press, 1988, p. 68.

10. Author interview, Txema Montero, Bilbao, July 2011; Casanova, Iker, *ETA 1958–2008*, Tafalla: Txalaparta, 2007, pp. 192–3.

11. Clark, *Negotiating with ETA*, p. 78.

12. Portell's contact, the former ETA member Juan José Etxabe, was killed five days later by the Triple A. Ibid., pp. 84–6 and de Otálora, Oscar B., 'La muerte del mensajero', *El Diario Vasco*, 29 June 2008.

13. In retrospect this and other assassinations by the BVE could be seen as a first 'dirty war'. Woodworth, Paddy, *Dirty War, Clean Hands: ETA, the GAL and Spanish Democracy*, New Haven and London: Yale University Press, 2002, pp. 44–53.

14. Domínguez Iribarren, 'El enfrentamiento de ETA', pp. 279–84.

15. Radical nationalism's anti-nuclear struggle began before the formation of HB.

16. Martínez, Isabel C., 'Treinta años del febrero más convulso', *El País*, 20 February 2011; Cercas, Javier, *The Anatomy of a Moment: Thirty-five Minutes in History and Imagination*, New York: Bloomsbury, 2011.

17. Author interviews, Jone Goirizelaia, Bilbao, July 2010; representative of Batasuna, Brussels, October 2010.

18. Clark, *Negotiating with ETA*, pp. 93–115.

19. Domínguez Iribarren, *De la Negociación a la Tregua*, pp. 221–9.

20. Clark, *Negotiating with ETA*, p. 115.

21. Gunther, Richard, 'The Spanish Socialist Party: from clandestine opposition to party of government', in Payne, Stanley G. (ed.), *The Politics of Democratic Spain*, Chicago: Chicago Council on Foreign Relations, 1986, pp. 25–43.

22. Shabad, Goldie, 'After autonomy: the dynamics of regionalism in Spain', in Ibid., pp. 122–32.

23. Balfour, Sebastian and Alejandro Quiroga, *The Reinvention of Spain: Nation and Identity since Democracy*, New York: Oxford University Press, 2007; Börzel, Tanja, *States and Regions in the*

European Union: Institutional Adaptation in Germany and Spain, Cambridge: Cambridge University Press, 2011, pp. 93–102.

24. Woodworth, *Dirty War, Clean Hands*, p. 66.
25. Ceberio, Jesús, interview with Felipe González, *El País*, 29 June 1997.
26. Clark, *Negotiating with ETA*, p. 57.
27. Uriarte, Eduardo, 'Consideraciones Sobre el Plan ZEN', *El País*, 9 August 1983.
28. Reinares, Fernando and Rogelio Alonso, 'Confronting ethnonationalist terrorism in Spain', in *Democracy and Counterterrorism: Lessons from the Past*, Art, Robert J. and Louise Richardson (eds), Washington, D.C.: United States Institute of Peace Press, 2007, p. 115.
29. Amnesty International, *Spain: The Question of Torture*, London: Amnesty International, 1985.
30. Domínguez Iribarren, 'El enfrentamiento de ETA', pp. 310–6.
31. Sola, Ramón, 'La cal viva no enterró la guerra sucia', *Gara*, 15 October 2008.
32. Cited in Woodworth, *Dirty War, Clean Hands*, p. 83.
33. 'El ministro del interior subraya que la oferta de diálogo "se enmarca en el ámbito policial, no en el político"', *El País*, 24 August 1984.
34. Aiartza, Urko and Julen Zabalo, 'The Basque Country: the long walk to a democratic scenario', Berlin: Berghof Conflict Research, *Berghof Transitions 7*, 2009, p. 231; Clark, *Negotiating with ETA*, p. 143.
35. Both men were released after being pardoned by Aznar. Del Riego, Marta, 'Barrionuevo, dos metros por tierra', *Vanity Fair* (Spain), August 2010, http://www.revistavanityfair.es/articulos/jose-barrionuevo-dos-metros-bajo-tierra/11294, last accessed 23 Apr. 2011.
36. See, for example, Zinkunegi, Joseba and Juan Jose Petrikorena, *Jon Anza El Último Crimen de Estado?* Tafalla: Txalaparta, 2010.
37. Domínguez Iribarren, 'El enfrentamiento de ETA con la democracia', pp. 296–324; Sánchez-Cuenca, *ETA Contra el Estado*, pp. 58–72.
38. Oreja Aguirre, Marcelino, 'Tres vascos en la política exterior española', Madrid: Real Academia de Sciencias Morales y Políticas, 24 April 2001, http://www.racmyp.es/docs/discursos/D51.pdf, last accessed 2 Apr. 2012.
39. See Casanova, *ETA 1958–2008*; Clark, Robert P., *The Basque Insurgents: ETA, 1952–1980*, Madison: University of Wisconsin Press, 1984; Domínguez Iribarren, 'El enfrentamiento de ETA con la democracia'; Domínguez, Florencio, *Dentro de ETA: La Vida Diaria de los Terroristas*, Madrid: Punto de Lectura, 2006; Heiberg, Marianne, 'ETA: Euskadi 'ta Askatasuna', in Heiberg, Marianne, Brendan O'Leary and John Tirman (eds), *Terror, Insurgency and the State: Ending Protracted Conflicts*, Philadelphia: University of Pennsylvannia Press, 2007; Reinares, Fernando, *Patriotas de la Muerte: Quiénes han Militado en ETA y por qué*, Madrid: Taurus, 2001.
40. Vasco Press, 'ETA ha modificado su estructura interna por motivos de seguridad', *El Correo*, 23 March 2006; Domínguez, Florencio, *La Agonía de ETA: Una Investigación Inédita Sobre los Últimos Días de la Banda*, Madrid: La Esfera de los Libros, 2012, p. 218.
41. In 2007 Fernando Reinares and Rogelio Alonso described the number of 'actual militants' as ranging from 'a few hundred in the late 1970s to several dozen by the turn of the century', Reinares and Alonso, 'Confronting ethnonationalist terrorism in Spain', p. 108. In 2012, Florencio Domínguez cited an internal document of ETA dating to the end of 2002—when the organisation was self-admittedly in 'crisis'—that reported 517 active members, with a further 514 in prison. Domínguez, *La Agonía de ETA*, p. 70.
42. Author interview, Patxi Zabaleta, Pamplona, July 2010.
43. Reinares, *Patriotas de la Muerte*, and Reinares, Fernando, 'Who are the terrorists? Analyzing changes in sociological profile among members of ETA', *Studies in Conflict and Terrorism*, 27, 6 (2004), pp. 464–88.
44. Aizpeolea, L.R. and J.A. Rodríguez, 'El actual jefe de ETA expulsó a los negociadores de la

tregua "por cobardes"', *El País*, 8 March 2010; Barberia, José Luis. 'Brechas en ETA', *El País*, 9 November 2008.

45. Aretxaga, Begoña, 'The intimacy of violence', in Zulaika, Joseba (ed.), *States of Terror: Begoña Aretxaga's Essays*, Reno: Center for Basque Studies, University of Nevada, 2005, p. 168.

46. Understanding the web of organisations that form the MLNV is complicated both by the opacity surrounding their functional and other relationships to one another, and their tendency to change both shape and name in response to illegalisation and other aspects of their prosecution by Spanish law. Different perspectives are given by Bullain, Iñigo, *Revolucionarismo Patriótico: El Movimiento de Liberación Nacional Vasco (MLNV)*, Madrid: Editorial Tecnos, 2011; Irvin, Cynthia J., *Militant Nationalism: Between Movement and Party in Ireland and the Basque Country*, Minneapolis: University of Minnesota Press, 1999; Muro, Diego, *Ethnicity and Violence: The Case of Radical Basque Nationalism*, New York and London: Routledge, 2008; and Portero, Daniel, *La Trama Civil de ETA*, Madrid: Arcopress, 2009.

47. Author interviews, Pamplona and San Sebastián, July and November 2010.

48. Author interview, Rafael Díez Usabiaga, San Sebastián, July 2010.

49. Author interview, Montero.

50. José Felix Azurmendi, in Iglesias, María Antonia, *Memoria de Euskadi*, Madrid: Aguilar, 2009, p. 99.

51. Figures from *Euskobarómetro*, 'Datos electorales País Vasco', http://alweb.ehu.es/euskobarometro/index.php, last accessed 29 Mar. 2011.

52. Danny Morrison, at the Sinn Féin annual conference in 1981. For an introduction to the complex relationship between radical nationalism in the Basque County and Irish Republicanism, see Irvin, *Militant Nationalism*.

53. Author interview, Eoin O'Brien, Dublin, October 2011.

54. Author interview, Txema Montero, Bilbao, July 2010.

55. Artexaga, Begoña, 'The death of Yoyes', in Zulaika, (ed.), *States of Terror*, pp. 147–62.

56. ETA communiqué of 31 June 1987, cited in Casanova, *ETA, 1958–2008*, p. 332.

57. Petxo Idoyaga, 'Anotaciones históricas', in 'ETA (1959–2009)', *Viento Sur*, 106 (November 2009), p. 50.

58. De Pablo, Santiago and Ludger Mees, *El Péndulo Patriótico. Historia del Partido Nacionalista Vasco*, Barcelona: Crítica, 2005, pp. 369–70.

59. Ibid. See also Muro, *Ethnicity and Violence*, pp. 67–90.

60. Llera Ramos, Francisco J., 'La transición y la autonomía actual', in de la Granja, José Luis and Santiago de Pablo (eds), *Historia del País Vasco y Navarra en el Siglo XX*, Madrid: Biblioteca Nueva, 2002, p. 119.

61. Ramón Jáuregui, in Iglesias, *Memoria de Euskadi*, pp. 247–8.

62. A further 39 per cent considered them to be 'manipulated by others'. Shabad, 'After autonomy', p. 149.

63. Xabier Arzalluz in Iglesias, *Memoria de Euskadi*, p. 1,129.

64. Author interview, Eduardo Madina, Madrid, February 2012.

65. Domínguez Iribarren, *De la Negociación a la Tregua*, p.53.

66. Aretxaga. Begoña, 'Of hens, hoods and other political beasts: what metaphoric performances hide', in Zulaika (ed.), *States of Terror*, p. 210.

67. Public display of the *ikurrina* was allowed only in 1977, two years after the Catalan national flag, the *senyera*. Muro, *Ethnicity and Violence*, p. 119.

68. Leader of Herri Batasuna cited in Shadad, 'After autonomy', p. 131.

69. Author interviews, San Sebastian and Vitoria, July 2010.

70. On 14 March 1985. Clark, *Negotiating with ETA*, pp. 154–5.

71. EA was not party to the anti-terrorist agreement and added a rider to the Pact of Ajuria Enea.

72. Domínguez Iribarren, *De la Negociación a la Tregua*, pp. 246–58; Reinares and Alonso, 'Confronting ethnonationalist terrorism', pp. 115 and 125.

73. 'Pacto de Ajuria Enea, Acuerdo para la normalización y pacificación de Euskadi', Vitoria-Gasteiz: 12 January 1988 http://www.elmundo.es/eta/documentos/pacto_ajuria_enea.html, last accessed 14 Jun. 2010.

74. *El Diario Vasco*, 20 January 1988, cited by Clark, *Negotiating with ETA*, p. 211.

75. Author interview, Alfredo Pérez Rubalcaba, Madrid, February 2012.

76. A point made by Rafael Vera in Reiss, Mitchell B., *Negotiating with Evil: When to Talk to Terrorists*, E-book, Open Road Integrated Media, September 2010, at 1,606.

77. Author interviews, Eugenio Etxebeste, *Antxon*, San Sebastián, July 2009; and Juan Manuel Eguigaray, Madrid, October 2009. Other sources for this account of the Algiers talks include Juan Manuel Eguigaray in Iglesias, Memoria de Euskadi, pp. 343–83; Casanova, *ETA: 1958–2008*, pp. 343–52; Clark, *Negotiating with ETA*, pp. 165–221; Domínguez Iribarren, *De la Negociación a la Tregua*, pp. 64–80; and Mees, Ludger, *Nationalism, Violence and Democracy*, London: Palgrave Macmillan, 2003, pp. 67–8.

78. Author interview, Etxebeste.

79. Clark, *Negotiating with ETA*, p. 201.

80. Sánchez-Cuenca, *ETA Contra el Estado*, p. 133.

81. Casanova, *ETA 1958–2008*, pp. 347 and 352.

82. Eguiagaray, in Iglesias, *Memoria de Euskadi*, p. 403.

83. Casanova, *ETA 1958–2008*, pp. 348–50.

84. Fonseca, *Negociar con ETA*, pp. 314–7; Reinares and Alonso, 'Confronting ethnonationalist terrorism'. p. 111. Author interview, Mercedes Gallizo, Zaragoza, September 2012.

85. Ley Orgánica Penitenciaria, 1979, ministry of the interior, http://www.institucionpenitenciaria.es/web/portal/documentos/normativa/LeyOrganica/, last accessed, 12 Jul. 2012.

86. Carmena gives a critical account of dispersión and the treatment of ETA's prisoners in general in Carmena Castrillo, Manuela, *Crónica de un Desorden: Notas para Reinventar la Justicia*, Madrid: Alianza, 1997, pp. 106–23.

87. Author interview, Eguiagaray.

88. In Iriondo, Iñaki and Ramón Sola, *Mañana, Euskal Herria: Entrevista con Arnaldo Otegi*, Bilbao: Gara, 2005, p. 28.

89. Hooper, John, *The New Spaniards*, London: Penguin Books, 1995, p. 62.

90. Casanova, *ETA 1958–2008*, p. 368.

91. Domínguez Iribarren, 'El enfrentamiento de ETA', pp. 381–4 and 393 and *De la Negociación a la Tregua*, pp. 108–19; Muro, *Ethnicity and Violence*, pp. 153–8.

92. A first-hand account of the crisis is given by Otegi in Iriondo and Sola, *Mañana, Euskal Herria*, pp. 33–6.

93. Author interview, Eugenio Etxebeste, *Antxon*, San Sebastián, February 2012.

94. Fonseca, *Negociar con ETA*.

95. In the 1960s Mitchell was part of a research team led by Dr. John Burton at University College, London which developed some of the foundational ideas of conflict resolution. John Paul Lederach is best known as a pioneer of the idea and practice of conflict transformation.

96. Author interview, Christopher Mitchell, Washington, DC, June 2011.

97. Author interview, Juan María Ollora, Vitoria, July 2011.

98. Author interview, Jonan Fernández, Aranzazu, February 2012.

99. Statement of Margarita Robles in *Guardia Civil* magazine, August 1994, cited by Domínguez Iribarren, *De la Negociación a la Tregua*, p. 102.

100. Author interviews, William Douglass, Reno, February 2009, and Fernández.

101. Author interview, Fernández.

102. Domínguez, Florencio, *Josu Ternera: Una Vida en ETA*, Madrid: La Esfera de los Libros, 2006, pp. 248–52 and *De la Negociación a la Tregua*, pp. 102–4.

103. Aiartza and Zabalo, *The Basque Conflict*, p. 27.

104. Otegi, in Iriondo and Sola, *Mañana, Euskal Herria*, p. 35.

105. Muro, *Ethnicity and Violence*, pp. 154–6.

3. AZNAR, COUNTER-TERRORISM AND ESTELLA-LIZARRA

1. Aznar, José María, Prologue, in Cosidó, Ignacio and Óscar Elía, *España, Camino de Libertad: La Política Antiterrorista para la Derrota de ETA, 1996–2004*, Madrid: Editorial Fundación FAES, 2010, p. 15.

2. Cebrián, Juan Luis, *El Fundamentalismo Democrático*, Madrid: Taurus, 2003, pp. 75–7. See also Núñez Sexias, Xosé-Manoel, 'From National-Catholic nostalgia to constitutional patriotism: conservative Spanish nationalism since the early 1990s', in Balfour, Sebastian (ed)., *The Politics of Contemporary Spain*, Oxford and New York, Routledge, 2005, pp. 121–45.

3. Domínguez Iribarren, Florencio, *De la Negociación a la Tregua: El Final de ETA?*, Madrid: Taurus, 1998, pp. 122–39.

4. 'Manifiesto de Euskadi ta Askatasuna a Euskal Herria', 15 April 2005, http://www.elkarri.org/pdf/AlternativaDemocratica.pdf, last accessed, 4 Mar. 2011.

5. Interviews, San Sebastián and Urrugne, December 2010. In a 2011 reflection on its history ETA considered the Democratic Alternative to have 'established the bases for a democratic process'. *Zutabe*, 113, cited in *Gara*, 20 April 2011.

6. Calleja, José María and Ignacio Sánchez-Cuenca, *La Derrota de ETA: De la Primera a la Última Víctima*, Madrid: Adhara, 2006; Domínguez Iribarren, Florencio, 'El enfrentamiento de ETA con la democracia', in Elorza, Antonio (coord.), *La Historia de ETA*, Madrid: Temas de Hoy, 2006; Reinares, Fernando and Rogelio Alonso, 'Confronting ethnonationalist terrorism in Spain', in Art, Robert J. and Louise Richardson (eds), *Democracy and Counter-terrorism: Lessons from the Past*, Washington, DC: United States Institute of Peace Press, 2007, pp. 105–32; Sánchez-Cuenca, Ignacio, 'Los espejos deformantes de ETA e IRA', *Cuadernos de Alzate* 33 (2005), pp. 137–53.

7. Gallego-Díaz, Soledad, 'Historia de un presidente satisfecho', *El País*, 26 January 2004 and Woodworth, Paddy, 'Spain changes course: Aznar's legacy, Zapatero's prospects', *World Policy Journal*, 21, 2 (Summer 2004), p. 8.

8. Centro de análisis y prospectiva, Guardia Civil, 'La kale borroka y la estrategia de ETA', 2002, http://www.guardia.civil, last accessed 9 Mar. 2011.

9. Aznar, José María, *Eight Years as Prime Minister: A Personal Vision of Spain 1996–2004*, Barcelona: Planeta, 2004, p. 165.

10. Cosidó and Elía, *España, Camino de Libertad*. Aznar wrote the book's prologue and the Fundación para los Analisis y los Estudios Sociales (FAES), of which he was president, published it.

11. Aznar, *Eight Years as Prime Minister*, p. 172.

12. Mees, Ludgar, *Nationalism, Violence and Democracy: The Basque Clash of Identities*, New York: Palgrave Macmillan, 2003, p. 111.

13. In December 1995 the Basque Parliament had passed a resolution urging the government to transfer all Basque prisoners to Basque prisons.

14. Jaime Mayor Oreja, in Iglesias, María Antonia, *Memoria de Euskadi*, Madrid: Aguilar, 2009, p. 928.

15. Gesto por la Paz described 8,150 different gatherings that took place as part of its mobilisation against violence in 1996. Gesto por la Paz, Chronology, 1996, http://www.gesto.org.cronologia1996.htm, last accessed on 9 Mar. 2011.

16. Aretxaga, Begoña, 'Before the law: the narrative of the unconscious in Basque political violence', in Zulaika, Joseba (ed.), *States of Terror: Begoña Aretxaga's Essays*, Reno: Center for Basque Studies, University of Nevada, 2005, p. 183.

17. Barbería, José Luis, 'El día que todos fuimos Miguel Ángel Blanco', *El País*, 8 July 2007.

18. 'Ellos han apretado el gatillo', *El Mundo*, 13 July 2007; Intxausti, A. and P.G. Damborena, 'Un grito unánime en Ermua: "¡A por ellos!" *El País*, 13 July 1997. The exception was Patxi Zabaleta, the leader of HB in Navarre, who condemned the assassination in strong terms. Patxi Zabaleta in Iglesias, *Memoria de Euskadi*, p. 1279.

19. Mayor Oreja, Jaime, *ABC*, 10 October 2007, cited in Cosidó and Elía, *España, Camino de Libertad*, p. 209.

20. In elections to the Basque Parliament the PP's share of the vote grew from 8.2 per cent in 1990, to 14.2 per cent in 1994, 19.9 per cent in 1998 and 22.9 per cent in 2001. *Euskobarómetro*, 'Datos electorales, elecciones autónomicas en el País Vasco', http://alweb.ehu.es/euskobarometro/index.php, last accessed 29 Mar. 2011.

21. Calleja, José María, *Algo Habrá Hecho: Odio Muerte y Miedo en Euskadi*, Madrid: Espasa Calpe, 2006, p. 113.

22. José Antonio Ardanza, in *Memoria de Euskadi*, p. 343; Author interview, Juan José Ibarretxe, Vitoria, July 2009.

23. In its internal bulletin, *Barne Buletina*, 67 (July 1993), cited in Domínguez Iribarren, *De la Negociación a la Tregua*, p. 114.

24. 'Ley 32/199, de 8 de octubre, de Solidaridad con las víctimas del terrorismo'. *Boletin Official Del Estado*, 242, Madrid, 9 October 1999, pp. 36050–2, http://www.boe.es/boe/dias/1999/10/09/pdfs/A36050-36052.pdf, last accessed 27 Mar. 2011.

25. UN Human Rights Council, 'Report of the Special Rapporteur on the promotion and protection of human rights and fundamental freedoms while countering terrorism, Martin Scheinin, Addendum: Mission to Spain', 16 December 2008, A/HRC/10/3/Add.2, paras 44–45; Rodríguez Uribes, José Manuel, director general de apoyo a víctimas del terrorismo, ministerio del interior, 'Sobre el terrorismo y sus víctimas', Fundación Victímas del Terrorismo, *Fundación 33*, Madrid: December 2010, pp. 54–5.

26. Author interview, Maixabel Laso, Vitoria, December 2010.

27. Foro de Ermua, 'Manifiesto por la democracia en Euskadi', 18 February 1998, http://www.elmundo.es/eta/documentos/foro_ermua.html, last accessed 18 Mar. 2011.

28. Balfour, Sebastian and Alejandro Quiroga, *The Reinvention of Spain: Nation and Identity since Democracy*, New York: Oxford University Press, 2007, pp. 83–91.

29. Savater, Fernando, 'Adiós a Ernest Lluch', *Perdonen las Molestias*, Madrid: Punto de Lectura, 2002, pp. 363–5.

30. Fundación Sabino Arana, *Información y Propaganda Ante el Conflicto Vasco*, Bilbao: Fundación Sabino Arana, 2001 and Ruiz Olabuenaga, José Ignacio, *Opinión sin Tregua: Viso y Denuestos del Nacionalismo Vasco 1998–1999*, Bilbao: Fundación Sabino Arana, 2001.

31. Illuminating accounts of this period are contained in Domínguez Iribarren, *De la Negociación a la Tregua*, pp. 171–81; Escrivá, Ángeles, *Maldito el País que Necesita Héroes: Como los Demócratas Acabaron con ETA*, Madrid: Ediciones Planeta, 2012; Mees, *Nationalism, Violence and Democracy*; and Zallo, Ramón, *El País de los Vascos: Desde los Sucesos de Ermua al Segundo Gobierno Ibarretxe*, Madrid: Fundamentos, 2001. The document agreed in September 1998 is variously referred to as the declaration, pact or agreement of Lizarra, Estella, Estella-Lizarra or—by members of the nationalist left—Lizarra-Garazi, with the name of the French Basque town (Garazi) where it was endorsed included as a reference to its embrace of the French Basque territories.

32. Further dissent came from a group of former ETA members called the Coletivo Sarobo, Domínguez Iribarren, *De la Negociación a la Tregua*, pp. 162–71.

33. Saldaña, J. J., 'Los nacionalistas vascos llaman a ETA/HB a sumarse contra el Estatuto', *ABC*, 19 October 2007.

34. 'Ardanza duda que haya suficientes motivos jurídicos contra la dirección de HB', *El País*, 9 October 2011.

35. Casanova, *ETA 1958–2008*, Tafalla: Txalaparta, 2007, pp. 425–6 and 'Garzón cierra "Egin" por ser "un instrumento del entramado delictivo de ETA-KAS"', *El País*, 16 July 1998.

36. 'Joint Declaration on Peace: The Downing Street Declaration', 15 December 1993, http://cain. ulst.ac.uk/events/peace/docs/dsd151293.htm, last accessed 18 Mar. 2011. Peter Brooke, the British Northern Ireland Secretary, made his 'no selfish or strategic interest' speech in November 1990.

37. Woodworth, Paddy, 'Gerry "Secretos" Adams", *Vanity Fair* (Spanish edition), December 2011.

38. Author interviews, Gorka Espiau, Vitoria, December 2008 and Jonan Fernández, Arantazu, February 2012. On Elkarri's approach to the Northern Ireland process, see Elkarri, 'Irlanda: una puerta a la esperanza', December 2007, http://elkarri.org/pdf/elkarrikasi_3_cast.pdf, last accessed 18 Mar. 2011.

39. Ollora, Juan María, *Un Vía Hacía la Paz*, San Sebastián: Erein, 1996.

40. The literature on the Irish peace process is extensive. See especially Bew, John, Martyn Frampton and Iñigo Gurruchaga, *Talking to Terrorists: Making Peace in Northern Ireland and the Basque Country*, London: Hurst, 2009; Cox, Michael, Adrian Guelke and Fiona Stephen (eds), *A Farewell to Arms? Beyond the Good Friday Agreement*, Manchester: Manchester University Press, 2006; Elliott, Marianne (ed.), *The Long Road to Peace in Northern Ireland*, Liverpool: Liverpool University Press, 2002; English, Richard, *Armed Struggle: the History of the IRA*, New York: Oxford University Press, 2005; Powell, Jonathan, *Great Hatred, Little Room: Making Peace in Northern Ireland*, London: The Bodley Head, 2008.

41. Zartman, I. William, 'The timing of peace initiatives: hurting stalemates and ripe moments', *The Global Review of Ethnopolitics*, 1, 1 (September 2001), p. 8.

42. Gurruchaga, Carmen, 'Proceso de paz: acto primero' and 'Proceso de paz: acto segundo', *El Mundo*, 20 September 1998; Gastaminza, Genoveva and Luis R. Aizpeolea, 'Así se negoció la tregua', *El País*, 20 September 1988; 'Una tregua histórica: la negociación secreta', *La Vanguardia*, 20 September 1998.

43. 'Plan Ardanza: Un acuerdo sobre el final dialogado', 1998, http://www.euskomedia.org/auna-mendi/8438/12806, last accessed 12 Mar. 2011.

44. On the 'distortion' by Basques of the Northern Irish process see Alonso, Rogelio, 'Pathways out of terrorism in Northern Ireland and the Basque Country: the misrepresentation of the Irish model', *Terrorism and Political Violence*, 16, 4 (2004), pp. 695–713, and Bew et al., *Talking to Terrorists*.

45. 'Texto integro de la Declaración de Lizarra', 12 September 1998, http://elkarri.org/pdf/Lizarra-Garazi.pdf, last accessed 23 Feb. 2011.

46. Otegi is quoted using the phrase 'Irish mirror' in Paddy Woodworth, 'Basque leader sees peace process as the way forward', *The Irish Times*, 31 October 1998. Zallo commented on the 'Stormont mirror in which everyone had to view themselves', *El País de los Vascos*, p. 55; Rafa Díez also referred to the 'Irish mirror' in an interview with the author in San Sebastián in July 2010.

47. For comparative analysis of Northern Ireland and the Basque Country, see Alonso, 'Pathways out of terrorism in Northern Ireland and the Basque cCountry'; Espiau Idioaga, Gorka, 'The peace processes in the Basque Country and Northern Ireland (1994–2006): a comparative approach', *ICIP Working Papers*, 2010/3, Barcelona: Institut Català Internacional per la Pau, May 2010; and Keating, Michael, 'Northern Ireland and the Basque Country', in McGarry, John (ed.), *Northern Ireland and the Divided World: Post-Agreement Northern Ireland in Comparative Perspective*, Oxford: Oxford University Press, 2001, pp. 181–208.

48. Cited in Powell, *Great Hatred, Little Room*, p. 312.

49. 'The Agreement reached in the multi-party negotiations', 10 April 1998, http://cain.ulst.ac.uk/events/peace/docs/agreement.htm, last accessed 12 Mar. 2011.

50. Arnaldo Otegi, in Iriondo, Inaki and Ramon Sola, *Mañana, Euskal Herria: Entrevista con Arnaldo Otegi*, Bilbao: Gara, 2005, p. 67

51. Ramón Jáuregui, in Iglesias, *Memoria de Euskadi*, p. 264.

52. L.R.A., 'Interior descarta la negociación política', *El País*, 17 September 1998; 'Aznar no será "insensible" a las expectativas de la tregua y consultará a los partidos democráticos', *El País*, 18 September 1998.

53. The proposed agreement from ETA, the response written on its reverse by the PNV and EA, and a further 'interpretation' by the PNV were published by *Gara* on 20 April 2000. The Spanish translation of the documents is available on http://www.elmundo.es/nacional/eta/tregua/ruptura/documentosgara.html, last accessed 23 Feb. 2011.

54. Mees, *Nationalism, Violence and Democracy*, p. 144.

55. Juan María Ollora and Joseba Egibar in Iglesias, *Memoria de Euskadi*, pp. 699–762; author interview, Joseba Egibar, San Sebastián, July 2009.

56. Egibar, in Iglesias, *Memoria de Euskadi*, p. 745.

57. *Euskobarómetro*, 'Datos electorales, elecciones autonómicas en el País Vasco', http://alweb.ehu.es/euskobarometro/index.php, last accessed 27 Feb. 2011.

58. Author interview, Javier Zarzalejos, Madrid, October 2009.

59. Romero, J. M. and J. A. Rodríguez, 'Lo que Aznar hizo por la tregua', *El País*, 24 March 2006.

60. Escrivá, *Maldito el País que Necesita Héroes*, pp. 216–7.

61. 'Diálogo de sordos', *El País*, 6 November 1998; author interview Zarzalejos, October 2009.

62. 'Acta de la reunión de miembros de ETA y tres representantes de Aznar', *Gara*, 1 May 2000 and 7 March 2006.

63. Mayor Oreja in Iglesias, *Memoria de Euskadi*, p. 942. The police surveillance of the emissary was discussed in the May 1999 meeting with ETA, as the 'Acta' reflects. See also de Diego, Enrique, 'La conexión San Egidio', *Epoca*, 23 September 2005.

64. 'Acta de la reunión de miembros de ETA y tres representantes de Aznar'.

65. Casanova, *ETA 1959–2008*, p. 446.

66. Domínguez, Florencio, *Josu Ternera: Una Vida en ETA*, Madrid: La Esfera de los Libros, 2006, pp. 268–73.

67. Egibar in Iglesias, *Memoria de Euskadi*, p. 747.

68. A report by *El Correo* reproduced by the Foro de Ermua documented forty-five members of ETA (twenty-eight in Spain and seventeen in France) captured during the ceasefire, http://www.foroermua.com/web/node/39861, last accessed 30 Apr. 2012; one article in *El País* described no arrests at all between 17 September 1998 and 9 March 1999, then thirty-one in Spain and thirty-nine in France during the remainder of 1999. Romero and Rodríguez, 'Lo que Aznar hizo por la tregua'. Domínguez, Florencio, *La Agonía de ETA: Una Investigación Inédita Sobre los Últimos Días de la Banda*, Madrid: La Esfera de los Libros, 2012, pp. 15–55.

69. Aretxaga, Begoña, 'Out of their minds? On political madness in the Basque Country', in Aretxaga, Begoña, Dennis Dworkin, Joseba Gabilondo and Joseba Zulaika (eds), *Empire and Terror: Nationalism/Postnationalism in the New Millennium*, Reno: Center for Basque Studies, Conference Papers Series, No. 1, 2004, pp. 164–9.

70. 'Comunicado del Presidente del Gobierno Vasco', *El País*, 28 November 1999, cited in ibid., p. 165.

71. 'La campaña arranca bajo la crispación provocada por el asesinato de Buesa', *El País*, 25 February 2000; Guenaga, Aitor 'Arzalluz critica el carácter "franquista" de los dirigentes del PP', *El País*, 11 March 2000.

72. Zallo, *El País de los Vascos*, p. 108.

73. Cited in Escrivá, *Maldito el País que Necesita Héroes*, p. 289.

74. Casqueiro, Javier and Anabel Díez, 'Aznar ningunea el pacto contra ETA del PSOE porque "no aporta nada" y solo busca publicidad', *El País*, 18 November 2000; 'El ejecutivo rechaza y descalifica la propuesta del PSOE para firmar un pacto contra el terrorismo', *El Mundo*, 18 November 2000.

75. 'Acuerdo por las libertades y contra el terrorismo', Madrid, 8 December 2000, http://www.elmundo.es/eta/documentos/pacto_libertades.html, last accessed 26 Mar. 2011.

76. Sen, Cristina, 'Aznar: la paz pasa por desalojar al PNV', *La Vanguardia*, 30 June 2000.

77. Charlemagne, 'Jose Maria Aznar', *The Economist*, 13 September 2001; See also, Cebrían, Juan Luis, 'El discurso del método', *El País*, 18 May 2001.

78. Running together, the PNV and EA won 42.4 per cent of the votes, and thirty-three seats in parliament, the IU-EB 5.5 per cent (three seats); the PP 22.9 per cent (nineteen seats); the PSE 17.8 per cent (thirteen seats); and EH 10 per cent (seven seats). *Euskobarómetro*, 'Datos electorales, elecciones autonómicas en el País Vasco'.

79. See, for example, Foreign and Commonwealth Office (FCO), 'Counter-Terrorism Legislation and Practice: A Survey of Selected Countries', FCO Research Paper, 2005, available at http://image.guardian.co.uk/sys-files/Politics/documents/2005/10/12/foreignterrorlaw1.pdf, last accessed 11 Sep. 2013, and Foley, Frank, *Countering Terrorism in Britain and France: Institutions, Norms and the Shadow of the Past*, Cambridge: Cambridge University Press, 2013.

80. Finn, John E., 'Counterterrorism regimes and the rule of law: the effects of emergency legislation on separation of powers, civil liberties, and other fundamental constitutional norms', in Crenshaw, Martha (ed.), *The Consequences of Counterterrorism*, New York: Russell Sage Foundation, 2010, pp. 41–2.

81. Ibid., but also, Cole, David and James X. Dempsey, *Terrorism and the Constitution*, London and New York: The New Press, 2006; Walker, Clive, *Terrorism and the Law*, Oxford: Oxford University Press, 2011; and Wittes, Benjamin, *Law and the Long War: The Future of Justice in the Age of Terror*, New York: Penguin, 2008.

82. Aznar, *Eight Year as Prime Minister*, pp. 120–1; Cosidó and Elía, *España, Camino de Libertad*, pp. 173–7.

83. Riding, Alan, 'The world: target; Europe knows fear, but this time it's different', *The New York Times*, 14 March 2004.

84. Guelke, Adrian, 'The Northern Ireland peace process and the war against terrorism: conflicting conceptions?', *Government and Opposition*, 12, 3 (2007), pp. 272–91.

85. Aznar, *Eight Years as Prime Minister*, p. 181.

86. Barbería, J.L. and M. González, 'España y Francia darán un salto cualitativo en su cooperación para erradicar a ETA', *El País*, 24 May 2000.

87. Figures from the Spanish ministry of the interior, in Cosidó and Elía, *España, Camino de Libertad*, p. 178.

88. Agreement in principle on a European Arrest Warrant (EAW) would be reached in December 2001, but only come into practice in 2004. Celaya, Fernando, 'The terrorist threat is being materially and normatively shaped by national and global institutions of law and order: Spain & beyond', *Athena Intelligence Journal*, 4, 1 (2009), p. 22.

89. Council Common Position of 27 December 2001 on the application of specific measures to combat terrorism, (2001/931/CPSP), Annex. Twenty-one out of twenty-eight persons included on the list were also identified as ETA activists.

90. Wilkinson, Isambard, 'Spain wants ETA political wing put on EU terror list', *The Telegraph*, 18 October 2001.

91. Author interview, Koldo Gorostiaga, Urrugne, December 2010.

92. 'GWOT assessment, Madrid feedback', US Embassy Madrid cable of 7 April 2005, posted on the website of *El País* as 'Cable sobre el terrorismo en España (2005)', http://www.elpais. com/articulo/internacional/Cable/terrorismo/Espana/2005/elpepuint/20110309elpepuint_16/ Tes, last accessed 27 Apr. 2011.

93. Cosidó and Elía, *España, Camino de libertad*, p. 189.

94. The memorandum of the conversation between Bush and Aznar would be published in *El País* on 26 September 2007.

95. Balfour and Quiroga, *The Reinvention of Spain*, pp. 175–83; Iglesias-Cavicchioli, Manuel, 'A period of turbulent change: Spanish-US relations since 2002', *The Whitehead Journal of Diplomacy and International Relations*, Summer/Fall 2007, pp. 113–29.

96. The figures cited in this paragraph are, unless otherwise stated, drawn from the ministry of the interior and cited in Cosidó and Elío, *España, Camino de Libertad*, pp. 105–20.

97. Centro de análisis y prospectiva, 'La kale borroka y la estrategia de ETA'.

98. Author interview, Patxi Zabaleta, Pamplona, July 2010.

99. Specific terrorist crimes and the penalties associated with them are established in articles 571– 579 of the criminal code. Many of the reforms referred to in this paragraph are contained in Ley Orgánica 7/2000 of 22 December 2000, *Boletín Oficial del Estado*, 23 December 2000, http://www.boe.es/boe/dias/2000/12/23/pdfs/A45503–45508.pdf, last accessed 24 Mar. 2011.

100. Ley Orgánica 5/2000 of 13 January 2000, *Boletín Oficial del Estado*, 14 January 2000, http:// www.boe.es/boe/dias/2000/01/13/pdfs/A01422–01441.pdf, last accessed 24 Mar. 2011.

101. Ley Orgánica 7/2003 of 30 June 2003, *Boletín Oficial del Estado*, 1 July 2003, http://www. boe.es/boe/dias/2003/07/01/pdfs/A25274–25278.pdf, last accessed 24 Mar. 2011. Art 76.2 is further discussed in Chapter 10, p.277.

102. UN Human Rights Council, 'Report of the Special Rapporteur' Martin Scheinin, Addendum: Mission to Spain', 16 December 2008, A/HRC/10/3/Add.2, paras 8, 9 and 10.

103. Amnesty International, 'Macroproceso 18/98 trial highlights flaws in Spanish counter-terrorism legislation', EUR/41/009/2009, 3 June 2009.

104. Portero de la Torre, Daniel, *La Trama Civil de ETA*, Madrid: Arco Press, 2008, p. 45.

105. Amnesty International, 'Macroproceso 18/98 trial highlights flaws'.

106. On the Egunkaria case, see Ramirez de la Piscina, Txema, Teresa Agirreazaldegi, Pedro Ibarra and Ramón Zallo, *Egunkaria: la Verdad de un Sueño*, San Sebastián: Tzarttalo, 2010.

107. Author interview, Jone Gorizeleia, Bilbao, July 2010.

108. Article 9 (2), Ley Orgánica 6/2002 of 27 June 2002, *Boletín Oficial del Estado*, http://www. boe.es/boe/dias/2002/06/28/pdfs/A23600–23607.pdf, last accessed 24 Mar. 2011. Ayres, Thomas, 'Batasuna banned: the dissolution of political parties under the European Convention of Human Rights', *Boston College International and Comparative Law Review*, 27, 1/3 (12 January 2004), pp. 99–113.

109. Informe del Gobierno para impulsar la ilegalización, 'Nota sobre los fundamentos para interponer demanda de declaración de ilegalidad de los partidos políticos Herri Batasuna, Euskal Herritarok y Batasuna, de conformidad con la Ley Orgánica 6/2002 de 27 de Junio, de partidos políticos', 12 August 2002, http://estaticos.elmundo.es/nacional/batasuna24.pdf, last accessed 26 Mar. 2011.

110. Juzgado Central de Instrucción No. 5, Sumario 35/02 Y, Auto, Madrid, 26 August 2002. http://estaticos.elmundo.es/especiales/2002/08/espana/batasuna/Integro.pdf, last accessed 26 Mar. 2012.

111. Author interview, Alfredo Pérez Rubalcaba, Madrid, February 2012.

112. Powell, Charles, 'ETA loses its voice', *The World Today*, November 2002.

113. 'Batasuna banned', *The Economist*, 29 August 2002.

114. Cited in 'Spain's press approves ban', *BBC*, 26 August 2002, http://news.bbc.co.uk/2/hi/europe/2217687.stm, last accessed 25 Mar. 2011.

115. Javier Ortiz, in 'La opinión de los intelectuales', in 'Batasuna: proceso de ilegalización', *El Mundo*, August 2002, http://www.elmundo.es/especiales/2002/08/espana/batasuna/intelectuales.html, last accessed 26 Mar. 2011.

4. THE BASQUE CRISIS: LOOKING FOR A WAY OUT

1. Barbería, José Luis and Patxo Unzueta, *Cómo Hemos Llegado a Esto. La Crisis Vasca*, Madrid: Taurus, 2003, p. 13.

2. Ibid., pp. 17–8

3. Elkarri, 'The Basque conflict', 2001, p. 8, http://www.elkarri.org/en/pdf/BasqueConflict.pdf, last accessed on 25 May 2011.

4. Author interview, Jonan Fernández, Arantzazu, February 2012.

5. Barbería, José Luis, 'Las "embajadas" de ETA', *El País*, 1 June 2008.

6. Iriondo, Iñaki, *Ibarretxe: Entre el Poder y el Querer*, Bilbao: Gara, 2009, p. 25.

7. 'Cronología del "caso Atutxa"', *El Correo*, 22 January 2008, http://www.elcorreo.com/vizcaya/20080122/politica/cronologia-caso-atutxa-20080122.html, last accessed 7 Mar. 2011

8. Author interviews, Txema Urkijo and Maixabel Laso, Vitoria, July 2009 and December 2010.

9. Basque Parliament, 'Informe relativo de la situación de todas las víctimas de la violencia generada en nuestro país', *Boletín Oficial del Parlamento Vasco*, Vitoria-Gasteiz, 18 May 2001.

10. 'Ibarretxe pide perdón a las víctimas del terrorismo', *El País*, 22 April 2007. Neither COVITE nor AVT attended the event—nor, more predictably, did representatives of the nationalist left.

11. Author interview, Juan José Ibarretxe, Vitoria, July 2009.

12. See Fisas, Vicenç, *Llegó la hora? Promesas de Paz Para el País Vasco*, Barcelona: Icaria, 2010 for an account of the evolution of the proposals made by Ibarretxe in this period.

13. Tremlett, Giles, 'Spain vows to block Basque referendum', *The Guardian*, 31 July 2001.

14. Ordozgoiti, Koldo, *El Futuro nos Pertenece: Memorias Políticas del Lehendakari Ibarretxe*, Irun: Alberdania, 2010, pp. 158–9.

15. The members of the Honorary Committee were John Hume, the Dalai Lama, Mairead Maguire, Rigoberta Menchú, Adolfo Pérez Esquivel and José Ramos-Horta, all Nobel Peace Prize winners; José Saramago, winner of the Nobel Prize for Literature; and Federico Mayor Zaragoza, Danielle Mitterand and Cora Weiss. 'Elkarri inicia la Conferencia de Paz expresando su reconocimiento a la participación ciudadana', Elkarri press conference, 1 October 2001, http://www/nodo50.org/elkarri.madrid/50mil.htm, last accessed 31 May 2011.

16. Elkarri VII General Assembly, 'Action Plan 2003–2005 I and II, The Bases and Role of Elkarri', 1 March 2003, p. 6, http://www.elkarri.org/en/pdf/BUILDING.pdf, last accessed 31 May 2011.

17. Fisas, *Llegó la hora?*, pp. 53–5; Càtedra Unesco sobre pau i drets humans, 'Ejercicio contrastes: recopilación del trabajo realizado desde Septiembre 2000 hasta Abril 2003', Escola de cultura de pau, Universitat Autònoma de Barcelona, mimeo.

18. 'Elkarri se ofrece a incluir a sus miembros en listas del PP y el PSE si lo necesitan', *El País*, 2 February 2002.

19. Arnaldo Otegi, in Iriondo, Iñaki and Ramón Sola, *Mañana, Euskal Herria: Entrevista con Arnaldo Otegi*, Bilbao: Gara, 2005, pp. 91–2.

20. Eguiguren, Jesús, 'Los tercios de flandes', *Cambio 16*, 17 October 2001, in Eguiguren Imaz, Jesús, *Los Últimos Españoles sin Patria (y sin Libertad)*, Seville: Cambio, 2003, p. 77.

21. Eguiguren, reproduced as 'Québec: el documento de la discordia', in ibid., pp. 93–135.

22. Savater, Fernando, 'Oxígeno para ETA', *El País*, 6 April 2002.

23. Aiartza, Urko and Julen Zabalo, 'The Basque Country: the long walk to a democratic scenario', Berlin: Berghof Conflict Research, *Berghof Transitions 7*, 2009, p. 32.

24. 'A scenario for peace in the Basque Country', 21 January 2002, Annex Document 2, in Aiartza and Zabalo, 'The Basque Country', pp. 56–8.

25. José Luis Barbería, 'Las "embajadas" de ETA'. Author interview, Batasuna representative Urrugne, France, July 2011.

26. Ibarretxe, Juan José, 'A new political agreement for coexistence', 27 September 2002, http://www.elkarri.org/en/pdf/Lehendakari_27092002_i.pdf, last accessed 31 May 2011.

27. Basque government, 'Propuesta de estatuto político de la comunidad de Euskadi', Ajuria-Enea, 25 October 2003. http://estaticos.elmundo.es/documentos/2003/10/estatuto_vasco.pdf, last accessed 6 Jun. 2011.

28. Keating, Michael and Zoe Bray, 'Renegotiating sovereignty: Basque nationalism and the rise and fall of the Ibarretxe Plan', *Ethnopolitics*, 5, 4 (November 2006), pp. 348–51.

29. Ibarretxe, 'A new political agreement for coexistence'.

30. Keating and Bray, 'Renegotiating sovereignty, pp. 347–64. See also Douglass, William A. and Pedro Ibarra Güell, 'A Basque referendum: resolution of political conflict or the promised land of error?', in Begoña Aretxaga, Dennis Dworkin, Joseba Gabilondo and Joseba Zulaika (eds), *Empire and Terror: Nationalism/Postnationalism in the New Millennium*, Reno: Center for Basque Studies, Conference Papers Series. No. 1, 2004, pp. 137–62; Muro, Diego, 'Territorial accommodation, party politics, and statute reform in Spain', in Bonnie N. Field (ed.), *Spain's 'Second Transition'? The Socialist Government of José Luis Rodríguez Zapatero*, London and New York: Routledge, 2011, pp. 78–81.

31. Leslie, Peter, 'Canada: the Supreme Court sets rules for the secession of Quebec', *Publius*, 29, 2 (Spring 1999), pp. 135–51.

32. Supreme Court of Canada, 'Reference by the Governor in Council concerning certain questions relating to the secession of Quebec', 161, Dominion Law Report (4th) p, 385.

33. Young, Robert A., 'A most politic judgment', *Constitutional Forum*, 10, 1 (1998), pp. 14–8.

34. Eguiguren, Jesús, 'Las enseñanzas de Quebec', in *Los Últimos Españoles sin Patria*, pp. 116–36.

35. Loughlin, John, 'New contexts for political solutions: redefining minority nationalisms in Northern Ireland, the Basque Country, and Corsica', in Darby, John and Roger Mac Ginty (eds), *Contemporary Peacemaking: Conflict, Peace Processes, and Post-War Reconstruction* (2nd edn), Basingstoke: Palgrave Macmillan, 2008, pp. 45–59.

36. Van Haelewyn, Mathieu, 'EFA in the fifth legislative period (1999–2004)', *European Free Alliance: Voice of the Peoples of Europe, The First Twenty-five Years (1981–2006)*, Brussels: European Free Alliance, 2008, p. 83.

37. Tremlett, Giles, 'Basque plan is treason, say critics', *The Guardian*, 27 October 2003.

38. PSE-EE, 'Más estatuto: propuesta socialista sobre el autogobierno', 2003, p. 6, www.berria.info/proposamenak/dokumentuak/PSE-EE.doc, last accessed on 28 May 2011.

39. This modification to the criminal code would be reversed by the government of Zapatero in 2004.

40. Otegi, in Iriondo and Solas, *Mañana, Euskal Herria*, p. 142. See also interview with ETA reproduced in Iriondo, *Ibarretxe*, pp. 116–9.

41. Arnoldo Otegi, cited in ibid., p. 133.

42. The criticism was somewhat cynical, in that the PP and PSE had on occasion used EH's vote to block Ibarretxe's budgets. Segura, Antoni, *Euskadi: Crónica de una Desesperanza*, Madrid: Alianza Editorial, 2009, p. 249.

43. Eguiguren Imaz, Jesús, *La Crisis Vasca: Entre la Ruptura y el Diálogo*, Seville: Cambio, 2004, p. 16.

44. PSE-EE, 'V Congreso Ordinario: Resoluciones', 30 October 2005, p. 11, http://www.socialistasvascos.com/upload/archivo_resvcong.pdf, last accessed 18 May 2011.

45. Zabaleta, Gemma and Deniz Istazo, *Con la Mano Izquierda: Una Nueva Política Frente al Colapso Vasco*, Irún: Alberdania, 2002.

46. Eguiguren Imaz, *La Crisis Vasca*.

47. Eguiguren, interview in Iglesias, Maria Antonia, *Memoria de Euskadi*, Madrid: Aguilar, 2009, p. 872.

48. Eguiguren, 'El sueño de un borracho', in *Los Últimos Españoles sin Patria*, pp. 220–4.

49. Accounts of the meetings in Txillare are given in Eguiguren, Jesús and Luis Rodríguez Aizpeolea, *ETA, Las Claves de la Paz: Confesiones del Negociador*, Madrid: Aguilar, 2011; Eguiguren's interview in Iglesias, *Memoria de Euskadi*, by Arnaldo Otegi in Iriondo and Sola, *Mañana, Euskal Herria*; in Jáuregui, Fernando and Manuel Ángel Menéndez, *El Zapaterato, La Negociación: El Fin de ETA*, Barcelona: Península, 2010; Munarriz, Fermin, *El Tiempo de las Luces: Entrevista con Arnaldo Otegi*, Bilbao: Gara, 2012; Murua Uria, Imanol, *El Triángulo de Loiola: Crónica de un Proceso de Negociación a Tres Bandas*, Donostia: Ttarttalo, 2010; and Gara, '2005–2007 proceso de negociación: en busca de un acuerdo político resolutivo', *Gara*, 2008. These paragraphs also draw upon the author's interviews with Jesús Eguiguren and Arnaldo Otegi in July 2009.

50. Gara, '2005–2007 proceso de negociación, p. 24.

51. Eguiguren, Jesús, 'Bases para un arreglo', in *Los Últimos Españoles sin Libertad*, p. 249.

52. Gara, '2005–2007 proceso de negociación', p. 27.

53. González, Felipe, 'El problema palestino: epicentro de la crisis internacional', *El País*, 11 May 2002; Eguiguren, 'Felipe González, Palestina y el país vasco', in *Los Últimos Españoles sin Patria*, pp. 225–8.

54. Huber, Konrad, 'The HDC in Aceh: promises and pitfalls of NGO mediation and implementation', Washington, DC: East-West Center, 2004; Sørbø, Gunnar, Jonathan Goodhand, Bart Klem, Ada Elisabeth Nissen and Hilde Selbervik, 'Pawns of peace: evaluation of Norwegian peace efforts in Sri Lanka, 1997–2000', Oslo: Norwegian Agency for Development Cooperation, 2011; and Whitfield, Teresa, 'Engaging with armed groups: challenges and opportunities for mediators', Geneva: Centre for Humanitarian Dialogue, 2010.

55. References to Colombia in this and the following paragraph draw on Arnson, Cynthia J. and Teresa Whitfield, 'Third parties and intractable conflicts: the case of Colombia', in Crocker, Chester A, Fen Osler Hampson and Pamela Aall (eds), *Grasping the Nettle: Analyzing Cases of Intractable Conflict*, Washington, DC: United States Institute of Peace Press, 2005, pp. 231–68, unless otherwise stated.

56. Both Spain and Germany had been involved in the peace process with the ELN conducted by Pastrana's predecessor, Ernesto Samper. Ibid., p. 253.

57. Author interview, Arnaldo Otegi, San Sebastián, July 2009.

58. Author interviews/conversations with outsiders involved in Basque issues including Andrea Bartoli, Brian Currin, William Douglass, Harold Good, Dennis Haughey, Nuala O'Loan, Alex Maskey, Roelf Meyer and Christopher Mitchell.

59. Author interview, Alex Maskey, Belfast, March 2011.

60. United Nations, 'Guidance for Effective Mediation', Annex to *Report of the Secretary-General on Strengthening the Role of Mediation in the Peaceful Settlement of Disputes, Conflict Prevention and Resolution*, New York: United Nations, A/66/811, 25 June 2012. There is, it should be noted, a healthy debate within the wider mediation literature regarding the relative benefits of a mediator's bias, impartiality or neutrality. See, for example, Smith, James D.D., 'Mediator impartiality: banishing the chimera', *Journal of Peace Research*, 31 (November 1994) pp. 445–50; Svensson, Isak, 'Who brings which peace? Neutral versus biased mediation and institutional peace arrangements in Civil Wars,' *Journal of Conflict Resolution*, 53, 3 (2009), pp. 446–69; and Zartman, I. William and Saadia Touval, 'International mediation', in Crocker, Chester A., Fen Osler Hampson and Pamela Aall, *Leashing the Dogs of War: Conflict Management*

in a Divided World, Washington, DC: United States Institute of Peace Press, 2007, pp. 437–54.

61. Quinney, Nigel and A. Heather Coyne, 'Talking to groups that use terror', *Peacemaker's Toolkit*, Washington, DC: United States Institute for Peace, 2011, p. 71.

62. Philipson, Liz, 'Engaging armed groups: the challenge of asymmetries', in Robert Ricigliano (ed.), 'Choosing to engage: armed groups and peace processes', *Accord Issue 16*, London: Conciliation Resources, 2005, pp. 69–71.

63. See Sørbø et al., 'Pawns of peace', p. 75, for the case of Sri Lanka.

64. See Rogelio Alonso's citation of this quote as the basis of criticism of outside 'experts' who defended a 'peace process' in the Basque Country. Ignatieff, Michael, *The Warrior's Honour*, London: Vintage, 1999, p. 104, cited by Alonso, Rogelio, 'Leaving terrorism behind in Northern Ireland and the Basque Country', in Bjørgo, Tore and John Horgan, *Leaving Terrorism Behind: Individual and Collective Disengagement*, London and New York: Routledge, 2009, p. 103.

65. This account draws on interviews the author and Cynthia J. Arnson conducted with diplomats and others involved in the Colombian peace process in New York and Bogotá in March and April 2002.

66. Statement by the EU Presidency in October 2000, cited in Centro de Investigación para la Paz, 'Colombia y Europa: el papel europeo en un futuro proceso de paz', *Papeles de Cuestiones Internacionales*, 83 (Autumn 2003), p. 3.

67. The FARC delegation visited Valencia and was received by the then head of the regional government (and later Aznar minister) Eduardo Zaplana as well as the PP judge Eloy Velasco, who prosecuted terrorism cases on the Audiencia Nacional. 'Cuando Zaplana recibió a Raúl Reyes', leveante-emv.com, 3 March 2008, http://www.levante-emv.com/secciones/noticia.jsp?pRef=3832_19_414785__Comunitat-Valenciana-Cuando-Zaplana-recibio-Raul-Reyes, last accessed 28 May 2011.

68. Jerez-Farrán, Carlos and Samuel Amago (eds), *Unearthing Franco's Legacy: Mass Graves and the Recovery of Historical Memory in Spain*, Notre Dame: University of Notre Dame Press, 2010.

69. Barbería, 'Las "embajadas" de ETA'.

70. This observation reflects conversations with former representatives of both Amnesty International and Human Rights Watch who asked not to be identified, as well as individuals in the Basque Country who have pushed for a more universal and transparent approach to human rights issues.

71. Behatokia, the Basque Observatory of Human Rights, linked several organisations of the nationalist left—TAT (Group Against Torture), Etxerat (Association of Relatives of the Politically Repressed), Eskubideak (Basque Solicitors Association) and Gurasoak (Association of Parents of Young Victims of the Repression) in an effort to promote communication with international bodies, non-governmental organisations and groups who work in the defence of human rights in order to publicise the violation of these rights in the Basque Country. http://www.behatokia.info/index.php?newlang=eng, last accessed 3 Jun. 2011.

72. Author interview, Eduardo Ruiz, Bilbao, July 2009. In 2010 a number of individuals of recognised independence formed the Asociación Pro Derechos Humanos, Argituz, to try to counter this tendency.

73. United Nations, 'Conclusions and recommendations of the Committee Against Torture: Spain', 23 December 2002, CAT/C/CR/29/3, para. 10.

74. Amnesty International's 2011 report on Spain began, 'Allegations of torture and ill-treatment by law enforcement officials persisted, and investigations into such allegations continued to be inadequate. Spain refused to abolish incommunicado detention despite repeated recommendations by international human rights bodies.' *Amnesty International Report 2011*, 'Spain', London: Amnesty International, 2011, pp. 299–301. See also, Council of Europe, 'Report to

the Spanish Government on the visit to Spain carried out by the European Committee for the Prevention of Torture and Inhuman or Degrading Treatment or Punishment (CPT) from 19 September to 1 October 2007', Strasbourg, 23 March 2011.

75. Author interview, Madrid, September 2012.
76. United Nations, Commission on Human Rights, 'Report of the Special Rapporteur on the question of torture, Theo van Boven, Addendum, Visit to Spain,' E/CN.4/2004/56/Add.2, 6 February 2004, para 29.
77. Landa Gorostiza, Jon-Mirena, 'La tortura en relación con la banda terrorista ETA: estado de la jurisprudencia penal. A la vez un comentario a la STS 2 noviembre 2011 (caso Portu y Sarasola)', *Jueces Para la Democracia*, 73 (2012), pp. 81–104.
78. United Nations, 'Conclusions of the UN Committee Against Torture after examining the fourth periodic report of Spain on the implementation of the Convention Against Torture', Official Records of the General Assembly, Fifty-eighth Session, Supplement No. 44, 2002, (A 58/44). para 60, and Terwindt, Carolijn, 'Were they tortured or did they make that up? Ethnographic reflections on torture allegations in the Basque Country in Spain', Oñati International Institute for the Sociology of Law, *Oñati Socio-Legal Series*, 1, 2 (2011).
79. Ayllón, Luis, 'España invita al relator de la ONU sobre la tortura para rebatir las denuncias etarras', *ABC*, 2 October 2003.
80. Author interview (telephone), Theo van Boven, July 2011.
81. United Nations, 'Report of the Special Rapporteur on the question of torture', para. 58.
82. Ibid., para 32.
83. United Nations, Commission on Human Rights, '*Notes verbales* dated 20 January and 2 and 22 February 2004 from the Permanent Mission of Spain to the United Nations Office at Geneva addressed to the Office of the United Nations High Commissioner for Human Rights', E/CN.4/2004/G/19, 4 March 2004.
84. Author interview, van Boven.
85. Berrocal, Salomé and Clara Fernández, 'Las elecciones legislativas de 2004. Un análisis de las encuestas y de la gestión comunicativa en la campaña electoral: su proyección en la decisión de voto', *Revista Doxa*, IV (May 2006), pp. 189–208.
86. *Zutabe* 100, cited by Domínguez Iribarren, Florencio 'El enfrentamiento de ETA con la democracia', in Elorza, Antonio (coord.), *La Historia de ETA*, Madrid: Temas de Hoy, 2006, p. 422.
87. Ibid., pp. 421–4. See also, Domínguez, Florencio, *La Agonía de ETA: Una Investigación Inédita Sobre los Últimos Días de la Banda*, Madrid: La Esfera de los Libros, 2012, pp. 106–19.
88. Jáuregui and Menéndez, *El Zapaterato*, p. 38.
89. Author interview, Gorka Espiau, Vitoria, December 2008.
90. Aguswandi and Judith Large (eds), 'Reconfiguring politics: the Indonesia–Aceh peace process', *Accord Issue 30*, London: Conciliation Resources, 2008, and Huber, 'The HDC in Aceh'.
91. This account draws on a conversation with Nancy Soderberg in October 2011 and the English version of a September 2008 paper written by William A. Douglass, describing his involvement with the HD Centre. The paper was kindly provided to the author by Douglass, and published in Euskera in the magazine *Argia* in November 2009.
92. Author interview, Julian Hottinger, New York, January 2012.
93. Author interview, William Douglass, Reno, February 2009.
94. Douglass, William A., paper, 20 September 2008.

5. ZAPATERO'S MOMENT

1. In early March, Instituto Opina found that 42 per cent of those consulted intended to vote for the PP and 38 per cent for the PSOE. 'Estimación de voto. Elecciones Generales 2004', *El País*, 4 March 2004.

2. Arnaldo Otegi, in Iriondo, Iñaki and Ramón Sola, *Mañana, Euskal Herria: Entrevista con Arnaldo Otegi*, Bilbao: Gara, 2005, pp. 109–15.

3. Crawford, Leslie and Joshua Levitt, '"A place in the history of infamy"—how the government's assumption and misjudgement shook Spain', *Financial Times*, 25 March 2004; Richburg, Keith B., 'Spain campaigned to pin blame on ETA', *Washington Post*, 17 March 2004.

4. Sánchez-Cuenca, Ignacio, 'Las elecciones de 2008: ideología, crispación y liderazgo', in Bosco, Anna and Ignacio Sánchez-Cuenca (eds), *La España de Zapatero: Años de Cambios, 2004–2008*, Madrid: Pablo Iglesias, 2009, p. 33. On *crispación* see Fundación Alternativas, *Informe Sobre la Democracia en España, 2007. La Estrategia de la Crispación* and *Informe Sobre la Democracia en España, 2008. La Estrategia de la Crispación—Derrota, Pero no Fracaso*, Madrid: Fundación Alternativas, 2007 and 2008.

5. Zartman, I. William, 'The timing of peace initiatives: hurting stalemates and ripe moments', *The Global Review of Ethnopolitics*, 1, 1 (September 2001), pp. 13–4.

6. Jáuregui, Fernando and Manuel Ángel Menéndez, *El Zapaterato, La Negociación: El Fin de ETA*, Barcelona: Peninsula, 2010, p. 16.

7. Grimond, John, interview, 'The second transition: a survey of Spain', *The Economist*, 24 June 2004.

8. Woodworth, Paddy, 'Spain's "Second Transition": reforming zeal and dire omens', *World Policy Journal*, 22, 3 (Fall 2005), pp. 69–80. See also, Field, Bonnie N. (ed.), *Spain's 'Second Transition'? The Socialist Government of José Luis Rodríguez Zapatero*, London and New York: Routledge, 2011.

9. Crawford, Leslie, 'Regions step up demands for autonomy', *Financial Times*, 15 June 2004.

10. Muro, Diego, 'Territorial accommodation, party politics, and statute reform in Spain', in Field (ed.), *Spain's Second Transition?*, pp. 76–8; Baldi, Brunetta and Gianfranco Baldini, 'La reforma del Estado de las autonomías', in Bosco and Sánchez-Cuenca (eds), *La España de Zapatero*, pp. 101–27.

11. Partido Socialista Obrero Español, 'La España plural: la España constitucional, la España unida, la España en positiva', Santillana del Mar, 30 August 2003, http://www.psoe.es/ambito/actualidad/docs/index.do?action=view&id=12209, last accessed 4 Jun. 2011.

12. See Balfour, Sebastian and Alejandro Quiroga, *The Reinvention of Spain: Nation and Identity Since Democracy*, New York: Oxford University Press, 2007, pp. 72–97 on the 'View from the left'.

13. Information on ARMH is available on its website: http://www.memoriahistorica.es. See also Cué, Carlos E., 'La última cuenta pendiente de la democracia', *El País*, 20 September 2004; Jerez-Farrán, Carlos and Samuel Amago (eds), *Unearthing Franco's Legacy: Mass Graves and the Recovery of Historical Memory in Spain*, Notre Dame: University of Notre Dame Press, 2010.

14. Wilde, Alexander, 'Irruptions of memory: expressive politics in Chile's transition to democracy', *Journal of Latin American Studies*, 31, 2 (1999), pp. 473–500.

15. Tremlett, Giles, *Ghosts of Spain: Travels Through Spain and Its Silent Past*, New York: Walker and Co., 2008; and Labanyi, Jo (ed.), 'The politics of memory in contemporary Spain', Special issue of *Journal of Spanish Cultural Studies*, 9, 2 (2008).

16. Tremlett, Giles, 'The grandsons of their grandfathers', in *Unearthing Franco's Legacy*, Jerez-Farrán and Amago (eds), p. 27; 'El jefe del gobierno español, José Luis Rodríguez Zapatero, un lider de optimismo blindado y con un profundo compromiso socialista', *Clarín*, 10 March 2008.

17. *El Mundo*, 22 June 2005, cited by Woodworth, 'Spain's "Second Transition"', p. 71.

18. Crawford, Leslie, 'Aznar stands by his claim of ETA link to bombs', *Financial Times*, 30 November 2004; Tremlett, Giles, 'Spanish right clings to bomb theory', *The Observer*, 28 November 2004.

19. Pettit, Philip, *Examen a Zapatero*, Madrid: Temas de Hoy, 2008 and, with José Marti, *A Political*

Philosophy in Public Life: Civic Republicanism in Zapatero's Spain, Princeton: Princeton University Press, 2010.

20. Cué, 'La última cuenta pendiente de la democracia'; Labanyi (ed.), 'The politics of memory in contemporary Spain'; Tremlett, 'The grandsons of their grandfathers', pp. 327–44

21. Amnesty International, 'España: poner fin al silencio y la injusticia', 18 July 2005, p. 65; Parliamentary Assembly, Council of Europe, 'Need for international condemnation of the Franco regime', Recommendation 1736, 17 March 2006.

22. Muro, 'Territorial accommodation, party politics, and statute reform', pp. 81–3.

23. Díez, Anabel, 'Zapatero declara el fin de la "oposición útil" y el inicio del "cambio responsable"', *El País*, 23 November 2003.

24. Documents related to the 'Cumbre Internacional sobre Democracia, Terrorismo y Seguridad', 8–11 March 2005 are available at http://cumbre.clubmadrid.org/, last accessed 29 Sep. 2010.

25. The human rights plan was approved on 12 December 2008, http://www1.mpr.es/uploads/media/pdf/3/ddhhen_1260787714.pdf, last accessed 24 May 2011.

26. Domínguez, Florencio, *La Agonía de ETA: Una Investigación Inédita Sobre los Últimos Días de la Banda*, Madrid: La Esfera de los Libros, 2012, pp. 127–35; Escrivá, Ángeles, *Maldito el País que Necesita Héroes: Cómo los Demócratas Acabaron con ETA Como los Demócratas Acabaron con ETA*, Madrid: Ediciones Planeta 2012, pp. 366–72; Rodríguez, Jorge A., 'Las horas finales del santuario de ETA', *El País*, 11 October 2004.

27. 'Históricos presos de ETA piden el cese de la lucha armada: "Nunca nos hemos encontrado tan mal"', *El Mundo*, 2 November 2004. See also *Diario de Noticias de Navarra*, 2 November 2004.

28. Otegi, in Iriondo and Sola, *Mañana, Euskal Herria*, p. 128.

29. ETA statement, 20 March 2004. Cited in Casanova, Iker, *ETA: 1958–2008, Medio Siglo de Historia*, Tafalla: Txalaparta, 2007, p. 475.

30. Author interview, Jesús Eguiguren, San Sebastián, December 2008.

31. Aizpeolea, Luis R., 'Así fue el diálogo con ETA', *El País*, 10 June 2007; Eguiguren, Jésus and Luis Rodríguez Aizpeolea, *ETA: Las Claves de la Paz*, Madrid: Santillana Ediciones Generales, 2011, p. 31; Jáuregui and Menéndez, *El Zapaterato*, p. 9.

32. Eguiguren and Aizpeolea, *ETA: Las Claves de la Paz*, p. 36.

33. 'Pluja seca: mediadors internationals al pais basc', *Catalan TV3*, 9 February 2011; Author interview, Gorka Espiau, Bilbao, July 2011.

34. Author interviews, San Sebastián and Urrugne, July 2011.

35. Domínguez, *La Agonía de ETA*, p. 156; Escrivá, Ángeles, 'ETA aceptó en febrero de 2004 mantener relaciones con el PSOE', *El Mundo*, 2 July 2006.

36. The experts included Harry Barnes (formerly of the Carter Center), Andrea Bartoli (Community of Sant'Egidio and Columbia University), Hurst Hannum (The Fletcher School, Tufts University), Julian Hottinger (Adviser to the Swiss government), Cynthia Irvin (Inter-American Center for Human Rights), Billy Leonard (Ulster University), Roelf Meyer (former government negotiator, South Africa), Christopher Mitchell (George Mason University), Kjell-Ake Nordquist (University of Uppsala), Carlos Villán Durán (Office of the UN High Commissioner for Human Rights), William Weisberg (Columbia University). Details of the Peace Conference available from Elkarri, 'Por la paz y el diálogo en el país vasco', *Boletín informativo*, 14 and 17 December 2004 and August 2005, http://www.elkarri.org/pdf/boletin14.pdf. and http://www.elkarri.org/pdf/boletin17.pdf, last accessed 3 May 2011.

37. This account draws on Carlin, John, 'Dirigentes de Batasuna acuden a suráfrica para adiestrase en negociaciones políticas' and 'El asesor surafricano de Batasuna', *El País*, 21 May 2006 and 11 December 2006 and author interviews, San Sebastián, July 2011 and July 2009, and Brian Currin, Belfast, March 2011.

38. Casanova, *ETA 1958–2008*, p. 475.

39. Gormally, Brian, 'Conversion from war to peace: reintegration of ex-prisoners in Northern Ireland', *Paper 18*, Bonn International Centre for Conversion and Initiative On Conflict Resolution and Ethnicity (INCORE), 2001; Shirlow, Peter, Jon Tonge, James W. McAuley and Catherine McGlynn, *Abandoning Historical Conflict? Former Paramilitary Prisoners and Political Reconciliation in Northern Ireland*, Manchester: Manchester University Press, 2010.

40. 'La qüestió penitenciària a la pau d'Irlanda: propostes per a un escenari de pau a Euskadi', 16–17 December 2004, mimeo. The seminar was organised by Vicenç Fisas and the Escola de Cultura de Pau and brought together a remarkably broad range of participants, including representatives of Batasuna.

41. Roelf Meyer was also a frequent visitor to the Basque Country from 2004 on, originally through Elkarri. Author interview (telephone), Roelf Meyer, August 2011.

42. Author interview, Alfredo Pérez Rubalcaba, Madrid, February 2012.

43. Author interview, Josep-Lluis Carod-Rovira, Barcelona, July 2011.

44. 'ETA anuncia una tregua solo en Cataluña y desata una tormenta', *El Mundo*, 18 February 2004.

45. An English translation of the proposal introduced at Anoeta, '*Orrain Herria, Orrain Bakea*', is included as Document 4, 'Now the people, now the peace' (Anoeta Proposal, Batasuna, 14 November 2004), in Aiartza, Urko, and Julen Zabalo, 'The Basque Country: the long walk to a democratic scenario', Berlin: Berghof Conflict Research, *Berghof Transitions 7*, 2009, pp. 59–65 and on the website Basque Peace Process, http://www.basquepeaceprocess.info/?page_id=486, last accessed 8 May 2012.

46. Otegi, in Iriondo and Sola, *Mañana, Euskal Herria*, pp. 123–6.

47. See also ETA statement in *Gara*, 28 October 2004 and Franco, M. Luisa G., 'ETA apoya por escrito la alternativa que Batasuna presentará al plan Ibarretxe', *ABC*, 28 October 2004.

48. Otegi referred explicitly to Alec Reid's frequent insistence that 'instead of settling differences with blows you have to do it at the negotiating table', in Iriondo and Sola, *Mañana, Euskal Herria*, p. 127.

49. 'Carta abierto de Arnaldo Otegi a José Luis Rodríguez Zapatero', *elmundo.es*, 15 January 2005; http://www.elmundo.es/elmundo/2005/01/15/espana/1105803659.html, last accessed 4 May 2011; 'Otegi emplaza a Zapatero a comenzar las negociaciones con ETA', *EFE*, 15 January 2005.

50. PSOE, 'Zapatero propone un "plan para todos" para que Euskadi logre su posición definitiva en el conjunto del Estado', 15 January 2005, http://www.psoe.es/saladeprensa/news/43875/page/zapatero-propone-plan-para-todos-para-que-euskadi-logre-posicion-definitiva-el-conjunto-del-estado.html, last accessed 15 Jun. 2011.

51. Author interviews, Eguiguren, December 2008 and Arnaldo Otegi, San Sebastián, July 2009.

52. Eguiguren and Aizpeolea, *ETA: Las Claves de la Paz*, p. 53.

53. Several individuals reported to the author conversations with Zapatero in 2005 and 2006 in which they had been 'shocked' by his confidence.

54. 'El gobierno debe impugnar el "plan Ibarretxe" ante el TC', *El Mundo*, 2 January 2005.

55. 'ETA avala a Batasuna en su propuesta de un diálogo político pero no rechaza la violencia', *el.mundo.es*, 16 January 2005, http://www.elmundo.es/elmundo/2005/01/16/espana/1105841461.html, last accessed 4 May 2011.

56. Casanova, *ETA: 1958–2008*, p. 481.

57. Cited in Murua Uria, Imanol, *El Triángulo de Loiola: Crónica de un Proceso de Negociación a Tres Bandas*, Donostia: Ttarttalo, 2010, p. 16. The interview is also discussed by Domínguez, 'El enfrentamiento de ETA con la democracia', in Elorza (ed.), *La Historia de ETA*, p. 434.

58. The sequence of letters and their contents is described by Jáuregui and Menéndez, *El Zapaterato*, p. 40.

59. Author interview, Karmelo Landa, Bilbao, July 2011.
60. Escrivá, *Maldito el País que Necesita Héroes*, p. 19.
61. Aizpeolea L.R. and P. Marcos, 'Política de puentes rotos', *El País*, 18 July 2005.
62. 'Zapatero y Rajoy se enfrentan con dureza por la lucha contra ETA', *El Mundo*, 11 May 2005; Valdecantos, C. and A. Díez, 'El PP se queda solo en su rechazo a la moción del PSOE que respalda el diálogo por la paz', *El País*, 18 May 2005.
63. 'Una amplia mayoría aprueba el diálogo con ETA', *El País*, 14 May 2005.
64. 'Texto de referencia: la estrategia antiterrorista, moción aprobada por el Congreso de de las diputados', *El País*, 18 May 2005.
65. Eguiguran and Aizpeolea, *ETA: Las Claves de la Paz*, pp. 60 and 77.
66. Ibid., p. 69.
67. Author interview, Eguiguren, December 2008.
68. Author interview, Alfredo Pérez Rubalcaba, Madrid, February 2012.
69. Eguiguren and Aizpeolea, *ETA: Las Claves de la Paz*, p. 79.
70. Douglass, William A., paper, 20 September 2008, mimeo, p. 10.
71. Cited in Domínguez, *La Agonía de ETA*, p. 161.
72. Author interviews, Eguiguren, December 2008 and Arnaldo Otegi, San Sebastián, July 2009.
73. Eguiguren, in Iglesias, María Antonia, *Memoria de Euskadi*, Madrid: Aguilar, 2009, p. 886.
74. Ibid., p. 888.
75. Eguiguran and Aizpeolea, *ETA: Las Claves de la Paz*, pp. 74 and 137.
76. 'Gobierno y ETA acordaron el alcance del alto el fuego y la declaración del Zapatero', *Gara*, 21 June 2007.
77. Author interview, Rubalcaba. Eguiguran and Aizpeolea say remarkably little about Rubalcaba's contacts with intelligence and security services, and less about the consultations with the French and Swiss authorities that must also have been necessary.
78. Eguiguran and Aizpeolea, *ETA: Las Claves de la Paz*, p. 139–42. The HD Centre's proposals are reproduced in the Annex, 'Propuestas del Centro sobre varios temas relacionados a la fase siguiente del proceso, según la solicitud de las delegaciones'.
79. 'Gobierno y ETA acordaron el alcance del alto el fuego y la declaración del Zapatero', *Gara*, 20 June 2007; Gara, '2005–2007 proceso de negociación: en busca de un acuerdo resolutivo', *Gara*, 2008. Eguiguran and Aizpeoloa published both the draft agreements reached in Geneva in July 2005 and those reached in Oslo in November, but not a single version of the final agreed text. 'Los Acuerdos de Ginebra' and 'Los Acuerdos de Oslo' in, *ETA: Las Claves de la Paz*, pp. 107–8 and 149–50.
80. 'Acuerdo entre ETA y el gobierno español (Ratificado en noviembre 2005)', Gara, '2005–2007 proceso de negociación', pp. 60–1.
81. Confusingly, reference to a commitment by ETA not to carry out extortion is included in Eguiguran and Aizpeolea's account of an 'Agreement on the ceasefire', but not included in their final version of what was agreed in Oslo. *ETA: Las Claves de la Paz*, p. 136.
82. 'Gobierno y ETA acordaron el alcance del alto el fuego y la declaración del Zapatero'.
83. Author interview, Rubalcaba.
84. Eguiguren and Aizpeolea, *ETA: Las Claves de la Paz*, p. 96.
85. Documento, 'Decálogo de la Fundación de Víctimas del Terrorismo para construir la paz', *elmundo.es*, 17 February 2006, http://www.elmundo.es/elmundo/2006/02/17/espana/114020 6217.html, last accessed 20 Jul. 2013.
86. 'A Catalan kerfuffle' and 'Bad echoes from the past', *The Economist*, 12 January 2006.
87. Brunetta and Baldini, 'La reforma del estado de las autonomías', pp. 109–11.
88. The case would be dropped after ETA's ceasefire was announced and then re-opened in 2008 in a blatantly political manipulation of the justice system. Iriondo, Iñaki, 'Caso Anoeta, un juicio político que estuvo parado entre 2006 y 2008', *Gara*, 6 November 2006.

89. Lázaro, Julio M., 'Magistrados del Supremo cambiaron su criterio de 2005 en la sentencia de Parot', *El País*, 2 March 2006. For the ruling of the European Court of Human Rights against the Parot Doctrine, see Chapter Ten, p. 279.

90. Eguiguran and Aizpeolea, *ETA: Las Claves de la Paz*, pp. 160–1.

91. Casanova, *ETA 1958–2008*, p. 488.

92. The communiqué is cited in Segura, Antoni, *Euskadi: Crónica de una Desesperanza*, Madrid: Alianza, 2009, p. 295.

93. ETA's statement was published in English in the *International Herald Tribune*, 22 March 2006

94. Only later would the seriousness of some of the attacks that had been thwarted in this period emerge. See Alonso, Rogelio, 'Falseando la voluntad asesina de ETA', *ABC*, 31 March 2007.

95. Benegas, Txiki, *Diario de una Tregua: Una Oportunidad Perdida*, Madrid: Espejo de Tinta, 2007, p. 11.

6. THE CEASEFIRE UNRAVELS

1. Pettyjohn, Stacie L., 'U.S. policy towards nationalist terrorist organizations', in Zartman, I. William and Guy Olivier Faure (eds), *Engaging Extremists: Trade-Offs, Timing and Diplomacy*, Washington, DC: United States Institute of Peace, 2011, p. 139.

2. See, for example, Merlos, Alfonso (ed.), *Rendirse ante ETA? 25 Voces Contra la Negociación*, Barcelona: Áltera, 2007. Merlos presents Spain's most popular weekly radio programme, 'La Mañana del Fin de Semana', broadcast on Radio COPE.

3. The Independent International Commission on Decommissioning certified that the IRA's weapons were beyond use in September 2005.

4. Moreno, Javier, Jesús Ceberio, Luis R. Aizpeolea, 'Entrevista, José Luis Rodríguez Zapatero, Presidente del Gobierno: "La democracia debe a las víctimas un pacto de memoria y apoyo"', *El País*, 26 March 2006. The 'Irish Republican Army (IRA) Ceasefire Statement', 31 August 1994 is available on the Conflict and Politics in Northern Ireland (CAIN) website of the University of Ulster, http://cain.ulst.ac.uk/events/peace/docs/ira31894.htm, last accessed 14 Aug. 2011.

5. Author interview, Alfredo Pérez Rubalcaba, Madrid, February 2012.

6. Author interview, Joseba Álvarez, San Sebastián, July 2010.

7. Information on the Basque Friendship group is available at http://basquefriendship.wordpress.com/about-the-friendship/, last accessed 14 Aug. 2011.

8. Eguiguren, Jésus and Luis Rodríguez Aizpeolea, *ETA: Las Claves de la Paz*, Madrid: Santillana Ediciones Generales, 2011, p. 193.

9. Author interview, Alex Maskey, Belfast, March 2011.

10. Carlin, John, 'Entrevista Gerry Adams, Presidente del Sinn Féin: "La negociación más difícil es siempre con el propio bando"', *El País*, 2 April 2006. 'ETA's armed struggle is over', *Irish Republican News*, 24 March 2006, http://republican-news.org/current/news/2006/03/etas_armed_struggle_is_over.html, last accessed 5 Sep. 2011.

11. Powell, Jonathan, *Great Hatred, Little Room: Making Peace in Northern Ireland*, London: Bodley Head, 2008, p. 314.

12. Otegi, in Munarriz, Fermin, *El Tiempo de las Luces: Entrevista con Arnaldo Otegi*, Bilbao: Gara, 2012, p. 37.

13. Domínguez, Florencio, *La Agonía de ETA: Una Investigación Inédita Sobre los Últimos Días de la Banda*, Madrid: La Esfera de los Libros, 2012, pp. 93–119.

14. Author interviews, Bilbao and San Sebastián, July 2010 and July 2011.

15. Author interview, Jesús Eguiguren, San Sebastián, December 2008.

16. Author interview, Rubalcaba. Duva, Jesús, 'El "commando Donosti" nació en vísperas de la tregua', *El País*, 8 April 2007.

17. Alonso, Rogelio, *Matar por Irlanda: El Ira y la Lucha Armada*, Madrid: Alianza, 2003, published in English as *The IRA and Armed Struggle*, Oxford and New York: Routledge, 2007; 'Los errores del proceso norirlandés', *El País*, 31 March 2006; 'Qué política antiterrorista frente a ETA? Lecciones desde la perspectiva comparada,' *Cuadernos de Pensamiento Político*, Octubre/ Diciembre 2007, pp. 95–120; and 'Leaving terrorism behind in Northern Ireland and the Basque Country', in Bjørgo, Tore and John Horgan, *Leaving Terrorism Behind: Individual and Collective Disengagement*, London and New York: Routledge, 2009, pp. 88–112. See also Bew, John, Martyn Frampton and Iñigo Gurruchaga, *Talking to Terrorists: Making Peace in Northern Ireland and the Basque Country*, London: Hurst, 2009.

18. Carlin, John, 'Las claves del caso irlandés', and 'El IRA entrega las armas', *El País*, 2 and 3 July 2006.

19. Author interview, Luis Aizpeolea, Madrid, December 2008.

20. Author interview, Eguiguren, December 2008.

21. Author interview, Rubalcaba.

22. The survey was conducted by Instituto Opina for *El País*. 'El 63.7% quiere que el PP colabore sin condiciones', *El País*, 26 March 2006.

23. Author interview, Aizpeolea, December 2008.

24. Aizpeolea, Luis R., 'La declaración del alto de fuego se fragúo en contactos en Oslo y Ginebra', *El País*, 24 March 2006. Other leaks would follow in a wide range of newspapers including *ABC*, *El Confidencial*, *Deia*, *Gara* and *El Mundo*.

25. Author interview, Arnaldo Otegi, San Sebastián, July 2009.

26. This point was made by Eduardo Madina, author interview, Madrid, February 2012.

27. See, for example, Hayner, Priscilla, 'Negotiating justice', in Darby, John and Roger Mac Ginty (eds), *Contemporary Peacemaking: Conflict, Peace Processes, and Post-War Reconstruction* (2nd edn), Basingstoke: Palgrave Macmillan, 2008, pp. 328–38 and Lekha Sriram, Chandra (ed.) and Suren Pillay, *Peace Versus Justice*, London: Boydell and Brewer, 2011.

28. Article 3.1 of Spain's civil code states that juridical norms will be interpreted, 'in relation to the context, the historical and legislative antecedents and the social reality of the time in which they have to be applied', http://noticias.juridicas.com/base_datos/Privado/cc.tp.html, last accessed 20 Aug. 2011.

29. Author interview, Javier Zarzalejos, Madrid, October 2009.

30. 'Conde-Pumpido pide a los jueces que "valoren la nueva situación"', *El País*, 22 March 2006.

31. Fernando Ruiz Piñero, President of the Basque High Court, interviewed in *El Correo*, 12 February 2006. See also Pradera, Javier, 'La vuelta de Garzón', *El País*, 5 July 2006.

32. Ramírez, Pedro J., 'Rodríguez Zapatero: "Con ETA no se hablará de política: primero la paz, luego la política"', *El Mundo*, 17 April 2006.

33. 'Entrevista íntegra de ETA en "Gara"', *El Mundo*, 14 May 2006.

34. Sola, Ramón, 'PSOE y Batasuna pusieron fecha al acuerdo resolutivo', *Gara*, 24 May 2007.

35. Cited by Alonso, 'Leaving terrorism behind', p. 102.

36. 'Rajoy anuncia en el Congreso que el PP rompe toda relación con el Gobierno', *El Mundo*, 7 June 2008.

37. 'El incumplimiento de garantías fue denunciado por ETA desde junio, y reiterado en diciembre', *Gara*, 22 June 2007. See also. Aizpeolea, Luis R., 'ETA exigió al Gobierno compromisos políticos en una reunión en julio', *El País*, 21 January 2007.

38. 'Gobierno español y ETA cerraron en febrero un acuerdo con compromisos y garantías', *Gara*, 10 July 2007.

39. 'Comunicado de Euskadi ta Askatasuna a la opinión pública española', Euskal Herria, June 2006, http://www.elpais.com/elpaismedia/ultimahora/media/200606/21/espana/20060621 elpepunac_1_Pes_PDF.pdf, last accessed 20 Aug. 2011.

40. Cited in 'El incumplimiento de garantías fue denunciado por ETA desde junio'.
41. Buesa, Mikel, 'ETA en "alto de fuego": nueve meses de actividad terrorista. Quinto informe de verificación de la violencia terrorista', *Documentos Foro de Ermua*. http://www.foroermua.com/html/descargas/5Informe_verificacion06 1231.pdf, last accessed 10 Sep. 2011.
42. Gara, '2005–2007 proceso de negociación en busca de un acuedo politico resolutivo', *Gara*, 2008, p. 12.
43. 'Declaración institucional de Zapatero para anunciar el inicio de contactos con ETA', *elpais.es*, 29 June 2006, http://elpais.com/elpais/2006/06/29/actualidad/1151569022_850215.html, last accessed 18 Aug. 2011.
44. EFE, 'Otegi: "La declaración de Zapatero es fundamental para resolver el conflicto"', *El País*, 30 June 2006.
45. Zapatero's statement, as it was claimed to have originally been agreed, is reproduced in Gara, '2005–2007 proceso de negociación', *Gara* pp. 62–3. ETA's complaints are described in 'El incumplimiento de garantías fue denunciado por ETA desde junio y reiterado en diciembre'.
46. Author interview, Otegi.
47. Yoldi, José, 'Garzón permite que el PSE y Batasuna se reúnan hoy, pero pide informes a la policía', *El País*, 6 July 2006.
48. 'PSOE y Batasuna pusieron fecha al acuerdo resolutivo', *Gara*, 24 May 2007. See also, Domínguez, *La Agonía de ETA*, p. 172; Eguiguren and Aizpeolea, *ETA: Las Claves de la Paz*, pp. 183–6, and Jáuregui, Fernando and Manuel Ángel Menéndez, *El Zapaterato, La Negociación: El Fin de ETA*, Barcelona: Península, 2010, p. 161.
49. 'ETA advierte en un comunicado que el proceso se encuentra "en crisis" y amenaza con "responder"', *El Mundo*, 18 August 2006.
50. 'Mensaje de ETA en el día del guerrero vasco', *elmundo.es*, 24 September 2006. On the shift within ETA in September, see Barbería, José Luis, 'París atribuye a ETA plena capacidad operativa', *El País*, 31 December 2006 and Domínguez, *La Agonía de ETA*, pp. 172–9.
51. Eguiguren and Aizpeolea, *ETA: Las Claves de la Paz*, p, 187. 'Detenido en Francia Javier López Peña, considerado "numero uno" de ETA', *Deia*, 21 May 2008.
52. For example, Zarzalejos, José Antonio, 'La tregua de ETA (1) De cuando la banda estaba derrotada', *ABC*, 24 September 2006.
53. Online news *20 minutos*, 'El Gobierno ordena recurrir todas las excarcelaciones de etarras', 14 June 2005. http://www.20minutos.es/noticia/31515/0/chaos/excarcelacion/etarras/, last accessed 18 Oct. 2011.
54. State Watch, 'Iñaki De Juana Chaos hunger strike raises the political temperature', 7 April 2007, http://www.statewatch.org/news/2007/apr/04spain-euskadi-juana-choas.htm, last accessed 15 Oct. 2011.
55. 'Algunas precisiones a las "Notas sobre medidas jurídicas que pueden adoptarse y de las situaciones y escenarios"', and, 'Análisis de las medidas jurídicas que pueden adoptarse y de las situaciones y escenarios' in Eguiguren and Aizpeolea, 'Anexos', *ETA: Las Claves de la Paz*.
56. Ibid., p. 187; 'El incumplimiento de garantías fue denunciado por ETA desde junio'.
57. Catan, Thomas, 'Blair backs talks with ETA', *Times Online*, 4 October 2006. Aizpeolea, L.R., 'Blair traslada a Zapatero su convicción de que el proceso de paz "merece la pena"', *El País*, 4 October 2006.
58. Eguiguren and Aizpeolea, *ETA: Las Claves de la Paz*, p. 195.
59. 'European Parliament resolution on the peace process in Spain', 25 October 2006, *Official Journal of the European Union*, 20 December 2006, http://eur-lex.europa.eu/LexUriServ/LexUriServ.do?uri=OJ:C:2006:313E:0165:0166:EN:PDF, last accessed 20 Oct. 2011.
60. Jáuregui and Menéndez, *El Zapaterato*, p. 172.

351

61. See the articles published in *El Mundo* and *El País* on 29 and 30 March 2011.

62. Surio, Alberto, 'La sociedad vasca se ha movilizado poco en favor del proceso de paz', *El Diario Vasco*, 29 January 2007.

63. 'Declaración de Ahotsak', 8 April 2006, included in annex to Murua Uria, Imanol, *El Triángulo de Loiola: Crónica de un Proceso de Negociación a Tres Bandas*, Donostia: Ttarttalo, 2010, pp. 229–30.

64. Goirizelaia noted that one member of the PP had attended Ahotsak's early meetings, until her party prevented it. Author Interview, Jone Goirizelaia, Bilbao, July 2009.

65. Further information on Ahotsak is available at http://ahotsak.blogspot.com/

66. Eguiguren's recollection, cited in Murua, *El Triángulo de Loiola*, p. 54.

67. Author interview, Otegi.

68. Murua, *El Triángulo de Loiola*, pp. 67–72. The following paragraphs draw considerably on Murua's account of the Loyola talks, as well as that given by Eguiguren and Aizpeolea in *ETA: Las Claves de la Paz*, pp. 200–17, and the author's interviews with Eguiguren, Otegi and Iñigo Urkullu, Bilbao, July 2011.

69. Murua, *El Triángulo de Loiola*, pp. 81–91.

70. 'Bases para el dialogo y el acuerdo político', in annexes to ibid.

71. In keeping with the Socialists' concern for respect for procedures, the document—which itself was to remain secret, in deference to the political sensitivities surrounding the issue of Navarre—outlined a complex sequence of actions for its implementation.

72. Batasuna's proposal of 8 November 2006 and the PSE's counter-proposal are reproduced in annexes to Murua, *El Triángulo de Loiola*, pp. 209–12.

73. Author interview, Otegi.

74. Author interview, Jesús Eguiguren, San Sebastián, May 2009; Eguiguren and Aizpeolea, *ETA: Las Claves de la Paz*, p. 217. Eguiguren recalled that he later heard Thierry complain about Otegi's lack of consultation with ETA during the negotiations at Loyola.

75. Basque government, Gabinete de Prospección Sociológica, 'Pacificación y proceso de normalización política', December 2006, http://www.euskadi.net/estudios_sociologicos, last accessed 10 Nov. 2011; on the reported ETA activity in France, see 'Interior cree que París exagera al hablar del rearme de ETA y crisis del proceso', *El País*, 21 November 2006.

76. Domínguez, *La Agonía de ETA*, pp. 179–90.

77. The PSOE video, 'La otra tregua: cómo actuó el PP cuando estaba en el Gobierno', is available at http://video.google.es/videoplay?docid=-1310133703581585695#, last accessed 3 Nov. 2011.

78. Sabino Arana Foundation, 'El proceso de paz hoy: condiciones para que sea irreversible'. Meeting notes at http://www.sabinoarana.org/sabinoarana/de/el-proceso-de-paz-de-hoy-condiciones-para-que-sea-irreversible.asp?nombre=2682&cod=2682&sesion=1, last accessed 24 Oct. 2011. Contributions made by three speakers are also cited in Woodworth, Paddy, 'The Spanish-Basque peace process: how to get things wrong', *World Policy Journal*, 24, 1 (Spring 2007), pp. 70–1.

79. Carlin, John, 'Los tropiezos del proceso' and 'El asesor surafricano de Batasuna', *El País*, 10 and 11 December 2006. Lanuza, Francisco Tomás y Valiente, 'Estamas locos?' *El País*, 13 December 2006. See also Alonso, 'Leaving terrorism behind', p. 103.

80. Zarzalejos, Charo, 'ETA declarará la tregua "en suspenso" y revindicará el robo de armas en Francia', *ABC*, 12 December 2006.

81. *Zutabe* 112, cited by Murua, *El Triángulo de Loiola*, p. 133.

82. 'Diciembre: "Dribling" el acuerdo político por parte del gobierno', Gara, '2005–2007 proceso de negociación', p. 35; Eguiguren and Aizpeolea, *ETA: Las Claves de la Paz*, pp. 220–1.

83. Aizpeolea, Luis R., 'Zapatero asegura que en un año España estará "mejor que hoy" en relación con el fin de ETA', *El País*, 30 December 2006.

84. 'Rubalcaba: "ETA ha roto el proceso, lo ha liquido y ha acabado con él"', *El País*, 2 January 2007.

85. Paddy Woodworth addresses the 'modelling' of the Barajas bombing on Canary Wharf in 'The Spanish-Basque peace process', p. 65.

86. Author interview, Otegi.

87. The reflection of Batasuna prepared for 'Reunión del 7/07' with the PSE is included in the annex of Eguiguren and Aizpeolea, *ETA: Las Claves de la Paz.*

88. *Gara*, 8 January 2007.

89. The statement was published in *Gara* on 9 January 2007 and is reproduced in Murua, *El Triángulo de Loiola*, pp. 240–2.

90. Author interview, Rubalcaba.

91. Otegi, in Munarriz, *El Tiempo de las Luces*, p. 65.

92. 'El Gobierno asegura que ETA "no ha logrado un solo objetivo"', *El País*, 16 June 2007; 'Política de ocultación', *ABC*, 20 June 2007 and Zarzalejos, Javier, 'El mito del final dialogado'. *Cuadernos de Pensamiento Político*, April–June 2007, pp. 13–5.

93. Ministry of interior, 'Lucha anti-terrorista contra ETA—VIII Legislatura (2006–2008)', http://www.interior.gob.es/prensa-3/balances-e-informes-21/lucha-antiterrorista-contra-eta-viii-legislatura-2004-2008-158, last accessed 15 Aug. 2011.

94. Lázaro, Julio M., 'El Supremo declara "organización terrorista" a Jarrai y eleva a 6 años las penas a 23 acusados', *El País*, 20 January 2007.

95. 'Carta de ETA al presidente del Gobierno español', annex to Murua, *El Triángulo de Loiola*, pp. 243–4.

96. Ramírez, Pedro J., 'Entrevista a José Luis Rodríguez Zapatero, Secretario General del PSOE y Presidente del Goberino', *El Mundo*, 13 January 2008.

97. Powell, *Great Hatred, Little Room*, p. 85.

98. Author interview, Rubalcaba.

99. In the midst of the uproar, *The Times* published a written interview with De Juana accompanied by a photograph of his emaciated figure. Catan, Thomas, 'The man whose fate is dividing Spain', *The Times*, 7 February 2007.

100. 'Rajoy llama a "defender España" ante cientos de miles de personas en Madrid', *El Mundo*, 11 March 2007.

101. Wikileaks cable, US Embassy Madrid, 'Spanish Interior Minister Rubalcaba on De Juana Chaos decision; ETA terrorism; key bilateral issues', 7 March 2008. http://www.elpais.com/articulo/espana/Otros/cables/caso/Couso/elpepuesp/20101207elpepunac_25/Tes, last accessed 29 Oct. 2011.

102. ANV had been formed in 1930 as a schism of the PNV and registered as a political party in 1977. It was a member of the electoral coalition Herri Batasuna between 1978 and 2001 and had remained a member of the MLNV.

103. Colli, Nieves and Pablo Muñoz, 'Garzón da vía libre a ANV pese a reconocer que puede ser "instrumentalizada" por ETA', *ABC*, 29 April 2007.

104. 'Reacciones al auto de Garzón sobre ANV', *www.elmundo.es*, 28 April 2007, http://www.elmundo.es/elmundo/2007/04/28/espana/1177782320.html, last accessed 4 June 2011.

105. Ekaizer, E. and J.M. Romero, 'Del Olmo investiga los contactos de un intermediario de ETA con el Gobierno', *El País*, 9 July 2007.

106. Murua notes that there are conflicting accounts of whether Thierry and Gómez Benítez met face-to-face in early May, or exchanged messages through the HD Centre. *El Triángulo de Loiola*, pp. 141–2.

107. The fullest accounts of these meetings are given by Eguiguren and Aizpeolea, *ETA: Las Claves de la Paz*, pp. 238–46, Murua, *El Triángulo de Loiola*, pp. 147–63 and Otegi, in Munarriz,

El Tiempo de las Luces, pp. 70–4. Murua's account, which contrasts Eguiguren's version of events with that given by Otegi, highlights the discrepancies between the two, while also drawing on the version of events given by ETA in the *Zutabe* it released in September 2007.

108. Author interview, Eguiguren, May 2009.
109. Author interview, Otegi.
110. 'Propuesta de ETA en mayo de 2007, in Murua, *El Triángulo de Loiola*, pp. 245–7. See also 'El PSOE dijo no al acuerdo político tras comprometerse ETA a desmantelar sus estructures militares como consecuencia del proceso', *Gara*, 24 June 2007.
111. Murua, *El Triángulo de Loiola*, p.157; Eguiguren and Aizpeolea, *ETA: Las Claves de la Paz*, p. 244.
112. Otegi recounted this anecdote to Eguiguren, who cites it in Ibid., p. 262.
113. Murua records Eguiguren's denial of the international authorship of the proposal, *El Triángulo de Loiola*, p. 159; Author interview, Otegi.
114. Powell, *Great Hatred, Little Room*, p. 12.

7. AFTERMATH

1. 'Comunicado integro del fin de la tregua de ETA', *elmundo.es*, 5 June 2007, http://www.elmundo.es/elmundo/2007/06/05/espana/1181008833.html, last accessed 12 Jun. 2012.
2. *Gara's* revelations were published in two waves, before and after the 27 May elections. They prompted other newspapers, including *El País* and *ABC*, to go public with what they knew.
3. Author interview, Alfredo Pérez Rubalcaba, Madrid, February 2012.
4. See, for example, Alonso, Rogelio, 'Leaving terrorism behind in Northern Ireland and the Basque Country', in Bjørgo, Tore and John Horgan, *Leaving Terrorism Behind: Individual and Collective Disengagement*, London and New York: Routledge, 2009, pp. 88–112 and Zarzalejos, Javier, 'El mito del final dialogado', *Cuadernos de Pensamiento Político*, April–June 2007.
5. Bosco, Anna and Ignacio Sánchez-Cuenca, 'Introducción', *La España de Zapatero: Años de Cambios, 2004–2008*, Bosco, Anna and Ignacio Sánchez-Cuenca (eds), Madrid: Pablo Iglesias, 2009, p. 11.
6. Otegi, in Munarriz, Fermin, *El Tiempo de las Luces: Entrevista con Arnaldo Otegi*, Bilbao: Gara, 2012, p. 100.
7. Eguiguren, Jésus and Luis Rodríguez Aizpeolea, *ETA: Las Claves de la Paz*, Madrid: Santillana Ediciones Generales, 2011, p. 248.
8. Imaz, Josu Jon, 'Euskadi, a la búsqueda de la paz', Foro Nueva Economía, Madrid, 29 November 2006, http://www.eaj-pnv.eu/documentos/josu-jon-imazforo-nueva-economia_6170.html, last accessed 15 Dec. 2011.
9. Fisas, Vicenç, 'El proceso de paz en el País Vasco', *Quaderns de Construcció de Pau*, 16, Barcelona: Escola de Cultura de Pau, September 2010; Woodworth, Paddy, 'The Spanish-Basque peace process: how to get things wrong", *World Policy Journal*, Spring 2007, pp. 65–73.
10. Zartman, I. William and Guy Olivier Faure (eds), 'Conclusion: when and how to engage', *Engaging Extremists: Trade-Offs, Timing and Diplomacy*, Washington, DC: United States Institute of Peace, 2011, pp. 285–6.
11. Author interview, Patxo Unzueta, Madrid, December 2008.
12. Author interviews, Kepa Aulestia and José Luis Zubizarreta, Bilbao, July 2009.
13. His remark was made during a television interview on 31 March 2006 with Pedro Piqueras of Telecinco. Video available at http://www.youtube.com/watch?v=yIG02XeRfvs, last accessed 5 Jan. 2012.
14. 'Zapatero irrumpe en el juicio de De Juana diciendo que el etarra es "favorable al proceso de paz"', *Libertad Digital*, 27 October 2006, http://www.libertaddigital.com/nacional/zapatero-

irrumpe-en-el-juicio-de-de-juana-diciendo-que-el-etarra-es-favorable-al-proceso-de-paz-1276 291278/, last accessed 5 Jan. 2012.

15. 'Rajoy insta a "mostrar las actas de las reuniones con ETA" y Zapatero le recrimina su "oposición al Estado"', *El País*, 3 July 2007; Aizpeolea, Luis R., 'Rajoy y las actas de ETA', *El País*, 4 July 2007.

16. Sánchez-Cuenca, Ignacio, 'ETA, obsesión nacional', *El País*, 19 July 2007.

17. Zarzalejos, José Antonio, *La Sonrisa de Julia Roberts: Zapatero y su Epoca*, Barcelona: Chronica, 2011, p. 34.

18. *Euskobarómetro*, November 2007, p. 56, http://www.ehu.es/euskobarometro/index.php?option= com_docman&Itemid=17, last accessed 15 Dec. 2011.

19. Ibid., p. 57.

20. Both published lengthy accounts of the process, Eguiguren's is contained in Eguiguren and Aizpeolea, *ETA: Las Claves de la Paz*, and Otegi's in Munarriz, Fermin, *El Tiempo de las Luces*. This section also draws on the author's interview with Otegi in July 2009.

21. Eguiguren and Aizpeolea, *ETA: Las Claves de la Paz*, p. 66.

22. Author interview, Otegi, July 2009.

23. Cited by Eguiguren and Aizpeolea, *ETA: Las Claves de la Paz*, pp. 250 and 254.

24. Otegi, in Munarriz, *El Tiempo de las Luces*, p. 37.

25. Aizpeolea, Luis R., 'Relato de un diálogo truncado', *El País*, 3 April 2011 and the numerous articles published in *El Mundo* and *El País* on 29 and 30 March 2011.

26. Domínguez, Florencio, *La Agonía de ETA: Una Investigación Inédita Sobre los Últimos Días de la Banda*, Madrid: La Esfera de los Libros, 2012, pp. 252–70. Escrivá, Ángeles, *Maldito el País que Necesita Héroes: Cómo los Demócratas Acabaron con ETA*, Madrid: Ediciones Planeta, 2012. Other accounts of the internal processes within ETA in this period are given in Barberia, José Luis, 'Brechas en ETA', *El País*, 9 November 2008; Segura, Antoni, *Euskadi, Crónica de una Desesperanza*, Madrid: Alianza, 2009, pp. 344–8; and Eguiguren and Aizpeolea, *ETA: Las Claves de la Paz*, pp. 248–63.

27. 'ETA warns violence will continue', *BBC News*, 9 September 2007.

28. Documents captured with Thierry, cited in Eguiguren and Aizpeolea, *ETA: Las Claves de la Paz*, p. 257.

29. Interview with ETA, *Gara*, 5 January 2008.

30. Alonso, Rogelio, Florencio Domínguez and Marcos García Rey, *Vidas Rotas: Historia de los Hombres, Mujeres y Niños Victimes de ETA*, Madrid: Espasa, 2010, p. 1175; Domínguez, *La Agonía de ETA*, pp. 199–202.

31. 'ETA declara "objetivo prioritario" al Gobierno de Patxi López', *El País*, 12 April 2009.

32. Aizpeolea, L.R. and J.A. Rodríguez, 'El actual jefe de ETA expulsó a los negociadores de la tregua "por cobardes"', *El País*, 8 March 2010.

33. The ministry of the interior lists sixty-seven alleged members of ETA detained between 6 June and 31 December 2007, eighty-six in 2008 and 124 in 2009; between 1 January 2007 and 31 December 2009 a further 195 people detained on charges related to *kale borroka*. Ministry of interior, 'Lucha anti-terrorista contra ETA—VIII Legislatura (2006–2008)', http://www.interior.gob.es/prensa-3/balances-e-informes-21/lucha-antiterrorista-contra-eta-viii-legislatura-2004-2008-158, last accessed 15 Aug. 2011.

34. Further details of these internal dynamics are given in Domínguez, *La Agonía de ETA*, pp. 252–70.

35. Agence France Press, 'Batasuna denuncia "una declaración de guerra" del gobierno español', 6 October 2007.

36. O.L.-J.M. Extarri-Aranatz, 'Más de 750 presos políticos por primera vez en 40 años', *Gara*, 10 November 2008.

37. Segura. *Euskadi*, p. 361.
38. Barbería, José Luis, 'ETA rompe en las carceles', *El País*, 10 October 2010.
39. Author interview, Mercedes Gallizo, Zaragoza, September 2012.
40. *Euskobarómetro*, November 2007, pp. 53 and 62.
41. 'Sectores de la izquierda abertzale critican la lucha contra el TAV porque "el tren se hará"', *El Correo*, 20 September 2009 and Barbería,'Las brechas en ETA'.
42. Author interview, Brussels, October 2010.
43. Europa Press, 'Miembros de AHT, entre ellos Iñaki Antigüedad, rechazan el asesinato de Uría, así como la "intervención de ETA"', *El Correo*, 5 December 2008.
44. Sola, Ramón, '"No negociarás", el primer mandamiento del candidato', *Gara*, 27 February 2008.
45. The PSOE won 43.9 per cent of the vote, and 169 seats in parliament in 2008, up from 42.6 per cent and 164 seats in parliament in 2004; the PP's vote rose to 39.9 per cent and 154 seats in 2008 from 37.7 per cent and 148 seats in 2004. Ministry of the interior, http://www.infoelectoral.mir.es/min/, last accessed 8 Feb. 2012.
46. '¿Adiós a la crispación?', *El País*, 24 July 2008.
47. Aizpeolea, L.R., 'Zapatero y Rajoy se unen contra ETA', *El País*, 24 July 2008
48. 'Zapatero: "No hay riesgo de crisis económica"', *20 minutos.es*, 4 February 2008, http://www.psoe.es/ambito/saladeprensa/docs/index.do?action=view&id=174741, last accessed 7 Feb. 2012.
49. 40 per cent supported an unconditional dialogue and 44 per cent dialogue only if it were conditioned upon ETA having abandoned the armed struggle first. *Euskobarómetro*, November 2007, p. 57.
50. Aizpeolea, L.R., 'El PNV rechaza el pacto PSOE-PP contra ETA porque "abandona el diálogo"', and Aizpeolea, L.R. and A. Diez, 'El PNV acepta el pacto contra ETA tras escuchar a Zapatero', *El País*, 25 and 29 July 2008.
51. Yoldi, Jose, 'La bola de cristal y los jueces del "lehendakari"', *El País*, 13 October 2008; Lázaro, Julio M. 'El Supremo archiva la causa contra López y Ibarretxe por reunirse con Batasuna', *El País*, 13 January 2010.
52. 'El PP vuelve a atacar a Eguiguren por la negociación con ETA', *El País*, 6 October 2008.
53. Imaz, Josu Jon, 'No imponer, no impedir', *Deia, El Correo, El Diario Vasco*, 15 July 2007.
54. Ley 9/2008, de 27 de junio, de convocatoria y regulación de una consulta popular al objeto de recabar la opinión ciudadana en al Comunidad Autónoma del País Vasco sobre la apertura de un proceso de negociación para alcanzar la paz y la normalización política, http://noticias.juridicas.com/base_datos/CCAA/pv-l9–2008.html, last accessed 12 Dec. 2011.
55. Woodworth, Paddy, 'Punto muerto', *Vanity Fair*, November 2008.
56. Cited in Altuna, Iñaki, 'Cuando Brian Currin recibió una carta de ETA?', *Gara*, 3 July 2011.
57. Ibid.. The second part of Altuna's account of the internal process of change within the nationalist left was published as 'La disyuntiva-trampa de Rubalcaba fracas', *Gara*, 10 July 2011.
58. Author interviews, Kepa Aulestia and Ander Landerburu, Bilbao, July and August 2009.
59. Otegi, in Munarriz, *El Tiempo de las Luces*, p. 17.
60. Ibid., pp. 84–99.
61. Iriondo, Iñaki and Ramón Sola, Interview with Arnaldo Otegi, 'La izquierda abertzale debe construir una estrategia eficaz para alcanzar un escenario democrático', *Gara*, 30 November 2008.
62. Iriondo, Iñaki, 'Un trabajo de meses y una fuerza militante única en Europa', *Gara*, 21 February 2010.
63. Altuna, 'Cuando Brian Currin recibió una carta de ETA?'.
64. J.M.G., 'Algo más que un sindicalista', *El País*, 14 October 2009.
65. Cited in Juzgado Central de Instrucción Diligencias previas proc. Abreviado 0000141/2009-PA, Auto (Caso Bateragune), p.10.

NOTES pp. [204–210]

66. Author interview, Eugenio Etxebeste, *Antxon*, San Sebastián, July 2009.
67. Author interview, former member of Jarrai, Urrugne, July 2011.
68. Author interview, San Sebastián, May 2009.
69. Electoral results from http://www.euskadi.net/q93TodoWar/eleccionesJSP/q93Contenedor.jsp ?menu=li_2_1_1&opcion=a&idioma=c, last accessed 8 Feb. 2012.
70. Aizpeolea, L. R., 'El 1-M fractura el apoyo a ETA', *El País*, 16 March 2009.
71. 'La izquierda abertzale iniciará una ronda de contactos con los agentes que "quieran construir un Estado para este país"', *Gara*, 16 March 2009.
72. 'Otegi afirma que la izquierda abertzale busca una solución al escenario de conflicto "con sinceridad y honestidad"', *Gara*, 18 March 2009.
73. Francisco José Llera Ramo, 'Aritmética y política', *El Correo*, 12 March 2009.
74. The *Euskobarómetro* poll of May 2009 found that the legitimacy of the new government was broadly questioned; 61 per cent of Basques were in disagreement with the pact reached between the PSE and PP; support for it was stronger among the PP (73 per cent) than PSE (43 per cent), http://www.ehu.es/euskobarometro/index.php?option=com_content&view=article&id =78&Itemid=14, last accessed 8 Feb. 2012.
75. Escrivá, *Maldito el País que Necesita Héroes*, p. 547.
76. Author interview, Jesús Eguiguren, San Sebastián, May 2009.
77. 'Entrevista a ETA', *Gara*, 25 May 2009.
78. Author interview, Eguiguren, May 2009.
79. Author interview, Rubalcaba.
80. Author interview, San Sebastián, July 2010.
81. Otegi, in Munarriz, *El Tiempo de las Luces*, p. 73.
82. Barbería, José Luis, 'Las "embajadas" de ETA', *El País*, 1 June 2008.
83. Information on the Fundación para la Libertad is available at http://paralalibertad.org/
84. Barbería, "Las "embajadas" de ETA'; Fundación para la Libertad, 'Informe Sudáfrica', 17–21 September 2007, mimeo. Author interview, Javier Elorrieta and Teo Uriarte, Bilbao, July 2010.
85. See for example, the Foundation's written response to UN Human Rights Council, 'Report of the Special Rapporteur on the promotion and protection of human rights and fundamental freedoms while countering terrorism, Martin Scheinin, Addendum: Mission to Spain', 16 December 2008, A/HRC/10/3/Add.2. 'La Fundación para la Libertad reclama en Naciones Unidas mayor implicación contra el terrorismo en el País Vasco', 10 March 2009, http://www.paralibertade.org/print.php?sid+26369, last accessed 5 Mar. 2012.
86. Author interview, Brian Currin, Belfast, March 2011.
87. Currin, Brian, 'Peaceful opposition politics in response to violent oppression', September 2008, mimeo.
88. The Mitchell Principles established that all involved in negotiations had to affirm their commitment: to democratic and exclusively peaceful means of resolving political issues; to total disarmament of all paramilitary organisations; to agree that such disarmament must be verifiable to the satisfaction of an independent commission; to renounce for themselves, and to oppose any effort by others, to use force, or threaten to use force, to influence the course or the outcome of all-party negotiations; to agree to abide by the terms of any agreement reached in all-party negotiations and to resort to democratic and exclusively peaceful methods in trying to alter any aspect of that outcome with which they may disagree; and to urge that 'punishment' killings and beatings stop and to take effective steps to prevent such actions. 'Report of the International Body on Arms Decommissioning', 22 January 2006, para. 20, http://cain. ulst.ac.uk/events/peace/docs/gm24196.htm, last accessed 12 Jul. 2013.
89. Author interview, Brian Currin, Bilbao, August 2009.
90. Cited in Diligencias previas proc. Abreviado 0000141/2009-PA, Auto (Caso Bateragune), 16 October 2009, p. 16.

357

91. Iniciativa Internationalista won 115,281 votes (15.89 per cent) in Euskadi and 22,985 votes (11.46 per cent) in Navarre, Elecciones Europeas 2009, *El País*, http://www.elpais.com/especial/elecciones-europeas/, last accessed 29 Apr. 2012.

92. Aizpeolea, L. R., 'López encabeza la última batalla', *El País*, 21 June 2009; 'ETA mata al jefe del Grupo de Vigilancias Especiales de la Policía española en Bilbo', *Gara*, 20 June 2009; Alonso, Rogelio, Florencio Domínguez and Marcos García Rey, *Vidas Rotas: Historia de los Hombres, Mujeres y Niños Víctimas de ETA*, Madrid: Espasa Libros, 2010, pp. 1,198–1,201.

93. This would be formalised in a document published the following year: Basque government, 'Convivencia democrático y deslegitimación de violencia', Vitoria-Gasteiz, 31 May 2010.

94. Author interview, Otegi.

95. Report of the Special Rapporteur, Mission to Spain, para. 14.

96. Press release issued by the Registrar, 'Chamber Judgment: Herri Batasuna and Batasuna v. Spain, Etxeberri and others v. Spain, Herritareen Zerrenda v. Spain', Strasbourg: European Court of Human Rights, 30 June 2009.

97. Author interview, Otegi.

98. Author interview, Jone Goirizelaia, Bilbao, July 2009.

99. Yoldi, José, 'Estrasburgo entierra a Batasuna', *El País*, 1 July 2009.

8. LEAVING VIOLENCE BEHIND

1. Aizpeolea, L. R., 'Es hora de cerrar la persiana', *El País*, 19 July 2009.

2. Author interview, Arnaldo Otegi, San Sebastián, July 2009.

3. De Zeeuw, Jeroen (ed.), *From Soldiers to Politicians: Transforming Rebel Movements After Civil War*, Boulder: Lynne Rienner, 2008.

4. The LTTE was the sixth armed group addressed by the project. Dudouet, Véronique, 'From war to politics: resistance and liberation movements in transition', *Berghof Report no. 17*, Berghof Research Centre for Constructive Conflict Management, April 2009, p. 18.

5. Author interview, Rufi Etxeberria, San Sebastián, July 2011.

6. Agencias, 'Rubalcaba dice que Batasuna condenará la violencia para intentar ser legalizada', *El Correo*, 4 August 2011.

7. Altozano, M., 'Otegi y Usabiaga gestaban un nuevo frente soberanista por orden de ETA', *El País*, 17 October 2009.

8. Aizpeolea, L. R., 'Rubalcaba: "Nadie va a hacer política y violencia a la vez"', *El País*, 15 October 2009.

9. Juzgado Central de Instrucción No. 5, Madrid, Diligencias previas proc. Abreviado 0000141/2009-PA, Auto (Caso Bateragune), 16 October 2009.

10. 'Egibar dice que quien detiene a Otegi y Díez no quiere que desaparezca ETA', *El Diario Vasco*, 15 October 2009; Zubizarreta, José Luis, 'ETA, la justicia y la política', *El Periódico de Catalunya*, 21 October 2009.

11. 'Rubalcaba: "El PNV está defendiendo en la calle una estrategia diseñada por ETA"', *EFE*, 17 October 2009.

12. Cited in, Diligencias previas proc. Abreviado 0000141/2009-PA, Auto (Caso Bateragune), p. 18.

13. Altuna, Iñaki, 'La disyuntiva-trampa de Rubalcaba fracasó', *Gara*, 19 July 2011; Domínguez, Florencio, *La Agonía de ETA: Una Investigación Inédita Sobre los Últimos Días de la Banda*, Madrid: La Esfera de los Libros, 2012, pp. 285–7.

14. Iriondo, Iñaki, 'Entrevista, Rufi Etxeberria, "Es tiempo de recoger el fruto de largos años de lucha y no para dejarlo perder"', *Gara*, 1 November 2009; Díéz, Rafa, Sonia Jacinto, Arnaldo Otegi, Arkaitz Rodríguez and Miren Zabaleta, 'Una foto y un futuro', 25 October 2009, *Gara*,

8 November 2009; 'Un primer paso para el proceso democrático: Principios y voluntad de la izquierda abertzale', *Euskal Herria*, 14 November 2009, http://www.gara.net/agiriak/20091115_adierazpena_gaztelera.pdf, last accessed 5 Jun. 2011.

15. Iriondo, Etxeberria interview; Sola, Ramón, and Iñaki Iriondo, 'Mediadores internacionales conocen la apuesta de Batasuna', *Gara*, 25 October 2009.

16. Escrivá, Ángeles, *Maldito el País que Necesita Héroes: Cómo los Demócratas Acabaron con ETA*, Madrid: Ediciones Planeta, 2012, pp. 576–7.

17. Otegi, in Munarriz, Fermin, *El Tiempo de las Luces: Entrevista con Arnaldo Otegi*, Bilbao: Gara, 2012, pp.143–4.

18. Author interview, Brian Currin, Belfast, March 2011.

19. Chico, Amaia, 'Batasuna y ETA saben que el éxito de su proyecto político depende del final de la violencia', *El Diario Vasco*, 29 October 2011.

20. Information on Lokarri's activities is available at www.lokarri.org.

21. 'La Fundación para la libertad denuncia el "discurso de parte" que usa el mediador Brian Currin sobre el conflicto vasco', *Europa Press*, 23 February 2010.

22. 'Clarificando la fase política y la estrategia', Euskal Herria, October 2009, pp. 35, 47, 49, and 54, http://www.gara.net/agiriak/eztabaidarakotxostena-eu-es.pdf, last accessed 6 Jun. 2011.

23. Sola, Ramón, 'La izquierda abertzale se compromete con un proceso pacífico y democrático', *Gara* 15 November 2009.

24. Cited in 'Home-info North of Ireland-Basque Country', 14 November 2009, http://www.info-nordirland.de/euskalherria/eh_new_135_e.htm, last accessed 6 Feb. 2010; Basque Friendship, 'Peace process in the Basque Country', 18 November 2009, http://www.berria.info/blogak/media/Friendship%20group.pdf, last accessed 6 Feb. 2010.

25. 'La izquierda "abertzale" aboga por negociar "en ausencia de violencia"', *EFE*, 15 November 2009.

26. I.C.M., 'Egibar ve un "cambio cualitativo" en la propuesta de la izquierda "abertzale" y propone explorarlo', *El País*, 17 November 2009.

27. Author interview, Joseba Egibar, Bilbao, December 2009.

28. Domínguez, Florencio, *La Agonía de ETA*, pp. 287–8.

29. 'ETA hace suyos los planteamientos expresados por la izquierda abertzale', *Gara*, 17 January 2011.

30. 'Zutik Euskal Herria', *Gara*, 16 February 2010. Iriondo, Iñaki, 'Un trabajo de meses y una fuerza militante única en Europa', *Gara*, 21 February 2010.

31. Author Interview, Etxeberria.

32. Gastaca, Juan M., 'Euskadi recibe con indiferencia las conclusiones de la izquierda "abertzale"', *El País*, 17 February 2010. Spain's interior ministry reported the arrests of 113 presumed members of ETA in 2010 (eighty-two in Spain, twenty-two in France and nine in other countries, only slightly down from the 124 arrested in 2009 (ninety in Spain, thirty-one in France and three in other countries). Eleven arrests were made in 2010 for *kale borroka*, down from twenty in 2009. Ministry of interior, 'Lucha antiterrorista contra ETA—IX Legislatura (2008–2011) http://www.interior.gob.es/prensa-3/balances-e-informes-21/lucha-antiterrorista-contra-eta-ix-legislatura-2008-2011-157, last accessed 7 Jun. 2012.

33. Zallo, Ramón, 'Una lectura de "Zutik Euskal Herria" de la Izquierda Abertzale', *Deia*, 20 February 2010.

34. Author interview, San Sebastián, March 2010.

35. Adams, Gerry, 'An end to violence for the Basque country', *The Guardian*, 26 February 2010.

36. Author interview, Currin, March 2011.

37. *Euskobarómetro*, November 2009, p. 25, http://www.prentsa.ehu.es/p251-content/es/contenidos/informacion/informes_gabinete_prensa/es_informes/adjuntos/EB%20Nov09%20baja[1].pdf, last accessed 7 Jun. 2012.

38. Author interview, Andoni Ortuzar and Joseba Egibar, Vitoria, March 2010.

39. 'Los tres detenidos en Catalunya también denuncien torturas', 'Los detenidos en Girona denuncian torturas e intentos de violación', *Gara*, 21 and 22 February 2010.

40. Author interviews, prisoner family members, San Sebastián, March and July 2010; Jone Goirizelaia, Bilbao, July 2010.

41. Author interview, Joseba Álvarez, San Sebastián, July 2010.

42. Ezker Abertzalea, 'Ante los graves hechos acaecidos ayer en Dammerie-Les-Lys', 17 March 2010, http://www.ezkerabertzalea.info./irakurri.php?id+3620, last accessed 17 Mar. 2010; Aizpeolea, L. R., 'El lamento "abertzale" es insuficiente', *El País*, 18 March 2010.

43. 'ETA subraya que el tiroteo se produjo contra su voluntad y que lo inició la policía francesa', *Gara*, 19 April 2010; 'Rubalcaba cree un "insulto a la inteligencia del común de los mortales" el último comunicado de ETA', *EFE*, 6 April 2010.

44. 'Brussels Declaration: Statement by International Leaders in Conflict Resolution and Peace Processes', Brussels, 29 March 2010, http://icgbasque.org/documents/brussels-declaration/, last accessed 6 Jun. 2011.

45. Rios, Paul, 'Editorial preventivo de El Correo', *Proceso de Paz blog*, Lokarri, 29 March 2011, http://paulrios.net/proceso-paz/editorial-preventivo-el-correo/, last accessed 29 Mar. 2010.

46. Alonso, Rogelio, 'ETA y los "pacificadores"', *El Diario Vasco*, 25 May 2010.

47. 'Los abogados de ETA detenidos pasaron a la banda información sobre Rubalcaba', *elmundo. es*, 15 April 2010, http://www.elmundo.es/2010/04/15/espana/1271329785.html, last accessed 13 Jun. 2012.

48. Aizpeolea, L. R. 'La izquierda "abertzale": reprocha a ETA ser un obstáculo en su objetivo', *El País*, 25 April 2010; Izquierda Abertzale, 'El camino y los pasos. La izquierda abertzale en marcha', 24 April 2010; and Sola, Ramón, 'La izquierda abertzale insta a ETA y al Gobierno español a responder de forma constructiva a la Declaración de Bruselas', *Gara*, 25 April 2010.

49. Author interview, Alfredo Pérez Rubalcaba, Madrid, February 2012.

50. This is hinted at in Zuloaga, J. M., 'ETA usa al centro Henry Dunant para enviar mensajes al Gobierno', *La Razón*, 27 July 2011, but was confirmed to the author by another source.

51. Powell, Jonathan, *Great Hatred, Little Room: Making Peace in Northern Ireland*, London: The Bodley Head, 2008, p. 5.

52. Interviews, San Sebastián, July 2009 and July 2010.

53. Author interview, Oscar Matute, Bilbao, July 2010.

54. 'Bases de un acuerdo estratégico entre fuerzas políticas independistas', 20 June 2010, http://www.gara.net/agiriak/20100620_euskalduna.pdf, last accessed 25 Jun. 2011.

55. C.E.C., 'El PP sugiere ilegalizar a EA, pero ajusta: "Solo si queda contaminada"', *El País*, 22 June 2010.

56. Author interview, Gorka Maneiro, San Sebastián, July 2010; Europa Press, 'Basagoiti cree que ETA podría anunciar una tregua en las próximas semanas para "colarse" en las urnas', *Deia*, 29 May 2010.

57. Author interview, Joseba Arregi, Bilbao, July 2010.

58. 'El "asesoramiento" de Brian Currin a la ilegal Batasuna podría acabar en los tribunales estadounidenses', *Euskadi Información Global*, 30 June 2010; 'El enigma Currin', *El Correo*, 26 September 2010; 'La AVT acusa el mediador Currin de "vivir a costa de las víctimas del terrorismo"', *Europa Press*, 22 August 2010.

59. 'ETA dice tener la "via Txusito" para relanzar el diálogo', *El Mundo*, 17 May 2010; 'El fantasma de la negociación con ETA alimenta la desconfianza del PP hacia los socialistas', *El Correo*, 18 May 2010.

60. Eguiguren, Jesús, 'Reflexiones y propuestas para un futuro de paz y convivencia', June 2010, later published in Eguiguren, Jésus and Luis Rodríguez Aizpeolea, *ETA: Las Claves de la Paz*, Madrid: Santillana Ediciones Generales, 2011, pp. 290–309.

61. Martínez, Isabel C., 'El "lehendakari" zanja el debate sobre Batasuna abierto por Eguiguren', *El País*, 19 June 2006.

62. Author interview, José Antonio Pastor, Bilbao, July 2010; See also 'El PSE cierra filas en torno a Eguiguren, pero aparca su propuesta de pacificación', *El Correo*, 22 June 2010.

63. Eguiguren, 'Reflexiones y propuestas', p. 293. See also, Aizpeolea, L. R., 'No es ningún dislate', *El País*, 19 June 2010; Zallo, Ramón, 'Paz y democracia o inmovilismo', *El Correo*, 23 June 2010.

64. Author interview, Mercedes Gallizo, Zaragoza, September 2012.

65. Aizpeolea, L. R., 'Un proceso a paso lento', and Ceberio Belaza, M. and M. Altozano, 'Siete internos de ETA acceden a permisos regulares y aspiran a la prisión atenuada', *El País*, 19 July 2010. See also Buesa, Mikel, 'Reinsertar a los presos de ETA? Una crítica de la política penitenciaria Española', *Cátedra de Economia del Terrorismo*, Universidad Complutense de Madrid, No. 9, September 2010,. http://www.ucm.es/info/cet/documentos%20trabajo/DT9CET_Reinsertar_presos_ETA_%20Critica_%20pol_%20penitenciaria.pdf, last accessed 8 Jun. 2012.

66. Europa Press, 'Basagoiti afirma que el PP no avala los movimientos de presos de ETA', *El Correo*, 20 July 2010.

67. Author interview, Patxi Zabaleta, Pamplona, July 2010.

68. Author interview, Rafael Díez Usabiaga, San Sebastián, July 2010.

69. 'El TC rebaja las aspiraciones de Catalunya en lengua, justicia y tributos catalanes', *La Vanguardia*, 28 June 2010; 'La constitución no conoce otra nación que la española', *El País*, 9 July 2010; Sánchez-Cuenca, Ignacio, '¿Quién tema a la nación?', *El País*, 23 July 2010.

70. Author interviews, Joseba Álvarez and Rafa Díez, San Sebastián, July 2010.

71. Zubizarreta, José Luis, 'Todo conseja cautela', *El Correo*, 31 October 2010; see also, Garzón, Baltasar, 'Escenario de paz sin trampas', *El País*, 14 November 2010.

72. Sola, Ramón, 'ETA anuncia que hace ya varios meses decidió no realizar acciones armadas y pide implicación a todos los agentes', *Gara*, 6 September 2010.

73. Minder, Raphael, 'Spain dismisses Basque truce announcement', *The New York Times*, 6 September 2010; 'Zapatero se muestra profundamente escéptico con el alto de fuego de ETA', *El Mundo*, 5 September 2010.

74. 'ETA, dispuesta a estudiar conjuntamente con los firmantes de la Declaración de Bruselas las compromisos a adoptar', *Gara*, 19 September 2010.

75. 'ETA ha dado un paso y tiene voluntad para dar otros nuevos', *Gara*, 27 September 2010.

76. 'La izquierda abertzale califica de "sabotaje a la nueva fase" la operación de la Guardia Civil', *Gara*, 15 September 2010.

77. 'Acuerdo para un escenario de paz y soluciones democráticas', Guernica: 25 September 2010, *Gara*, 26 September 2010.

78. 'Sin más evasivas', *El Correo*, 26 September 2010.

79. Sola, Ramón, 'La marcha de Bilbo altera a PSOE, PP, y también a Urkullu', *Gara*, 4 October 2010.

80. Martínez, Isabel C., 'El PNV exige a ETA el "cese definitivo" de la violencia', *El País*, 27 September 2010.

81. Aizpeolea, L. R., 'Rajoy y Urkullu tratan sobre el fin de ETA en seis reuniones secretas', *El País*, 10 October 2011.

82. 'Gobierno, PSOE y Batasuna desmienten reuniones entre socialistas y "abertzales"', *El País*, 29 October 2010. That the meeting did take place was confirmed to the author in interviews conducted in the Basque Country in late November 2010.

83. Carlin, John, 'Entrevista, Arnaldo Otegi: "La estrategia independentista es incompatible con la violencia armada"', *El País*, 17 October 2010.

84. EFE, 'Zapatero: "Los pasos de Batasuna no van a ser en balde"', 20 October 2010.

85. 'Basagoiti pide poner a EA en cuarentena cuatro años para ver si optan por la democracia', *El Mundo*, 27 October 2010.

86. 'Eguiguren admite ante el juez que conocía la declaración de Anoeta', *elmundo.es*, 12 November 2010, http://www.elmundo.es/elmundo/2010/11/12/espana/1289557570.html, last accessed 4 June 2011.

87. Carlin, 'Entrevista, Arnaldo Otegi'.

88. Sola, Ramón, 'El nuevo proyecto de la izquierda abertzale nace con fuerza y anuncia que sus estatutos cumplirán con la ley', *Gara*, 28 November 2010.

89. Author interview, San Sebastián, November 2010.

90. 'Basagoiti rechaza un encuentro con el mediador sudafricano Brian Currin', *ElConfidencial.com*, 18 October 2010, http://www.elconfidencial.com/espana/basagoiti-rechaza-encuentro-mediador-sudafricano-brian-20101018-70609.html, last accessed 24 Jun. 2012.

91. 'Otegi, en transición', *El País*, 17 October 2010.

92. 'History of the International Contact Group', http://icgbasque.org/mandate, last accessed 24 May 2012.

93. Goikoetxea, Agustín, 'Brian Currin, ilusionado al presentar el mandato de Grupo de Contacto' and 'El Grupo Internacional de Contacto asume el "mandato" de la normalización política', *Gara*, 13 November 2010. The prospect of endowing the commission with responsibilities for verification had first been raised in September. See Aizpeolea, L. R., 'Mediadores internacionales piden una comisión para verificar el alto de fuego', *El País*, 20 September 2010.

94. 'Urkullu pide a Currin "discreción" sobre la mediación con ETA', *EFE*, 11 November 2011. Author interview, Joseba Egibar, Vitoria, December 2010.

95. 'Rubalcaba rechaza el papel de los mediadores porque "no hay ni habrá diálogo"', *El Correo*, 13 November 2010.

96. 'Pagazaurtundua advierte de que las víctimas del terrorismo no quieren acabar siendo "víctimas de la paz"', *El Correo*, 27 May 2010.

97. 'Principios rectores para un modelo de fin de ETA sin impunidad', *Fundación*, 33 (December. 2010).

98. Domínguez, Florencio, *La Agonía de ETA*, pp. 294–8.

99. 'Declaración de ETA', 8 January 2011, http://estaticos.elmundo.es/documentos/2011/01/10/comunicado_eta.pdf, last accessed 10 Jan. 2011.

100. See, for example, Soto, Iñaki, 'Entrevista, Brian Currin', *Gara*, 11 January 2011; 'Cospedal: "Es una pausa, no una renuncia"', *El País*, 10 January 2011.

101. Iriondo, Iñaki, 'Quien mantiene la violencia tema la verificación internacional', *Gara*, 11 January 2011.

102. For a detailed account of this activity see Gara, *Anuario 2011: Un Nuevo Tiempo*, Bilbao: Gara, 2012.

103. Zallo, Ramón, 'Sortu o el ave fénix', *Deia*, 9 February 2011.

104. Article 3, Statutes of Sortu, 8 February 2011, http://elpais.com/20110209elpepunac_3_Pes_PDF.pdf, last accessed 10 Feb. 2011.

105. Guadilla, David, 'El lunes fue el primer día de la paz en Euskadi. Esto es irreversible; ya no hay marcha atrás', *El Correo*, 9 February 2011.

106. Author interview, Iñigo Urkullu, Bilbao, February 2012.

107. Abogacia general del Estado, 'Recursos acumulados 6 y 7/2002. Procedimiento de ejecución. Sortu.' Madrid, 3 March 2011.

108. Council of Europe, 'Report to the Spanish Government on the visit to Spain carried out by the European Committee for the Prevention of Torture and Inhuman or Degrading Treatment or Punishment (CPT) from 31 May to 13 June 2011', CPT/Inf (2013) 6, Strasbourg, 30 April 2013.

109. Aizpeolea, L. R., 'Zapatero advierte que Sortu no será legal hasta que ETA desaparezca', *El País*, 9 March 2011; 'Sortu: "Nuestra legalización no puede estar sujeta a batallas políticas"', *Gara*, 10 March 2011.
110. Tribunal Supremo, Auto definitivo con voto particular [Sortu], Sala Especial Art. 61 L.O.P.J. 30 March 2011, p. 214, http://www.cadenaser.com/espana/articulo/voto-particular-considera-ilegalizacion-sortu-basa-citas-parciales-conjeturas/csrcsrpor/20110401csrcsrnac_5/Tes, last accessed 2 Jul. 2012. ·
111. Ibid., pp. 273–4.
112. Rios, Paul, 'Cuarentena más corta', *Proceso de Paz blog*, 24 March 2011; 'Sortu, por ahora, no', *El País*, 24 March 2011.
113. ETA communiqué, 26 March 2011, Gara, *Anuario 2011*, p. 8.
114. Garea, Fernando, 'El jefe de Gobierno con la peor valoración ciudadana, según el CIS', *El País*, 2 April 2011.
115. Aizpeolea, L. R., 'Relato de un diálogo truncado', *El País*, 3 April 2011 and the numerous articles published in *El Mundo* and *El País* on 29 and 30 March 2011.
116. Lázaro, Julio M., 'La Abogacía asegura que Bildu obedece al plan de ETA para colarse en las instituciones', *El País*, 27 April 2011.
117. Guadilla, David, 'López pide al Constitucional que defienda los derechos de los candidatos de Bildu', *El Correo*, 4 May 2011.
118. Author interview, Urkullu, February 2012.
119. Goikoetxea, Agustín and Aritz Intxusta, 'Bilbo y Iruñea, puntos neurálgicos de una "noche mágica"', *Gara*, 7 May 2005.
120. 'Rajoy afirma que el fallo de Bildu es un "paso atrás" en la lucha contra ETA', *El País*, 6 May 2011.
121. 'Las víctimas en la calle por que Bildu no esté el 22-M', *ABC*, 14 May 2011.
122. Author interview, Santi Merino, San Sebastián, July 2011.

9. VIRTUAL PEACEMAKING

1. Election results from the ministry of interior, http://elecciones.mir.es/resultados2011/99MU/DMU14999CM_L1.htm, last accessed 12 Jul. 2012.
2. Author interview, Rufi Etxeberria, San Sebastián, July 2011.
3. Barbería, José Luis, 'Listo para el gran "sprint"', *El País*, 3 July 2011.
4. Otegi, Arnaldo, Rafa Díez, Sonia Jacinto et al., 'La razón vasca', *Gara*, 17 July 2011.
5. Gabilondo, Iñaki, 'Hay que ganar a ETA la batalla del relato', *La Voz de Iñaki*, 6 September 2011, http://elpais.com/elpais/2011/09/05/videos/1315210619_870215.html, last accessed 8 Sep. 2011.
6. 'Final sin proceso', *El País*, 4 September 2011.
7. Author interviews, San Sebastián, July 2011.
8. Fisas, Viçenc, 'Gestionar el final de ETA', *El País*, 29 August 2011.
9. International Crisis Group, 'Colombia: peace at last', *Latin America Report No. 45*, Brussels and Bogotá, 25 September 2012, p. i.
10. See, for example, Zuloaga, J. M., 'ETA usa al centro Henry Dunant para enviar mensajes al Gobierno', *La Razón*, 27 July 2011. This report was promptly denied by Antonio Camacho, the minister of the interior.
11. Author interview, Martín Garitano, San Sebastián, July 2011.
12. Bildu won 313,151 votes, or 22 per cent, in municipal elections and 316,272 votes, 22.18 per cent, of the votes in elections for the Juntas Generales in Álava, Guipúzcoa and Vizcaya and the parliament in Navarre. Gara, *Anuario 2011: Un Nuevo Tiempo*, Bilbao: Gara, 2012, pp. 34–6.

13. Aralar, which fared poorly in the elections, remained outside Bildu but would join it in Amaiur to contest the general elections in November.

14. Author interview, Leopoldo Barreda, Bilbao, July 2011.

15. García, Andoni, 'Rosa Díez compara el acceso de Bildu a los ayuntamientos con la llegada del nazismo a Alemania', *El Mundo*, 11 June 2011. *Euskadi Información Global* began a blog titled 'Despachos desde el infierno Bildu' ('Dispatches from Bildu-hell'). http://territoriobildu. blogspot.com, last accessed 16 Sep. 2011.

16. Author interview, Etxeberria, July 2011.

17. Author interview, Oscar Rodríguez, Vitoria, July 2011.

18. Author interview, Odón Elorza, San Sebastián, July 2011.

19. Auto Caso Bateragune, cited in Cuadra Lasarte, Sabino, 'Bateragune: el maligno son ellos', *Gara*, 27 June 2011, and Zallo, Ramón, 'Bateragune y el Huracán Ángela', *Deia*, 18 September 2011.

20. Author interview, Batasuna lawyer, San Sebastián, July 2011.

21. Author interview, Alfredo Pérez Rubalcaba, Madrid, February 2012.

22. Accounts of Otegi's testimony are given in: Sola, Ramón, 'Otegi indica al Estado que los hechos les dan la razón y que debe adaptarse', *Gara*, 28 June 2011; 'Otegi: Una bomba nos destroza y nos deja sin credibilidad para generaciones', *El País*, 27 June 2011.

23. 'Díez afirma que Otegi, él y otros impulsaron el debate en la izquierda abertzale', *Gara*, 27 June 2011.

24. The case against the editor and journalists of *Egunkaria* was dismissed on 12 April 2010 and that against the councillors and members of Udalbiltza on 20 January 2011.

25. Author interview, Gorka Espiau, Bilbao, July 2011.

26. Sentencia No. 22/11, Audiencia Nacional Sala de lo Penal, Sección 4, 16 September 2011, http://www.elpais.com/elpaismedia/ultimahora/media/201109/ 16/espana/20110916elpepunac_1_Pes_PDF.pdf, last accessed 20 Jul. 2012.

27. 'Otegi el terrorista', *ABC*, 18 September 2011.

28. M. O., 'El "lehendakari" ve riesgo de convertir en "víctima" a Batasuna y hacerle la campaña', *El País*, 19 September 2011.

29. Pradera, Javier, 'Incoherencias lógicas', *El País*, 20 September 2011. See also Yoldi, José, 'La paradoja de los 10 años en carcel', *El País*, 20 September 2011; Zallo, 'Bateragune y el Huracán Ángela'.

30. Cited in M. O., 'El "lehendakari" ve riesgo de convertir en "víctima" a Batasuna'.

31. Author interview, Iñigo Urkullu, Bilbao, Feb. 2012. A detailed, but somewhat different version of the events that are described below is given by Aizpeolea, L. R., 'ETA decidió su fin en julio', *El País*, 23 October 2011.

32. Domínguez, Florencio, *La Agonía de ETA: Una Investigación Inédita Sobre los Últimos Días de la Banda*, Madrid: La Esfera de los Libros, 2012, p. 299.

33. EFE, 'Urkullu cree "insultante" que ETA se arrogue el papel de velador del proceso', *Noticias de Álava*, 13 July 2011; EFE, 'Urkullu avisa a Bildu de que el tiempo para pedir a ETA su fin se acaba en otoño', 17 July 2011.

34. 'Legalizada o ilegalizada, no puede ser un actor político', *El País*, 18 September 2011.

35. Author interview, Etxeberria.

36. Author interview, Brian Currin, Bilbao, July 2011.

37. 'Pluja seca: mediadors internationals al Pais Basc', *Catalan TV3*, 9 February 2011; Currin, Brian, 'Elegir la paz en el País Vasco', *Le Monde Diplomatique*, 188 (June 2011).

38. De la Quintana, Vicente, 'Brian Currin, mediador demediado', *Fundación para la Libertad*, June 2011, mimeo. During July 2011 several analysts interviewed by the author referred in critical terms to Currin's article; one shared a copy with particularly offending passages highlighted.

39. Author interview, Currin, July 2011.
40. Soto, Iñaki, 'Un proceso no puede ser eternamente unilateral', *Gara*, 13 July 2011.
41. Author interviews, Bilbao and San Sebastián, July 2011.
42. Author interviews, Rubalcaba; Urkullu; representatives of the nationalist left, San Sebastián, February 2012.
43. Aizpeolea, L, R., 'El final de ETA, en punto muerto', *El País*, 4 September 2011.
44. Soto, Iñaki, 'Entrevista a ETA: "Euskadi Ta Askatasuna nunca será una amenaza para el proceso de resolución política"', *Gara*, 11 November 2011.
45. Otegi, in Munarriz, Fermin, *El Tiempo de las Luces: Entrevista con Arnaldo Otegi*, Bilbao: Gara, 2012, p. 202.
46. Guadilla, David, 'López abre la puerta a una acercamiento de presos y a cambios de la política penitenciaria', *El Correo*, 29 September 2011; 'Las bases del "lehendakari"', *El País*, 29 September 2011.
47. Vasco Press, 'ETA acusa al Estado de incumplir pactos que el banda admite que nunca adoptó', *El País*, 4 April 2012. Author interviews, San Sebastián, February and September 2012.
48. Author interview, Urkullu, February 2012.
49. Maniikkalingham, Ram, 'Launch of the International Verification Commission', Bilbao, 28 September 2011, http://www.ivcom.org/en/documents, last accessed 2 Jan. 2012.
50. 'ETA acepta colaborar con la Comisión Internacional de Verificación', *Gara*, 2 October 2011.
51. Aizpeolea, L. R., 'La vuelta de Josu Ternera', *El País*, 19 April 2009.
52. Rodríguez, Jorge A., 'ETA cuenta ahora solo con 50 terroristas libres y en activo', *El País*, 4 September 2011.
53. Etxerat, 'Informe para el Grupo Internacional de Contacto', 2011, p. 2, mimeo.
54. Author interview, San Sebastián, July 2011.
55. Ceberio Belaza, Mónica, 'Las líneas rojas para los presos', *El País*, 10 October 2011.
56. 'El Colectivo de Presos anuncia que incidirá en el nuevo escenario', *Gara*, 24 December 2010.
57. Author interview, Eugenio Etxebeste, *Antxon*, San Sebastián, February 2012.
58. Author interview, representative of Etxerat, San Sebastián, July 2011.
59. Gorospe, Pedro, 'Los presos de ETA y la izquierda "abertzale" reclaman un paz "sin vencedores ni vencidos"', *El País*, 25 September 2011.
60. Garea, Fernando, 'El PSOE ve un "paso muy importante" y el PP ninguna novedad', *El País*, 23 September 2011; Sola, Ramón, 'El PSOE ve un paso "inédito" y asume que habrá que hablar de la dispersión', *Gara*, 25 September 2011; Zubizarretta, José, 'La penúltima pieza del puzle', *El Diario Vasco*, 25 September 2011.
61. Author interview, Eduardo Madina, Madrid, February 2012.
62. Murua Uria, Imanol, *El Triángulo de Loiola: Crónica de un Proceso de Negociación a Tres Bandas*, Donostia: Ttarttalo, 2010, pp. 95–100
63. Conciliation Resources had facilitated a workshop in San Sebastián in April 2011 for the Basque movement for civil and political and social rights (the successor of Adhierazi EH that from July 2011 would become known as Eleak). The Berghof Foundation published Aiartza, Urko, and Julen Zabalo, 'The Basque Country: the long walk to a democratic scenario', Berlin: Berghof Conflict Research, *Berghof Transitions 7*, 2009 and hosted a number of workshops involving participants from the nationalist left and representatives of other groups involved in transitions away from armed violence.
64. Aizpeolea, 'ETA decidió su fin en julio'; Lokarri, *Conferencia Internacional para Promover la Resolución del Conflicto en el País Vasco*, Donostia-San Sebastián, March 2012.
65. Woodworth, Paddy, 'Gerry "secretos" Adams', *Vanity Fair*, December 2011.
66. Author interview, Ramón Jáuregui, Madrid, February 2012.
67. Sola, Ramón, 'Powell: "No hay conflicto que no se resuelva con liderazgo y con riesgo"', *Gara*, 12 October 2011.

68. Villapadierna, Ramiro, 'Kofi Annan consultó a Moncloa', *ABC*, 23 October 2011.
69. 'Jesús Eguiguren: "Los socialistas hemos perdido la oportunidad de abanderar la paz"', *El Periódico de Catalunya*, 19 October 2011.
70. 'Declaration by International Leaders', Donostia-San Sebastián, 17 October 2011, http://icg-basque.org/documents/, last accessed 17 May 2012.
71. Muñoz, U., 'Blair, Carter y Mitchell expresan su apoyo a la Declaración de Aiete', *Deia*, 20 October 2011.
72. 'Francia exige el fin de la violencia', *El País*, 19 October 2011.
73. Fernández, Juanfer, 'El PSE critica la Declaración de Aiete asuma la "jerga de los abertzales radicales"', *El Mundo*, 18 October 2011; Pradera, Javier, 'Eufemismos y ambigüedades', *El País*, 19 October 2011; Reyero, I. and J. Pagola, 'Los "mediadores" compran la "paz" que venden ETA', *ABC*, 20 October 2011.
74. 'Pagazaurtundua: "En el final de ETA estamos en juego como país de tramposos o respetuosos con la Ley"', *ABC*, 20 October 2011.
75. Basagoiti, Antonio, 'Carta abierta de Basagoiti a Kofi Annan', *ABC*, 19 October 2011; EFE, 'Basagoiti critica que "la declaración es inaceptable para cualquier demócrata"', *El Correo*, 17 October 2011.
76. 'González Pons: "Adams no tienen ni puñetera idea del conflicto con ETA"', *ABC.es Video*, 16 October 2011, http://www.abc.es/videos-espana/20111016/gonzalez-pons-annan-adams-1220891494001.html, last accessed 1 Nov. 2011.
77. 'El Gobierno dice no sentirse concernido por el comunicado: "Nos parece un papel más"', *El Mundo*, 18 October 2011.
78. 'Declaración de ETA', 20 October 2011, Gara, *Anuario 2011*, p. 85.
79. 'Talking to Alfredo Rubalcaba, Socialist candidate for Spanish prime minister', *The Washington Post*, 28 October 2011.
80. Author interview, Rubalcaba.
81. Garea, Fernando, 'Zapatero reconoce la labor de todos los presidentes de la democracia', *El País*, 20 October 2011.
82. Ramírez de Ganuza, Carmen, 'Rajoy: "Es una gran noticia porque no ha habido ningún tipo de concesión política"', *El Mundo*, 20 October 2011.
83. PSOE, 'Declaración de Rubalcaba sobre el comunicado de ETA', Madrid, 20 October 2011, http://www.psoe.es/saladeprensa/news/610327/page/declaracion-rubalcaba-sobre-comunicado-eta.html, last accessed 12 Jun. 2012.
84. Aizpeolea, L. R., 'Zapatero frena las peticiones de Urkullu para los presos antes del 20-N', *El País*, 27 October 2011.
85. See special edition of *El País* exploring the end of ETA's violence. 'Y Después qué?', *El País*, 23 October 2011.
86. See, for example, articles in Gara, *Anuario 2011*, pp. 83–9.

10. UNFINISHED BUSINESS

1. Cited in Tremlett, Giles, 'Baltasar Garzón trial opens in Spain', *The Guardian*, 31 January 2012.
2. Author interview, San Sebastián, February 2012.
3. Alonso, Rogelio, 'El estado contra ETA: entre la derrota policial y la victoria política', *Cuadernos de Pensamiento Política* 34, FAES, April–June 2012, pp. 139–70.
4. See, for example, Dayton, Bruce W. and Louis Kriesberg (eds), *Conflict Transformation and Peacebuilding: Moving from Violence to Sustainable Peace*, London: Routledge, 2008; De Zeeuw, Jeroen (ed.), *From Soldiers to Politicians: Transforming Rebel Movements After Civil War*, Boulder: Lynne Rienner, 2008; Dudouet, Véronique, 'From war to politics: resistance and liberation

movements in transition', *Berghof Report no. 17*, Berghof Research Centre for Constructive Conflict Management, April 2009; and Heiberg, Marianne, Brendan O'Leary and John Tirman (eds), *Terror, Insurgency and the State: Ending Protracted Conflicts*, Philadelphia: University of Pennsylvannia Press, 2007.

5. Navarro, Vicenç, 'La necesidad de una segunda transición', *Pensamiento Crítico*, 17 June 2012, http://blogs.publico.es/vicenc-navarro/2012/06/17/la-necesidad-de-una-segunda-transicion/, last accessed 25 Jul. 2012.

6. Centro de Estudios de Opinión, *Baromètre de Opinió Política*, Generalitat de Catalunya, 27 June 2012, http://www.ceo.gencat.cat/ceop/AppJava/pages/home/fitxaEstudi.html?colId=412 8&lastTitle=Bar%2Fmetre+d%27Opini%F3+Pol%EDtica+%28BOP%29.+2a+onada+2012, last accessed 11 Sep. 2012.

7. Author interview, San Sebastián, February 2012.

8. Martínez, Isabel C., 'López da por hecho el "consenso" en cambios de política penitenciaria', *El País*, 9 January 2012; 'López planteará a Rajoy acercar presos, el tercer grado y excarcelar a los enfermos', *El País*, 10 January 2012.

9. Author interview, Alfredo Pérez Rubalcaba, Madrid, February 2012.

10. González, Cayetano, 'Qué política antiterrorista tiene Rajoy?', *El Mundo*, 4 September 2012.

11. 'Acuerdo parlamentario sobre la gestión del final de ETA', *El País*, 21 February 2012; Author interviews, Leopoldo Barreda and Ramón Jáuregui, Madrid, February 2012.

12. Basque government, 'Sociómetro Vasco 48—fin del terrorismo', March 2012, p. 16, http://www.lehendakaritza.ejgv.euskadi.net/contenidos/informe_estudio/sociometro_vasco_48/es_soc48/adjuntos/12sv48_es.pdf, last accessed 9 Oct. 2012.

13. CIS Estudio no. 2917, 'Barómetro de Noviembre', Centro de Investigaciones Sociológicas, November 2011, p. 10, http://datos.cis.es/pdf/Es2917mar_A.pdf, last accessed 9 Oct. 2012.

14. Author interview (written), Patxi López, March 2012.

15. Author interview, Oscar Rodríguez, Vitoria, February 2012. While Patxi López dismissed the international role as 'minimal' (written interview with the author, March 2012), the International Verification Commission developed a fluid and useful relationship with Rodolfo Ares.

16. Author interviews, Leopoldo Barreda, Madrid, February 2012; Ignacio Cosidó, Madrid, September 2012; Javier Zarzelejos, Madrid, February 2012. This view has also been expressed by the *El Mundo* correspondent Angeles Escrivá, in *Maldito el País que Necesita Héroes: Cómo los Demócratas Acabaron con ETA*, Madrid: Ediciones Planeta, 2012, p. 633.

17. Ministry of the interior, 'Lucha contra el terrorismo de ETA—X Legislatura', http://www.interior.gob.es/documents/10180/1210364/TABLA +DETENIDOS+ETA+Y+VIOLENCIA+CA LLEJERA+%2817-II-2014% 29.pdf/9d6b856b-5c5b-46ba-846f-42c39c0139fa, last accessed 2 Mar. 2014.

18. Author interview, Ignacio Cosidó, Madrid, October 2012.

19. Author interview, Ciboure, February 2012.

20. Lokarri, 'Lokarri's newsletter about the Basque peace process', March 2012, p. 6, http://lokarri.org/files/File/PDF/Lokarri%20newsletter%20March%202012.pdf, last accessed 26 Apr. 2012.

21. Cited in Basque Friendship brief, 'Aiete Conference, A Road-map for peace in the Basque Country, 29 Mar. 2012', http://basquefriendship.files.wordpress.com/2012/04/29–03–2012-aiete-ep.pdf, last accessed 4 Jun. 2012.

22. International Verification Commission (IVC) report, 26 January 2012, http://www.ivcom.org/en/documents/document/fecha/2012/01/26/informe-de-la-comision-internacional-de-verificacion-civ/, last accessed 14 Apr. 2012.

23. 'Rajoy: "Espero la disolución de ETA, pero no me voy a mover"', *Gara*, 14 May 2012; 'El ministro de interior no reconoce "ninguna legitimidad" a la Comisión Internacional de Verificación', *EFE*, 5 May 2012.

24. Author interview, Cosidó.

25. Pérez, Fernando J., 'Noruega expulse a Ternera y otros dos jefes de ETA al no avanzar el desarme', *El País*, 3 March 2013; Terradillos, Ana, 'Noruega deja de dar cobijo a la dirección política de ETA', *Cadena SER*, 3 March 2013, http://www.cadenaser.com/espana/articulo/noruega-deja-dar-cobijo-direccion-politica-eta/csrcsrpor/20130305csrcsrnac_1/Tes, last accessed 10 Jul. 2013.

26. 'Comunicado íntegro de ETA', *Libertad Digital*, http://www.libertaddigital.com/c.php?op=imprimir&id=1276485941, last accessed 28 Jun. 2013.

27. Author interview, Urkullu, February 2012.

28. EP, 'Currin cree que no tiene sentido pedir la disolución de ETA y que incluso podría ser "un riesgo"', *Deia*, 21 April 2012.

29. Vasco Press, 'Basagoiti dice que sin facilitadores como Currin "hoy probablemente ETA no existiría"', *El Correo*, 23 April 2012.

30. Cited in R.S., 'Ares remarca el cese total de ETA ante nuevas insinuaciones de Fernández', *Gara*, 29 May 2012.

31. Mora, Miguel, 'Sarkozy considera "deseable" el acercamiento de presos de ETA', *El País*, 1 March 2012.

32. 'Comunicado de ETA a la sociedad francesa', 22 February 2012, *Gara*, 9 March 2012.

33. 'ETA nombra una delegación para entablar un "diálogo directo" con los gobiernos español y francés', *Gara*, 16 May 2012.

34. Spain-France Summit 'Joint statement', 10 October 2012, http://www.lamoncloa.gob.es/NR/rdonlyres/BC7403A6–842A-4EDE-814C-6CC9DFD1ECDF/216706/JointPressStatement22ndSpainFranceSummit.pdf, last accessed 22 Oct. 2012.

35. EP, 'La líder "abertzale" critica la detención de la etarra que comunicó el alto de fuego', *El País*, 29 October 2012; R.S., 'Madrid y París escenifican su rechazo a Aiete deteniendo a Izaskun Lesaka', *Gara*, 29 October 2012.

36. 'ETA anuncia que está buscando formas de abrir vías de diálogo', *Gara*, 10 July 2012.

37. Efe, 'Fernández defiende no haber negociado con ETA: "El tiempo nos da la razón"', *El Mundo*, 9 August 2012.

38. Weinberg, Leonard, 'Italy and the Red Brigades', in Art, Robert J. and Louise Richardson (eds), *Democracy and Counterterrorism: Lessons from the Past*, Washington, DC: United States Institute of Peace Press, 2007, pp. 25–62.

39. Della Porta, Donatella, 'Leaving underground organizations: a sociological analysis of the Italian case', in Bjørgo, Tore and John Horgan, *Leaving Terrorism Behind: Individual and Collective Disengagement*, Oxford and New York: Routledge, 2009, pp. 66–87.

40. Von Tangen Page, Michael, 'A "most difficult and unpalatable part": the release of politically motivated violent offenders', in Cox, Michael, Adrian Guelke and Fiona Stephen (eds), *A Farewell to Arms? Beyond the Good Friday Agreement*, Manchester and New York: Manchester University Press, 2006 (2nd edn), pp. 201–11.

41. Author interview, Eugenio Etxebeste, *Antxon*, San Sebastián, February 2012.

42. See Chapter Three, p. 92–3.

43. Author interview, Mercedes Gallizo, Zaragoza, September 2012.

44. Author interview, Eduardo Madina, Madrid, February 2012.

45. Sola, Ramón, 'Respetar los derechos de los presos traería un cambio evidente', *Gara*, 13 April 2012.

46. Angeles Pedraza, 'Estamos en contra de la aplicación de la "via Nanclares" a los presos de ETA', 20 April 2012, Asociación Víctimas del Terrorismo, http://www.avt.org/comunicados-y-noticias/ngeles-pedraza-estamos-en-contra-de-la-aplicacion-de-la-via-nanclares-a-los-presos-de-eta/745, last accessed 19 Oct. 2012.

47. Author interview, San Sebastián, September 2012.

48. Landa, Jon, 'Presos: exigencias éticas y jurídicas', *Diario Noticias de Gipuzkoa*, 4 March 2012.

49. Art. 76.2, Ley Orgánica 7/2003 of 30 June 2003, *Boletín Oficial del Estado*, 1 July 2003, http://www.boe.es/boe/dias/2003/07/01/pdfs/A25274–25278.pdf, last accessed 24 Mar. 2011.

50. It had accepted the demand for the release of three prisoners and rejected nineteen; twenty-two cases were admitted for further consideration. 'Informe Mensual', Asociación Etxerat, May 2012, http://www.etxerat.info/fitxategia_ikusi.php?id_fitxategia=3554, last accessed, 12 Jul. 2012.

51. Ceberio Belaza, Mónica, 'El Gobierno facilita el acercamiento de presos para acelerar el fin de ETA', *El País*, 26 April 2012.

52. Efe, 'Mayor Oreja compara el plan de reinserción de Rajoy con el proceso de paz de Zapatero', *La Gaceta*, 26 April 2012.

53. 'Rajoy: "El Gobierno no ha cambiado su política antiterrorista"', *elperiodico.com*, 26 April 2012, http://www.elperiodico.com/es/noticias/politica/rajoy-gobierno-cambiado-politica-antiterrorista-1712483, last accessed 16 Jul. 2013.

54. 'Declaración del Colectivo de Presos Políticos Vascos a la Ciudadanía Vasca', *Euskal Herria*, June 2012, *Gara*, 2 June 2012.

55. Author interview, Jesús Loza, Vitoria, September 2012.

56. Author interview, Fernando Etxegaray and Nagore Mujika, Bilbao, September 2012.

57. Marcos, José, 'La línea dura del PP arremete contra el Constitucional y hasta plantea eliminarlo', *El País*, 21 June 2012.

58. European Court of Human Rights, press release issued by the Registrar of the Court, 'Unlawfulness of detention extended by the retroactive application of a change in the case-law', Strasbourg, 10 July 2012.

59. 'Fernández defiende no haber negociado con ETA'.

60. Minder, Raphael, 'Spain assails European Court's ruling on ETA prisoner', *The New York Times*, 9 August 2012.

61. On the 'Bolinaga case' see, 'Huelga en la carcel', *El País*, 14 August 2012; Ollé Sesé, Manuel, 'La controvertida libertad de Bolinaga', *El País*, 7 September 2012; Woodworth, Paddy, 'Harsh criticism as Spain's government moves towards early release of dying ETA prisoner', *The Irish Times*, 20 August 2012.

62. Ceberio Belaza, Mónica, 'Insinuar ahora que hemos cedido al chantaje sirve a los intereses de ETA', *El País*, 18 October 2012.

63. 'Las víctimas exigen un cambio de Rajoy contra ETA en dos marchas', *El País*, 8 September 2012.

64. Author interview, Isabel Urkijo, Bilbao, February 2012.

65. Author interview, Gorka Landaburu, San Sebastián, February 2012.

66. Egaña, Iñaki, 'La memoria de los nuestros', in Joxean Agirre (coord.), Prologue, *No les Bastó Gernika: Euskal Herria 1960–2010*, Andoain: Euskal Memoria Fundazioia, 2010, p. 9. Ormazabal, Sabino, 'Intentos dados en la historia reciente y pasos a dar en el futuro', October 2012, http://www.vientosur.info/spip/IMG/pdf/Intentos_y_pasos_dados_Sabino_Ormazabal.pdf, last accessed 25 Oct. 2012.

67. Iniciativa 'Gleencree', 'Declaración íntegra de víctimas de diferentes violencias', San Sebastián-Donostia, 16 June 2012, http://www.eitb.com/es/noticias/politica/detalle/907110/declaracion-victimas-texto-iniciativa-glencree/, last accessed 20 Oct. 2012.

68. Basque government, 'Decreto de declaración y reparación de las víctimas de sufrimientos injustos como consecuencia de la vulneración de sus derechos humanos, producida entre los años 1960 y 1978 en el contexto de la violencia de motivación política vivida en la comunidad autónoma del País Vasco', 2 June 2012, mimeo. In 2000 the Human Rights Commission had prepared a report addressing all the victims of violence, but its 'global' approach to victims led

it to be rejected by the PSE and PP. In 2008 a new report by the human rights office addressing violence by state security forces, parapolice forces or extremists was again rejected by the PSE and PP. A third report—that proved the basis for the new decree—was finally approved by the parliament in December 2010.

69. Egiari Zor, 'Manifestua Egiari Zor. documental fundacional', May 2012, http://www.egiarizor. org/?id_kat=2&lang=es, last accessed 2 Oct. 2012.

70. Ormazabal, 'Intentos dados', p. 2.

71. 'Ponencia para la paz y convivencia del Parlamento Vasco', July 2012, http://www.bakeola.org/ archivos/experiencias/58_es_Principios%20y%20compromisos%20-%20Ponencia%20Paz%20 y%20Convivencia.pdf, last accessed 4 Sep. 2013. Vasco Press, 'El Parlamento vasco sella los principios básicos para la convivencia en Euskadi', El Correo, 13 July 2012.

72. Argituz, 'El largo camino hacia una política pública de víctimas incluyente y respetuosa con todas las víctimas', October 2011, mimeo.

73. Author interview, Maite Papagazaurtundua, Logroño, February 2012, and COVITE, on 8 February 2012, cited by Ormazabal, 'Intentos y pasos dados', p. 2.

74. Izquierda abertzale, 'Viento de solución', 26 February 2012, http://gara.naiz.info/agiriak/ 20120226_ezkerab.pdf, last accessed 20 Jul. 2013.

75. Agirre, No les bBastó Gernika, p. 184.

76. Author interview, Eugenio Etxebeste, Antxon, San Sebastián, September 2012.

77. The government drew on the work of Proyecto Retorno to develop legislation. Universidad del País Vasco, 'Informe Final: Proyecto Retorno', San Sebastián-Donostia, September 2011, http:// www.interior.ejgv.euskadi.net/contenidos/informacion/informe_retorno/es_info/adjuntos/ Retorno%20Informe%20final%206%20JLC.pdf, last accessed 30 Mar. 2012.

78. Otegi, in Munarritz, Fermin, El Tiempo de las Luces, Entrevista con Arnaldo Otegi, Bilbao: Gara, September 2012, p. 210.

79. Izquierda abertzale, 'Viento de solución' and Iriondo, Iñaki, 'La izquierda abertzale da otro paso para transitar a la paz', Gara, 27 February 2012.

80. 'Sin disolución, nada', El País, 27 February 2012.

81. Particularly active in this effort was Lau Haizetara Gogoan, a platform of pro-nationalist left NGOs that worked on issues related to the recuperation of memory.

82. Bono, Ferran, 'Valencia lanza una Comisión de la Verdad sobre el franquismo', El País, 10 February 2007.

83. Landa Goroztiza, Jon-Mirena, 'Bases para la puesta en marcha de una Comisión de la Verdad en Euskadi', Dirección de Derechos Humanos, Basque Government, Vitoria-Gasteiz, 31 March 2009.

84. Otegi, in El Tiempo de las Luces, pp. 200–1.

85. Author interview, Loza.

86. Author interview, Etxegaray and Mujika.

87. Agirre (coord.), No les Bastó Gernika, p. 145.

88. Altozano, Manuel, 'Luz y taquígrafos contra la tortura', El Pais, 23 September 2012.

89. Amnesty International, 'Adding insult to injury: the effective impunity of police officers in cases of torture and other ill-treatment', 14 November 2007, EUR 41/006/007.

90. Council of Europe, 'Report to the Spanish Government on the visit to Spain carried out by the European Committee for the Prevention of Torture and Inhuman or Degrading Treatment or Punishment (CPT) from 19 September to 1 October 2007', CPT/Inf (2011) 11, Strasbourg, 25 March 2011.

91. Altozano, 'Luz y taquígrafos contra la tortura'; Landa Gorostiza, Jon Mirena, 'La tortura en relación con la banda terrorista ETA: estado de la jurisprudencia penal. A la vez un comentario a la STS 2 noviembre 2011 (caso Portu y Sarasola)', Jueces Para la Democracia, 73 (2012), pp. 81–104.

92. 'Tortura', in Agirre (coord.), *No les Bastó Gernika*, pp. 123–61.

93. Author interviews, former ETA prisoners, San Sebastián, February and September 2012.

94. Gómez, Manuel V., 'El paro en España supera el 25% por la primera vez en la historia', *El País*, 26 October 2012.

95. 'El 52% de los catalanes está a favor de la independencia', *El País*, 11 September 2013.

96. Blanchar, Clara, 'Rubalcaba pide una "reforma federal" para acabar con la "crisis territorial"', *El País*, 15 September 2013; Garea, Fernando, 'La España federal como medicina', *El País*, 28 September 2012.

97. Zallo, Ramón, 'Catalunya en *on*, Euskadi en *standby*', *El Correo*, 18 September 2013.

98. Gómez, 'El paro en España'.

99. EH Bildu, 'Programa electoral', September 2012, http://ehbildu.net/es/elecciones/parlamento-vasco-2012/programa-electoral, last accessed 28 Oct. 2012.

100. *Euskobarómetro*, May 2012, p. 41, http://www.ehu.es/euskobarometro/index.php?option=com_docman&task=doc_view&gid=337&tmpl=component&format=raw&Itemid=17, last accessed 28 Oct. 2012.

101. 'Basagoiti alerta de un pacto de PNV y CiU para "romper España"', *El País*, 10 October 2012.

102. Gastaca, Juan Mari, 'Urkullu: "Más autogobierno es más bienestar"', *El País*, 19 October 2012.

103. For different perspectives on the evolution of the nationalist left during 2012 see the monthly columns of Iker Casanova carried by *Gara* and their critique by Fermín Santxez, 'Iker Casanova: del marxismoo-socialismo de ARGALA a los brazos del PNV, de la Revolución Socialista Vasca al Estado Burgés Vasco....', *Euskal Herria Sozialista*, September 2012, http://euskalherriasozialista.blogspot.com/2012/09/iker-casanova-del-marxismo-leninismo-de.html, last accessed 30 Oct. 2012. Information on Sortu is available in English as well as Euskera, Spanish and French at http://sortu.net/en.

104. Otegi, in *El Tiempo de las Luces*, p. 19.

105. Ibid., p. 198.

106. Basque government, Resultados electorales, Parlamento Vasco 2012, http://www.euskadi.net/q93TodoWar/eleccionesJSP/q93Contenedor.jsp?menu=li_2_1_1&opcion=a&idioma=c. last accessed 1 Jul. 2013.

107. Aizpeolea, L. R., 'ETA plantea disolverse si el Gobierno cambia la política penitenciaria', *El País*, 30 October 2012.

108. 'Urkullu: "Tiene que ser normal dialogar entre ideologías opuestas"', *El País*, 30 January 2013.

109. Terradillos, Ana, 'Ram Mannikkalingham: "No tenemos ninguna información de que ETA vaya a desarmarse"', 20 February 2013, http://www.cadenaser.com/espana/articulo/ram-manikkalingam-tenemos-informacion-eta-vaya-desarmarse/csrcsrpor/20130220csrcsrnac_39/Tes, last accessed 15 May 2013.

110. In addition to Lokarri and Bake Bidea, these organisations included Ahotsak, Cátedra Unesco de Ciudania, Convivencia y Pluralismo, Fundación Etikarte and Basque youth of distinct social sensibilities as the forum's backers, and the Berghof Foundation, Conciliation Resources, the European Association of Lawyers for Democracy and the International Contact Group as international collaborators, www.forosocialpaz.org/entidades-organizadores, last accessed 23 Jul. 2013.

111. Basque government, Propuesta, 'Plan de paz y convivencia 2013–16', Vitoria-Gasteiz: Secretaría General de Paz y Convivencia, Gobierno Vasco, 11 June 2013.

112. Mirena Landa, Jon, 'Informe de derechos humanos: el proceso y la intención', *Deia*, 16 June 2013; Carmena, Manuela, Jon Mirena Landa, Ramón Múgica and Juan María Uriarte, 'Informe-base de vulneraciones de derechos humanos en el caso vasco (1960–2013)', Vitoria-Gasteiz: Gobierno Vasco, June 2013, http://www.eitb.com/multimedia/documentos/2013/06/14/1145758/INFORME-BASE-PDF.pdf, last accessed 25 Jun. 2013.

113. 'El PSE dejará la ponencia de paz si Bildu no asume el "suelo etíco"', *El Correo*, 4 September 2013.

114. Iriondo, Iñaki, interview with Julen Arzuaga, 'El "suelo ético"' está decidido por mayoría, vamos ya a trabajar por la paz', *Gara*, 8 September 2013.

115. The experts and rapporteurs included Christine Bell (University of Edinburgh), Colm Campbell (Transitional Justice Institute, University of Ulster), Andy Carl (Conciliation Resources), Silvia Casale (Committee against Torture of the Council of Europe), Véronique Dudouet (Berghof Foundation), Mark Freeman (Institute for Integrated Transitions), Brandon Hamber (International Conflict Research Institute, INCORE), Priscilla Hayner (Geneva Call and Truth Commission expert), Robert McBride (South Africa), Kieran McEvoy (Queen's University, Belfast), Martin Snodden (Northernspring, Northern Ireland) and Aaro Suonio (former Chief of Cabinet of the Commission on Disarmament in Northern Ireland). 'Programa', Foro Social, 14–15 March 2013, available at http://www.forosocialpaz.org/programa/, last accessed 12 Jul. 2013.

116. Sola, Ramón, 'El Foro Social pone doce raíles para que el proceso continué avanzando', *Gara*, 28 May 2013.

117. Lokarri, 'Recomendaciones', http://www.forosocialpaz.org/recomendaciones/recomendaciones-2/, last accessed 12 Jul. 2013.

118. 'ETA hará llegar su aportación a los promotores del Foro Social', *Gara*, 15 July 2013; Chávarri, Inés, 'Urkullu vuele a reclamar a ETA su desarme y disolución', *El País*, 30 August 2013.

119. 'De ETA solo se espera su disolución', *ABC*, 24 August 2013.

120. Efe, 'ETA está dispuesta a iniciar la entrega de armas antes de Navidad', *El País*, 12 September 2013.

CONCLUSION: WHAT CAN WE LEARN FROM THE BASQUE CASE?

1. 'Statement of the International Verification Commission', Bilbao, 21 February 2014, http://www.ivcom.org/en/home/, last accessed 3 Mar. 2014.

2. Abaitua, Alberto, 'PNV y PSE respaldan a la comisión que el PP desdeña', *Deia*, 24 February 2014.

3. Aizpeolea, Luis R., 'A ETA le pierde la retórica', *El País*, 1 March 2014; González, Santiago, 'Hacer un Manikkalingam', *El Mundo*, 24 February 2014; Juarasti, Jon, 'Verificaciones', *ABC*, 2 March 2014; Rivas, Javier, 'ETA dice que sellará todos sus arsenales tras el fiasco de los verificadores', *El País*, 1 March 3014.

4. 'ETA confirma el proceso iniciado con la CIV con el objetivo de "sellar hasta el último arsenal"', 1 March 2014, http://www.naiz.info/eu/actualidad/noticia/20140301/eta-confirma-el-proceso-iniciado-con-la-civ-con-el-objetivo-de-sellar-todo-su-armamento, last accessed 4 Mar. 2014

5. Powell, Jonathan, 'Eta needs Spain's help to puts its arms beyond use', *Financial Times*, 4 March 2014.

6. J.M.G., 'Urkullu se muestra dispuesto a abrir un "diálogo" con ETA para "hablar de paz"', *El País*, 28 February 2014.

7. European Court of Human Rights Press Release, 'The Court delivers its Grand Chamber judgment in the Del Río Prada case', ECHR 307, 21 October 2013.

8. Cué, Carlos E. and Francesco Manetto, 'Rajoy cede ante el sector duro del PP', *El País*, 27 October 2013.

9. Cué, Carlos E., 'Las dos derechas se cruzan en una protesta de víctimas con abucheos al PP', *El País*, 27 October 2013.

10. '"Reconocemos el sufrimiento y daño multilateral generados"', *El País*, 28 December 2013.

11. Statement, 'Ex-componentes del EPPK excarcelados en los últimos tiempos', 4 January 2014, http://www.naiz.info/eu/hemeroteca/gara/editions/gara_2014–01–04–06–00/sections/1, last accessed 4 Jan. 2014.

12. Pérez, Fernando J., 'Interior responde a ETA: "Lo único que nos interesa es su disolución"', *El País*, 3 January 2014.

13. 'Gorroño reitera a la AN que el premio a Otegi valora su esfuerzo por la solución', *Gara*, 14 September 2013.

14. Lokarri, 'Lokarri critica la injustificable operación contra Herrira', Bilbao, 30 September 2013, http://www.lokarri.org/index.php/es/actualidad-lokarri/prensa/lokarri-critica-injustificable-operacion-contra-herrira, last accessed 30 Sep. 2013.

15. Mathieson, David, 'Madrid's dangerous attempt to distort the history of the Spanish Civil War', *The Guardian, Comment is Free*, 6 June 2013, http://www.guardian.co.uk/commentisfree/2013/jun/06/madrid-history-anti-fascist-resistance, last accessed 10 July 2013.

16. Plataforma Comisión de la Verdad, 'Informe al Comité de NNUU sobre Desapariciones forzadas', November 2013, http://tbinternet.ohchr.org/_layouts/treatybodyexternal/SessionDetails1.aspx?SessionID=889&Lang=en, last accessed 3 Mar. 2014.

17. Paris, Roland, *At War's End*, Cambridge: Cambridge University Press, 2004; Richmond, Oliver, *The Transformation of Peace*, Basingstoke: Palgrave, 2005.

18. Author interview, Alfredo Pérez Rubalcaba, Madrid, February 2012.

19. As recounted to Xabier Arzalluz by Javier Corcuera. Arzalluz, Xabier, *Así Fue*, Madrid: Foca, 2005, p. 152.

20. Domínguez, Florencio, 'Inmovilismo eficaz', *El Correo*, 27 August 2013.

21. Heiberg, Marianne, Brendan O'Leary and John Tirman (eds), *Terror, Insurgency and the State: Ending Protracted Conflicts*, Philadelphia: University of Pennsylvania Press, 2007, p. 12.

22. Crenshaw, Martha, 'How terrorism declines', *Terrorism and Political Violence*, 3, 1 (1991), pp. 69–70.

23. Cronin, Audrey Kurth, *How Terrorism Ends: Understanding the Decline and Demise of Terrorist Campaigns*, Princeton and Oxford: Princeton University Press, 2009, p. 8.

24. Crenshaw, 'How terrorism declines', p. 80; Cronin, *How Terrorism Ends*, p. 141.

25. Heiberg et al., *Terror, Insurgency and the State*, p. 2 and p. 390.

26. Dudouet, Véronique, 'From war to politics: resistance and liberation movements in transition', *Berghof Report no. 17*, Berghof Research Centre for Constructive Conflict Management, April 2009, p. 26.

27. McCartney, Clem, 'From armed struggle to political negotiations: Why? When? How?', in Ricigliano, Robert (ed.), 'Choosing to engage: armed groups and peace processes', *Accord Issue 16*, London: Conciliation Resources, 2005, p. 31.

28. Cronin, *How Terrorism Ends*, p. 187.

29. Jaramillo, Sergio, 'Texto de la conferencia que el Alto Comisionado para la Paz dictó en la Universidad Externado', *El Tiempo*, 13 May 2013.

30. Finn, John E., 'Counterterrorism regimes and the rule of law', in Crenshaw, Martha (ed.), *The Consequences of Counterterrorism*, New York: Russell Sage Foundation, 2010, pp. 33–93.

31. Quinney, Nigel and A. Heather Coyne, 'Talking to groups that use terror', *Peacemaker's Toolkit*, Washington, DC: United States Institute for Peace, 2011, p. 16. See also Heiberg et al., *Terrorism, Insurgency and the State*, p. 417 and Pettyjohn, Stacie L., 'US policy towards national terrorist organizations: isolate or engage?' in Zartman, I. William and Guy Olivier Faure (eds), *Engaging Extremists: Trade-Offs, Timing and Diplomacy*, Washington, DC: United States Institute of Peace, 2011, pp. 144–54.

32. Author interviews, Bilbao and San Sebastián, September 2012, including a representative of the Colombian social movement Marcha Patriótica visiting the Basque Country. See also

International Crisis Group, 'Turkey: the PKK and a Turkish settlement', *Europe Report No. 219*, Brussels and Ankara, 11 September 2012, p. 34.

33. Powell, Jonathan, *Great Hatred, Little Room: Making Peace in Northern Ireland*, London: The Bodley Head, 2008, p. 315.

34. Gago Anton, Egoitz, 'The analysis of the framing process of the Basque peace movement: the way *Gesto por la Paz* and *Lokarri* changed society', *ICIP Working Papers* 2012/1, Barcelona: Institut Català Internacional per la Pau, January 2012.

35. Author interviews, Urrugne, July 2011 and San Sebastián, February 2012.

36. Author interview, Eugenio Etxebeste, *Antxon*, San Sebastián, February 2012.

SELECTED BIBLIOGRAPHY

Aiartza, Urko and Julen Zabalo, 'The Basque Country: the long walk to a democratic scenario', *Berghof Report no. 7*, Berlin: Berghof Conflict Research, 2009.

Agirre, Joxean (Coord.), *No les Bastó Gernika: Euskal Herria 1960–2010*, Andoian: Euskal Memoria Fundazoa, 2010.

Alonso, Gregorio and Diego Muro (eds), *The Politics and Memory of Democratic Transition: The Spanish Model*, New York and London: Routledge, 2011.

Alonso, Rogelio, 'Pathways out of terrorism in Northern Ireland and the Basque Country: misrepresenting the Irish model', *Terrorism and Political Violence*, 16, 4 (2004), pp. 695–713.

———, Florencio Domínguez and Marcos García Rey, *Vidas Rotas: Historia de los Hombres, Mujeres y Niños Víctimas de ETA*, Madrid: Espasa Libros, 2010.

Aretxaga, Begoña, *States of Terror: Begoña Aretxaga's Essays*, Zulaika, Joseba (ed.), Reno: Center for Basque Studies, University of Nevada, 2005.

Aznar, José María, *Eight Years as Prime Minister: A Personal View of Spain*, Barcelona: Planeta, 2004.

Balfour, Sebastian and Alejandro Quiroga, *The Reinvention of Spain: Nation and Identity Since Democracy*, New York: Oxford University Press, 2007.

Bosco, Anna and Ignacio Sánchez-Cuenc, (eds), *La España de Zapatero: Años de Cambios, 2004–2008*, Madrid: Pablo Iglesias, 2009.

Carmena, Manuela, Jon Mirena Landa, Ramón Múgica and Juan María Uriarte, 'Informe-base de vulneraciones de derechos humanos en el caso vasco (1960–2013)', Vitoria-Gasteiz: Gobierno Vasco, June 2013.

Casanova, Iker, *ETA 1958–2008: Medio Siglo de Historia*, Tafalla: Txalaparta, 2007.

Clark, Robert P., *The Basque Insurgents: ETA, 1952–1980*, Madison: University of Wisconsin Press, 1984.

——— *Negotiating with ETA: Obstacles to Peace in the Basque Country, 1975–1988*, Reno and Las Vegas: University of Nevada Press, 1990.

Conversi, Daniele, *The Basques, the Catalans and Spain: Alternative Routes to Nationalist Mobilisation*, London: Hurst, 2nd edn, 2000.

———— 'The smooth transition: Spain's 1978 constitution and the nationalities question', *National Identities*, 4, 3 (2002), pp. 223–44.

Cosidó, Ignacio and Óscar Elía, *España, Camino de Libertad: La Política Antiterrorista Para la Derrota de ETA, 1996–2004*, Madrid: Editorial Fundación FAES, 2010.

Crenshaw, Martha (ed.), *The Consequences of Counterterrorism*, New York: Russell Sage Foundation, 2010.

Cronin, Audrey Kurth, *How Terrorism Ends: Understanding the Decline and Demise of Terrorist Campaigns*, Princeton and Oxford: Princeton University Press, 2009.

Dayton, Bruce W. and Louis Kriesberg (eds), *Conflict Transformation and Peacebuilding: Moving from Violence to Sustainable Peace*, London: Routledge, 2008.

De la Granja, José Luis and Santiago de Pablo (eds), *Historia del País Vasco y Navarra en el Siglo XX*, Madrid: Biblioteca Nueva, 2002.

De Zeeuw, Jeroen (ed.), *From Soldiers to Politicians: Transforming Rebel Movements After Civil War*, Boulder: Lynne Rienner, 2008.

Domínguez Iribarren, Florencio, *De la Negociación a la Tregua: el Final de ETA?* Madrid: Taurus, 1998.

———— *La Agonía de ETA: Una Investigación Inédita Sobre los Últimos Días de la Banda*, Madrid: La Esfera de los Libros, 2012.

Douglass, William A. and Joseba Zulaika, 'On the interpretation of terrorist violence: ETA and the Basque political process', *Comparative Studies in Society and History*, 32, 2 (April 1990), pp. 238–57.

Dudouet, Véronique, 'From war to politics: resistance and liberation movements in transition', *Berghof Report no. 17*, Berlin: Berghof Research Centre for Constructive Conflict Management, April 2009.

Eguiguren Imaz, Jesús, *Los Últimos Españoles sin Patria (y sin Libertad): Escritos Sobre un Problema que no Tiene Solución (Pero sí Arreglo)*, Sevilla: Editorial Cambio, 2003.

———— *La Crisis Vasca: Entre la Ruptura y el Diálogo*, Seville: Cambio, 2004.

———— and Luis Rodríguez Aizpeolea, *ETA, Las Claves de la Paz: Confesiones del Negociador*, Madrid: Aguilar, 2011.

Elorza, Antonio (coord.), *La Historia de ETA*, Madrid: Temas de Hoy, 2006.

Escrivá, Ángeles, *Maldito el País que Necesita Héroes: Como los Demócratas Acabaron con ETA*, Madrid: Ediciones Planeta, 2012.

Field, Bonnie N (ed.), *Spain's 'Second Transition'? The Socialist Government of José Luis Rodríguez Zapatero*, London and New York: Routledge, 2011.

Fisas, Vicenç *Llegó la hora? Promesas de Paz para el País Vasco*, Barcelona: Icaria, 2010.

———— 'El proceso de paz en el País Vasco', *Quaderns de Construcció de Pau*, 16, Barcelona: Escola de Cultura de Pau, September 2010.

Fonseca, Carlos, *Negociar con ETA: Del Proceso de Argel de Felipe González a la Paz Dialogada de Rodríguez Zapatero*, Madrid: Temas de Hoy, 2006.

Heiberg, Marianne, Brendan O'Leary and John Tirman (eds), *Terror, Insurgency and the State: Ending Protracted Conflicts*, Philadelphia: University of Pennsylvannia Press, 2007.

Ibarra Güell, Pedro, *La Evolución Estratégica de ETA: De la 'Guerra Revolucionaria' (1963) a la Negociación*, San Sebastián-Donostia: Kriselu, 1987.

Iglesias, María Antonia, *Memoria de Euskadi*, Madrid: Aguilar, 2009.

Iriondo, Iñaki and Ramón Sola, *Mañana, Euskal Herria: Entrevista con Arnaldo Otegi*, Bilbao: Gara, 2005.

Irvin, Cynthia J., *Militant Nationalism: Between Movement and Party in Ireland and the Basque Country*, Minneapolis: University of Minnesota Press, 1999.

Gara, '2005–2007 proceso de negociación: en busca de un acuerdo político resolutivo', *Gara*, 2008.

Keating, Michael, 'Northern Ireland and the Basque Country', in *Northern Ireland and the Divided World: Post-Agreement Northern Ireland in Comparative Perspective*, McGarry, John (ed.), Oxford: Oxford University Press, 2001, pp. 181–208.

Keating, Michael and Zoe Bray, 'Renegotiating sovereignty: Basque nationalism and the rise and fall of the Ibarretxe Plan', *Ethnopolitics*, 5, 4 (November 2006), pp. 348–51.

Mees, Ludger, *Nationalism, Violence and Democracy: The Basque Clash of Identities*, New York: Palgrave Macmillan, 2003.

Morán, Gregorio, *Los Españoles que Dejaron de Serlo: Cómo y por qué Euskadi se ha Convertido en la Gran Herida Histórica de España*, Barcelona: Editorial Planeta, revised edn, 2003.

Munarriz, Fermin, *El Tiempo de las Luces: Entrevista con Arnaldo Otegi*, Bilbao: Gara, 2012.

Muro, Diego, *Ethnicity and Violence: The Case of Radical Basque Nationalism*, London and Abingdon: Routledge, 2010.

Murua Uria, Imanol, *El Triángulo de Loiola: Crónica de un Proceso de Negociación a Tres Bandas*, Donostia: Ttarttalo, 2010.

Payne, Stanley G., *Basque Nationalism*, Reno: University of Nevada Press, 1975.

Powell, Jonathan, *Great Hatred, Little Room: Making Peace in Northern Ireland*, London: The Bodley Head, 2008.

Reinares, Fernando, *Patriotas de la Muerte: Quiénes han Militado en ETA y por qué*, Madrid: Taurus, 2001.

Roberts, Adam, 'The "War on Terror" in historical perspective', *Survival*, 47, 2 (Summer 2005), pp. 101–30.

SELECTED BIBLIOGRAPHY

Tremlett, Giles, *Ghosts of Spain: Travels Through Spain and Its Silent Past*, New York, Walker and Company, 2008.

Watson, Cameron, *Basque Nationalism and Political Violence: The Ideological and Intellectual Origins of ETA*, Reno, Nevada: University of Nevada, Center for Basque Studies, Occasional Papers Series, No. 14, 2007.

Woodworth, Paddy, *Dirty War, Clean Hands: ETA, the GAL and Spanish Democracy*, Princeton: Yale University Press, 2002.

———— 'Spain's "Second Transition": reforming zeal and dire omens', *World Policy Journal*, 22, 3 (Fall 2005), pp. 69–80.

———— 'The Spanish-Basque peace process: how to get things wrong', *World Policy Journal*, 24, 1 (Spring 2007), pp. 65–73.

Zallo, Ramón, *El País de los Vascos: Desde los Sucesos de Ermua al Segundo Gobierno Ibarretxe*, Madrid: Fundamentos, 2001.

Zartman, I. William and Guy Olivier Faure (eds), *Engaging Extremists: Trade-Offs, Timing and Diplomacy*, Washington, DC: United States Institute of Peace, 2011.

Zulaika, Joseba, *Basque Violence: Metaphor and Sacrament*, Reno: University of Nevada Press, 1988.

Zulaika, Joseba and William A. Douglass, *Terror and Taboo: The Follies, Fables and Faces of Terrorism*, New York and London: Routledge, 1996.

INDEX

379

INDEX

INDEX

221, 224, 227, 251, 254–6, 266, 269, 275–81, 285–6, 296–7; public opinion of, 43, 58, 85, 155, 166, 181, 186, 199, 213, 236, 289, 195, 303, 315; recruitment to, 62–63, 195; reintegration of ETA-pm, 55–7, 66; relations with Batasuna, 64, 160–1, 163, 174, 177–80, 182, 192, 199, 201–5, 207, 210, 216–21, 228, 230–1, 248, 314; relations with MLNV, 52–3, 56, 63–64, 74, 78, 80, 86; relations with PNV, 52, 67–70, 72, 74, 91–2, 94–6, 221; relations with Sinn Féin, 182, 184–5, 207, 318; response to Aiete Conference, 251; response to Brussels Declaration, 224–5, 229, 234; response to Social Forum, 292; 'road map' (2011), 248, 251–2, 266, 269, 317, 319; structure of, 61–2, 190–2, 195; targeting of PP councillors, 88–9; targeting of military/police personnel, 29, 43. 54, 59, 71–3, 84, 187, 194, 198, 212; targeting of PSE, 96; ties to FARC, 125; Tour de France route bombing (2007), 194; view of electoral results (2004), 141; Txiberta meeting with PNV, 74; view of Ibarretxe Plan, 116–17; Zaragoza barracks bombing (1987), 71, 84, 94; *Zutabe*, 129, 179

Euskadiko Ezkerra (EE): 57, 121; formation of, 32; members of, 56, 58

Euskal Herria: 90, 92, 95, 141, 145–6, 171, 180, 251, 257, 264, 299; aspirations for independence of, 26–7, 171; concept of, 2, 23–4, 119; demands for recognition of, 80, 111, 117, 119, 176

Euskal Herria Bildu (EH Bildu): 282–3, 291–2, 298; electoral performance of (2012), 16, 288–9; members of, 288

Euskal Herritarrok (EH): 94–95, 110–11; formerly HB, 92; renamed Batasuna, 99

Euskal Memoria: 281; report (2010), 30, 283; views on torture, 286

Euskera (language): 2, 23–4, 31–2, 35–6; 41, 48, 62–3, 83, 118–9; recognition as official language, 26–7; repression of, 37, 40

Eusko Ikaskuntza (Society of Basque Studies): 257

Eusko Langileen Alkartasuna (ELA): 86, 89

Euskobarómetro: personnel of, 27; research conducted by, 29, 197, 221, 228

Ezker Batua (United Left): 28, 219, 287

Falange Española Tradicionalista de las Juntas de la Ofensiva Nacional y Sindicalista (Traditionalist Spanish Phalanx of the Juntas of the National Syndicalist Offensive): case brought against Garzón, 222; formation of, 39

Falcone, Giovanne: 82

Faure, Guy Olivier: 190; *Engaging Extremists* (2011), 19, 190

Fernández, Jonan: 87–8, 130, 316; Basque commissioner for peace and coexistence 290; director of Baketik, 282; director of Elkarri, 76

Fernández Díaz, Jorge: 273, 275, 290; Spanish interior minister, 270, 279

FIFA World Cup (2010): significance of Spanish victory in, 69

First of October Anti-Fascist Resistance Group (GRAPO): 30, 271, 275

Fisas, Viçenc: 111, 242–3

Fluxá, Ricardo Martí: Spanish state secretary for security, 93

Foro de Ermua: 85, 95; lawsuit filed against Ibarretxe (2006), 168

Forum for National Debate (2005): 142

Foundation for the Victims of Terrorism (FVT): 156, 234

Fraga, Manuel: founder of AP, 49

France: see also Iparralde (French Basque Country) 2, 10, 23, 32, 41, 95, 124, 162, 289, 318; Bidart capture of ETA leadership at, 5, 15, 53,

INDEX

INDEX

INDEX